Agency and Consciousness in Discourse

Self–other dynamics as a complex system

PAUL J. THIBAULT

continuum
LONDON • NEW YORK

Continuum International Publishing Group
The Tower Building   15 East 26th Street
11 York Road   New York, NY 10010
London
SE1 7NX

British Library Cataloguing-in-Publication Data
A catalogue record for this book is available from the British Library.

ISBN: 08264 7426 8 (hardback)

Library of Congress Cataloging-in-Publication Data
A catalog record for this book is available from the Library of Congress.

Typeset by RefineCatch Ltd, Bungay, Suffolk
Printed and bound in Great Britain by
MPG Books Ltd, Bodmin, Cornwall

Contents

List of Figures

List of Tables

Preface

This is a further development of my last book *Brain, Mind, and the Signifying Body* (Thibault 2004a). That book was a first step in an overall attempt to rethink meaning-making activity from the perspective of the body-brain system – the signifying body – embedded in its ecosocial semiotic environment. As I pointed out in the epilogue to that project, the key themes included activity, agency, body-brain system, contextualization, cross-coupling, differentiation, dynamic open systems, ecosocial environment, embodiment, individuation, meaning-making, metafunctions, multimodality, process, scalar hierarchy, self-organization, specification hierarchy, system, timescales, topological, trajectory, typological, and value.

Against this same backdrop of concerns, this book explores the ways in which agency and consciousness are created and enacted in and through transactions between self and other. The transactions between self and other are seen as the central notion in the development of an adequate explanation of both agency and consciousness. I argue that it is necessary to reconnect body-brain processes and interactions to the social and discursive practices which directly act upon and affect our body-brain systems in meaning-making activity. To achieve this goal, it is necessary to construct an integrated picture of the semiotic integration of meanings across many different space and timescales and how these linkages relate to the structure of agency and consciousness.

The closely related issues of agency and individuation are also explored in relation to early (pre-linguistic) infant semiosis, as well as in relation to children's symbolic play around the age of 4–6 years. The ability of individuals to internally recognize and appraise their own actions and states of consciousness – i.e. the possession of a moral conscience based on ethics and values – is also explored in relation to the interpersonal dimension of all acts of meaning-making. This ability is itself connected to the development of a self-referential viewpoint on the basis of the transactions between self and other along the individual's historical–biographical trajectory. The development of a self-referential perspective is central to consciousness. In the present book, I discuss this notion by connecting a theory of ecosocial semiotic systems to thinking about consciousness as a complex adaptive system on many different levels of brain–body–world relations.

A central theme of the book is the ways in which new emergent levels of organization come into existence *between* already existing scalar levels at the same time that existing levels are reorganized by the emergence of the new levels. I show how Halliday's account of the emergence of language from protolanguage in the infant is compatible with this view, whilst at the same time giving it a few new twists. The final section of the book continues this discussion, but gives it a new focus. In this section, I consider some of the ways in which metaphor raises fundamental questions about the relationship between semiotics and the dynamics of complex self-organizing systems. Metaphor, I suggest, can help us to understand how the complexity of such systems arises from the emergence of new levels of organization over their history. These issues are discussed in relation to language, visual images, and other semiotic modalities.

During the course of the present endeavour, I visit and critically evaluate the work of linguists, psychologists, biologists, semioticians, and sociologists in order to draw upon and reconstitute their insights while developing my own. Some of the key players include Basil Bernstein, Mikhail Bakhtin, Robert de Beaugrande, James J. Gibson, Michael Halliday, Ruqaiya Hasan, Walter Kauffman, Lakoff & Johnson, Jay Lemke, Jean Piaget, Stanley Salthe,

Colwyn Trevarthen, Lev. N. Vygotsky, and others. In particular, I suggest how they can all assist in the development of a semiotic theory of agency and consciousness and their formation across diverse scalar levels of semiotic and material organization.

Michael Halliday, Ruqaiya Hasan, and Jay Lemke deserve a very special mention for their generosity and support – both intellectual and personal – over very many years.

I also wish to express my profound appreciation to the following friends and colleagues for their support and their willingness to listen to, discuss and provide forums for my ideas: John Alexander, Anthony Baldry, Marco Battacchi, Olga Battacchi, Jim Benson, Kjell Lars Berge, Paul Bouissac, Stein Bråten, Tony Brennan, Magda Cortelli, Stephen Cowley, Fan Dai, Kristin Davidse, Ersu Ding, Andrew Goatly, Bill Greaves, Michael Gregory, Guowen Huang, Marcel Kinsbourne, Lisa Leung, Marc Lorrimar, Eva Maagerø, Jim Martin, Kieran McGillicuddy, Blair McKenzie, Ng Lai Ping, Carlo Prevignano, Duane Savage-Rumbaugh, Susan Savage-Rumbaugh, Zhang Shaojie, Jared Tagliatela, Godfrey Tanner, Amy Tsui, Theo van Leeuwen, Eija Ventola, and David Wallace.

To my daughter, Ilaria, many thanks for allowing me to use so many of the materials that I have analysed in the book and for providing so much of the inspiration for this study.

I also thank my family for all their love and support and for the infinite ways in which they have enriched my life.

All my gratitude to Maggie, for your courage and wisdom, for believing in me, and much more. And to Marc, for your recognition and constant interrogation: only a significant other can achieve that!

Ordy, thanks again for all your inspiration and encouragement. Thanks for helping me to find the agency to go on! I can think of no better demonstration of co-agency in action than your love.

My editor, Jennifer Lovel of Continuum, provided invaluable technical and practical advice and support throughout all stages of this project. Many thanks, Jenny, for making it all happen so efficiently and professionally.

Bologna,
February 2004

For my daughter, Ilaria

1

Introduction

A word is a microcosm of human consciousness.

Lev Vygotsky (1986 [1934]: 256)

1 Semiosis is a microcosm of human agency and consciousness

Many readers will recognize this quotation from Vygotsky as the final sentence of his essay "Thought and word", the final chapter in Vygotsky's influential book *Thought and Language* (1986 [1934]). In taking these concluding words of Vygotsky as the point of departure for the present study, I would like to suggest that the study of language (and other meaning systems) cannot or should not be divorced from the scientific inquiry into the nature of human consciousness and agency. Typically, linguistic inquiry is taken as the primary goal and the study of consciousness, selfhood, and agency are seen as secondary or derived modes of inquiry with respect to that goal. In some respects, the present book will seek to reverse that perspective. I shall suggest that linguistics can serve as a valuable, though hardly complete, tool that can be useful in the study of the concepts mentioned above.

The primary goal of the present study is to elucidate the notions of agency and consciousness and to use linguistics and discourse analysis, among other things, to pursue that goal. Moreover, I shall also suggest that any theory of language or of semiosis in general that cuts itself off from a serious theoretical reflection on the ways in which the study of human meaning-making activity relates to human consciousness and agency simply fails to account for the very nature and purposes of language (Halliday 1995). Nor is it enough to analyse the lexicogrammatical and semantic units and relations in and through which agency and consciousness are construed and enacted in discourse as linguistic data that can be separated from the agency and the consciousness of the people who use language. Instead, it will prove necessary to connect language and other modalities of semiosis with the body-brain system which is the ground and reference point for all of our engagements with and perspectives on the world. Language and other semiotic modalities are truly a microcosm of human consciousness and agency and cannot be separated from these without failing to understand the nature of human meaning-making activity (see also Wertsch 1995).

Consciousness, as I argued in *Brain, Mind, and the Signifying Body* (Thibault 2004a), is a highly specified meaning-system in the perspective of the self. This argument remains central in the present study. Rather than assuming that consciousness pre-exists meaning as its precondition, I propose that meaning cannot be separated from consciousness just as consciousness cannot be separated from the action trajectories of agents. As we shall see, consciousness, agency, and action are all internally linked to each other by meaning-making activity. As in the previous study, the notion of the trajectory provides a way of thinking about the ways in which consciousness and agency are integrated to the trajectory of the self on diverse space-time scales. In making this move, we can also begin to grasp the dialogical-interpersonal basis of consciousness and its implications more fully, rather than persisting with the view that consciousness is the unique and monological property of the individual mind *per se*. The fundamental and constitutive role of the other and of the other's meanings in the formation of consciousness comes more clearly into view once we take this step.

2   Alterity is a primitive intrinsic value that motivates self–nonself relations and meaning-making activity

Gibson (1986 [1979]) shows that infants first perceive the most schematic and hence topological properties of the dynamic body movements of others. These movements and their cross-modal correlations with auditory inputs (vocalizations), visual inputs (e.g. faces) enable infants at a very early age to link the stimulus information from these various sources to a unified bodily source and to orient to this source as a resource to lock into for the purposes of semiosis (see also the work of Johnson and Morton (1991) on the way in which neonates orient to and perceive the human face). The principle of the other – the nonself – is not only a property of the human dyads which characterize all stages of human social development. It is also an affordance – perhaps the most fundamental one of all – of the ecosocial semiotic environment which the individual inhabits. It is a material and semiotic resource in and through which action, interaction, and, therefore, self-organization can take place. This observation suggests that the ontological basis of our bio-social being is the principle of alterity. The ambient flux (the nonself) is not a passive and objectified exterior which we simply process as information. It affords the principle of alterity. Alterity is the very basis of the active and dialogical orientation in and through which a self-referential perspective self-organizes in and through the self's engagements with the nonself.

According to Flohr, subjectivity is intrinsic to the very high rate of assembly formation of neuronal nets in the human brain. The occurrence of subjectivity can thus be explained as:

> . . . the necessary result of representational and metarepresentational processes. Nerve nets with a high rate of assembly formation can produce more and more complex, and thus qualitatively different, representations than nets with a lower formation rate. Nets with a high formation rate will automatically generate active metarepresentations of internal states, the complexity of which will be limited by the complexity of the physical tokens generated per time. At a sufficiently high formation rate such systems will develop self-referential, intro-spective, metacognitive activities. In such systems an inner perspective will automatically develop. Subjectivity arises necessarily in nerve nets with high rates of assembly formation.
> (Flohr 1991: 258)

Flohr's brain-focused account remains tied to the individual biological organism. In the eco-social conceptual framework of the present study, we would do well to substitute Flohr's term "subjectivity", whenever it occurs in the above quotation, with the more properly dialogical concept of "intersubjectivity". This substitution is more than a mere changing of the terms: it entails a fundamental reconstitution of the principles at stake. Subjectivity arises necessarily in and through our dialogical relations with the other. The formation of an "inner perspective", as Flohr expresses it, depends on the generating of active meta-representations, not of subjective states *per se*, but of the self's axiological-affective and dialogical orientation to the nonself, or the other.

However, the formation of an inner, self-referential perspective is not a uniquely individual and subjective affair. The research on early infant semiosis by Trevarthen (1978, 1998) and Bråten (1992, 1998, 2002) shows that infants have an inborn capacity to attune to and to lock into more senior others such as parents and their meanings. This inborn capacity for inter-personal engagement with and attunement to others in primary intersubjectivity is a primitive value bias (Edelman 1992: 119–121; Edelman and Tononi 2000: 105, 174). Such a value bias specifies the kinds of environmental information that the infant needs and how to get it in order that the infant is nudged along certain developmental pathways that are typical of his or her kind. The attunement to others as a source of meanings is an adaptive modification which ensures the further development of the child. In the first instance, the infant orients to the saccadic nature of the prosodies of others' movements and vocalizations. From the infant's perspective, these prosodies are iconic signs of affect, motivation, and interest (chapter 3, section 1). These prosodies can in turn be related to the 40 Hz event-related EEG changes which humans and other organisms undergo in different "focused arousal paradigms" (Flohr 1991:

256). Flohr explains that the neural substrate of focused attention "is the coherent activity of assemblies in specific or multisensory circuitry" (1991: 256). He also notes that the objects to which attention is directed "not only elicit behavioural reactions, but are also different subjectively" (1991: 257). Attention and attention seeking activity are necessarily dialogic. Moreover, they implicate the self's axiological-affective orientation to the particular object of attention. Attention is never disinterested.

In the case of human infants, the child attunes to significant adult others in his or her environment in order to obtain information that will contribute to his or her further development. The infant actively orients to and seeks contact with others through the deployment of a range of proto-semiotic activities which are functional in getting adults to respond to them at the same time that adults have a range of activities which are adapted to their tuning into and engaging with babies. Bråten's (1992, 1998, 2002) notion of the virtual other whereby infants' preverbal capacities are adapted to and attuned to the other and his or her responses now receives support from the recent findings concerning the role of mirror neurons in the recognition of reciprocal processes of attunement in the action and speech of others (Rizzolatti and Arbib 1998; Rizzolatti, Craighero, and Fadiga 2002). Rizzolatti, Craighero, and Fadiga (*op. cit.*) have shown that in the course of their interpersonal engagements with others, the agent's motor system simulates the other's activity as if the agent (the self) were virtually performing the other's activity. Mirror neurons suggest that the biological initiating conditions that underlie the dialogical processes of mutual attunement to each other's actions in human social interaction are themselves properties of the organism *qua* dynamic open system in relation to the higher-scalar ecosocial environment in which the transactions between individuals take place (chapter 8, section 4).

How does the combined complex of biological and ecosocial semiotic relations which are involved selectively attend to and de-locate the social semiotic action formations from the "outer" social domain and then selectively re-locate these in a specialized inner perspective of the self? Self-awareness may be an evolutionary innovation which first arose out of a growing social need to know the other – to share his or her perspectives – as someone who is more than a merely instrumental companion in the hunting and gathering of food. In more recent times, this dialogically refracted "self-awareness" has been progressively channelled by a whole battery of socio-discursive technologies of the self which foster social practices of "introspection". These technologies include: (1) the religious and later the psychoanalytical practices of the confession as a means of "revealing" "inner" truths about the self; (2) the pedagogical practices of reading aloud, followed by the transition to silent reading, which are functional in the construction of a pedagogical subjectivity in the elementary school; (3) the religious practices of silent prayer and communion with a transcendental (social) other, and so on.

All of these social practices foreground the dialogical act of looking at and gauging the self through the eyes of some real or imaginary social or cultural other. A further question to ask is: How are such thoroughly social and discursive technologies implicated in the co-evolution and the co-construction of complex relations of co-contextualization between the biological and the social semiotic dimensions of our embodied social being?

A good starting point in attempting to answer this question is the pre-linguistic semiosis of infants. Early infant semiosis reveals the critical importance of the other human being in the emergence of consciousness and agency in the human individual. The next section takes up this thread in our overall argument.

3 Brain activity regulates body–world relations at the same time that body–world relations organize and shape body-brain systems and functions

Consider the following discussion and related example from Halliday (1993):

> . . . typically, at 0;3 to 0;5 (years;months) babies are "reaching and grasping", trying to get hold of objects in the exterior domain and to reconcile this with their awareness of the interior domain (they can see the objects). Such an effort provokes the use of a sign, which is

then interpreted by the adult caregiver, or an older child, as a demand for explanation; the other responds in turn with an act of meaning. There has been "conversation" before; but this is a different kind of conversation, in which both parties are acting symbolically. A typical example from my own data would be the following, with the child at just under 0;6 (Halliday 1984a: 2):

There is a sudden loud noise from pigeons scattering.
Child [lifts head, looks round, gives high-pitched squeak]
Mother: Yes, those are birds. Pigeons. Aren't they noisy!

(Halliday 1993: 95)

The infant perceptually picks up information about an environmental event – the scattering pigeons – and responds to this event. The perceptual information that is picked up by the infant is then relayed as specific afferents from the receptor organs through specific thalamic nuclei to the primary cortical projections areas in the brain (Flohr 1991: 248). The neural networks that are activated as topological representations of spatio-temporal activity stand in no fixed or necessary relation to the external events that they are connected with. Instead, patterns of activity in real time generate multimodal correlations of stimulus information from various information sources. In this way, time-dependent categories of experience are built up that can be generalized to and integrated with other experiences in the past and the future. These categories are not symbols in the head, but patterns of activation of neural networks that can be contextually integrated with past, present, and possible future experiences in newly contingent ways. They stand in no fixed relation with environmental events and in this sense they can be said to be symbolic.

I have previously argued (Thibault 2004a: 241–246) that the infant's earliest pre-linguistic engagements with his or her immediate here-now environment in the dyad evidence proto-metafunctional characteristics. Language (not protolanguage) is **internally** organized along metafunctional lines. The metafunctional organization of language form is an order parameter (Haken 1984, 1988; Thibault 2004a: 245) which enslaves and entrains the component parts of language form to its principles of organization. At the same time, it provides context-sensitive principles that are internal to language itself and which relate language to its ecosocial and bodily contextual environments along a number of diverse, but interrelated, parameters. The full significance of this argument for the emergence of the metafunctional organization of language from the infant's protolanguage is developed in chapter 2, section 10. The metafunctions show how previously looser environmental constraints in relation to protolanguage are entrained to the internal organization of language and re-organized as intrinsic linguistic constraints on language form and function. The proto-metafunctional character of the infant's vocalization in Halliday's example will be discussed below. The metafunctional organization of language will be a recurrent theme in the following chapters. A few words about the metafunctions are therefore in order to clarify the meaning of this term before returning to the above example.

The relationship between the internal organization of language form – e.g. its lexicogrammar – and meaning has led Halliday and others working within the systemic-functional framework to postulate the existence of a small number of diverse functional regions known as the metafunctions in order to explain the always fluid, dynamic, and contextualized nature of the ways in which language forms relate to meaning in context. According to Halliday (e.g. 1979a), the content stratum of language – viz. its lexicogrammar and semantics – is internally organized in terms of a small number of very general functional regions which are simultaneously inter-woven and configured in the internal organization of lexicogrammatical form. These functional regions correspond to the experiential, interpersonal, textual, and logical dimensions of lin-guistic meaning, respectively. Experiential meaning interprets the phenomena of the world as categories of experience, as configurations of, for example, clause-level process-types (actions, events, states, and so on), the participants that take part in these, and the circumstances that may be attendant upon them. Experiential meaning relations are realized in the grammar as particulate or part-whole structures which are based on the principle of constituency. Interpersonal meaning is concerned with the grammatical resources for organizing language as interaction (cf. speech acts, dialogic moves), the expression of attitudinal and evaluative orientations (modality), and the taking up and negotiating of particular subjective positions in discourse. Typically, interpersonal meaning is expressed by field-like prosodies rather than particle-like segments. Textual meaning is concerned with the organization of language into semantically coherent text in relation to its context. It is concerned with the distribution of information in text, continuity of reference, and lexico-semantic cohesion. Textual meanings tend to be realized by wave-like peaks of prominence. Logical meaning is concerned with relations of causal and temporal interdependency between, say, clauses. Logical meanings are realized by recursive structures which add one element to another so as to build up more complex structures.

The proto-metafunctional character of the child's vocalization can be described in the following terms. The infant's vocalization:

1. directs the attention of both members of the dyad to a given phenomenon of experience (the pigeons) such that both infant and mother can be said to be coordinated in a joint frame of attention whereby they attend to the given phenomenon *qua* experience; in this sense the infant's utterance has proto-experiential characteristics;
2. requires both members of the dyad to see the other as taking up reciprocal, dialogically coordinated roles, which I shall gloss here as "requiring the other to attend to the particular phenomenon of interest" (infant) and "responding to and engaging in joint attention to phenomenon" (parent); in this sense, it is proto-interpersonal;
3. gives shape, texture and unity to the space-time of the dyad relative to the points of action operated by the two participants and the perspectives that these afford; in this sense, it shows proto-textual characteristics.

What we see here is how, given certain conditions, a relatively incoherent system – the infant and his mother were not previously engaged in a specific dialogic exchange – may spontaneously cohere. Information is then more constrained as more subsystems (movement, protolinguistic vocalization, language, gaze, point gesture, posture, and so on), interact with each other as new higher-order boundary conditions now modulate the previously looser, less coherent arrangement in the form of the dyad which is constituted by the interaction of the two participants. Moreover, these early protolinguistic activities of infants show very clearly the cross-modal basis of their utterances, as well as the link between perception and semiosis. In the above example, the infant correlates movement (head turning), auditory and visual inputs (the scattering of the pigeons), and his vocalization. This correlation is achieved on the basis of the dynamical features which link all these modalities to the same phenomenon in the infant's spatial-temporal purview as the infant jointly orients to the given phenomenon *qua* sharable experience.

In this way, we may see how perception directly contributes to the emergence of semiotic (e.g. linguistic) activity. Repeated experiences in time – both real time and from one occasion to another – of orienting to particular phenomena and using the cross-modally correlated resources of perception, action, and vocalization to jointly coordinate that orientation with others suggest that the separation between language, perception, and action (movement) is unwarranted. Perception and action both entail categorization on the basis of the reentrant mapping of cross-modal inputs from diverse information sources. Moreover, the accumulated experience of particular bodily orientations to and perceptions of phenomena, in conjunction with more senior partners in proto-dialogue, provides a basis for the emergence and development of linguistic categories. In such a view, there is no dichotomous separation between categories obtained through direct perception and abstract linguistic knowledge, seen as independent of specific sensori-motor modalities.

The child's body-brain activity is integrated to and entrained by higher-scalar arrangements that progressively take on the shape of the metafunctions as the system self-organizes in time. That this is not merely an artifact of the theoretical perspective itself is borne out by the way in which the mother contextually integrates the child's vocalization in ways that correspond to all three of the parameters described above. That is, she (1) attends to the same environmental event *qua* phenomenon of (shared) attention and experience; (2) she responds to the infant as a partner in dialogue in which both participants are assigned reciprocally defined and dialogically coordinated speaking and listening positions; and (3) both participants and their contributions cohere into a larger whole whose texture and unity on its space-time scale, where the perspectives of both participants come into play, is made possible both by lower-scalar initiating conditions on their (smaller) space-time scales and higher-scalar boundary conditions or constraints on their (larger) space-time scales. All three space-time scales are seamlessly interwoven into the event and contribute to its semiotic cohesion and texture in space-time.

The child orients to the adult member of the dyad as an agent who is able to bring about desired outcomes in the world on the child's behalf. We can call this the proto-imperative orientation. In this case, the outcome is to draw the mother's attention to the pigeons. The child at this stage in his development is unable explicitly to represent his own relationship to the pigeons to others. His protolinguistic vocalization is devoid of any capacity for experiential categorization in this sense. More precisely, he is unable to explicitly represent his own interpretation of the event to others. Interpretation for the infant is highly implicit and sensori-motor or procedural. The child can attend to the perceived phenomenon in the situation, but he cannot explicitly interpret his attending to it to others. However, the child's squeak is directed at the mother as the socially relevant other in the dyad who is able to provide such an interpretation.

In other words, the child directs the squeak at the mother, who is interpreted as an agent who is able to attend to the same phenomenon (the pigeons, in this case) and to respond to it. The point is that the child is in possession of an implicit or procedural understanding of the other (the mother) as an **intentional agent** who is able to bring about the outcome desired by the child. In this sense, the child has an implicit point of view, based on sensori-motor imagery, at the same time that he is an explicit point of action owing to the indexical capacity of the squeak to point to or indicate the particular phenomenon of interest and to secure the mother's interest. The child perceives the given situation, utters the squeak, engages the mother and therefore directs the mother's attention to the same phenomenon. In other words, the child's action acts on the mother and her focus of attention such that the two agent's attention is focused on the same phenomenon.

Trevarthen (1978) has pointed out that infants have an in-built ability to orient to other persons as subjectivities and to distinguish them from inanimate objects from the very earliest stages of their life. It is on this basis that infants can orient to others as agents who can bring about the desired goals of the infant at the same time that the co-agency of infant and parent which is constructed in and through the exchange jointly accesses (attends to) the same phenomenon of experience. The infant's ability to do this even at a very early age before the onset of language is based on his or her ability to interpret the other as an agent who is able to stand in the requisite relationship with the world. As I said before, this interpretation is entirely implicit or procedural and not at this stage liable to explicit representation in a shareable format. Instead, the child utters a protolinguistic vocalization which functions indexically to direct and to coordinate the mother's attention to the relevant feature of the situation. Protolinguistic utterances are indexical in the sense that their meaning and relevance are situation-dependent at the same time that the knowledge of the situation is based on implicit procedure. The child attends to and interprets iconic-indexical aspects of the mother's activity as indicative of her stances on the world. In this way, the infant can direct the mother's attention (gaze, body orientation, pointing, and so on) and interpret the mother and the given phenomenon as being linked by a shared vector of interest or attention. However, the infant cannot explicitly represent the other's attending to the object.

What we see here is much more than the infant's orienting to and interpreting the other. Rather, the infant attends to and interprets in sensori-motor imagery a protolinguistic format that may be schematized as follows: [OTHER-VECTOR-WORLD]. That is, the child interprets an entire action schema, connecting the other to the world, with its implicit categories and relations. In time, such schemas become sensitive to and therefore come to classify a variety of different situation types and the participant roles in these, as well as the subjective stances of the participants on the situation and each other's roles in it. When these schemas are explicitly represented in thought before this occurs in language, the infant has developed the capacity to reflect on and to interpret such schemas off-line. In this way, these off-line or unsituated representations in thought can themselves become objects of conscious attention and reflection. Thus, the child's interpretation of the other's relations to the world is an interpretation of a domain of experience based on the dyadic relation between "you" and "me", where the focus is on the child's interpretation of the **other** or the "you" as an agent who can enact certain kinds of relations with the world so as to bring about the infant's desired goal.

This relation, based on the above schema, can be expanded and represented as follows: [I WANT [*YOU-ACTION VECTOR-DESIRED OBJECT/ACTION*]], where the italics indicate the domain of explicit interpretative focus and representation in contrast to the child's own agency and selfhood, which is not at this stage the focus of interpretation. This comes later. The point is that it is the focus on and interpretation of proto-interpersonal formats involving OTHER-VECTOR-WORLD relations that pave the way for and later make possible the focus on the self and the self's own relations to the world. At the present stage, the child has implicit proximate intentions which inform and motivate the squeak as the beginning of an action trajectory that extends from the child's immature body-brain system into the environment and engages with the other in the way already described. At the same time, the child has no means of explicitly representing himself as the source of the trajectory and its effects in the world. However, this other-centred interpretation of agency and its relations to the world forms the basis for the eventual closing of the loop on the "me" sector of the loop. Consequently, a meta-level self-perspective arises which is able to interpret the self, its own agency, and, hence, its own viewpoints and how these relate to the world, including the ways in which others see the self.

The closing of the loop on the "me" sector gives rise to the following kind of schema. In this schema, the focus is on the interpretation of the self and the self's relations to the world and how others see the self's relations to the world, as follows: [SELF-VECTOR-WORLD]-OTHER. Both (self)consciousness and agency in the self emerge in this way. Agency implies that the self is a point of action at the same time that the self has viewpoints and perspectives that inform and modulate the action trajectories that are sourced at the self. Consciousness implies that the self has viewpoints and that these viewpoints can be focused on particular phenomena or on the actions that the self performs in the world. The child's protolinguistic vocalization in our example is an action in this sense. As such, it is explicit, whereas the child's representation of his self's relation to the world (the pigeons, say) is entirely implicit. The latter, as we saw above is based on imagistic, procedural, and sensori-motor representations.

Importantly, the action schemas described above are not just action, but **interaction**. In both cases, they are constituted by a dialogically organized loop, though the focus is different in the two cases – on the other in the first instance and on the self in the second. The importance of the dialogical nature of this loop cannot be underestimated. This importance can be explained as follows: the child's very earliest models of agency, his or her organized viewpoints, and his or her focused attention on particular objects organize action trajectories. These trajectories, which have their source in the agent, are not, in the first instance, based on sensori-motor representations of physical agency in the physical world, or of the agent's engagements with the physical world (cf. Lakoff and Johnson 1999; see chapters 10 and 11). Rather, the dialogic closure that is characteristic of the primary intersubjectivity in the early months of the infant's life gives rise to and stimulates the emergence of action schemas which have their basis in the **interpersonal** transactions between infant and more senior others in the dyads in which the infant participates. Consciousness and agency emerge in the individual in and through the individual's transactions with others – especially more senior, enculturated others – such that the body-brain dynamics of the infant are, over time, entrained to and reorganized by these transactions.

The transformation of the other-centred focus to a self-centred one goes hand in hand with the self's emerging awareness of its own perspectives and interpretations of its own relations to the world (see above). Agency and consciousness are increasingly grounded in the self and its viewpoints. In the former, other-centred perspective, which is characteristic of the proto-imperative mode, the action trajectory is grounded in the here-now and I-you of the dyad. Thus, the action trajectory is grounded, in the sense of being located with respect to the speech event, as occurring simultaneously with the speech event in the here-now as well as being "desired" by the speaker. It is also simultaneously grounded as being tied to the "you" – the second person other – in the transaction as the agent who will carry out the action. It will be remembered that self-representations at this stage are entirely implicit in procedural or sensori-motor representations and cannot be explicitly represented to the self (or the other). The shift in focus to the self also means a shift in grounding such that the action trajectory is tied to the "I" in the here-now of the speech event.

The emergence of a self-perspective therefore entails the capacity to tie one's action trajectories to the here-now-I perspective as a point of reference – viz. a point of view and a point of action – in relation to the ground of the speech event. The self's consciousness and agency are therefore internally linked to both the here-now and to the I-you of the speech event. The indexical nature of the child's protolinguistic utterances means that these utterances are always simultaneous with the here-now dimension without the possibility of their being encoded as temporally removed from the ground either in the past or in the future. Likewise, the action trajectory can only be grounded in relation to the I-you of the dyad; it cannot at this stage be tied to third persons outside the speech event and in relation to which the self can take up viewpoints and adopt or propose courses of action. These two possibilities come later with the emergence of the triadic perspective that is characteristic of secondary intersubjectivity and its proto-indicative mode of intersubjectivity.

The "outward directed" character of secondary subjectivity, as illustrated in Halliday's example, brings about an "extension" and an "enlargement" of the child's *Umwelt* (Harré 1990: 300). This expansion is afforded by the expanding material and semiotic resources at the child's disposal. Without these resources, the child would remain in the semiotically compressed world of "you and me". The move into secondary intersubjectivity entails a fundamental reorganization of the dyad. What might this imply for the self-organization of the infant as an internally complex social being?

In Flohr's terms, self-organizing associative nets in the brain create topological representations of spatio-temporal patterns (events, objects, and so on) in the world. Such patterns are matter-energy flows and perturbations which impact upon the consciousness of the individual. These topological representations are not, of course, endowed with any pre-given semantic or "cognitive" content. Nevertheless, these dynamical processes on their scalar level (neural activity) are contextually integrated with bodily activities and discourse-level meanings and events on their very different scalar levels. Perceptual and other categories are not stored at particular locations in the brain as copies of the things they represent (Edelman 1992).

The grounding of the action trajectory in the speech event is afforded by the body-brain system's constructions of the environment – the dyad – in which it is immersed and in which it participates, rather than some absolute external yardstick (Damasio 1996 [1994]: xviii). What is it that enables mother and child jointly to focus on the same phenomenon? How does the self and the agency that is sourced at the self emerge? On what basis? I suggested above that self emerges from an initial focus on otherness. In my view, the emergence of self and therefore of consciousness and agency has its basis in what I have elsewhere referred to, following Bråten (1992, 1998), as the dialogic closure that characterizes the mother–infant dyad in primary intersubjectivity (see Thibault 2000a). The dyad that links mother and infant is itself a self-organizing system with its own internal dynamics. It is the system as a whole which individuates along its temporal trajectory and not just its lower-scalar component parts. The dialogic closure of the dyad means that the dyad is a stable, self-organizing system that is successively organized and reorganized into a more complex and finely differentiated system. Moreover, the dialogic closure of the dyad constitutes a **social** environment in which the affect-laden meaning exchanges between mother and infant take place.

Contrary to the embodied realism of Lakoff and Johnson (e.g. 1999), I do not think that the physical transactions between an infant and its environment provide the primary impetus for development and individuation. Instead, the infant's transactions with the mother are socially organized and constrained from birth. In agreement with Trevarthen (1978, 1998) and Bråten (1992, 1998), I argue that these social transactions and therefore the initial orientation to the other provide both the environment and the stimulus for the emergence of consciousness, agency, self, and so on. The same argument applies, in my view, to the later emergence of metaphor (see chapters 10 and 11). As we saw above, the earliest action formats that emerge are based on these interpersonal-social transactions between mother and infant. The challenges and complexities of these social engagements require the honing of skills and powers of interpretation that are considerably more complex than those required by the physical environment. Furthermore, the inherently dialogic nature of the dyad and hence of the ways in which mother and infant orient to and interpret each other's actions from their respective points of view itself provides the basis for the emergence of the ability to interpret others and the self, the relations between self and an increasingly wide range of different others, and the ability to reflect reflexively and to interpret self–other relations across increasingly greater space-time scales in ways that do not depend on the immediate here-now material context.

The action trajectories of the self are routed not only through the internal dynamics of the self; they are also routed through the others with whom the self interacts. In the dyad, dialogically organized forms of social interaction and the affective links between mother and infant that these entail provide the self with ways of relating to the other. Thus, the infant, say, learns to interpret the mother's actions, affective dispositions, intentions, and so on, as ways in which the mother relates to the world. The infant also comes to understand that he or she has a repertoire of actions and categories that enable him or her to harness others – initially the mother – in order to achieve the infant's desires and goals, as we saw above. The infant's emerging selfhood does not result in the first instance from the infant's relations to the world, but, rather, from the infant's efforts to act upon and to interpret the other's relations to the world. Thus, the action trajectories which link the other (e.g. the mother) to the world along some vector of, say, interest, attention, emotional response, and so on, provide a basis for the development of interpretive schemas of action and reflection which link different domains in some kind of relationship. The linking of these domains is based on forms of intelligence that are stimulated and developed by specifically **social** transactions rather than physical ones. Metaphor itself can be seen as arising at a later developmental stage out of this prior ability (chapter 11, section 2.2).

The infant's initial orientation to the other, along with the structured contributions that both mother and infant make to the dyad, is a form of adaptive activity. More complex forms of organization evolve in and through this activity as the infant system progressively differentiates itself from the mother and develops the capacity to interpret the world from the point of view of the self, rather than the other. The system becomes more and more individuated. The emergence of the self entails the system's increasing differentiation into a more complexly organized system on many levels of organization in which new functions and components emerge. These properties have important implications for the notions of consciousness, self, agency, meaning, point of view, and the action trajectories which are sourced at particular agents in relation to their points of view at the same time that these same trajectories interact with those of other agents on diverse space-time scales.

The mother-infant dyad is a system that allows interpretation and meaning-making to occur. In Peirce's terms, such a system is a thirdness. The individual interpreter is a firstness. The interpretation of the signs he or she encounters is a secondness. Interpretation takes place through the agency of the interpreter *qua* firstness. In this way, selfhood – viz. agency and consciousness – develops as a result of the interpreter's discovery of the thirdness that emerges through the process of interpretation of the signs *qua* secondnesses that it encounters. The dyad as a whole affords these processes of reciprocal interpretation at the same time that it affords the expansion and evolution of the infant's Meaning System. From the infant's perspective, the dyad allows social transactions to take place such that the infant's body-brain dynamics are in time entrained to the cultural dynamics that the mother alone is connected to in the earliest stages of primary intersubjectivity.

Rather than a dichotomy or opposition between the biological and cultural facets of the child's development, the dialogic closure of the dyad affords social transactions which mediate between and reorganize the biological and cultural levels of organization (Thibault 2000a). These processes of reorganization give rise to the progressive emergence along the individual's trajectory of iconic followed by indexical followed by symbolic modes of meaning-making. This semiotic progression is a developmental sequence which has important implications for the emergence of agency and consciousness in the individual, as we shall see in later chapters. The semiotic progression outlined here can be thought about in terms of the specification hierarchy of integrative levels proposed by Salthe (1993: 52–74).

A specification hierarchy in the sense defined by Salthe entails a hierarchical arrangement of levels of generality of statement (Salthe 1993: 66). A specification hierarchy comprises a series of integrative levels in which the more highly specified levels are progressively nested within the less specified. The more specified levels both (1) correspond most closely to the macroscopic phenomena of human experience and perception and hence our viewpoints and perspectives; and (2) act as boundary conditions or constraints on the less specified levels (Salthe 1993: 67). A specification hierarchy provides a multiplicity of interrelated perspectives on a given phenomenon. The progression from "most general" to "most specific" implies a discursive ordering of our experience of some object.

Two examples of specification hierarchies are: (1) physical → chemical → biological → social semiotic → individual psychological; and (2) vertebrate → mammal → primate → human. In both examples, the progression from "most general" to "most specified" entails a progression from "most simple" to "most complex" (Salthe 1993: 68), or from more vague or less defined to more detailed and more specified. The lower integrative levels are the foundation on the basis of which more highly specified levels may be described. For example, all biological organisms that we know of obey the laws of physical nature, without, however, being explanatorily or causally reducible to these. As I shall show in more detail in chapter 3, the progression from iconic to indexical and symbolic modes of semiosis can be seen as a specification-integration hierarchy in this sense and can accordingly be related to the development of consciousness in the individual (see also Thibault 2000a: 301–303; Thibault 2004a).

Figure 1.1 shows the two-way or transitive nature of the relations among levels in the specification hierarchy. Thus, a lexicogrammatical unit in language is a symbolic sign at the same time that it also has iconic and indexical properties and functions. A linguistic sign can therefore be analysed at different integrative levels (Salthe 1993: 64) because the given sign has more general

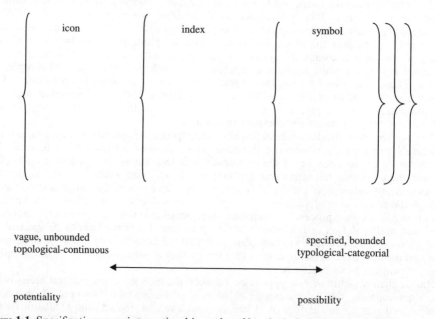

icon   index   symbol

vague, unbounded   specified, bounded
topological-continuous   typological-categorial

←——————————————————————————→

potentiality   possibility

Figure 1.1 Specification-cum-integration hierarchy of iconic, indexical, and symbolic modes of semiosis, seen as a system of integrative levels extending from the most general to the most specified properties

and more specified properties (Thibault 2004a: chap. 3). The symbolic level is the innermost class, as Figure 1.1 shows. The outermost class (iconic) is therefore conceptually subordinated to the innermost class (symbolic). Conceptual subordination means that there is a system of nested levels of degrees of specification going from the outermost to the innermost (Salthe 1993: 64).

This progression corresponds to the developmental sequence of semiosis in the infant such that the most specified stage cannot be reached until the prior stages have been traversed. Each level of the hierarchy indicates the semiotic-categorial reach of the sign-maker at any given stage of his or her development. Moreover, the logical transitivity of the relations among levels means that the acquiring of a new level does not mean that the prior levels have been transcended. Rather, the acquisition of a new stage means that the prior stages are re-organized and integrated to the new perspective. An agent with symbolic capacities integrates the prior iconic and indexical capacities and perspectives to the new capacities and perspectives afforded by the symbolic level.

4 Brain activity is contextually integrated to and participates in discourse

The cognitive-representational model of knowledge presupposes some form of isomorphism between the "real" external world and the knowledge the system has, or acquires, of this. I should like to propose an alternative model, which is, in part, based on Varela's notion of "organized closure". This model starts from quite a different premise, which may be defined as constructivist. Instead of the language of stimuli which the organism receives from the outside as instructions to be acted on, we have a view of the individual as an active explorer of his or her environment. In the cybernetic model, data, stimuli, and so on, have to be taken from the environment and assembled, or processed, as information through some process of association.

In the area of visual perception, Gibson (1986 [1979]) has proposed an alternative to this view. Gibson argues that organisms can discriminate information in their environment in species-specific ways which are relevant to their further development and survival in their ecologically specific niche. Gibson's point is that while there may, to some extent, be an innate, biological basis for this, much of what is perceptually learned occurs through the organism's active exploration of its ecological niche. This process of "active exploration" is not an individualistic one. Rather, it takes place through the necessarily dialogic and intersubjective structures of action and recognition which are potentially available to the individuals who inhabit a specific niche. Such a niche, in the case of the human species, is always a socially and historically specific cross-coupling of the physical-material and the semiotic-discursive domains (Lemke 1995a, 1995b).

Material-phenomenal experiences are the result, in the first instance, of our perceptual pick up, in Gibson's sense, of matter-energy flows and perturbations in the ambient flux. The various perceptual systems are transducers which selectively attend to variants and invariants in the ambient flux, which are in turn construed as information about environmental events. The stimulus energy that excites or stimulates the receptors can be said to stand in an indexical relation to the corresponding change that is brought about in the receptors whenever they are so excited. This indexical relation is a requirement of what Salthe (1993: 178) calls the "fittingness of receptors to external stimuli". However, once this information has entered the central nervous system, it is no longer indexical. Instead, it is at least potentially symbolic because it no longer stands in any necessary relation to external events.

The relevant system of relations is hierarchically organized in terms of three levels. The three-level hierarchical system which I have derived can be formalized as follows:

L+1   Environment of animal *qua* system of interpretance which brings into relation (mediates) animal and its affordances and provides the higher-scalar principles whereby these affordances and their relation to the animal can be interpreted in ways that afford perception and action;

L   The focal level of the animal's engagements with the affordances that it encounters in its environment;

L–1   The biological and other physical-material properties of organisms **and** environmental affordances that enable them and predispose them to engage in transactions with one another and selected aspects of their environment.

The material correlation between the stimulus energy and the response it causes or stimulates in a receptor is a particular configuration of matter-energy flows on level L–1. This correlation is indexical. Such matter-energy flows on this level are not detectable by the observer system on level L+1. Nevertheless, these flows do constitute information on the microscopic level of L–1 interactions that affords its re-organization on level L as information about environmental events that is salient and meaningful to a higher-scalar perceptual system involving the body-brain in its environment on level L+1. The information on this level is already potentially symbolic for the reasons given above.

We do not hear sound waves or see light rays as such, although these stimulate the receptors and are transduced into neural activity in the central nervous system. What we do perceive is information about some macroscopic environmental event that is relevant to us and which in some way affords us possibilities for action and meaning relative to the macroscopic environment in which we live. In Gibson's view, there is information in the world that affords its pick up by the infant by virtue of the dynamical relation that links infant to the environment. In this view, the infant is pre-adapted to orient to and explore its ecosocial semiotic environment in the form of the mother–infant dyad in order to obtain information from it, rather than being in possession of knowledge from the outset. The intrinsic value biases of the infant pre-adapt the infant to explore the environment, and it is in the process of this exploration that categorization and conceptual structures are built up.

Stimulus energy stimulates the receptors (e.g. the retina, the inner ear, and cochlea), but this is not the same as the stimulus information that light and sound give us about environmental objects and events (Gibson 1986 [1979]: 54–55). Stimulus information acts on an entire higher-scalar perceptual system, whereas stimulus energy (e.g. sound waves, light rays) stimulates the lower-scalar receptors. We do not perceive stimulus energy as such. Three-level hierarchy thinking provides a useful tool for thinking through the levels of relations involved here (see Salthe 1993: 36–46; Lemke 2000a: 183–185; Thibault 2004a).

Stimulus energy exists on a lower-scalar level (L–1) of matter-energy interactions than those that the organism is equipped to pick up and respond to. At the same time, level L–1 material interactions, which stimulate the receptors, thereby producing particular microscopic patterns of interaction between, for example, the light energy which enters the retina and the rods and cones in the retina of the eye, afford possibilities of their being reorganized on the next highest level L as macroscopic information which is interpretable from the perspective of the organism as information about salient environmental events. That is, the information on level L is interpretable as having semiotic salience within some system of interpretance on level L+1.

The system of interpretance that is in operation provides the organism with resources for contextually integrating the stimulus information that is picked up by the organism with environmental events in ways that are relevant to its activity and survival in its environment. It is in this way that the organism develops a repertoire of possibilities in its *Innenwelt*, in the form of patterns of neural activation, for both interpreting its environment, as well as for responding to it.

The activity of the brain regulates body–environment relations and interactions. Information that is picked up about events on the immediate here-now scale can thus be contextually integrated with information about past experiences at the same time that it constitutes a resource for interpreting and responding to possible future events. Stimulus information is macroscopic information that is salient for an organism in its ecological niche, relative to some system of interpretance in which such information is relevant and meaningful for organisms that operate that particular system of interpretance. It provides information about, or, more precisely, it can be interpreted by, an organism from the perspectives the environment makes available to that organism, as a phenomenon that affords the organism possibilities for meaning and action.

The same basic logic applies to both perception and social semiosis. Thus, the vocal tract activity of a speaker is an environmental event which provides listeners who operate the same higher scalar system of interpretance with acoustic information about the source of that event – the speaker's vocal tract activity and other bodily states – at the same time that the listener is able to integrate this information with a meaning that relates to some context on some other space-time scale beyond the immediate one in which the acoustic event was produced by the speaker's vocal tract activity. In this way, the signifying body is contextually integrated, though the mediating activity of semiosis, to meanings across diverse space-time scales.

Semiotic activity requires no prior representation of signs within some pre-existing system. The structure of semiotic activity self-organizes in relation to its ecosocial environment. There is no single locus of control in the form of internal programmes, competences, or plans. Rather, control is distributed along the entire trajectory that loops between organism and its ecosocial environment. The ambient flux of matter, energy, and information flows include both the self and the nonself and there is no a priori distinction between the two. Such distinctions are the result of the boundaries which are constructed in and through the exchanges of matter, energy, and information between the self and its environment and the consequent reorganization of the self's internal dynamics. Bateson (1973a [1972]: 287) has pointed out that in any system which has "mental characteristics", no part has unilateral control over the whole. Such characteristics are immanent in the whole (Thibault 1986a; Whitson 1997).

Three-level hierarchy thinking shows that lower scalar biological initiating conditions, such as the many degrees of topological freedom of the vocal tract, or of hand-arm movements, provide affordances and their own material constraints, without entailing a central programme that controls the entire system. A higher scalar system of interpretance in the ecosocial environment imposes boundary conditions on the kinds of organism–environment transactions that can occur on the intermediate level. Meaning-making activity is a result of the dynamical interplay of processes on all of these different levels such that the structure of the activity is shaped by the way it interfaces with the body-brain system, on the one hand, and with the ecosocial semiotic environment, on the other.

5 An outline of the arguments in this book

This book is divided into four parts. Each part is assigned a short title, which serves as a guide to the principle concerns of the chapters that belong to that part. Part I is entitled "Meaning and Discourse"; Part II "Agency, Otherness, and the Self"; Part III "Consciousness"; and Part IV "Metaphor and System Complexity". There is a logical relation of implication between the concerns of these four parts at the same time that the arguments in each part are conceptually integrated with each other. Thus, discourse and meaning are the backdrop against which the self and its agency emerge in and through the self's engagements with otherness. Consciousness, I argue, is a highly specified meaning-system in the perspective of the self. It can only emerge in individuals as a result of the self's agency along its trajectory at the same time that consciousness and its meanings entrain and modulate the agent's action trajectories. In order to think through the implications of this tangle of considerations, the old dualistic and mechanistic models and metaphors will no longer suffice. The two chapters in Part IV draw out some further implications for the dynamic systems thinking which has been a guiding thread throughout the entire study, as well as the previous study (Thibault 2004a). Metaphor and its explanation is central here. In discussing metaphor in this perspective, I shall also take issue with some of the central tenets of the "embodied realism" of Lakoff and Johnson (1999).

How can we connect consciousness and agency in the self with the higher-scalar level of the ecosocial semiotic system and its meanings? Chapter 2 explores some solutions to this question. In chapter 2, I argue that all forms of social semiosis are characterized by three very general parameters which are only analytically, though not constitutively, separable dimensions of all acts of meaning-making. The three aspects are as follows: (1) indexical meaning-making practices; (2) intertextual meaning-making practices; and (3) meta-discursive meaning-making practices (Thibault 2003a). I explore ways in which these three parameters can help us to construct an overall picture of the semiotic integration of meanings across many different space-and timescales.

Hans Bühler's (1990 [1934]) work on linguistic deixis provides a fertile point of entry into the question as to how bodily activity and the orientation of the body in its external environment are linked to the structure of consciousness. I also draw on Bakhtin's (1981) theory of social heteroglossia to consider the ways in which intentional, individuating acts of meaning-making (semiogenesis) are always a selective reenvoicement, to use Dore's (1989) term, of the diversity of social voices that constitute the system of social heteroglossia in a given community. This insight also proves suggestive for considering how specific voices and their associated values, when re-envoiced by social agents in their own inner self-referential perspective, are attractors which are embodied in the landscape of the individual's semantic neurological space. This has important implications for the analysis of how intentions, motivations, and affective orientations are channelled by the agent's identification with specific axiological positions in the ecosocial system.

The four chapters in Part II take up different aspects of this last point. Chapter 3 is concerned with the closely related issues of agency and individuation. The focus of this chapter is early infant semiosis. Its point of departure is the dialogic closure (Bråten 1992, 1998; Thibault 2000a) that is characteristic of the mother–infant dyads in the phase identified by Trevarthen (1978, 1987, 1992, 1998) as "primary intersubjectivity". In interacting with each other, the two members of the dyad give rise to the dialogic closure whereby emergent order and organization become discernible by virtue of the contextual constraints operating on level L+1. These considerations form the backdrop for a discussion of how individuals not only undergo developmental change, but they also individuate.

The case for the distinction between development and individuation is convincingly put forward by Salthe (e.g. 1993: 147–151). Development has to do with perceived regularities of change, seen as instantiations of the type. Development is predictable. Individuation, by contrast, is the irreversible accumulation of historical-biographical experiences, meanings, and so on, as a result of contextual contingencies – both material and semiotic – that are both internal to the organism and external to it. It is, by definition, unpredictable. Individuation refers to the accumulated processes in time that leave their mark on the self's trajectory and hence distinguish one's self from other selves. These considerations lead naturally and logically enough into questions of agency. The emergence of a self-referential perspective will be seen to be crucial here. A self-referential perspective is a historically emergent property of the individuating trajectory of a self-organizing system.

In chapter 4, I suggest that the interactive play of children around the age of 4 to 5 years provides an environment in which the child's ability to think beyond the here and now and to imagine and hypothesize alternative situations and realities, as well as the self's links to both past situations and possible future ones is greatly enhanced. In the play context, children at this stage greatly increase their capacity to see things from the other's point of view and also see that others have different desires, intentions, and viewpoints. In this way, the child learns to interpret things from the point of view of the other, as well as to posit in language and in imagination alternative relations between other and world and between self and world. In the process, the child learns (1) that others are selves with their own points of view and points of action and (2) that other selves are distinct from one's own self. Social intelligence is therefore massively expanded in this stage and with it the capacity to think and reason in ways that are the prototypes of metaphorical thinking itself. The expanding capacity to see things the way an increasing diversity of others see things goes hand in hand with an expanding ability to create semiotic links and trajectories between self and others on ever larger space-time scales.

In chapter 5, which is an extended reflection on the nature and significance of what Piaget (e.g. 1959) and Vygotsky (1986 [1934], 1987 [1934]) referred to as egocentric speech, I argue that this form of discourse is about the turn to the interpretation of the self and the self's relations to others in the context of the social processes in which the self participates. Egocentric speech is a process of self-interpretation, self-monitoring, and self-commanding which is focused on the self's relations to the world. These self–world relations are becoming increasingly differentiated from other–world relations at the same time that they are becoming increasingly less dependent on the here-now scale. The self constructs self–world–other relations in terms of the self's take up and negotiation of the interpersonal semantics of propositions and proposals and the modalized stances that one can adopt towards these. Thus, the self and its agency can be enacted and negotiated in and through the self's relations to and stances towards propositions and proposals, now seen as explicitly manipulable in the perspective of the self as a point of action. At the same time, the re-envoicement of actions and points of view in the self-perspective represents the progression towards and the further differentiation and elaboration of an inner self-referential perspective.

Chapter 6 focuses on the developing capacity mentioned above to create semiotic links across an increasing diversity of space-time scales. I also show in this chapter how the child learns to re-envoice in the perspective of the self the perspectives that the world affords. Metaphor in sound plays a key role in this process in the case that I shall consider in that chapter.

The three chapters in Part III move the question of consciousness centre stage. In chapters 7 and 8, the emergence of a self-reflexive perspective is a central theme. In agreement with Bogdan (2000: 148–149), I begin chapter 7 with the argument that a "state" of consciousness is a relation between self and world; it is not a state *per se*. The problem is to explain how (human) consciousness is recognizable in a given system of interpretance by self and others as a relation between self and world in the perspective of the self who undergoes the particular experience. In this perspective, acts of consciousness (1) can be represented as having Meaning System contextualization relations in some system of interpretance; and (2) are constrained by the supersystem (Interaction System) transactions in which they are embedded (Lemke 1984a: 120–121; Thibault 2004a: 264–267).

With these considerations in mind, I develop a critique of the notion of intrinsic non-inferential awareness. This critique serves as the springboard for an account of the relationship between the notions of consciousness and conscience that is inspired by an insightful discussion of Natsoulas on the inter- and intra-personal dimensions of these two notions. Harking back to chapter 2, we will see that the perspectives and associated values which the self acquires along its trajectory are selective re-envoicements of voices and their associated values in the system – the state space – of social heteroglossia of some community. We shall see how the ability to internally recognize and appraise one's actions and states of consciousness – i.e. the possession of a conscience – means that higher-scalar contextual constraints embody ethics and values, along with the possibility of selecting from an increasingly differentiated repertoire of moral values, which impose constraints on the lower-level dynamics of our own states of consciousness and our own action trajectories.

Chapter 9 moves Lemke's (1999) Principle of Alternation to centre stage. In chapter 9, I begin with the problem of how the organism as a whole mediates the interaction on the lower-scalar level of the perceptual pick up of stimulus information about its environment by means of the dynamics of **higher**-scalar sensori-motor and neural dynamics. I argue that when this occurs the organism is responding to and adapting to information about a given environmental event on the basis of a system of interpretance which is stored in its central nervous system. This internalization of a higher-scalar system of interpretance is a consequence of the ways in which the organism's own trajectory has entrained its internal dynamics to those of the higher-scalar ecosocial system in which the organism is embedded.

I then analyse, with reference to the lexicogrammar of a wine-tasting text, how each new emergent level serves to reorganize one type of semiotic information from the level below it as another type for the level above it. The linguistic construal of taste and smell in a wine-tasting text serves as a useful sounding board for this discussion. Once these basic principles have been established, the remainder of this chapter is mainly concerned with showing how the mapping of semiotic functions onto organizational scales has dynamical implications for the emergence of consciousness. I then postulate, on the basis of the Principle of Alternation, six different levels of closure across the diverse organizational scales involved in order to explain the emergence of (self)consciousness. These levels range from the notion of material closure to what I call self-referential closure. Following the logic of the three-level hierarchy (see section 3), a further development in this chapter is an investigation into how new emergent levels of organization come into existence *between* already existing scalar levels. I show how Halliday's account of the emergence of language from protolanguage in the infant is compatible with this view.

Part IV is about metaphor. Chapters 10 and 11 continue the discussion of the Principle of Alternation, but give it a new focus. In these chapters, I consider some of the ways in which metaphor raises fundamental questions about the relationship between semiotics and the dynamics of complex self-organizing systems. Metaphor, I suggest, can help us to understand how the complexity of such systems arises from the emergence of new levels of organization over their history. Metaphor is a newly emergent level of organization in the dynamics of the system which functions to reorganize variety on the level below as meaning for the level above. In this way, both the semiotic and the dynamical closure of system levels are reopened to allow the development and evolution of greater complexity.

The theory of metaphor advanced by Lakoff and Johnson is critically discussed in the light of theoretical alternatives that I propose in relation to linguistic and non-linguistic semiotic modalities. I conclude that language and other semiotic modalities emerge from the primordial many degrees of freedom of the prior, sensori-motor based modalities of semiosis which constitute our earliest, always embodied, always semiotically mediated, transactions with the topological richness and variety of the physical-material processes and flows of the world in which we are immersed. By the same token, language and the other modalities alluded to here are seamlessly and dynamically interwoven with the primordial many degrees of freedom of our topologically mediated material interactivity with the world.

PART I
Meaning and Discourse

2

The Semiotic Mediation of Consciousness in Social Meaning-making

1 The diverse semantic scales of meaning-making

Symbolic consciousness implicates much greater space-time scales than the organismic one *per se*. This fact can be explained in terms of the nested hierarchy of iconic, indexical, and symbolic modes of semiosis (chapter 1, section 3). As we have seen, this hierarchy of integrative levels implicates progressively larger scales as one proceeds from the innermost to the outermost levels of the hierarchy. Symbolic meaning-making in particular is based on the production of discourse. The production of discourse implicates processes on a number of very different scales ranging from the organismic to the ecosocial. The production of discourse is not confined to spatial scales of metres within the immediate purview of the organism, or to timescales of the order of the composition of the successive clauses which constitute a given text production. This characteristic of discourse production means that human consciousness is itself extended and transformed by the possibilities which texts afford for the semantic or semiotic integration of meanings across many different space- and timescales. Linguists who have worked on the semantics of discourse have demonstrated how discourses consist of a hierarchy of units at the semantic level (Hasan 1996a: 117). Hasan has proposed the semantic unit message, as follows:

> Seen from above [i.e. from the contextual level], it is the smallest significant semiotic action that an interactant might take in the context of an interaction so as to affect its character . . . On the basis of these enquiries, I would propose a four-unit rank scale at the semantic level; moving from the largest to the smallest these are: text, rhetorical unit, message and text radical.
>
> (Hasan 1996a: 117–118)

Hasan's hierarchy of semantic units shows that meanings in texts are made on a diversity of semantic scales that cannot be made on the scale of a single message unit. A further dimension of this question concerns the semantic scales that are built up over very large-scale (inter)textual spans that go beyond the relatively short text spans typically analysed by linguists. This question addresses the kinds of semantic scales that are built up in time over the reading of an entire book, but it also concerns the semantic scales that are built up over the months and years of interaction between, say, the members of a family unit or between two friends, or over the historical-biographical or lifespan trajectory of an individual.

I have elsewhere (Thibault 2003a) proposed three generalized parameters which are characteristic of all forms of social meaning-making, as follows:

i.   indexical meaning-making practices;
ii. intertextual meaning-making practices;
iii. meta-discursive meaning-making practices.

These three parameters are analytically, though not constitutively, separable dimensions of all social meaning-making. The fundamental question at stake here is: how can these three parameters of social meaning-making help us to explain the semiotic integration of meanings across many different space- and timescales? How is human consciousness extended and transformed in the way suggested above? The three parameters I am proposing specify a number of very general meaning-making strategies that apply to all modalities of semiosis. That is, I shall argue that they can provide us with a conceptually unified framework for theorizing the semiotic mediation of consciousness in ecosocial networks of human activity across diverse space-time scales.

2 Indexical meaning-making practices and the semiotic grounding of consciousness

Consciousness is always grounded relative to an intentional source, or a viewpoint, which I define in terms of the notion of SELF (chapter 7). It is always connected to multiple spatial, temporal, and other contextual connections and the trajectories of selves which may extend near or far in space and time. These connections and trajectories function to give texture to our experience of the world and our place in it. The linguistic notion of texture (Halliday and Hasan 1976) is our starting point here (see also Hasan 1999). Texture refers to the properties of discourse which produce both intra-textual and extra-textual coherence. The notion of texture provides insights into the ways in which all forms of semiosis, wherever they are situated in terms of the presupposition-cum-specification hierarchy of icon, index, and symbol, constitute a many levelled trajectory comprising richly interconnected patterns of relations. These patterned relations do not only give the unfolding semiotic event *qua* discourse a felt sense of coherence and wholeness, but they also extend this same sense of coherence and wholeness into the contextual environment in which the discourse is functioning. The textured nature of semiotic events can only be adequately accounted for in terms of the dynamic, open, and complex nature of the relations between semiotic acts and their contexts. They cannot be adequately accounted for in terms of fixed rules or principles of logical induction. Instead, the textured character of the multi-levelled and intricate relations that ground us in our trajectories in space, in time, in society, and in culture, emphasizes the instantial nature of meaning-making and of consciousness itself.

The instantial dimension of meaning-making highlights the need for a renewed understanding of the specific, the particular, the situated nature of our being and embodiment, and of difference and variation. For these reasons, the textured nature of semiosis has important implications for our discussion of consciousness. Higher-order consciousness, in particular, which is constituted by and embedded in contexts of meaning-making extending across and integrating very many diverse space-time scales, cannot be explained in terms of universal or abstract regularities which transcend particular contexts. Consciousness has a phenomenology (Seager 1999: 126); it has depth and breadth in time and space. For this reason, we can say that it is grounded in a richly textured pattern of interconnecting relations, potentially implicating many space-time scales, which give to our experience a sense of being grounded in larger, textured wholes of which we are a part. A different kind of scientific explanation – a different kind of science – is, therefore, required. An ontology of social being worthy of its name must know how to reinstate the centrality of the individual's meaning-making trajectory and the centrality of time to the individuation of the trajectory. This calls for a very different scientific approach from one which seeks to factor out all of those messy details which make us individuals in the name of abstract, de-contextualizing principles of scientific reason and generalization.

Grounding can be seen in terms of a specification hierarchy comprising iconic, indexical, and symbolic modes of grounding. In the first instance, consciousness is iconically grounded in terms of one's relation to the world on the basis of one's physiology and perception. Grounding is, in the first instance, perceptual-motor in character. It is based on the body-brain's mediate relation to its physical-material milieu, including feelings and sensations on the surface of the body, as well as those which are sensed as originating from within the body. This type of grounding is based on proprioception and exteroception; it provides information about the environment, as well as the body-brain's movement in the environment (kinaesthesis). Information is, thus, provided concerning such variables as the vertical and horizontal axes of the world, the gravitational frame of reference, and awareness of the frame of the body, "which has its own axes of reference, head-to-foot, right-to-left, and front-to-back" (Gibson 1983 [1966]: 67). Information is also obtained concerning spatial displacement, as in locomotory movement from place to place, distance, and velocity (Gibson 1983 [1966]: 67–8). Finally, information is obtained concerning change of direction of movement.

The most basic form of grounding of the body-brain is in relation to the surface of the earth – to gravity and the ground or other surface of support (Gibson 1983 [1966]: 59). This type of iconic grounding affords the body-brain possibilities for orienting to its environment. This most primary or basic form of grounding is not, however, merely a passive sensation which is imposed on the organism by external forces. Importantly, organisms actively orient to and move (locomote) through their physical-material environment. Active exploration through efferent output produces re-afferent input, which yields positive feedback. Such self-caused activities and movements mean that the organism's internal dynamics interact with stimulus information which is obtained from the environment. This information is, as Gibson (1983 [1966]: 31) points out, intrinsic to the flow of the activity itself, rather than extrinsic to it. In the first instance, the body-brain's orientation to gravity and the surface of support – the ground – provides stimulus information concerning the most basic forms of orientation, viz. the direction up/down and the plane of the ground (Gibson 1983 [1966]: 59). Importantly, Gibson points out that the body-brain's orientation to these two factors depends on "the most basic type of perception on which other perceptions depend, that is, the detection of the stable permanent *framework* of the environment" (1983 [1966]: 59). It is this stable and permanent framework of the environment and the individual's conscious awareness of his or her being situated in it that constitutes the basis of a textured field to which the individual relates and orients. For this reason, it is a most primary form of iconic being-in-the-world. The iconic signs generated by this primary form of grounding provide necessary information about the environment relative to the organism's relationship to it (see chapter 1, section 3).

True indexicals are signs which are contiguous with some contextual value. Ocular pointing with one's arm to indicate some distant location to one's interlocutor, relative to a textured orientational framework of spatial relations, is one example of a true index. Thus, addresser and addressee are grounded within a contingent, occasion-specific orientational framework which serves to orient perception and action. As I see it, the relationship of contiguity between indexical sign and contextual value entails a further differentiation of the relationship between self and world with respect to the much more primordial vagueness and sense of wholeness or at oneness that characterizes one's iconic grounding in the world. With respect to the vaguer sense of self-world which is entailed by iconic grounding, indexical grounding represents a further closing of the loop comprising me-indexical sign-world-you. Here we have awareness of the self selectively attending to and interacting with specified contextual values in the orientational field shared by addresser and addressee.

Indexical relations create trajectories which extend beyond the self so as to link signs to events, objects, other persons, and so on, relative to an intentional source on the here-now scale. Indexical signs are context specific; they function to ground sign-types in situation-specific ways by pointing to or otherwise specifying the relations between sign-tokens and selected aspects of the context in an organized deictic field (Bühler 1990 [1934]: 93–95). In doing so, they ground acts of meaning-making in relation to the dynamical attractor which originates at an intentional source. Pure indexicals can only occur as act-tokens. In establishing a relation of contiguity between indexical sign and some contextual value, as in the case of pointing gestures to indicate direction or location, the indexical creates a trajectory such that there is a reduction of possibilities relative to an intentional source. Indexicals are probabilistic, in contrast to the necessary character of icons. They are probabilistic because their context-dependent vectorial nature means that the occurrence of an indexical sign either presupposes or entails, to use Silverstein's (1976) terminology, a relationship with some other object, event, or contextual value. The occurrence of an indexical sign thus increases the probability of co-occurrence of some such object or event which is internally related to it. For example, the indexical act of pointing and the object or location which is indicated by the point now enters into a simple redundancy relation.

The relational and contextually patterned nature of meaning and experience can be described in terms of the principle of metaredundancy which Lemke (1984a: 117–119; 1984b: 64; 1984c: 35–39) has developed on the basis of the earlier proposals of Bateson concerning meta-communication and meta-learning (e.g. 1973b: 102–111). Redundancy refers to the likelihood or the probability with which two items, say, connect or combine to form a larger patterned whole or relation (see chapter 3, section 5; see also Thibault 2004a: 26–30 for further relevant discussion). Consider, for example, the co-occurrence of a pointing gesture and the object or location in the visual-spatial purview of the interactants which is the target of the point (see Thibault 2004b: 113–115 for discussion of pointing gestures). A redundancy relation exists between the combination of point and the object pointed to when not all possible combinations of points and objects are possible. When such a redundancy relation exists, this means that the point and the object (or the word and the gesture) mutually predict each other's co-occurrence. There is a better than random chance of their combining or occurring together as part of a still larger contextual pattern or relation. Thus, the point and the object pointed to are redundant with (redound with) each other in the sense that the occurrence of one predicts the probability of its being combined with the other in some context.

This relationship of contextual co-dependency or redundancy is what enables a coordinated indexical field to emerge. The redundancy relation between object pointed to and indexical pointer thus alters the probability distribution which the indexed object had in the overall phase space of probabilities prior to the enacting of the indexical relationship. In doing so, this leads to the emergence of higher-order contextual constraints – meta-redundancies – as a consequence of the closure of positive feedback (Juarrero 1999: 174). In altering the probability distribution as a result of the indexical sign-token, intentionally sourced and directed indexical signs function as self-organizing attractors for the flow of meaning along a vector from source to completion of act.

Textual products and records can, therefore, be seen as extensions of the agent's own embodiment. They extend from the agent's internal dynamics along a trajectory out into the ecosocial environment. When philosophers and psychologists say that consciousness is intentional or that it is "about something", I believe they are drawing attention to the ways in which the internal dynamics of acts of consciousness in agents constrain the trajectory which loops out into the ecosocial environment so that specific aspects of the trajectory can be related back to or attributed to the act of consciousness. Whilst the vagueness that characterizes iconic semiosis makes it difficult or problematic to assign a particular behaviour to a conscious source, indexicality, on the other hand, fully specifies the relationship between a conscious source and the meaning-making trajectory which can be attributed to it on the here-now scale. The specification of the source of indexical signs does not mean that iconic semiosis cannot be related to a conscious source. The point is, rather, that the diffuse, topological-continuous character of iconic semiosis and its associated bodily dynamics support a very broad and shallow attractor basin. The many degrees of freedom of iconic semiosis give rise to very many vague and indeterminate possibilities for meaning (Salthe 1993: 162), as well as giving rise to a narrower range of less determinate acts that are recognizable as such in a given system of interpretance. It is doubtful at this (iconic) stage that we can talk about consciousness as being semiotically determinate. The internal dynamics of the newborn are semiotically underdetermined. Because of this initial topological-continuous vagueness, it is difficult to ascribe to these dynamics a specific action trajectory relative to an intentional source (see chapter 3, section 5 and chapter 9, section 9). In this regard, it is interesting to note how both caregivers and, indeed, psychologists, linguists, and others, attribute mental states, intentions, and so on, to the newborn. Of course, the relationship between the semantic categories used by parents and psychologists and those of the newborn are not symmetrical. Instead, the mother, in interacting with the infant in the dyad, is the infant's main link to the higher-scalar ecosocial level where categories like [INTENTIONALITY] reside. For this reason, the senior member of the dyad, *qua* repository of higher-scalar ecosocial resources and practices, is inserted into a relationship with an individual who is in some respects a lower-scalar being.

Indexicality introduces discrete variation into the primary semiotic landscape of iconic, topological-continuous variation. Iconicity, as we have seen, is necessarily tied to inner and outer states of the body-brain. It is embodied in the internal dynamics of the organism from the very outset of its existence. Iconicity embodies the body-brain's primordial tendencies to orient towards saccadic, pulsing and rhythmic qualities in the other and at the same time to exhibit such tendencies in their own bodies as a result of their own internal dynamics. These internal dynamics, too, are context-sensitive and are themselves further entrained by the emergence of higher-order constraints in the form of the indexical followed by the symbolic modes. In onto-genesis, the very many degrees of freedom of the primary iconic mode – its near equiprobable semiotic landscape – are soon re-organized by virtue of the ongoing interaction between the internal dynamics of the organism, its in-built value biases, and the world. Thus, the primary ecosocial environment of the mother–child dyad, along with the surrounding physical-material world, provides affordances with which the internal dynamics of the newborn engage. The resulting interactions and their ongoing history of development lead to the reorganization of the initial, purely iconic dynamics, thereby bringing about increasing differentiation in the form of, say, discrete variation as indexicality emerges. As we have seen above, the establishing of an indexical relationship means that the probability distribution of some act is altered. The emer-gence of indexicality means that lower-scalar topological-continuous (iconic) variation is entrained into the higher-scalar dynamics of indexical contextualizing relations. These con-textualizing relations in turn act as boundary conditions on the lower, iconic level. As the work of Halliday (1975, 1993), Painter (1984), and Oldenburg (1987) on child language devel-opment in the systemic-functional approach shows, the move into grammar, and hence the emergence of symbolic semiosis, occurs as the stratum of lexicogrammatical organization is dynamically assembled in and through the body-brain's interactions with its ecosocial environ-ment, leading to the self-organization of lexicogrammar with its complex metafunctionally organized semantic regions (section 10 below).

Lemke's (1999) theory of semiotic alternation is the best tool that I know of for theorizing this overall process. With reference to the three-level hierarchy discussed in chapter 1, section 4, we can say that an indexical sign at level L is reorganized (not transcended) at the symbolic level of lexicogrammar (level L+1). Indexical signs are entrained into the higher levels of organization along with the massively expanded possibilities that characterize the phase space of the sym-bolic mode of natural language. This is the case, I believe, with the deictic elements in natural languages. Natural language deictics have both indexical and symbolic aspects and are not, therefore, pure indexicals. In the case of deictics, the indexical constraints at level L are inte-grated into the system of symbolic constraints at level L+1. Consequently, they now have a much more expanded phase space of symbolic possibilities for meaning-making on space-time scales beyond the here-now scale of pure indexicals.

If what I have said above has any validity, then it should have interesting things to tell us about the notion of consciousness and the relationship of consciousness to neural activity in the brain. In terms of the hierarchy of icon, index, and symbol, indexicality is the intermediate level. We have seen how, in the case of language, this level (L) semiotically reorganizes the many degrees of topological-continuous freedom of the iconic level (L–1) as digital, typological-categorial distinctions on the symbolic level (L+1).

Indexicality – cf. "grounding" (Langacker 1987: 126–128) – refers to the fact that all semiotic forms and their functions in discourse contribute in some way to the ongoing enactment and maintenance of the wider situational context of which these forms are a constitutive part. From the instantial perspective of discourse, there is not, then, some special class of semiotic forms whose function it is to indicate the context. Instead, all the forms used in conjunction with each other function in various ways to enact and to specify the overall discourse event. From the point of view of discourse, the distinction which is sometimes upheld between context-independent symbolic signs and context-dependent indexical ones is meaningless. All of the semiotic forms which are co-deployed in some communicative event serve a plurality of semi-otic functions in that event. In so doing, they act on and affect each other in complex and multiple ways which function to enact and maintain that event in time.

Consciousness implies an individual system which is in some sense separate from its sur-rounding milieu. Consciousness entails boundaries that indicate or signify the distinction between "self" and "nonself". In the early stages of infant semiosis these boundaries are vague and ill-defined. The proto-self exists in a wash of iconic vagueness in which the individual system is only weakly distinguished from its surroundings. However, the processes of development and individuation along a time-bound trajectory bring about internal-symmetry-breaking choices. As a result of these choices, fields of organization emerge as internal control parameters for the creation of boundaries and constraints which lead to the creation of an organized field of relations. The emergence of symbolic-symmetry breaking generalizes across the phase space of a given ecosocial system through the action of the ordering field it creates.

The emergence of indexicality reorganizes the iconic mapping of topological-continuous variation onto topological-continuous variation as a digital distinction. The distinction between a given percept and a contextual value which is assigned to it in relation to the more global schema in which the percept occurs is an example of indexicality. Iconic vagueness corresponds to Peirce's category of Firstness. It is concerned with being and potentiality. Indexicality entails the creating of a boundary or a distinction between Firstnesses. In so doing, Secondness emerges. Secondness is concerned with here-now actuality and with individual existence, hence the creating of the distinction between self and nonself. The emergence of indexical distinctions amounts to the creation of order, which, in turn, leads to the further ordering of the relevant milieu. The indexical distinction requires two control parameters, x and y, where x is the external object which is perceived, or better, the ambient information which is picked up about this object in the environment, and y is the internal control parameter, which corresponds to the activities in the central nervous system which create the meaning that x has for the observer. The order parameter is the distinction between x and y which specifies for the individual the semiotically mediated relevance of the x/y distinction as being significant for action (Salthe 1993: 176–179). Here we see the transition from the potentiality of iconic vagueness to the actuality and specificity of indexicality. In turn, the semiotically salient distinctions of indexicality pave the way for the emergent generalities of symbolic meaning-making. Thirdness entails the mediation of instantiated sign-tokens by an ordered field of systemic regularities, which have the status of a habit or law for Peirce. Thus, sign-tokens with this status can be replicated from one occasion of use to another. The ensuing regularity allows for self-reference: a symbolic field of possibilities – cf. Saussure's (1971 [1915]: 155–166; 1993: 326–336) system of values – constitutes the Thirdness in and through which symbolic signs can be construed.

3 The deictic field of language and the texturing of consciousness

Linguistic deictics do not simply refer to entities objectively located in Newtonian space-time. Systems of deixis are used to refer to a participant or circumstantial element whose identity is contextually recoverable. In English, the relevant resources include demonstratives, the definite article, pronouns, comparatives and the phoric adverbs *here, there, now, then*. Deictics are not pure indexicals; they have symbolic dimensions of meaning in addition to their indexical ones for establishing text-internal links between the different parts of a given text, as well as text-external links between elements in the text and selected aspects of the context. For example, the experiential categories that are realized by deictics are symbolic, rather than indexical. Deictics do not simply point to something which is already there in the (con)text; deictics also symbolically construe their referents in terms of experiential categories such as spatial orientation, gender, time, and so on. Deixis is fundamental to the question of the relationship between language and higher-order consciousness because it is the resource which grounds, to use Langacker's term, the unfolding text in relation to the here-&-now act of speaking. Bühler has aptly formulated the textual (deictic) and experiential (symbolic) functions of the deictic terms as follows:

> They [deictic words], too, are symbols (and not only signals); *da* and *dort* (there) symbolize, they name an area, they name the geometrical location, so to speak, that is, an area around the person now speaking within which what is pointed to can be found; just as the word *heute* (today) in fact names the totality of all days on which it can be spoken, and the word *I* all possible senders of human messages, and the word *thou* the class of all receivers as such. But one difference still remains between these names and the other naming words of language; it

lies in the fact that they expect their meaning to be made definite from case to case in the deictic field of language and in what the deictic field is able to provide for the senses.

(Bühler 1990 [1934]: 104–105)

There are two important notions in Bühler's discussion. First, Bühler points out that deictics are "made definite from case to case". That is, deictics function to ground the symbolic categories of meaning in specific contexts. In doing so, they enable social agents to orient both to each other as well as to selected aspects of the context. Deixis operates in both the nominal group and the verbal group in this sense. Insofar as consciousness is concerned with "relating global input to its contextual conditions" (Baars and McGovern 1996: 91) and guiding the mechanisms of selective attention and awareness, the linguistic systems of deixis would appear to play a key role in these processes.

The starting point for Bühler's discussion of deixis is the three-way distinction he makes among the following three modes of deixis: (1) ocular demonstration, or deixis which is connected to sensory cues, as when one points with one's finger so as to indicate some object in conjunction with the use of a given deictic word; (2) the use of the same deictic words to point anaphorically in discourse which is removed from perceptual cues; and (3) imagination-oriented deixis. While each of these modes is increasingly removed from any reliance on perceptual cues, Bühler (1990 [1934]: 95) points out that perceptual cues are never entirely transcended even in the second and third modes referred to here. The three modes of deixis postulated by Bühler are thus seen to be a little integration hierarchy in their own right. This last point suggests a fruitful point of entry into the question as to how deixis functions as a system of resources for integrating and orienting discourse participants on the basis of the ways in which their bodies are situated in relation to the cross-couplings of physical-material and semiotic-discursive activities and processes in the ecosocial system. It further suggests that deixis is intimately linked to and is a further development of the ways in which the experiencing and the semiotic body, including its location and extension in space, is connected to its environment. These connections are the result of the perceptual, conceptual, and semiotic models that emerge as a consequence of the body-brain's transactions with its ecosocial environment.

Psychologists of perception such as Gibson (1983 [1966], 1986 [1979]) and Handel (1989) in the ecological tradition have pointed out that perception entails the pick-up of stimulus information about environmental events. Such events and the stimulus information which specifies them are not to be confused with the proximal stimulus such as the vibration in the eardrum or the light waves entering the retina of the eye. The information about environmental events specifies that event. Part of this process consists of specifying the objects and events which are perceived and experienced as existing beyond the body and in relation to the observer's embodied point of observation. Thus, stimulus information in the environment specifies the location of some event in relation to the point of observation occupied by the observer, as well as the nature of the event. Bühler's first deictic mode – viz. oracular demonstration – vividly draws attention to the ways in which deixis functions to cross-couple individuals to context-bound activity, including perceived aspects of the material world. In this way, perceptual exploration and the selective attending to aspects of the world, along with the cross-coupling of these to the deictic categories of language, produce specific trajectories of conscious attention and awareness.

The anchoring or grounding functions of deixis suggest a key role for the deictic systems of language, and their analogues in other semiotic modalities, in the construction and functioning of higher-order consciousness. Deixis has the following functions:

1. Deixis cross-couples consciousness to and entrains it in relation to its context-bound activities. Consciousness is always realized in situation-specific ways. It is not an intrinsic property of some lower-scalar physical brain processes; rather, it is the product of the body-brain complex in specific contexts with specific dynamic properties that emerge in and are grounded in a deictic field which bestows texture and wholeness on the self's experience of the nonself; conscious experience is not confined to the self *per se*, but is always

constructed in and through the self's relationship to the nonself within some organized and textured deictic field.

2.   It is a resource for selectively attending to and focusing on and, hence, exercising selective control over features of the environment so that these will be brought to the conscious attention of discourse participants.

3.   It can help in the recruiting of sensori-motor systems in ways that help to organize and execute voluntary actions by virtue of the ways in which they provide access to spatial, perceptual, participant, and other domains.

4.   Deictics index domains of participation such as the egocentric, altercentric, and sociocentric (addresser–addressee) zones as intentional sources of action and of consciousness.

5.   By selectively drawing on and orienting to available information and by specifying whether knowledge is shared or not, deictics enable knowledge and information sources to be indexed and recruited in ways that facilitate and enable decisions to be made during the course of some unfolding action. They therefore provide resources for reflecting on and consciously monitoring the flow of information and knowledge in discourse.

6.   In grounding discourse and its participants within a specific deictic field of orientation, deictics help to reduce situational indeterminacy and hence ambiguity in perception and understanding.

7.   Deictics help in the adaptation to novel contexts through their facilitation of conscious involvement and on focusing attention on the solving of problems and on learning.

8.   In delimiting and defining the relations between agents and selected aspects of their *Umwelt*, deictics specify trajectories which link participants and practices across diverse space-time scales.

9.   Deictics coordinate and jointly establish intentionally directed reference to "objects" in discourse and provide resources for the intersubjective monitoring of interactants' understandings of what is being referenced (Hanks 1996: 233).

10.   The embedding of deictics in social practices which predispose agents to act, perceive, and understand in certain ways on the basis of their embodiment, habitual coding orientations or habitus, or cultural values means that deictics play an important role in organizing the trade-off between adaptiveness and flexibility, on the one hand, and the standardization of activity as routine, on the other.

4   Karl Bühler's theory of the deictic field of language

Bühler's work is enormously suggestive because it shows how the individual's integration into the deictic field is, in the first instance, connected to perceptual cues in the ecosocial environment of interactants. For example, he refers to the deictic function of the expression stratum of spoken language:

> Products of the human speech organs also have a *spatial quality of origin* for every hearer, and as a rule they are easily distinguished from other noises as products of the human voice. Moreover, they have an *individual character*, which we are familiar with because we have a vital interest in it and practise recognition our whole life long; we can individually and correctly assign such an individual character to a few dozen or hundred of the most familiar speakers around us. We recognize our closest acquaintances and quite a few other people easily and reliably from their voice.
>
> Our speaker at the place not visible to us counts on his *here* being unmistakeable by virtue of the quality of origin and his *I* by virtue of the personal character of his voice, and he does this because he has grown used to it in normal speech situations. Whoever calls out *here* in a group of people when his name is read is entitled to expect that the receiver of the sound will be able to find the sender of the sound with his eyes by the quality of origin of his *here*. The hearer looks where he hears the sound coming from and optically recognizes the speaker there. The blind cannot do this, they must rely on their ears alone to achieve similar ends; and that is what the person calling from the place out of view expects from the normal

hearer: not always in vain, as we all know, because we are all quite skilled in these operations, which are so often required of us.

(Bühler 1990 [1934]: 106)

Bühler's observations resonate very well with Gibson's ecological theory of perception. Deixis can be seen as emerging from, as well as being founded upon, the body-brain's orientation to and essential material unity with its ecosocial environment, including other conspecifics. For example, in Gibson's theory, the human listening system is a bilateral system comprising two ears fixed on either side of a mobile head (1983 [1966]: 75). This system actively orients to acoustic events by picking up the direction of the event and its source at the same time that it identifies the nature of the event. Furthermore, vocal gestures *qua* vocal tract gestures, rather than mere indexes of the internal states of the organism, are oriented to and specify something within the shared perceptual purview of both addresser and addressee. In this regard, Bühler (1990 [1934]: 113) speculates on the goal-oriented character of the voice. That is, the voice does not only index the origin of the sound and the individual identity of its speaker; it is also modulated and adjusted in terms of loudness, directionality, and other parameters so as to select and engage the attention of a specific addressee. Bühler postulates, in the first instance, the basic categories of *here*-deixis and *I*-deixis, as follows:

> For it can be seen in the use of every acoustic communicative signal that two factors are relevant in it, namely *first* its (spatial) source quality and *second* its integral acoustic character. From a psychological perspective, the acoustic signs of language rank among the acoustic communicative signals. For the sighted receiver of a signal there is nothing more natural than that he should turn towards the sound source. In the case of verbal communicative signs, the source is the speaker and is at the position of the speaker. The word *here* and the word *I* both require this reaction, or at least they suggest it. To that extent their function as deictic words is identical. But then the intention (or the interest) that they recommend splits, so that they capture the position and surrounding circumstances of the sender in the one case and the sender himself with a physiognomic or pathognomic gaze in the other. A *here* contains the invitation to follow the one direction of interest at the parting, an *I* the invitation to follow the other. That is the most general and most nearly presuppositionless analysis that can be given. It is (by the way) as objectivistic an analysis as possible, one that does not pay closer attention to the speaker's experience at all.
>
> (Bühler 1990 [1934]: 125)

These two categories contribute to the formation of their respective deictic fields in different ways. *Here*-deixis functions both to draw the listener's attention to the speaker as the source of the vocalization and to direct the latter's attention to some object of reference within the perceptual purview of speaker and listener. *I*-deixis functions, like *here*-deixis, to direct the listener's attention to the source of the sound (the speaker), but differs in that it also functions to focus the listener's attention on the speaker and his or her individual identity, as indexed by the individual speaking voice. From the perspective of *I*-deixis, the sound of the speaker's voice is a projection of energy and information into the ecosocial environment. When Bühler says that the voice directs the listener's attention to the source of the voice in terms of a "physiognomic gaze", I believe that this observation by Bühler shows how the drawing of the listener into the speaker's sphere creates a dyadic relation between the two. The dyad constitutes a compression of the many fluctuating matter, energy, and informational variables which are at play. It is the system as a whole – more specifically, the supersystem transactions that constitute the dyad, not the speaker or the listener *per se* – which is attracted to some preferred configuration out of the many possible ones. The dyad is an "order parameter" which enables the system to self-organize. Previously "separate" entities – self and nonself – are brought into a dialogic relationship with each other. The dialogic mode is an attractor state, i.e. self and nonself are attracted to certain states rather than others. These states define the degrees of difference – i.e. the degrees of freedom – of the system, though in ways which fluctuate according to changing contextual parameters.

It is not difficult to see here how the primordial and necessary condition for the emergence of consciousness is founded upon the dialogic or proto-interpersonal orientation of self to non-self. The resulting "dialogic closure" (see chapter 3, section 1 and chapter 9, section 6.1.5) entrains and compresses the many degrees of freedom of the system such that the re-entrant connectivity of neural groups creates a meta-representation (see chapter 1, section 2) in the brain of the self's always dialogic relations to the nonself. Thus, self-awareness and a sense of self emerge as a result of the reentrant mappings of the dialogic closure imposed by the dyad. The self is always construed and constructed in and through its constitutive relations to the nonself. These proto-interpersonal transactions are iconic and topological in character. This behavioural variability of the system means that, initially, the self has no meta-perspective on its own primordial experiencing. There is no sense of a self which is "separate" from nonself. The drawing of this boundary comes later with the emergent sense of the experiencing of one's own experiencing (Lemke personal communication). This experiencing of one's own experiencing occurs at a logically higher-order of contextualization than the experience. It entails the development of meta-perspectives on one's own dialogically constituted experiences and, hence, the constructing of boundaries between self and nonself. These boundaries are increasingly typological-categorial (digital) and represent the first stage in the overflowing of experiential categories into the world. By the same token, there also emerges a proto-textual or proto-deictic field whereby the initial wholeness of proto-interpersonal transactions between self and nonself is maintained.

The first category (*here*) discussed by Bühler in the above quotation constitutes a deictic field which is focused on spatial relations; the second category (*I*) is oriented to participant relations. Bühler's insistence on the mixed symbolic and indexical functions of deictics – both names and signals in his terminology (see above) – shows how deictics do not simply index an already existing and presupposed contextual value or entity. Rather, in selectively attending to aspects of context within the relevant deictic field, they also symbolically construe or create the relevant contextual parameters. Thus, spatial deictics such as *here* and *there* do not simply refer to an already existing set of spatial relations; they symbolically construe these in discourse with reference to the relative positions of addresser and addressee. Deictics, like all other linguistic signs, are semiotic in nature and function. They are, thus, implicated in semiotic practices of selective contextualization whereby spatial, temporal, participant, perceptual, and discursive relations are construed and constructed in discourse by selectively focusing on some aspects of the spatial-temporal purview of the participants, some aspects of the jointly enacted participant relations, some perceived entities and events, and so on, so as to make these meaningful as a part of a particular whole, i.e. the particular deictic field which is constituted on a given occasion of discourse. The two basic categories initially postulated by Bühler show how deixis is more than a simple material pointing to entities in an objective physical world. Rather, deixis entails socially meaningful action whereby semiotically salient relationships are constructed between some part of the overall context and some other part in relation to an overall ecosocial semiotic system and its values. The pointing or indexical practices implicated in the use of deictics are embedded within networks of interlinked practices across potentially many differ-ent space-time scales in the overall ecosocial system. They constitute and indicate the trajector-ies of agents' participations in social meaning-making practices (see also Hanks 1996: 242). These trajectories may extend no further than the immediate here-now context of the per-ceptual purview of discourse participants, or they may range over far greater space-time scales.

Bühler (1990 [1934]: 117–118) also postulates what he calls "the here-now-I system of subject-ive orientation". This system is the means whereby spatial, temporal, and participant modes of access are unified by their relationship to the first person source of these deictics. The phenom-enology of the use of these deictics in our social meaning-making practices shows that these accord with our everyday conscious experience as being localized either within our body or in the external world. Thus, the deictic systems of natural language are a further elaboration of the already existing perceptual and conceptual categorizations which are embodied in primary consciousness. This fact suggests that higher-order consciousness is constituted within a deictic field which cannot be localized within the brain of the individual. Deixis works on, shapes, and extends exteroceptive and proprioceptive perceptual experience. It gives texture to our experience of the phenomenal world. It does so through the creating of trajectories which extend beyond individual body-brains so as to link participants to their perceptual purview, to activities, to each other, as well as to wider systems of networks of activities in the ecosocial system as a whole. In English, the contrast between *here* and *there* organizes space in terms of that which lies within the speaker's sphere and is, hence, immediately graspable (*here*) and that which lies beyond this, perhaps corresponding to the addressee's sphere (*there*).

Bühler's second category of anaphoric deixis is concerned with the achievement in discursive interaction of textual cohesion. Textual cohesion is based on patterns of co-occurrence of sign-tokens such that the occurrence of a given sign-token will enable text users or participants to predict the occurrence of some other sign-token elsewhere in the same text. That is, a given sign-token, in its text-making function, indexes or points to the location of some other sign-token, and vice versa. Such endophoric relations in texts refer to the set of text-internal indexical relationships known as co-textuality (Halliday and Hasan 1976; Hasan 1980; Martin 1992a: chapter 3; Silverstein 1997; McGregor 1997). A second type of indexical relationship is that which occurs when some sign-token in the text points to something outside the text in its context of situation. This second type of indexical relation, in selectively linking the text to its context, contributes to the sense of the appropriateness of the fit between text and context. This indexical fit between textual signs and selected aspects of the context is what is known as exophoric text-context relations. The fact that deixis allows text users to "reach ahead and back" in texts clearly demonstrates the intentional character of deixis. The constitution of a deictic field entails a trajectory that can only be generated through the reduction of field possibilities relative to an intentional source. The constitution of a deictic field in discourse is organized in relation to larger-scale activity structures in which the deictic field is embedded. It therefore provides a way of channelling meaning along a trajectory which can be sourced at some agent. The deictic field is a set of contextually grounded constraints resulting from positive feedback. The dialectic of presupposition-and-entailment, in specifying or enacting intersubjective reality in the course of the unfolding discursive event, represents the dynamic changes in the probability distribution of the action as a whole as it occurs in time. The deictic field functions as a control parameter whereby alternative possibilities – spatial, temporal, perceptual, interactional, and so on, – are constrained and made possible by the unfolding dynamics of the deictic field. The achievement of a stable textual cohesion – i.e. the processes of entextualization – is thus grounded in the individual (not generic) use of deictic tokens. This cohesion suggests that (con)textually grounded and intentionally sourced deictics are attractors of self-organizing semiotic-material dynamics and cross-couplings. These cross-couplings, in constraining the interplay of fluctuating variables within the self-organized discursive space-time, point to the higher-order genre-based practices and conventions whereby the given instance takes on a recognizable form (see Andersen 2000; Hasan 1985).

What of Bühler's third category, viz. imagination-oriented deixis? Bühler poses the question as to what happens when the pre-linguistic cues available to perception are not available to accompany the use of deictic words:

> The matter changes with one blow, it seems, when the narrator leads the hearer into the realm of what is absent and can be remembered or into the realm of constructive imagination and treats him to the same deictic words as before so that he may see and hear what can be seen and heard there (and touch, of course, and perhaps even smell and taste things). Not with the external eye, ear, and so on, but with what is usually called the "mind's" eye or ear in everyday language and, probably for the sake of mere convenience, in psychology, too. It seems that the conditions must be different there because those pre-linguistic deictic clues that are indispensable for ocular deixis are not available in imagination-oriented pointing. One who is being guided around the phantasy product in imagination cannot follow with his eyes the arrow formed by the speaker's outstretched arm so as to find something *there*; he cannot use the spatial source quality of the voice to find the place of a speaker who says *here*; in written language he also does not hear the vocal character of an absent speaker who says *I*. And still, these and other deictic words are offered to him in great variety in a visual account of absent objects, and they are sometimes offered by absent narrators, too. One

must only look at the first page of any travel diary or a novel to find rough confirmation of this claim. To be sure, the psychological niceties of it require rather more reflection so as to be understood scientifically.

(Bühler 1990 [1934]: 141–142)

The answer to Bühler's question lies in the dually deictic and symbolic character of deictic expressions, as well as in what Gibson has defined as non-perceptual awareness (1986 [1979]: 255–256). I will start with the latter notion. Gibson points out that perceiving means being aware of the surfaces, events, and so on, of the environment and one's position in it relative to an observer position (1986 [1979]: 255). Gibson argues that remembering, fantasizing, wishful thinking, imagining, and related activities mean being aware of environmental events which existed in the past or which could exist, or which are outside the realms of possibility. In all these cases, Gibson argues, the traditional hypothesis of "mental imagery" does not explain what is going on. Instead, Gibson hypothesizes that in such cases "a perceptual system that has become sensitized to certain invariants and can extract them from the stimulus flux can also operate without the constraints of the stimulus flux. Information becomes further detached from stimulation" (1986 [1979]: 256).

Both perception and non-perceptual awareness are a result of dynamical self-organization in time which takes place in and through the individual's interactions with its environment. Environmental events, surfaces, and so on, are, in this view, context-bound affordances and constraints on what can be perceived. The information which is provided by the environment is not a static given; nor does it act on the individual in the manner of externally imposed Newtonian forces. Both perceptual and non-perceptual awareness are constructed and modified as a result of the individual's interactions with his or her environments. Even when the adjustment loops for active perception (looking around, listening, haptic exploration, and other perceptual modalities) are not operative, as in non-perceptual awareness, attractor basin landscapes capture the effects of the time-bound sensitization of the individual to perceptual invariants which have been decoupled from the stimulus flux and embodied within the individual as information about possible, remembered, or imaginary events. It is the decoupling from the stimulus flux which enables the individual to posit hypothetical and imaginary situations as different from or alternative to actual ones. However, decoupling is not an all-or-nothing matter; there is decoupling to varying degrees. Imagination may be grounded in and, therefore, close to current perception while at the same time positing alternatives to this. These alternatives always relate to the perceptual scene in the here-now. For this reason, they are still grounded in this. Imagination may also be of images, scenes, and so on, which are completely decoupled from current perception. In the latter case, the imagined situation is no longer constrained by or grounded in the stimulus flux of current perception. Perceptual invariants, decoupled from the stimulus flux, are manipulated and rearranged as possible situations and scenes or even as totally fantastic ones. However, in these situations, deixis still functions to ground and to orient participants in relation to an orientational field based, in the final analysis, on perceptual invariants.

It is clear, then, that an individual can locate and orient him- or herself in an imaginary or fantasy environment in the "mind's eye", so to speak, using the deictic resources of language and other semiotic systems. As Bühler points out, imagination-oriented deixis is not as far removed from deixis based on perceptual clues as it may first seem. This last point brings me back to the first point made above. The dually indexical and symbolic character of the deictics means that individuals can deploy these linguistic resources in order to symbolically construe a given deictic field at the same time that these symbolic categories are grounded in the deictic field relative to an intentional source such as the "here-now-I" field of subjective orientation (see above). In other words, the semiotic resources of the language system are selectively cross-coupled with perceptual invariants which have been embodied and stored in the individual's *Innenwelt*.

In the following section, I shall examine a second analytically separable dimension of the higher-scalar ecosocial constraints which operate on agents and their meaning-making activities, viz. the systems of intertextual meaning-making practices of some community.

5 Intertextual meaning-making practices and the entraining of individuals to ecosocial semiotic values and constraints

Many researchers in cognitive science and discourse analysis refer to the extra-communicative background information or knowledge, the frames, or the higher order schemata and mental representations which discourse participants draw on and use in order to make appropriate interpretative inferences. The use of these notions raises two orders of problem. First, these notions are not, analytically speaking, close enough to the order of discourse to be really useful. However, they do refer to a most important dimension of all social meaning-making, and one which is not specifiable at the level of, say, lexicogrammar *per se* in the linguistic system. Secondly, there is a danger that the notion of background information or knowledge is reified as an abstract psychological property of the individual, one which is not connected to discourse and context in a principled way. In other words, an essentially social order of meaning relations is seen as simply already existing "in" the minds of individual members of the culture in question. With this in mind, I shall now propose an alternative to the notion of background information – one which puts social meaning-making at the centre of the picture. My point is that the various notions mentioned above are grounded in a mentalistic discourse, which is individual-centred and consequently unable to provide solutions to the theoretical questions that are central in the present study. Both new questions and new answers are required.

The central question to tackle is: how do discourse participants construe meaningful relations between one occasion of discourse and some other? Or, how does one occasion of discourse serve as the context for the interpretation of another? We do not interpret or understand texts and discursive occasions in isolation from other texts and other situation-types that are available in a given community. The patterns of connections across texts have both typical and individual aspects. The former refers to the typical ways in which patterned connections are construed between texts in a given community of practice. The latter refers to the ways in which individuals create to varying degrees, along their life trajectories, unique networks of patterned connections among texts that are context-dependent and hence contingent on their life experience. In this way, the networks of connections that are embodied in individuals may differ from those of other individuals according to individual experience and historical accidents. The individual thus creates in his or her brain global networks of associations among texts and text-types which are stored in memory and which can be dynamically re-activated according to the requirements of specific contexts. The individual's neural networks are dynamically entrained by their trajectory through a given culture's networks of intertextual relations. These processes of entrainment occur through the participation of the person in the relevant meaning-making practices. Thus, individuals and their internal dynamics are entrained into the appropriate ways of interpreting the particular kinds of texts which are relevant to some community of practice (Lave 1997; Lemke 1997; Walkerdine 1997).

The networks of intertextual connections that are created in the individual's brain emerge as a result of the fact that an individual's trajectory is embedded in both historical-biographical time, as well as in a structured higher-scalar ecosocial semiotic environment. It is by means of such higher-scalar contextual constraints, built up through ongoing exchanges between the individual and his or her ecosocial environment, that individuals internalize their ongoing engagements with the culture's meaning systems. In time, the latter come to constitute boundary conditions that act on and constrain the agent's possibilities for meaning-making. Higher-scalar intertextual constraints are built up by positive feedback as the agent creates networks of meaningful connections along his or her trajectory. These connections are integrated with the internal dynamics of individuals. Individuals are consequently entrained to the patterns and dynamics of a culture's higher-scalar meaning systems. In other words, the connections that are established between the system's internal dynamics and its environment set up redundancy or metaredundancy relations between the system's dynamics and the environment (Lemke 1997: 41; Salthe 1993: 118). This contextual integration of the individual's internal dynamics to the ecosocial semiotic environment has the effect of embedding both the agent and the environment in a higher-order supersystem of contextualizing relations which regulate the relations between the two. It is in this way that the patterns of intertextual connections which are typical of a given culture's various domains of practice are hooked up to the internal dynamics of individuals: the individual's trajectory is always linked to and embedded in the higher-scalar ecosocial semiotic level.

Human agents who engage in dialogically coordinated linguistic or other semiotic interaction produce discourse, which is itself embedded in and is often the direct product of meaning-making activity. Texts can be seen as the semiotic products and records of acts of higher-order or symbolic consciousness. In this perspective, they can be seen as that part of the control loop of acts of higher-order consciousness which constitutes its external structure, as projected into the ecosocial environment in which the interaction takes place by means of the efferent impulses that bring about what Gibson (1983 [1966]: 46) calls performatory activity, i.e. articulatory or other potentially significant sensori-motor activity. The making of discourse – spoken or written – does not usually require deliberate planning or conscious decisions about which choice to make at every stage along the way of the unfolding text's trajectory; rather, the making of discourse is spontaneous in the sense that it is not driven by pre-programmed cognitive, mental, genetic, or other causes (Salthe 1993: 80). The discourse loops through the internal dynamics – motor control, affect, memory, semantics, and so on – of the agent as well as out into the context of situation and context of culture. In doing so, the discourse is constrained by higher-order boundary conditions or constraints in the form of intertextual systems of, for example, thematic relations, axiological orientations, and genre structures (Lemke 1985; Thibault 1986b, 1989). These intertextual systems are context-sensitive systems which emanate from the context of culture. These higher-order contextual constraints provide the unfolding text with principles of organization, as well as indications as to how it is to be interpreted and in relation to which social situation-types. These higher-order systems of intertextual systems do not prescribe rigid models of text-structure. Rather, as context-sensitive feedback, they alter real-time probability distributions in response to specific contextual contingencies as the discourse unfolds in time. It is this continual honing of context-sensitive intertextual constraints during the dynamic unfolding of the discourse that enables a specific trajectory to be carved out for the text. The logo-genetic trajectory of the discourse is the result of the interaction among the internal dynamics of the agent, initial conditions, and the ongoing adjustment to fluctuations in the specific parameters of the context of situation in which the discourse unfolds and which it, in part, enacts or constitutes.

With respect to the agent's internal – neurological, motor, and so on – dynamics, the discourse is not a reflection or a representation of something prior in the brain. Nor is there any need to explicitly form a thought or idea which must then be "coded" into linguistic form. To suggest that language is simply a public, conventional code for the externalizing and communicating of one's inner, private thoughts and feelings is to miss the entire point. Meaning is both "inside" and "outside" the brain. The dichotomy suggested by the distinction between the public and private domains is simply beside the point. To use Peng's (1994: 124) term, vague "proto-meanings" in the brain do not in themselves entail a proximate decision to create discourse in, for example, speaking or writing activities through the making of specific linguistic choices. It is not the case that the agent must formulate a specific linguistic choice in order to translate the proto-meaning into a specific linguistic realization. Instead, it is the interaction between the vague possibilities of the proto-meaning in the brain, other aspects of the agent's self-organizing inner dynamics (motor control, motivation, affective orientation, and so on), the emergent properties – both physical-material and semiotic-discursive – of the specific context of situation, along with the higher-order context-sensitive intertextual constraints, that shifts the probabilities of the attractors within the agent's inner dynamics such that linguistic choice A rather than B or C is made. Proto-meaning is, in relation to the choice of A, a broad attractor basin comprising potentially very many vague possibilities for meaning-making. Moreover, these possibilities may encompass a range of different semiotic modalities and their possible combinations in actual discourse. A particular decision to act in some way is but one possible option in a self-organizing phase space in the culture's metasystem of possible options for meaning. The metasystem is the structured system of semiotic alternatives (Lemke 1984b: 63); it specifies the meaning potential which can be accessed in a given context of culture or context of situation. In systemic-functional theory, these systems of alternatives are specified using the notation of the system network (see Fawcett 1988). The choosing of a particular option forges a narrower, steeper valley within this phase space. However, there is no need to infer a proximate decision which then pushes the choice one way rather than some other. The making of a given choice is the result of the interactions among many different factors, both inside and outside the individual, as the event unfolds in time.

Halliday and Matthiessen claim that in logogenesis, there is a "*move from potential to instance* (from system to text);" (1999: 382; emphasis in original), which can be described as a cline of instantiation. The stratified resources of language can be specified as a cline of instantiation, moving from the potential of the context of culture to the sub-potential of particular sub-cultural situation-types to specific instantial values of field, tenor, and mode in a particular context. The focus of interest of these authors is the linguistic system. I would propose, in ways I believe to be complementary to the linguistic focus of Halliday and Matthiessen, that the honing of a particular semiotic-discursive trajectory in logogenesis can be viewed as a dynamical landscape. In this perspective, the vague possibilities of proto-meaning are a very broad basined attractor space of low specification, though rich in possibilities based on memories, personal experience, and so on. The fact that I have a particular historical-biographical trajectory which has taken me through one or more contexts of culture means that my neurological semantic space is very broad. The moment that I engage in semiosis in response to some semiotic or material contingency, the semantic space self-organizes so as to narrow the range of possibilities. If we track through the proposed cline of instantiation, we may see how vague initial decisions in the broad basined proto-meaning in my mental space are, in the first instance, narrowed down by my perception and understanding of the social situation-type. This has the effect of further steepening the attractor space of my dynamical semantic landscape to a more restricted set of possible pathways through the topological semantic space.

Thelen and Smith (1994: 60) point out that there are no codes or programmes which drive this process. Instead, the system self-organizes as a function of both its intrinsic dynamics and its sensitivity to contextual conditions. Thus, "the attractor regime is only determined as the system is assembled through the slaving of its order parameter" (Thelen and Smith 1994: 60). A further narrowing of the attractor space occurs when I begin to instantiate a specific discursive production. At this point, contextually specific meanings and their realizations are selected from the available networks of options in meaning. Even so, there is no absolute rigidity about this process. The realization of a given intention along a logogenetic trajectory can take place in various ways. The semiotic resources may be co-deployed and assemble in various ways, according to specific situational contingencies, or in accordance with the particular subjective inclinations and preferences of the agents involved. Thus, the semiotic resources used are able to assemble into other stable multimodal regimes. It is this ability of multimodal semiotic resource systems to "soft-assemble" as Thelen and Smith (1994: 60) express it, that helps to explain the extraordinarily labile and adaptive nature of such systems in the face of varying personal, material, and semiotic contingencies.

Following earlier work by Lemke (1983, 1985, 1990a) and myself (Thibault 1986b, 1989, 1990, 1991a), I shall discuss these questions in the following section in terms of the *intertextual meaning-making practices* (IMMPs) of some community.

6 Lemke's theory of intertextual thematic formations

Individuals are entrained to the meanings and values of a particular ecosocial system on the basis of their apprenticed participation in specific cultural activities, which mediate their interactions with others in the same culture. The semantic valences of the words and other lexico-grammatical forms so learned are neither context-free nor fixed in their meaning. Instead, we learn the meaning potential of terms in relation to their semantic valences in specific sets of texts which are typical of a given culture or some part of it. We learn the meanings of linguistic items in relation to what Lemke (1983: 160–161) has defined as intertextual thematic formations (ITFs). To quote Lemke:

... words do not have definite meanings of their own; rather, the meaning of a word is only approximately invariant in relation to its semantic valences to (usually a small set of) other words *in a specific set of texts*. That set may form a register (Halliday 1964, Lemke 1982[1] and citations on register therein), or have some narrower relation to the set of social contexts to which its texts regularly occur. What may be invariant over almost all texts are the abstract, *taxonomic* relations of words as *lexical* items (not as *fully* semantic items). Thus *warm / cold* may be a *lexical* contrast-pair that are always in *some* kind of semantic contrast (i.e. taxonomic antonymy), but different thematic systems, and their texts, map or impose on this pair quite different semantic contents and semantic relationships, as in "a warm/cold day" vs. "a warm/cold look". What logicians wish to isolate as the exceptionality of "metaphor" is the normal semantic mode of language use, the concrete operation of the principle that all meaning is context-dependent.

(Lemke 1983: 160–161; italics in original)

Different intertextual thematic systems, the texts which instantiate them, and the social practices in which these are enacted may specify different semantic relationships and different semantic contents for the same lexicogrammatical form. The learning of particular semantic contents and semantic relationships occurs on the basis of the semantic registers and intertextual sets which instantiate particular kinds of thematic relations. Semantic neural space embodies, as it were, different semantic relationships and different semantic contents that derive from different thematic formations, even for the same abstract lexical item. The semantic schemas that generalize the meaning of instances at higher levels of schematicity constitute a very broad region of semantic state space. By the same token, the context-dependent nature of semantic relations means that each specific instance that is encountered and learned in its specific context registers context-sensitive differences. These differences are identified in the continuously varying semantic state space (Elman 1995: 199). Specific differences, Elman points out, are characteristic of different learning contexts.

The social practices in which individuals are embedded create common forms of participation and common forms of meaning-interpretation which are distributed across the members of that social group. Therefore, the development of linguistic and other forms of semiosis in the individual has a type-specific dimension. For this reason, the developmental trajectories of individuals are constrained by common factors to which their neural and bodily dynamics are entrained. This does not mean that the language system is the same for all individuals. Instead, the trajectories of individuals through the networks of socio-cultural practices which constitute their experience always have, as Lemke (1997: 48–49) has pointed out, an individuating dimension on account of the unique experiences which individuals undergo along their particular life trajectories. For this reason, the networks of associations whereby a given individual in some community assembles and elaborates, in his or her brain the language system and associated practices of that community, is never entirely identical from one individual to another.

Intertextual thematic formations in the work of Lemke (e.g. 1983, 1985) are neither systems nor structures; they have both paradigmatic and syntagmatic elements, they are both resources and ways in which resources typically get deployed to make a certain meaning about some topic. They are both **intra**-textual and **inter**-textual. Intertextual thematic formations are typical patterns of register-specific semantic relations among register-specific semantic items that recur from text to text. They are characteristic of a particular discourse community, and usually of a particular "opinion group" or value orientation within the community. When we recognize one of these patterns, we tend to say that the two texts are talking about the same topic from the same point of view or evaluative orientation. However, there is no implication that the same semantic pattern is always realized by exactly the same lexicogrammatical forms. An ITF is also typically associated with a particular value-orientation or evaluative viewpoint toward the topic. For this reason, the notion of value-orientation has been built into the definition of thematic formation. A thematic formation, or some fragment of this in a given text, is, under this definition, a realization of a particular social voice in Bakhtin's (1981) sense. The notion of

---

[1]   See Lemke (1985 [1982])

voice refers to a typical social value orientation on some topic; a given discursive or textual voice is situated in the system of social voices – the system of social heteroglossia – in some discourse community. Seen in this way, the notion of an ITF captures the fact that, in social meaning-making, there are typical associations, or contextual redundancies, between value orientations and topics. Therefore, the experiential, interpersonal, and textual dimensions of meaning-making are not neatly separable in actual discourse. Specific associations among different kinds of metafunctional selections are, in turn, redundant with higher scalar levels such as discourse genre.

Genre is a construct whereby we can specify the typical syntagmatic structuring of a discourse – how it unfolds as a Recount, a Narrative, an Argument, and so on. Genre is not just a matter of Mode, or the logical and textual metafunctions, but also of how experiential meanings are made in texts above the levels of clause and clause complex. Typically, a text does not make meanings belonging to just one thematic formation. By the same token, these meanings are not random either. Gregory (1995, 2002) has shown how the various phases and sub-phases of a text are lower-scalar levels of organization which are characterized by a fair degree of semantic homogeneity. But when we move from one phase or sub-phase in a text to the next, this local (phasal) semantic homogeneity itself shifts so that we find ourselves shifting from, say, one thematic formation to some other. We may still be in the same higher-scalar discourse genre overall, but we also move, at lower-scalar levels, from one micro-level theme to another, as well as enacting particular logico-semantic relations between them. Thematic formation relations themselves are built up by small-scale lexicogrammatical relations that are repeated in the development of cohesive chains of textual items. The thematic formation is construed by the cross-chain relations afforded by the lexicogrammatical choices made in the text.

ITFs are realized in texts by specific lexicogrammatical selections. Whereas register is a paradigmatically based construct, an ITF sits somewhere between language system *qua* system of differences and text. ITFs are abstractions from the linear succession of elements in a text. Given their abstract status, they can be realized by very many different selections at the lexicogrammatical level. Moreover, the linear sequencing of clauses and clause complexes in some text is not criterial for the definition of an ITF. This does not, however, exclude the fact that different kinds of logical sequencing between clauses impose their own semantic ordering on text development, as shown by semantic relations between clauses such as CAUSE-CONSEQUENCE, MOTIVATION-ACTION, and so on. Importantly, ITFs combine ideational and attitudinal-evaluative meaning, as pointed out above, in order to realize social voices. In their lexicogrammatical realizations, they therefore may combine experiential selections at clause (e.g. Actor-Process-Goal) and group levels (e.g. Epithet-Thing in the nominal group) with interpersonal selections such as modality and evaluative lexis. These possibilities are more concretely discussed in the following section.

7 An analysis of the interaction of thematic patterns and genre in an instance of mother–child interaction

The following text is a transcription of a spoken dialogue between a mother and a four-year-old child. It provides insights into how children learn and build up knowledge about the world through their linguistic interactions with them. Children do not acquire knowledge about the world by passively observing it, or through their personal experience alone. Instead, adults provide children with access to information through their linguistic interactions with them. Children need this kind of interaction with adults in order to expand and elaborate their knowledge beyond that provided by direct observation and personal experience.

1. **Child**: Do cars go faster than horses? [noticing rider in park]
2. **Mother**: Yes [busy driving]
3. **Child**: No, look [points to horses galloping next to traffic jam]
4. **Mother**: Not all the time; cars don't go faster all the time, but they can go faster than horses can

5.   **Child**: If we have a race . . .
6.   **Mother**: Yes, in a race, cars will beat horses

> *Source*: Clare Painter, unpublished child language data, University of Sydney

Contextual note: In this exchange, the child is aged about four years. Mother and child are in the car, which the mother is driving.

Dialogically, the text illustrates a particular kind of global organization, as shown in Table 2.1. There is an alternation of different kinds of question, statement, and command, each one responding to and interpreting the other or some aspect of the extra-linguistic situation. There is also a passing of terms such as "cars", "horses", "yes", "no", and so on, between the two participants. On each occasion, the meaning of the specific item does not remain static, but is dynamically reoriented to the context as it unfolds in time. There are also modal verbs such as "can" and "will", which indicate a particular shift in the speaker's evaluation of or attitude towards the thematics of the moves in the conversation. What we have here is the dialectical unfolding in time of a discussion about the relative speed of cars and horses. This dialectic is achieved through the interaction of specific discourse moves (statements, questions, and so on), interpersonal relations, and extra-linguistic situational factors which are relevant to the meaning of the text. The organization of the text as a sequence of initiating and responding discourse moves is shown in Table 2.1.

Table 2.1 Moves and their semantic description in mother–child exchange

Text of dialogue	Semantic interpretation of discourse move	Lexicogrammatical realization
1. Child: Do cars go faster than horses? [noticing rider in park]	Asking mother for yes/no information (on basis of direct observation)	yes/no interrogative
2. Mother: Yes [busy driving]	Mother gives positive response, thus confirming the proposition in the child's question	positive polarity
3. Child: No, look [points to horses galloping next to traffic jam]	Child contradicts mother's thesis and draws her attention to observable evidence for his position in order to infer a false generalization	negative polarity + imperative
4. Mother: Not all the time; cars don't go faster all the time, but they can go faster than horses can	Mother corrects child's incorrect generalization and gives correct generalization	negative polarity ("not", "no") + statements linked by "but"
5. Child: If we have a race . . .	Child seeks confirmation of mother's generalization through a specific instance	if-clause of condition specifying specific circumstance ("a race")
6. Mother: Yes, in a race, cars will beat horses	mother takes up and confirms instance ("yes, in a race") and completes child's argument with specification of generalized consequence ("cars will beat horses")	positive polarity + modalized statement

In this exchange between mother and child, we see how a thematic formation linking participants such as "cars" and "horses" to particular kinds of processes such as "go faster", "have a race", and "beat" in relation to the relative speed of the two kinds of participants mentioned in the given circumstance "in a race". The thematic relations are created by the semantic relations in the individual clauses and the relations between these clauses. Thus, the thematic items CAR, HORSE, GO, BEAT, and FASTER are semantically related to each other by a variety of means in the lexicogrammar of the clauses which realize the thematic items. In move 1, *cars* is a noun which is related to the circumstance of Manner: Comparison *faster than horses* by the Material: Action Process *go*. The same thematic relation is taken up by the mother in move 4, where the relationship is qualified by the Temporal Circumstance *not all the time*. The mother's qualifying use of this circumstance, along with her use of the modal *can* in move 4, serve to orient the discourse away from specific instances – specific cars and horses – to CARS and HORSES as types of participants which typically behave in certain ways according to the meanings of the thematic formation that is being activated here. Thus, her use of *can* in the final clause in move 4, signals that CARS and HORSES are being contrasted as different types of participants which can be expected to behave differently with regard to their overall speed capabilities in a thematic formation in which the relative speed of the two types is being compared. In move 6, by contrast, the mother's modal evaluation of the proposition that is being evaluated and argued about here shifts to the high modal *will* of certainty and prediction. This shift is in keeping with the law-like force of the general conclusion she is drawing in the process of her completing the CONDITION and CONSEQUENCE structure referred to above. The individual clauses in the text do not say that CARS and HORSES are different kinds of participants, for example machine versus animal. Nevertheless, it is possible to fit the examples cited above to a more general thematic relation in which the basic semantic pattern is:

MACHINE-IS-MORE POWERFUL-THAN-ANIMAL

What was not immediately obvious to the child on the basis of his initial observation of the horse in the park in comparison to the stationery car in the traffic jam, is that his observation and the false generalization he makes on the basis of it can be assimilated to a common thematic formation in terms of which the observed phenomenon can be made sense of.

The final exchange between child and mother in moves 5 and 6 is also an instance of the elementary genre of Logical Inference. The basic genre consists of two functionally related parts in a larger whole. The larger whole consists of the clause complex which combines the two clauses in this example into a larger-scale semantic structure which may be glossed as CONDITION^CONSEQUENCE. The *if*-clause spoken by the child specifies some condition, and the mother's *then*-clause completes this semantic structure by indicating the consequence which logically follows from the condition which is indicated in the *if*-clause. Clause complex relations such as the *if . . . then* structure in the above example are elementary genre structures. These elementary or primary genres provide the resources whereby conceptual thinking and logical reasoning characteristic of higher mental activity are organized. The *if . . . then* structure of the clause complex is a lexicogrammatical resource which enables the specific semantic relation of CONDITION^CONSEQUENCE to be constructed between the thematic items that are realized by the experiential semantic relations in the two clauses in question. In this example, the two parts of the structure are jointly constructed by child and mother in and through the dialogic turn-taking process. The mother completes the genre structure that is initiated by the child, in the process creating the required semantic relation between the thematic items in the child's *if*-clause and her *then*-clause. Dascal (2002: 43–53) has made a distinction between language as "environment, resource and tool of cognition" that is relevant here. The above example and related discussion show that the systemic properties of language – e.g. the semantic patterns of its thematic formations and the lexicogrammatical resources for combining clauses into larger complexes such as the CONDITION^CONSEQUENCE semantic relation – constitute a higher-scalar semiotic environment. Elementary discourse genres such as Logical Inference constitute ready-made resources that are used as technological artifacts for the purposes of carrying out specific mental operations such as reasoning about the behaviour of phenomena in the world.

The mother's superior knowledge of both the relevant thematic relations and the genre structure for reasoning about them in a logically coherent way provides the necessary scaffolding in and through which the child's own powers of reasoning and thinking are enhanced and developed. The semantic relations of the thematic formations are resources for organizing our knowledge of the phenomena of experience as information that can be accessed, retrieved, and taught to others by activating the relevant networks of thematic relations. Moreover, the genre structure that is realized by the *if . . . then* clause complex is a linguistic tool which is deployed in order to facilitate logical reasoning about the phenomena of the world and how these phenomena can be expected to behave in determinate circumstances, as in our example. Finally, language constitutes a higher-order semiotic environment – a system of interpretance. It both provides the meaning-making resources which make exchanges such as the above instance possible at the same time that language is the environment which semiotically mediates and further specifies non-linguistic thought. It does so by integrating thought to its own system of semiotically salient differences, as well as to the activities through which these differences are given sequential and logical forms of organization.

Thus, elementary genres such as the CONDITION^CONSEQUENCE relation that is realized by clause complexes of the *if . . . then* sort, are more than just formal linguistic expressions for expressing and giving shape to "inner" thought. Instead, they are activity-structure types which, when enacted in speech and writing in contextually appropriate ways, are artifacts for harnessing the agency of their users – jointly child and mother in our example – such that they are able to control the flow of events and their consequences in ways which go beyond the immediately perceptible here-&-now. Genres *qua* artifacts are semiotic technologies which are used to perform mental tasks and operations such as reasoning, rational thinking, conceptualization, and so on.

Thus, the dialogic exchange between child and mother in moves 5 and 6 functionally coordinates, by means of the CONDITION^CONSEQUENCE activity structure, (1) observed events in the world (e.g. the child's observation of the horse); (2) a determinate situation here construed in move 5 as a non-specific instance (CONDITION); and (3) the general CONSEQUENCE that can be expected to arise when the given condition is met. Thus, we see how the *if . . . then* clause complex is a semiotic tool whereby future or probable races between cars and horses are integrated into immediately present semiotic activity – the discussion between child and mother – in the form of the clause complex relation that they jointly construct in the exchange (moves 5 and 6).

The lexicogrammatical resources used therefore constitute the "mental" entities which are manipulated as formal logical operations. They do not simply reflect previously existing cognitive operations, but are themselves the cognitive operations, whether in "inner" semiosis (cf. "thinking") or "outer" semiosis (cf. "talking") (see also Ono and Thompson 1995). Such semiotic technologies play an important role in integrating the here-now dyad exchange between child and mother to larger-scale processes of socio-cultural learning. The larger-scale processes are taking place across many similar instances of parent–child interactions. They also reflect the patterns of informal teaching and learning that are typical of a particular culture or subculture (see, for example, Hasan 1996b [1986] for an important analysis and theoretical discussion of the emergence of "semantic consistencies" in mother–child interactions). These "semantic consistencies" emerge as a consequence of higher-scalar constraints that are typical of the ways in which different subcultures and social groups orient to the material and semiotic resources that are available to them (Bernstein 1971, 1990).

8 The context-sensitive and probabilistic nature of intertextual thematic formations

ITFs are, above all, **inter**textual. A particular ITF can be instantiated in a single text, or in some wider intertextual set, which may comprise just a few texts or very many texts. However, the fact that ITFs can be instantiated in single texts, or perhaps more accurately, specific texts may instantiate or activate a more abstract ITF does not mean that the ITF so instantiated is limited to any specific lexicogrammatical selection in that text. Lemke (1985) points out that ITFs are distributed across very many lexicogrammatical selections in a text. Consistent cross-linkages between cohesive chains of items (Hasan 1980) in a given text put certain kinds of items in a consistent semantic relationship with other items. In this way, a given cohesive chain is construed as realizing a consistent pattern of thematic development in a text. The lexicogrammatical resources whereby these cross-chain relations are established and maintained in texts include the clause level experiential semantic relations of Actor-Process, Medium-Process, Senser-Process, and so on, and group level relations such as Epithet-Thing. Individual chains realize a thematic-semantic item which contributes to the development of the ITF. It is the consistent patterning of cross-chain relations which leads to the instantiation and further development of some thematic formation in a given text.

In discourse, interactants, as the analysis in the preceding section shows, jointly contribute to the building up of different thematic formations. They do so by enfolding different thematic formations into the texts they produce by, for example, creating thematic ties in particular clauses between items from different formations. ITFs tend to be regularly repeated across many different textual instances on different occasions by the members of that community who use those particular thematic formations. Not all members in a community use all of the same formations or all of the same formations in the same way. Cohesive harmony, as described in the work of Hasan (1980), is the product of the ways in which ITFs are built up and developed in particular texts. Furthermore, because the same word may occur in a plurality of differing ITFs, with different semantic valences according to the ITF in which it occurs on a given occasion, Lemke's original notion of thematic system analysis also shows why de-contextualized notions of lexical meaning such as synonymy, hyponymy, antonymy, and so on, as defined in classical lexical semantics (see Lyons 1977), are inadequate. ITF analysis clearly shows that collocational relations between lexical items are constrained by the ITF in which the item occurs. The recognition of intertextual constraints on collocation patterns is an important development because the ITF analysis can reveal the **typical** semantic relations with which a given item collocates in some ITF. More precisely, collocation patterns are restricted to the typical semantic relations realized by experiential relations in the lexicogrammar of, say, the clause or nominal group which realizes these. This emphasis on typical semantic relations therefore avoids the problem of unlimited associations between items. The networks of thematic relations which are activated in symbolic neural space are constrained by the grammar: lexicogrammatical patterns and relations act as dynamic attractors and repellers which constrain the possible trajectories which can be made through this space (see also Elman 1995: 199, 208, for a similar observation). Elman, like Halliday, also draws attention to the probabilistic nature of the lexicogrammatical processes involved: the semantic valences of lexicogrammatical forms vary according to the specific ITFs which are activated in a particular context.

Elman (1995) has developed a connectionist model of the ways in which lexicogrammatical items are semantic attractors. Like intertextual thematic formations, Elman's (1995) connectionist semantic networks are both context sensitive and probabilistic. The context sensitive nature of networks allows for the ways in which the same word, in different contexts, may exhibit different, even subtly different, semantic contents. This variation is explained by the ways in which the semantic state space of different contexts attracts different semantic valences of the given item such that meaning and context are built into the linguistic form from the start. In such a view, the postulated distinction between "what a brain intrinsically knows" and "how it is socialized" becomes irrelevant (see Cowley 2001). According to Elman, language processing, rather than operating on context-free representations, as in the traditional formalist conception of the lexicon, can be seen as taking place in a dynamical system. To quote Elman:

> The lexicon is viewed as consisting of regions of state space within that system; the grammar consists of the dynamics (attractors and repellers) which constrain movement in that space. ... this approach entails representations that are highly context-sensitive, continuously varied, and probabilistic (but, of course, 0.0 and 1.0 are also probabilities), and in which the objects of mental representations are better thought of as trajectories through mental space rather than things constructed.
>
> (Elman 1995: 199)

Rather than rules as abstract formal knowledge which constrain how lexical items are combined to form syntactic units, I find it more useful to view language on the scale of the individual body-brain as networks of associations comprising ordered hierarchies of terms (see also Elman 1995: 207). Gee (1992: 45–49), for example, has pointed out in his own use of connectionist modelling of semantic potential in the individual mind-brain that the individual does not have stored language rules. Instead, the individual has networks of associations in their brains which can be deployed in specific contexts. The networks of associations stored in the individual's brain are not meaning as such, but a meaning potential – cf. Peng's proto-meaning – which can be selectively activated and contextualized in relation to other semiotic modalities, the material world, and our bodies. This meaning potential is a topologically organized phase space in the way defined by Elman (1995). Thematic formations are (inter)textually specific networks of semantic relations. They provide resources whereby "knowledge" and "information" concerning determinate domains of human experience are assembled, organized, and stored in distributed ways across the entire network of relations. These networks of semantic relations provide a resource in which the inner semiosis of "thinking", "reasoning" and other "cognitive" operations can take place. For instance, Lemke (1990a) shows how the conceptual distinctions relevant to the learning of physics in the high school classroom are based on highly specific thematic formations of the kind discussed here. Different semantic contents and relationships are defined by their relations of nearness and farness to each other in this phase space. It is the different thematic formations that we have learned that specifies the relative location of particular items in this space. In this way, different items can form networks of associations with other items in the phase space, though not all in the same way or to the same degree. The meanings we enact in our social meaning-making practices through our use of the resources of particular ITFs do not then have a prior existence apart from the ways in which we enact them through the various semiotic and material resources at our disposal. The networks of associations in our brains are, from this point of view, not meanings, but a meaning potential. We selectively contextualize the meaning-making possibilities of this potential in the process of our meaning-making activity. Thus, bodily activity is integrated with the higher-scalar system of interpretance in and through the jointly enacted social activities whereby meanings are made in context-specific ways. There is no logical, temporal, or ontological priority for the thematic formations or for the social formations relative to the acts of doing that make meaning. It is in such doings that our body-brains are integrated with the meaning-making acts in which meaning is made. Meaning has no existence prior to this. Instead, it is constituted in and through the cross-couplings of semiotic and material resources whereby meanings are made along a time-bound trajectory.

Individuals learn the meaning potential of specific items on the basis of the value which that item has in relation to other items in an ordered hierarchy of linguistic relations that comprise a language system. Our biology provides us with a basic set of intrinsic values from the very beginning of our existence. In this way, our further development and individuation is selectively nudged down some preferential pathways rather than others along an epigenetic trajectory (Edelman 1992: 46–47; Thelen and Smith 1994: 142–143). These intrinsic biological values ensure that the organism has a basic level of neural organization at birth. The presence of these values means that the individual is already equipped to interact with the world in some ways rather than others which are essential for its further development and survival. The individual's participation in the ecosocial semiotic practices of particular socio-cultural networks means that his or her neural and bodily dynamics are further entrained to the systems of values which are intrinsic to the meaning-making resource systems to which the individual has access in his or her culture (Thibault 2000a). For example, the systems of contrasting values which define, at a very high level of schematicity, a particular language system contextually entrain the individual's lower-scalar body-brain dynamics to the dynamics of the high-scalar language system. These values are not random, but reflect the distribution of the semiotically salient terms which comprise a particular semiotic system. However, individuals are not determined by the higher-scale dynamics in any simple or unilinear way. Nor are these values and their distributions exactly the same for all individuals. These values are neither static nor merely formal; on the contrary, they are dynamic, context-sensitive features of language and other semiotic resource systems as self-organizing systems. The point is, rather, that the individuals in a given socio-cultural formation interact with each other and with their material environment in ways which are mediated by socio-cultural systems of semiotic values. Thus, the individual's own body-brain dynamics are entrained to and self-organize along their trajectory. The semantic valences which linguistic and other semiotic forms have in a particular semiotic system constitute seman-tic attractors which reorganize the intrinsic dynamics of the individual system. In this way, the networks of associations of neurological connections which constitute the meaning potential in our brains is calibrated and weighted by the value-laden semantic relations among items in a particular language or intertextual thematic formation within that language.

9 Social heteroglossia as a dynamical field of attractors and repellers and the individual's re-envoicement of voices and values

Bakhtin's (1981) concept of social heteroglossia draws attention to the diversity of social meaning-making practices in a particular community. Bakhtin's term heteroglossia designates the diverse categories of social agents and the diverse social viewpoints associated with these. The differential access to and use of the meaning-making resources of the community give voice to different social positions, the social interests and values associated with these, and the different social practices and discourse genres associated with these. A given text is always produced and articulated within the wider system of social heteroglossia which operates in a given community in a given historical period. No text can stand "above" or "outside" the system of social heteroglossia. This means that all texts, in varying ways and to varying degrees, give voice to a plurality of discursive voices which speak through the text and which respond to or anticipate other discursive voices – past, present, and future. In this way, discursive voices are construed by texts as standing in varying relations of opposition, alignment, cooptation, and so on, to each other (Thibault 1991a: 43–44).

Importantly, Bakhtin (1981: 265) also points out that individual identity and intentionality are always voiced in and through the heteroglot, multi-voiced, multi-styled, and even multi-languaged diversity of heteroglossia, rather than through a unitary and normative language system which gives expression to the "unity of an individual person realizing himself in this language" (1981: 264). The individual's linguistic and other semiotic acts are neither con-strained by nor do they emanate from a unitary and homogeneous linguistic or other semiotic system. The self-organizing semantic space which is embodied in the individual's neurological dynamics is therefore constrained by the higher-scalar dynamics of the heteroglossic diversity of discursive practices with which the individual's trajectory engages in the course of their life-span as well as logogenetically on particular occasions of meaning-making. Different, even conflicting, social voices and their associated values are higher-scalar attractors within the overall intertextual space of heteroglossia. Intentional, individuating acts of meaning-making (logogenesis) are always a selective reenvoicement, to use Dore's (1989) term (see chapter 4, section 5; chapter 5; chapter 6), of the diversity of social voices that constitute the system of social heteroglossia in a given community. Higher-order consciousness, as we have seen, means (1) that the individual is less dependent on physical-material cross-couplings and more attuned to semiotic-discursive cross-couplings; and (2) that the individual is situated at the intersection of diverse scalar orders. The symbolic character of higher-order consciousness means, then, that individuals, as complex, self-organizing systems, are increasingly de-coupled from both physical-material cross-couplings *per se*, as well as from the scalar homogeneity of the here-now scale. They act from points of view which are, to a large extent, constituted in and through the symbolic resources afforded by higher-order consciousness, rather than by lower-level organic functions *per se*. Individuals are thus able to access a greatly expanded range of symbolic possibilities for intending, acting, deciding, and so on.

Bakhtin's notion of social heteroglossia is useful to the present inquiry because it shows how we need to understand the wider field of intertextual relations within which individual trajector-ies are constituted and negotiated. In selectively engaging or negotiating with diverse social voices and their values and in reenvoicing or adaptively modifying these in their own internal dynamics, agents construe intentions and then enact them as a flow of goal-seeking activity. Action is thus seen to be a function of the agent's affective identification and alignment with and ideological positioning in relation to some voices rather than others in the overall system of social heteroglossia. Insofar as individual identity and personality are a function of the complex interactions along an individuating trajectory between the agent's internal dynamics, the history of his or her engagements with the system of social heteroglossia, and the contingencies of the particular context of situation in which the agent finds him- or herself, it is possible to say that specific voices and their values which the agent has reenvoiced and internalized are attractors which are embodied in the landscape of the individual's semantic neurological space. Thus, intentions, moral judgements, decisions, and so on, are formulated in and through the voices afforded by this semantic space. The successful formulating and executing of a decision can be said to depend on the particular decision's being aligned with those voices whose attractor space is strong enough to ensure that the intention flows through into meaningful action. The clarity or otherwise of a given decision therefore depends on the robustness of the attractor space of the particular voice(s) in terms of which it is formulated and the extent to which this voice is able to resist being co-opted or neutralized by the attractor spaces of other voices which are opposed to it or which conflict with it within the self-organizing neurological semantic space of the individual.

The notion of "voice", as first defined by Bakhtin, suggests a certain robustness for a given meaning which derives from the meaning-making practices of some community. For a particular voice to be present or activated in the neurological semantic space of the individual presupposes the social meaning-making practices in and through which the individual came to assimilate that particular voice into his or her internal dynamics. The fact that a particular voice can be said to occur "inside" the individual's neurological semantic space should not distract us from the fact that these meanings could not exist if they were not integrated by the supersystem transactions in which the individual participates in the higher-scalar ecosocial system. The robustness that I mentioned above further implies that a given voice must be able to cross the threshold of consciousness. This means that the individual can activate it so that a given voice can function as an attractor in and through which meaningful action is realized. Particular thematic meanings are associated, by virtue of their position in their ITFs, with particular values. These values can act as motivational attractors whereby particular action trajectories get coupled to particular voices. Voices function as value attractors. As participants engage in discourse, they effect particular courses of action, or make particular textual choices; at the same time, they are aware of the responses of their co-participants. In this way, particular stable evaluative orientations and agents' investments in these are linked to particular thematic meanings in the ITFs of the community. The system of social heteroglossia can be viewed as a field of voices – dynamic attractors and repellers in the terminology of dynamic systems theory – in which social agents move and position themselves in the course of their meaning-making activities. The system of social heteroglossia is a dynamic field of attractors and repellers in the form of the diverse social voices and the associated values that constitute it. Individuals, in forging their particular trajectories through this field, construct their identities according to the ways in which they align with, conflict with, co-opt, and so on, particular voices in the overall system of heteroglossia.

An important aspect of discourse in the early work of both Bakhtin (1981) and Vološinov (1973 [1930]) is its multi-voiced or polyphonic character. Discourse acts *qua* tokens are not the instantiations of a single type. Instead, they usually entail selections from a plurality of overlapping, even contradictory, contrast sets which cannot be reduced to a single, determinate meaning in a given context (Lemke 1984b: 84; Thibault 1991a: 103–110). Furthermore, scalar heterogeneity means that a given act may be contextualized in relation to other meanings, other acts, other discourses, and so on, which existed or will exist or which occurred or will occur on very disparate space-time scales (Lemke 2000a, 2000b; Thibault 2000a; chapter 6, section 1 below). Thus, a given discourse voice can evoke, usually implicitly, contextualizing relations across diverse space-time scales that can become relevant to its meaning. The multi-accented character of discourse voices also refers to the ways in which a given voice may embody a plurality of differing, even conflicting or contradictory, value orientations. Given my view that consciousness is historically emergent along an individuating trajectory, we can argue that the contradictory nature of the voices that exist in neurological semantic space is the motor of irreversible change as contradictions among voices and their value-orientations are subordinated to the higher-level action trajectories which integrate them.

10 Meta-semiotic meaning-making practices, stratification, and the emergence of symbolic levels of neural organization

Halliday (1993: 98) points out that the emergence of lexicogrammar – at age 1.3 in the case of Nigel, the child studied by Halliday – makes it possible for the child to take the step into generalization, "whereby the principle of naming evolves from 'proper name', which is not yet a sufficient condition for a grammar, to 'common name', which is the name of a class" (1993: 98). The move into a stratified linguistic system with a lexicogrammar goes hand-in-hand with a move to a new level of consciousness. It is the recursive nature of language as a stratified system which makes this possible. Rather than responding to the here-now environment and its immediate extensions on the basis of iconic and indexical signs, the recursion of the newly emergent symbolic level means that these lower levels of conscious experience may be symbolically re-construed and reintegrated to the higher symbolic level of consciousness. In this way, information obtained from here-now environmental samplings may be integrated to the categories of the symbolic level without the immediately prior here-now stimulation simply being replaced by the symbolic level. The symbolic level leads to the emergence of the child's ability to generalize, to classify, and to outclassify experience (Halliday 1993: 98–99) owing to the fact that the child now has access to the names of **classes** of phenomena. This access provides the child with a symbolic resource whereby subjective experiences can now be symbolically classified and integrated in long-term memory. The emergence of further levels of recursion – stratification – in the form of discourse level forms of organization and genre structures provide the child with additional resources for integrating phenomena which have been named and classified in long-term memory into specific social activity-types and discourse genres. It is only through these higher levels of recursion that the child is able to deploy the newly acquired symbolic resources in order to control and direct the flow of environmental events. In other words, the child is increasingly integrated into activity structures and discourse genres which provide him or her with resources for directing action from an intentional source in and through the social practices of the culture.

Recursion means that what Zelazo (1999) calls "minimal consciousness", the contents of which are presumably based on perceptual-motor and conceptual categorization, is able to be decoupled from the here-now of perception and symbolically re-construed in terms of the class names which the emergent lexicogrammar begins to make available to the child. Zelazo (1999: 98) also points out that minimal consciousness is, by definition, intentional, i.e. in Brentano's (1973 [1874]) sense of being conscious of something. In my terms, this is equivalent to the earliest consciousness experience of one's own experience (see above). The symbolic memory which is afforded by recursion means that the body-brain complex begins to de-couple from the immediate here-now so that the child is able to act independently of proximate stimulus information.

The emergence of lexicogrammar also means that the prior opposition between language as action and language as reflection is now combined such that every utterance "involves both a choice of speech function (i.e., among different kinds of doing) and choice of content (i.e., among different realms of understanding)" (Halliday 1993: 100). The development of this newly emergent principle of intrinsic functional diversity therefore means that the child has symbolic resources both for construing experience and for enacting social relations – both kinds of meaning now simultaneously realized in the same lexicogrammatical form. That is, he or she has symbolic categories of both experience and action which can be de-coupled from the immediate here-now and stored in long-term memory. In this way, the child's internal dynamics are coupled with symbolic categories which can be inserted into working memory and used to reflect on environmental information which is picked up in order to orient to and guide acting at one remove from proximal stimuli, i.e. at a meta-level. It is the emergence of this meta-level that enables toddlers to formulate self-commands that allow them to organize and control the intentional flow of their actions with respect to both events and things in the world and themselves (Zelazo 1999: 113; Vygotsky 1986 [1934]: 31; chapter 5, sections 6, 7).

Prior to the emergence of a stratified linguistic system with a lexicogrammar, the child's acts of meaning are construed in what Halliday (1975) and other researchers have termed protolanguage. Halliday describes protolanguage as follows:

> This stage when children are construing their signs into sign systems, the protolanguage, typically extends somewhere in the range of 0;8 to 1;4, and it is associated with freedom of movement. Semantically, the systems develop around certain recognizable functions (the **micro-functions**, as I have called them): instrumental and regulatory, where the sign mediates in some other, nonsymbolic act (e.g., "give me that!", "sing to me!"); interactional, where the sign sets up and maintains an intimate relationship ("let's be together"); and personal, where the sign expresses the child's own cognitive and affective states (e.g., "I like that", "I'm curious about that"). There may also be the beginnings of an imaginative or play function, a "let's pretend!" sign, often accompanied with laughter (Halliday, 1975, 1978a, 1979b).
>
> (Halliday 1993: 96)

The change from protolanguage to language is an abrupt one, which those close to the child recognize as a discontinuity (Halliday 1993: 96). The interfacing of lexicogrammar between semantics at one end and phonetics at the other takes the prior protolinguistic system far from equilibrium so that the relative disorderliness internal to protolanguage – it cannot create information – is abruptly shifted to a new macroscopic regime of organization so that the new system reduces its own internal rate of entropy production (Prigogine and Stengers 1985 [1984]). The emergence of lexicogrammar between the prior levels of semantics and phonetics constitutes a local sink of macroscopic order whereby pattern and organization now come into view. The interfacing of lexicogrammar with semantics and phonetics means that previously uncoupled micro-functions are now correlated at the same time that they are reorganized. Each of the previously discrete meanings is now entrained into a global principle of pattern and organization so that they are related to each other as parts of a wider system of relations. Halliday has described this process as follows:

> Perhaps the most important single principle that is involved in the move from protolanguage into mother tongue is the **metafunctional** principle: that meaning is at once both doing and understanding. The transition begins with an opposition between utterance as action (doing) and utterance as reflection (understanding); I have referred to this as the opposition of two macrofunctions, "pragmatic/mathetic". This is transformed, in the course of the transition, into a combination whereby every utterance involves both choices of speech function (i.e., among different kinds of doing) and choice of content (i.e., among different realms of understanding). In the grammar of the mother tongue, each clause is a mapping of a "doing" component (the interpersonal metafunction) and an "understanding" component (experiential metafunction) (see Halliday, 1983; Oldenburg, 1987; Painter, 1984, 1989).
>
> We can summarize this as shown in Table 2 [renamed Table 2.2]. In Stage 1, content$_x$ and content$_y$ do not overlap and there are no combinations of prosody$_a$ with content$_y$ or prosody$_b$ with content$_x$. Stage 2 shows the beginning of clause and group structures, the grammar's construction of processes and entities. In Stage 3 the mood is now also grammaticalized, the nondeclarative then evolving into imperative versus interrogative.
>
> (Halliday 1993: 100–101)

Language is a self-organizing system which reorganizes, in the transition from protolanguage in the individual, by altering its own control parameter. This process is not efficiently caused by prior mental or cognitive programs (e.g. Chomsky's Language Acquisition Device) which reside in the individual's genes from the outset and which oversees this process. Genetic initiating conditions do not determine or cause this process. Rather, these conditions are entrained and shaped to ecosocial semiotic boundary conditions on higher-scalar levels. Language *qua* semi-

Table 2.2 Halliday's stages in development of the metafunctional principle

Stage 1 (Early transition)		Examples	
Either:	Doing ("pragmatic"), ↓ [prosody$_a$ + content$_x$]	$\overline{\text{more}}\ \overline{\text{meat}}$	"I want more meat!"
Or:	Understanding ("mathetic") ↓ [prosody$_b$ + content$_y$]	$\overline{\text{green car}}$	"That's a green car."

Stage 2 (Mid-transition)			Examples	
$\left\{\begin{array}{l}\text{Doing}\\ \text{Understanding}\end{array}\right.$	$\left.\begin{array}{l}↓\ \text{prosody}_a\\ ↓\ \text{prosody}_b\end{array}\right\}$ +	any content	$\overline{\text{mummy}}\ \overline{\text{book}}$	"I want mummy's book!"
			$\overline{\text{mummy}}\ \overline{\text{book}}$	"That's mummy's book!"

Stage 3 (Late transition)

Mood system (Speech functions)	$\left\{\begin{array}{l}\text{Nondeclarative}\\ \\ \text{Declarative}\end{array}\right\}$	Transitivity system + (Process types)	$\left\{\begin{array}{l}\text{Material}\\ \text{Mental}\\ \text{Relational}\end{array}\right\}$

otic system is an instance of a genuinely autopoetic system in which nonlinear positive feedback plays a fundamental role in the shift from the high internal entropy of protolanguage to the low internal entropy of language. In Halliday's description of the early stages of the development of the metafunctional principle when the shift to language proper has occurred, we see how positive feedback, in the form of autocatalytic cycles (see Kauffman 1993: 369–404), drive this process of self-organization. Thus, the combination of prosody$_a$ and prosody$_b$ with any content in Stage 2, which was not the case in Stage 1, activates a process – an autocatalytic cycle – such that the combination of prosodies (expression) with contents in regular and stabilized patterns itself acts as a catalyst. In this way, positive feedback loops amplify a fluctuation which occurs at the moment of the transition from protolanguage and which causes a new mode of internal organization – the metafunctional principle – to emerge. Previously discrete components such as the prosodies and contents mentioned by Halliday now cohere around some value which is internal to the system itself.

The progression from stage 1 to stage 3 in the development of the metafunctional principle reveals the progressive internal differentiation and complexity of the system as it self-organizes into a multilevel hierarchy – i.e. stratification – such that new functional components and systemic relations emerge. The system of values or differences internal to the language system self-organizes into complexly differentiated hierarchies of functional regions and relations. Thus, the stratified combination of particular prosodies with contents catalyses further combinations, which, in turn, catalyse still others, until the loop is closed as new levels of systemic organization emerge. It is this organizational closure, as Maturana and Varela (1980) have termed it, which autocatalysis brings about and which leads to this process of increasing internal differentiation and semiotic complexity. In turn, this means that the system itself is progressively differentiated with respect to its surroundings, such that it acquires its own individuating characteristics as it unfolds along its time-bound trajectory. The individual's cross-coupling to an emergent stratified linguistic system means, above all, that consciousness is increasingly de-coupled from its prior iconic and indexical modes and is now increasingly symbolic.

The newly emergent global principles of organization that the language system manifests establish a new relationship between the individual's internal dynamics and the supersystem transactions in which he or she participates in the ecosocial system. The entraining of the individual's neural dynamics to the multidimensional semantic space of the new system establishes a qualitatively new, symbolic relationship between the individual's internal dynamics and his or her relationship to the world on account of the individual's cross-coupling to the content and expression levels of organization. This results in a new type of relationship between the individual and the ecosocial semiotic environment.

I pointed out in my earlier book, *Re-reading Saussure*, that Saussure had already understood that a putative language system in which all of the terms or values intrinsic to it are equiprobable, that is, totally random, without any discernible principles of order and pattern, would be equivalent to a situation of maximal degrees of freedom in which no constraints operated (Thibault 1997: 284). Such a situation would ensure that no meaning could be construed from the resulting disorder. However, a language system is not like this, as Saussure well understood. Instead, a language system comprises regular or typical patterns of what Saussure referred to as syntagmatic and associative groups. On this basis, principles of order and pattern are features of the language system's internal organization. This means that there are constraints on the ways in which the values constituting the system are organized into recognizable functional regions and relations. Thus, the system of values in the system is not organized in an equiprobable fashion; rather, it is skewed so that the constraints which are in operation ensure that the many degrees of freedom of the system of pure values can function as a meaning-making potential that can be instantiated in specific contexts.

Halliday (1991: 42) points out that a linguistic system is inherently probabilistic in nature. This requires a paradigmatic, or systemic, orientation to the study of lexicogrammar, rather than an exclusive focus on structure. The point is, as Halliday argues, that the grammatical systems of a language have to be represented as choice, "since probability is the probability of 'choosing' (not in any conscious sense, of course) one thing rather than another" (1991: 42). In a significant adaptation of Shannon and Weaver's mathematical theory of information, Halliday (1991) has been able to make use of the large-scale computerized analysis of linguistic corpora in order to strengthen the validity of his arguments concerning the inherently probabilistic nature of grammar and the relevance of the Shannon–Weaver model to this. Here is how Halliday has characterized his thinking on this question:

> Frequency in text is the instantiation of probability in the system. A linguistic system is inherently probabilistic in nature. I tried to express this in my early work on Chinese grammar, using observed frequencies in the corpus and estimating probabilities for terms in grammatical systems (1956, 1959). Obviously, to interpret language in probabilistic terms, the grammar (that is, the theory of grammar, the "grammatics") has to be paradigmatic: it has to be able to represent language as *choice*, since probability is the probability of "choosing" (not in any conscious sense, of course) one thing rather than another. Firth's concept of "system", in the "system/structure" framework, already modelled language as choice. Once you say "choose for polarity: positive or negative?", or "choose for tense: past or present or future?", then each of these options could have a probability value attached.
>
> Shannon – Weaver, in their *Mathematical theory of communication* (1949), had provided a formula for calculating the information of a system, which I used in an exploratory way for a paper, "Information theory and linguistics", in 1968. This was a valuable concept for linguistics; but structuralist linguistics had dismissed it because they had no paradigmatic model and had therefore attempted to relate it to representations of syntagmatic structure, to which it has no relevance at all. Information is a property of a system (in the Firthian sense); not of its individual terms. The system with maximum information is one whose terms are equiprobable; any skewness (departure from equiprobability) involves a reduction in information. Hence a minimally redundant system network would be one in which all systems tended towards equiprobability.
>
> (Halliday 1991: 42)

The incorporation of redundancy in the linguistic system in the form of the skewing of probabilities means that the choice between, say, positive or negative polarity or between past, present, and future tense may have probability values attached. In other words, the choice of one term rather than some other in the systems of POLARITY and TENSE occurs less than randomly. Each choice has its typical probability skewing, which is a way of saying that its probabilities have been pre-set by the internal constraints operating within the language system. The tendency for language and other semiotic systems to evolve away from equiprobability in favour of (meta) redundancy suggests that such systems incorporate intrinsic constraints on the probability distributions of their terms (values) independently of specific instantial contexts of use. Some examples provided by Halliday are the following:

> On the basis of what little counting I had done, I suggested a bimodal distribution. The hypothesis was that systems tended towards one or other of just two types, (i) equiprobable and (ii) skew, with the skew tending towards a ratio of the order of magnitude of ten to one (which I represented for obvious reasons as nine to one, i.e. 0.9/0.1). This corresponds to one interpretation of the concept of marking: type (i), the equiprobable, have no unmarked term, while type (ii), the skew, have one of their terms unmarked. Expected examples of each type, in English, would be:
>
> (i)   equiprobable (0.5/0.5)
>   number: singular/plural
>   non-finite aspect: "*to*"/"*ing*"
>   process type: material/mental/relational
>   nominal deixis: specific/non-specific
>   verbal deixis: modality/tense
> (ii) skew (0.9/0.1)
>   polarity: positive/negative
>   mood: indicative/imperative
>   indicative mood: declarative/interrogative
>   voice (verbal group): active/passive
>   declarative theme: subject-theme/other theme
>
> (Halliday 1991: 44–45)

The probability distributions of the terms in the system mean, for example, that if one chooses within the grammatical system NUMBER, there is an equiprobability that the terms SINGU-LAR or PLURAL will be chosen. Likewise, if one chooses within the system of POLARITY, the probability that one will choose POSITIVE in contrast to NEGATIVE is skewed by a factor of 0.9 to 0.1. These and the other probability distributions referred to above refer to the given term's intrinsic probability within the language system. However, terms do not occur on their own, independently of their patterns of co-occurrence with other terms. Their probability also depends on the larger-scale grammatical and discourse structures and the intertextual formations in which they occur. In other words, the selection of particular terms is the realization of higher-order principles of patterning at the levels of, say, group/phrase or clause in the grammar. There are, then, further levels of constraints operating beyond those of the prior probabilities of the terms in the system that make typical or regular lexicogrammatical patterns emerge.

The emergence of typical lexicogrammatical patterns corresponds, as I mentioned above, to the presence of global principles of organization in the language system. This means that there are limitations on the possible combinations of the elements which comprise the system. However, these limitations on the possible variety of forms in the language have the advantage of permitting a vast number of different meanings to be made across very many different contexts of use. For example, the combination of a choice from among a small number of possible basic mood options (e.g. declarative, interrogative, imperative) with one of the choices in the transitivity system (e.g. material, behavioural, mental, verbal and relational processes) provides for a greatly expanded potential to mean in different contexts. In this case, the inter-functional solidarity (Martin 1991) across metafunctions means that different functional regions in the language system are synchronized within the same lexicogrammatical form, such that the previously separate micro-functions of the child's protolanguage are now brought together into a more complexly differentiated lexicogrammatical form – for example, the clause – which allows the newly emergent language system to access a greater variety of states than could the prior, protolinguistic system.

Halliday's illustration (see Table 2.2 in the citation above from Halliday 1993: 100–101) of the stages in the development of the metafunctional principle in the early phases of the child's entry into language shows how the co-patterning of prosody$_a$ and prosody$_b$ with "any content" (Stage

2) functions as a catalyst which increases the probability of further differentiation (Stage 3), where the mood system combines with the transitivity system. The systematic co-patternings of prosody$_a$ and prosody$_b$ with "any content" alters the prior probabilities of Stage 1, where the two prosodies were co-patterned with two disjoined contents. The new systematic combinations that emerge in Stage 2 have skewed the previously operating probability distributions and in ways which pave the way to the new possibilities of combination in Stage 3. Stage 1 is characterized by the either/or independence of one micro-function from other (i.e. the pragmatic and mathetic). Stages 2 and 3, on the other hand, show the emergence of increasing dependence at the same time that the probability distributions are altered.

The significance of the metafunctional principle lies in the fact that choices in one metafunction are internally related to and affected by choices in other metafunctions. A given metafunctional choice constitutes the context for the interpretation of the others in the meaning of the clause, text, or whatever, as a whole. This is a very different perspective from the prevailing view in linguistics that interpersonal and textual meanings are extrinsic to language form and, therefore, only externally related to experiential content (see Thibault and Van Leeuwen 1996). In showing how these meanings, too, are incorporated into lexicogrammatical form, it is possible to show in a more principled way how the current state of the system depends on its history. Halliday's analysis in the Table 2.2 shows how positive feedback loops of autocatalysis incorporate the time-bound effects of the individual's trajectory into the internal organization of language as a stratified semiotic system. Specifically, his example refers to the ontogenetic time whereby the various stages illustrated above are shown to be dependent on prior ones. However, the same point refers to all fractal levels of an individual's trajectory – from the logogenetic time of text instantiation to the ontogenetic time of development to the much slower and larger timescale of the evolution of the ecosocial semiotic system within which the individual's trajectory is embedded. To go back to a point made by Salthe and Lemke, the system only exists and only has its identity as a trajectory-in-time such that the system's past is incorporated into the system's present. This is true of all three levels of time mentioned above.

Consciousness has been repeatedly talked about as if it were a thing. However, our discussion of consciousness as a trajectory draws attention to the ways in which consciousness is constrained by its own history. Its behaviour is dependent on the contingencies – material, semiotic, and historical – which led to its creation and ongoing maintenance in time. Furthermore, positive feedback loops mean that the system's present and future are dependent on its being embedded in its contexts. The emergence of the metafunctions during the child's move into the fully stratified language system represents the shift into a new form of internal organization whereby the individual body-brain complex is integrated into new boundary conditions which relate it to its contexts. The inter-functional solidarity among the diverse semantic regions in the lexicogrammar of language leads to a more highly differentiated system whereby social semiotic hierarchies and semantic variation are created.

Once the autocatalytic loop represented by Stage 2 in Halliday's example closes, we have a phase change, as seen in the emergence of more clearly delineated metafunctional regions (e.g. mood and transitivity) in Stage 3. At this stage, top-down contextual constraints emerge as a constraint on the lower-level metafunctional components. These top-down constraints function as the boundary conditions for the choice of metafunctional components at the level below. Importantly, the two levels are systematically and internally related to each other. Following Kauffman (1993: 384–385), we can say that the mutual action of prosodies and contents to produce new formal sequences builds up constraints, as revealed by the relations between the newly emergent metafunctional components. The point is that the catastrophic shift – the discontinuity – from protolanguage into language entails the self-organization of the metafunctional diversity discussed earlier. The previously discrete micro-functions of protolanguage, in the processes of their re-organization, become interdependent. As I pointed out above, selections in one metafunction affect selections in the other. It is this which leads to the formation of top-down constraints – e.g. from context to text – in addition to the constraints already in place at lower levels. These downwardly acting constraints mean that the lower-level parts can only have their meaning and identity in relation to the whole.

The new constraints, acting downwards, alter the probability distributions of the lower levels,

and hence their degrees of freedom. Hasan's (e.g. 1996b [1986]) work on mother–child interaction in Sydney (Australia) shows how the interaction itself shapes the ways in which children
learn and the kind of knowledge they have. The different patterns of reasoning that her research
showed to exist in a systematic way in the interactions in lower-class and middle-class homes
shows how these different orientations to meaning or semiotic styles and, consequently, the
different ways in which their consciousness is constituted, are a consequence of the contextually
determined probability distribution of the kinds of linguistic selections typically made, along
with their typical patterns of combination. Different probability distributions of options in
meaning, themselves the instantiation of higher-order coding orientations, entrain both the
child's ways of making meaning as well as his or her internal dynamics. Thus, the systematic
orientation along one's historical-biographical trajectory to some ways of making meaning
rather than others within a particular society means that those meanings and associated practices become part of the way in which the individual is integrated into larger organism-
environment supersystem transactions (Lemke 1984b: 63).

The transition from protolanguage to language is a bifurcation, which further hones the
organism's integration with its ecosocial environment. The emergence of the metafunctions
means that many diverse space-time scales can be incorporated into the internal dynamics of
the individual. The stratified and recursive nature of language reorganizes these dynamics such
that the metafunctional interfacing of the individual body-brain and the ecosocial semiotic
environment leads to the self-organizing of a qualitatively different mode of organization. This
new mode of organization has significant repercussions for the organization of consciousness in
the individual. We have already seen that the de-coupling of "minimal consciousness" from the
here-now scale marks the beginning of the development of self-consciousness and reflective
consciousness. This goes hand in hand with an increase in the variety of the meaning options
available to the individual system, now seen as the emergence of higher-order contextual constraints from the lower-order components of the prior system. It is the synchronization and reorganization of the previously discrete micro-functions which enables more complex forms of
organization to emerge by virtue of the stratification of the language system into semantics,
lexicogrammar, and phonology or graphology. With respect to protolanguage, the new system
constitutes an expansion of the prior system's phase space. Bottom-up enabling constraints
create new possibilities for symbolic meaning-making – i.e. an expanded system of metafunctionally organized options in meaning – which the individual can access. This expansion of
symbolic meaning potential means that many diverse space-time scales can now be accessed
in ways that the previously iconic and indexical modes of protolanguage, confined as they are
to the here-now scale, cannot. The emergent metafunctional organization of language has
capacities that the other levels do not have.

Again, following a suggestion in Kauffman (1993: 394), the couplings among elements in this
emergent metafunctional organization are not defined by external criteria. The cross-coupling
of metafunctional components within lexicogrammatical form is defined according to intrinsic
principles of organization (Halliday 1979a). Couplings of prosodies and contents, as seen
above, attain a contextual adaptiveness, which is dependent on their exchanges with the higher-
scalar ecosocial environment. In this way, they co-evolve with other combinations (e.g. mood
and transitivity) through processes of mutation, recombination, and selection. Halliday's
analysis, as discussed above, shows that metafunctional couplings are governed by criteria
whereby the action (interpersonal) component of one micro-function acts on the content
(experiential) component of another. Both the grammar and its dynamical self-organization in
neural semantic space is an open, dynamic, self-organizing system. Such systems are "always
out of equilibrium, always adapting, rather than falling to simple dynamical attractors"
(Kauffman 1993: 394).

The interfacing of a metafunctionally organized lexicogrammar between the levels of content
and expression in the earlier protolanguage imposes second-order constraints on the system as
a whole. In this sense, it limits the system's degrees of freedom. I have argued, following
Kauffman, that the global order of lexicogrammar is an autocatalytic system, the integrity of
which is maintained through its continual transactions with its ecosocial semiotic environments.
Importantly, the metaredundancy relations in operation select which environmental elements

can enter the system. It is the interdependency of the internally organized metafunctional components, along with their context sensitivity, which makes this possible. The metafunctions mutually act on and constrain each other, thereby maintaining the system's integrity. Because the components of the system are constrained by intrinsic criteria, this allows for the emergence of higher-order context-sensitive semantic components which, in turn, constrain the lexicogrammatical level. It is this semantic level which interfaces with context (Halliday 1978b: 123, 130–133). These top-down constraints limit the ways in which lexicogrammar can behave. By the same token, the metafunctional organization brings together previously separate microfunctions into a new system, with massively expanded meaning-making potential.

The emergence of symbolic levels of neural organization means greater degrees of freedom, along with the potential for the higher-order semantic space to organize in ways not predicted by the lower levels. Small differences in initial conditions may lead to major differences as the trajectory unfolds in time. Higher-order or symbolic consciousness is a semantic space whose emergent properties are the experiential manifestation of self-organizing body-brain dynamics in dialogue with their ecosocial environment along a time-bound and historical trajectory.

In the final section of this chapter, I shall explore this question in relation to the notion of reference.

11 Life as a referent: iconic, indexical, and symbolic dimensions

Rather than rules as abstract formal knowledge which constrain how lexical items are combined to form syntactic units, I find it more useful to view language on the scale of the individual body-brain as networks of associations comprising ordered hierarchies of terms. Individuals learn the meaning potential of specific items on the basis of the value which that item has in relation to other items in an ordered hierarchy of linguistic relations that comprise a language system. Individuals learn meanings on the basis of their apprenticed participation in specific cultural activities which mediate their interactions with others in the same culture. The semantic valences of the words and other lexicogrammatical forms so learned are neither context-free nor fixed in their meaning. Instead, we learn the meaning potential of terms in relation to their semantic valences in specific sets of texts which are typical of a given culture or some part of it. As we saw above, meanings are always mediated and made in and through particular intertextual thematic formations. Different intertextual thematic formations, the texts which instantiate them, and the social practices in which these are enacted may specify different semantic relationships and different semantic contents for the same lexicogrammatical form. The social practices in which individuals participate create common forms of participation and common forms of meaning interpretation which are distributed across the members of that group. It follows that the development of linguistic and other forms of semiosis in the individual has a type-specific dimension. The developmental trajectories of individuals are constrained by common factors to which their neural and bodily dynamics are entrained. However, we also saw that the language system is never exactly the same for all individuals. Instead, the trajectories of individuals through the networks of socio-cultural practices which constitute their experience always have, as Lemke (1997: 48–49) has pointed out, an individuating dimension on account of the unique experiences which individuals undergo because of their particular life histories. For this reason, the networks of associations whereby a given individual in some community assembles and elaborates in her brain the language system and associated meaning-making practices of that community is never entirely identical from one individual to another.

For all the common patterns of meaning-making which typify a given community and which constrain its members, there are also the historically specific trajectories of particular individuals through the common patterns, such that these can be experienced and re-elaborated in ways unique to particular individuals and their specific circumstances. Take linguistic reference, for example. The ability to refer is often taken to be one of the crowning achievements of the symbolic mind. In this view, "what is referred to" is mapped onto internal cognitive representations in the brain. This view assumes the autonomy of language as a system of forms housed in an individual's mind. On the other hand, the view that reference is semiotically mediated activity leads to a very different view. In such a view, reference is an act of selective re-contextualization of linguistic forms, other semiotic resources of the human body such as gaze, prosody, facial expression, pointing, and so on, the specific interests and motivations of the agents involved, the social activity jointly engaged in, and the physical-material world.

On the other hand, reference in the Cartesian view is founded on the concept of world-as-machine: reference, in this perspective, is a device for picking out some bit of "reality" from the ensemble of bits that comprise a world which is essentially external to us. The Cartesian view of reference is based on the non-semiotic assumption that there is a world "out there" to be referred to. In this view, language reflects that superior reality. Furthermore, words are the objects of formal processing in this view. Formal rules operate on words: once acoustic and phonetic processing has taken place, their internal representations are stored and accessed for retrieval from storage. Once such retrieval takes place, the internal representations of words are combined by rules to form abstract syntactic units. But I have suggested above a different, internalist view of reference as a means of interpreting and categorizing the phenomena of the world through the semiotic mediation of language and other semiotic resources. This semiotic mediation is by definition intersubjective through and through.

Symbolic reference can only occur when the child has the massively expanded meaning potential afforded by lexicogrammar. In order to see how this works, we need to understand the stratified nature of the relation between the grammatical class "noun" and the name the noun realizes. I shall now discuss this. In terms of Deacon's (1998[1997]: 79–101) referential hierarchy comprising iconic, indexical, and symbolic modes of reference, a noun is a grammatical word class which is **iconically** related to the name of some category of "Thing" in a given language (Halliday 1988: 28–29). The distinction between "noun" as a grammatical class item and "name" as the meaning which this grammatical class realizes helps us better to sort out the distinction between the grammatical form "noun" and its semantic function. A noun symbolic-ally names a semantic type-category of thing; it does not, as such, have any referring function. The iconic nature of the relationship between the two simply refers to the natural or non-arbitrary character of the relationship between grammatical form and semantic function, viz. nouns name categories of human experience – specifically, categories of Thing – which are recognized within a given language system.

The referring function of the noun only becomes apparent when a given noun is grounded by the grammatical resources of the nominal group. Take the nominal group *that damn medal* in the clause *I've never worn that damn medal*. The noun *medal* is simply the name of a category of Thing in English. There is an iconic relationship between this noun and the category it names. At this iconic level, discourse participants simply recognize the relationship between noun and thing named. They do not have to engage in algorithmic rule-governed procedures for assigning a meaning to the grammatical form. However, it is only within a nominal group such as *that damn medal* that the noun refers to a specific medal. Both the deictic *that* and the attitudinal Epithet *damn* are relevant here. The common noun *medal* merely specifies a type-specification of a Thing. It is not tied to specific instances of the type-category. The resources of the nominal group enable the type-specification to be instantiated as a specific instance of the particular type-category. The nominal group, as linguists such as Halliday (1994 [1985]: 180–190), Lan-gacker (1991: chapter 2) and Davidse (1997) have shown, allows specific things to be referred to in some discourse context according to a number of semantic parameters. In our example, these are as follows: (i) type specification, expressed by the Thing element in the nominal group ("medal") and the non-determining modifier ("damn"); (ii) instantiation, expressed by the determiner "that"; and (iii) grounding, also expressed by the determiner "that".

The indexical functions of the various resources mentioned here therefore serve to specify a particular instance of the Thing in some discourse context. Only in this way can a particular instance of the Thing be tracked through some discourse event or text such that it is understood as referring to the same participant. Indexical grounding in discourse by means of the various categories of deixis entails socially constrained meaning-making activity in which the recognition of the named category is achieved through its grounding in culturally thick networks of activities and practices. In this way, the semiotic salience of the entity referred to is more readily grasped on account of its cultural association with an abstract semiotic value of a given term. The symbolic value – the semantic valence of the term – means that the iconic recognition of the named category is more readily grasped on account of the symbolic value which the noun has acquired as the name of a thing in relation to a symbolic system of the names of other things in a given language.

Nevertheless, the deictic and other items referred to here are not pure indexes. They also have symbolic functions by virtue of their belonging to a system of contrasting terms, each with their semantic valences deriving from their place in that language system. Thus, the type-specification function of the Thing element *medal* contrasts with other categories in an ordered hierarchy ranging from maximally schematic to maximally specifying, as shown in section 6. The determiner *that* has both symbolic and indexical functions. It is part of a system of symbolic possibilities because it contrasts with other terms such as *this*, *those*, and so on, in a **system** of contrasting terms. In this way, *that* does not merely index the occurrence of a particular Thing in some context. It also specifies a deictic value that symbolically construes the spatial and/or attitudinal relation between the speaker and the medal as [DISTAL] rather than [PROXIMATE]. The attitudinal relation is further reinforced in our example by the attitudinal meaning conveyed in the word *damn*, which both indexes the speaker's relationship to the Thing and symbolizes a category of attitude or affect in contrast with other possible selections, for example *precious*, *valuable*. The point of this discussion is to suggest that reference involves processes of semiotic mediation which integrate the iconic, indexical, and symbolic facets of the lexicogrammatical resources of the nominal group.

Reference is a semiotically mediated relationship between the deployment of these resources in some context and the referent so created. This means that reference involves both the instantiating and categorizing functions of the nominal group. Referents are specifiable, as Bruner (1999: 335) has pointed out, by their functions in discourse. To be a referent means being integrated into the texture of some discursive event. The resources of the nominal group come into their own here. Not only do these resources ground referents in textured discourse events, but they also identify them as being instances of such-and-such a category at the same time that attitudinal or affective (interpersonal) orientations to them are organized by these same resources. The clause I have used as an example here was spoken by Bob Kerrey, as reported in the *International Herald Tribune* dated 28–29 April 2001, p. 1, with reference to the Bronze Star medal which he had been awarded "after he led a squad that killed more than a dozen unarmed women and children during the Vietnam War" (*IHT*). The referent in question is embedded in a controversial, affect-charged historical context in which Kerrey's actions as leader of a Navy Seal Squad in the Mekong Delta have been questioned. The resources of lexicogrammar enable the bringing together of the interpersonal and the experiential dimensions of the referent – cf. Bruner's (1999) instrumental and epistemic intentions. In this way, the referent emerges as an intentional object of dialogically coordinated semiotic activity in which addressers and addressees can both orient to the referent as an object of experience at the same time that this is embedded in the unfolding interpersonal exchange between interlocutors. What we see here is how reference functions in interlinked networks of ecosocial processes across different space-time scales. This interlinking of different semiotic scales is reflected in the contextual integration of the iconic and indexical functions of reference to the symbolic function.

That is, there is no epistemically private mental domain to start with. Instead, the body-brain is a smaller-scale system which creates order, pattern, and meaning through its transactions with the larger-scale ecosystem in which it is embedded (Lemke 1997: 42). The specific forms of closure whereby a sense of a self and self-consciousness emerge in individuals are no exception to this. Reference, like any other form of meaning-making, always occurs in a network of relations involving both biological and social semiotic processes and the particular forms of cross-coupling between these that characterize particular social groups. In this view, a given language *qua* system of relations is structured in ways which enable its users to create referents in discourse. Reference cannot be reduced to specific uses of these resources *per se*.

The increase in the system's redundancy – i.e. the tendency to evolve away from equiprobability – means that the meaningful variety of the system also increases as the system becomes more highly organized along metafunctional lines. This increase in meaningful variety means that the system's determinacy also increases.

PART II
Agency, Otherness, and the Self

3

Agency and Intentionality in Early Infant Semiosis

1 The timescales of development and individuation: preliminary questions

The formation of pre-linguistic, cognitive, and linguistic mechanisms does not take place on short timescales. Short-term events such as the interactive encounters between caretakers and infants contribute to the creation of these longer-term processes. However, it is the longer-term processes, and the ways in which these integrate the short-term ones, that constitute the reality of human cognitive and (pre)linguistic development. We still know very little about how such integration across timescales takes place. This integration requires two fundamental shifts in perspective. First, the individual is only definable as a sub-system operating in some larger-scale ecosocial semiotic system. Secondly, the individual is only definable in dynamical terms as a trajectory which both develops and individuates through its interactions with its environment – social and material – along its temporal (lifespan) trajectory (Salthe 1993; Lemke 2000a; Thibault 2000a).

The development of semiosis in humans therefore requires integration across timescales. What we think, feel, say, and mean in this particular micro-encounter, with a given caretaker, in this dialogic position, and so on, is integrated with processes and relations on larger space-time scales by processes of memory-governed meaning-making. Crucial here are the ways in which, for example, affective stances emerge and develop on timescales that are greater than that of the single micro-encounter, which may last mere seconds or minutes. Such affective dispositions are created by the individual's participation in typical child rearing and other practices over much longer timescales. Moreover, they appear to be linked to socio-economic, educational, nutritional, and other factors along the individual's temporal trajectory. Aside from "universal" genetic factors, we can enquire as to how, for instance, socio-economic and nutritional factors shape the epigenetic environment whereby gene information is elicited along an individual's trajectory.

In this perspective, we can consider the principle of dialogic closure (Bråten 1992, 1998) and how it functions in bringing about the emergence of meaning in infants (Thibault 2000a; Cowley *et al.* In press). Here, the focus is on the ways in which dyad transactions in which infant and caretaker jointly participate are transformed in the infant's developing neurological dynamics. There is a continuous exchange between the infant's internal neural and motor dynamics and the activities which take place in the caretaker–infant dyad as a whole (Perinat and Sadurní 1999). In the process, the proto-meanings which are elaborated in the child's mind are projected back into the dyad and further modified, and so on. Emergent patterns of meaning-making in the dyad on the here-now scale become the basis for the emergence of more complex patterns on larger scales. On its own scale, the dyad itself is an individual with its own history. At the same time, it has features which are typical of the larger-scale developmental processes in a given community. The essential point here is the self-organizing nature of the process, which is fed by the reciprocal contributions of both infant and caretaker. Relevant questions to be addressed here include: (1) How does the caretaker–infant dyad itself develop as an individual in primary intersubjectivity? (2) How is its development typical of its kind in a given socio-cultural community? (3) How is it constrained and enhanced by processes operating on larger space-time scales? (4) How do specific body-brain dynamics, in combination with the particular positions taken up in dialogue by caretaker and infant, along with the use of particular social and material resources on the here-now scale of dyad interaction, contribute to this development?

2 Early infant semiosis and the dyadic regulation of the body-brain system

The actions and behaviours of the individual are not the doings of the solitary and autonomous individual. According to the logic of three-level hierarchy thinking (chapter 1, section 4), individual agents always interact with other agents and entities on the same scale of the L level here assumed to be focal. This level is the world which we perceive with our perceptual systems and in which we act, move around, and interact with others (see Gibson 1986 [1979]: 8–10). Above all, it is the world in which we interact with and modify the actions of others at the same time that they interact with and modify our own actions. Colwyn Trevarthen has shown that in the first developmental stage of intersubjectivity (primary intersubjectivity), i.e. 0 to 2 months after birth, mother and infant participate in proto-conversation whereby "dialogic closure" is enacted and maintained by the reciprocal exchange of feelings and affect.

Studies of semiotic development in pre-linguistic infants by Bråten (1992, 1998, 2002), Halliday (1975, 1978a, 1992), Kaye (1984 [1982]), Trevarthen (1992), and others have shown that in the very earliest moments of the infant's life, mother and infant reciprocally act on each other in ways that link them together as a dyad. In the process of adapting to each other, there emerge higher order patterns which regulate the possible ways in which the two members of the dyad can interact with each other. The resulting dialogic closure of the mother–infant dyad therefore consists of emergent order and organization at level L+1. The order and organization at this level is no less consequential for individual behaviour than the neuroanatomical and neuropsychological capabilities within the individual organism. Here is Trevarthen on the ways in which 2-month olds typically interact with their mothers:

> The mother is usually alert to any new focus of the infant's attention and she responds quickly. She detects the baby's glance to one side and reveals in her speech that she interprets it as a sign that the "utterance" to her is going to be "about something in the baby's mind", possibly the germ of an "idea" about their shared world. In this way fundamental syntactic forms, particularly a basic articulation between control of direct interpersonal contact and redirection of interest to a collateral "referent" or "topic", may be detected in the cyclic patterning of protoconversation, and also given a place in the emotional "melody" of an utterance.
>
> (Trevarthen 1992: 105–106)

In this passage, Trevarthen shows that the constraints arising from the reciprocal exchange of elementary signs at level L constitute emergent patterns at the level L+1 of the dyad in the form of "fundamental syntactic forms". Such emergent patterns at the level of the dyad in turn act on and impose boundary conditions on the actions of the individuals – mother and infant – at the level below. Trevarthen's research emphasizes the socioaffective character of these early exchanges between infant and mother. The relationship of "dialogic closure" means that mother and child are engaged in a dyadic system of reciprocal affective stimulation and response to stimulation. For example, the mother's facial expression communicates positive affect – e.g. interest and motivation – towards the infant; this communication on the part of the parent arouses positive affect in the infant, and the positive affect so aroused is, in turn, communicated back to the mother by the infant's facial expression. The resulting "dialogic closure" is an emergent property of the individual contributions that mother and infant make to the ongoing exchange of meanings between them.

In the period from 3 to 6 months, the infant begins more actively to explore its surroundings. With increasing use of body-action and object-manipulation, the infant begins to detach itself from the mother and to explore its surroundings. The affective transactions between infant and mother both function as a secure reference point for the infant at the same time that they also function to further motivate the child's interest in and desire to explore the world beyond the mother–infant dyad. The mother thus stimulates the infant to sample the information- and meaning-rich environment. In so doing, she acts as an external regulator of the infant's developing brain.

Importantly, approximately 83% of the development of the prefrontal cortex takes place post-natally in the first two years of the infant's life. In other words, brain and language co-develop in the course of both development and individuation (see Deacon 1998 [1997]). The infant's developing prefrontal cortex is attuned to the output from the mother's right hemisphere. This process has its origins in the very first socioaffective exchanges between mother and infant in primary intersubjectivity.

However, the mother is more than simply an external regulator of the child's developing brain. The central point is that the body-brains of both mother and infant are **mutually** (dialogically) regulated and entrained by the interactions between them. Thus, the mother's face, gaze, and smile arouse pleasure in the infant. In turn, the infant instigates acts of, for example, smiling in order to obtain a pleasure-giving response from the mother. The mutual give-and-take of these early dyadic exchanges draws attention to the fact that the child is being inserted into and is learning to participate in jointly made and sustained activity structures. In the process, he or she is learning to take up specific positions in the dyad as well as to orient to the other from these positions. In other words, the infant is learning to participate in the prototypes of what will later become the fully-fledged semiotic genres and social activity-types of the community (see section 5).

The importance of the infant's participation in these early forms of activity with the mother and their consequences – both biological and social – for the child's development have been shown by Shanker (1996). Shanker (1996) points out that a number of recent studies of the aetiology of social deficits in autistic children suggest that the autistic child's inability to participate in these socioaffective exchanges may adversely affect the neurological mechanisms whereby such affective bonds are created in the course of these exchanges. Thus, the normal development of the cortico-subcortical circuitries in the prefrontal cortex will be impaired. Such impairment means that "the connections that are programmed to form between the limbic system and the prefrontal cortex will not be adequately developed and differentiated" (Shanker 1996: 25). It is the consequent failure of the prefrontal system to "control and modulate the operations of the orbitofrontal cortex" (Shanker 1996: 25) that leads to the social deficits which, in autistic children, tend to manifest themselves towards the age of 3. Progress has been made in the therapeutic rehabilitation of autistic infants by rebuilding the socio-affective links with the infant. Shanker reports on the success of therapies such as LOVAAS, OPTION, and TEACHH in helping children to adjust to their hypersensitivities. These same therapies can also help caregivers not to "overstress the child's fragile visual, tactile, or auditory systems" (Shanker 1996: 26). In doing so, it has been possible to assist autistic children to participate in the dyadic exchanges so essential for the development of the corticolimbic centres.

3 Movement, consciousness, and proto-intentionality in infant semiosis: Trevarthen's account

Trevarthen (1978: 100) argues that the newborn is predisposed, from the very outset of its existence, to experience what Halliday has called "the contradiction between the two primary modes of experience, the material and the conscious" (1992a: 20–21). Trevarthen observes that "neonates move the parts of their body in coordination with external events in patterns that proves that there is far more intrinsic unity and variety of intention in the untutored brain than Piaget assumes in his pioneer study (1953)" (1978: 121–122). The first shaping of consciousness occurs in the dyadic space-time of primary intersubjectivity relative to an embodied point of action. The rhythmic periodicities consisting of matter, energy, and meaning flows in the dyad organize space-time relative to some point of action in relation to which the movement is centred and coordinated. Trevarthen has made the following pertinent observation concerning the ocular orienting and pre-reaching arm extensions of 2- or 3-month olds:

Each of these highly coordinated, synergistic and periodic movement patterns is purposive in the sense that it has a clear shape adapted to the performance of an ultimate conscious operation (looking to see, reaching to grasp and manipulate), but all of them may be produced in elaborate and far from random form when there is no actual object present to serve as goal. All are (in outline) of the same form as adult movements which are clearly voluntary.

(Trevarthen 1978: 123)

These regular movement patterns are related to an emergent sense of a point of action as the source of proto-intentionality which orients to and acts on the world (the nonself). Thus, patterns of body movement are organized in intersubjective and socially cooperative ways which constitute the basis of the action trajectories that are sourced at the self. From the neonate's perspective, the distinction between self and nonself is a fuzzy or vague one; it is based on topological-continuous variation, rather than the typological-categorial distinctions that are the characteristic mode of organization of the grammar and semantics of natural language. The linguistic glosses "self" and "nonself" that I have used should not distract us from this important point. My point is that the movement patterns of looking, grasping, and manipulating described by Trevarthen entail a proto-self in interaction with the immediate environment beyond its body. The notion of the proto-self does not mean that the newborn is consciously aware of this distinction as anything more than a vague continuum of topological-continuous differentiations. Such activities involve a reentrant loop extending along a trajectory from the child to the object which is the focus of interest or attention and then back again to the child's body-brain. It is this loop, including both efferent and afferent elements, which constitutes the neonate's primitive conscious awareness (reentrant loop) of his or her doing/being-in-the-world as a purely topological, pre-polarized whole. At this early stage, consciousness is just this entire loop, which is embedded in the flows of matter, energy, and meaning of the dyad as a whole. It is not until later that the reentrant connectivity of neural groups creates a meta-loop that closes the first-order loop in the dyad on the "me" sector such that an awareness of self as a point of action and awareness emerges (section 5). The topological differentiation between the two sectors therefore constitutes the basis for their further differentiation as two poles of experience and meaning in the further development and individuation of the dyad (section 7).

Trevarthen notes that in primary intersubjectivity "the activities directed to persons, and highly responsive to them, are different in form and in coordination from those directed to objects" (1978: 125). Primary intersubjectivity is the phase in which "the prototype of diadic communicative interaction" emerges. This fact suggests that the interpretation of others is an inbuilt evolutionary priority. Adult and infant engage in reciprocal acts of meaning exchange. There is a fundamental difference with respect to the way the infant orients him- or herself to other kinds of objects, such as inanimate ones. What makes the infant respond to other social beings – other embodied subjectivities – in its social purview? How does this differ from the ways he or she responds to other classes of inanimate object? Here is Trevarthen's explanation:

How, physically, could the infant mind identify persons? What features of their behaviour are diagnostic of them? Intentional behaviour has a number of features that are not shared with inanimate things, and so an intentional agent may be equipped to respond to others like itself. To control complex movements the brain organizes patterns of motor output which detect themselves as well as their effects that are reflected back from the world as reafference. Given an unchanging, stable environment, the best way to move with control is in preprogramed, ballistic steps. All intentional movements have a saccadic (stepping) quality. Inanimate movement runs downhill, oscillates in simple ways, bounces, but it does not surge in self-generative impulses. Anything that tends to make unprovoked bursts of rhythm, like a spot of reflected sunlight, seems alive. This rhythmical vitality of movement is the first identifier of live company.

When the circumstances of intention are changing, complex, or uncertain, the brain must accurately distinguish self-made change in sensory signals from effects caused from outside. Awareness of the world is facilitated by a special sensitivity to one's own pattern of action. In a society of intentional agents each may detect the output of acts of others, as if they were produced by each agent itself. I believe that animal communication evolves by adaptation of the self-detecting, ego functions of the subject-agent, an adaptation that serves to pick up the effects of others with like subjectivity.

(Trevarthen 1978: 130)

The infant has an inbuilt and selective sensitivity to the field-like surges of energy which are characteristic of the movements and articulatory activity of other animate beings, especially conspecifics. The rhythmic and saccadic nature of these patterns of movement consists of continually changing energy states, corresponding to a charged field of articulatory or other movement variables. Such patterns are structured in terms of a field of relations of continuously changing topological variation. This continuous topological variation is quite different from the typological distinctions whereby segmental units such as phonemes and syllables are distinguished in speech on the basis of the differential position of the articulators. Speech prosodies such as rhythm, intonation, and so on, are examples of the topological variation characteristic of the charged fields that indicate the presence of another subjectivity in Trevarthen's account.

Such prosodies are based on body movement and have to do with the dynamic ebb and flow of energy in the system as a whole. As Bateson observes, this perspective "must compare change to change and use the result of *that* comparison to account for the next step" (1980: 120). From this point of view, it is the dynamic ebb and flow of, for example, body movement which works to reduce or increase (topological) difference in the system. This principle is based on the analogue (topological) principle of quantity (Bateson 1980: 123).

It is this dimension of social meaning-making which attunes the infant to the presence of another human being. Prosodies of the voice and the body directly interface with the ebb and flow of bodily energy, which is why they are so closely bound up with dynamic and vectorial energy and movement in ecosocial space-time. Meaning-making is an intersubjective process; it requires some shared bodily orientation along some vector of interest or attention. Trevarthen notes that "acts of orienting and attending may . . . give continuous data on the curiosity, recognition, or motivation, that the subject has for surroundings" (1978: 131). The energetic ebb and flow of vocal and other prosodies and their vectorial control (or lack of) provide interactants with a great deal of very often unconscious information concerning the level of attention, interest, engagement, and so on, of the other party to the interaction. From this point of view, such information is iconically related to the energy flows to which these interpretations relate.

The notion of iconicity that I referred to above does not mean that there is a visual resemblance between representamen and object. Peirce's notion of icon draws attention to mathematic signs and diagrams, in which the "similarity" is based on more abstract principles (Nöth 1990: 122). In the present case, continuously variable energy flows in the system are interpreted as continuously variable flows of attention, interest, engagement, and so on. Attention, affect, and so on, are mapped onto continuous quantitative variation in body movement or vocal activity such as duration, pitch intensity, and volume. The relation between the two levels is iconic in the sense that two topological modes are mapped onto to each. Continuously varying flows of energy in the system signify continuously varying degrees of attention, interest, motivation, and so on. Furthermore, it is the affect, motivation, interest, or motivation which is consciously attended to, rather than the energy flow itself. Gendlin's notion of "implicit felt meaning" (1962: 66–67), whereby we feel the meaning of something as a felt sense which is associated with a particular sign or experience, is relevant here. The implicit yet felt quality of this kind of meaning relates to the iconic dimension of semiosis, which involves the immediate felt recognition of the given phenomenon.

4 A comment on Trevarthen's ascription of intentionality to the infant

Trevarthen refers to the intentional movement patterns of the neonate in ways which I think warrant closer critical examination. The attribution of intentionality to self and others is based on indexical and symbolic signs, though these signs are not necessarily linguistic in nature. Specification hierarchy thinking is useful here. Intentionality in the human case is the most highly specified category which we use as a descriptor for human actions relative to the inter-personal moral orders within which intentional acts are seen as occurring and in terms of which they may be understood. In terms of the specification hierarchy, the neonate's looking at, grasping, and so on, of objects, belongs to a category of a much more general and vaguer logical class than does the intentionality that we apply to mature human individuals. That is, the neonate progresses from the much more general and fuzzier, or less specified, category of proto-intentionality to the highly specified category of intentionality which we recognize and which is built into the semantics of natural language as a typological-categorial distinction. The specifi-cation hierarchy, as Salthe (1993: 89) points out, is also an implication hierarchy. In the same way that society implies biology, which implies chemistry, and so on, we can say that the highly specified typological category of intentionality that we use in the case of the mature individual implies much more general, less specified forms of proto-intentionality which reach right back to the vaguest topological differentiations characteristic of very early infant semiosis. This argument does not alter the fact that the meaning-making practices of adults do attribute intentions to the child as if the child had a mind to which such intentions can be attributed. However, the infant is a lower scalar being; he or she cannot access these perspectives. Rather, the adult's practices derive from and reflect the more highly specified categories of the ecosocial semiotic system which the adult alone accesses during the period of primary intersubjectivity in question here.

5 Proto-genres and semiotically mediated agency in the indexical phase: some reflections on Perinat and Sadurní's interpretation of Piaget

In Piaget's second and third sensori-motor stages, indexes are a constitutive part of global schemas whereby the child discriminates objects and events by means of indexical signs which are themselves inseparable parts of a whole, i.e. from the child's perspective. For the child, there is a sensori-motor connection, which is indexical in character, between some elemental percept and the larger situation of which the index is a constitutive part. The following example is adapted from Piaget (1946), as discussed by Perinat and Sadurní (1999: 56).

PARENT PUTS BIB ON CHILD / CHILD ASSOCIATES THIS WITH BEING
ADMINISTERED AN UNPLEASANT SYRUP

/ = is contextually redundant with

The indexical association can be represented, as shown here, as a redundancy relation between the two components of the situation. In this way, the bib and the unpleasant syrup function as contexts for each other's interpretation. The occurrence of one part of the relations predicts to a high degree of probability the other part. The indexical association of the two entities in this way is itself dependent on some second order metaredundancy relation which defines the context-type in which the relata on the first level are typically associated with each other. In the present example, the second order contextualizing relation pertains to the higher-order structures and relations at the level of the dyad in which the particular transaction between mother and infant is embedded.

Initially, the child's sensori-motor immaturity means that the child is unable to respond indexically to the mother's indexes. Perinat and Sadurní (1999: 64–65) point out that mothers typically enact sequences of actions in relation to particular objects while the child looks on. The mother shows the child various possible ways of responding to the object. She then tries to get the child to perform the same action. This particular activity sequence may be schematized as a proto-genre structure, comprising an ordered sequence of stages, as follows:

1. MOTHER SHOWS OBJECT TO CHILD
   ↓
2. (MOTHER NAMES OBJECT)
   ↓
3. CHILD SHOWS INTEREST
   ↓
4. MOTHER INDICATES PROTOTYPICAL USE OF OBJECT
   ↓
5. MOTHER PROPOSES COURSE OF ACTION WITH RESPECT TO OBJECT

In the early stages, the child is not able to coordinate his or her actions with the mother's actions. In any case, unlike Trevarthen, I do not think that intentions are a pre-existing part of the child's mental equipment. In the early states, the action schema mentioned above provides a model which builds **possible** dialogical responses on the part of the child. That is, the mother adopts and takes up both the adult and the child positions in this action sequence and acts them out for the child. This fact suggests that the mother is adapted to attune to and respond to the infant's actions *qua* dialogically motivated responses to her signs. The transactions between the mother and the infant are reciprocal and therefore dialogic. The child is not a mere passive onlooker, but an active participant. The initial value settings of the newborn provide him or her with implicit structures of communication which enable him or her to participate in and interpret the adult's signs, though not from the point of view of the much more highly specified structures of the adult. Rather, the child acquires implicit structures which gradually increase in specification in time through the exchanges of matter, energy, and meaning in the dyad. These implicit structures, in modifying and resetting the initial value wash, provide a basis for the progression to yet more specified structures.

For instance, the child's demonstration of interest is an active response, which has the function of eliciting a further dialogic response from the mother. In the process, the proto-dialogue structure which links the two participants is transformed over time on the basis of the complementary responses of both participants in the dyad. Thus, primitive elements of dialogue are built into the newborn's value setting from the outset. The infant is both sensitive to and equipped to access the more specialized forms of dialogue which the mother *qua* teacher system provides in the immediate environment of the dyad. In time, the repeated use of such schemas, along with the variation from one deployment to another, provides the child with principles of regularity on which memory is built on the basis of the intertextual links that are built up over the different occasions in which the activity is engaged.

The guiding mechanism here is the principle of dialogic closure (Bråten 1992; Thibault 2000a). Within the boundary conditions established by the activity structure, a loop is established which links the two participants in a closed circuit of a flow of differences (Bateson 1973a [1972]: 285–291). The mother's actions function as indexes of possible courses of appropriate action and therefore of points of action for the infant to take up and enact within the constraints provided by the dyad. The indexical signs which the infant interprets enable him or her to build up an internalized repertoire of action schemas. As the above schematization shows, the mother's activity indicates possible responses on the part of the child. Moreover, the child's responses also index his or her degree of understanding of the unfolding activity so that the mother can adjust her actions accordingly.

The child comes to construe the mother's contributions to this schema as indications of her expectations as to how to act. Moreover, her interpreting the child's actions, including physical bodily movements, as components in a larger-scale activity, helps to provide the child with the resources for actively taking up of points of action in the unfolding activity. It is important to point out here that mother and child share meaning and perspective only up to a certain point. The basis of their dyadic exchanges is indexical, as I pointed out above. For this reason, they can be said to share a core of indexical meanings and relations which they jointly enact. By the same token, the mother also acts symbolically (e.g. linguistically) such that both caretakers and outside observers can link her actions to wider cultural meanings and values. That is, the mother is the agent who is, at this stage, connected to the higher-scalar system of symbolic meaning-making possibilities. She can make links beyond the here-now of the dyad to other space-time scales that are not available to the infant in the here-now scale of the dyad.

Halliday (1993) has written of the "interpersonal gateway" to the ontogenesis of meaning in the child. How, then, does the dialogic closure of the kind of interpersonal interaction between mother and infant discussed above help to bring about the emergence of meaning in infants during the course of their interactions with adults? I have already mentioned the asymmetry between the perspectives of the infant and adult participants with respect to the interaction that occurs between them. In the early stages, mothers and infants do not have access to the same system of symbolic meaning-making possibilities. Nor do they perceive the signs in the inter-action in the same way. As Perinat and Sadurní (1999: 67) point out, many aspects of the adult's behaviour are not construed as signs by the infant, though this situation progressively changes. Take the case of a simple indexical relationship of the kind identified by Piaget in the sensori-motor stage of the child's development. As I said before, this entails a relationship between an elementary percept and some environment object or event within the child's purview. The relationship is a topological one. But what makes this a sign for the child? The perceiving of *x as y*, as in the case of the child who produced an indexical association between the bib and the unpleasant syrup (see above), is an essential step in the emergence of agency and the action-trajectories which can be sourced at agents. This is so because this elementary act of perception (a form of indexical association) means that the action is routed through the individual's semiotically organized neural landscape. Thus, higher-level intentions act as top-down, neuro-logically organized, semiotic constraints on lower-level sensori-motor realizations as action.

In this way, the lower-level sensori-motor implementation of an action trajectory comes to be more and more constrained by higher-level context-sensitive semiotic constraints. Only when sensori-motor activity is so routed can it be construed as purposive and appropriate to the situation. The elementary percept (e.g. the bib) which is construed as an index of something refers to some environmental phenomenon. The given environmental phenomenon functions as the final cause (cf. object of desire) of the action trajectory. This object-in-itself cannot function as an indexical sign for the perceiver. The infant, say, must **perceive** the bib as contiguous with some contextual value (e.g. unpleasant syrup) in order for it to be the object of a particular course of action. In other words, the child constructs a first-order redundancy (contextual) relation between the bib and this unpleasant association on the basis of some still higher-order contextual relation. Thus, intentionally directed awareness and the goal-seeking activity which is directed towards some object are made possible by processes of semiotic mediation (Vygotsky 1986 [1934]; Cole 1996: chapter 4), which link what is inside the organism to what is outside it. This process takes place in and through the signs that agents construct in their activity in order to integrate inside and outside. In terms of the presupposition-cum-implication hierarchy of icon, index, and symbol, such processes of semiotic mediation can be seen to operate at all levels of the hierarchy in the emergence of both consciousness and agency.

Figure 3.1 illustrates the principle of dialogic closure and its function in bringing about the emergence of meaning in infants. The *a* part of the loop represents the adult's contribution to the ongoing infant–adult dyad. Many of these contributions are responses to actions from the child whereby he or she actively seeks needed information from the social environment afforded by the mother–infant dyad. The *b* part of the loop represents the interpretation of the infant's contributions by the adult. That is, in responding to the infant's acts, the adult interprets the infant's contributions *as if* they were signs. From the infant's perspective, they are not symbolic signs in the adult sense, but actions (indexical signs) which serve to elicit responses from the other (Perinat and Sadurní (1999: 67). The *c* loop represents the transforming of these transac-tions in the infant's developing neurological dynamics such that there is a continuous exchange between the infant's internal neural dynamics and the activities which take place in the dyad as a whole. In the process, the proto-meanings which are elaborated in the infant's brain are projected back into the dyad and further modified, and so on. The essential point here is the self-organizing nature of the process, which is fed by the reciprocal contributions of both infant

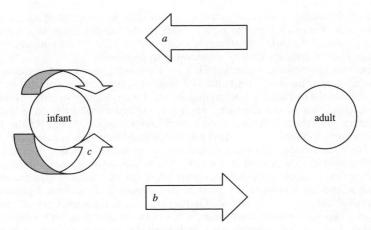

Figure 3.1 The principle of dialogic closure and its role in early infant semiosis; adapted from Perinat and Sadurní (1999: 67)

and mother. A self-organizing system is a dynamic open system which responds to environmental information by reorganizing its own internal dynamics and structure (Lemke 1995a [1993]; Maturana and Varela (1980; see also section 7).

6 Halliday's account of early protolanguage

The processes of meaning-exchange which occur in the infant–caretaker dyads that are characteristic of early protolanguage are not the result of the mere adding together of the infant and caretaker, seen as two separate and individual systems. The specific interaction which occurs between them enacts a unitary system, which has its own higher-scalar structures and dynamical processes. The unitary and systemic character of the dyad suggests that the structure of emergent consciousness in the infant is contextually integrated with the structures of the infant –caretaker dyadic system. Importantly, shared semiotic and material resources mediate the transactions between the two partners in the dyad. The processes which take place in the dyad serve to build up new structures, including those of consciousness and agency. The infant is an active member of the dyad: infants have their own resources for dialogically engaging with adults (Bogdan 2000: 33). In my view, this explains why the proto-imperative mode of goods-and-services (action) exchange appears before the proto-indicative mode in child protolanguage, as noted by Halliday (1975: 18–21, 37). I shall return to this point in chapter 5, section 7.

The proto-indicative mode of interaction is concerned with the intersubjective sharing and exchange of **linguistically** constituted information. In early protolanguage, the infant's vocal and other gestures frequently have a proto-imperative function of acting upon and eliciting a response from the adult member of the dyad. The infant uses these gestures in order to structure interpersonal exchanges with adults. The infant gets the adult to respond to his or her protolinguistic sign-making by providing input which will contribute to the infant's further development. The adult interprets the child's gesture as meaningful from the perspective of the higher-scalar ecosocial meanings which only the adult has access to. In so doing, the adult supplies the child with epigenetic structures, meaning, and values that contribute to his or her further development. This process is possible because the adult member of the dyad has already been integrated to these same higher-scalar contextualizing relations on account of that individual's prior participation in the same kinds of type-specific developmental trajectories.

In the exchange between Nigel and his mother concerning the scattering pigeons that I discussed in chapter 1, section 3, it is the mother's integration to the higher-scalar level of cultural meanings and practices which allows her to interpret the child's utterance from the standpoint of the culture's meaning systems. In this way, the lower structural order of the child's utterance is regulated by the higher order of the mother's linguistic response. The relatively low order of the child's protolinguistic sign and the high order of the adult's linguistic sign stand in a complementary dialogic relationship to each other.

The child's very high-pitched squeak in Halliday's example generates relative disorder which elicits its regulation by the adult's response. The adult's response, which is elicited by the child's utterance, reduces the disorder by interpreting the child's vocalization in terms of the culture's meaning systems. That is, the adult imports order into the dyad at the same time that the disorder generated by the child's lower-order contributions is exported away (Lemke 1984c: 45). However, the notion of lower order does not imply that the child's contribution is without meaning. The child's protolinguistic contributions to the infant–caretaker dyad are meaning-ful from the points of view of both infant and adult. Needless to say, they both have different standpoints for the reasons mentioned above. The child's mental resources are pre-cultural and protolinguistic and are limited to the primary consciousness of perceptual phenomena and early forms of elementary social relations. On the other hand, the adult's mental resources are cultural and linguistic; primary consciousness has been integrated to higher-scalar symbolic consciousness. Halliday has proposed that protolinguistic meaning emerges in humans (and some other primates) as a consequence of the contradiction between the material and the conscious, which Halliday (1992: 20) defines as "the two primary modes of experience", as follows:

> In humans, meaning develops, in the individual, before the stage of language proper; it begins with what I have called "protolanguage". So where does this mammalian experience come from? It probably evolved out of the contradiction between the two primary modes of experience, the material and the conscious. Material processes are experienced as "out there"; conscious processes are experienced as "in here". We can see in observing the growth of an individual child how he or she construes this contradiction in the form of MEANING. The child constructs a sign, whereby the one mode of experience is projected on to the other. In my own observations this took the form of what I called "v.h.p.s." (very high-pitched squeak), Nigel's first sign that he produced at five months old; I glossed it as "what's that? – that's interesting". In other words, Nigel was beginning to construe conceptual order out of perceptual chaos: "I am curious (conscious) about what's going on (material)". This impact of the material and the conscious is being transformed into meaning by a process of projection, in which the conscious is the projecting and the material the projected.
>
> (Halliday 1992: 20–21)

It is interesting to note Halliday's interpretative glosses on the five-month-old child's very high pitch squeak. It would be superficial, in my view, to dismiss this as Halliday's reading too much into the child's vocalization. Rather, the fact that adult's do so interpret children's protolinguis-tic gestures is itself an essential part of the functioning of the transindividual structures which regulate the dyad and the subsystems (child and adult) that participate in it. By the same token, it constitutes an important recognition that the child's utterance is meaningful, though not, as I said before, to the same level of specification that the adult's symbolic contributions are. More-over, the child is recognized as having his own agency and, hence, his own active role to play in getting adults to do what he wants them to do. That is, adult caretakers are pre-programmed *qua* caretakers to respond to infants in ways that contribute to their further development at the same time that infants are pre-programmed to socialize adults, as Bogdan (2000: 33) usefully expresses it, to get them to do what the child wants. Furthermore, this requires that the infant is in possession of interpretative schemas such that he or she is able, again from his or her perspective, to predict the effects of his or her protolinguistic utterances on the adult partner and therefore to predict the kind of response the adult will give. Initially, the ability to predict is limited to the here-now scale of the indexical signs characteristic of early protolanguage. For example, it is the reiterated use of such signs over many different occasions that allows for the emergence of a proto-imperative category. In time, this category is integrated to the inner perspective of the self so that it can be used in the off-line planning and imagining of the effects and consequences of one's interpersonal engagements with others. The fact that the imperative orients its users to a not-yet-attained, though desired, future suggests that the imperative is of fundamental importance in structuring this ability to plan and anticipate off-line (see chapter 5, section 7).

The pre-programming I have in mind here has to do with the genetically inbuilt values with which the infant is endowed from the outset. The two modes of projection – viz. "I think" and "I want" – postulated by Halliday derive from values of this kind. These two protolinguistic modes function to provide conscious access to the domain of the nonself on the two different timescales of "how things are" (here-now) and "how things ought to be" (beyond the here-now in some possible future). Furthermore, the ontogenetically prior emergence of the proto-imperative mode, with its orientation to the future, goes hand-in-hand with the child's focus on the other as a source of actions and meanings to be interpreted from the child's point of view.

The fact that the proto-imperative mode emerges first seems to bear out this interpretative focus on the other, rather than on the self. The infant's task is to figure out what others mean as well as how his or her actions will effect what others mean. That is, the proto-imperative mode focuses on and facilitates conscious access to the meanings and perspectives of the other on account of its function of getting others to respond in desired ways and therefore of predicting how they are likely to respond. In so doing, the infant is an agent who activates complementary epigenetic meanings and structures in the adult member of the dyad. On the here-now scale of the example discussed here, the two partners have perceptual access both to each other and to the phenomenon which is (jointly) attended to. Nevertheless, the future-oriented character of the proto-imperative mode requires the infant to integrate not just the (still relatively small) space-time scales which are implicated by indexical perception-action routines, but also the scales of self and other in dialogic communion with each other. This integration arises from the fact that the proto-imperative focuses on conscious access to and interpretation of the other as a mind which is a source of intentions, perceptions, and so on, and which relate to and integrate with the world that is shared by the two members of the dyad.

It is doubtful that distinctions such as that between the proto-imperative and the proto-indicative modes are as clear cut for the child as the linguistic glosses might make them appear from our perspective as adult interpreters. These glosses derive from the semantic categories of the adult language system in which typological-categorial distinctions are used to interpret the much vaguer and topological-continuous variations characteristic of the infant's perspective. In the infant's perspective, the socioaffective exchanges characteristic of early primary intersubjectivity show very many degrees of topological differentiation which are not yet connected up on the basis of a smaller number of variables and connection weights as a system. These connections will not occur until the infant learns to reduce these many degrees of freedom of this topological variation to a smaller number of interconnected typological distinctions, as defined by the systems of interrelated values internal to a language or other semiotic system. Thus, the less specified topological differentiations operated by the infant in the first three months or so, in particular, probably mean that the infant does not recognize a clear distinction between the "you-me" and the "it" domains of experience that begin to emerge in early protolanguage.

The development of a more outward perspective in the period from 0.3 to 0.6 months, as the child's increased sensori-motor maturity enhances his or her ability to explore beyond the dyad, goes hand-in-hand with the appearance of protolanguage. In Halliday's example, as discussed above, the child's high-pitched squeak is an interpersonal (dialogic) response to a perceptual phenomenon. The squeak simultaneously indexes its speaker as the conscious projector of a meaning which results from the child's construal of the information picked up about the material event (the pigeons) that impacts upon his consciousness at the same time that it indexes the event as a projected phenomenon which is experienced in the child's consciousness. However, the distinction between these two poles of the one overall experience – viz. the projecting and the projected – is not a sharply defined or polarized one. The difference between self and nonself is not yet sharply defined.

The child's vocalization indexes and hence accesses an awareness of his acting and perceiving in the world where the world is not yet sharply differentiated from a strong sense of self. The indexical meaning-making which is characteristic of the child's early protolanguage is centred on others, rather than on the self (Bogdan 2000: 173). Both child and adult engage in joint perception-action routines. The child's memory is procedural and therefore based on the short timescales afforded by the indexical sign-making that is characteristic of such routines. As noted above, the child is engaged in interpreting and predicting the responses of the other on this short timescale. For this reason, the child's self is closely linked to and defined by these still largely only implicitly defined relationships with the other. The indexical nature of the child's perspective means that it is limited to the very short timescales of here-now perception-action routines and procedural memory. Indexical consciousness at this early protolinguistic stage is, then, a form of semiotically mediated consciousness which has not been integrated to the inner perspective of the self by virtue of the closing of the loop on the "me" sector (chapter 5, section 14). The child's squeak, for instance, loops from his neural dynamics out into the environment of the dyad. In so doing, it entrains flows of matter, energy, and meaning in response to the environmental event with which he engages through the use of this sign. The child's sign in effect accesses simultaneously both the perceptual phenomenon of the pigeons scattering and the other's (the mother's) joint (interpersonal) engagement with this phenomenon. Thus, the child's indexical consciousness amounts to a consciousness of (1) other conspecifics with whom one can interpersonally engage for the purpose of interpreting and predicting their responses; and (2) phenomena of perceptual experience outside the you-me experiential domain which can be jointly accessed and attended to by the use of these same signs.

These two points suggest that the indexical consciousness characteristic of early protolanguage involves the introjection of the projected into the projecting, where that which is projected is a topologically less specified fusion, to borrow Halliday's term, of both "the other" and the phenomena of experience as an elementary content of consciousness. In this way, both proto-interpersonal and proto-experiential meanings enter into the formation of consciousness. Indexical consciousness is therefore seen as comprising a semiotic trajectory extending from the infant's developing neural dynamics into the ecosocial semiotic environment so as to jointly access both the other and the world. It does so in ways which leave the boundary, so to speak, between the projecting self of primary consciousness and the projected domain as only weakly insulated. The onset of early protolinguistic sign-making leads to a first, weak polarization of "self" and "nonself" by virtue of the fact that indexicality enhances the child's ability to attend to (point to) phenomena beyond his or her body. Nevertheless, the attending to phenomena still occurs within the immediate here-now scale. It also enhances the infant's capacity to integrate the phenomena attended to in his or her internal dynamics through the processes of semiotic mediation between the projecting and projected domains that indexical meaning-making affords (section 5 above). At this stage, the child's neural dynamics and the indexical signs which constitute these processes of semiotic mediation are not able to access and reflect upon the sense of self as an object of consciousness. This capacity comes later and depends on the symbolic resources of higher-order consciousness. However, it is wrong to think that there is no differentiation. The relationship between the projecting and projected domains may be schematized as shown below. In this schema, the arrow signifies the projection of the phenomenal-material domain "out there" into the conscious domain ("in here"):

PROJECTING CONSCIOUSNESS INDEXES AWARENESS OF ← [PROJECTED PHENOMENON OF PERCEPTUAL EXPERIENCE]

In terms of the infant's neural dynamics, the relationship between the projecting and the projected domains is constituted by the reentrant looping or mapping of the multimodal sensorimotor inputs in the material domain (the projected) into the domain of proto-consciousness (the projecting). The resulting higher-order neural maps lead to the emergence of the proto-self's topological immersion in, rather than clearly defined separation from, the projected phenomena of conscious awareness. In metaredundancy terms, this may be expressed as follows:

neural maps of projecting consciousness/projected multimodal sensory inputs deriving from ambient flux//topological-indexical awareness of our acting/being-in-world as an undivided whole

According to the perspective indicated by these contextualizing relations, "self", "other", and "world" are not yet clearly differentiated as typological distinctions in the way that they are in the semantics of adult language. Instead, these differentiations are based on topological-continuous variation. For this reason, they are considerably vaguer and fuzzier than the typological-categorial distinctions made in the semantics of natural language.

There is a danger in all this that we will put too much emphasis on the producer *per se* of the squeak. Nigel's high-pitched squeak, it should not be forgotten, is itself a response to an environmental event. Without wishing to debate which comes first, it is important to bear in mind the mediating function of the higher-scalar dyad, which is the means by which the infant is brought into contact with selective aspects of his or her environment or *Umwelt*. The stimulus information which the child picks up about an environmental event – the scattering of the pigeons – is an indexical sign of that event. That is, an indexical sign of an external material event impacts upon the child's peripheral and central nervous systems. The indexical sign is introjected and elaborated in the child's central nervous system as a developing theory about its surroundings, including events such as the one referred to here. Consciousness is generally treated as an autonomous property of the individual. But we have seen that individual, *Umwelt*, and *Innenwelt* are part of a single larger-scale system, which is organized on different scalar levels. Consciousness is "autonomous" in the sense that it shows properties of functional closure. The notion of "autonomous" does not mean, however, that the individual agent and the biological organism that supports the agent is a closed system. Instead, agents and organisms are embedded in a system comprising higher-scalar levels which modulate them at the same time that symbolic consciousness in particular is able to attend to the higher (and lower) levels in ways which are meaningful to the individual consciousness in question.

The fact that Nigel responds to an environmental event with his protolinguistic squeak means that he has a developing, if only highly implicit, theory of such events in his immature central nervous system. The development of such a theory depends on the existence of such events in the first place which constitute the *Umwelt* of the child, along with other conspecifics. The child responds to and interprets selected aspects of this *Umwelt*. These aspects are not random. Rather, they exhibit potential regularities and systematic features for the members of a particular *Umwelt*. In this view, Nigel's neuroanatomical and sensori-motor capabilities are initiating conditions on level L–1. The existence of a stable environment rich in information affords its perceptual pick; action responses to such events constitute boundary conditions on level L+1, as specified by the three-level hierarchy. These boundary conditions therefore allow for the closure in which consciousness, at this particular developmental stage, can occur. Gee (1992: 51) has said that the brain and the networks of associations that are stored in it are tools which individuals can use to make meanings with others in social contexts (see also Harré and Gillett 1994: chapter 6). Thus, the individual puts the neural activities of the brain to use according to the demands of particular contexts. In the process, he or she responds to and interprets events in the environment, in the process acquiring new, at times unique, experiences which alter the networks of associations in the individual's brain.

The stimulus information about some environmental event which the child picks up is transduced by the child's central nervous system into networks of neural activity. Unlike the indexical sign (the stimulus information), this neural activity stands in no necessary relationship to an external event (Salthe 1993: 176). Thus, the networks of associations in the brain's neural activity relate the given input to memories of other inputs in a proto-symbolic way because these have no necessary relationship to outside events. Furthermore, they are the tool – the resource – which can be deployed on this occasion or on some other occasion to produce a response to this or some other event. In this way, the networks of associations serve as a higher-scalar system of interpretance whereby models – systems of meanings – are built up such that the individual can respond to external events in **meaningful** ways. Such resources serve as the basis – partly set by the genetically inherited value wash and partly developed through the child's individuating trajectory – for the child's production of (as here) protolinguistic signs which have proto-metafunctional properties, as shown in Table 3.1 (see also chapter 1, section 3). The child's squeak does not stand in a necessary relationship to the particular external event which he attends to. Instead, there is a proto-symbolic transduction from networks of proto-meanings

Table 3.1 Proto-metafunctional interpretation of Nigel's high-pitched squeak uttered at 0.6 months

Perspective adopted —————— Metafunction	Interpretation of Nigel's perspective	Halliday's glosses
proto-experiential	projects environmental event (scattering of pigeons) as a phenomenon of perceptual experience which is consciously accessed and attended to by utterer	domain of material experience: the rest (them, it) outside the you-me domain
proto-interpersonal	engages and orients to other (mother) in order to engage her attention and response; prosodics iconic to interest, affect, and motivation	"I think" mode as reflective or proto-indicative orientation to the material, viz.
		I am curious (conscious) about what's going on (material)
proto-textual	the squeak *qua* articulated sound locates utterer as source of the utterance in a proto-deictic field defined by the dyad; the indexical sign enacts a trajectory which loops from the body-brain dynamics of the child out into the here-now environment so as to index the perceived event as a contextually salient value, thereby contributing to the creation of texture and wholeness in which the field of conscious awareness is defined	distinction between "in here" and "out there"

in the central nervous system to the articulation of the vocal gesture, which is projected into the external environment (the dyad). However, it is important to point out that the proto-symbolic nature of these proto-meanings does not mean that they exhibit the typological-categorial distinctions characteristic of the semantics of natural language. Rather, the networks of associations of proto-meanings in the brain are topological-continuous differentiations which are only later reorganized at higher levels as linguistic meanings. What is indexical is the squeak *qua* sensori-motor act. From the listener's (e.g. the mother's) point of view, there is an essential fit between perceptual information about an event sourced at the child and the auditory systems equipped to pick this up. From the speaker's point of view, the same squeak is indexical insofar as there is an essential fit between modulated vocal tract activity and the resultant sound which is projected into the environment.

However, the squeak is interpreted as a dialogic response to an external event in which the responses and interpretations of others are of considerable importance and interest. Furthermore, the proto-meanings that are stored and networked in the brain's neural activity stand in no fixed or determinate relationship to particular external events. Instead, they are beginning, with the onset of protolanguage, to be connected up as a system of semiotic values defined by the interrelations among the terms in the linguistic or other semiotic system (chapter 2, section 10; chapter 5, section 15). It is in this sense that we can understand Halliday's account of the emergence of a protolinguistic sign system in Nigel. The squeak is an act unfolding along a trajectory from an agent, who is its source. The infant seeks to impose his own value-laden categories on his surroundings, including the caretakers with whom he usually interacts. So, the child creates a sign in the proto-indicative mode. In doing so, he accesses the situation and its possible meanings.

Infants at the age in question can access a certain range of classes of environmental events on account of their species-specific neurological and sensori-motor capacities. Such events are affordances, in Gibson's (1983 [1966], 1986 [1979]) sense, in relation to which the categories which the child has in his central nervous system can be selectively (contextually) deployed so as to create patterned relations or contextual redundancies between value categories in the central nervous system and instances of particular classes of events in the *Umwelt*. That is, these stored value categories enable the information about external events which is picked up to be contextualized in appropriate ways so that the child can selectively respond to these events. The child's capacity to respond therefore depends on a developing repertoire of proto-meanings and the value-making associations among them. This repertoire is elaborated in his central nervous system as an implicit theory – a system of interpretance – concerning the possible ways in which one can respond *qua* conscious agent to specific environmental contingencies by means of contextually relevant action trajectories. The child can thus make choices from an initially limited repertoire of protolinguistic and other signs. The deployment of these signs in particular contexts produces a cascade of possibilities, including the sought-for responses and interpretations of others. The responses and interpretations of others are then collected by the emergent self. The self therefore creates increased possibilities for choice from an expanding system of symbolic values.

This relationship can be expressed in proto-metafunctional terms, as shown in Table 3.1. The terms I have used here represent an analytical attempt to interpret the protolinguistic meanings as seen from the child's perspective in the exchange.

I said earlier that the protolinguistic sign produced by the child in Halliday's example introjects an elementary content of consciousness comprising the full range of proto-metafunctional meanings mentioned (section 6; see also chapter 1, section 3). Moreover, these signs comprise jointly enacted and interpreted responses to events in the purview of the members of the dyad. The squeak *qua* meaningful sign is an event on the same scale as the person who enacts it and the persons who interpret it. Individuals do not perceive sound waves or light waves. These forms of energy occur on a lower-scalar level, which is not the point of reference for the ecological scale of the inhabitants of the particular *Umwelt*. Thus, consciousness rubs up against the question as to how the objects of consciousness and consciousness can be on different scalar levels. Gibson (1986 [1979]: 10), for instance, has pointed out how we can imagine phenomena on scales that we cannot access by means of the perceptual systems which we use to observe phenomena on our own ecological scale. The emergent metafunctional basis of the protolinguistic meanings that infants make provides some clues as to how the relations between object of consciousness and the system of interpretance are incorporated into the structure of consciousness. This link between object of consciousness and the system of interpretance suggests that there is a self-referential relation between conscious observer and object of consciousness, which is reflected in the semiotic character and structure of consciousness. In Table 3.2, I try to make explicit the connections between higher-level entities such as the structure of human consciousness and the lower levels from which it emerges. Thus, it is possible to see how consciousness contextually completes lower integrative levels at the same time that the latter are connected to the (higher-order) consciousness which models them (Salthe 1993: 49).

Table 3.2 Specification hierarchy, showing the categorial reach of symbolic consciousness across its lower integrative levels

Type of (semiotic) mediation	Relevant discourse	Type of system
space, time, matter, energy; scalar homogeneity; no memory mediating different space-time scales	physics	subatomic particles to the Universe; attoseconds to light years
chemical reactions; self-organization	chemistry ecology	molecules abiotic systems
memory mediates across scales; matter, energy and information exchanges	biology	cells, organs, systems of organs; organism
organism-environment transactions; creation of organism's *Umwelt* and *Innenwelt*; CNS-PNS-environment interface	biology	perception-action relative to species-specific environmental affordances on scale of reality to which the species has adapted and on which scale it picks up information about salient environmental events relevant to its transactions with the environment; access to environment including conspecifics based on perception-action or situated exchanges in here-now; information in form of perceptual invariants and variants in ambient array
Innenwelt of organism topological-continuous differentiation in socioaffective exchanges	infant-caretaker dyad in primary intersubjectivity; type-specific developmental trajectory	
indexical semiotic mediation: protolanguage in human infant and some other mammals	society; self-world-other triad; emergence of "mind" as object of semiotic engagement and access; type-specific developmental trajectory	situated interpretation of and engagement with nonself based on indexical signs on here-now scale; other-centred and weak polarization of self-nonself; here-now projecting of material into the projected, i.e. PROTO-SELF CONSCIOUSLY projects [MATERIAL ENVIRONMENTAL EVENT as elementary semiotic content]

early symbolic mediation in later protolanguage	culture: entraining of individual to higher-scalar symbolic resources of ecosocial system; type-specific apprenticeship to cultural practices (school, family, peers, media, trades, professions, etc.)	unsituated interpretation of nonself-world transactions, not necessarily accessible by perception; embedding of others' projections into one's own perspective, i.e. SELF [NONSELF PROJECTS WORLD]
language and other symbolic systems	emergence of self-reflexive consciousness which is able to access self as an object of conscious awareness; individuating trajectories and individual psychology, seen as a time-bound historical-biographical integrity which selectively integrates lower level integrative levels to its more highly specified level by virtue of the historical contingencies and unique experiences which characterize the cascading/collecting dialectic of its trajectory; semiotic performance texts and their entextualizations	meta-self projects other-as-self projecting one's self as an object of conscious awareness which can be symbolically accessed and interpreted; $METASELF_1$ projects [OTHER $SELF_2$ projecting $SELF_1$] such that $METASELF_1$ is able to access and interpret one's self from the perspective of others ($SELF_2$)

7 The conscious and the material domains as the two primary modes of experience: implications for the self

Halliday's discussion of the two primary modes of experience, viz. the conscious and the material, shows that signs are constructed in child protolanguage through the projection of the material mode of experience onto the conscious mode (section 6 above). Halliday further writes that "this impact of the material and the conscious is being transformed into meaning by a process of projection, in which the conscious is the projecting and the material the projected" (1992: 21). The material domain is the ambient flux of stimulus information. This domain does not passively impact on the individual's consciousness in the form of forceful physical impacts. The individual selectively attends to the stimulus information in the ambient energy of its environment. The conscious domain is the domain of the self and its inner, self-referential perspectives. Both the points of view and the points of action of the self are understood as having this domain as their source.

Living systems maintain their own structural integrity and organization over time by exchanging energy with their environment. A large part of this energy is exchanged through food intake, respiration, and the organism's activity. Some of the ambient energy in which the organism is constantly immersed provides stimulus information for the organism about environmental events (Gibson 1986 [1979]: 57). Structured ambient energy provides the organism with information about events in its environment. However, the pick up of this information is not a passive process. It is not, as Gibson explains, merely a question of stimulus energy "stimulating" or exciting the receptor cells so that they will fire. Rather, organisms actively and selectively orient to environmental events.

The pick up of stimulus information from the environment requires the organism actively to explore its environment so that stimulus information may be obtained by an entire perceptual system (Gibson 1986 [1979]: 53). Both the organism and its environment are co-adapted to each other. They are not separate entities, but are constitutive components of a still larger system of relations. There is a relationship of complementarity between the two: the organism is adapted to a particular environment just as a particular environment implies a particular organism (see Gibson 1986 [1979]: 8). The environment is not the same for two different species. In the human case, the ecosocial semiotic environment – cf. the context of culture – implies human agents who are co-adapted to that environment, including its possible meanings, activity structures, participant roles, and so on.

When organisms obtain stimulus information about environmental events from the ambient energy which surrounds them, the information so obtained is, in turn, interpreted by the neuronal systems within the organism's central nervous system. This process of interpretation is work which the organism performs on the information that it has obtained about the given environmental event. The organism may then decide to respond to the environmental event in the form of, say, the child's protolinguistic squeak in Halliday's example. That is, the organism dissipates some of the energy that it expends in interpreting the information within its neuronal networks in the form of a response which it projects back into the environment as an (elementary, in Halliday's example) act of meaning.

Human beings are open, self-organizing systems in common with all other biological systems. Self-organizing systems consist of many different components on many different scalar levels of organization. These components have the potential to interact with each other in very many different, complex, and nonlinear ways across the diverse levels of the system's organization. The obtaining of adequate supplies of energy from the system's environment allows for the emergence in self-organizing systems of new properties and now forms of pattern and order that were not previously apparent. In the human case, the obtaining of information about environmental events, including most crucially the meanings that circulate through the social networks in which humans participate, leads to the elaboration, in time, of very complex patterns of neuronal activation. The obtaining of meanings from the ecosocial semiotic environment alters the internal global neural landscape of the individual. Patterns of neural activation emerge which dominate and modulate the activity of the system as a whole. In the human case, the system as a whole and its actions are slaved to the inner self-referential perspective of the self and its viewpoints. In my view, it is more appropriate to say that meanings that originate in the ecosocial semiotic environment are re-envoiced in the inner perspective of the self, rather than saying that they are internalized (see chapter 5, section 1).

Thus, the material or "out there" domain in Halliday's account comprises stimulus information about environmental events. The conscious or "in here" domain is the inner self-referential perspective of the self and its relationship to its own body image. The outer surface of the body and the perceptual systems located on this surface constitute the interface between the two domains. Stimulus information that is obtained about environmental events is introjected into the conscious domain of the self and its inner perspectives through the mediating agency of the body. In this case, there is a process of introjection, in which information about the material or "out there" domain is introjected on to the conscious mode of the self, or the "in here" domain.

In the case of the child's high-pitched squeak, the conscious domain of the self and its inner perspectives produces an interpretation of and a response to the environmental event in the way described above. The squeak is a bodily act that is projected into the ecosocial environment of the child such that others (e.g. parents) can interpret it and respond to it as a meaningful act. They are able to do so because the squeak does not have a definite or fixed meaning already attached to it. Rather, the child's squeak is, in the first instance, a material environmental event which makes available stimulus information that others can orient to and interpret in environmentally and contextually relevant ways. When others pick up this stimulus information, they orient to the event as a meaningful act that has been projected from the child's self-perspective.

The squeak has no necessary connection to external environmental events. This fact means that it has to be attended to and interpreted by observers in contextually relevant ways. Once again, we see how the child's act of projection, like the prior act of introjection discussed above, entails bodily activity which mediates between the two domains of the conscious and the material discussed by Halliday. Furthermore, observers interpret the squeak as providing information **both** about the child's own body (a somatic event) and about some salient environmental event that the squeak can be related to (an extra-somatic event). Thus, the observer connects the squeak both to a projecting source of consciousness to which a meaning can be attributed and to an environmental event that the child wishes to express a meaning about. The sign is made at the intersection of these two modes of the conscious and the material because selves, including both the producer of the sign (e.g. the child) and observers (e.g. parents) who interpret it, are able to integrate the physical signal (e.g. the child's squeak) to some context. In this way, the squeak, say, is construed as meaningful in that context. Both producers and observers do so through their own interpretative activity such that the resulting sign is meaningful in the perspectives of the selves – again producers and observers of the squeak – in the conscious domain.

The concept of the sign may be defined as follows. A sign is always made through the contextual integration in the perspective of the SELF of the two modes of conscious experience – the conscious and the material – at the interface between the body-brain system and its external environment. Bodily activity always constitutes this interface between the two domains. Signs are always for someone. That is, signs are always made and are meaningful in the perspectives of the selves who make them in and through their meaning-making activity. Different selves can take up the perspectives afforded by particular signs.

Table 3.3 shows the different components of these processes, as seen from the perspective of (1) the introjection into consciousness of information about the external environment; and (2) the projection from consciousness of information into the environment. In both cases, the body is the interface between the two modes. The exchange of information across this interface in both directions – i.e. from organism to environment and from environment to organism – necessarily entails that when information crosses this interface, it is modified.

For example, the organism does not directly perceive the given material event. Instead, the information about this event which the organism picks up is perceived as chemical and other changes that occur within the organism. On the one hand, the information that the organism picks up about some external event brings about changes in the internal structure of the organism. This general principle can be applied, with varying degrees of specification, to all living

Table 3.3 The sign as the contextual integration of the conscious and material modes with the body-brain as the interface between SELF and environment, showing how signs arise through (1) the self's interpretation of environmental events and (2) the self's responses to environmental events

Role of consciousness	Introjection of information from environment (nonself)	Projection of information into environment (from self)
Source of information		
self	consciousness responds to information about external event	consciousness projects information into external environment
nonself	information about external event is picked up by body-brain	body-brain projects information into external environment
	sign of external event	sign of body

systems. In the human case, the internal structure of the organism is organized around the notion of SELF, with its meanings and inner self-referential perspective. Therefore, the changes that information about external events brings about in the internal structure of the organism take place in the perspective of the SELF and its meanings at the same time that these changes are interpreted in that perspective. This perspective is, of course, the conscious domain. Consciousness enables the individual organism to selectively orient to and attend to environmental events as phenomena of experience at the same time that consciousness enables the organism to modulate and regulate the changes that take place within it in the perspective of the self. By the same token, consciousness also allows the organism to respond to environmental events by projecting actions back into the environment in ways that adapt and modify the environment to suit the needs of the organism and the perspectives which consciousness affords it.

The definition of the sign as a relationship between, for example, a signifier and a signified truncates and distorts beyond recognition the real nature of the processes and relations involved in the making of signs. In my view, the definition of the sign must take into account the following factors: (1) the relationship between the conscious and the material domains; (2) the role of the body as interface between the two domains; (3) the perspective(s) of the selves without which there would be no sign; and (4) the meaning-making activity as dynamic, time-bound loop which integrates all of the previously mentioned components to its trajectory.

The infant's squeak is part of a dynamic loop of activity which extends from the body-brain system of $SELF_1$ (the infant) out into the external environment to the body-brain system of $SELF_2$ (the mother). The squeak is a vector. It has a source (the speaker) and it is directed to some phenomenon of interest or attention (the scattering pigeons). The vectorial character of the squeak is indicated both by the squeak's cross-modal connections with other perceptual-action modalities (e.g. pointing, gaze, body movement) and by the infant's interest or excitement, which is iconic to the energy level of the infant system.

The squeak integrates the two participants – infant and mother – to a particular phenomenon of experience that the two members of the dyad attend to. It also integrates the two participants to each other in the sense that the squeak dialogically coordinates the actions of infant and mother such that they can jointly orient both to the event and to each other. In this sense, both participants orient to each other as selves with viewpoints that can be made accessible to the other self through the process of taking up positions in dialogue.

The structure [Scattering Pigeons ∧ Squeak] is a component of an overall trajectory. This trajectory exhibits proto-metafunctional features as follows. First, the scattering of the pigeons is a Subject-like entity about which a proto-proposition is predicated by the squeak. If we assume for present purposes that the squeak is proto-declarative, then the scattering of the pigeons is the phenomenon about which a proto-proposition is made in the form of the squeak. In this sense, we can say that the squeak is proto-interpersonal. Secondly, the squeak is a vector which draws attention to the pigeons as a phenomenon of experience in the world outside the mother–infant dyad. In this perspective, the squeak orients the two participants to the pigeons as an experience which they can jointly attend to and share. In this sense, the squeak is proto-experiential. Thirdly, the squeak is part of an action trajectory which enables various previously unconnected or only more loosely connected factors to cohere as part of an action trajectory. Information is more constrained as more and more somatic and extra-somatic subsystems of infant, mother, and environment cohere along the action trajectory that they jointly enact in conjunction with external events. The action trajectory, as it self-organizes, creates a unity and coherence of experience in the space-time of the dyad. In this sense, the squeak is proto-textual.

Figure 3.2 illustrates the proto-metafunctional character of the squeak in terms of a number of parameters whereby this sign contextually integrates both the participants and the experienced phenomenon to its trajectory. The two-way arrows link the scattering of the pigeons to the participants as a jointly attended to and experienced phenomenon of experience, along with the subsequent linguistic construal of this in the identifying clause *those are birds pigeons* by the mother. The contributions of both participants modify and extend each other's contributions as well as the environmental event which instigated the dialogue in the first instance. Thus, the child's squeak is an engagement with and a further development of that event just as the mother's response to the child's squeak is also an engagement with and a further development of the child's utterance in relation to the environmental event. Figure 3.2 therefore illustrates a lattice-like structure in which semiotic complexity and depth are built up over the time span of the dialogue at the same time that the inner perspectives of the participants are also modified.

The observations I have made in the preceding paragraph show that it is the contextual integration of the squeak with its environment, including the two members of the dyad, which reveals its protometafunctional character. The squeak is, in this sense, a protolinguistic sign which lacks the internal differentiation into different semantic functions that is characteristic of linguistic signs (see chapter 2, section 10). In language, the metafunctions are forms of intrinsic linguistic organization which, however, function to integrate language to context along a number of different, though interrelated, parameters. The internal organization of language reflects this principle. In protolanguage, there is not the same kind or degree of internal organization. Nevertheless, protolanguage too reflects principles of contextual integration in which we can discern the vague outlines of the metafunctions that emerge with the onset of language.

The child's protolinguistic vocalization is a context-sensitive response to an environmental event. However, this vocalization does not occur on its own. Rather, it emerges from the dynamic

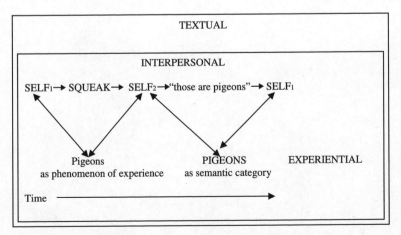

Figure 3.2 Proto-metafunctional coordinates of infant's dialogically organized protolinguistic utterance trajectory

interactions among the child's perceptual pick up of information about an environmental event, patterns of neural activation in his brain, including mental imagery and his felt state of excitement about or interest in the event that he has observed. In this sense, the squeak is motivated by affective or volitional factors, which both motivate it and give it its vectorial quality. The squeak is motivated by and dynamically interacts with all of these factors. It is also motivated by the infant's desire to obtain a response from the adult member of the dyad. Clearly, language cannot be tied to thought in the infant's case. There is no inner speech to give shape to thought. The tying of language to thought and to mental imagery occurs later, as we shall see in chapter 5, when I discuss egocentric speech. The squeak can also be understood as an externalized tool in and through which the infant elicits a response from his mother at the same time that the mother's more elaborate linguistic response provides the infant with a basis for the linguistic categorization of things and events in the world.

Individuals are immersed in their ecosocial semiotic environment and its meanings. It is often said that no two individuals can undergo the same conscious experience. Consciousness is unique to the individual in this sense. Nevertheless, the possible trajectories through the ecosocial semiotic environment, along with its discourse genres, activity-structure types, and dialogue structures, constitute a set of possible points of action and possible points of view that different individuals can take up and occupy at different times. Insofar as the ecosocial semiotic environment persists on a larger timescale than do the actions of any given individual, different individuals traverse similar trajectories through their joint participation in the discourse genres, social activities, and dialogue structures of the ecosocial semiotic system.

In this way, different individuals, on different occasions, can observe and interpret the phenomena of experience in their environment from the perspective of their own self in the "in here" or conscious domain, though in ways that are accessible to the consciousness of other selves. This does not mean that all individuals have the same experiences or that they traverse all the same trajectories through the ecosocial semiotic system. Rather, all participants are regulated by the same higher-scalar system of interpretance, which both constrains and enables the possible points of action and points of view that are available to participants for acting on and interpreting events in their environment. This last point will be central in chapter 4.

4

Agency, Consciousness, and Meaning-making in Children's Play

1 The reconstitution of language and experience in symbolic play

Play involves a de-location of activities from their original contexts and their re-location in new contexts. Children's symbolic play is a step along the road towards the child's capacity for increasing generalization and abstraction. Play is a form of fantasy or "as if" behaviour. It is proto-metaphorical because it entails the simultaneous mapping of different domains of meaning, action, and experience (see chapter 11, section 4). Play goes further than mere imitation. Imitation allows for duplication of action, although it does not show the same capacities that play exhibits for the abstraction and generalization of the recontextualized principles that are distilled in play across different domains. Play embodies both the sensori-motor acting out of activities in other contexts as well as processes of symbolic abstraction and generalization of the essential or idealized elements of social practices from their original contexts into the ludic context.

The child's entry into symbolic play involves a reconstitution of the symbolic resources (e.g. language) at his or her disposal. This reconstitution, in turn, involves a reconstitution of experience. Symbolic play provides access to a new form of decontextualizing and recontextualizing activity in which the knowledge and the participant roles which are embodied in activity as procedural knowledge – i.e. "how to" knowledge in specific contexts – are transferred to and generalized to other contexts and experimented with. If human meaning-making activity is a decentring towards otherness, towards complementarity in the social agent's relations with others, towards the meanings to which we are adapted through our phylogenesis and onto-genesis to respond to and interpret in the world of the nonself, then symbolic play can be seen as doubly significant here. In play, children both take up and respond to the meanings and actions of generalized cultural Others (e.g. adult roles, actions, meanings) at the same time that, in their play, they interact with and respond to specific others (e.g. their peers) in their pursuit of the affective commitments and the identity projects that are specific to the play realm.

Harré (1983: 247) has used the term "autonomous precursor world" to suggest the dual character of play. On the one hand, the participant roles and the social activities that children act out in play – e.g. preparing meals, playing mothers and babies, and so on – are recontextualizations of roles and activities deriving from the adult world. In this sense, play is a precursor world in Harré's sense. On the other hand, children have their own projects, affective commitments, and rules whereby the play world is constructed, maintained, and negotiated. In this sense, it is autonomous with respect to the adult world. In this way, play permits forms of activity which are intimate without being serious. Adult roles and activities are recontextualized according to the identity projects, the affective commitments, and the rules of the autonomous pretend world of children's play.

In taking a further step towards abstracting from the concrete and in generalizing from the specific in symbolic play, children learn to attend to experience in a qualitatively different way. That is, the child is able to look at knowledge of the knowing how or procedural kind at one remove, i.e. with enhanced powers of abstraction and generalization with respect to imitation. Symbolic play embodies an implicit meta-level system of reflection on and observation of action whereby the rules of the (adult) actions acted out in play, as well as the rules of the autonomous world, are subject to increasing powers of explicit reflection.

2 Introducing the play episode: analytical preliminaries

The text to be analysed below is a transcript which I made from the taped dialogue of two young girls, both of whom were aged 04;10 at the time. (See Appendix I.) This dialogue took place in the bedroom of one of the two girls one Saturday afternoon in November 1989 in Bologna (Italy). One of the girls, Elena, has come to visit the other, Paola, for the afternoon. The scene takes place in Paola's bedroom, where the tape recorder was concealed. For most of the time, the bedroom door was kept rigorously shut, as if to demarcate the strong insulation of the girls' play and the space – both physical and symbolic – in which this occurred from the adult world. During the period concerned, the two girls attended the same class at pre-school, as they had done for the previous two years. The parents of the two girls were also known to each other and the two girls frequently visited each other in the period in question.

The particular episode that I shall analyse in the next section features a play scene which was regularly enacted by the two girls. Typically, Paola took up the discursive position of the mother, while Elena took up that of the baby. Thus, a number of social discourses of child-rearing practices, and, in particular, the genres of parental control of children, are negotiated. This does not mean that other factors are not also relevant and significant. Certainly, many things are going on in this episode, which was just one of a number of intertextually related ones, which I collected over a period of several months. Unfortunately, space does not allow me to discuss everything which is relevant or interesting, or to explore the intertextual relations with the other episodes which I have recorded and transcribed.

In the analysis, I shall start by referring to the lexicogrammatical and genre features which are deployed. I shall then go on to discuss the processes of "re-envoicement" whereby features of adult talk that derive from the wider contexts of situation and context of culture of the play episode are renegotiated and transformed. The analysis is subdivided into a number of sub-units, which correspond to the various discourse phases (Gregory 2002) which I have identified in the analysis. Gregory's concept of phase refers to the ways in which particular stretches of discourse may be characterized by an overall micro-registerial "consistency and congruity in the selections that have been made from the language's codal resources" (2002: 321). Such phases may be continuously or discontinuously realized in stretches of discourse. My analysis accepts Gregory's formulation, but will also bring out some further implications, which are not addressed in Gregory, for the ways in which discourse activity is related to the high-scalar ecosocial system in which such activity is always embedded.

The meta-grammatical terminology which I have used is based on Halliday (1994 [1985]). Appendix I to this chapter consists of a transcription of the entire text, with English language glosses. Appendix II is a detailed linguistic analysis of the textual transcription in Appendix I. Appendixes I and II can be cross-referenced with each other, as well as with the discussion in the main part of this chapter.

3 Connecting the play episode to the context of culture of the participants

The two girls' regular meetings over a period of months constitute a distinctive interpersonal moral order. Children's autonomous social worlds, as constituted in play, entail their own norms and practices at the same time that they appropriate and transform adult meanings and practices for the purposes of the autonomous precursor worlds that are constructed in play. In their autonomous precursor worlds, children allocate roles to self and to others in particular activities. They also negotiate and dispute moral norms for the regulation of conduct and the allocation of these roles, display personality attributes, and engage in projects which are autonomous with respect to the rules and the aims of the adult world.

Moreover, the play situation and its interpretation depend on a wider system of cultural meanings and practices, which are not necessarily made fully explicit in any given episode. In the episode to be analysed in this chapter, the two girls both jointly and individually interpret and contextualize texts, songs, social activities, particular situations, objects, and so on. They do so by connecting these to other texts and other situations both in the autonomous precursor world of the children, as well as in the wider context of culture in which the children are also apprentice participants in a range of different social practices and their associated subject and agent positions. In their play together, both their autonomous precursor world and the wider context of culture are interwoven so as to create networks of connections among social practices, texts, objects, and so on, in both domains.

The two girls come from similar social backgrounds – professional middle-class parents – so that they orient to many experiences and meanings in very similar ways. We can see in the analysis of the play episode created by the two children that the common culture that they both orient to is interwoven with the particular activities that they engage in during the episode. At the same time, the meanings, texts, activities, objects, and the bodies of the two girls themselves index other cultural practices and meanings that are relevant to the meaning of any given phase of the episode.

The networks of connections among specific activities, texts, meanings, participants, discourse genres, social institutions, communities, and so on, are the basis on which meanings are made on any given occasion. The connections made are not simply between the two participants as they engage in particular forms of dialogue and take up particular positions in particular activities. They are also between, for example, text and individual, text and social practice, individual and social practice, and so on.

In the episode under consideration here, the various phases of the overall episode selectively orient to and create connections among different aspects of the social networks that the children participate in, as shown in Table 4.1.

As Table 4.1 indicates, the overall organization of the play episode is quite heterogeneous. There are many interacting variables from the social networks that the two girls participate in. By the same token, the movement or progression of this particular play episode from one phase to the next does not occur in accordance with any pre-determined plan or cause. While we can say that, overall, the episode is recognizably an instance of children's play, this observation does not in itself explain the quite considerable semiotic heterogeneity of the episode.

Each phase can be seen as an attempt to approximate local shifts in the potential of the episode overall as it unfolds and individuates in time. That is, each phase is a local change of state in relation to some parameters as the overall system self-organizes in time. If we assume that the trajectory of the episode as a whole started with Paola's opening bid in phase 1, when she sought to negotiate the allocation of play roles with Elena, then we can say that the trajectories of both Paola and Elena converge on particular dynamical patterns that constitute the attractors of the system and its temporal trajectory.

The individual contributions of the two girls to the opening dialogue in phase 1 self-organize into jointly made activity to which the two girls orient from their respective points of view. Each move and each sub-move by each of the speakers as they engage with and respond to each other contribute to the making of the activity. Thus, each person's contribution converges on the attractor that constrains the activity of the emerging system as a whole. In this way, the trajectory of the episode is given shape and directionality in time. Attractors are not transcendent with respect to the lower-scalar activities of the two girls. Rather, attractors themselves self-organize in time in the sense that they embody the constraints constituted by the interaction between lower-scalar activities and the overall context in which the activity takes place.

However, the analysis of the specific phases, as described in Table 4.1, shows that there is considerable fluctuation from phase to phase as the episode unfolds along its trajectory. The transition from phase 1 to phase 2 can, at first sight, appear random. Why does Paola suddenly import the song she had learned at pre-school when the two children were previously discussing, in phase 1, the rules and the allocation of participant roles for their play session as mother and baby girl? The transition from phase 1 to phase 2 is signalled by the use of the adversative conjunction *ma* in the utterance *ma potevi anche cantare*. The sing-song intonation, culminating on the word *cantare*, which characterizes Paola's mode of utterance here, is also relevant. That is, the utterance is almost sung, as if in anticipation of the song which she then sings. Its specific rhythmic and intonational properties already contain characteristics that anticipate the song.

The play episode as a whole is a complex system in which the individual trajectories of the participants do not follow a pre-determined path. Instead, their trajectories may be attracted to

Table 4.1 Description of phases and the relevant aspects of the social networks that are selectively invoked in each phase in the Paola–Elena play episode

Phase	Aspects of social networks invoked	Description of phase
1	Friendship between the two girls as manifested in their playing together; Parenting roles with respect to mother–daughter roles and relations	Establishment and negotiation of rules and allocation of roles according to the norms of the autonomous precursor world; Orientation to metalevel of *giociamo* ("let's play") and *facciamo finta* ("let's pretend"); Orientation to joint agency: "we".
2	Pre-school context of song learned through activities in that context; Both girls attended the same pre-school and therefore shared the same kind of experiences	Paola in play role as mother imports song learned (by both girls) from pre-school and proposes to Elena in her play role as baby girl that she could sing it; Paola, in singing the song, re-situates herself in relation to it as the song is de-located from pre-school context and re-located in play context as part of a proposal for action that she makes to Elena; The adversative conjunction *ma* ("but") which begins her utterance shows that the song is being proposed to Elena as a possible alternative activity to the previously proposed one of playing mothers and babies; Interweaving and connecting of pre-school and parenting contexts; Orientation to agentive capacity (*potevi*)
3	Pre-school activity of song learning and the teacher who taught it to them	Joint orientation of both girls to the source of the song in the pre-school context and the teacher as the agent responsible for their learning it; Teacher–pupil roles invoked; Both girls position themselves in relation to both the song and the teacher; Orientation to source (causal regress) of capacity: *imparata*
4	Family life and parent roles; preparing a meal in the kitchen	Paola engages in pretend activity of preparing a meal (for Elena); orientation of Paola to the activity and associated role of meal preparation and associated objects (oil, salt); Orientation to self-command of task-oriented activity

| 5 | Birthday party interwoven with playing out of mother and baby roles | Orientation to social norms and activities associated with the providing of food to one's birthday party guests; In play, Elena-baby urging Paola-mother to ensure that the baby's birthday party is adequately catered for |
| 6 | Family life and parent roles; preparing food in the kitchen | Paola engages in pretend activity of preparing food in the kitchen, as in phase 4; orientation of Paola to the activity and associated role of food preparation, possibly now in relation to the party that was discussed in phase 5; Orientation to self-command of task-oriented activity as in phase 4 |

other meanings, other activities, other texts, and so on, in the overall social networks of the two participants and in ways that go beyond the specific episode. Thus, in phase 2, Paola accesses a social activity and relevant text (the song) that exists within the overall landscape of the social networks that she participates in at that stage in her life. This landscape embodies attractors that the system can access. The landscape and the likelihood that some attractors rather than others will be accessed in the creating of a given trajectory is a probabilistic one.

My point is that there is nothing in the prior phase 1 that can necessarily predict the transition to the different activity and situation that becomes newly and contingently relevant to the trajectory of the play episode as a whole in phase 2. We can, however, say that the pre-school context, along with its associated texts, activities, participants, and so on, constitutes a particular attractor and therefore a potential state which the system – a given play episode in this case – can access as it unfolds in time. In the present context, this observation is undoubtedly reinforced by the fact that both girls can readily access the same attractor. Given that the pre-school is such a regular feature in the weekly lives of both girls, this is hardly surprising. In other words, the pre-school context is itself a potential attractor that has a high probability of being accessed in play that takes place at home. The meanings, texts, activities, and so on, associated with pre-school themselves become a source of meaning and hence of variability of meaning in the play context.

4 Reconstituting Harré's theory of agency in relation to interpersonal meaning

In Harré's theory of personal being, an agent is a being who is in possession of dispositions or tendencies to act in ways that influence and change the world around him or her, including most importantly other social beings (1983: 190). The exercise of a tendency in action is what Harré calls an "influence". Harré argues that someone "is a perfect agent relative to some category of action when both the tendency to act and the release of that tendency are in the power of that person" (1983: 190). In my view, tendencies or dispositions to act are constituted in discourse by modalizing operations of various kinds.

The range of modalities in a language can be related to agentive tendencies or dispositions that discourse participants attribute to themselves and to others. These processes of attribution take place when social agents are negotiating both the location of agentive tendencies at particular person-places in the social order and the release or activation of these tendencies as particular courses of action. The agent's possession of a given tendency or disposition to act means, in the present framework, that the agent has been modalized to act in relation to one of a number of different possible areas of validity that correspond to the different kinds of modalities that exist in a given language. For our present purposes, I shall refer to three very general categories of modality which will be useful in the analyses that I develop in this chapter. These categories are INCLINATION, CAPACITY, and MORAL NECESSITY, as discussed in the following paragraphs.

Inclination

The socio-semantics of CONATION (trying, endeavouring, striving, and so on) and VOLITION (intending, wanting, willing) are unified by the semantic domain of Inclination in the present account.

Harré (1983: 201–202) notes that conation is rarely linked to the question of agency in socio-psychological studies. On the other hand, CONATION and VOLITION are very closely related, socio-semantically. Both are sub-categorizations of what Habermas (1984 [1981]: chapter 3) calls cognitive-instrumental (purposive-rational) action. In action of this type, the agent is oriented to achieving some end or goal through the rational assessment of the certainties and risks involved and the egocentric calculation of the strategies required to attain the desired goal or end, along with possible unforeseen consequences (Habermas 1984 [1981]: 285). Conation falls into the subcategory of cognitive-instrumental action called INSTRUMENTAL by

Habermas, i.e. the plans, attempts, strivings, and so on, of the agent follow technical and procedural rules of action for intervening in and acting upon "a complex of circumstances and events" (Habermas 1984 [1981]: 285). Such circumstances and events can include the rational assessment and/or co-optation of those factors, which both facilitate and/or hinder the attainment of the desired end. On the other hand, volition is oriented to SUCCESS, because the agent's intentions, decisions, wants, and so on, are based on criteria of rational choice for "influencing the decisions of a rational opponent" (Habermas 1984 [1981]: 285).

The grammar of conation relates to the way in which planning, trying, and succeeding entail the rational assessment of the certainties that a given aim will be attained through a particular action trajectory. The attainment of the aim requires the rational application of procedures which this area of meaning expresses, as in the grammar and semantics of, say, planning, trying, succeeding, and so on.

Overall, INCLINATION has a systemic reactance with the "high" end of the scale of modality, i.e. in the area of "certain" and "always". Inclination entails a model of agency in which the agent seeks, from a socially ratified and recognized person-place, to control the certainties and/or permanencies of the objective world through the imposition of a rational plan or will. In terms of the regress of causal explanation, this area of modalization has a systemic reactance with the semantics of "motivation", concerned with "causing the agent to want".

Capacity

Halliday (1976 [1970]) separates "ability" and "permission" into two distinct categories. The first is an intrinsic modulation; the second, which Halliday, subcategorizes under "necessity", is extrinsic. This distinction suggests that there are two distinct *cans*. I prefer to talk in terms of just one for reasons that I shall now explain. While I am not denying that these glosses serve a purpose, I am assuming that the use of the same grammatical form *can* to express permission and ability is, in fact, motivated by an underlying functional semantic unity. In this case, the relevant criterion is no longer the distinction between "ability" and "permission", but the socio-semantic location of particular agentive capacities. Are these intrinsic to the agent, or are they derived from some external source? Thus, the clause *I can swim* expresses an intrinsic subjective competence or capacity of the *I* whereas a clause such as *you can come in now*, which is subclassified by Halliday as "permission", is not, in my view, concerned with a separate semantics of "permission" as opposed to "ability". Instead, in clauses of this kind, the speaker delegates or transfers the relevant agentive capacity to the addressee. The "granting of permission" is, then, a process of transferring a given modal capacity from one social being to another. In the clause, *Can I help you?*, which typically functions as an opening move in a goods-&-services type transaction or, SERVICE ENCOUNTER genre, the speaker (the shop assistant) is not simply offering a service. Instead, the speaker is also seeking the relevant modal capacity, or the authority to release it, from his or her addressee (the customer). The speaker is seeking to empower him- or herself through the acquisition of the relevant modal ability or competence from the relevant other in the social encounter. There are not, then, two separate *cans*, but one. The difference is not one of "ability" vs. "permission", but of the socio-semantic location and re-location of agentive powers and capacities in the social order.

Halliday's network places "permission" in the same semantic area as NECESSITY, which is concerned with the regulation of the other (see below). My decision to place both "ability" and "permission" in the semantic domain CAPACITY is motivated by the fact that the relevant validity claim is not concerned with moral rightness and wrongness, as would be the case for MORAL NECESSITY (see below), but with the social location and delegation of, the access to, and the distribution of agentive capacities. In the first instance, it is the capacities themselves and the agent's right to them which are being regulated in the semantic area of CAPACITY. CAPACITY is a single area of socio-semantic potential; it includes the semantics of knowing, getting to know, learning, ability, and permission. The relevant causal regress has to do with what "caused the agent" to know, or to possess some skill or ability, variously defined as forms of modal competencies or capacities, which are intrinsic to the agent. These capacities can be questioned (doubted, disbelieved, disagreed with, and so on), but their socio-semantic location and definition as intrinsic properties of agents is not in itself brought into question.

Meanings in the general semantic area of CAPACITY have a systemic reactance with the "low" end of the scale of modality, i.e. with "possible" and "sometimes", as evidenced by the semantic overlap of meanings in the area of "possibility", "ability", and "permission" in the auxiliary verb *can*. From this point of view, we are concerned with the conditions of possibility whereby an agent is able to perform some action, i.e. to make that action possible. These conditions of possibility are located at particular person-places in the ecosocial semiotic system. Agents may sometimes possess the relevant capacity by virtue of their being located at the appropriate person-place, and sometimes not. The relevant causal regress is concerned with the conditions of enablement whereby an agent comes to be in possession of some capacity or some possibility to act.

Moral necessity

The area of meaning which I refer to as MORAL NECESSITY is concerned with the moral-practical domain, rather than with causal necessity in the physical world. In the domain of Moral Necessity, we are not concerned with the allocation and release of agentive capacities, but with the regulation of the self and others with reference to norm conformative validity claims. These claims have to do with criteria of moral rightness and wrongness, goodness and badness, duties, obligations, responsibilities, their imposition and enforcement. The conditions of their enforcement may be connected to institutionalized power claims and sanctions, but this is by no means always the case. The point is that the speaker's demand for goods-&-services is met (rather than refused and challenged) by the addressee if, from the point of view of both parties to the interaction, the conditions for what Habermas (1984 [1981]: 298) calls intersubjective recognition of the speech act are fulfilled. Both addresser and addressee thereby bind themselves in a form of agreement to the conditions (duties, obligations, responsibilities) for the fulfilment of the command, request, and so on. I am not saying that this is necessarily or even usually a symmetrical or reciprocal process. The bottom line in moral necessity is always power.

The modal category of Moral Necessity integrates into a single area of semantic potential both moral-normative and moral-practical reason. The former includes meanings that have to do with moral approbation and disapprobation. Speakers may position themselves and others at person-places which are the locus of claims to do with goodness and badness, or rightness and wrongness, relative to some particular norm. These meanings thus foreground the possibility for making such claims and for disputing them as a means to establishing, maintaining, and changing social norms to do with ethics, morality, and value judgements.

Modalities in the area of Moral Necessity are concerned both with self-regulation and the regulation of others. Such modalizations are extrinsic – the agency or the source of the modulation conditions or constrains the social actor from the outside. In giving an order or making a request, the speaker, as the agent who imposes the modalization on the addressee, is inviting the addressee to be inclined to do something. The relevant criterion is "moral necessity" (Harré 1983: 30), rather than physical force or the efficient causality of forceful impacts. The processes of intersubjective recognition and negotiation between the two agents may motivate the addressee to take up and to adopt (or not) a position of compliance or assent through a process of modal investment in and identification with both the position which is made available and with the normative discourses which sanction this position.

At the tendency stage, the addresser imposes an expectation to conform to some norm on the addressee. The tendency may be released at some future stage. In this way, the addresser can "count upon", or "rely upon", the addressee to do what is required. The addresser seeks to control the regularities of actions and events from a particular person-place. From this person-place, there emanates a controlling field, which functions to define and to control what is "probable" and "usual". In other words, the agent seeks to control the probabilities, usualities, and the expectations concerning the actions of other social beings by locating them at person-places which conform to the field of probabilities and expectations which the relevant norms have established. These norms include expectations as to what is usual, what is right, what is required, what is allowed, and so on, for social beings to do and be. Thus, the addresser is located at a person-place from which there extends a controlling field of probabilities and/or expectations. This controlling field can extend into the past, whereby agents are constrained by past regularities, as the oblique modals such as *should, would,* and so on, suggest. It can also extend into the future. In the latter case, the agent seeks to control the probabilities of future actions, and so on. For example: *it is necessary* (for you) *to do* ... The semantics of moral necessity, by extending their control of the field of probabilities and expectations into both past and future, thereby "compel" agents to act according to a moral logic of what is **necessary** precisely because the relevant norms have "always been" and "always will be". The relevant reactances in the system of modality are in the median area of "probably" and "usually". Similarly, the relevant causal regress has to do with "what it is necessary to do" in order to bring some state of affairs into line with the relevant expectations concerning what is probable and usual.

Thus, persons and particular categories of persons in the social order are locations for actual and potential modal tendencies to act in certain ways in relation to particular moral or other criteria that establish if and when a given action is an act of a certain type. Persons are locations in the "primary structure" (Harré 1983: 76) in the sense that they are physical locations without inner complexity. However, real human beings, as Harré (*op. cit.*) points out, attribute inner complexity both to themselves as well as to other beings in the social order. This inner complexity includes the attribution of intentions, motivations, and reasons for acting in certain ways. Harré (*op. cit.*) refers to this inner complexity as the "secondary structure".

Harré (1989: 32) has also drawn attention to the problem of intractability when answers to questions such as "How is agency possible?" are sought on the basis of causal explanations, rather than being grounded in "the grammar of authorization explanations". Such a grammar is always derived from the systems of axiological and ethical orientations in a culture which define what Harré has called interpersonal moral orders (Harré 1983). Harré (1989: 32) draws attention to the intractability of attempting to map the language of causal explanations on to human actions. The latter have their basis in the interpersonal moral orders in which social agents, their possibilities for action, and their rights, responsibilities and ethical commitments, and so on, are defined.

The causal species of explanation critiqued by Harré is founded on the language of forceful impacts between objects in the physical world (see chapter 8, section 8). It is the language of efficient causality. In this view, it is assumed that epistemically private mental states and intentions cause people to act in the same way that, in the physical world, one object, when it collides with a second object, causes the second object to move. Harré points out that the activities of warranting, explaining, and justifying their actions on the part of social agents are "authorization explanations". Explanation of this kind ground the understanding of a particular action that someone performs or intends to perform in the interpersonal moral orders of that culture, rather than in the language of physical causation. Such explanations cannot be understood in terms of physical causality. For this reason, attempts to explain human agency in these terms are intractable. Instead, we need a different kind of framework, which grounds human agency in the kinds of meanings that connect individual body-brain systems to their ecosocial semiotic environment at the same time that these meanings modulate and guide their action trajectories.

It is possible, in my view, to extend Harré's critique in ways which connect with the interpersonal dimension of meaning and, therefore, with the interpersonal enactment and negotiation of agency in discourse. This connection can help us to construct a unified account of the relations between given social act-types, the lexicogrammatical (and other semiotic) selections which realize these, and the intertextually retrievable interpersonal moral orders in terms of which agents ground their actions and their understandings and explanations of these same actions. In this way, we can show how any given dialogic move is connected to the wider intertextual formations in and through which a given interpersonal moral order and its meanings shape and guide human actions along specific trajectories.

In the following section, I shall analyse in some detail the deployment of the interpersonal linguistic resources by the two girls in the process of their allocating and negotiating agency with respect to self and other.

5 The take up and negotiation of agent positions in the play episode: an analysis

Phase 1

In the imperative clause *giociamo a mamma*, Paola selects the implicit first person plural Subject (*noi* = inclusive we) as the entity which is held modally responsible for carrying out the proposed action. In terms of the present theory, the use of the imperative clause in this utterance is a case of co-agency at work. The speaker is an agent who is in possession of a particular volitional tendency or desire to bring about a particular not-yet-achieved state of affairs in the world. The speaker, in uttering the imperative clause, seeks to transfer this volitional tendency to act to the addressee *qua* potential second agent. That is, the speaker, in selecting the addressee as Subject, positions the addressee at a particular person-place in the array of person-places in the secondary structure. The speaker seeks to position her addressee as a potential agent who is willing and, therefore, in possession of the required volitional tendency for carrying out the action desired by the speaker.

In my terms, this is a modalizing operation whereby the speaker transfers or delegates to the addressee *qua* modally responsible Subject in the clause the modal power or tendency that is required to perform the action. In other words, the speaker seeks to recruit, align, or modally conjoin the addressee to a particular modalizing operation, which is enacted through the uttering of the clause in question. Thus, when agents linguistically act on others to influence them or to change them in some way, or to get them to carry out a particular course of action, we can say that the speaker is attempting to bring about a particular kind of modalizing operation on the addressee, or to modalize the addressee in a particular way (chapter 8, section 3).

In actual fact, nothing is transferred from one person to another in the transaction. Instead, the speaker seeks to modally conjoin the addressee to the modal orientation of the speaker's proposition or proposal. In this way, addresser and addressee are oriented to the proposition or proposal and hence its possibilities for further action or thinking in similar ways, though always from their respective viewpoints. Modality is one of the linguistic resources for grounding or making a proposition or proposal finite by relating it to an evaluative framework – e.g. a choice of modality – that both addresser and addressee can jointly orient to.

Insofar as the system of modality in particular languages is a set of possible ways of orienting to and evaluating propositions and proposals in discourse, we can say that the speaker's modalizing operation seeks to orient the addressee in a particular way with respect to some proposition or proposal. Speakers, in deploying particular modalizing operations, act on the consciousness of others to change or to influence this – i.e. by modalizing the addressee's consciousness such that the addressee is modally aligned or oriented to the proposition or proposal in some way. Bakhtin has written of the "active and responsive understanding" (1986: 75) of the other to whom the speaker's utterance is always directed in discourse. Modalizing operations in discourse, as ways of acting upon and influencing the consciousness of others, can be understood in precisely this sense.

In uttering the clause, the speaker positions herself as an agent in possession of a particular volitional tendency. At the same time, she also positions herself as someone who is authorized or legitimated in the local interpersonal moral order as an agent who is entitled to make such claims on other persons. The example shows that the structure of agency is more complex than Harré's description implies. This is so in the sense that it is more correct to say that agency typically involves two (or more) agents in a relationship of co-agency.

The structure of the co-agency involved in the example considered above may be modelled as follows:

AGENT$_1$ (SPEAKER) WANTS TO PLAY WITH AGENT$_2$ (ADDRESSEE)
↓
AGENT$_1$ SEEKS TO LOCATE AGENTIVE TENDENCY (WANTING TO PLAY) AND ITS RELEASE AS PROPOSED ACTION AT AGENT$_2$ BY PERFORMING MODALIZING OPERATION ON AGENT$_2$
↓
AGENT$_2$ TAKES UP A PARTICULAR MODALIZED ORIENTATION TO THE PROPOSED ACTION IN HER RESPONSE
↓
AGENT$_2$ PERFORMS OR REFUSES TO PERFORM THE PROPOSED ACTION

Agent$_1$'s "wanting to play" may appear to be a case of an epistemically private mental state or intention that causes her utterance. However, a very different explanation can be made without entailing the kind of mental determinism that this model of causation requires. Instead, the "regress of causes" that can be postulated in terms of the willingness, the intentions, or the desires, and so on, that motivate the given act, are **meanings** that both parties to the transaction can access and negotiate in order to explain or to understand the reasons for the speaker's proposal. Such meanings are always made in relation to more abstract and more general inter-textually adduced norms, principles, or conventions that can, if desired, be made explicit and further negotiated on any given occasion (see Habermas 1984; Hasan 1992a; Thibault and Van Leeuwen 1996).

Generally speaking, these norms, principles, and conventions take the form of the validity claims that are recognized in the particular interpersonal order. Agents draw on and use these norms to warrant their own actions as well as those of others. Such warranting takes place with reference to interpersonal moral criteria which regulate the assignment and distribution of rights and responsibilities in the performing of various classes of social action.

Phase 2

In this phase, Paola's utterance *ma potevi anche cantare* locates a particular modalized capacity at Elena *qua* person-place. Paola therefore recognizes Elena as being in possession of both the requisite capacity and the conditions for its release, i.e. as a particular kind of action that is lexicalized by the verb *cantare* in this clause. That is, Elena is recognized as having an intrinsic subjective capacity which affords possibilities for various kinds of action – i.e. singing in this case – in the interpersonal moral order that is relevant here. In the play situation, Paola, in her role as pretend-mother, delegates to Elena, in her role as pretend-baby-girl, the possibility of releasing or enacting the capacity in question as an appropriate form of action.

Again, we see that the declarative clause that Paola uses to express her modalized proposition necessarily implicates co-agency. In this case, the addresser (Paola) seeks to conjoin or align her addressee (Elena) to the modal evaluation of the proposition that the choice of the modal verb *potevi* implicates. In this clause, the implied (ungrammaticalized) Subject is the second person singular pronoun *tu*. Elena is thereby designated as the co-agent who is made modally responsible for the proposition in the clause and therefore for performing the action specified by the proposition. Paola positively evaluates the possibility of Elena being in possession of this capacity at the same time that she positions Elena in the discourse as being authorized to release this capacity as a given course of action.

In the present example, the relevant interpersonal moral order is a blend of the play situation and the pre-school that the two girls attended at that time. Paola, in her role as pretend-mother, delegates the responsibility for the release of the given capacity as action to Elena as the baby girl. At the same time, Paola recognizes the source of this capacity in the pre-school environ-ment that the two girls share. Paola's own singing of the song is itself a release of the same capacity *qua* modalized possibility for action that she has previously recognized in Elena. In the present context, it may serve as an example to guide or instruct Elena at the same time that the song explicitly evokes the pre-school context in which it was learned.

Phase 3

In phase 3, the relevant causal regress, pertaining to the learning of the song from the pre-school teacher, is itself made the focus of the question and answer sequence in this phase. Phase 3 shows that the two girls are quite capable of engaging in this kind of meta-level discussion with regard to the source of a particular intrinsic capacity that they possess in relation to the relevant interpersonal moral order. In so doing, they evoke criteria concerning the assignment and distribution of agentive capacities to particular person-places. They also reveal an understanding of the social processes whereby such capacities are transformed from one agent to another in the learning process. This last point shows that they also have some understanding of the learning process itself as the means through which particular capacities are acquired.

Phase 4

The egocentric speech that Paola uses in this phase shows the role of language in her self-constitution as agent whereby both a point of action and a point of view are reflexively sourced at the same person. This phase and the relevance of egocentric speech to the theory of agency and consciousness that I am developing in this book will be discussed in a more sustained and complete way in chapter 5. Egocentric speech can be seen as part of the self-organizing process whereby a self is constituted in symbolic neural space as individual consciousness. In this way, the integral link between individual consciousness and agency becomes evident. Thus, the body is integrated to the brain's representation of the body in the image of the self at the same time that higher-order consciousness enables semantic attractors to emerge which direct and modulate bodily activity along determinate action trajectories in the fulfillment of specific intentions, the exercising of particular capacities, and the following of particular moral norms. Consciousness is thus able to posit specific goals as well as harness bodily activity in connection with selected aspects of the ecosocial environment in the attainment of these goals.

The individual draws on and re-envoices the meaning-making resources of the ecosocial semiotic system in the construction of his or her own agency. In the present case, the child selectively draws on and co-deploys language and other material and semiotic resources. Thus, the manifestation and exercise of agency in the individual has a necessarily historical and collective dimension. The self constructs its agency through the process of adaptively modifying and re-envoicing the resources of the higher scalar ecosocial semiotic system to the perspectives of the self. Following the logic of three-level hierarchy thinking (see chapter 1, section 4), the self, which necessarily implicates both agency and consciousness on the intermediate level L, is an emergent consequence of the interactions between the lower level L–1 and the higher level L+1. Thus, there is a reorganization of the biological initiating conditions on level L–1 of the individual body-brain system through the interactions between L–1 relations and processes and the higher-scalar system of interpretance on L+1 that the agent (the self) on level L accesses. This reorganization results from the kinds of self–other transactions that the self engages in on level L.

Meanings are stored in the much more stable and more slowly changing structures and dynamics of the higher scalar ecosocial semiotic system, rather than in the individual body-brain systems in and through which meanings are enacted in contextually specific ways. The interaction between levels L+1 and L–1 thus allows for the emergence of more highly complex intermediate level systems (e.g. selves) that are able both to maintain themselves over time and to increase their own self-complexity in and through their own self-activity. These processes are informationally (semiotically) constrained by the higher scalar level of the ecosocial semiotic system. The constraints emanating from the L+1 level harness and channel level L–1 processes at the same time that level L processes are enabled by material structures and processes in the individual body-brain system on level L–1. Moreover, the self's selecting and modulating of this information as action trajectories that can be sourced at the self also requires the self's capacity functionally to evaluate this information and the resulting trajectories that are generated from the perspective of the self.

Paola's episode of "egocentric speech" involves both the acting out, through her sensori-motor activity, of knowledge which is embodied in specific activities (e.g. preparing a meal) and a simultaneous linguistic activity which both describes and guides her embodied performance. This acting out in the pretend context of a particular culturally recognized participant role in a determinate social activity-type ("preparing a meal") is itself a move in the process of abstracting from procedural knowledge. At the same time, her linguistic activity both experientially construes the activity by naming it and its component parts at the same time that she interpersonally enacts it in the form of the self-commands which guide and shape her own activity.

In this way, the language she uses is both an on-line (situated) naming of the activity and its enactment from the perspective of the self. The self is, dually, the source of the experiential categories used and the point of action for the activity performed in the point of view of the self. Egocentric speech can, therefore, be seen as playing a crucial role in the self-organization of the semantic state space within the perspective of the self. The individual's bodily activities are increasingly constrained by and originate in meanings and values that can be sourced at and integrated to the perspective of a self *qua* agent. Such an agent is able, in generalizing and abstracting from implicit embodied procedure, to develop and to reflect upon an expanding repertoire of alternatives from which the agent chooses in the process of undertaking a given course of action.

Egocentric speech illustrates the process whereby the ecosocial semiotic environment is selectively imported into the organism's internal body-brain dynamics in ways which constrain and enable the activity potential of the body-brain system *qua* self. A self, as I pointed out earlier, is necessarily endowed with the properties of both agency and consciousness. In the example under discussion here, the child both directs her own activity (interpersonal) at the same time that she names it (experiential) in the perspective of herself. As the action schema below shows, she does so in ways that enact, guide, and modulate her action trajectory to its conclusion. The modulation of the trajectory is semantically consistent with the capacities, volitions, and moral necessities that she has elaborated in the perspective of her self as an agent with particular points of view and particular possibilities for action in the relevant interpersonal moral orders. The child's activity in this phase can be schematized as follows:

1. AGENT CAN PREPARE MEAL (POSSESSES REQUISITE CAPACITY AND POWER OF ITS RELEASE) ↓
2. AGENT WANTS TO PREPARE MEAL (HAS INCLINATION/VOLITION AND POWER OF ITS RELEASE) ↓
3. AGENT NEEDS TO PREPARE MEAL (MORAL NECESSITY: SOCIAL NORMS) ↓
4. AGENT SEEKS TO LOCATE AGENTIVE TENDENCY (WANTING TO PREPARE MEAL) AND ITS RELEASE AS PROPOSED ACTION AT SELF BY PERFORMING MODALIZING OPERATION ON SELF (SELF-COMMAND) (*un pò di olio*)

    ↓

5. AGENT TAKES UP A PARTICULAR MODALIZED ORIENTATION TO THE PROPOSED ACTION IN HER RESPONSE (*ch ch*)

    ↓

6. AGENT PERFORMS THE PROPOSED ACTION

The above sequence of stages in part reflects the sequential structure of the activity as it unfolds in time. In particular, this is true of parts 4 to 6, which refer to those stages of the activity that are realized by linguistic and other means. Parts 1 to 3, on the other hand, represent an analytical reconstruction of the "causal regress" of capacities and intentions that can be postulated as underlying a given act. Thus, the performing of the action presupposes (1) that the agent is in possession of the requisite knowledge, competence, or skill to perform it (CAPACITY); (2) that the agent wants or intends to perform the action, which is, therefore, under the agent's control (INCLINATION/VOLITION); and (3) that the action is referable to and accountable in terms of some locally relevant moral order of moral-normative and moral-practical reasoning

(MORAL NECESSITY). In this case, the relevant moral order would refer to the norms for the preparation and serving of meals for one's children and/or one's birthday party guests (see also chapter 8, section 2).

In the philosophical and psychological literature, stages 1 to 3 in the above sequence would be treated as a causal regress of psychological attributes. As such, these attributes are said to cause human action. However, a more valid alternative explanation is that stages 1 to 3 refer to **meanings** that act as contextual constraints on the activities of the individual body-brain system. The emergence of such meanings in the perspective of the self alters the probability distribution of the neural and sensori-motor dynamics of the body-brain system such that some possibilities for acting and meaning are possible whereas others are not. Thus, volitions, capacities, and moral reasons for acting in certain ways rather than others are the phenomeno-logical equivalent of the probability distribution of the meanings in symbolic neural space that regulate the individual's activity. Neural and sensori-motor dynamics are entrained to these meanings such that the activities of individuals, including their interactions with others, are more likely to go down some possible trajectories, rather than others, according to the social networks in which the individual has participated.

Thus, capacities, volitions, and moral necessities are not psychological attributes of indi-viduals that "cause" action in individuals in the sense of forcefully impacting on them. Instead, they are ecosocial semiotic meanings to which the internal dynamics of the individual *qua* (potential) agent are entrained. The individual's entrainment to these higher-scalar meanings therefore creates certain kinds of persistent interdependencies between the individual body-brain system and the higher-scalar ecosocial semiotic environment. The interaction between these two levels leads to the emergence of persons or selves with agentive powers and capacities, along with the power to release these powers and capacities as appropriate courses of action in determinate contexts. The agent's capacities, volitions, and moral necessities are, then, mean-ings, which, in entraining the dynamics of the body-brain system to the dynamics of the higher scalar ecosocial environment, attune the dynamics of the former to the latter.

Persons *qua* agents accordingly self-organize in response to contextual contingencies that require them to act as agents. Thus, capacities, volitions, and moral necessities are collected by selves as the result of their own cascading activities. In this way, they increase in semiotic complexity as a result of the meanings that they have acquired along their trajectory and elaborated as patterns of . . . of neural activation (Salthe 1993: 173). They, therefore, evolve perspectives *qua* selves such that these perspectives are referable to the self as being in control of and responsible for the points of action and points of view that can be sourced at the self. It is with reference to these points of action and points of view that individual agents can act in the world and produce effects in the world. These effects can be sourced at the self, as well as explained in terms of the self's points of view relative to some interpersonal moral order (chapter 7).

Phase 5

In clauses 22–23c, the speaker, Elena, is pretending to be the little girl who is talking to her mother, as played by the other child, Paola. In her role as speaker, Elena seeks to modalize her listener (Paola) to take up a particular modal stance in relation to the proposition that she expresses in clause 22. The use of the first person inclusive plural form (I + YOU) as implied Subject of this clause shows that the speaker seeks to conjoin her listener to herself as Subject. Thus, the meaning SPEAKER + LISTENER is grammaticalized as a composite Subject with reference to which the proposition can be affirmed by the speaker. The modulation *dobbiamo* ("we must") lies in the semantic domain that I glossed as MORAL NECESSITY in section 3 above.

In this way, the proposition uttered by Elena in clause 22 references a system of higher-order norms of rightness, appropriateness, and so on, in connection with norm conformative validity claims that specify the moral-practical conditions and reasons whereby certain courses of action are adopted. In this case, Elena, as speaker, seeks to bind both herself and Paola in a

	dobbiamo	fare	la mente	mamma
SPEAKER	Subject: 1st Person Plural Inclusive + Finite: Modality: Moral Necessity	Predicator	Complement	Vocative
	Mood: Grounding of Proposition in Person Deixis (*noi*) and modality (obligation)	Residue: Specification of Action to be performed		
Agent in possession of power to release relevant disposition or tendency	Subject as co-agent consisting of speaker and addressee in whom the tendency is modally invested such that the Subject is authorized to carry out the action specified in the Residue			

Figure 4.1 The structure of joint agency in the clause *dobbiamo fare la mente*

form of agreement as to the conditions that are necessary for the fulfilment of the action that is lexicalized in the Residue of this clause, i.e. *fare la mente* ("make the mint") as a not-yet-achieved action, but one which the two participants must achieve according to the norm that Elena evokes here. The uttering of this particular clause, rather than the undertaking of some other possible course of action (linguistic or otherwise), constitutes a reduction of possibilities in the particular context as it dynamically unfolds and develops along its trajectory. Thus, the proposition is linked to intertextually retrievable validity claims in relation to which a speaker's intention can be identified as the source of the proposition. In this case, the speaker evokes specific moral-practical norms for justifying her intention to get the action mentioned in the clause done.

Now, intentions, in the present theoretical framework, are not epistemically private mental states that stand behind action in a separate "mental" realm and cause action. Rather, they are meanings which we attribute to ourselves and to others in the processes of discursive activity. In the present example, the evoking of higher-order principles of the norm conformative kind serves to identify the speaker's intention in the uttering of the given proposition as one which is oriented to the achieving of the specified course of action. The intention as such is not explicitly grammaticalized in this particular utterance. However, it is possible to infer the intention on the basis of the semantics of the utterance in its contexts. The intention is itself a semantic construct that the utterance indexes for the participants in the context of situation in the course of their meaning-making activity. Moreover, the intention, which, in this case, can be glossed as "recruit listener to carry out action with speaker", can be realized by any number of different linguistic or other strategies. Here, the intention and the proposition that instantiates the intention is grounded in a validity claim of the norm conformative kind.

The important point is that the utterance articulates a particular trajectory in semantic state space at the same time that it is finalized. That is, the utterance is determined by the possibility of the other's responding to it, or of "assuming a responsive attitude toward it" (Bakhtin 1986: 76). Meaning-making activity is always dialogically organized in relation to some other. The other may be concrete or abstract, general or specific, present or absent, near or far in time, and so on. The point is that utterances anticipate and are therefore finalized, as Bakhtin says, in order that the other can respond to them. Language is decentred on the other; human beings are not oriented to the interpretation of things *per se* in the world, but to the interpretation of the network of meanings in which they are immersed. This network of meanings is the primary human reality.

Paola's response in clauses 24–25b illustrates the criteria of active responsive understanding, to use Bakhtin's formulation, which I referred to above. That is, in her utterance, she takes up a specific evaluative orientation with respect to Elena's prior utterance. In so doing, she is integrated to the same overall action trajectory. Elena's initial utterance constitutes a semantic attractor, which is taken up and responded to positively by Paola. In the ensuing development of the discourse, both participants are entrained to the same overall semantic trajectory. All the lower-scalar components of the interaction are enslaved to the same overriding semantic principle, which modulates their individual contributions. Each participant's moves in the dialogue make a local contribution to the sustaining of the semantic trajectory in question until it, too, achieves some kind of local resolution or closure such that the intention is fulfilled. In the present case, this occurs in clauses 28a–c in Phase 6 when Paola returns to the pretend activity of preparing the food for the party.

Because of the mentalistic baggage that accompanies the term intention, it is important to clarify that, in the present context, intentions refers to goal-seeking activity rather than to epistemically private mental states. Wilden points out that human communication is founded on "the elevation of the lack (the goal) from simple absence, which is analog, to NEGATED PRESENCE, which must be digital," (1980 [1972]: 431) (see chapter 8, section 12). Elena's dialogic move in clauses 22–23c posits the activity of making the mint for the paddle pops as a demand which is to be fulfilled in conjunction with the other, rather than as a simple absence such as the bodily need for food or drink. The further point is that her demand is symbolically constituted in language. For this reason, it is digital rather than analogue. Her desire that the mint for the paddle pops be prepared is a second-order semantic constraint which exists in the context. It entrains the activity of the two participants to its higher-scalar dynamics because each participant's utterance making activity is constrained as a consequence of the constraints emanating from the higher-scalar level to a much narrower pathway of possibilities as the unfolding trajectory moves from one state to another.

There are two things to keep in mind here. First, the linguistic and other semiotic resources used are formal causes that serve to entrain and integrate each participant's activity to the higher-scalar trajectory. Secondly, the desired or anticipated outcome – the goal – of getting the mint made is a final cause that marks the end point of the trajectory. If the trajectory achieves the desired goal, rather than being prematurely truncated or deviated in some other direction by some other attractor, then we can say that it has achieved a local semantic closure or resolution in the sense that the end point is semantically congruent with the prior intention. The idea of semantic congruency here means that the action's trajectory, as it unfolds in time, both embodies the semantic content of the intention at the same time that it is modulated by it all along the duration of its trajectory (Juarrero 1999: 193).

In the move realized by clauses 22–23c, Elena both gives her point of view on the proposition and seeks to position Paola to take up a similar point of view in order that the desired action is carried out. In clauses 22 and 23c, she uses modalizations from the semantic area of moral necessity – *dobbiamo* (22) and *bisogna* (23c) – to align herself to the norm conformative validity claims that are being indexed here at the same time that she seeks to align her addressee, Paola, to these same norms of behaviour.

In clauses 24–25b, Paola's response to Elena positively aligns itself with the former speaker's discourse by positively evaluating the truthfulness of the propositions expressed by Elena. In this sense, Paola expresses her agreement with what Elena says and therefore, by implication, her willingness to be recruited to the course of action desired by Elena. Clauses 25a–b realize a projecting clause complex in which the addressee (Elena) is sourced as the Senser of the mental process *sai* (know) in the projecting clause, as follows:

[TU + sai che	[quello che stai dicendo è proprio vero]]
PROJECTING CLAUSE	PROJECTED CLAUSE: hypotaxis
Senser + Mental Process	

Paola, in her response, positions her addressee as the source of the hypotactically projected thought in the projected clause. In so doing, she projects her own evaluation of what Elena had previously said as if it were Elena's evaluation as well. While the evaluation in the projected clause is undoubtedly Paola's, the use of this particular grammatical strategy positions Elena as being similarly aligned with respect to Paola's evaluation. The strategy used by Paola can be seen as a meta-cognitive one of monitoring her interlocutor's (semantically construed) thoughts by imputing to her interlocutor her own evaluation of what her interlocutor said. In this way, Paola checks that Elena is able to see the proposition in the projected clause from the same point of view.

In clauses 26a–b, Elena again evokes the domain of norm conformative action through the third use of a modalization – again, *bisogna* – from the semantic area of moral necessity. Thus, each use of these modalizations shows how the further development of the trajectory that I discussed above continues to be modulated by the meanings that can be traced back to the source of the trajectory. In this case, Elena has aligned and motivated her intention in terms of meanings concerned with moral necessity. Each successive use of *dobbiamo* (22) and *bisogna* (23c, 26a) continues to provide information about the source at the same time that it constitutes its further development. In this sense, the ongoing development of the trajectory is consistent with the meaning of the intention that is attributable to Elena as the source of the trajectory.

Clause 27 again indicates Paola's active agreement with the propositions expressed by Elena and therefore her (Paola's) assent to the projected proposed by Elena, as well as the norm conformative reasons she has adduced for motivating this project.

In clauses 28a–c in Phase 6, Paola takes up and resumes the activity of preparing the pretend meal that she had begun in clauses 19a–20d in Phase 4.

6 Consciousness, agency, and the negotiation of self–other relations in and through propositions and proposals

Consciousness in all of its forms is a consequence of the self's dialogically coordinated engagements with the nonself, i.e. with the environment to which the organism is adapted. The relationship between self and nonself is one of complementarity: the individual is decentred with respect to the world in which the individual is immersed and which is meaningful for the individual. Thus, individuals, from the outset, are oriented to interpreting the world of the nonself in ways that are meaningful to the self. The distinction between self and nonself goes through various stages of specification, which I have schematized in terms of iconic, indexical, and symbolic modes of consciousness (see chapter 1, section 3). The increasing specification of each of the various modes of consciousness allows for ever more elaborate means for localizing the world of the nonself and therefore for objectifying it.

The fact that consciousness is, from its earliest stages in the ontogenesis of the individual, founded on a semiotic relationship between self and nonself means that the structure of consciousness is proto-propositional or propositional from its inception in the individual. An individual has consciousness (1) when the phenomena of experience constitute a sufficiently large field that can be selectively attended to; (2) when the self is connected to the field of the phenomena of experience and is related to the system of terms which enable this field to exist and to be attended to; (3) when the self selectively orients to and acts on this field using the logical operations of propositions and proposals such that the use of these modes of action and interaction allows one to perform operations on the given field whereby the field is unified with respect to the self. In this way, the self sees itself as the source of these propositions (or proposals) and of their consequences in the world of the nonself.

Consciousness is the product of these operations on the world, including the inner world that pertains to one's self. Acting on the world propositionally means that the self is reflexively positioned as both a point of action and a point of view in relation to the wider field of the phenomena of experience. The individual is therefore able to construct hypotheses about the world. Such is the nature of the interpersonal semantics of propositions and proposals in natural language. The self is reflexively connected to a given language or languages, to others, to the objects and events of the ecosocial environment, to the phenomena of experience, by virtue of the interpersonal semantics of propositions and proposals.

The progression from iconic to indexical to symbolic modes of consciousness in ontogenesis is an increase in the individual's information capacity due to increasing semiotic differentiation and specification (Salthe 1993: 80; Thibault 2000a: 298–303; 2004a: 226–227). Formally, this is a spontaneous cascade. With the help of specification hierarchy thinking, we have seen in chapter 3 that, in ontogenesis, the individual collects the effects of its own cascading in the process of integrating holistically, as Salthe (1993: 80–81) observes, the effects of all previous stages. Thus, iconic consciousness is integrated to and reorganized by indexical consciousness and the results of this integration – call it iconic-indexical consciousness – are in turn integrated by symbolic consciousness. In this way, the holistic character of the system is maintained as each stage integrates and reorganizes the prior stages in the formation of iconic-indexical-symbolic consciousness. Specification hierarchy thinking tells us that symbolic or higher-order consciousness stands in a unified relation of semiotic implication with respect to iconic, indexical, and iconic-indexical modes of consciousness. The prior stages are systemically subordinated to the later stages in a hierarchy of both implication and specification.

The increasing semiotic specification and complexity of symbolic consciousness means that the distance or the separation between self and nonself is increased. This means that the nonself is increasingly objectified in relation to the self. This increasing objectification can be seen in the semantics of proposals. Proposals realize the teleological positing of a goal in the mind of the speaker. They achieve this by acting on the consciousness of the addressee in order to bring the latter's activity into line with the speaker's teleologically posited goal (Lukács 1980 [1978]: 1–46), as expressed in the proposal. In the first instance, the proposal mediates the distance between the speaker and the posited goal at the same time that, in acting upon the consciousness of the addressee, the proposal brings about a second mediated series between the addressee and the posited goal. The coming into being of these mediated series takes place because the symbolic relation between the language of the proposal and the posited goal entails a semiotic distancing of the phenomena of experience from the self. It is in this way that the posited goal can exist in the consciousness of two social agents (addresser and addressee) in the organization and coordination of a temporal sequence of operations that is directed to the attainment of the posited goal. That is, language, in the form of the proposal, enables the posited goal to be shared and attended to as the common possession of the two consciousnesses that are implicated in the series of operations required to bring about the goal. Proposals are used to posit goals that exist in the consciousness of the speaker by directing and coordinating matter-energy flows in the physical-material domain in order that the desired goal be attained.

At the moment of uttering a proposal, the posited goal has a modal status of *irrealis*: the proposal constitutes a hypothesis in the speaker's consciousness about a desired, though not-yet-attained, state-of-affairs. The desired state-of-affairs is, in actual fact, a particular conjunction of semiotic and material factors to which a particular socially recognized value is attached by the speaker. The proposal entails a complex interaction between the social constraints that regulate the proposal and therefore the social relations between addresser and addressee, on the one hand, and the social value that is invested in the posited goal or outcome of the transaction, on the other. The point is that the end product of this process is the end product of a linguistically mediated labour process. As such, it is the product of this process which is deemed to be of value (Lukács 1980 [1978]: 75).

The fact that a goal can be posited in the speaker's consciousness prior to its execution as a specific form of action already entails the separation between speaker and immediate physical-material environment that arises through the semiotic mediation of this relation. Thus, the not-yet-attained goal is a meaning that the speaker posits in his or her consciousness as a possible future outcome of the proposed action. In this sense, it has a hypothetical character. The proposal enables the speaker to raise him- or herself above the immediate material environment and to construct hypotheses concerning possible courses of action in relation to that environment. The meaning in the speaker's consciousness is, of course, distinct and separate from the material outcome of this process. At the same time, the meaning in the speaker's consciousness guides and modulates the activity all along its trajectory until the final outcome is reached in the form of a grounded instantiation of the proposed action that was specified in the imperative clause. Again, the action proposed in the clause and the material instantiation of this as a particular form of activity are distinct. The distinctive character of the two facets of the overall activity can be seen in the following example, which is taken from a KLM advertisement:

> Spending the Miles you earn (which never expire) is easy and more rewarding than ever. To find out more or to join the program online, visit www.klm.com. And start counting down all the benefits you'll gain as a member.

In the example from the KLM advertisement, the proposed action (*you*) *visit www.klm.com*, can be posited by different addressers on different occasions to different addressees. The symbolic categories of the utterance stand in no necessary relation to particular addressers and addressees or to particular actions and events on particular occasions. Rather, these categories can be acted on and responded to by many different individuals on different occasions. The text of the KLM advertisement is a dually semiotic-material artifact that can be integrated to the activities and to the body-brains and therefore to the consciousnesses of different addressers and addressees on different occasions. Proposals illustrate very well an essential social dynamic in which one agent acts on and seeks to influence the consciousness of another social agent with a view to achieving the desired goal. In this way, a linguistically mediated social relation emerges. Once this happens, the subjectivity and, therefore, the consciousness of the addresser and addressee are transformed by virtue of the fact that consciousness is mediated by a social relation with a social other (see Lukács 1980 [1978]: 73). The social and dialogical character of this relation also means that the speaker always has the potential to be the object of others' teleological positings and therefore to be positioned as the modally responsible Subject of actions proposed by other speakers.

In general, we can say that proposition and proposals entail the following considerations:

- The SPEAKER takes up an attitude towards to the proposition or proposal at the same time that he or she positions him- or herself as the source of the proposition or proposal;
- The dual aspect of propositions and proposals referred to in the preceding point entails and fosters a self-reflexive attitude towards one's self as the source of propositions and proposals and their meaning;
- Propositions and proposals are always oriented to and adjusted in relation to the other to whom they are addressed;
- This process of adjustment further entails that the speaker of the proposition or proposal orients to the other as a self who is able to take up similar attitudes and orientations to the proposition or proposal and to respond accordingly;
- The propositional way of orienting to the world beyond the self that language makes available poses the problem of the hypothetical character of human knowledge, as shown in the whole range of resources for modalizing this orientation (e.g. certain, uncertain, doubtful, possible, probable, believable, unbelievable, and so on); the modal orientation of propositions and proposals can therefore be seen as the articulation of the attempt to close the "gap" between desire and goal. Thus, Elena's clause 22 in the analysis in the previous section postulates this modalized gap between her desire that the mint be made, on the one hand, and the fact that at the moment of her utterance, the mint is not yet made, on the other.

The gap between desire and posited goal is constituted by the semiotic-material friction that resists or stands in the way of the completion of some goal-seeking trajectory (chapter 8, section 1). I have argued elsewhere (Thibault 1995) that propositions are oriented to the negotiation and overcoming of semiotic friction or difference; proposals are oriented to the negotiation of semiotic-material friction or difference. Agency, as we have seen, entails both a point of action and a point of view from which certain effects derive and in relation to which these effects can be sourced. An agent, as both point of action and point of view, is the result of semiotic and material constraints: it is like a semiotic-material figure against the ground (the friction) of all the things that resist and oppose its projects (Salthe 1993: 99). In deploying propositions and proposals, agents make choices from a system of possibilities. They do so in ways that generate particular goal-seeking (actional) trajectories by means of particular configurations of modalizing operations in relation to particular goals.

The motivation for language just is, in this view, the generalized semiotic-material friction that generates goal-seeking actional trajectories that are sourced at particular agents in relation to future goals that have been posited. Such trajectories are the social work that is required in order to complete some context – both semiotically and materially. Social work involves the release of energy, its entrainment and modulation by meanings that are sourced at some agent, and the coordinating of semiotic-discursive and physical-material processes and flows. In so doing, it is not language *per se* which is produced, but context. The agent's positing of future goals, the commanding of the resources required for their achievement, and the harnessing and channelling of causal complexes in the physical world constitute adaptive modifications of the ecosocial environment in ways that are semantically consistent with the goal itself.

The fact that both propositions and proposals are modalizing operations means that they are oriented to the domain of the hypothetical – to what could be, what should be, what isn't, what will be, and so on. The hypothetical stance therefore entails friction. That is, it entails difference – semiotic and material – between the agent's modalized stance and the domain of the nonself (secondness) that the agent (firstness) rubs up against, in the process discovering the difference between the two. Thus, the world, including others, does not conform to the agent's wishes, desires, judgements, and so on. For this reason, agents enact semiotic trajectories for achieving a local resolution in some context between the way things are and the way the agent wants them to be. In the process, the agent draws on and discovers patterns of possibilities in thirdness (Thibault 1999a: 28–29). Therefore, the order and complexity of the world is revealed through the agent's negotiations with and discovery of the differences between its perspectives and those of the nonself, including the world of other selves, with their potentialities for action and the perspectives which inform these.

7 Agency, learning, and the zone of proximal development

The developments discussed in the previous paragraph pave the way for the appropriation of this same dynamic to the inner self-referential perspective of the self (see chapter 5). The self commands, guides and directs his or her own activity in and through the selective specialization to the inner perspective of the self of the same social semiotic resources that are deployed in external social relations between the self and others.

In my view, egocentric speech, as we see in the example that is analysed in section 5 (Phase 4), is a transition phase that illustrates precisely this dynamic (see chapter 5). It is part of a process of developing increased powers of abstraction whereby the self is increasingly differentiated from others at the same time that the self learns to take on an increasingly differentiated range of socio-discursive positions in relation to an increasingly differentiated range of social others that go beyond the early mother–infant dyads of pre-symbolic semiosis. The play context plays a key role in the development of such powers of abstraction. Children, in the fantasy world of play, attempt to take up and to negotiate a wide range of adult positions and their corres-ponding practices. At the same time, the play context insulates them from the existential consequences of self-revelation and the instrumental consequences of task-oriented activity.

Paola's activity of preparing the pretend meal in Phase 4 of the play episode analysed above is a cascade: both experiential and interpersonal differentiations are involved in the process of building up additional semiotic complexity in the perspective of the self. Experientially, the child differentiates classes of things and actions involved in the preparation of the meal – e.g. oil, crushing, and so on – by naming them. Interpersonally, she positions herself and her imaginary interlocutor in specific participant and speech roles both in relation to each other as well as in relation to the activity itself.

This little episode therefore shows Paola engaging in a fantasy version of an adult social practice with its social differentiation of roles (meal preparer and server, recipient of meal, mother, baby girl) and social division of labour. The child also collects the effects of this activity and integrates them holistically to her self-perspective. She therefore acquires ever more differentiated self-perspectives along with ever more differentiated points of action from which she can control and regulate the flow of social activities in the course of her further development and individuation as a social agent.

The present example is part of a larger-scale episode of play between Paola and Elena. As a distinctive phase in that larger-scale episode, it is clearly related to it at the same time that it has its own phase-specific characteristics. In particular, Paola's episode of egocentric speech is a further selective recontextualization of some of the things that are going on between herself and Elena in the wider play episode. For example, Paola had previously assigned to herself the role of pretend-mother in phase 1. Paola and Elena, in their respective play roles in phase 5, discuss relevant norms for the preparation of Elena's birthday, including, most importantly, the requirement that the guests be provided with something to eat. In phase 6, Paola then resumes the preparation of the pretend meal that she had started in phase 4. Seen in this slightly larger context, phase 4 can be seen as the first specific development in the overall episode of the mother role that Paola had assigned to herself in phase 1, when the two girls negotiated their respective play roles. It will be remembered that, in phase 1, Paola had introduced the topic of eating, though this was neither completed nor further developed at that point (see her uncompleted clause 6b). Phase 4 may, therefore, be seen as the first development of this topic and associated activities now that the role relations have been established in phase 2.

Moreover, phase 4 anticipates the discussion in phase 5 between the two girls in relation to the party. There are both co-thematic and co-actional ties between these two phases. Thus, in phase 4, Paola rehearses in egocentric speech the relevant thematic and actional meanings through her direct participation in the pretend activity. In phase 5, the two girls engage in a meta-level discussion of the appropriate norms and courses of action concerning the provision of meals for one's birthday party guests. In this phase, Elena has introduced the topic of her birthday for the first time such that this new thematic material provides further impetus and direction for the preparation of the meal. In phase 6, Paola does not simply resume the activity she began in phase 4. Rather, she now puts into operation the matters she and Elena talked about in phase 5.

To recapitulate: the discussion in the previous paragraph shows how an activity ("eating"), which Paola had proposed in a tentative and incomplete way in phase 1 (clause 6b), is taken up and further elaborated by her in phase 4 in the way I discussed above. Paola's self-instigated phase 4, in turn, constitutes a zone of proximal development, in Vygotsky's sense, for the further development of its meanings in phase 5. In my view, this possibility applies here to both self (Paola) and other (Elena). Even though Elena does not participate in phase 4, she is not a passive bystander, but an active and attentive observer of her pretend-mother's sayings and doings. Phase 4 therefore provides Elena with the semiotic material which she extends and elaborates in her dialogue with Paola in phase 5. Thus, phase 5, which is initiated and primarily developed by Elena, is, in this point of view, a further recontextualization and development of phase 4 meanings and activities.

We see how each child provides resources in and through which they develop and deepen each other's capacities for operating and understanding the relevant meanings and activities by building up a pool of shared knowledge and experience in their jointly made and negotiated play. The meta-level discussion that Elena initiates in phase 5 is another little zone of proximal development that allows for further joint learning and understanding to occur. In this case, it does so by bringing about a shift to a higher level of jointly negotiated understanding through the meta-level discussion of the norms and practices involved and how they relate to the activity which is focused on here. Vygotsky (1986 [1934]; also see Wells 1999: 323–324) drew attention to the ways in which peers, no less than more senior others such as parents, teachers, older siblings, and so on, can constitute semiotically mediated environments for each other's learning and development.

Similarly, Paola's singing of the song learned at pre-school in phase 2 is another kind of zone of proximal development, which she evokes in relation to a proposed course of action. As we saw earlier, the song then leads, in the following phase, to a meta-level discussion of the conditions of its learning. The song is a "knowledge product" (Bereiter 1997: 296–297), which is shared by the two girls. As such, the song is a text that is the result of situated processes of knowledge building in the pre-school activities that the two girls then go on to discuss in phase 3. Both girls, as I suggested before, orient to this knowledge product on an individualistic basis at the same time that they use it as an occasion for the further exploration of the basis on which they learned it. Knowledge products are artifacts – textual and material – that result from situated knowledge-building activity. Their status as products and artifacts means that they can be accessed on other occasions so as to create occasions for further learning and understanding (see also chapter 6, section 13).

The pretend meal activity in phase 4 is an instance of situated or on-the-fly knowledge building: the pretend meal, the activity performed, the objects (real and pretend) that Paola integrates to this activity can be seen as constituent parts of a knowledge object that she creates in and through her self-activity. This object is, to be sure, more ephemeral in some respects as compared to the song by virtue of the fact that the song can be traced back to a textual record (e.g. the musical score and/or repeated occurrences of its prior performance in the pre-school context) whereas Paola's pretend meal is based on a contextually contingent conjunction of material and semiotic resources. However, the difference, in my view, is one of degree, rather than of kind.

The fact that Elena can observe Paola's pretend meal preparation and then further develop it in the way described above, along with the fact that Paola can then resume the meal in the light of Elena's contribution (phase 5), shows that both children adaptively and creatively respond to, modify, and retroactively recontextualize each others' prior contributions. They do so in ways which suggest that, in the play context, the meanings and actions of one or the other participant can be taken up and responded to as knowledge products which provide further occasions for knowledge construction and learning.

We also get some tantalizing glimpses in the episode analysed in this chapter of the ways in which classroom identities and their associated affective investments are re-articulated in relation to other cultural sites such as peer group play and the child's positioning of herself in fantasy in relation to adult roles and practices, such as those in our example. This re-articulation also shows that much of the learning process is concerned with the learning of social identities and their associated affective investments – e.g. mother, baby, meal preparer, and so on – that are central to the child's development, yet are completely disjoined from the learning that takes place in the classroom. Play therefore shows very powerfully how the learning of abstract theoretical principles and concepts can be effectively harnessed to the negotiation of meanings, values, activities, and identities that very young children can use to find solutions to problems and answers to questions in and through their own situated or on-line knowledge-building activity (see Bereiter 1997: 297).

The knowledge-building processes – i.e. the various forms of meaning-making activity – are constituted in the practices of some community. The knowledge products which result from these processes afford various possibilities for further knowledge building on other occasions (Bereiter 1997: 295). Knowledge building is always a form of situated learning which arises in and through the co-deployment on their timescale of available semiotic and material resources. The knowledge products which result from these processes are, for example, various forms of text, semiotic artifacts of different kinds, and computer records of participants' interactions with computers, the internet, and so on. Knowledge objects are theories, interpretations, presentations, and so on, which have an objectified status and which can be compared to and otherwise related to other knowledge objects on other space-time scales (Bereiter 1997: 296–297). Rather than assuming that all learning is reducible to internalized cognitive mechanisms, we see how the participants, in play, produce and work with such knowledge objects as a central aspect of the learning process on different scalar levels of semiotic organization (see also chapter 6).

The particular episode of play has its own unique trajectory over time at the same time that it is embedded in larger-scale patterns that are typical of a particular culture or community and which constrain and sculpt its trajectory. Therefore, it is important to connect the messy, heterogeneous, and complex details of real time, always multimodal activities on their timescale, with the emergent patterns of global organization that become evident on the developmental timescale where learning takes place. In this way, "knowing" and "learning" are seen to be seamlessly interwoven with real-time meaning-making activity, rather than being seen as pertaining to two disjoined research traditions of the psychological and the semiotic.

5

Egocentric Speech and the Re-envoicement of Others' Meanings: Dialogue, Genre, and the Emergence of the Self

1 Re-envoicement versus internalization and appropriation

Children's discursive productions "re-envoice" meanings, discourse-level features, tones, intonations, rhythmic patterns, and so on, in the contexts of situation and the context of culture that they participate in (Dore 1989). Bakhtin's (1981) notions of "voice" and "dialogicity" are relevant here (see chapter 2, section 9). The relevant unit of analysis in this perspective is genre, rather than formal linguistic units such as the sentence (see chapter 2, section 7). The term re-envoicement was proposed by Dore (1989) to explain the ways in which children's interactions with others are involved in a constant process of dialogic negotiation with others' discourses and therefore with the meanings that are negotiated and made in these discourses (see Bakhtin 1986: 89), rather than with purely formal linguistic units. Bakhtin (*op. cit.*) referred to the "process of *assimilation* – more or less creative – of others' words (and not the words of a language)" in this general sense. Children learn language through their participation in and entrainment to the forms of organization, the meaning relations, the positioned-practices and their corresponding semantic voices of the various discourse genres and social activity-types in and through which they interact with others. In so doing, they learn to take up positions in and selectively to re-envoice the meanings and values of others in the system of heteroglossia of the wider context of culture as their own meanings. There is, then, no direct, unmediated contact with an abstract language system; the language system that the self elaborates is always mediated by these processes of the selective re-envoicement of others' meanings.

In chapter 4, we saw how apprentice-participants in particular meaning-making activities attempt to take up and to negotiate discursive positions which are at times in conflict or contradiction with respect to other voices which the child operates. The re-envoicement of others' meanings can only happen in and through the jointly constructed and socially constrained and enabling genre performances which children participate in. In this view, it is illogical to talk about how children learn or acquire sentences, as if this were the goal or main point of language development. It is illogical because lexicogrammatical units and relations are never encountered in a direct or unmediated way. Rather, lexicogrammatical units and relations are local resources in and through which global discourse patterns and relations are constructed in contextualized meaning-making activity. Our awareness of lexicogrammar is always mediated by the larger-scale forms of discourse organization which are assembled through the co-deployment of smaller-scale lexicogrammatical units and structures. To say that language development is primarily concerned with the learning of sentences is to confuse the categories and assumptions of linguistics with the very different activities in which children participate.

The notion of re-envoicement is preferred to the notions of "internalization" (Vygotsky 1986 [1934]) and "appropriation" (Rogoff 1995) for the following reasons:

1. The term re-envoicement draws attention to the ways in which the meanings that individuals make in and through the activities they participate in are always situated in the diversity of social voices of the wider system of social heteroglossia of a given culture (Bakhtin 1981; chapter 2, section 9);

2. The different points of view, social interests, role positions in social activities, and so on, operate distinct voices from the diversity of meaning-making practices that constitute the

system of social heteroglossia in a given community. Discourse voices both articulate a thematic content as well as a value orientation to this thematic meaning at the same time that they take up and/or imply stances of alliance, opposition, co-optation, and so on, with other voices in the system of heteroglossia; no voice is ever neutral or value-free in this sense (chapter 2, section 9);

3. Individuals are always positioned in the system of social heteroglossia in relation to its social points of view and values. The meanings that individuals make in particular activities always re-envoice meanings and values in the system of heteroglossia;

4. The meanings that we give voice to and the positions we take up and/or respond to in the system of social heteroglossia include rhythms, intonations, tones of voice, and so on. The textual voices that we operate index our degree of affective attunement with or alienation from particular voices and alignments of voices in the system of social heteroglossia. Re-envoicement also refers to the articulatory (embodied) dimension of giving voice to meanings and not only its lexicogrammatical and semantic dimensions. Therefore, the notion of re-envoicement, like that of appropriation (Rogoff 1995), emphasizes the importance of activity. By the same token, re-envoicement draws attention to the embodied character of meaning-making. We do not understand and respond to meanings solely on the basis of the semiotic relations that we construe between the different parts of the activity in relation to the systems of paradigmatic alternatives that are relevant to the contextualization of the unfolding text or discourse event. We also understand and respond to meaning on the basis of the physical-material relations and processes with which these semiotic relations cross-couple and whose flows they entrain. Meanings are made not only in the local context of the here-now event; they are also cross-coupled to physical-material flows and processes on other spatio-temporal scales beyond the immediate here-now context;

5. The discourse voices that the child takes up and adaptively modifies as his or her own voice extend the child's own regulatory mechanisms. For example, the child's participation in Teacher Question^Student Answer^Teacher Evaluation activities does not only provide the child with knowledge of a particular thematic content. It also initiates the child into particular forms of social activity and their associated participant roles, along with the evaluative and affective investments associated with these roles. Thus, the child is implicitly taught models of authority, deference, and a particular way of relating to the thematic content, as well as a particular kind of social-interpersonal relationship with the teacher. The thematic content of the exchange is explicit, whereas these other aspects are much more implicit, though no less real;

6. Re-envoicement allows us to theorize how a self-referential inner perspective self-organizes in and through the self's engagements with and re-envoicements in the perspective of the self of the meanings of the nonself.

2 Egocentric speech, interpersonal meaning, and the development of self-reflexivity

The ability to posit an imaginary object in and through the symbolic resources of language and then to integrate this object to a particular activity requires powers of symbolic abstraction and interpretation (chapter 4, section 1). These powers exist on a second-order or meta-level relationship that allows the agent to view his- or herself as standing in a particular relation to the object in question. Egocentric speech is, then, a situated or on-line form of reflexive interpretation of the self's linguistically mediated relations to the phenomena of experience. The relationship is situated (on-line) because the child's use of language remains closely tied to the immediate situation and activity in which the child is engaged, as distinct from the much more abstract and de-contextualizing forms of semiotic activity that are independent of the immediate physical-material situation. This relationship may be schematized as follows:

SELF → PROPOSITIONAL RELATION TO → WORLD

The propositional nature of this relationship means that (1) the object in the world that is attended to is experientially construed as a meaning that can be shared with others; and (2) the speaker takes up a modalized propositional attitude or stance which can also serve to orient the other to the proposition and/or its referent situation in a common framework of evaluation.

Unlike perceptual acts, the propositions and proposals of language are dialogically organized acts: they anticipate responses from others at the same time that they contribute to the formation of larger-scale genre structures and social activities. In the example of egocentric speech that I shall analyse in detail in section 12 below, the child appropriates dialogic structures involving changes of speaker and their turns in dialogue. In doing so, she interprets herself and her own activity to herself in and through the same kinds of genre resources that are used to account for herself and to enact her interpersonal relations with other selves. She does so through the adaptive take up and modification, or re-envoicement, of the same genre resources that she uses to negotiate her social relations with others in play, pre-school, and home activities. The interpersonal nature of propositions and proposals in language necessarily entails the enactment of self–world–other relations in the perspective of the self. The self, as I remarked above, has points of view, as well as being a point of action. The fact that propositions and proposals involve self–world–other relations presupposes that these relations can be reflected on at a higher level within the perspective of the self who is the source of the proposition or proposal and its effects in the world.

In this way, the self can explicitly and reflexively relate itself to its own perspectives and actions – to its own experiential construals of and interpersonal takes on the world. Thus, egocentric speech involves a focus on the self in relation to both the world and to other selves. This two-fold focus is evident in the ways in which objects in the world are selectively attended to and integrated to the activity at the same time that others, not directly participating in the dialogic loop of egocentric speech, may be addressed or otherwise referred to. In the example to be analysed in section 12, this occurs when Paola uses the pronoun *te* (second person; singular; familiar) to address the imaginary interlocutor (the pretend baby) for whom she is preparing the meal.

This focus also enables the individual to select and increasingly to specialize those responses which form the basis of further adaptive modification. Egocentric speech marks a particular phase in the necessarily dialogical processes of the self-organization of the self. The child selectively re-envoices the meanings of the ecosocial semiotic system in the process of taking up agent positions in and through the system's genre structures and social activities. He or she also provides information to the group about his or her own social performance at the same time that he or she seeks further guidance from the group. The child, in other words, provides information to the dyad about the processes of the development of his or her implicit self-regulatory structures at the same time that he or she obtains information from the dyad in the course of his or her development. Egocentric speech is not about the development of the self's powers of self-reflexivity in any individualistic sense. Rather, the essentially dialogic nature of this processes points to the ways in which the self reflexively connects to the higher-scalar ecosocial semiotic system. Egocentric speech, in this view, is a moment in the processes of self-organization and self-reference in and through which the self emerges and individuates along its trajectory.

From the interpersonal point of view, egocentric speech is not necessarily directed to a specific other. This does not mean that it is not directed to some generalized addressee. Instead, the boundaries between self and other are not yet fully defined. The child has not yet drawn the lines in a fully determinate way around the self as social agent who is in possession of certain socially recognized and authorized dispositions and tendencies to act. These dispositions and tendencies are distributed across and located at particular person-places in particular interpersonal moral orders as is the agentive power to release these in self and other. Agency means having the capacity to project such powers from some point of action. It means having the capacity to entrain matter, energy, and meaning flows through discourse and to project these beyond the self in socially meaningful ways. Without this capacity, one is not an agent. Agency and the limits to agency are socially learned through just such a process of projecting beyond the boundaries of the self.

If agency is a social achievement arising out of a specific synthesis of the unities of self-monitoring, autonomy, and autobiography, as Harré (1983) has proposed, I would like to suggest that egocentric speech is part of a social semiotic process in which the child struggles to give voice to his or her own "inner self activity" in order to confront what lies "outside" of him or her, not only in the objectified world, but, above all, in the interpersonal moral orders in which agents are created, recognized, and enabled. Egocentric speech is an attempt to re-envoice the social semiotic resources for construing agency (experientially) and enacting agency (interpersonally) in self and other in order to give voice to one's own "inner self activity" as a social being. It is not just language in the abstract which is appropriated from the social world; it is particular voicings and their positioned-practices in the social order.

Egocentric speech in the young child is therefore part of the child's struggle to become a social being. The dialogic moves which are deployed as self-commands in egocentric speech are re-envoiced from the relevant interpersonal moral order (see the analysis in section 12). The child names, evaluates, directs, and comments on his or her own activity. Egocentric speech thus connects the child in a self-reflexive mode to the ecosocial semiotic environment. The child is thus able to attain an axiological-ethical orientation to him- or herself as a developing social agent in relation to the moral orders in which he or she acts and means.

In the present chapter, I shall develop the arguments presented in this section in relation to Vygotsky's pioneering contribution to our understanding of egocentric speech in the child's development.

3 Genre, dialogue, and the self-regulation of the individual

The relevant system of relations for the purposes of my analysis in this chapter is not the individual, but the discourse genres and activity-structures in which individuals participate and in which, through their participation, they are positioned. Discursive voices, prosodies, bodily dispositions, and so on, are in constant movement and flux in the overall ecosocial semiotic system of which they are components. The relevant system is defined, minimally, in terms of three-level hierarchy thinking as follows: (1) on level L–1 the meaning-making affordances of the individual organism; (2) the activity-structures and discourse genres in which individuals participate and are positioned on level L; and (3) the larger scale ecosocial semiotic system of constraints and possibilities in which the interactions among the individuals in and through the activities they participate in are interpreted and have the meanings that they do. A system of this kind is a dynamic, open system; it freely exchanges matter and energy, and through these, information-meaning, with its environment(s), at the same time that it maintains its overall identity and structural integrity. Dynamic open systems, in order to maintain themselves, must undergo constant change of this kind.

Importantly, systems of this kind also exchange **structure**. Information exchange is explicit; the exchange of structure is implicit (Lemke 1984d: 10–12). Our analysis can attempt to show what implicit (unconscious) structural principles underlie the particular system under study (chapter 8, section 5). The relevant questions are: (1) What are the higher-order (more implicit) contextualization principles which organize and coordinate the flows of matter, energy, and information-meaning in a given system?; (2) How do local (e.g. clause level) units and structures contribute to these more global patterns of organization?; (3) How do children "learn" these structures?

The pre-linguistic dyads which are evident from the very earliest stages of the child's interactions with others are the very beginnings of the development of genre (chapter 3, section 5). Bakhtin's (1986) distinction between "primary" and "secondary" genres is useful here. Primary genres are made up of minimal dialogic interacts such as Statement^Response, Question^Answer, Command^Compliance, Offer^Acceptance of Offer, and so on (see also chapter 8, section 1). They are the raw discursive material of which more complex genres are made up, though they may also function in their own right as complete social activity-structures. The carat sign "^" designates a change of speaker in the exchange. Bakhtin (1986: 76) recognized that it is the "change of speaking subject" in such exchanges which is the critical factor in creating the internal coherence and stability, and hence the social relevance, of such exchanges across the separate turns or moves of the individual speakers.

Genre, as the most global level of discourse patterning and organization, acts as a functional interface between the lower level (lexicogrammatical and other) resource systems that are co-deployed and the physical-material processes which are always cross-coupled with semiotic-discursive ones in semiosis. In this way, the speaker is always dually constituted as a materially embodied being and a socially positioned subject-agent. Genre is the organizing principle whereby such cross-couplings are dialogically coordinated and entrained in the exchange process.

Genre, as the most global level of patterning and organization that we typically recognize in discourse, similarly regulates these processes by coordinating and channelling in socially relevant ways the cross-couplings of the material and the discursive. The "lower" level units – e.g. grammatical units and structures of various kinds and on various levels of organization – are the micro-level resource systems which are assembled into larger-scale units of social action (cf. genres, texts, social activity-structures, discourse formats). These resource systems only have fully contextualized social meaning by virtue of their deployment in the making and enacting of larger-scale activities in particular contexts.

In this view, children do not "acquire" a set of formal syntactic structures. Instead, they are recruited, from the very earliest stages, into the dialogue structures and processes of the meaning-making activities in which they participate. These structures and processes are discourse-level forms of social action into which the child is inserted and in relation to which he or she is required to take up some agent positions rather than others. It is through the child's participation in and growing mastery of an increasingly wide range of different discourse-types, or genres, that he or she is both positioned in the cultural order and develops to be a mature member of the species and of the culture. Children's dialogues are processes of matter, energy, and information-meaning exchange. It is through these processes of exchange that dynamic open systems develop. At the same time, these same exchange processes also regulate both the individual's internal principles of structural organization (self-organization) and the individuals who participate in them (self-regulation).

The processes of re-envoicement entail exchanges of voices, messages, tones, intonations and rhythmic patterns, and so on, between the activities of individuals and the larger scale ecosocial semiotic system in which the individual participates and in which the activity is embedded. These processes of selective re-envoicement both integrate the child into the larger-scale ecosocial system at the same time that they provide the individual child with genre structures and functions which are powerful extensions of his or her regulatory mechanisms.

4 Vygotsky's theory of egocentric speech and ludic communication

In selectively attending to and taking up meanings which circulate in the ecosocial environment of the child, and which regulate his or her structures and processes, the child, in egocentric speech, orients his or her performance both to the self and to the other. First, the child learns how to position him- or herself in particular social activity-structures. This positioning entails a selective response to meanings in the child's environment. Secondly, the child's performance, which is audible to onlookers, becomes a way of displaying his or her emerging agentive powers and capacities at the same time that he or she can obtain appropriate corrective feedback and guidance from others.

Play provides the appropriate level of intimacy in which such structures may be safely "experimented" without the attendant existential risks (chapter 4). Vygotsky has interpreted children's play as follows: "Three- to five-year olds while playing together often speak only to themselves. What looks like a conversation only turns out to be a collective monologue" (1986 [1934]: 232). Again, it is the lack of a clear notion of dialogicity and, therefore, of otherness, which is problematic in Vygotsky's explanation. Moreover, I would suggest that the play environment itself facilitates the use of egocentric speech on account of the increased powers of abstraction that symbolic play and its meanings entail (see chapter 4, section 1). Vygotsky concludes his brief discussion of the "collective monologue" functions of play with the claim that egocentric speech derives "from the lack of differentiation of speech of oneself from speech for others, [which] disappears when the feeling of being understood, essential for social speech, is absent" (1986 [1934]: 233).

Goffman (1981: 95–96), in his discussion of Vygotsky's interpretation of the self-guidance (cf. self-monitoring) functions of what Goffman calls "self-talk", provides a different interpretation. In Goffman's account, the child's self-talk is a response to the norms of the local moral order. According to Goffman, self-talk "discounts" the child's actions should the child fail to display him- or herself as a competent member of the moral order. Goffman (1981: 96n_{12}) also refers to the work of Cook-Gumperz and Corsaro (1976), whose interpretation is even more other-oriented than Goffman's. According to Cook-Gumperz and Corsaro, self-talk "cues other interactants to what is presently occurring as well as provides possibilities for plugging into and expanding upon the emerging social event" (1976: 29; cited in Goffman 1981: 96n_{12}).

In the ludic situation, there is heightened intimacy at the same time that there is a focus on social norms, their definition, redefinition and transgression. In ludic communication, norms are explored without existential pressures and risks. The absence of existential pressures may explain the capacity for children to generate their play sessions over quite lengthy time spans, frequently lasting many hours. In the ludic domain, intimacy is heightened and self-consciousness is inhibited. The latter, if allowed to enter, would, in turn, allow the serious to enter as well. Of course, children cannot (and do not) remain in the ludic situation indefinitely. The overall dynamics of the ecosystem, require, at some stage, that children leave the ludic situation and move into some other form of communicative experience. Typically, this occurs when adults intervene so as to call the situation to order in one way or another. Thus, the child is directed into other, more practical or task-oriented activities which need to be undertaken. Activities such as "taking the visitor home", "getting ready to go out", "having a bath", "preparing for the meal", to name but a few, are typical. These interventions on the part of adults are not mere external perturbations on the ludic space-time which the children have created. Such interventions have their function in the overall dynamics of the ecosystem. If play continually experiments and calls into question and even transgresses moral order norms, then the overall dynamics of the ecosystem require that, at some stage, a new equilibrium be restored. The establishment of a new equilibrium can only occur if the child exits the ludic situation and effects a transition to some other type of communicative experience in the overall communicative ecosystem.

Vygotsky has noted the functional connection between egocentric speech and one's "being understood" (1986 [1934]: 233) in the play situation. According to Vygotsky, this functional connectedness springs from "the lack of differentiation of speech for oneself from speech for others" (1986 [1934]: 233). My hypothesis is that egocentric speech is important in the development of the child's situated capacity to view him- or herself as standing in a particular relation to the nonself. In egocentric speech, the child engages in a form of situated interpretation of his or her own activity at the same time that the child's discourse is integrated with and participates in the enacting of that same activity. The key notion here is that the child represents her own activity to herself at the same time that she enacts it.

Take the locution *un pò di olio* in the example that I first considered in chapter 4, section 5 (see Appendix I). In the imaginary play context, this nominal group experientially construes an imaginary object – the pretend oil – and in so doing it creates it as an imaginary object for conscious reflection and action. However, the nominal group and the imaginary object are distinct, even though the latter is not given to perception because of its pretend status. Its pretend status does not alter the fact that it is integrated with other aspects of the overall activity such as the child's action of sprinkling the pretend oil onto the pretend meal that she is preparing. The fact that it is a pretend object means that a higher level of abstract thinking is involved than would be the case if the child were attending to some real cooking oil in her perceptual purview. In the latter case, the child's act of perception allows the child to see the object in the world. If the nominal group specified a grounded instance of a certain quantity of oil within the child's perceptual purview, then that too would be a first-order relationship between the linguistic token and the material object. The use of language rather than perception *per se* would entail a significant increase in the child's powers of abstraction. Nevertheless, the relationship between perceptual and/or linguistic act and material object is, in both cases, a first-order one. As such, both perception and language can function, to different degrees of specification, to focus on and selectively to attend to objects as phenomena of conscious experience. In this view, I can use both perception and language to be conscious of objects in the world.

The principle difference with respect to the present example lies in the fact that the pretend status of the oil must mean that the child has developed the capacity to represent herself as standing in a particular relationship to the pretend oil. There are two aspects to this question. First, she has developed the capacity to interpret herself as having a point of view which is centred on herself as the source of her interpretations of and perspectives on the phenomena of experience that she attends to. Secondly, she has also developed the capacity to interpret herself as a point of action in relation to which particular courses of action can be attributed and from which they can be **semantically** controlled. These two aspects go together and can readily be assimilated to the metafunctional view of language and of semiosis in general that is central in this study. As I shall show in detail in section 15 below, the notion of semantic control is crucial here.

5 The linguistic characteristics of egocentric speech

Vygotsky identified a number of lexicogrammatical features which are foregrounded in both egocentric speech and inner speech. These features include omission of the subject, the foregrounding of predication, and a highly elliptical relationship between these forms and the speech situation (Vygotsky 1986 [1934]: 236). In doing so, he draws attention to various forms of linguistic "abbreviation" in both egocentric and inner speech. My proposal is that the orientation to the here-and-now in egocentric speech has more than an accompanying or monitoring function. Most importantly, it is concerned with the child's social location in the modalized space – time of the dyad. In the "abbreviated" forms which characterize egocentric speech (and inner speech), a central function is the "outward" (explicit) expression to both self and others of the child's positioning of him- or herself at particular person-places in the relevant interpersonal moral order. The "abbreviated" forms which Vygotsky associated with the transition to "inner speech" are a function of the child's development of a more stable social orientation in relation to these norms at the same time that they reflect the progressive autonomy of the child's mental processes.

As the child stabilizes his or her social positioning in the activities in which he or she participates, the need for explicit, "non-abbreviated" linguistic expression, which functions to provide clear reference points, diminishes. The "abbreviation" of inner speech reflects a high degree of semantic condensation at the same time that the lexicogrammatical forms are reduced to a minimum. These characteristics of inner speech are a function of the specialized inner context in which it is used. There is no requirement in this context that inner dialogues and their meanings be made explicit to specific others in social discourse. Rather, these meanings are specialized to the highly specific context of the inner self-referential viewpoints of the self and the others to whom the self relates in that context (see Thibault 1998a). In any case, the abbreviated and highly condensed characteristics of inner speech should be seen as one extreme point of a cline of possibilities whereby language is used, to varying degrees of explicitness, to complete or to make fully explicit the context in which it is to be understood. The differences with outer speech, as far as this point is concerned, are a matter of degree, rather than one of kind.

The shift into the phase of egocentric speech in our example is also evident in the voice prosodics. The rhythm, tempo, voice quality, and timbre of the child's speech all change with respect to the preceding phase in the overall play episode that I analysed in chapter 4. Cook-Gumperz (1992: 186) has also commented on what she calls "formulaic pause fillers" in the play activities of young children. These pause fillers, writes Cook-Gumperz, "could be considered to represent drinking, pouring, or soothing sounds, hh .. shh .. .. shh". According to Cook-Gumperz, lexical and prosodic "pause fillers" have a status somewhat akin to the concept of "formula" in Albert Lord's (1960) study of the ability of the performers of epic poetry, i.e. "to

create spontaneous, rhythmically fast and complex narrative poems and songs in long narra-
tives" (Cook-Gumperz 1992: 180; see also Cook-Gumperz 1986, 1991). In the case of the
lexicalizations which children invent, the formula, Cook-Gumperz argues, resolves difficulties
"in actually finding words or adequately lexicalizing". There are two problems with this
interpretation.

First, Cook-Gumperz takes some unspecified adult norm as the external yardstick for meas-
uring the presumed lexical inadequacies of the children in her study. Thus, an external norm is
imposed, which inhibits inquiry into the meaning-making practices that are specific to the peer
group culture of young children (chapter 4, section 1). There is no good reason to assume that
adult linguistic and social norms are the appropriate ones for understanding what is going on
in the "autonomous precursor worlds" of children (Harré 1983: 247; chapter 4, section 1).
Secondly, the assumption of an external norm fails to account for the fact that children make
meanings in ways which are specific to these "autonomous precursor worlds", rather than
attempting, imperfectly, to copy or to imitate adult meanings and forms. This view fails to
account for the ways in which it is the dynamics of the ecosystem itself at any given stage
which prepare the child's transition to the successor stage. There is no telos of a normative
adult model towards which the child, perfectly or imperfectly, strives in a progression of
naturalistically defined developmental stages.

6 Egocentric speech, practical activity, and the self's emergence as agent

According to Vološinov, inner speech is always oriented to some other in the social order (1976
[1927]: 79). When, in the developing individual, these orientations become more stabilized in
relation to the practices and ideologies of society, the need for their outward and explicit (non-
abbreviated) expression may diminish. That this is not unique to infant behaviour is shown by
the ways in which people use egocentric speech (cf. Goffman's self-talk) when the stability
of one's social orientation is (momentarily) disrupted (Goffman), or in certain pathological
conditions (Vološinov).[1]

For Vygotsky (1986 [1934]: 33), Piaget saw egocentric speech as being "a reflection of the
child's egocentric thinking". For Vygotsky, it is a question of the child's "becoming an agent of
realistic thinking". Vygotsky defined "realistic thinking" as follows:

> Piaget argues that "things do not shape a child's mind". But we have seen that in real
> situations when the egocentric speech of a child is connected with his practical activity,
> things do shape his mind. Here, by "things" we mean reality, neither as passively reflected in
> the child's perception nor as abstractly contemplated, but reality that a child encounters in
> his practical activity.
>
> (Vygotsky 1986 [1934]: 39–40)

Vygotsky makes the connection between the "shaping of mind" and "practical activity", yet the
underlying assumption remains a cognitive-representational one. First, Vygotsky does not theorize the nature of practical activity, which remains an underdeveloped assumption with respect

---

[1] In any case, there are different degrees and different kinds of internal dialogue, as the founder of
transactional analysis, Eric Berne, pointed out:

> In the first degree, the words run through Jeder's head in a shadowy way, with no muscular move-
> ments, or at least none perceptible to the naked eye or ear. In the second degree, he can feel his vocal
> muscles moving a little so that he whispers to himself inside his mouth; in particular, there are small
> abortive movements of the tongue. In the third degree, he says the words out loud. The third degree
> may take over in certain disturbed conditions so that he walks down the street talking to himself, and
> people turn their heads to watch and are likely to think he's "crazy". There is also a fourth degree,
> where one or other of the internal voices is heard as coming from outside the skull. This is usually the
> voice of the parent (actually the voice of his father or mother) and these are hallucinations. His Child
> may or may not answer the Parental voices, but in any case they affect some aspects of his behavior.
> (Berne 1988 [1974]: 273–274).

to the external processes which act on and shape "inner" mental reality. Secondly, he has nothing equivalent to the notion of the propositional relation to show how the child develops a self-reflexive interpretation of his or her own actions and experiences through his or her participation in dialogical-interpersonal processes of meaning-making. The key concepts in Vygotsky remain those of "mind" and "thinking", and so on.

In the analysis in chapter 4, I drew attention to the ways in which, in the incidence of Paola's egocentric speech that I first considered there, the child is outwardly verbalizing the cross-coupling of the semiotic-discursive and the physical-material domains while enacting the pretend activity sequence. It is the cross-coupling of the two domains which constitutes the activity sequence. In the analysis, I placed some emphasis on the interpersonal semantic selections for this reason. I should now like to extend and deepen the significance of the observation I made then in connection with the grammatical distinction between the indicative and imperative moods.

Halliday (1975, 1978a, 1992) points out that the exchange of goods-&-services precedes the exchange of information in ontogenesis. Proto-imperative mood precedes proto-indicative mood. The semantic distinction between goods-&-services exchange (proposals) and information exchange (propositions) derives from this basic opposition in the interpersonal grammar of Mood. Halliday (1992) relates this distinction to the one which Malinowski (1923, 1935) made between action (cf. goods-&-services exchange) and reflection (cf. information exchange). However, reflection is also a form of action. With this point in mind, we shall now proceed to propose an alternative to Vygotsky's outside-to-inside theory of the social formation of mind. Practical activity, Vygotsky claims, shapes mind and thinking. Vygotsky continues to privilege the latter.

In my view, it is a mistake to assume that the distinction between "practical activity" and "thinking", on the one hand, and "action" and "reflection", on the other, correlates in any direct way with the outer/inner distinction. It is this reasoning, along with the corresponding directionality of the causal fit from the outside to the inside, which leads Vygotsky to postulate that practical activity "shapes" mind. Activity is on the outside; thinking on the inside. Let us now proceed to an alternative view.

Vygotsky (1986 [1934]: 29–30) showed that the coefficient of egocentric speech, as he puts it, increased in the experimental contexts in which he set children specific tasks and then introduced some material obstacle to the successful completion of the task. The task might take the form of a drawing activity in which the child was confronted, unexpectedly, with having no paper, no pencil, or no colour with which to complete the task to hand. In other words, the child encounters semiotic-material friction, which must be overcome. In the tasks that Vygotsky refers to, the child uses language to coordinate and entrain matter and energy flows in the physical-material domain. Vygotsky does not direct our attention to this aspect, but focuses, instead, on a more intellectualistic notion of "problem solving".

My point is that the child must learn how to cross-couple the available semiotic-discursive and physical-material resources in order to create, enact, and sustain a given social activity-structure. Language and other semiotic resource systems are cross-coupled with the physical-material in order to achieve this. Language functions contextually to complete, to resolve, or to "finalize" (Bakhtin 1986; Vološinov 1983) the physical-material world in order to perform the social work to hand (McGillicuddy, personal communication: 1991). Language does this by organizing and entraining physical-material processes in socially and discursively specific ways. Language is a resource for negotiating, resolving, or finalizing what Vološinov (1983: 116–117) has called the "friction" (cf. difference), which is both semiotic and material, between the "word" and the "non-verbal environment" (see also Thibault 1995). Such negotiation takes place through the interpersonal enactment of propositions and proposals in discourse.

Vygotsky's interpretation, in my view, is too one-sidedly intellectualistic; it is too centred on the formation of the child's emerging "higher mental functions". I should like to put forward another interpretation, which takes account of the arguments I made in the previous paragraph. Social meaning-making, as I pointed out above, always occurs at the intersection of the material and the discursive. In egocentric speech, the child gives voice to the cross-coupling of the two domains. This cross-coupling always occurs, as I pointed out above, in and through particular socially organized activity-structures and in relation to specific "points of action" in these. The child gives his or her own voice to his or her participation in the social activity, whose regularities he or she is learning to control and to channel in socially productive ways.

In practical activity, the child encounters material and semiotic differences, or friction, which must be negotiated and resolved. The child's egocentric speech gives voice to his or her embodied participation in some emerging social activity-structure. The child struggles to negotiate and to give voice to his or her location at some person-place, relative to a given interpersonal moral order. It is from such person-places that the child learns to control the regularities of social events. The point is the child's emerging and developing sense of a socially recognized "point of action" relative to which he or she can centre his or her own embodied participation in the flux of matter, energy, and information flows in meaning-making activity. A social agent is an embodied social being whose location at the relevant person-place enables the agent to control and to coordinate flows of matter, energy, and meaning in activity. For example, in the semantic interact *un po' di olio* ∧ *chh chh*, which I analysed as SELF-COMMAND ∧ COMPLIANCE TO COMMAND in the analysis in chapter 4, the prosodically realized COMPLIANCE finalizes this exchange. The child gives voice to both speaking positions. She gives voice to her own embodied participation in the cross-coupling of the semiotic and the material and its dialogic negotiation and finalization in discursively simulated self–other transactions. That is, in her egocentric talk, the child simulates and enacts the complementary moves of both self and other. Her first move both anticipates the simulated response of the other at the same time that her non-linguistic vocalization *chh chh* simulates the dialogically coordinated response (Compliance) on the part of the other that the first move requires.

In egocentric speech, the child gives outward verbal expression to this emerging sense of agency. It is not a matter of a transition from "outer" activity to "inner" thinking. Instead, it is a question of the child's ability to centre him- or herself in relation to socially available points of action. This centring is always a social achievement, rather than an innate capacity, in any case. Now, I am not saying that the child addresses specific others when using egocentric speech. Both Piaget and Vygotsky understood very clearly that this is not the case. Egocentric speech is, contrary to the term first used by Piaget, not ego-centred in any monologic or autistic sense; it is always addressed to the self-as-other, or to some generalized notion of the other. The other in question is always pertinent to the social group that the child participates in. For Vygotsky, the process is essentially a cognitive one in the child's progression from inter-mental to intra-mental thought. However, Vygotsky's account does not explain that the interpersonal grammar of self-willing, self-command, and self-control is also re-envoiced in the perspective of the self in the formation of the self as an agent in discourse.

In the next section, I shall explore the significance of the distinction between the imperative and indicative modes in relation to the interpersonal enactment of action and reflection as two ways of orienting to self and others.

7 The imperative and indicative modes and the learning of the reflexive interpretation of self and other

Why does the imperative orientation emerge prior to the indicative one in child language development? The answer to this question has to do with the fact that the imperative is other oriented. Initially, the infant does not control the flows of matter, energy, and information in the dyad from a stabilized point of action in the perspective of the self. Moreover, he or she has no self-reflexive capacities for viewing either others or oneself as selves who are able to reflect upon their own actions and interpretations from the perspective of the self. This comes later. In the early stages of (mother–infant) dyad formation, others (e.g. the mother) are viewed as agents who can do things that the infant wants and needs. Only later does the child learn, through the same processes of exchange and counter-transference, to locate him- or herself at those person-places in and through which he or she can delegate particular agentive capacities to self (cf. Offers) and to others (cf. Commands) in the dyad.

The indicative orientation, by contrast, is oriented to the self. The self initially emerges out of the developing capacity of the individual to take up the position of the other in the dyad (Mead 1934; Habermas 1984 [1981]). At first, as seen from the point of view of the imperative orientation, it is the other who is the source of agentive capacities. In the further development of this distinction, the self learns to identify with the other and, self-reflexively, to take up these positions for him- or herself. Children's egocentric speech, as both Piaget and Vygotsky correctly understood, in spite of the differences in their theoretical positions, is an orientation to ego, to the self. Nevertheless, both miss the mark in their explanations.

In the imperative orientation, the other is the focus of the self in the sense that the other can perform actions on the self's behalf so as to fulfil the self's needs and wants. In this perspective, the other is seen as a point of action for meeting the self's demands. In the indicative orientation, the focus is on the other as an agent of reflection. That is, the speaker shares some experience with the other. In so doing, the speaker presupposes that the other is also a self who is able to jointly share in this experience with the speaker as well as to orient to the speaker's evaluative or affective stances to the experience in similar ways. All this is so before the emergence of language, as the joint attention-sharing activities between adults and infants in primary intersubjectivity demonstrate (chapter 3).

All joint attention-sharing activities in early infant semiosis entail this proto-indicative orientation. The attention-sharing stance of the proto-indicative entails true intersubjectivity as opposed to the more instrumental stance of the proto-imperative. The former requires a joint orientation not only to the given shared experience, but also to each other as agents who can reflect on the experience from their respective perspectives as selves. On the other hand, the proto-imperative orientation entails an orientation to others as agents who can be manipulated in ways that will bring about some desired change in the causal nexus of events in the physical-material world. In this perspective, there is no requirement that self and other jointly orient to a given phenomenon as shared experience.

Rather than prior representations of action and mental schemas within the organism, the appropriation of genre structures to the inner self-referential perspective of the self means that higher-order or linguistically mediated thinking is achieved in and through the relation between the self's intrinsic neural dynamics and dynamical ecosocial semiotic relations and processes. For present purposes, this relation can be explained as follows. In the brain, distributed networks of patterns of neural activity create connections across the entire network. The selection of patterns of neuronal activation depends on feedback from sources of information in the "outer" and "inner" environments of the organism. Rather than prior representations or schemas, it is the distribution of activity across the whole network which categorizes experience. In Edelman's (1989, 1992) theory, the whole network evolves on the basis of experience. Evolving patterns of neural activation are intrinsic properties of the organism. These intrinsic properties interact with extrinsic factors in the child's ecosocial environment such as the genre performances that the child participates in. The resources for action and meaning afforded by discourse genres interact with and entrain patterns of neural activity to their own dynamics.

In this way, they contribute to the emergence of thinking and reasoning. Thinking is a self–world relation in which complex control is achieved through the relationship between intrinsic properties of the organism and extrinsic properties of its environment. The self-organizing character of networks of neural activation means that the organism does not respond to contextual contingencies on the basis of fixed programmes, which would be impossible. Rather, the neural network is itself adapted to respond to such contingencies through its patterns of activation and their interconnections in the network itself. Thus, the child's participation in genre performances creates feedback loops that inform the self about self–other relations, the meanings associated with these, and their negotiation in discourse. The child's repeated participation in and positioning in some kinds of genre performances and their meanings over time creates stable categories of the self-in-relation-to-others. In this sense, the child re-envoices meanings that circulate in her ecosocial semiotic environment.

The child's participation in genre performances also provides feedback about sensori-motor processes: discursive activity is also bodily activity. Lexicogrammatical and discourse-level patterns of organization are cross-coupled to sensori-motor processes in complex ways such that the feedback relations provide information about bodies, meanings, and features of the ecosocial environment in complexly interrelated ways that cross-cut the traditional dichotomy between bodily processes and semiotic ones. Semiotic processes are never disembodied and purely mental. Instead, the processes of re-envoicement that children engage in involve the cross-coupling of and the establishing of equivalence relations among sensori-motor, discourse, and environmental systems and relations on diverse timescales.

In this perspective, thinking can be viewed as the re-envoicement of genre structures and performances in the inner perspective of the self who interprets and reflects upon self–environment relations in this same perspective. The appropriation of genres to this perspective can only occur through the child's active participation in dialogue. Dialogue is founded on the interpersonal take up and negotiation of propositions and proposals *qua* discourse activity. It is in this way that the child learns the propositional attitude, which necessarily entails the reflexive interpretation of self and other in the perspective of the self.

8 Indicative mood, reflection, and the development of dialogical thinking

Flohr (1991: 258) points out that the development of neural networks with a "sufficiently high formation rate" will lead to systems with a self-referential, inner perspective (see also chapter 1, section 2). Furthermore, the plasticity of genres and dialogue structures (see Bakhtin 1986: 79) ensures a high degree of flexibility and possibilities for the adaptive modification of the resources afforded by discourse genres to the very many diverse situations that the self encounters. In this view, symbolic or linguistically mediated thinking may be defined as the unsituated, self-reflexive meta-level interpretation of self–world–other relations in the perspective of the self. Thinking of this kind arises in and through the self's re-envoicement to its own self-referential perspective of the genres and social activity-structures of the ecosocial semiotic system. Rather than saying that genres are "internalized" in the individual, it is more correct to say, in the first instance, that the body-brain system's dynamics – neural and sensori-motor – are entrained to the very different dynamics of discourse processes on their scalar level. On this basis, the brain evolves patterns of neural activation that categorize experience in ways that enable the individual to respond to and reflect upon new experiences and new situations in contextually appropriate ways.

The reflective mode of the proto-indicative, as we saw above, differs from the proto-imperative mode because the latter entails an objectivating and instrumental view of the other as an agent in action. The emergence of the proto-indicative provides the self with resources for responding to contextual contingencies on the basis of a range of discretionary responses that he or she can adaptively modify to new situations. The capacity for creative and adaptive modification is a very different kind of ability from the automatic and pre-programmed responses of the kind that are based on efficient causality or stimulus and response models. Dialogue and the ability to anticipate and respond dialogically do not work on the basis of such models. The emergence in the individual of the proto-indicative orientation enables the individual to participate in truly dialogic processes. This does not mean that, whenever one uses imperative mood, one is always limited to an instrumental view of others. The point I am making is an ontogenetic one. Thus, the adult, who is in possession of the full system of grammatical mood, including both the indicative and imperative modes, has the possibility of reflecting on proposals as well as propositions in ways that are not available to the infant, who is limited to the proto-imperative mode in the early stages of his or her development. Moreover, the development of the indicative mode enables the individual to develop a truly dialogic mode of thinking whereby the self is able to respond self-reflexively to new contingencies by considering and evaluating alternatives, their consequences, and so on, as well as being able to see things from the other's point of view, rather than according to automatic, pre-programmed schemas (see also Ilyenkov 1977 [1974]: 49).

In this sense, thinking is an **activity** performed by a spatially and temporally embodied being, rather than the internal "cause" of some external action (Ilyenkov 1977 [1974]: 34). Thinking is not separate from the body; it is not a separate essence which interacts with the body. Instead, thinking is a specific relation of a determinate embodied being to the mode of its own action (Ilyenkov, *op. cit.*). Genres are, then, extensions of the body-brain system. In the development of the individual, they are both the means for recruiting, co-opting, and instructing apprentice-participants into the social practices of some community and for organizing higher-order forms of thinking (chapter 2, section 7). For this reason, genres increase in both complexity and specificity in the processes of human development and individuation (Thibault 1998b).

In egocentric speech, the child gives outward expression to the construction and deployment of those ecosocial semiotic resource systems which transform the initial contact with the friction or opposition posed by a recalcitrant material world into an organized dialogic response in the self-reflexive perspective of the self. These semiotic resource systems are the social means in and through which the child learns to reflect on and to contemplate the appropriate response which any given situation and its contingencies may require. The child develops an emerging mastery of the possible dialogic responses to such contingencies. This developing mastery means that the child draws on and further elaborates the available resource systems so as to critically reflect on possible dialogic responses according to the material and semiotic contingencies of any given situation. In so doing, the child learns actively to modify these in the course of his or her further development. The learning and fine-tuning of this ability, in turn, leads to the elaboration of alternatives by virtue of the increasing diversification of genre structures which the growing demands of a widening range of social situations entail.

Higher-order or symbolic thinking is, then, the capacity of the agent to adapt and modify the available social semiotic resource systems to new circumstances in the inner self-referential perspective of the self. Thinking is not some disembodied cognitive process. Thinking always entails the cross-coupling of the self with the ecosocial semiotic system across potentially very many space-time scales. Egocentric speech, in this point of view, is the outward verbal expression of the child's transition to critical reflection. It is the social achievement of an agent who is learning to centre his or her identity in relation to specific person-places in particular interpersonal moral orders. It is the social achievement of an individual who is learning to centre his or her own embodied being to the mode of its own activity. Once this is achieved and stabilized, normally between the age of seven and eight years, the incidence of egocentric speech falls away sharply.

9 Egocentric speech, self-awareness, and identity

In Vygotsky's conception, egocentric speech is a transition stage to inner speech or verbal thinking. The social is, thereby, relocated in the mind of the individual. In the present account, egocentric speech is an adaptive modification of the ecosocial semiotic resources whereby the individual gives "outer" expression to the motives which inform its activity. It is a stage in the developing self-awareness of the individual. Self-awareness, as Vološinov (1976 [1927]: 86) observed, is always "an act of gauging oneself against some social norm, social evaluation". Vološinov has written:

> In becoming aware of myself, I attempt to look at myself, as it were, through the eyes of another person, another representative of my social group, my class. Thus, self-consciousness, in the final analysis, always leads us to class consciousness, the reflection and specification of which it is in all its fundamental and essential respects. Here we have the objective roots of even the most personal and intimate reactions.
>
> (Vološinov 1976 [1927]: 87; emphasis in original)

Egocentric speech is the child's re-envoicement of how others in the social group see him or her. The child is learning how to turn into speech his or her own positioning in the social group at the same time that he or she learns to see him- or herself as others do. Once this acquires, as Vološinov (1976 [1927]: 89) has put it, "formulation, clarity, and rigor" – i.e. when the child's position in the dyad is stabilized and self-awareness is achieved – there is little need to give continual outward expression to this. Egocentric speech does not, however, just disappear with the passing of this stage. Instead, it goes underground, as it were, only to resurface in those moments when the dialogic relation between self and social group loses its clarity. Goffman's (1981) notion of "self-talk" also goes in this same general direction.

Harré (1983: 265) has argued that the individual constructs a (folk)-theory of self through the transformation of the locally available theories of self in the *Umwelt*. Egocentric speech, in my view, is part of the ongoing process of constructing and stabilizing an emerging self-identity. The above discussion suggests that this process has at least three aspects, which are always constituted out of the adaptive modification – the re-envoicing – of the available social semiotic resources. These three aspects are:

1. The individual is always spatio-temporally located at some cross-coupling of the physical-material and the semiotic-discursive in the modalized space-time of the dyad;
2. This location, in turn, becomes a point of reference in relation to which the individual, through his or her participation in dialogic processes of matter, energy, and information exchange, elaborates criteria of self-organization and self-reference. In this way, the individual does not only extend and further develop his or her own regulatory mechanisms in relation to the group, but his or her own internal complexity as well (Harré 1983: 75). It follows from this that members of the social group attribute criteria of internal complexity to self and to other;
3. The criteria of self-organization and self-reference cited in 2 (above) are themselves select-ive and adaptive modifications of the available material and social semiotic resources, including the theories of "self", in the local culture. Such theories are always immanent in the social praxis of the members of particular cultures, social networks, and so on.

10 Egocentric speech and the dialogical negotiation and emergence of a self-referential perspective

Vygotsky focuses on the ways in which the child learns to transfer "social, collaborative forms of behavior to the sphere of inner-personal psychic functions" (1986 [1934]: 35). To explain this transition, Vygotsky postulates three linguistic stages in the child's development. These are: (1) social speech; (2) egocentric speech; and (3) inner speech. He proposes a developmental frame-work for explaining the transition that the child makes from social speech to inner speech. In social speech, language functions are less differentiated (Vygotsky 1986 [1934]: 35). Around the age of three years, the second stage, that of egocentric speech, emerges. Vygotsky relates the emergence of this stage to the child's developing capacity for self-regulation. Egocentric speech, Vygotsky argues, "does not merely accompany the child's activity; it serves mental orientation, conscious understanding; it helps in overcoming difficulties; it is speech for oneself, intimately and usefully connected to the child's thinking" (1986 [1934]: 228). If, in social speech, the boundaries between self and nonself are not yet clearly differentiated, then the self-regulatory function of egocentric speech marks an important moment in the child's organization of the self-nonself distinction. As the above quotation shows, Vygotsky recognized that this process has important adaptive value. That is, egocentric speech semiotically mediates the child's adap-tive modification of his or her ecosocial environment in the satisfaction and organization of personal needs and desires.

Egocentric speech is especially interesting to Vygotsky because it represents in audible and hence observable form an intermediate stage between social speech and inner speech. Ego-centric speech has the same psychological function as silent inner speech, though the former is not yet fully internalized. Internalization takes place around the age of seven years. It is for this reason that egocentric speech provides the analyst with a unique opportunity to study the transition from social speech to inner speech and the consequent organization of the child's intra-psychic functions.

Vygotsky contrasts his explanation of the transition from social to inner speech to that of Piaget. In Piaget's account, internal and essentially "autistic" states of the child are gradually externalized through the child's developing linguistic capacities (Vygotsky 1986 [1934]: 34). Piaget has made the following observations on egocentric speech:

> This talk is egocentric partly because the child speaks only about himself, but chiefly because he does not attempt to place himself at the point of view of his hearer.
>
> The child talks to himself as though he were talking aloud. He does not address anyone.
>
> (Piaget 1959: 9)

For Vygotsky, on the other hand, it is the speech practices in which the child participates in the social world which are gradually internalized. In the process, inner speech is not simply outer speech which is relocated in the mind of the individual. As a specialized use of language, inner speech is also a transformation, or a recontextualization, of external speech into the specialized speech genres of "internal" language activity.

Vygotsky argues that egocentric talk:

> does not long remain a mere accompaniment to the child's activity. Besides being a means of expression and a release of tension, it soon becomes an instrument of thought in the proper sense – in seeking and planning the solution of a problem.
>
> (Vygotsky 1986 [1934]: 31)

Vygotsky contrasts his account of the transition from egocentric speech to inner speech with that of Piaget as follows:

> In our conception, egocentric speech is a phenomenon of the transition from interpsychic to intrapsychic functions, i.e., from the social, collective activity of the child to his more individualized activity – a pattern of development common to all the higher psychological functions. Speech for oneself originates through differentiation from speech for others. Since the main course of the child's development is one of gradual individualization, this tendency is reflected in the function and structure of his speech.
>
> (Vygotsky 1986 [1934]: 228)

Table 5.1 compares the positions of Piaget and Vygotsky in relation to egocentric speech.

Inner speech and outer activity are not separate activities, but part of a single holistic activity. The one does not cause the other. Rather, they are both contextually integrated with each other

Table 5.1 Comparing Piaget and Vygotsky on egocentric speech

Piaget	Vygotsky
egocentric speech is manifestation of child's solipsism or "egocentricity"	egocentric speech is the transition between external inter-psychological functions and internal intra-psychological ones
egocentric speech withers away as a result of the child's socialization	egocentric speech does not die out but "goes underground" as inner speech; this is a result of the increased differentiation between the self-regulative, planning function of speech and speech for interpersonal engagement with others
non-social, individualistic	social basis and origin of egocentric speech
	inner speech sets up an internalized self–other relation which functions as the interiorized social regulation of one's actions

as part of a larger-scale semiotic trajectory. In Vygotsky's account, inner speech breaks the chain of external stimulus – internal response – external reaction. Such accounts, which are based on pre-determined cognitive or other formal schema, are characteristic of mechanistic explanations of human action. The epigenetic and self-organizing nature of the individual's relations to the ecosocial semiotic environments means that the individual is continually able to adapt to new circumstances, and in ways not predicted by such schema. This fact bespeaks the individual's capacity for self-reflexivity. Speech for oneself, to use Vygotsky's turn of phrase, is speech which allows the individual to reorganize his or her responses to outer phenomena on the basis of a capacity for the critical contemplation of alternative courses of action and their future consequences. Inner speech is actively oriented to the external or internal environments of the individual. It represents an emergent, rather than a pre-given, capacity for adaptively modifying our actions so that we can respond to the environment in a reflective, rather than in an automatic or mechanistic, way. The individual, as a self-organizing social being, does not respond to the contingencies of social life on the basis of pre-wired or pre-determined internal cognitive schema. The inner and outer domains are a unity. This is so because the forms of silent verbal thought (inner speech) are also the forms of our outer linguistic and other semiotic activity. Both use the resources of language; they are not two distinct languages. Rather, inner verbal thought is a highly specialized deployment of the resources of language in the particular contextual domains in which it operates.

Vygotsky's materialist conception of this relation emphasizes the individual's capacity to plan and to alter his or her activities according to individual needs and desires. Piaget's formal schema, on the other hand, as his interpretation of egocentric speech as being essentially asocial and autistic shows, severs the internal link between formal cognitive operations and material human activity. His interpretation of egocentric speech assumes that abstract formal schemas operate through individuals. For Vygotsky, on the other hand, inner speech is a means for actively reflecting on and altering our material and social environments through embodied social action and thought.

According to Vygotsky, "... egocentric speech appeared when a child tries to comprehend the situation, to find a solution, or to plan a nascent activity" (1986 [1934]: 30). Vygotsky also points out that egocentric speech "does not long remain a mere accompaniment to the child's activity. Besides being a means of expression and a release of tension, it soon becomes an instrument of thought in the proper sense – in seeking and planning the solution of a problem" (1986 [1934]: 31). Nevertheless, Vygotsky's claim that language is "an instrument of thought, especially as the transition from egocentric speech to inner speech is completed" remains in the cognitive-representational mould (see also Hasan 1992b). A further problem with Vygotsky's theory is that it still relies to some extent on a dichotomy between the social and the individual. The causal fit, for Vygotsky, is very much from the "outer" social processes to the "inner" workings of the individual psyche (1986 [1934]: 134, 136, 228). In my view, a more distributed account is required (see below). I shall now consider some of the implications of the following passage for the arguments advanced so far:

> Our experiments showed highly complex changes in the interrelation of activity and ego-centric talk. We observed how egocentric speech at first marked the end result or a turning point in an activity, taking on a directing, planning function and raising the child's acts to the level of purposeful behaviour. What happens here is similar to the well-known develop-mental sequence in the naming of drawings. A small child draws first, then decides what it is he has drawn; at a slightly older age, he names his drawing when it is half-done; and finally he decodes beforehand what he will draw.
>
> (Vygotsky 1986 [1934]: 31)

In Vygotsky's account, the child gradually internalizes external activities in the development of higher mental functions. Yet, Vygotsky uses a causal-deductive model of explanation, which fails to overcome the society/individual and outer/inner dualisms. The emphasis, in the final analysis, remains individual development. What is missing is any conception of the dyad, seen as a specialized instance of the exchange processes in and through which dynamic open systems develop and regulate their internal structure and the activities that organize them. A child, to go back to Vygotsky's example, does not just "draw first", and so on. Instead, the child is integrated into the practices of the social group through dialogical-interpersonal processes of interaction and exchange with its members. It is an essential part of the child's further development that he or she is integrated into the practices of some group. It is the group which provides the child with the material and semiotic resources for deciding "what it is that he has drawn", and so on. This process can only occur through genre performances, which integrate participants into the ways of the group. This integration has two consequences. Firstly, the system of relations, structures, and processes which constitute the group (minimally, the dyad) are maintained. Secondly, these same regulatory processes are not, in turn, simply "internalized" or "appropriated" from the outside, in the child's development. The same processes which integrate the self into the group also extend the regulatory mechanisms of the individual and, therefore, the individual's agency.

Thus, the child is integrated into the ways of drawing, playing, speaking, and so on, of the group. These various social doings constitute information about some environment, or *Umwelt*, in which the members of the group act and interact. The child's egocentric speech is the child's taking up of meanings (cf. voices) which circulate in the relevant ecosocial environment. The child selectively attends to and takes these up in ways which bind or identify the child with particular social voices. I prefer to use Dore's (1989) term re-envoicement to describe this process because the child never simply replicates meanings already in circulation. Instead, any instance of subjective (modal) investment in these meanings always brings about their adaptive modification (Lemke 1984d: 13). In some way, the processes of subjective investment always interferes with the "object" that is invested in. The voices that circulate in the given socio-cultural context constitute specific guidelines for further development. Egocentric speech, as Vygotsky well recognized, is a critical transition point in the further development of the child. The child, to be sure, does not randomly pick up meanings in its environment. Instead, the regulatory structures and processes of the group shape and channel the child's semiotic transactions in terms of a set of preferred developmental pathways, which Waddington (1977) referred to as "chreods". Yet, I do not think egocentric speech can be properly explained as a transitional moment in the passage to thought *per se*. In this sense, Vygotsky's conception remains too monologic.

My point is that Vygotsky lacks a clear notion of the **interpersonal** semantic structures and processes which coordinate and entrain the dyadic processes of exchange that I discussed in section 2 above. Vygotsky (1986 [1934]: 228) emphasizes the "transition from the social, collective activity of the child to his more individuated activity", but the central problem, already identified, of the social/individual split remains unresolved. Vygotsky (1986 [1934]: 230), in emphasizing the increasingly "independent" and "autonomous" functions of egocentric speech, leaves no room for the crucial function of the other in the co-emerging of self and other.

In my view, egocentric speech is very much oriented to the other; it is concerned with the emergence of a self-referential perspective on the relations between self and nonself. In selectively attending to and taking up meanings which circulate in the ecosocial semiotic environment, and which regulate his or her structures and processes, the child, in the egocentric stage, is orienting his or her performance both to the self and to the other. Firstly, the child learns the means for subjectively locating him- or herself at particular positioned-practices, as constituted by the activities of the group. This subjective take up of particular participant roles and positioned-practices is, in other words, a selective response to environmental meanings. Secondly, the child's performance, which is audible to onlookers, becomes a way of displaying his or her emerging powers and capacities at the same time that the child seeks appropriate corrective feedback and guidance responses from the other members of the group.

The problems in Vygotsky's account may be summarized as follows:

- outside to inside causal view;
- social/individual dichotomy;
- not free of a representational view of mind;
- language is still defined in syntactic-semantic terms, rather than in terms of its multimodal integration with the sensori-motor activity of the body.

11 Egocentric speech, indexical and symbolic modes of semiosis, and the development of the metaredundancy contextualization hierarchy

Piaget (1940; see also Kinsbourne 2000) showed that the infant's very earliest uses of language to refer to phenomena in his or her environment appear not to differentiate between the word and the phenomenon that the word refers to. The two are experienced as a single, undifferentiated whole; words are holistically seen as being attributes of the particular phenomenon. The relationship between the two is one of indexical necessity. Later, the child learns to differentiate the two such that the same word acquires a symbolic potential to be used in combination with others words in different contexts. The symbolic potential of words means that words name type-categories of things (nouns), processes (verbs), qualities (adjectives), and so on. Type-categories can then be linked to specific instances in particular contexts by means of the grammatical resources of instantiation.

This enhanced symbolic potential means that different higher-order or metaredundancy (contextualizing) relations constrain the first-order redundancy relation between word and its referent according to the diverse contexts in which the word is used to refer to a given referent. For example, in the infant's egocentric speech, the linguistic utterance, the given phenomenon of experience that the infant perceives, the infant's attending to the experienced phenomenon through visual tracking, movement of the head and body, the action strategy the child adopts through control of the limbs for reaching, pointing, and so on, afford the child a varied repertoire of reentrant, multimodal takes over the course of the infant's trajectory as to how percepts are differentiated and attended to. In selectively contextualizing the phenomena of experience as instances of semiotically salient categories that are recognized and interpreted in a given ecosocial system, linguistically mediated activity in both inner and outer speech constitutes a powerful resource for specifying and stabilizing the flux of experience such that it can be attended to and manipulated in consciousness.

In the earlier indexical phase, no distinction between the first-order and the second-order contextualizing relations has yet emerged (chapter 3, section 5). This is so because the contextual relationship between word and referent in the infant's discourse is a holistic one of topological-continuous variation: word and referent merge with each other to form an as yet undifferentiated whole. Class and member, or schematic category and its instantiation, are not yet distinguished. The infant has not, at this stage, developed the higher-order or meta-contextualizing relations which enable him or her to recognize and interpret a particular instance as belonging to a given class of objects or events rather than to some other. The subsequent development of the symbolic meaning-making potential of language goes hand in hand with the capacity to "logically type" the relationship between word and referent as being of a certain logical class, or as being a use of language which is appropriate to some types of situation and not others.

Bateson's theory of redundancy provides a formal means of distinguishing the different levels of abstraction, corresponding to the different Logical Types, of the metaredundancy contextualization that are implicated in the development of this capacity (chapter 2, section 2; chapter 3, section 5). Class and member are, therefore, discontinuous the one with the other because they belong to different levels of abstraction (Bateson 1973c [1972]: 174). The infant who topologically merges word and referent as a single undifferentiated whole has not yet developed the higher-order contextualization relations which enable him or her to make the appropriate differentiation: the word is seen as being on the same level of logical typing as the object that it refers to, rather than being of a higher logical type. The infant's access to the symbolic possibilities of language, on the other hand, means that first-order objects, actions, and events, which the child observes in the world, can now be interpreted and categorized as instances of symbolic categories in language. This ability becomes possible only when the infant and his or her internal neural dynamics are entrained to the higher-scalar systems of symbolic categories of a given language system and its patterns of use in social activity. The emergence of the capacity to distinguish word from object, and hence, to name and categorize that object as an instance of such and such a semantic (or other) category greatly enhances the individual's ability selectively to make some aspects of the environment which surrounds the individual salient for the purposes of attending to it in consciousness. In this way, the given object is construed as an instance of a particular category of experience at the same time that it can be oriented to as having a particular value and, therefore, a particular potential for action.

12 Egocentric Speech and the Emergence of Agency

12.1 An example of egocentric speech in children's play: an analysis

In section 12 below, I shall analyse in detail the brief episode of egocentric speech that I first analysed in chapter 4 in relation to the overall play episode in which it occurred (see Appendix I) as a distinct discourse phase. In the analysis below, the focus and emphasis will be different. I shall be concerned, above all, with the ways in which egocentric speech and its analysis can contribute to our understanding of the emergence of agency in relation to the inner self-referential perspective of the self who is the source of this agency. The notion of re-envoicement will continue to be relevant here. The analysis below is a further development of the more theoretical discussion in the preceding sections of this chapter.

The overall context of the play episode from which this brief stretch of Paola's egocentric speech is taken involves the two girls playing "mothers and babies", with Paola as the mother and Elena as the baby (see chapter 4, section 5). In the excerpt below, Paola is preparing a pretend meal for the baby. At this point, she has broken off the previous dialogue with Elena and becomes involved in the pretend activity of preparing the meal for the baby.

(1) un po' di olio ^ (2) chh chh
(3a) questo è l'olio (3b) se ti serve ^ (4) chh chh
(5) e l'olio . . .
(6) vado a prendere il sale . . .

English language gloss

[1. a little oil ^ 2. chh chh // 3. this is oil if its useful to you ^ 4. chh chh 5. and oil . . . 6. I'll go and get the salt (breaks off activity and goes out of bedroom to kitchen)]

Summary of multimodal meaning-making resources co-deployed

(1) language; (2) significant contrast in voice prosody, volume, and rhythm with respect to previous exchange with Elena; (3) non-linguistic vocalization "chh chh", which has a synaesthetic value in the discourse (Van Leeuwen 1999: 142–144); (4) body movement / sensori-motor activity, e.g. shaking hand to sprinkle pretend oil onto meal she is preparing; (5) material and pretend objects integrated into activity, e.g. the oil and various kitchen utensils.

The analyses in Figures 5.1 and 5.2 show that the episode of egocentric speech under consideration here consists of two complete dialogic turns, or semantic interactants. The first of these comprises units (1) and (2); the second, units (3a)–(3b) and (4). In units (1) and (2) the speaker first issues a self-directed command to add some oil to the pretend food which she is preparing. The non-linguistic response "chh chh" realizes her self-compliance to this command. Bakhtin's (1986) notion of genre finalization is useful here. The sequence Command^Compliance is an elementary speech genre comprising these two parts (chapter 8, section 1). The addressee's Compliance to the command, whether verbal or non-verbal or both, finalizes the command by resolving the friction – the difference – between the initial state of affairs and the desired outcome. Bakhtin points out that genres such as Command^Compliance are stable forms which enable the "accidental and non-repeatable" contingencies and obstacles of every-day situations to be resolved in and through socially recognizable forms of action. Thus, the

un	po' di	olio	chh chh
Deictic: Non-specific	Pre-qualifier: numerative: quantifier	Thing: countable substance	
Dialogic move: Self-command			Dialogic move: Compliance / Completion of Activity
New – Rheme			

Figure 5.1 Metafunctional analysis of instance of egocentric speech; dialogic turn coordinating linguistic and other resources

questo	è	l'olio	se	ti	serve	chh chh
Identified/Token	Process: Identifying	Identifier/Value		Medium	Process: Material	
Mood: Declarative						
Theme + Given		Rheme + New				
Offer				Motivation for offer		Acceptance

Figure 5.2 Metafunctional analysis of semantic interact in an instance of egocentric speech

child's spontaneous and improvised cooking activity is organized in and given determinate shape in and through socially stable forms as a particular genre performance.

The second sequence of units, viz. (3a)–(3b) and (4), consists of the discourse semantic relationship Offer-Motivation for Offer^Acceptance. In (3a), the speaker offers the oil to the imaginary addressee, who is specified by the pronoun *ti* in clause (3b). Clause (3b) provides a motivation for the offer ("if you need it"). Unit (4) expresses the addressee's response, again in the form of Acceptance to the invitation implicit in the offer. Once again, we have a stable generic form, which provides a resolution to the local friction that is generated between the positions of addresser and addressee in the exchange.

In both cases, the addresser and the addressee are the same individual, who deploys these two dialogic interactants (cf. Bakhtin's primary genres) to channel her action down a particular trajectory towards a desired goal. In both cases, she takes up the speaking positions of both participants in these two semantic interactants, viz. the agent who issues the command and/or offer and the one who complies with or accepts these. That is, she articulates the Command in (1) and the Offer in (3a–3b) to herself as the addressee; she then responds by taking up the position of the other (the nonself) in the non-linguistic responses which ensue. Figure 5.2 illustrates the dialogic structure of this utterance.

In the episode of egocentric speech that I am analysing here, the child in question invokes, through the specific linguistic choices, her body movements, and non-linguistic vocalizations, intertextual links with a culturally recognizable activity-structure Preparing a Meal in the Kitchen. This activity can itself be broken down into a number of smaller constituent parts. The use of specific linguistic choices, the use of specific objects, the performing of specific physical activities, all have their meaning by virtue of their relations to other components of the activity, as well as to the activity as a whole. Furthermore, each linguistic choice, each object, each action, and so on, is selected against a background of alternatives in a contrast set of possible choices that could be made at various stages in the unfolding activity.

In this case, the construction of these meanings occurs in the child's pretend play, rather than in the preparation of a real meal in a real kitchen. The child has learned, both through her observation of and participation in relevant cooking activities with the mother and father in the kitchen, through story books, and other intertextual sources in the context of culture, the basic meanings associated with the activity of Preparing a Meal in the Kitchen. Furthermore, she has learned these meanings and activities through symbolic resources which intertextually invoke the relevant activity-structure type. There are no real cooking ingredients or utensils, no real kitchen, and so on, in this particular sequence, which takes place in her bedroom while playing with her friend. Instead, the child substitutes vocalizations such as "chh chh" for other choices that would normally serve to enact the activity in question. The process of metaphorical trans-categorization (Halliday and Matthiessen 1999: 242–244) across diverse material and semiotic domains enables the child to build these symbolic links between the two domains, viz. the play situation with her friend and the cultural activity of Preparing a Meal in the Kitchen (see chapter 11, section 4).

12.2 Re-envoicing the social semiotic

The child's discourse puts into operation a small fragment of a wider discourse formation, which is common to a potentially large number of texts in the community in which she lives. A discourse formation is characterized by particular intertextual thematic and axiological meaning relations, which both define and express the meanings typical of that discourse forma-tion. The present example shows a very high degree of thematic condensation on account of the foregrounding of New information at the same time that Given information tends to be omit-ted. The thematic formations that are adduced in the example and the heteroglossic relation of semantic alliance between them are the following:

/OIL: CULINARY: ADD OIL TO FOOD; POSITIVE EVALUATION/

$\updownarrow$

allied to

$\updownarrow$

/OIL: CHILD REARING: GENDERED DIVISION OF LABOUR IN HOME:
MOTHER PREPARES FOOD FOR BABY; POSITIVE EVALUATION/

A heteroglossic relation of alliance is construed between the two formations referred to here. Both formations are positively valued insofar as they are construed as compatible with each other and, therefore, mutually reinforcing. The child marshals the resources of these two the-matic formations in order to re-envoice a particular social voice to her own inner self-referential perspective. This social voice speaks from a particular viewpoint in the community into which she is being apprenticed. The construal of the heteroglossic relation of complementarity between the /CULINARY/ and /CHILD REARING/ formations constitutes this social voice, which the child re-envoices and invests in as her own.

The lexicogrammatical characteristics of the episode are in conformity with those identified by Vygotsky (e.g. 1986 [1934]: 236; section 5 above). Wertsch (1991: 41–42) has pointed out that these features refer, in actual fact, to the distinction between given and new information that has been made in modern functional and discourse-based grammars. Wertsch argues that the term "subject" in Vygotsky's account really refers to given information; the term "predi-cate" to new information. This clarification helps to explain the high degree of thematic con-densation that is evident in egocentric speech, along with the often implicit, presuming nature of the ties between this kind of discourse and its context of situation.

However, I would argue that the omission of Subject and the Finite element in the verbal group in the present example can be further explained in terms of the interpersonal functions of these items in the clause. Interpersonally, this utterance is concerned with the negotiation in its speech situation of a proposed self-directed action. Instead of a full imperative clause such as *metti un po' di olio* ("[you] put a little oil"), in which the Subject function is grammaticalized in the morphology of the verbal group, both the Subject and the verb process are ellipted in the present case. The significance of this ellipsis can be explained in interpersonal grammatico-semantic terms as follows.

The Subject grounds the clause in terms of person deixis (Davidse 1997: 9). The proposed action in the verb is grounded with reference to its grammatical person, viz. first person, second person, or third person. Imperative clauses lack the feature of Finiteness that is characteristic of declarative and interrogative propositions. In other words, the proposed action in an imperative clause is not grounded in the here-&-now of the speech situation in the same way that a proposition is grounded because the verb in an imperative clause lacks precise tense specification. Nevertheless, this does not mean there is no location in time with respect to the time of the utterance. In the case of proposals, the time is the future time of a not-yet-realized-action, which is desired by the speaker and which the speaker seeks to oblige the listener to carry out. As Davidse (*op. cit.*) points out, the interpersonal functions of Subject and Finite tie propositions and proposals to the I-here-now reference point – the ground – of the speech situation. These observations can help us to clarify the absence of the Subject in the present example as follows.

Given that the Subject in the present example is the second person speaker-as-addressee in the here-&-now of the speech event, the proposed action in this clause *qua* instance of egocentric speech is located with respect to its ground by being tied to the self as **both** the first person speaker of the proposed action and the second person addressee of the proposed action. Given this situation, in which first person self and second person other are the same individual, there is no need to tie the proposed action to its ground by explicitly specifying the grammatical person of the Subject. The dialogical loop consisting of the I-you-now-here frame of reference is intrinsic to the speaker's perspective and for this reason it requires no further grammatical specification. Instead, the focus is on the nominalized Object *un po' di olio* because it is this grammatical Object, as well as the pretend entity which it designates in the referent situation of the discourse, that is brought under the Subject's control by virtue of its being held in the scope of the imperative clause as an object to be manipulated and integrated to the child's self-activity. Self-talk, to use Goffman's term, is very much integrated into self-activity and its perspectives.

I shall explain this last point by pointing out first that the discourse is concerned with the negotiation along an action trajectory of an emergent self–nonself dialogic structure. In the process, the child orchestrates and re-envoices various social voices from the perspectives of both self and other. In the closed loop of relations which defines and generates this perspective, it is not necessary, from the child's viewpoint, to make explicit all of these co-textual and contextual links because they are taken as given in the context and are in no need of lexico-grammatical specification. In my view, this is the reason why egocentric discourse frequently ellipts both Given information and the Subject-Finite functions. From the self-referential point of view of the self, there is no need to spell these out; only the new information needs to be introduced into the discourse situation as that which is relevant to the ongoing negotiation of the self–nonself relation. Furthermore, the ground of the proposed action is the I-you-here-now perspective of the self as **both** addresser and addressee. From this perspective, there is no need to make this point of reference explicit because this pole of self-consciousness is taken for granted and the focus is on the other pole, viz. the object of conscious attention and manipulation in the activity.

13 Genre as social activity structure-type

The thematic formations and heteroglossic relations which we have analysed in section 12.2 above are enacted by an unfolding multimodal activity-structure, which has a particular Generic Structure Potential (GSP). The GSP of a text or occasion of discourse consists of a sequence of functional elements which define the various stages of the unfolding activity structure (Hasan 1985). Such a structure is said to be "generic" because it is typical of, or in some way indexes, a particular genre formation that is regularly enacted in the community. Furthermore, the genre formations of a community are redundant with particular intertextual thematic formations. That is, some genres rather than others are more typically associated with particular thematic and axiological meanings, deriving from their ITFs (see chapter 2, section 7).

For example, the text-types and activity-structures associated with recipes, the preparing of meals, and such like, are likely to express thematic and axiological meanings from the ITF which I have glossed in section 12.2 above as /CULINARY/. From this point of view, the child's activity creates a co-actional tie both with the kinds of social activities associated with the preparation of meals, along with the text-types (e.g. recipes) that are frequently embedded in and used in these activities. The child's agency is enacted by virtue of her taking up and situating herself as the performer and controller of such an activity. Each stage in the unfolding generic structure of the text is realized by discourse-level semantic elements of the kind identified by Mann *et al.* (e.g. 1992) as rhetorical structures such as Problem-Solution, Cause-Consequence, and many others. In the episode analysed here, the rhetorical structures used include Self-Command^Compliance and Offer-Motivation^Acceptance. The generic structure is an emergent property of the interactions among the child's internal dynamics, the activity-structure in which she positions herself, and her intertextual knowledge of the thematic and axiological meanings associated with these activities.

A genre is a regular repeatable pattern of use of the available semiotic resources in a given community. Genres are activity-structure types which are recognizable in a given community. The notion of text is derived from and secondary to that of activity structure. This is so because texts – e.g. written linguistic texts – are always embedded in and produced in and through structured social activities, including the practices of writing or composing (and reading) a written linguistic text (see chapter 6). Spoken genres are typically best represented as multimodal activity-structures in which language is combined with selections from other semiotic resource systems in the process of enacting a particular instance of the genre in question. Genre is not, then, reducible to the notion of text-type *per se*. This last point does not exclude the fact that written and other printed genres are typically defined in terms of specific *text*-types. Genres *qua* text-types are also multimodal integrations of language, spatial layout, visual images, and so on, on a treated surface such as the page.

However, texts differ from social activity-structures in the sense that texts may be the products and/or records of social activity-structures, or they may be selectively embedded in such activity structures across different space-time scales (see chapter 6, section 1). This orientation to the written object text may be a defining characteristic of our Western cultural notions of text, i.e. text is a semiotic product or record, which can be de-located from one space-time scale and re-located in another (cf. the notion of a semiotic object text in Thibault (1994). Thus, different space-time scales are integrated by virtue of the symbolic possibilities which texts afford for their de-location and re-location across different space-time scales. However, there is also a material aspect of this de-location and re-location. That is, the object text *qua* material artifact can be materially re-located as well.

The two dimensions – semiotic and material – are complementary. From the performance perspective, activity-structures are more ephemeral, though these too can be recorded by various technological means (transcription, video and audio recording, CD-ROM, and so on) and re-played and re-enacted on different occasions as either products or records which stand in some kind of semiotic relation of homology to the conditions of their original enactment (Thibault 1991a: 73–74; Thibault 1994). In any case, the text is not reducible to its material substrate(s) *per se* on level L–1 of the three-level hierarchy. Thus, the black marks forming patterns of letters on a printed page are semiotically reinterpreted at level L as potentially meaningful patterns which can be assigned a contextualized meaning according to the semiotic practices and categories available in a given system of interpretance on level L+1. Similarly, the physical-material patterns of activity on the hard disk of a computer are translated by means of electrical energy into patterns of sound and light produced by the monitor and audio system of a multimedia personal computer. These patterns of sound and light are, in turn, interpretable as a multimodal semiotic performance text which the computer user can interact with and interpret.

The dialogic exchange units or elementary genres which I have examined above are discourse level semantic units. They specify types of social action. These small-scale activity sequences, or mini-genres, are integrated into the unfolding action trajectory as a whole. They are not defined by clauses or other lexicogrammatical units *per se*. Instead, they constitute an intermediate level which mediates between lexicogrammar and discourse. There is no simple, one-to-one realizatory fit between lexicogrammar and the larger-scale discourse units that lexicogrammatical units realize. This principle is, of course, central to the systemic-functional understanding of the relationship between form and meaning in discourse. Action is better stated in terms of semantic, rather than lexicogrammatical, criteria. The episode as a whole is not easily assimilated to any specific genre model. The analysis of the episode shows that the child has developed the capacity to harness the resources of the mini-genres deployed so that these are integrated to the higher-scalar semantics of the intention which guides her action trajectory as a whole. To explore this question, I shall focus now on the interpersonal enactment of agency in the episode, rather than on its experiential construal. In doing so, I shall consider how the mini-genres and their constituent discourse moves, as discussed above, are integrated to the overall semantic structure of the intention which semantically structures and modulates the trajectory as a whole from its inception to its conclusion.

In the episode under consideration, the child produces a SELF-COMMAND, realized by the nominal group shown in Table 5.2. It is clear from other aspects of the multimodal activity sequence that this has the function of directing and coordinating the child's own sensori-motor activity, i.e. adding the pretend oil to the imaginary recipe. As a Command, the utterance sets up expectations as to what will be or what should be the case in relation to the point of action occupied by the child, i.e. the desired change in the material world. The point is that the vocalization "chh chh" and the associated manual-brachial movement of sprinkling the oil on the meal are routed through higher-order, context-sensitive semantic constraints which constrain and direct the (bodily) action along a particular trajectory. In this case, the dialogically coordinated roles of addresser (self) and addressee (other) are the same person. The element SELF-COMMAND expresses the speaker's PROXIMATE INTENTION, seen as sourced at the child as a point of action.

The semantic item Proximate Intention may, therefore, be seen as the first stage in the action trajectory. It is important to emphasize here that this is a semantic function in the discourse. It has nothing to do with the logic of external efficient causes, which are seen as the drivers of action in the classical account. The point is that the Proximate Intention is a semantic structure, which functions as a dynamical attractor in a prior semantic space. Proximate Intentions entrain both semiotic and material, including bodily, processes, along a trajectory such that the frequency distribution of the semiotic-material cross-couplings and their entrainings along this trajectory is taken in a determinate direction. The intention is a semantic structure in symbolic neural space which guides and modulates the action all along its trajectory. The idea that an intention modulates and guides an action all along its trajectory to the completion of the action does not preclude the possibility that Proximate Intentions by agents may be resisted or contested by other agents along the way. In our example, the non-linguistic vocalization "chh chh" realizes the fulfilling of this intention as an action, and, hence, the further enacting of its trajectory in the ecosocial environment of the dyad.

However, the semantics of agency typically entails a number of other steps. These further steps are not always or necessarily explicit in the discourse. The second of these is the providing of some Reason for the exercising of one's agency (see also Hasan 1992a). In our example, this is supplied by the composite unit comprising clauses 3a and 3b. In this declarative clause complex, the child establishes a condition in the form of a motivation "se ti serve" for the offer "questo è l'olio". Semantically, this structure provides a Reason for the child's action in (1). In this case, the child-as-mother is also anticipating the probable user of the pretend meal she is preparing, i.e. the "baby" in their pretend play. The third and fourth steps are not explicitly realized in this text. They are, however, intertextually recoverable. These two steps can be defined as the more general Principle on which the Reason is based. The Reason given is specific to the particular proximate intention, which is realized in the first part of this activity. Particular Reasons are, in turn, based on more general Principles. In this case, the practice of adding oil to this particular recipe derives from more general principles such that oil is commonly added to very many meals in the particular culture in question. This general Principle does not, however, preclude some discretion in this matter on the part of specific individuals and their personal tastes and requirements. Finally, the generalization underlying the Principle is grounded in some Validity or Warrantability Claim. Such claims provide an ultimate justification for the particular action relative to the practices and expectations of the interpersonal moral order (Harré 1983; see also Prodi 1987) in which the action is carried out and interpreted. In this particular case, the grounding of the Validity Claim appeals to the culinary and gastronomic practices of Italian culture and, hence, to gastronomic norms which are socio-cultural in nature. The semantic structure of the child's unfolding action trajectory in the above instance of egocentric talk may be analysed as follows:

1   PROXIMATE INTENTION: Self-command^Compliance: un po' di olio ^ chh chh
2   REASON: Offer-Motivation^Compliance: questo è l'olio se ti serve ^ chh chh
3   (PRINCIPLE): oil is normally used in cooking
4   (VALIDITY CLAIM): this is a culinary or gastronomic requirement

( ) = not explicitly realized in text, but intertextually adduced or recoverable as culturally relevant semantic patterns

The above analysis draws attention to the ways in which agents semantically organize and modulate their action trajectories in the self-referential perspective of the self. In the individual, global context-sensitive constraints in the form of self-organizing neurological dynamics based on meaning constrain sensori-motor activity. In this way, sensori-motor activity is integrated to and, hence, channelled and directed along a goal-seeking action trajectory by these same top-down semiotic constraints. Importantly, these top-down self-organizing neurological constraints do **not** function after the fashion of unilinear efficient causes. The principle at work here is entirely different from Humean regularity empiricism, which is based on the notion of constant conjunctions of events and their (efficient) causes (Juarrero 1999: 48–49). The meanings which self-organize in the brain as intentions, desires, conscious awareness of and attention to objects, and so on, are not a separate soul which kick starts the body into action after the fashion of externally related causes and events. Instead, these meanings modulate the action *qua* action along its entire trajectory, which loops outside the individual and into the ecosocial environment of other individuals, objects, events, and so on. The relationship among these diverse factors is a time-locked, dialogical, and internalist one. The action trajectory emerges as a result of the time-bound interactions between the individual's internal dynamics and the context of situation which the child's discourse creates or enacts. Action does not uniquely originate from within the agent; action is distributed across and emerges from the complex interaction of many variables on diverse scalar levels of organization both inside and outside the organism.

In this context, we can return to the question of agency. Salthe offers the insight that agency is an "operational sign" of the emergence of a self-referential perspective (1993: 159). A self-referential perspective is a historically emergent property of the individuating trajectory of a self-organizing system. A self-referential perspective implies a perspective or viewpoint, which also enables other viewpoints to be recognized in a given ecosocial system of relations. Furthermore, Salthe points out that "[agents] cause historical events that contribute to the individuation of other systems" (1993: 159; Thibault 2004b). They do so along their individuating trajectory, both logogenetically and ontogenetically. That is, agency is distributed along an entire action trajectory, which loops through the self-organizing neurological dynamics at its source and out into its ecosocial environment in the way described above. In the early stages of infant ontogenesis, the child's perspective is limited to the topological-continuous variation and the indexical meanings of primary and secondary intersubjectivity, respectively. Indexicality entails the emergence of means-end schemas, as first observed by Piaget (1952) (see chapter 3, section 5). Indexicality entails procedural memory. The enhanced sensori-motor coordination of this stage affords the ordering of means-end schemas, as well as increased attention to environmental objects and events (Cole 1996: 194; Perinat and Sadurní 1999: 70). Adult and child share an indexical core which forms the basis of the child's emergent agency.

Nevertheless, the child member of the dyad does not yet access the higher-scalar level of the symbolic meanings and values of the wider context of culture. The adult's access to these symbolic meaning-making possibilities mediates the child's indexical sign-making just as it helps to restructure it. However, it is the symbolic level which permits access to and trajectories through the wider systems of intertextual connections and social practices in a given culture. Only in this way can co-thematic, co-actional, and co-axiological links (Lemke 1985) be formed with other texts, other activities, other values in the culture at large (see chapter 2, section 5). That is, symbolic semiosis, unlike the prior indexical mode, invokes intertextual possibilities which ramify beyond the here-now scale of indexical relations.

Symbolic semiosis and its intertextual possibilities in discourse mean that the agent and its effects in the world are linked to an increasing diversity of semiotically integrated space-time scales (chapter 6). Egocentric speech requires "tertiary intersubjective understanding" (Bråten 2002: 288), which is only possible when the child has access to the possibilities of discourse. Access to these possibilities means that the meanings and the perspectives of both self and other and the capacity to identify with others can be both experientially construed and reflected on and interpersonally enacted in and through socially determinate discourse genres that are shared with others. Egocentric speech affords such possibilities for simulating one's own and others' meanings and perspectives in the perspective of the self at the same time that it participates in the further honing and elaboration of the self. The following section will take up this last point.

14 The emergence of a self-referential perspective: the closing of the meta-loop on the "me" sector of the dialogic loop

The child uses the symbolic possibilities of language to project specific meanings from a point of action which is centred on herself as agent. This centring of the self involves a self-referential perspective on one's self as the agentive source of these acts. The child symbolically projects from a point of action – from her own embodied (self-)consciousness – an imaginary nonself (a second in Peirce's terms) with which her agentive firstness engages. However, the fact that this is an imaginary symbolic projection in the transition phase usually referred to as egocentric talk really shows, in my view, that the child's emergent perspective as an agent and, hence, as a point of action from which certain individuating effects can flow is a symbolic projection of her awareness of her self as being defined in and through her interaction with the nonself, i.e. other people, objects, and so on, in the world of the nonself. In this sense, the child is decidedly not a little Cartesian! That is, she symbolically projects a self-referential perspective on the whole dialogically organized loop comprising, in our example, me-dialogic move-pretend oil-dialogic move-me-as-you such that the pretend oil is construed as being "out there" in contrast to the "in here" of the "me" sector of the loop.

Vygotsky theorized that egocentric speech is a necessary transition phase preceding and preparing for the emergence of the intrapersonal higher-order mental functions (section 6). He regarded egocentric speech as central in the gradual transition between years 4 and 7, approximately, from interpersonal (inter-mental) to higher-order intrapersonal (intra-mental) functions. This transition can only take place through the symbolic meaning-making resources of language for it presupposes an off-line freeing of mental activity from the on-line or here-now character of indexically situated mental activity. The higher-order mental (intrapersonal) functions may be seen to emerge when the reentrant connectivity of neural groups creates the meta-loop that closes the loop on the "me" sector of the dialogic loop described above.

Following Bateson's (1973a [1972]: 288) famous description of the man felling a tree with an axe (chapter 9, section 6.1.5), I propose that the child projects a dialogic move – i.e. *un po' di olio* – from the "me" perspective. In turn, this move leads to a response from the discursively simulated perspective of the nonself – i.e. the *chh chh* of the oil being sprinkled on the meal – as construed, of course, by the self. This response, in turn, leads to a further dialogic move from the perspective of the self – i.e. *questo è l'olio se ti serve* – and so on. This little episode of egocentric talk consists of a self-corrective loop, which is enacted by the entire system of relations, as glossed above. In Bateson's terms, transforms of (semiotically salient) differences are transmitted around the entire dialogically closed loop. It is this total system which is "mental" in character, rather than some arbitrarily de-limited part of it such as the "me" sector *per se*.

The symbolic projection of the child's self-referential perspective onto the whole dialogically organized loop can be schematized as follows:

ME → DIALOGIC MOVE → PRETEND OIL → DIALOGIC MOVE → ME

Still more schematically, these specific choices may be represented as follows:

ME → SYMBOLIC RESOURCES → NONSELF → SYMBOLIC RESOURCES → ME

Figure 5.3 schematizes the relations among the various components of this dialogic loop, as well as the closing of the emergent meta-loop on the "me" sector of the entire loop. In this way, we can see that the dialogic character of these relations is not replaced by a monologic perspective with the transition to the higher mental functions. Rather, it is interiorized and correspondingly reorganized and re-envoiced in the further structuring of the self's emergent consciousness and agency.

In Figure 5.3, the *a* component refers to the "me" sector of the self. The *b* component is, for example, the linguistically realized dialogic move *un po' di olio*, which is uttered from the perspective of the self. The *c* component is the symbolically projected object – the oil – in the domain of the nonself. The *d* component is the dialogic response to her move in the *b* component. Here, the child may be seen as enacting, by means of the non-linguistic vocalization "chh chh", the dialogic response to and uptake of the nonself *qua* response to her own action on the pretend oil. She participates in what the simulated other is doing, though from the standpoint of the self. The *e* component is the meta-loop which reentrantly closes the entire first-order loop comprising *a-b-c-d* on the "me" component. That is, the entire first-order loop is re-envoiced in terms of this newly emergent self-referential perspective and its meanings and viewpoints on the meta-level *e*. The emergence of this level further suggests that the self-as-agent instigates events which contribute to its own individuation from the perspective of the emergent meta-level.

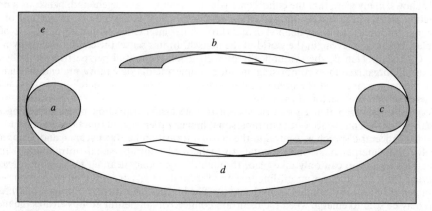

Figure 5.3 The closing of the meta-loop on the "I" sector of the dialogic loop in the transition from egocentric talk to inner speech and the higher, intrapersonal mental functions

15 Value, self-organizing context-sensitive constraints, and the semantic honing of the agent's action trajectory

The system of semiotic values, viz. the systems of semiotically salient differences in some community, is a system of context-sensitive constraints. Each level of organization in the system

is a further system of contextual constraints whereby, in the case of language, complex phonological, graphological, lexicogrammatical, semantic, and discourse patterns of organization
emerge. The terms that belong to a given system of values, viz. semiotically salient differences,
impose internal constraints on each other. They are, therefore, internally related to each other.
Each stratum of semiotic organization contextually constrains the lower levels and, therefore,
their probabilities of co-occurrence. Top-down discourse-level and genre-level patterns of
structure and organization are higher-scalar contextual constraints which enable lower-scalar
lexicogrammatical and expression (phonological, graphological) level systems and structures
to self-organize into more complex and differentiated wholes. The emergence of these more
complex global structures enables the system to access an increased variety of states along
its logogenetic and individuating trajectories. The system of values which are intrinsic to a
language system means that some semantic states are more probable than others (chapter 2,
section 10). Further levels of contextual constraints, such as those emanating from the higher-
scalar intertextual formations and genre formations that are in operation (chapter 2, section 6),
impose further constraints on the probabilities of some patterns occurring, rather than others.
For this reason, the intertextual formations themselves are not extrinsic to the lexicogrammatical choices which are made; instead, they are co-patterned in terms of contextualizing relations
which form a larger-scale system of relations (chapter 2, section 6). Thus, the higher-scalar
intertextual formations and genre formations are part of the individual agent's context and
are, therefore, imported into the internal body-brain dynamics of the agent for the reasons
discussed in chapter 2, section 6.

In the case of the episode analysed here, the child's choice of the nominal group *un po' di olio*
can be seen as the lexicogrammatical realization of a semantic structure, which I have glossed as
Proximate Intention. In so doing, the lexicogrammatical choice embodies a number of semantic
constraints in experiential, interpersonal, and textual meaning, which all operate at the level of
the lexicogrammatical selection made. There is, then, an experiential construal of a given phenomenon of experience as an intentional object, which is consciously attended to. There is also
a correlated mode of action with respect to this object. Specifically, an arbitrary instance of a
given type-category of semantic Thing (*olio*) is both symbolically and indexically grounded as
an (imaginary) object of conscious experience at the same time that the lexicogrammatical
choice also coordinates and enacts the child's dialogic orientation to this object as a particular
discourse move.

The metafunctional organization of the whole thus imposes constraints on the component
parts of the whole such that the various parts are systematically and internally related to
each other (see chapter 2, section 10). Once this kind of metafunctional semantic closure
takes place, then higher-scalar context-dependent constraints act upon the first-order constraints that transitivity choice a exerts on interpersonal choice y, and so on. The emergence of
these higher-scalar constraints, whereby the experiential, interpersonal, and textual selections
are now realized as a single global configuration, alters the prior probability distribution of its
components and, hence, its degrees of freedom. The newly emergent patterns of organization
on the higher-scalar levels just *are* the change in probability of the relations among the lower-
scalar components such that action and understanding are themselves constrained. Thus, the
emergence of an action trajectory centred on the child's self as point of action is the phenomenological manifestation of this skewing and re-skewing of the probability distributions of
values on lower-scalar levels. The semantic choice acts as a dynamic attractor which entrains all
of the lower-level components – both semiotic and material – along a particular trajectory
(section 14 above).

The higher-scalar intertextual formations which are activated are not external to the child
(section 12.2). They are selectively contextualized facets of the context of culture with which the
child is systematically interrelated along her trajectory. For this reason, the regular, typical
contextualizing (metaredundancy) relations that are created and elaborated between the child's
internal dynamics and the context of culture build up context-dependent and time-bound
interdependencies between the two. The child's internal dynamics are, in this way, entrained to
those of the higher-scalar ecosocial semiotic dynamics in which she is embedded in time.
Agency is not, therefore, explainable in terms of the child's mechanistic or forceful interactions

with the environment *per se*. Instead, agency is dependent upon the higher-scalar constraints emanating from the intertextual formations and genre formations and the ways in which these self-organize in the internal dynamics of the individual. Agents are robust precisely because the higher-scalar contextual constraints ensure that the conditional probability of a particular lower scalar component will persist and behave in regular and predictable ways under determinate contextual constraints.

Children learn through their apprenticed participation in social meaning-making practices (Lave 1997; Walkerdine 1997). Moreover, they are positioned in particular ways within the networks of relations and the possible trajectories through these practices that define a given community or sub-community. In this way, complex contextual redundancies are built up between the child's internal (neural and sensori-motor dynamics) and the world by virtue of the child's entraining to certain patterns rather than others through his or her active, always situated, participation in and selective re-envoicement of cultural networks of meaning-making. The emergence of a self entails the closure of a self-referential perspective whereby individual agency becomes possible. This closure means that a self-nonself system has self-organized and that this system, in turn, imposes further contextual constraints on its lower scalar components. The imposition of such constraints allows for the further closure of a self-referential perspective on the "self" component in response to and as a consequence of the re-organization on the emergent meta-level of persistent dialogic exchanges between self and nonself over time.

Patterns of neural activation in the brain are therefore context dependent in accordance with the probability distributions of values which characterized the organism's initial conditions, along with those to which it is entrained along its trajectory. In other words, no two individuals have exactly the same intrinsic dynamics as their initial conditions. The individual's intrinsic dynamics are then entrained to higher-scalar ecosocial semiotic dynamics through ongoing matter, energy, and meaning exchanges with the environment such that positive feedback imports pattern and organization into the organism's internal dynamics. Saussure, it will be remembered, had talked about each individual as having a *langue individuelle* in his or her brain. The language system is built up as a system of value-laden connection weights and patterns of patterns of pattern . . . of connection weights in the individual's brain. It is a multidimensional semiotic space, which is distributed across very large scale patterns of neural connections, as well as involving very complex attractors. It is these attractors, in symbolic neural space, which function as a higher-scalar system of interpretance for giving meaning to lower-scalar states and processes. The vast number of linguistic and other semiotic values and their connections which are networked in the brain, along with the individual's being embedded in a time-bound trajectory, mean that (1) no two individuals have exactly the same system of values in their symbolic neural space and (2) individuating states and meanings in specific contexts, and according to the individual's own internal (psychological) dynamics, are manifestations of the complex and adaptive nature of the brain as a dialogically organized meaning-making organ-in-process.

6

Agency in Action: from Multimodal Object Text to Performance in the Building of Semiotic Bridges between School and Home

0 Preliminary observations on the episode to be analysed and its transcription

In this chapter, I shall analyse in detail a single episode in which a six-year-old girl enacts a solo performance in the form of a pretend concert recital before an imaginary audience. Her performance consists of songs, sounds, and other textual materials taken from her school copy book. She produced the copy book materials in school classroom activities that took place in February and March 1991. At the time of her solo performance, the girl in question was aged 06;04 and attended her second year of elementary school in Bologna in Italy. The episode took place on Saturday, 20 April 1991 at around 10.00 am. The child was alone throughout the entire performance, which occurred at home in her bedroom. The entire episode was recorded by the author of the present study. Moreover, the child also recorded her own solo performance with the use of a hand-held microphone and audiocassette recorder while she performed before her imaginary audience, whom she frequently addresses during her performance.

The entire episode, which is in Italian, is transcribed in Appendix III. The Italian text is glossed in English and supplemented with notes and analytical observations on salient features of the activity. Furthermore, in the transcription, I have divided the episode into a number of phases, consisting of the specific activities and orientations that characterize a given phase. Throughout the transcription, the utterances and other units in the child's performance have been numbered for easy cross-referencing so that they can be linked to the analysis and discussion in this chapter.

Selected relevant pages from her copy book are also re-produced in Appendix IV. The pages in question refer in particular to phases 9 and 10 of the episode. Appendix IV is a double-page spread from the girl's copy book. The two pages are dated 25 February and 28 February 1991, respectively. Throughout the discussion in this chapter, I shall refer to these pages as Appendix IVa and IVb, respectively. For reasons of space, it is not possible to reproduce here all of the material from the copy book that the child utilizes and refers to during her performance. The analysis and discussion below will focus on the pages of the copy book that are reproduced in Appendix IV in relation to the transcription in Appendix III in connection with the child's vocal performance of the classroom sounds which are transcribed and commented on in the relevant pages of the copy book (Appendixes IVa and IVb). The primary focus of the discussion and analysis below will therefore be on sound as a meaning-making resource and its recontextualization across other semiotic modalities and domains of social practice.

An English translation of the Italian text is provided in Appendix III.

1 The emergence of meaning across diverse timescales

In play between children, as well as between children and adults (e.g. parents), we can observe, over time, emergent patterns and processes. New discourse patterns emerge, new groupings of playmates, new alignments of the roles they negotiate in play. We can observe particular ways of relating to favourite toys, typical sayings and intonations, meanings specialized to the play group. All of these and much more become, in turn, the raw material for complex new patterns to emerge. We also see individuating patterns that are unique to a particular child. We also see patterns in the way the child orients to school, as well as in the contexts that bridge between the home and school domains. There are typical patterns in the ways the child interacts with her parents, grandparents, and so on.

The patterns of meanings and actions that we associate with a given individual contribute to our sense of that person's identity, including the ways in which he or she is construed as being different from other individuals. By the same token, individuals, for all their distinctive and idiosyncratic features, participate in the typical patterns of meaning-making activity of the social networks of which the individual is a member (chapter 4, section 3). These social networks include the typical patterns of the classroom, play with peers, family life, and so on. These typical patterns shape the development of all individuals who participate in their practices.

An individual is only definable in terms of his or her historical-biographical trajectory. We can ask how the individual both individuates and develops as a typical instance of its kind. What constraints on still larger timescales constrain its trajectory? The episode under consideration here has its own component processes and constituent units that are characteristic of its particular timescale. These processes and units include the bodily activities of the child in relation to the objects that she uses during this episode, e.g. the cassette recorder and hand-held microphone, the school exercise books, and so on. These dually semiotic and material artifacts are embedded in and participate in processes on timescales that go well beyond the here-now event in which the child uses them.

Lemke (2000b: 281–282) points out that an artifact is a product of larger-scale and longer-term processes (e.g. of writing, editing, manufacture). Artefacts are participants in processes on these scales. By the same token, artifacts are also small-scale participants in small-scale events such as the episode under consideration here. In the present case, the copy books that the child uses in her performance participate in at least three timescales that I shall single out as relevant to our analysis. The relevant timescales in descending order of magnitude are: (1) the status of the copy books as material artifacts that are manufactured for the purpose of being sold as blank copy books to be used by (mainly) school children; (2) the classroom activities that occurred several months (February) before the present analysis and which led to the production of the texts – written and visual – that the child has written up in her copy book; and (3) the child's solo performance of the texts in her copy book at home some months later (April).

To understand how these artifacts are both participants in short-term events such as the episode under consideration and, at the same time, the products of processes on larger timescales, we need to distinguish, following Lemke (2000b), the following two principles that regulate semiotic relationships across different space-time scales:

1. Timescales on different levels are seen as distinct from one another. Thus, different timescales are separable. For example, events on one level are buffered from events on faster, smaller-scale events by longer-term regulatory processes on intermediate levels of (biological) organization. In this perspective, events and processes on large timescales have little or no effect on normal human activity;
2. Processes on long timescales produce effects on much shorter timescale activities and processes. This is the case in human meaning-making activity and is the basis for human semiotic integration across timescales. In this perspective, processes on very different timescales are interdependent.

Human meaning-making activity links longer-term processes and shorter-term ones by means of semiotic-material artifacts such as book, toys, computers, and so on. The material characteristics of these artifacts function as signs for an interpreting system that belongs to processes on very different timescales than that of the event or activity in which the interpreting takes place. In this view, we can consider the ways in which texts circulate in social networks and as they do they participate in many different small-scale situations. In the present example, the child's exercise book has participated in short-term activities in both the classroom and at home. The text's overall movement in the network constitutes a functional cycle of activity on a larger timescale than any of the constituent activities.

In the present case, the constituent activities include:

1. The bodily activities of inscribing the written words and visual images in her copy book as visual traces on a treated surface (the copy book page);
2. Participating in the classroom discourses of discussing and attending to the different kinds of sounds that are distinguished;
3. The visual scanning and interpreting of the visual traces in the process of reading them;
4. The integration of the words and images in the child's copy book text to their re-enactment as a multimodal semiotic performance text in her bedroom involving the integration of written words, visual images, the copy book itself as object that can be manipulated, the hand-held microphone and cassette recorder, her body and its movements and gestures, the performing in song, imitated sounds, and language of the text.

The child's copy book and the linguistic and visual signs that she has written or drawn in it, along with the meaning-making potential of her own body, afford this kind of semiotic integration across diverse time scales. For example, in the performance text, she re-enacts sounds in a pretend question and answer sequence in which she takes up and re-envoices both the teacher's voice and respective positions in the discourse as well as the voices and positions of the pupils. The exercise book is a semiotic-material affordance that enables this kind of solo re-enactment. That is, the exercise book materially links events separated by months which took place in school and at home. The events so linked participate in processes on a much longer timescale as compared to the short-term processes of writing and drawing in her copy book or its re-enactment in her bedroom on the Saturday morning in question.

The words she uses, the participant roles she takes up in the various activities, the discourse patterns, the conventions of visual semiosis, and so on, all have a much longer history than does this particular exercise book, its unique linguistic and visual patterns, and the child's unique re-enactment in the form of her solo performance before a pretend audience. The processes that produced the exercise book, the visual, musical, and discourse-linguistic patterns, and the classroom sounds and noises that she gives voice to, all intersect through the semiotic mediation of both the book and her body as a material-semiotic performance on the timescale of her re-enactment in her bedroom one particular Saturday morning in April 1991.

2 The distribution of participant roles in the experiential space-time of the activity: an analysis of the location and distribution of consciousness across the "inner" and "outer" domains in relation to verbal and mental processes

The Performer / Singer and Presenter – Audience / Listener relations frame the whole episode. Paola regularly punctuates her own performance with utterances which directly construe in their experiential grammar the relationship between herself as Performer and Presenter and her imaginary interlocutor as Audience and Listener. Verbal processes, which construe the participant roles of Sayer, Receiver, and Verbiage, are foregrounded in her performance (see Appendix III). Verbal processes construe dialogic processes between the Sayer and the Receiver. The third participant function, the Verbiage, specifies the semiotic event or text that is communicated when the Sayer and the Receiver interact. In the episode, the Verbiage is very often referred to with a demonstrative pronoun such as *questo* ("this"), rather than being fully lexicalized. For example: (2) *adesso vi canto una canzone* (NOW + YOU: PLURAL + I-SING + A SONG). The experiential structure of the clause is as follows: Temporal Circumstance + Receiver + Sayer-Process: Verbal (fused) + Verbiage.

The fact that the speaker does not typically make the Verbiage in her clauses lexically explicit indicates the extent to which she assumes the objects she refers to are already available in the context of situation and are therefore able to be recovered by her imaginary addressee. Furthermore, the reference of these items is always cataphoric; they anticipate the given song and its performance by the speaker as something which is about to occur in the upcoming discourse context. The following examples illustrate this:

adesso vi canto una canzone (2)
ve la canto tutta allora (17)
adesso adesso vi canto questa (19)
adesso vi canto questo (33)

In all of these examples, the clauses construe the speaker's activity of singing a song to her audience. Singing is a type of verbal process. The act of singing involves three participant roles. For example, in (2) there is the participant who sings, i.e. the first person singular *io* ["I"]; the participant to whom she sings, i.e. the second person plural *vi* ["you"]; and what is sung, i.e. *una canzone* ["a song"]. These three participant roles conform to the schematic model of verbal processes in which the participant functions of Sayer (Singer), Receiver, and Verbiage are respectively realized by the three items mentioned above.

The positioning of the child as Sayer (Singer) of the various songs that she performs during the episode is itself a part of a wider chain of semiotic activities linking participants across different space-time scales. There are a number of ways in which these might be reconstructed, depending on the starting point that one wishes to posit. Following some suggestions in Hasan (1998: 219–220; see also Thibault 2002: 76–77) concerning the ways in which verbal processes act upon and modify the consciousness of the Receiver of the Sayer's Verbiage, the following possible chains of semiotic activities involving the re-contextualization of verbal processes into mental processes can be considered:

SOMEONE WRITES A SONG → SOMEONE READS THE SONG → SOMEONE SINGS THE SONG → SOMEONE LISTENS TO / HEARS THE SONG → SOMEONE APPRECIATES / UNDERSTANDS THE SONG

THE TEACHER TEACHES A SONG → THE PUPIL LISTENS TO THE SONG → THE PUPIL COPIES THE SONG IN HER COPYBOOK → THE PUPIL REFLECTS ON THE SONG → THE PUPIL LEARNS THE SONG → THE PUPIL SINGS THE SONG → THE AUDIENCE LISTENS TO THE SONG → THE AUDIENCE APPRECIATES/RESPONDS TO THE SONG

THE SONGWRITER WRITES A SONG → THE PUPIL READS THE SONG → THE PUPIL LEARNS THE SONG → THE PUPIL SINGS THE SONG → THE AUDIENCE LISTENS TO THE SONG → THE AUDIENCE APPRECIATES AND RESPONDS TO THE SONG

Verbal processes act upon and potentially transform the consciousness of the Receiver. In this perspective, the Receiver can be re-construed as the Senser in the mental process that results from the transformation of the Receiver's consciousness. The child's re-envoicement of the various songs that she sings in her performance requires both her active attending to and responsive understanding of the songs and an audience that is able to appreciate and understand them. In the child's performance, the audience is the imaginary one that she creates and projects through her own semiotic activity as the second person plural Receiver, as we see in the above clauses.

There is one clause in which she orients to her audience as actively and appreciatively responding to one of the songs she sings. This is the interrogative clause (22) and associated tag questions, *vi è piacuta, vero?si?* The interrogative clause *vi è piacuta* is a mental process clause of the kind that Halliday classifies as "affection". Mental processes of the affection kind construe affective and aesthetic responses to particular phenomena. The experiential structure of clause (22) is analysed as in Table 6.1.

Table 6.1 Experiential analysis of the interrogative clause + tag, showing Process and Participant roles

vi	è piacuta	[la canzone]	vero?
Senser	Process: Mental: Affection	Phenomenon [implicit]	tag
YOU: PLURAL	PLEASED: THIRD PERSON SINGULAR: FEMININE	THE SONG	right?

In the mental process clause in Table 6.1, the speaker construes her audience as the Senser on whom the implied Phenomenon, which is recoverable in the context, has a positive impact. In other words, utterance (22) de-locates the audience from the public realm in which the audience was construed as the Receiver of the song which she sings in Phase 3 and re-locates the same audience in the private domain as the Senser who undergoes a subjective mental experience and appraisal of the text, now re-construed as the implied Phenomenon of this mental process clause.

The interrogative mood of the clause signals that the speaker is actively seeking to know the impact of the song on her imaginary audience in the way that singers at live concerts frequently interact with and directly address their audience. This interpretation is supported by the tag question, which shows that she is asking the audience to verify the appreciative response that the speaker assumes. The speaker then follows this dialogic move with a further move, *sì?* ["yes?"], with rising intonation. In the present context, this move is interpreted as the speaker's acknowledgement of an imaginary and unverbalized positive response that she receives from her audience. The meaning of this move could be glossed as "really?" in English. Thus, the speaker not only enquires as to the response of her audience in the interrogative clause + tag in (22); she then imagines a positive response from her audience, which she acknowledges in the minor clause *sì?*, which follows the tagged clause.

The discussion in the preceding paragraph shows that the child is able to position her audience as a collective (plural) participant who is both an active listener and therefore Receiver of the verbal process of singing at the same time that the audience mentally responds to the song with appreciation as a Senser. It follows that the child also positions herself not only as Singer, but also one who is able to attend to and engage with the audience's response. In clause (22), the audience is construed as the Senser of an inner mental process, which is the consequence of a prior semiotic or verbal process. In this way, the child constructs a relationship between her verbal process of singing *qua* public act and the inner domain of mental appreciation and response in her audience.

There are a number of verbal processes in which the child is the Sayer of acts of saying, rather than the Singer of songs. In Phase 8, she turns her attention in clause (44) to the sound scripts in her copy book (see Appendix IVa; see also sections 6 and 7 below) that she performs in this phase. As with the previous examples, clause (44) announces her intention to perform the designated items by grounding the utterance in the present time of the unfolding performance. Each mention of *adesso* ["now"] becomes the point of departure for the performance of a new item. Clause (78) also fits this same general pattern.

adesso vi dico questi (44)
adesso vi leggo tutto (78)

There are two instances of verbal processes in which the Receiver role is not present. These are as follows:

questo nome è un po' difficile e quindo non lo dico (67)
tutti abbiamo detto la frase "sulla finestra c'era un piccione" (80)

In both of these cases, the focus is on the Verbiage and on the Sayer's relationship to or performance of the Verbiage. In (67), she comments on the difficulty of pronouncing the name "Serge Prokofiev" and cites this as her reason for not saying it after her initial attempt had proved unsuccessful. The focus is on her role as Sayer in relation to the Verbiage, rather than on the audience as Receiver of the Verbiage, which the audience is expected to attend to. In this clause complex, she provides both an evaluation of her own performance and her reason for not bringing this particular performance off. Thus, the verbal process here monitors her own relationship as Sayer to a piece of text – the Verbiage – that she is unable successfully to re-envoice in her solo performance.

On the other hand, in clause (80), the Sayer is a collective "we" comprising the members of her class, including the speaker. In this clause, she positions herself as a member of that particular classroom community. She then construes the collective Sayer as having said the Verbiage in question, which is a piece of text belonging to a prior classroom activity, which is recorded in her copy book. As with (67), see previous page, there is no Receiver role in this clause. Again, the focus is on the Sayer's relation to the Verbiage as someone else's text – either taught by the teacher or written in a textbook. In this case, the Verbiage has been successfully re-envoiced by the collective Sayer of the classroom. As the previous utterance (79), which is a section title that she reads from the copy book, explains, the focus in this section is on listening to and attending to one's own voice.

Other examples, in which either the self or the audience is de-located from one semiotic realm (the verbal) and re-located in another (the mental), include the following mental process clauses:

guardate che è troppo bella che la voglio proprio registrare (8)
adesso sentite il fruscio de . . . ascoltate la carta (14)

Clauses (8) and (14) are second person plural (*voi*) imperatives which the speaker uses to direct the addressee's attention to the particular phenomenon. Clause (8) draws attention to the song she has just mentioned in (7) and therefore to the speaker's aesthetic evaluation of the song in the remainder of this utterance. The two imperative clauses in (14) require the audience to attend to the sound of the paper, which the speaker then crumples with her hands to produce a crackling sound. These two clauses require the addressee to "hear" (*sentite*) and then "listen to" (*ascoltate*) the sound of the paper being crumpled. More particularly, the speaker creates an interactive context in which her addressee is invited to attend to a specific auditory event. This context is created by the relationship between the utterance, the speaker, and her audience, the speaker's physical action of crumpling the paper, the crackling sound that this action produces, and the naming of this event by means of the nominal group *il fruscio della carta*.

Listening is active. The speaker's shift from "hearing" to "listening" is interesting here. Listening is an activity in which the listener actively attends to the given phenomenon in the context of the cross-modal relations between diverse semiotic and perceptual modalities. In the present case, these modalities include auditory perception, looking at something, performing a physical action, producing a linguistic utterance which orients both addresser and addressee to the auditory event at the same time that the utterance names it. The processes in (8) and (14) are behavioral or mental processes that are concerned with perception. Behavioral processes such as *guardate* ["look at"] and *ascoltate* ["listen to"] are not only more activity oriented. They also indicate that the Behaver is an active perceiver who is in control of the act of perceiving. They contrast with their mental process counterparts *vedere* ["see"] and *sentire* ["hear"], in which the Senser has less control over the Phenomenon.

The Senser's lack of control over the Phenomenon is characteristic of mental processes of the perception kind in which the Phenomenon is construed as a first-order Phenomenon that exists on the same level of reality as the Senser (see Davidse 1991: 294). The speaker dialogically engages with the imaginary audience in order to create a context in which the latter orients to a particular auditory event. Both parties are able to see and hear the event as part of the first-order reality in which the interaction takes place. The Phenomenon thus has high reality status at the same time that the Senser or Behaver can directly interact with it.

In the following two clauses, the act of perception is construed as the work of a joint first person inclusive plural Senser. The two examples below refer to the joint perception of their respective first-order Phenomena, as in (73) and (79), which the child reads from her copy book:

abbiamo visto il film di "Pierino e il Lupo" (73)
ascoltiamo le nostri voci (79)

The child thus re-envoices her own relation to this joint Senser as a participant in shared perceptual experiences that took place in the public domain of the classroom.

Other mental process clauses consist of processes of the cognition subtype, as in the following:

impariamo ad ascoltare (48)
sì perchè ad occhio chiuso possiamo riconoscerli (62)
conosciamo altri strumenti musicali (65)

With respect to mental processes of perception, mental processes of cognition entail a greater degree of the Senser's control over the Phenomenon. Thus, in (48), the mental process of cognition *impariamo* ["let's learn"] in this first person inclusive plural imperative clause entails a Senser who has active control over the Phenomenon. In (48), the Phenomenon is a projected meta-Phenomenon. As Davidse (1991: 292–294) points out, second-order or projected meta-Phenomena have lower reality status than non-projected first-order Phenomena which the Senser can perceive and otherwise physically engage with. In (48), the projected meta-Phenomenon is construed as the purpose of the collective act of classroom learning of the first person inclusive plural Senser in the projecting clause *impariamo*. Thus, the activity of listening is construed as a purposeful activity which can be learned and therefore enhanced through education, experience, conscious reflection, expertise, and so on.

Similarly, the mental process of cognition *riconoscere* ["recognize"] in clause (62) is construed as a modalized capacity which the first person inclusive plural Senser of the classroom group can deploy and control in the absence of information from other modalities such as the visual ("ad occhio chiuso") so that she is able to cognitively process the given Phenomenon in the correct way. Thus, the cognitive process of correctly recognizing the sounds in the absence of visual information is one over which the Senser has a high degree of control. In this example, the auditory perception of the sounds has been transformed into internal cognitive processing for the purposes of their correct identification.

The mental process clause (65) also fits the same pattern. The collective Senser's knowledge of the given Phenomenon is a group knowledge that is derived from the shared classroom experience. Again, the Senser is in control of the Phenomenon – the knowledge of the musical instruments that are evoked here. Clauses (48), (62), and (65) are all written in the child's copy book. In each case, they specify a group position or a joint Senser – i.e. the members of the class as a whole, rather than specific first person singular egos. It is the joint Senser which has access to and control over the requisite cognitive capacities. These cognitive capacities are therefore located in and distributed across the public domain of this collective Senser, rather than in the purely private domain of the individual "I" as Senser. In the present context, the child, in her performance, re-envoices this collective position and identifies with it, rather than separating herself off from the group and taking up a purely individualistic and ego-centered stance. That is, she re-envoices the collective cognitive capacities as being distributed across the group, rather than as her private possession.

The one exception to this pattern is the following mental process of cognition:

questa me lo ricordo anche da sola (27)

In this case, the speaker construes herself as Senser in the individual act of remembering the song which she is searching for in her copy book at the moment that she utters clause (27). She then sings the song in question in phase 6. This clause takes place in a context of self-monitoring of her own activity of searching for the song at the same time that she provides aesthetic appraisal of it. The cognitive act of remembering is, in the present case, oriented to her capacity as solo performer before her imaginary audience. The act of singing the song in phase 6 (see 30) is a de-location of an individual cognitive capacity (remembering) from the private domain of individual consciousness and its re-location in the public domain as a sung performance to her imaginary audience.

On several occasions, the speaker uses relational clauses of attribution to express aesthetic evaluations of the songs which she sings. The following examples occur in the episode:

guardate che è troppo bella che la voglio proprio registrare (8)
no questa è bella (16)
adesso più avanti adesso più avanti c'è ne un'altra che è bella (27)

Like the mental process clause of affection (22) that I discussed above, these three attributive clauses relate speaker and imaginary audience in a shared context of aesthetic appraisal and therefore of shared values for judging and appreciating the songs that she sings. These clauses also display a self-monitoring function as the speaker gives voice to the criteria according to which a particular song, rather than some other, is selected for performance whilst she searches through her copy book. In (16), the "no" is a self-command: she directs herself to pause at this point and to break off the search while she appraises the song as one that is worthy of performance. In (27), something similar occurs when, during the act of searching in the copy book, she anticipates a song that she has not yet come to as being worthy of performance. In this case, the aesthetic judgement serves to orient her own search activity so that she can zero in on the particular song, which she then decides to perform.

The significance of these evaluative utterances lies in the way that they evoke a set of aesthetic values and judgements and standards of appreciation that are shared by her and her imaginary audience. At the same time, the mental attributes [*bella* in all three cases] in these clauses are inner cognitive orientations that anticipate and orient her activity in some directions, in terms of some choices, rather than others. Thus, attitudinal orientation is a prelude to action, a motivator of it, as well as being a modulator of the action along its trajectory.

Figure 6.1 does not represent a fixed grid of relations. Harré suggests that the orthogonal can help us to illustrate that the developmental process "would typically involve a time-dependent displacement of attributes through the three-space" (1983: 44). Each of the three regions can vary independently relative to the others. For instance, the region "Action – Inner Domain" specifies how verbal processes act on and can induce changes in the consciousness of the Receiver. The egocentric speech of young children occurs in the region "Action – Outer

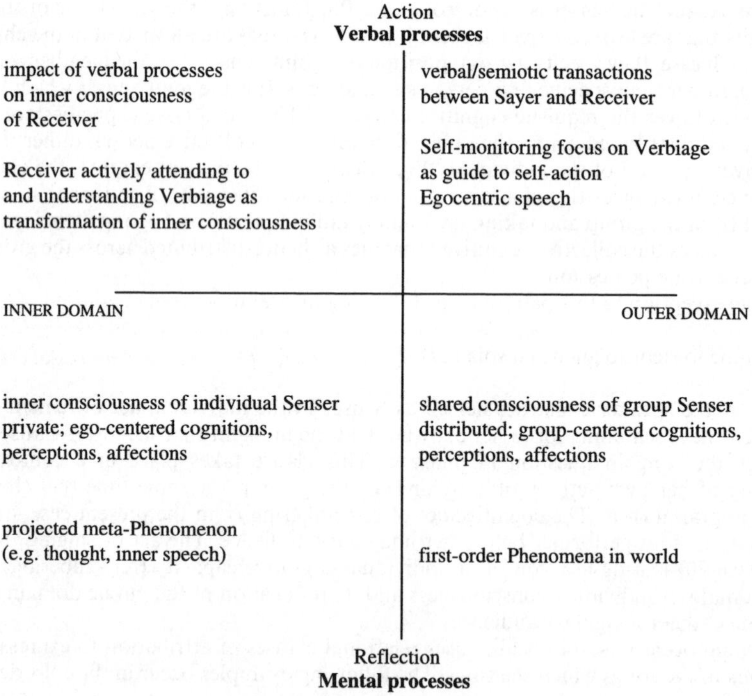

Figure 6.1 The intersection of the Action/Reflection and the Outer/Inner distinctions; represented as a three-dimensional space for understanding the experiential construal, location, and distribution of consciousness in relation to verbal and mental processes

Domain" (see chapter 5). According to the principle of time-dependent displacement, ego-centric speech is later re-located in the region "Reflection – Inner Domain" as inner speech. Mental processes of learning, knowing, and so on, can be distributed across a social group in the region "Reflection – Outer Domain" before they are re-located as ego-centred inner processes in the region "Reflection – Inner Domain". First-order Phenomena in the region "Reflection – Outer Domain" can impact on the consciousness of a Senser and be introjected as second-order meta-Phenomena in the region "Reflection – Inner Domain". Mental processes in the region "Reflection – Inner Domain" can be verbalized as the Verbiage of some Sayer in the region "Action – Outer Domain" just as verbal processes in the "Action – Outer Domain" can either mediate the transaction of the Verbiage between a Sayer and a Receiver, or focus on the Sayer's own activity as in self-monitoring and egocentric speech.

3 Agency, viewpoint, and the locus of control of the activity

What is the locus of control in the child's activity? Is the child the sole agent in the activity? Some of the dialogic moves in Paola's speech are directed towards securing the interest and attention of her imaginary audience. Other moves are directed towards her own activity and her role in it. The moves in this second category relate to the control and evaluation of her activity. Yet other moves provide her aesthetic and affective evaluations of the materials – e.g. particular songs – in her own performance. Overall, the entire episode shows little evidence of pre-planning. Rather, it is spontaneous, though it is difficult to say that the entire episode is constructed on the basis of her self-regulatory activities alone.

The evidence provided by my own analysis indicates that the activity is also entrained by the genre conventions and the meaning-making affordances of the copy book and the other arti-facts that she integrates to the activity or to some part of it (e.g. the microphone, the cassette recorder). In other words, the child is not the sole locus of control and therefore of agency for the unfolding activity. The agency and therefore the regulation of the activity are distributed across various participants – human and nonhuman – on different space-time scales. Import-antly, the discourse is very much centred on Paola as the first person performer of a range of participant roles (Sayer, Singer, Commentator) in relation to the second person plural Receiver, Audience, and so on, that her discourse indexes through the pronominal and other lexicogram-matical resources used (see section 2).

The child's dialogic relation to the imaginary other of her pretend audience also plays an important role in the entraining and regulating of the activity as it unfolds along its trajectory. The imaginary other – the audience – whom the child addresses is anticipated and responded to because the child has internalized in her neural dynamics models of genre structures and therefore of dialogic moves – both initiating and responding – that enable her to entrain her bodily dynamics to the constantly fluctuating and changing nature of the activities that she constructs in real time.

Salthe (1993: 214–215) points out that the much faster dynamics of such internal models with respect to the slower dynamics of the external environment enable organisms to rapidly "mobilize" their internal models in ways that anticipate possible environmental contingencies. The development of internalized genre models of how to participate in various forms of dialogically coordinated interaction with an increasingly varied and specified array of real, specific, non-specific, and imaginary others provides the individual with more and more resources for tuning into more and more kinds of selves in an increasingly diverse range of social situation-types.

In the present case, the child appears to be relatively well integrated to the possibilities of this kind of genre performance such that the overall specificity of the activity is maintained as she moves from the performance of one song to another. This specificity of activity in the real time of its performance contrasts in some ways with the play episodes involving Paola and Elena 18 months earlier (see chapter 4), where more activities, goals, and performance roles are compet-ing with each other. Thus, the integration of the genre models to the child's internal dynamics is a new integrative level which allows her to access new possibilities at the same time that the system as a whole is reorganized by the emergence of the new level of agency that the new models afford her.

Paola attempts to re-envoice, to varying degrees of success or integration, various genres of joint participation. These genres include: (1) Teacher-Pupil Interrogation, e.g. 38–42, 53–54, 61–62; (2) Performer-Audience, e.g. 1–3, 6–7, 14–15, 16–17; (3) Lead Singer-Other Vocalists, e.g. 5; and (4) Cooperative Group Activities with Classmates, e.g. 48–49. For example, in both phase 9 and phase 10, Paola's reading from the copy book shows her attempting to re-envoice the teacher's classroom voice of interrogation of the pupils. The clause *cosa intendiamo per suoni e rumori?* (falling intonation in (53); rising intonation in (54)) attempts to re-enact the teacher's voice of interrogation of the class. The pupils are required (1) to reproduce the question in their copy books and (2) to respond to the teacher's question in the classroom. Paola, in her solo performance, attempts to re-envoice the teacher's voice. However, the hesitation in her voice and the repetition of the utterance with the two different intonation contours indicate her lack of complete mastery of and identification with the agent position that this type of position requires. In (54), she corrects herself in order to replay the utterance with the intonation that is typically associated with utterances of this kind.

In phase 10, there is a further example of the same kind of attempt to take up the position of the teacher, as in the utterance *anche gli strumenti musicali hanno un timbro* (falling intonation in (60); rising intonation in (61)). In both cases, Paola's first attempt to re-envoice the teacher's voice does not work. She gets the intonation wrong on the first attempt, which is in each case the falling intonation that is typical of a statement. In the second attempt, she then corrects this to the rising intonation that is characteristic of teacher interrogation. The child's reading aloud is an effort or a struggle, which is both semiotic and material, to inscribe herself within the bodily *habitus* of the rhythms, intonations, vectors, and so on, of the teacher voice.

In her attempt to integrate her own activity to the genre of Teacher-Pupil Interrogation and therefore to re-envoice its meanings and discursive positioning, we can point out that, in her first attempt to ask a Teacher Question, the intonation she uses is at cross-purposes with the meaning of this type of discourse move and the category of speaker who typically operates it. The difficulty that she evidences in re-envoicing this meaning and the performance role that it entails shows that her own activity and possibilities for agency are little integrated to the possibilities afforded by the teacher position in this kind of dialogue.

Overall, the episode, when viewed synoptically as a completed temporal trajectory, does not exhibit any global staged, goal-oriented genre structure. Rather, it integrates a diversity of genre structures to its dynamics at the same time that a good deal of recursivity is in evidence as the child moves from one song performance to another, each time preceded by her announcing the new item to her audience.

On a number of occasions, she interrupts the flow of the performance activity to correct her own activity, to comment on or to evaluate it, to assess her own role in its performance, to correct herself when she makes a mistake or changes her mind about the choice of text or the direction of the activity. In these moments, we obtain clues concerning the meta-level evaluation of herself, her activity and her performance role in it from the perspective of the self. In this way, we get valuable insights into her self-positioning as agent and her affective commitments to the roles and activities she engages in, as well as to the others implicated in the activity. These insights can, I believe, help us better to understand the learning and developmental processes in and through which children integrate new possibilities for action and meaning to the perspective of their selves at the same time that such processes of integration bring about the global reorganization of the system as a whole. It is in this way that the self can tune into and access new possibilities, which, in their turn, prepare the way ahead to the next developmental or learning stage.

4 The semiotic integration of pictorial, graphological-typological, and linguistic resources in the child's copy book

The text of the copy book is a recontextualization in language, visual image, and graphological-typological resources for indexing specific sorts of classroom sounds and noises that are typically associated with the classroom environment that the child participates in (Appendix IVa and IVb).

On the left page (Appendix IVa), a series of framed vignettes depict typical events and their participants, along with the sounds or noises that are produced by these events. The overall page works to classify different sounds on the basis of both their acoustic properties and the participants – human and nonhuman – that produce them. This page relates each of the individual illustrations both to each other and to the handwritten caption "*I suoni e i rumori dentro la scuola*" ["The sounds and noises inside the school"] as members of an overall taxonomy (see Kress and Van Leeuwen 1996: 81). Each individual illustration is a subordinate component in this taxonomy. The superordinate meaning is specified by the verbal caption. Each illustration comprises a schematic drawing and a visual-graphic script item. In each case, the image specifies the participant – human or nonhuman – that is the source of the sound and the script item is the sound that the participant produces. The participants are indifferently human and nonhuman. In terms of visual transitivity, the various illustrations uniformly depict a Participant(s)^Process relationship through the integration of the image and the written script. The illustrations are without background detail and provide only the most essential or schematic detail without perspective. All of these features foreground the classificatory function of the overall illustration. The emphasis is on the timeless and objective qualities of the depicted items (Kress and Van Leeuwen 1996: 81). On this page, we can see, therefore, how a diverse collection of auditory events is recontextualized in a multimodal text comprising visual images, language, and visual-graphic script items so as to produce a general classification. With the exception of the superordinate caption, the items on this page use non-linguistic resources to create the meanings of this page.

The right-hand page (Appendix IVb) is a table in which different sounds are classified in terms of the two columns headed "sounds" and "noises", respectively. This classification implies a positive versus negative evaluation of certain categories of sounds. In the table, the two categories and their corresponding evaluations are explicitly and strongly separated from each other by the visual organization of the table into the two columns. On the other hand, this classification and evaluation is only weakly implied by the visual display on the left-hand page. The meanings that the table makes possible are, in part, organized in relation to the left page and its meanings, though the principles of organization and meaning-making are different on the two pages. The table is a further stage in the overall processes of recontextualization and abstraction with respect to the visual-verbal texts on the left page. In this case, a superordinate linguistic item, *Che cosa intendiamo per . . .* ["What do we mean by . . . "] is integrated to the headings of the two columns of the table, viz. *suoni* ["sounds"] and *rumori* ["noises"], in order to form the question: *Che cosa intendiamo per suoni [e] rumori?* ["What do we mean by sounds [and] noises?"]. This integration of the linguistic text to the headings of the two columns in the title provides a link both to the meanings of the left-hand page at the same time that these meanings are integrated to the table on the right-hand page. In the way, the table provides a response to the question and therefore further defines the terms "sounds" and "noises".

The table *qua* visual genre is closely related to written language (Lemke 1998a; Thibault 2001: 294–295). Whereas the illustrations on the left-hand page build up a visual thematic formation in which Participant-Process relations are specified for each item as visual co-hyponyms, and related to the superordinate thematic item in the title, the items in the two columns of the table are thematically underspecified. That is, they are semantically highly condensed and require more interpretive work to relate them to their thematic formations. Each item in any given column is a nominal group which stands in a hyponymic relation to the superordinate term at the heading of its respective column, as well as in a co-hyponymic relation to the other subordinate items in the same column. At the same time, the items in each of the two columns stand in a relationship of semantic contrast or opposition with each other.

The Participant-Process relations that were depicted on the left-hand page are nominalized by the items in the table. This process of nominalization means that they are reclassified through the process of naming them by the use of abstract terms in their respective nominal groups in the table (Halliday 1993: 98–99). The illustrations on the left-hand page thus provide a principle of mainly visual classification. The illustrations are knowledge objects which the child can use and elaborate in various ways in other contexts. They can become the objects of further reflection prior to the recontextualization of these visual meanings into the still more abstract meanings of the nominal group. The visual images, for all their schematic and recontextualizing features, are still tied to sensori-motor representations of the classroom events that are the source of the sounds under consideration in ways that the nominal groups in the table are not and cannot be.

The semantic orientation of the nominal group is towards reality as thing, rather than to process (Halliday 1993: 111). The nominal groups in the child's table are instances of grammatical metaphor in which Participant-Process relations are re-construed as things. In this way, they are transformed into abstract things which can be reflected on and manipulated in discourse. In most of the nominal groups in the child's table, the Thing item is the Participant, whereas the Process is a post-qualifying item which further specifies the Thing in terms of some quality which is attributed to the Thing. The focus in these nominal groups is therefore on the Participant which is the source of the sound (the Process). The following two examples from the table illustrate this trend:

la porta che sbatte ("the door that slams") → PARTICIPANT=THING (la porta) + PROCESS=QUALITY (sbatte)

la matita che scrive ("the pencil that writes") → PARTICIPANT=THING (la matita) + PROCESS=QUALITY (scrive)

This emphasis contrasts with the way that we attend to and parse auditory events. In this case, the listener attends to the Process – the auditory event – and, on this basis, identifies the Participant which is the source of the event. In the visual images on the left-hand page, the multimodal text, consisting of visual image and the visual-graphic script, recontextualizes the sound event in terms of both visual and auditory invariants. The picture and the script, respectively, integrate these invariants as a single multimodal experience of the original event in terms of an arrested visual-graphic array. This array consists of visual and auditory invariants that have been extracted from the ambient flux of stimulus energy and displayed as a frozen array. Table 6.2 re-constructs, albeit in schematic form, the transformations that are involved as the original classroom auditory events are recontextualized by the texts on the left and right pages in Appendix IVa and Appendix IVb, respectively.

The processes of abstraction and generalization of the original sound acts and sound events in the classroom environment mean that the child is using other semiotic modalities (depiction, graphology, language) to make the sounds selected the object of conscious attention and re-coding. In so doing, the child's attention is drawn to the acoustic and contextual properties of specific sounds, as well as to their meanings and values in these contexts. In this way, the child is made aware of the potential for sound to be a semiotic resource, rather than mere noise in the physical environment (see Van Leeuwen 1999: 1–9). Both the visual and linguistic re-contextualizations of these sounds and their performance by the child, as her own sound acts, are all ways of semiotically re-constituting the original sound events in a variety of different semiotic modes that afford possibilities for abstraction and for re-envoicement in her own voice.

Abstraction involves classification, categorization, and schematization such that sound events can be understood and reflected on. Re-envoicement means that the sound events can be assimilated to the child's own embodied perspectives and produced as sound acts of the child's own body, rather than being experienced as extra-somatic events "in" the environment of the child. Her choice of a hybrid situation exhibiting characteristics of both the classroom and the concert performance before a live audience illustrates the child's efforts to create activities in which the sounds themselves are tools for action and reflection in relation to activities that the child herself creates in the processes of making the sounds meaningful to her.

Table 6.2 Multimodal recontextualizations of original auditory event, showing principles of recontextualization and the shifts in experiential focus that each recontextualization entails

Attention parameters	Nature of phenomenon attended to	Experiential focus	Perceptual-semiotic modality
Object			
original sound event in classroom	ambient array of environmental stimulus energy	auditory event [+ source of sound]	multimodal time-bound perceptual event in classroom environment
depiction on left-hand page	frozen array of arrested visual and optical variants traced on left page	Participant as Performer/Causer (visual)+Process (script)	multimodal text based on sensori-motor representations and their classification according to visual-linguistic principles
presentation in table on right-hand page	nominal group as name of phenomenon in table	Participant-as-Thing + Process as post-qualifier or quality of Process	multimodal text in which abstract principles of linguistic naming and classification are integrated to the visual semiotics of the table

5 The school copy book as semiotic-material artifact

The copy book is a manufactured artifact that is important to the overall meaning-making process for a number of different, though interrelated, reasons. First, it affords the preparation of the page as a treated surface on which graphic traces can be permanently recorded with the use of a suitable tracing tool such as a pen, pencil, or crayon. Secondly, the portability of the copy book means that it can be carried from one location to another (e.g. from school to home). Thirdly, it can be used in various ways – added to, consulted, read, revised, and so on – over time such that it affords the integration of activities on different timescales. Fifthly, the portability of the copy book goes hand in hand with its size as an object that is readily integrated both to the embodied activities of the child such that it affords easy physical manipulation and integration to particular architectural features of the classroom and home environments (e.g. placing the copy book on a desk or classroom bench for the purposes of working with it, turning the pages, holding it in one's hands, and so on).

The material page is much more than a physical medium. Rather, the page plays an important mediating role in a number of different ways. The material page mediates the following activities:

1. the child's act of tracing visual invariants onto the page, therefore the relationship between the act of tracing, involving hand-arm-joint-eye kinaesthesis (Gibson 1986 [1979]: 275), and the visual invariants that he or she traces onto the page;
2. the possibility of transporting visual-graphic traces from place to place;
3. the possibility of accessing the visual-graphic traces over time;
4. engaging in shared classroom activities involving the teacher and other pupils on the basis of a shared stock of visual-graphic traces;
5. the visual scanning of the visual traces and hence the correct bodily orientation towards the page;

6.   the possibility of re-enacting or performing the visual traces as vocalizations;
7.   the possible syntagmatic arrangement of visual traces and therefore possible ways of tracing in terms of factors such as the top-bottom and the left-right spatial organization of the page; it also affords possibilities for the local bunching of items, the spreading of items, the spatial juxtaposition of items (e.g. images and script items), and so on;
8.   in relation to 7 (above), the page therefore specifies possible ways in which spatially juxtaposed and organized items are to be visually scanned, read, or otherwise interpreted;
9.   the "installation" (Harris 2001 [2000]: 85–88) of visual-graphic traces as potential signs that can be integrated to activities of one kind or another and therefore contextualized as meaningful;
10.   the cross-modal integration of scripts of various kinds, including written language, with visual images (drawings, photographs, tables, graphs, diagrams, and so on) on the basis of the visual-graphic and spatial characteristics of both the visual traces and the spatial character of the page as their material support;
11.   the construction of reading paths in and through which aspects of the visual-graphic traces and their particular spatial arrangements on the page can be contextualized as time-bound meaning-making activity.

The page as material artifact of particular manufacturing processes therefore affords the integration of visual-graphic traces with various kinds of activity. It is in and through such contextualizing activity that these traces are made into signs. Independently of such activities, these traces are potential sign-making material, rather than being fully contextualized signs. The traces afford sign-making; they are not signs as such. The traces become signs when the semiotic-information potential of these lower-scalar physical marks is integrated to and reorganized by higher-scalar semiotic processes and relations in and through some contextualizing activity (see chapter 9, sections 1, 3).

6 Sound events and sound acts

Sound events in a busy and noisy classroom environment often overlap and compete with each other. In her copy book, the child classifies various sounds in relation to the events that produce these sounds. This classification creates knowledge and expectations about environmental events, their sources and the sounds produced and their acoustic properties in the given environment (Handel 1989: 209). Some of these sound events are produced by extra-somatic physical events (e.g. the slamming door); others are produced by human vocal articulation (e.g. the teacher's "ssss"); still others are produced by the actions of some part of the human body (e.g. the sounds of shoes on the floor as someone walks). In all the examples depicted in the child's copy book, the sounds are clearly related to the child's embodied experience of the environment that surrounds her. The sounds she refers to do not simply designate a physical environment *per se*. Rather, they are all constitutive elements of the social environment of the classroom. As such, they are meaningful in that context.

The sounds that the child has classified in her copy book are themselves recontextualizations of the sound events and their specific acoustic properties in terms of the visual semiotics of depiction, language, and the typological-graphological conventions for indexing environmental sounds in writing. The child's re-enactment of these environmental sounds with her own voice is itself a further recontextualization, not only of the original sound events that have been experienced and discussed in the classroom activities involving teacher and pupils, but also of their multimodal visual-linguistic representation in the copy book. In the first case, the acoustic properties of the sound events in the classroom are used as a basis for classifying different types of sounds in relation to the environmental events with which they are associated. In the case of the child's re-enactment of these sounds with her own voice, the resulting sounds both index the original environmental events and associated sounds at the same time that they identify the speaker (the child) as the source of the performed sounds, as well as indicating features of her age, sex, and physiology.

The sounds that the child produces do not directly imitate the acoustic properties of the original sound events; rather, they index some of their salient acoustic properties through the use of the voice, along with their contexts of production and reception. Both the drawings in the copy book and the performing of these sounds constitute acts of categorization and classification along different parameters and in relation to the different semiotic modalities used – visual depiction and language in one case; vocalization in the other. The various parameters and modalities have quite different relations to the child's body. In the first case, the child visually scans words and images and integrates them to produce a complex sign about a prior acoustic event in its environmental context. In the second case, the child produces vocalizations that re-enact, as body performances, sounds that are in some cases produced by extra-somatic means (e.g. a door slamming) at the same time that she hears the sounds that she so produces.

The sounds that we perceive in the environment constitute a continuous acoustic stream (Handel 1989: chapter 7). They can, however, be analysed by the ear into a number of different events and their sources (Handel 1989: 182). Listeners construe relationships among different components of the acoustic wave at any given point in time. They also construe relationships among different parts of the wave at different moments in time. The listener's construal of sound events does not mean that listeners will always arrive at the same conclusion as to the true nature of an event or its source. Importantly, the perception of sound events is shaped by subjective perceptual factors, as well as by social conventions and values.

Both the visual-graphological representations of the sound events and sound acts in the child's copy book, as well as her performances of the various sounds, make each of the sounds selected for attention focal in ways that are not necessarily the case in the environment of the classroom. In that environment, sounds overlap; some are more prominent than others, in the foreground, others are in the background, others are somewhere between these two possibilities. In selectively attending to these sounds and in isolating them from the acoustic environment in which they occur, the child is making them the focus of interest in ways that are not necessarily the case when they are heard in their original environment.

The sounds are also contextualized in terms of a range of social meanings and values that they have in the context of the sources of their production and their reception in the classroom. Moreover, the environmental sounds that the child vocalizes in her own performance are integrated to the rhythmic characteristics of that performance. Thus, extra-somatic sounds, as well as those produced by others (the teacher or fellow classmates), are recontextualized in terms of the rhythms generated by her own performance. These rhythms emerge from the body of the person such that events on very different timescales are integrated to the rhythms of the child's body. Rhythm involves movement, regularity, the grouping of weaker elements with stronger elements to produce groups of elements, and timing. The natural rhythms of the body are modulated by rhythms that derive from specific genres of song and speech performance on different scalar levels, including the rhythms of the whole activities in which these take place.

The rhythms of the child also indicate the extent to which she is emotionally integrated to the particular *habitus* of bodily dispositions that characterize the various contexts that she engages with in the episode. The child's rhythms, intonations, and tones of voice tell us a great deal concerning her positive involvement in the activities, rather than, for example, a detached or faltering one. In this way, we can gauge her emotional or affective connectedness to the social activities and contexts as well as to the meanings that are made in these. In other words, she exhibits a high degree of what Scheff (1997: 171) calls emotional "attunement" to the feelings that bond individuals to each other in particular forms of social organization and social relations. This form of connectedness is the most fundamental form of social bond and is the basis of the dyads that connect mother and infant in early infant semiosis (see chapter 3).

7 Written script and vocal performance

In the child's drawings in Appendix IVa, the child has inserted written sequences such as "CI!!CICEECI!!", "SSSS!!", "SBAM. BABAM", "SDENDEDEN", "TACTACTAC", "FFFFEE", "FSCI FSCI", "DRIIIIIIIIN!!", "LA, LA, LAL!", "SGRR!!", and "SCLAC!" to indicate the sounds that are associated with each of the pictures. She invents or utilizes a script that uses the familiar notation of the Italian alphabet. However, the script items that she creates are integrated to the evocation (indexing) of non-linguistic sound events and sound acts, rather than to familiar linguistic items such as words, sentences, and so on, in Italian. The environmental sounds so evoked, the written script items, and their vocal performance are all closely integrated activities.

The environmental sounds and their vocal re-enactment influence the way they are written as script items at the same time that the way they are written influences the way they are vocalized by the child. The script assimilates some of the principles of alphabetic writing at the same time that none of the items, as I mentioned above, are words of Italian or any other language. Other features of this script include the use of punctuation marks such as the exclamation mark, the comma, and the full-stop. The repetition both of individual letters (e.g. I in DRIIIIIIIN) or letter clusters (e.g. TACTACTAC) is also functional in this script. Spacing between clusters (e.g. FSCI FSCI) and the local bunching of repeated notational items such as letters to form a single cluster (e.g. SSSS or FFFFEE) are also featured. The written script, which makes use of familiar notational items, nevertheless has a distinctive and effective visual organization.

By the same token, the script also provides cues concerning its vocal performance. These performance cues to some extent draw on the practices for integrating writing with spoken Italian. The phonology of standard Italian provides the template for their pronunciation following the models for Italian phonemes and syllables. Other features of the script signal a continuous, unbroken sound with a constant dynamic range (SSSS!!); the lengthening of a particular sound (e.g. IIIIIII in the item DRIIIIIIIN); a pause or a break in the sound flow (e.g. SBAM. BABAM); or the rapid, uninterrupted repetition of the same sequence of sounds (e.g. TACTACTAC).

These examples show that graphical-visual differences in the written script can be integrated to the practices of the oral performance of the script and therefore to the practices of performing phonic differences that are meaningful in the vocal performance. For example, the local bunching of the same graphic item in SSSS specifies the continuous nature of the sound to be produced. On the other hand, LA, LA, LAL! specifies the rhythmic patterning of this sequence as a potential group of sound items in which the third item is lengthened and emphasized as the strong or salient member of this rhythmic group.

The script items produced by the child are written signs. Their nearest intertextual analogue as script items are the visual-graphic items that are used to index particular sounds and sound effects in comic strips. Like their comic strip analogues, they are integrated with visual images in ways that further specify their meaning in relation to the scenes depicted in their respective images. In both cases, there is a cross-modal tie with the source of the sound which is evoked by the script item in some aspect of the visual image. For example, SSSS!! is placed in a speech balloon and therefore indicated as a projected vocalization of the teacher. This item is the only script item which is placed in a speech balloon even though some of the other sounds that the script items relate to are clearly the products of human vocal activity (e.g. CI!!CICECI!! BLA!BLA! to indicate everyone – pupils and teacher – all talking together). The distinction may be explained by the fact that the teacher's SSSS!! is the voice of authority in the classroom: it is a vocalization that seeks to discipline and impose silence on the class. For this reason, it is uniquely sourced at the teacher as a kind of quasi-speech act in a way that the cacophony of indistinct vocal sounds evoked by CI!!CICECI!! BLA!BLA! is not.

The discussion in this section shows that the script items provide indications as to how a given item can be integrated to segmental features such as syllables – vowels and consonants – of Italian phonology and to specific features of voice dynamics such as loudness, duration of segments, rhythm, tempo, and so on. By the same token, the script items cannot be integrated to lexicogrammatical units and structures of the Italian language. The script items are not linguistic items, although they exhibit some language-like properties in their visual-graphic organization. Moreover, their spoken forms exhibit some language-like properties insofar as they have segmental features such as syllables. Nevertheless, the fact that both segmental features and features of voice dynamics can be uncoupled from language, as well as being uncoupled from each other and then re-coupled in different ways according to the different kinds of activities to which these features are integrated, suggests that the speaking voice – not necessarily spoken language as such – is decomposable into a number of distinct sound modalities.

Moreover, spoken language is an activity which combines and integrates these modalities in language-specific, genre-specific, and performance-specific ways. At the same time, these same modalities can be combined and integrated in other ways, in other activities, to give rise to sound performances of the human voice such as the one recorded here, which is not linguistic. The vocal tract activity of the human voice is not therefore the source of a single sound modality. Rather, it affords the multimodal integration of a diversity of sound modalities according to the activities on other semiotic scales with which vocal tract activity is integrated and which, in turn, modulate the activity of the vocal tract.

8 The activity-dependent nature of the contextualization of the written script

In the present example, the visual-graphic traces are potentially able to be contextualized as signs in and through the following activities:

1. silent reading;
2. linking the script items to familiar environmental sounds and correlated situations;
3. linking the script items to the depicted scene in the corresponding picture and therefore relating the script item to the participants and situations depicted, including the source of the sound event or sound act;
4. linking the script items and the sounds they potentially evoke to the linguistic items in the table on the second page and hence to the principles of classification and evaluation that the table expresses;
5. the partial integration of the graphic differences in the script to phonetic differences in spoken Italian, as well as to phonic differences that pertain to non-linguistic vocalizations;
6. the re-envoicing of the script items and other features of the copy book (song, language) as embodied vocal performance.

The activities listed above can be interrelated to each other in many possible ways as parts – often simultaneous – of more complex activities which require the integration of different activities. In producing meaningful signs in and through her activity, the child integrates her own embodied here-now activity of visual scanning and reading aloud with other activities and other participants across diverse space-time scales. The above considerations should make it clear that I do not assume there is any sort of original relation between a given script item and the sound event in its physical-acoustic environment. Instead, there is a process of activity-dependent recontextualization across different domains and practices. This process may be schematized as follows as one which can go in any number of different directions, as suggested by the two-way arrows:

CLASSROOM SOUNDS ↔ DISCUSSION OF CLASSROOM SOUNDS IN CLASS ↔ DRAWING AND WRITING ABOUT SOUNDS IN COPY BOOK ↔ CONTEMPLATION AND REFLECTION ON THESE IN SILENT READING AND SCANNING ↔ RE-ENVOICEMENT AS EMBODIED VOCAL PERFORMANCE

Now, the environmental sounds that are heard in the classroom exhibit a wide range of acoustic properties at the same time that they emanate from a variety of different sources. Moreover, these sounds, like speech sounds, are experienced as a continuous acoustic stream with a particular duration (Handel 1989: 185–190). Nevertheless, the use of the child's graphic script to evoke or to index particular sounds in the classroom environment, as well as to afford their possibilities of performance, says a lot about the way that written scripts based on alphabetic principles reshape our conceptualization of sound itself.

Vygotsky points out that writing requires the child to take a more deliberate, conscious, and analytical view of speech. Writing requires the child to "take cognizance of the sound structure of each word, dissect it, and reproduce it in alphabetical symbols, which he must have studied and memorized before" (Vygotsky 1986 [1934]: 181–182). Olson (1995) and Harris (2001 [2000]: 207–209) likewise point out that alphabetic writing systems, far from being a record or a representation of speech, as in the orthodox and generally accepted account, provide a means of shaping our understanding of speech. Thus, it is alphabetic writing in this account which provides the conceptual models for thinking about the continuous stream of speech sounds as consisting of discrete linguistic units such as words (Harris 2001 [2000]: 208). We can adapt this way of thinking to the child's script.

For example, the visual-graphic sequence SSSS!! consists of the repetition of the same discrete element – the graphic item "S" – along with the two uses of the exclamation mark. The combination of these discrete items in the sequence produces a larger-scale discrete visual-graphic unit, viz. SSSS!! This visual-graphic sequence therefore treats the sound as a discrete unit in contrast with other discrete units. In the acoustic environment of the classroom, the sounds that one hears are, as I pointed out before, a continuous stream that can, however, be parsed by the ear as different sounds produced by different sources. Here, we see how the child's script, which derives from the alphabetic script, provides a model for thinking about sounds as discrete entextualized entities that can be contemplated as visual-graphic objects at the same time that they can be used as a script for the purposes of their vocal performance.

Both the visual-graphic unit and the teacher's vocalization are, when appropriately contextualized, signs. In the graphic sequence SSSS!!, the repetition of S in the sequence is iconic of the continuous and lengthened nature of the sound over the time in which it is vocalized, rather than the continuous repetition of the same sound. The placing of the two exclamation marks at the end of the sequence may serve as both a marker of emphasis or of force at the same time that it indicates the imperative status of the vocalization as one which the teacher uses to impose silence on the class.

If this visual-graphic unit is integrated with its vocalization, then the unvoiced sound [s] can be seen to evoke the idea of silence or stillness. The very quiet release of air that characterizes the vocalization of this sound is therefore iconic to the action of requiring the members of the class to be silent. This shows how the act of producing a given sign, in this case by modulating the vocal tract to produce the unvoiced [s], is iconic to the process of acting on others. Thus, doing things to the voice semiotically mediates doing things to others.

In the sequence TACTACTAC, the repetition of the letter cluster TAC without spacing between each cluster again produces an integrated visual-graphic unit. In this case, the indexed sound is treated as a discrete unit that can be segmented into three occurrences of the smaller segment TAC, itself seen as a discrete unit. Again, the written script and its alphabetic notation impose a particular interpretation on the acoustic signal. This interpretation has little or nothing to do with the stream of acoustic energy as such. Rather, the written script proposes units of analysis on various levels – individual script item (T), clusters of these (TAC), and the whole sequence – that depend on a particular interpretation of the script as visual-graphic unit. The units of analysis proposed by the script therefore suggest different levels of the event and possible ways of attending to these levels.

9 The phonetic characteristics of the sounds

As a sound sequence, TAC is transcribed in phonetic notation as [tak]. The sound [t] is an unvoiced plosive. The sudden release of the air stream that is characteristic of plosives, along with the unvoiced quality of this sound, expresses the abrupt nature of the sound in question. At the same time, its unvoiced quality indicates that the sound in question is not loud and intrusive, but soft and unobtrusive. The sound [a] has the features [open] and [back]. The mouth and oral cavity are relatively open at the same time that the sound is produced back in the mouth. This sound therefore yields properties of largeness and distance. The final sound in this sequence [k] is an unvoiced plosive that is produced in the back of the mouth in contrast to the middle position of [t] at the beginning of this sequence. This movement from middle to back position is iconic to the sound going farther away from the listener. It therefore implies the listener's perspective on the sound event and its source, i.e. the sound metaphorically construes the person as walking away from the listener. To sum up, we could say that the explosiveness of [tak] is abrupt or sharp at the same time that it is receding away from the listener. The repetition of TAC suggests the regular, periodic sequence of stronger and weaker beats – the metre – of this sound.

The visual-graphic unit DRIIIIIIIIN!! is yet another visual-graphic unit like those already considered. In this case, the repetition of the graphic unit "I" is iconic to the duration of the indexed sound, suggesting the lengthening of the sound. The two exclamation marks again suggest emphasis and force.

Phonetically, the sound is represented as follows: [drɪn]. The sound [d] is a voiced plosive. As we saw above, voiced plosives are sudden, abrupt sounds. The feature [voiced] places the sound on the loud end of the loud-soft continuum. The sound [r] is a kind of semi-fricative. It involves constriction of the air stream as well as friction, as the air passes through the constricted space of the oral cavity and mouth when it is released. The combination of [d] with [r] at the beginning of this sound therefore indicates a loud abrupt sound, which has a grating quality. The sound [ɪ] has the features [frontal], [high], and [closed]. The sound is produced in the front of the mouth. This feature can suggest proximity to the listener. The feature [high] can suggest height. The feature [closed] suggests smallness. Such a sound is sensed as close to the speaker, as well as being sharp and intrusive. Finally, the sound [n] has the features [voiced], [nasal], and [resonant]. The oral cavity captures the sound and allows it to resonate within its confines, rather than be expelled outside the mouth. Overall, the sound [drɪn] combines all of these qualities to produce the acoustic effect that probably needs no further elaboration here.

All of the examples discussed above, as well as the others in the child's copy book, show a complex relationship between the visual-graphic unit, the environmental sound that is indexed, and the vocalization that the child produces in her performance. Following Harris (2001 [2000]: 91–92), we can say that features of a particular notation (the letters) get integrated to a script in the activity of producing the visual-graphic units in question. These units mediate potential relations that can be constructed through other activities that integrate the visual-graphic sequence to the given environmental sound or to its performance as a vocalization. This integration can be schematized as follows:

ENVIRONMENTAL SOUND ↔ VISUAL-GRAPHIC UNIT ↔ VOCALIZATION

In so doing, visual-graphic units such as SSSS!!, DRIIIIIIIIN!!, and so on, raise important and interesting questions in connection with both sound and visual-graphic units as meaning-making resources, as well as for the cross-modal relations between them. As Olson and Harris have argued, the written word brought about a major change in our ways of thinking about spoken language such that speaking came to be modelled on writing. This observation obviously has important implications for our conceptions of literacy, especially for the kind of multimodal literacy that is at issue in the text and its performance that I have been considering here.

What kind of literacy might be at stake here? With respect to the visual-graphic units under consideration here, I would single out the following ways in which these units enable the child to orient to and to conceptualize the environmental (classroom) sounds that she has attended to, as follows:

1.   the listener learns to attend to acoustic phenomena in her environment and to parse these into distinct events that are propagated from a given source that can be identified and classified by, for example, visual or linguistic means;
2.   the listener is induced to consider the environmental sound as a phenomenon that can be de-located from its physical context and considered as a discrete unit or sequence of discrete units on analogy with alphabetic writing;
3.   visual-graphic units such as DRIIIIIIIIN!! are scripts that provide indications as to how the reading of the script can be integrated to its performance as a vocalization;
4.   features of a particular notation consisting of letters and punctuation signs are integrated

to a script for the production of visual-graphic units that can serve to index specific sounds;

5.   visual-graphical units like SSSS!! and DRIIIIIIIIN!! are a form of writing that can be integrated to the semiotics of visual depiction in order to specify a sound that is sourced at one or more of the depicted participants in the visual scene.

10 Meaning, text, and performance

The written text – the child's copy book – is a record of a prior set of discursive events which took place in the classroom activities involving teacher and pupils. It is a recontextualization in words and images of some set of classroom events. The copy book is a recontextualization of speaking turns, textual voices (in Bakhtin's sense), and of genres of action and interaction. The child's performance in her bedroom is, in turn, a new, situationally contingent recontextualization of the textual records which she has previously produced; it is an activation and orchestration of diverse material and semiotic resources in order to enact a performance event. This process necessarily involves the child's selective re-envoicing of some aspects of the "original" event.

Meaning-making in vocal performance is also achieved in and through and channelled by the graphological-visual, lexicogrammatical, and discourse levels of a written text. The reader, in interpreting the written text, discovers, through the use of her voice, that dimension of the grammar which no grammar has been able to explain adequately, i.e. grammar as a labile instrument of discourse organization and of the distribution of meaning.

For the young child, reading aloud is an important resource available to him or her for becoming aware of the organizational powers of rhythm. The reading aloud of a text is not *the* rhythm of a text; nor is it its mere reproduction. Rather, it is one of the possible enactments of the rhythm of the text. The reading aloud of a text requires the reader's active interpretation. In the process, the text becomes his or hers: reading aloud is itself a process of re-envoicement, rather than one of mechanical reproduction. The reader uses the resources of the voice to produce a discourse meaning which is reflexively connected to and embodied in one's self. It is the point of contact between language, discourse, and the embodied subjectivity/agency of the reader. Reading aloud, in this sense, places the child in the condition necessary for the development of his or her autonomy with respect to the organization of discourse. What resources does the voice have for making meaning and for transforming rhythm into embodied performance? These resources include: characteristics of timbre; the search for pauses; the exploitation of timbre; the placing of stress; and the selection of a melodic contour.

Moreover, there is a relationship between the performance of a given reading and the graphic-visual, lexicogrammatical, and discourse levels of organization of the written text. These resources include: visual-graphic script organization; spatial layout; paragraphs; punctuation; and the integration of visual images with language. Aside from the units and structures on various levels of organization that are "given" by the text, there are also those that the reader imposes interpretatively. The reader *qua* performer recognizes and interprets the dynamic relations between lexicogrammatical units and relations. In the process, he or she "feels" dynamic links and forces which are "cemented" together in the temporal flow of the discourse in his or her performance. Moreover, the rhythms and prosodies of the spoken voice constitute a dynamic energy, which is experienced as a moving force whenever a linguistic unit is uttered. The spoken performance – the giving voice to a linguistic form – is also a dynamic relationship between this performance energy and (1) the other layers of meaning which are configured in the text and (2) the embodied agency of the performer in relation to his or her audience. Meaning-making has a material and sensual quality in this sense.

The materiality of the meaning-making performance can be explained by the relations between the energy of the performance and its materiality. This energy has directional vectors which extend beyond the utterance (and the speaker) and into the ecosocial environment, in the process producing a resonating density of significance. This energy, in order to be effective and not merely redundant and "empty", must be brought under control; it must be effectively harnessed and synchronized with (1) the other dimensions of the utterance's meaning potential; and (2) with the bodily dispositions and *habitus* of the participants in the performance.

Sound is a mode of literacy (Van Leeuwen 1999). It involves the child in processes of both listening and learning to listen to, describing and classifying, and of performing selected sounds. The child's performance shows that not all societies and not all individuals within a given society have the same orientation towards the dominant literacy – writing. In the present example, there is an orientation to and an exploration of aurality: bodily pleasure and desire are not excluded.

From this point of view, the child's copy book text is not a record of a merely individual performance, but of a collective one. It is a discursive map of a classroom literacy event. The copy book is itself a re-envoicement in other semiotic modalities of this event. By the same token, as we have seen, this textual record also affords the child's bodily performance of the episode which I have analysed in this chapter. The performance tests the child's variable cap-acity to give adequate voice to specific agent positions and the material and semiotic resources that such positions command. I pointed out in this regard the difficulty the child had in her attempt to re-envoice the teacher's voice of interrogation (section 3 above). The voice of the teacher is a monitoring and controlling voice. The teacher is the one who interrogates and watches over the class, as well as being the agent who is invested with the moral authority to do so. The child's attempts to re-envoice such positions are very often far from intellectualistic; they also involve the child's watching and listening, moving and staying still, speaking, be spoken to, and being silent and, more generally, of entraining, in and through their activity, their own bodily dynamics to the larger-scale dynamics of an entire *habitus* of bodily dispositions and practices.

11 Sound metaphor

Vocalizations such as [drɪn] are sound metaphors. A given auditory event and the source that produced it in its environment and a given vocal tract gesture of the kind involved in the articulation of [drɪn] are mapped on to each other as a complex metaphorical structure in which the two domains – auditory event and vocal tract activity – are hybridized. Thus, vocal tract activity uses the topological resources of the vocal tract to map meaningful sounds in the environment of the listener onto the listener's vocal tract gestural activity. In the case of [drɪn], the environmental sound of a school bell ringing has been mapped onto a particular configur-ation of vocal tract activity to yield an instance of a sound metaphor.

Sound metaphor thus involves the re-articulation of a sound event in one domain – in the listener's environment – in terms of another domain, viz. the oral cavity and the vocal tract activity that is associated with it in the production of speech sounds. As in all cases of meta-phor, the resulting metaphor is a hybrid phenomenon in which two different domains are combined or mapped, the one onto the other. The resulting combination of the two domains gives rise to a complex meaning that cannot be reduced to the mere sum of the two domains that were combined to produce the metaphor. Clearly, both the environmental sound and the vocalization have their own distinctive properties: the one cannot be reduced to the other. The metaphorical meaning of the vocalization is schematized in Figure 6.2.

The articulation of speech sounds occurs in the oral cavity as a result of vocal tract gestural activity. Terms such as [open], [closed], [voiced], [unvoiced], [plosive], and so on, are systemic values which correspond to particular regions within this space. The combination of a number of terms, e.g. [frontal], [high], and [closed] in the vowel [ɪ], is an articulatory region that is specified in terms of a number of intersecting dimensions in the overall topological space of the system of sounds of a given language. A system of this kind is the phonology of a given language. Thus, the phonological values that intersect in [ɪ] define [ɪ] as a particular articula-tory region, along a number of different parameters such as those mentioned above. These phonological values are congruently related to particular positions in the vocal tract.

Environmental sounds such as the sound of a school bell ringing or the sound of someone's shoes as the person walks across a hard surface belong to distinct classes of identifiable sounds.

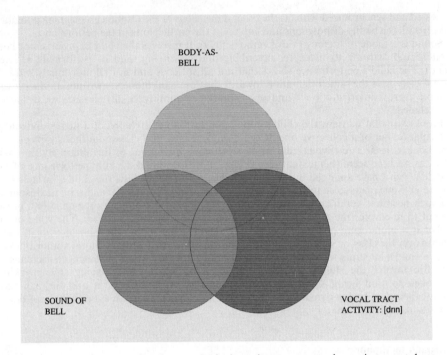

Figure 6.2 Sound metaphor showing topological continuum among the environmental acoustic event, articulatory (vocal tract) activity, and vocalization

For example, there are classes of sound that pertain to mechanical actions, the flow of liquids, the sound of solids scraping or rubbing against each other, gaseous flows and emissions, paper, wood, metal, electronic devices, tools, actions of various kinds, and so on (see Gibson 1983 [1966]: 89). Moreover, the vibratory events (the sounds) that the listener picks up enable the listener to identify the source of the sound – the mechanical disturbance – that produced the sound event (Gibson 1983 [1966]: 89). Environmental sounds are meaningful to the observer in relation to the environmental events that they enable the listener to identify, orient to, and respond to. Gibson points out that the meaningful sounds in the listener's environment vary in much more complex ways than in duration, pitch, loudness, and volume (Gibson 1983 [1966]: 87). Gibson comments as follows:

> Instead of simple pitch, they [meaningful sounds, PJT] vary in timbre or tone quality, in combinations of tone quality, in vowel quality, in approximation to noise, in noise quality, and in changes of all these in time. Instead of simple loudness, they vary in the direction of *change* of loudness. In meaningful sounds, these variables can be combined to yield higher-order variables of staggering complexity.
>
> (Gibson 1983 [1966]: 87; italics in original)

Sound is potential stimulus information that can function for the listener to specify or provide information about environmental events. However, the information in the vibratory event does not consist of pure tones, simple duration, or simple loudness. These are abstractions; they do not provide information about ecological events (Gibson 1983 [1966]: 87). To quote Gibson:

> It is the pattern of the relative intensities of the different frequencies that are harmonics (i.e. whole multiples) of the fundamental frequency. The spectrum has to be sustained for some time interval to be realized, of course, but it is not a tone. It should be thought of as a

relational pattern, a configuration, not as a set of absolute frequencies, for the pattern is *transposable* with a shift of absolute frequencies. This fact is demonstrated in music by the equivalence of chords with a shift in key, and in speech by the equivalence of vowel qualities with a shift from male to female voice. The information in a sound spectrum seems to be given by the frequency ratios, not by the frequencies as such.

(Gibson 1983 [1966]: 87–89; italics in original)

The human ear evolved to pick up relational patterns of frequencies, rather than pure tones, and to distinguish different patterns. The relational patterns of frequencies that characterize and identify a school bell ringing specify acoustic invariants that are characteristic of that event or class of event and its source. The listener picks up and responds to an auditory array – a set of invariants that specify an event and its source – rather than acoustic energy. In learning to attend to and to discriminate features in the array, the listener can also learn how to transpose or to transcategorize them to some other domain (Halliday and Matthiessen 1999: 242). Trans-categorization from one domain to some other is important to the present discussion for the following reason. According to Halliday and Matthiessen, transcategorization is a feature of the grammar of every language. In the grammar, transcategorization involves the transfer of an item from one grammatical class to another, e.g. *snake* (noun) → *snake* (verb).

In my view, transcategorization can also apply to sound events. Thus, a given class of environmental event such as a school bell ringing can be transposed to a given class of articulatory event such as the vocalization [drɪn]. Transcategorization of this kind means that certain acoustic invariants of the environmental event are attended to and extracted from the auditory array and then transferred to and re-articulated by the different resources of the vocal tract. This process is not copying or imitation because the process of metaphorical transcategorization involves the shifting of auditory invariants from one class of auditory event (environmental) to another (articulatory).

In the case of [drɪn], a mechanical event and the auditory invariants associated with that event are transcategorized as an articulatory event and its invariants. Metaphorically, a given environmental event or class of event is treated as an entextualized sign when it is transcategorized as a vocalization. The vocal tract has constructed a semiotic object by transcategorizing auditory invariants such as direction of change of loudness, rate of change of loudness, abruptness of beginning and end, rate, rhythm, sequencing, timbre, combinations of tone quality, and so on, of the environmental event into articulatory invariants such as those already mentioned in the analysis of [drɪn] above.

We saw earlier that particular sounds such as [ɪ], [d], and so on, can be described as packets of features. Particular features such as [frontal] or [closed] in the sound [ɪ] were seen to have metaphorical potential. Thus,

(a) [frontal] → proximity   or   (b) [closed] → smallness

Frontal vowels are pronounced forward in the mouth, with the highest point of the tongue lying beneath the hard palate (Abercrombie 1967: 68; Van Leeuwen 1999: 146–147). Vowels with the feature [close] are pronounced with mouth closed or nearly so and the oral cavity correspondingly reduced in size (Van Leeuwen 1999: 147). In (a), the phonetic value [frontal] has been mapped onto the spatial domain of proximity. In (b), the phonetic value [closed] has been mapped onto the domain of physical size. Phonetic values are, of course, pure abstractions. They do not occur on their own as particular sounds. Instead, they specify particular parameters of articulation in conjunction with other parameters such as those that instantiate the schematic (phonemic) category [ɪ].

Table 6.3 shows some aspects of the relationships between the congruent and metaphorical domains of sound events.

Environmental events constitute the congruent domain because of their derivational priority (Halliday and Matthiessen 1999: 235). Environmental events such as school bells ringing and the sounds of shoes impacting against the floor inspire the vocalizations that derive from them, rather than the other way round. Environmental events are also congruent with respect to the

Table 6.3 The transcategorization of the congruent domain of environmental events to the metaphorical domain of articulatory events (gestures)

Congruent domain	Metaphorical domain
informational invariants of environmental events in various domains, e.g. spatial, auditory, visual invariants	articulatory/phonetic features, e.g. [plosive], [frontal], [voiced]
components (of environmental events)	specific speech sounds, e.g. [d], [s], [ɪ]
environmental events + source, e.g. school bell ringing	vocalization, e.g. [drɪn]

relationship between the vibratory event and its source. Thus, the sounds made by the various classes of mechanical action, for example, specify their sources, usually without too much confusion or ambiguity, although errors in judgement can and do occur. In such cases, the environmental (vibratory) event and the information it specifies for the listener is congruently related to its source.

In the case of vocalizations such as [drɪn], the environmental event, to be sure, specifies the speaker as the source of the vocalization. However, the metaphorical transcategorization or mapping across domains is not about the relationship between speaker and vocalization, but about the relationship between the environmental event that inspires the vocalization and the information that the vocalization specifies both about that class of event and about the act of articulation itself. Obviously, vocalizations such as [drɪn] specify schematic informational invariants of the environmental event that inspires them, rather than the acoustic details of such events.

The metaphorical power of the vocalization lies in the way it brings together these two previously disjunctive domains. Thus, environmental events in ecosocial space-time beyond the body are re-conceptualized and re-enacted within the very different space-time of the oral cavity and its dynamics within the body. It is in this way that the resulting vocalizations are introjected into the ecosocial context as semiotic acts that can be sourced at the body of the speaker at the same time that they construe links between the speaker's body and the given class of extra-somatic environmental event. In this way, children learn how to re-envoice extra-somatic environmental events as meaningful acts that extend from the individual body-brain system back into the environment at the same time that they are sourced at and evaluated within the perspectives of the selves who are implicated in the dialogic act of their re-envoicement as meaning.

12 Agency, individuation, and self-organization: body dynamics, action, and the building up of viewpoints in the perspective of the self

Agents, as self-organizing systems, build up categories of action performances, letting each occasion make its mark so that they can individuate even as they progressively narrow the scope of their possibilities in the course of their further development. This is not, of course, the same as being merely battered into shape by external forces. Such a view would exclude criteria of internal complexity and agentive determinability. In the process of collecting feedback from its own participation in action performances, the self comes more clearly into focus.

The three-level scalar hierarchy view (chapter 1, section 4) shows us that the focal level L of individual participation dynamics is made possible by lower-level L–1 resources and affordances – the body, rhythm, posture, movement, and so on, – at the same time that these are governed by higher-order boundary conditions on level L+1 such as the overall organization of the activity. Lower-level bodily processes of the individual do not regulate the higher-order formations. They do not even interpret these. Rather, they are embedded in and entrained by a higher-order system of meaning-making practices. The micro-level resource systems and their deployments must necessarily be interpreted at the level of the macro-systemic perspectives of participants. The micro-level realization systems of action do not in themselves have viewpoints.

Indeed, the term viewpoint is, in some ways, misleading. It implies a fixed point of observation in space-time. In action, on the other hand, a viewpoint implies a vector. It cannot be relegated to a fixed point source. This is so because there can be no privileged point through which any single micro-level system, seen in isolation, moves. Rather, the notions of meaningful variety and point of view can only be built up on the basis of multiple contextual redundancies across the various multimodal systems that are co-deployed along the entire space-time trajectory of the action performance. Their effect is always multiplicative, rather than linear and additive (Bateson 1973d [1972]: 319–320; Lemke 1998a). A point of view always entails a dynamic trajectory in the space-time of the particular action performance. The meanings that have been elaborated in the perspective of the self flow into and modulate the action all along its trajectory. It is in this sense that a "viewpoint" is more correctly seen as a vector. For example, particular interpersonal orientations – evaluative stances, modalizations, and so on *qua* the expression of particular viewpoints in discourse – are vectors which have their source in the perspective of the self and which flow into and modify or modulate action from that perspective.

An action performance is a semiotically delimited domain of space-time, which the action models through specific cross-couplings of semiotic-discursive and physical-material resources. In some ways, the logic of scalar hierarchies places us in a dilemma. How can individual participants regulate action formations, with their higher-order boundary conditions and constraints? The point is that individual participants selectively construe locally constrained environmental information as meaningful or semiotically salient to the action performance itself. The sources of this information include the other (nonself), the material environment, and so on. Self and other – the participants, indifferently human and nonhuman – provide potential information about how the interaction may develop and unfold in space-time. That is, participants in their own bodily and other resources embody information which is potentially semiotically salient. The making available of information in this way is not in itself interpretation (meaning-making), but it provides a basis for enacting and interpreting action, both locally and globally. The semiotic affordances of the body, the material environment, and so on, generate local contributions to the unfolding action. Likewise, the other responds in ways which jointly create the action.

Bodily processes – gesture, posture, movement, voice, rhythm – configure and covary in relation to events in the surrounding *Umwelt*. As such, these cross-modal semiotic configurations together, not separately, work as a model of the world, which generates appropriate courses of action. There can be no reduction from the performing of an action to any of the lower-level processes and principles that are involved. In a given society, there are many different kinds of meaningful activity. These are not all based on the same principles, so there can be no privileged reduction of action to combinations of privileged physical, mental, or other parameters. The category of "performing or participating in a meaningful social activity" is an emergent category, relative to an observer. That is, all of the lower-level principles and processes involved are gathered together by some higher-scalar principle which integrates them as an action performance. This is one good reason as to why criteria for defining action cannot be reduced to the lower-level neurophysiological and other mechanisms of the individual organism, which are among the initiating conditions of an action (see above). Even if action had but one material embodiment in a given culture, there would still be the semiotic properties and viewpoints of an observer-agent, which regulate the physical principles and processes involved.

As seen from the perspective outlined above, sound metaphor arises as a result of the ways in which an embodied observer/interpreter perspective re-construes particular classes of auditory (or other) events in his or her environment from the perspective of the observer's own embodied participation in the world. In this way, the secondness (otherness) which firstness (self) engages with in the world, is mapped onto and hybridized with the perspectives of the self and its possibilities for meaningful action. At the same time, the metaphorical models which the self collects in her own perspective are returned to the environment in and through the self's own cascading activity. In transcategorizing the world in terms of the self's own possibilities for action and meaning, auditory events in the world are mapped onto the perspectives afforded by vocal tract activity. Thus, the self harnesses this activity to adjust to and to re-envoice the world in terms of its own embodied perspectives.

Consider the vowels [u] and [a] in the Italian words *acuto* and *grave* in (76) and (77) in the transcription (Appendix III, Phase 13). In uttering these two words in her performance, the child modifies their pitch patterns, especially the vowel segments in each word, so that the speech melody of these segments is iconic to the sounds of the two musical instruments referred to in her discourse – the flute and the bassoon, respectively. Furthermore, the child, in her performance, accentuates her voice dynamics when uttering these two words in order to high-light this effect. The vowel [u] in *acuto* is characterized by the features [close or high], [back], and [rounded]. The tongue is close to the roof of the mouth or positioned high in the mouth; the main part of the tongue is positioned back in the mouth; and the lips undergo anticipatory rounding as the lips are brought forward during articulation. The word *grave* is characterized by the features [open or low], [back], and [unrounded]. Thus, in [a] the tongue is far from the roof of the mouth; the main part of the tongue is positioned back in the mouth; the lips are unrounded, i.e. pulled back or spread. The combination of features associated with [u] produces more constriction of the vocal tract, whereas [a] is characterized by less constriction. The higher degree of vocal tract constriction, together with the lip rounding, itself a form of constriction, that are associated with [u], mean that tongue, teeth, and lips create a more restricted articula-tory space than is the case with [u]. The information provided by the position of these organs in relation to each other is both haptic and visual.

The haptics of the mouth provide information about the shape of the articulatory space involving the vocal tract and the lips, just as the muscles of the lips also provide movement information about the shape and position of the lips. Thus, there is an equivalence of spatial information provided by the two perceptual modalities – the haptic and the cinesic – concerning the shape of the articulatory space during the articulation of the two vowels. The restricted space that is associated with [u] in contrast to the less restricted space associated with [a] can be mapped onto our haptic experience of the shape of material objects in the external world through haptic exploration with the hand.

Haptic exploration of objects by the hand may or may not be linked with visual information, depending on whether the observer is able to see the object or not. Thus, the restricted articula-tory space is mapped onto our experience of the surfaces of objects with sharp protuberances in contrast to the surfaces of objects which are even or flat, without protuberances. In turn, the vibration modes of the different articulatory positions of the two vowels result in different modes at different relative frequencies in their respective auditory events. The pick up of this auditory information about the different frequencies of the vibration modes, along with correl-ated visual inputs from observing the speaker's lip movements, gives rise to the perception of sounds which are "sharp" in contrast to sounds which are "flat" on analogy with the sharpness or the flatness of the surfaces of objects, as revealed by haptic exploration.

The resulting analogies across perceptual modalities, along with the cross-modal integration of information from different sources in perception, suggest that perceptual categorization, prior to conceptual and semiotic categorization, already provides a basis for the metaphorical transcategorization of sensori-motor categories before the emergence of conceptual metaphors. Metaphor is quite literally "in the flesh" in ways that provide a basis for more abstract metaphorical structures in conceptual thinking and in language (Lakoff and Johnson 1999).

The processes of metaphorical transcategorization across the different perceptual domains mentioned above may be re-constructed as follows:

(1) haptic/visual information about the degree of protuberance of the surface of an environmental object → (2) haptic/movement information about the degree of restriction of the articulatory space and the shape which this restriction defines in the vocal tract → (3) auditory/visual information about the differences in the vibration modes of different auditory events produced by musical instruments (flute and bassoon) → (4) auditory

information about the differences in the vibration modes of different auditory events deriving from articulation.

The chain of metaphorical transcategorizations from one domain to some other domain shows how perceptual information about an environmental event in (1) is transposed to the domain of the proprioception of one's own vocal tract activity. Proprioception is, in turn, transposed to the perceptual domain of musical events in (3). In turn, (3) is transferred to the domain of auditory events resulting from vocal tract articulation in (4). Thus, the metaphorical movement is from (1) the concrete shape of extra-somatic physical objects to (2) the abstract somatic shape of the articulatory space that is created by the intersection of different parameter values in the oral cavity to (3) the abstract auditory shape of musical sounds to (4) the metaphorical shape of the sounds that are produced by this activity. The reconstruction which I have proposed above is not conceptual, but perceptual. Figure 6.3 illustrates how this process operates across domains (1) and (2).

Edelman's (1989, 1992) theory of reentry provides a way into understanding the nature of the metaphors I have proposed. This understanding is consistent both with the neuroanatom-ical functioning of the brain and the structure and function of metaphorical relations (see also chapter 11, section 3). The notion of reentry in Edelman's theory refers to the interconnections among diverse perceptual and motor sources of stimulus information during the activity of, for example, perceptual exploration. Reentry explains the biological basis of the multimodal cor-relations among diverse information sources arising from different perceptual modalities. For example, the haptic exploration of an object with one's hand involves information from a diversity of sources. These sources include the tactile information that is picked up by the skin about the feel of the object, the movement of the hand as it explores the surface of the information, the visual information that is provided through the visual scanning of the object, and the movements of the eye muscles involved in visual scanning. The perception of an object is a multimodal activity in which stimulus information from diverse sources, activating different groups or populations of neurons in the brain, is correlated during the real-time experiencing of the object. That is, the information from touching the object, the information from the move-ment of the hand–arm system in the haptic exploration of the object, the visual information, and the information from the eye movements, in the visual scanning of the object, are all correlated in order that a coherent experience of the perceptual event is experienced as it unfolds in real time.

Reentry is the process whereby the input to the central nervous system from different sources of stimulus information activates patterns of neural firing in different groups of neurons. Thus, one set of neural impulses transmitted from the skin activates patterns of neural firing in relation to information that the skin transmits concerning the size, shape, texture, consistency, and so on, of the object. Another group of neurons receives information from the visual system, another group receives information from the exploratory (mechanical) movement of the hand – arm system, another from the muscles of the eye movement system, and so on. The experience of exploring the object with one's hand occurs in time. As the hand moves over the object, the person experiences a particular distribution of stimulus information from the various sources such that touch, seeing, movement, and so on, are all coordinated to provide a coherent, temporally unfolding experience of a perceptual event.

The inputs from these diverse information sources and the patterns of neural firing that they activate in diverse groups of neurons are correlated by the formation of neural connections that are formed among the diverse neural groups. The connections among the diverse neuronal groups thus form a higher order neural network in which the patterns of activation of the diverse neuronal groups are linked to form a still higher-order network of neurons. This higher-order network categorizes the experience and therefore the object experienced as being of a certain kind. Repeated experiences of the same or similar objects lead to the formation, on still larger timescales, of similar patterns of activation of diverse neuronal groups and, therefore, to the building up of higher-order networks that are consistent across larger timescales that go beyond the timescale (real time) involved in any given perceptual experience of a particular object on a particular occasion. The consistency of patterning is selective: patterns of activation

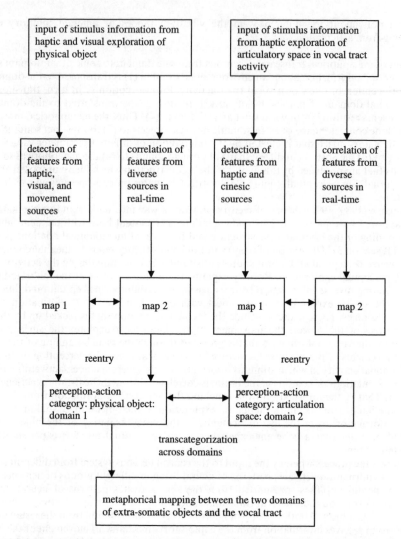

Figure 6.3 Metaphorical transcategorization across perceptual domains, showing the transcategorization of perceptual information about the concrete shape of extra-somatic physical objects (congruent) to the abstract somatic shape of the articulatory space that is created by the intersection of different parameter values in the vocal tract (metaphorical)

(neural firing) arising from the experience of particular phenomena, along with the fact of the correlation of the information from diverse sources, leads to consistent patterns of feature correlation. In this way, perceptual categories are elaborated in the brain on the basis of the real-time perceptual exploration of phenomena in the world.

From the perspective of the embodied participant in action, vocal tract gestures are proximate activities of the neuroanatomical and physiological capabilities of the body. Such capabilities provide a repertoire of essentially lower-level biological constraints or initiating conditions on these dynamical transformations. Yet, vocal tract activity is also modulated by higher-level constraints on these transformations. These higher-level constraints derive from the ecosocial environment. The cross-coupling of these two orders of constraints sets up a system of possibilities that the system may be said to anticipate in many ways in any given action performance.

What we see here is how, given certain conditions, a relatively incoherent system – the child and the various objects she uses were not, before the episode in question, co-deployed in a specific activity – may spontaneously cohere. Information is more constrained as more and more somatic and extra-somatic subsystems (e.g. the meaning-making affordances of the child's body, the copy book, school text books, the cassette recorder, the hand-held microphone, her voice dynamics, rhythm, intonation, language, and so on), interact with each other as new higher-order boundary conditions now modulate the previously looser, less coherent arrangement so as to give rise to the episode which I have transcribed. Self-organization can, therefore, be expressed in semiotic terms as follows: it entails an increase in agency as determined by or relative to some viewpoint. A viewpoint is carried by the meaningful variety a system can generate; this meaningful variety increases as the system becomes more organized. A system that begins with some initial redundancy, however vague and ill-defined, can become something more. That is, it can increase its determinability relative to some observer. The principle of cohesion as mentioned above represents a fundamental statement of the principle of redundancy.

The newly emergent activity and its meanings reflect the constraints of an ecosocial semiotic level of organization which the child accesses. Nevertheless, this does not mean that the level of the "autonomous precursor world" (see chapter 4, section 1) has been transcended. If this were the case, then the logic of the ecosocial semiotic integration of Paola into the more highly specified adult level would be abrogated. The child does not transcend prior levels of activity and meaning. Rather, these undergo significant and adaptive modification along some parameters as the result of the emergence of constraints of a qualitatively new kind. In this way, she attains new integrative levels of action and meaning (Salthe 1993: 213). This process can be understood in terms of the logic of specification hierarchy thinking.

13 Multimodality, learning, and the development of knowledge through the agent's own meaning-making activity

The chain of recontextualizations of the sounds across a variety of perceptual and semiotic modalities on a number of different, though seamlessly interrelated, timescales takes place because of the mediating role of the body-brain system. In each case, we can say that the body-brain system participates in a loop of meaning-making activity which runs through the ecosocial semiotic environment on some timescale(s) (Thelen 1995). The child hears a variety of sounds in the classroom environment on the here-now scale. The experience of these sounds is stored as mental images of these perceptual events in the brain's neural activity. These experiences are then discussed and reflected upon in further classroom activities. On the basis of these discussions and the teacher's instructions, the child, along with her classmates, produces externalized visual-graphic script items, drawings, and written linguistic text about the sounds. This loop of activity in turn loops back on the "original" sounds heard in the classroom such that the drawings, texts, and scripts are further modified and elaborated.

The specific material characteristics of these items *qua* potential signs, or affordances for meaning-making activity, impinge on the body-brain in specific ways. These same characteristics also afford further possibilities for cross-modal meaning-making or contextualizing operations to be performed, which create more complex multimodal arrangements and potential signs for their contextualizing in still further cycles of meaning-making activity. Each cycle or loop of meaning-making activity involves processes of mental imaging, producing external texts or objects in various modalities, and reflecting on and acting upon these. The processes of action-reflection on external semiotic-material artifacts afford further recontextualizations and hence further meanings in and through our integration of these external artifacts to yet more cycles of action-reflection.

In so doing, the agent creates artifacts that, through further processes of their adjustment, adaptive modification, adding to, and so on, both support and afford deeper levels of perceptual discrimination, understanding, and interpretation through the multiplying effect (Bateson

1973d [1972]: 319–320; Lemke 1998a) of the increasingly dense and resonating layers of meaning that loops of activity across more and more timescales make possible (Miettinen 1999). Semiotic-material artifacts – cf. Bereiter's (1997) "knowledge objects" – such as the pages in the copy book and the textbooks used by the child are not mere memory records or stores of prior occasions of meaning-making. They are not mere records of classroom activities and discussion. Instead, they mediate the integration of more and more layers of meaning-making in an increasingly dense and resonating synergy of meanings across more and more timescales in the processes of the child's knowledge building. Our semiotic-material artifacts and their associated technologies are an integral and intrinsic part of the ecosocial semiotic environments that loop from the body-brain system into the same environment and back again. As such, they are part of the resources in and through which what we habitually call thinking and reasoning take place.

The child, in her activity, puts the focus on the copy book as "knowledge object" in Bereiter's sense. The focus is on what she does with the knowledge objects that she works with, rather than with what goes on inside her head. The continual loops of meaning-making activity that link the copy book *qua* knowledge object to more and more layers of meaning and interpretation across more and more space-time scales put the emphasis on how such objects are used in activity for the creation of more knowledge and understanding. It is important here to study in detail such occasions because they can help to show us how individual differences and variability are the source of new forms, new meanings, and new knowledge, both in the real time of particular occasions of meaning-making, as well as in the ontogenetic time of development. In the episode that I have analysed, the child explores new possibilities and she does so in new ways that would not be possible in the school classroom.

The copy book is a semiotic technology which is meshed with the body-brain system in and through the child's activity. The copy book affords possibilities of dialogic uptake and further development in other modalities of its meaning-making potential. The readiness with which the child exploits this potential suggests that the copy book constitutes a user friendly environment for this kind of scaffolding of her own semiotic development and hence of her own capacities for reflection and action across diverse space-time scales and semiotic modalities. The body-brain system is a dialogical system: the dialogic possibilities of diverse semiotic resources and of the genres that give social shape and direction to these resources suggest that the body-brain and the multimodal meaning-making resources of our educational technologies best co-adapt to each other and therefore co-individuate when these essentially dialogical possibilities of our semiotic-material artifacts are understood and enhanced so as to optimize the fit between the two. The dialogic potential of the copy book pages entails a contextual complementarity between the body-brain system and the meaning-making activities that are afforded by the copy book and which enhance the body-brain's own powers of action and reflection.

The social networks that the child participates in constitute an attractor basin for the meaning-making trajectories that the child constructs. The dialogical structures and processes – the genres – in which she participates are re-envoiced as processes of action and reflection of the self. In this way, these same dialogical processes and genres become embodied as thought. The child's here-now activity in her performance is built on other texts and other activities on other timescales in the past at the same time that it constitutes a basis for future meaning-making activity. The child's performance can be related to Rogoff's (e.g. 1995) notion of "participatory appropriation", whereby individuals and the activities they participate in are inseparable from each other. In Rogoff's account, the individual's participation in an activity is itself a transformative – cf. recontextualizing – process in which appropriation is "the change resulting from a person's *own participation* in an activity, not to his or her internalization of some external event or technique" (Rogoff 1995: 153; italics in original).

In my view, the child's dialogic engagement with the copy book is more than just an "appropriation"; instead, it is a more complex process of disarticulation (or de-location) from one context and re-articulation (or re-location) in some other context (see Thibault 1991a: 105–106 for some critical remarks on the concept of appropriation). That is a further reason why I prefer the term "re-envoicement" (chapter 5, section 1; see also section 4 for discussion). The child engages in a dialogue with the copy book; she selectively takes up and negotiates its meaning-making potential as a series of dialogic moves or acts at the same time that she reflects on and evaluates these same moves. Importantly, she evaluates her own performance and therefore her own positioning as a participant in her own activity. The term re-envoicement is suggestive and, to my mind, preferable here because it allows us more accurately to grasp that the child is not simply reconstructing in her own mind particular correlated patterns of features (Gee 1997: 244) through her own activities. Instead, she is embodying action-reflection through her own rhythms, intonations, tones of voice, and so on, such that her body-brain itself is sculpted to the material dynamics of her own bodily activity.

The brain is, in the first instance, a regulator of sensori-motor activity. In re-envoicing meanings in the perspective of the self, the self – a firstness – builds its meanings in internal (embodied thought) as well as in external activity in active response to the semiotic-material resistances or friction of secondness in the world. That is, the self adaptively modifies its own body-brain and shapes it according to the others that it encounters and interacts with in the world of the nonself. In doing so, the self develops meta-level perspectives and evaluations on its own activity such that it is able to direct the very shaping of its own actions in developing responses to others. In this self-referential perspective, the body is shaped, adjusted, and modified, so to speak, in order to achieve desired interactional effects on others (chapter 5, section 15). The self does things to others by doing things to its own body-brain such that the body-brain is the object of the self's own dialogically oriented and coordinated activity.

If meaning or thinking were mainly or essentially patterns of correlated features of the ideational kind (cf. Gee's 1997: 243 "midlevel situated meanings"), then something important would still be missing from our account of how the body-brain re-envoices meanings in its ecosocial environment in the perspective of the self. The ways in which the self shapes or modifies the body in its activity indicate how the self intends the sign so produced is to be taken interactively by the other at the same time that it indicates the self's subjective stance on or evaluation of the same sign and of the referent situation with which it is co-contextualized.

For example, a speaker can deform or shape the neuromuscular activity of the vocal tract in ways that create major shifts in pitch across a given lexicogrammatical domain in some discourse context. The major pitch contour – the intonation – that is created holds a given lexicogrammatical domain – e.g. a clause – in its scope and shapes it in order to achieve a particular dialogically oriented effect on the other and/or to signal the speaker's evaluative or affective stance on the proposition or proposal in the clause (see McGregor 1997: 64–67). The nonsegmental resources of voice dynamics such as rhythm, timbre, voice quality, intonation, and so on, are all vocal resources that can be used – usually in some kind of complex synergy with each other – to achieve particular interactional effects or to indicate particular subjective evaluations in this sense.

Such re-shapings or modulations of vocal tract activity are often co-contextualized by neuromuscular deformations of, for example, the superficial skeletal muscles of the face and the modification of the erectile vascular tissues such as the lips and the lower eyelids or the contractions of the frontalis, corrugator supercilii and the procerus muscles (Bouissac 1999: 10) to yield facial expressions such as raised or lowered eyebrows, and so on. All of these bodily activities – either together or separately – are ways in which the body regulates – both voluntarily and involuntarily – the body's sensori-motor activity in response to external and internal environmental events, including, most importantly, the actions – actual or anticipated – of other selves (see also chapter 5, sections 6 and 14).

More precisely, it is the brain's assembling of a very high rate of formation of nerve nets in and through the brain's own patterns of neural activity that gives rise to an inner self-referential perspective (see chapter 1, section 2). It is this neural activity, corresponding to the self perspective, which regulates the body's dynamics to the higher-scalar dynamics of the self perspective. It is in this sense that the self shapes and deforms bodily activity in its dialogically coordinated responses to the other, rather than being mechanistically stimulated to act by external forces impacting on the body from the outside. It is in this sense that the body-brain re-envoices meanings that the self collects from the ecosocial environment in the course of its own cascading activity as its own meanings, in its own voice, in the self-referential meta-perspective of its own self.

PART III
Consciousness

7

Reflexive (Self-)consciousness, Conscience, and the Dialogical Basis of Intrapersonal Moral Consciousness

1 Consciousness is a relation between self and world, not access to a state

Psychologists and philosophers often speak of the non-inferential access that the self has to its own states of consciousness (e.g. Carruthers 1996: 202–203; Natsoulas 2000a: 329). Non-inferential access contrasts with the inferential or interpretive access that each of us has to others' states of consciousness. Bogdan (2000: 148–149) points out that the flaw in this account rests on the assumption that higher-level thinking (meta-representation) provides non-inferential access to lower-level thoughts such that conscious awareness of this thought results. However, states of consciousness may indicate the presence of a given mental state or thought, but, Bogdan observes, "this internal sense can not yield the recognition of the relation that the state has to the world" (Bogdan 2000: 148–149). A state of consciousness is a relation between self and world; it is not a state *per se*:

> Conscious reflexivity presupposes the representation of mind-world relations and therefore cannot emerge from merely having and registering internal states.
>
> (Bogdan 2000: 149)

The view that conscious reflexivity emerges from the having and registering of internal states *per se* assumes that (self-) consciousness contextualizes itself. In other words, consciousness occurs within its own domain. But this does not explain how (human) consciousness is recognizable in a given system of interpretance by self and others as a relation between self and world in the perspective of the self who undergoes the particular experience. In this perspective, acts of consciousness (1) can be represented as having Meaning System contextualization relations in some system of interpretance; and (2) are constrained by the supersystem (Interaction System) transactions in which they are embedded (see Thibault 2004a: 264–267). Consciousness emerges, in the first instance, in the supersystem transactions between individuals and selected aspects of their environments, which are dynamically integrated to the *Innenwelt* perspective of the self. The transactions between self and nonself in the supersystem are regulated by higher-scalar constraints which become re-envoiced in the perspective of the self. Furthermore, these supersystem transactions are contextualized by a higher-order Meaning System. A self-referential perspective is seen as an essential component of a mind which has consciousness. The distinction between first person and third person accounts of consciousness may be seen, in part, as being concerned with whether self-reference should be excluded or not from the description of consciousness. Notions such as intrinsic awareness and non-inferential access show that self-reference is an essential feature of any definition of consciousness. However, these notions assume that self-reference is reference to internal states *per se*. Thus, one has inner awareness of or non-inferential access to some states in one's own stream of consciousness. Following Natsoulas (2000a), this view may be characterized as follows.

The stream of consciousness consists of states of consciousness that are the first person perspectives or viewpoints on other states of consciousness in the same stream. The stream of consciousness thus consists in a SELF which views or experiences other components of the stream of consciousness as thoughts, feelings, phenomenal awareness, and so on, which are directly experienced by the SELF as its own experiences. This duality in the stream of consciousness means that consciousness or a state of consciousness dually consists in the self who has the experience and that which is experienced by the self. By the same token, the experiencing self is also able to experience the self's own experiencing of a given experience. Consciousness involves what Natsoulas calls "a duality of perspective" (2000a: 330). First, there is an "outward orientation" to the object of consciousness. Secondly, there is an "inward orientation", which is constituted by the experiencing self's possessing an inner awareness of its own state of consciousness (Natsoulas 2000a: 330; see also Battacchi 1998).

In this view, self-reference occurs internally between different states of consciousness within the one overall stream of consciousness. But this view does not include self-reference between the Meaning System and the supersystem transactions of the Interaction System which constitutes and sustains the Meaning System. It is a view which limits self-reference to components of the Meaning System, thereby denying the link between states of consciousness and the world (Bogdan 2000: 149). The problem can be solved when we make explicit the link between consciousness and the supersystem transactions in which consciousness is embedded and from which it always derives and which it self-reflexively interprets in the perspective of the self. As we shall see, this means that self-reference must be made between states of consciousness and the (internalized) self–nonself supersystem transactions to which such states are always related. Rather than a theory of consciousness which is concerned, above all, with intrinsic states *per se*, we shall be concerned with consciousness as a resource for actually acting in and/or for imagining acting in and relating to the world from the perspective of the self. In this way, the self-perspective which necessarily informs consciousness is a self which is embedded in the supersystem transactions which inform its perspective. (Self-)consciousness connects these supersystem transactions between self and nonself to the Meaning System in the individual's *Innenwelt* at the same time that it includes itself in its own domain. In this way, consciousness can be applied to and can be used to view its own self–nonself transactions through its own self–nonself transactions. This is possible because each level of consciousness is about a certain kind of self–nonself transaction or relationship in the specification hierarchy of supersystem transactions that inform the perspective of the self (see the discussion of the emergence of the meta-loop in chapter 5, section 14).

According to Natsoulas (2000b: 142), there is no alternative to physical monism as an explanation of consciousness. In contrast to mind–body dualism, which says that brain processes and mind processes are irreducible, the one to the other, Natsoulas argues that mental states are brain occurrences because:

> beyond all of their third-person properties *qua* occurrences in the brain, mental states possess no other properties, in my view. Mental states must be different from brain occurrences that are not mental, but their difference does not consist in their instantiating any non-physical properties.
>
> (Natsoulas 2000b: 142).

In my view, the issue is not one of dualism versus monism. Dualism would transcend materialism by postulating the incommensurability of mind occurrences and brain occurrences. In this view, metasystem (mind) and supersystem (brain) are explanatorily disconnected. Dualism remains unable to say how mind is immanent in the matter, energy, and information exchanges among different parts of the brain, as well as between the body-brain system and its environments. Therefore, self-reference pertains to mind or metasystem categories *per se*. I make this claim on the assumption that the term "mind" is a reification of the meanings that are stored and elaborated in an individual's *Innenwelt*. For this reason, it is appropriate to say that mind is a metasystem category because it consists of and is accountable for in terms of the contextualizing relations that connect forms, meanings, actions, and events to each other and in recognizable, type-specific ways in a given Meaning System.

Monism suggests that any other explanation other than that some brain occurrences just *are* mental occurrences on account of the physical characteristics of those particular kinds of brain occurrences, seems to suggest that a physical system cannot refer to itself on account of its irreducibly third person properties. Yet, we know that self-reference is at the very foundation of (self-)consciousness. Self-reference is made possible by the autorecursion of increasingly higher-scalar meta-representations and reinterpretations across diverse scalar levels of lower-scalar levels of brain organization (chapter 1, section 2; chapter 9, sections 3, 6). Dualism preserves a notion of the soul or mind (self), though it is unable to explain the connection between, say, mind and brain. In dualism, self-reference is to meta-system processes. Monism rules out self-reference, or autorecursion, between Meaning System and supersystem, by claiming that physical brain occurrences just *are* mental occurrences. That is, mental occurrences are supersystem processes *per se*. Monism remains unable to account for the following two facts: (1) Physical brain processes are reorganized on higher levels as meaningful experience in the perspective of a self; and (2) self-reference is made between the higher-scalar categories of the metasystem – the system of interpretance – and the lower-scalar supersystem processes that instantiate these.

Moreover, it is not enough to say that the higher levels of neural organization referred to in the preceding paragraph are just the same old physical brain processes re-described in some other non-physical terms. The point is, rather, that higher-scalar brain dynamics emerge from lower levels and have properties that cannot be inferred from the lower levels. The neural dynamics of the self and the system of interpretance which provides the self with its categories and, therefore, informs its viewpoints is a pattern of organization of brain dynamics that is qualitatively different from lower-level patterns. Moreover, the higher levels behave in correspondingly different ways with respect to the lower levels without, on the other hand, being materially divorced from them. In terms of the three-level hierarchy view, the self and its system of interpretance are boundary conditions or constraints on lower levels. Furthermore, the higher level is necessary in order to explain the specific causal effects which arise from symbolic neural space in the entraining of lower-level neural and sensori-motor dynamics to the meanings of the self (chapter 5, sections 14–15). After all, it is the self to whom we attribute these meanings and not the lower-scalar neuro-muscular processes which enact the meanings of the self and project them beyond the body into the ecosocial environment as articulatory or other gestural activity of the body.

The categories of Peircean semiotics are useful here. In the immature system, the infant proto-interpreter is predisposed to certain kinds of dyadic engagements with the nonself on account of the inbuilt values which selectively nudge him or her along certain developmental trajectories, rather than others. The infant's dyadic engagements with others (persons, objects, and so on) will be assumed to be the focal level (L) for the purposes of the present discussion (chapter 3). Above this focal level, there is the L+1 level of the structure of the dyad and the system of interpretance in which this is embedded. Below the focal level, there is the immature infant body-brain system on level L–1. The brain is not, in the early stages, able to distinguish and refer to a self that is clearly differentiated from nonself. There is in this stage no clear differentiation of self and other. Instead, the relation between the two is based on topological-continuous variation. In Peircean terms, the infant interpreter is a firstness who engages with the nonself *qua* secondness. In the process, he or she discovers and constructs higher-level thirdness in the form of the system of interpretance which mediates and makes possible the transactions between first and seconds. In actual fact, we have seen that, for the infant, secondness is historically primary (chapter 1, section 3). Its sense of self – its firstness – and the differentiation of self from others emerge in the course of the proto-self's engagements with the secondness of others. Moreover, the construction of thirdness in the process of doing so enables the increasing differentiation of different kinds of selves and others and different kinds of self–other relations.

It is not difficult to translate this understanding into the semiosis of brain processes themselves. Thus, the dyadic engagements between proto-firstness and secondness yield reentrant mappings of the multimodal disjunctive samplings from these two sources of information, i.e. "in here" and "out there" (chapter 3, section 7). These reentrant mappings lead to the creation of higher-order neural maps based on the value-laden categories that are, over time, built up through the disjunctive samplings of information from "in here" and "out there". In this way, higher-scalar perspectives and viewpoints are created for interpreting lower-scalar reentrant mappings from the two sources mentioned above. The higher level is constructed over a much greater timescale than the much faster reentrant samplings of the dyadic engagements between "in here" and "out there" on the here-now scale. This difference in timescales reflects the fact that the relevant ecosocial semiotic system can only exist on the basis of the kinds of dynamical processes and relations (individual, institutional, societal, and so on) that exist over much greater space-time scales than the specific transactions that occur on the focal level L of the self and its immediate material environment (chapter 6, section 1). Categories emerge and are stored on the higher-scalar level of the neural maps which interpret lower-scalar samplings of environmental events. Furthermore, the internalization of the ecosocial semiotic scale requires neural connectivity on a far greater scale than do the lower-scalar samplings because it is on the higher level that a system of interpretance is gradually built up and elaborated in the inner perspective of a self. This system of interpretance and the self that is associated with it require many more interconnected neural networks in long-term memory than do the lower-scalar transactions that are interpreted in the self-perspective as particular experiences of the self on particular occasions.

We see here how the three-level hierarchy can be used to interpret brain processes as internalized semiotic processes in the perspective of a self who experiences and interprets these same processes as well as being a constitutive part of them. The inner perspectives and viewpoints that are associated with the self in consciousness are a firstness. Yet, the objects of consciousness with which the self transacts and forms particular relations are forms of secondness which require interpretation by means of a system of interpretance which mediates and makes possible these transactions. In this view, the observer's brain and the world of the nonself co-develop (and co-individuate). That which is experienced in consciousness develops in concert with the self-perspective on account of the dialogical character of the relations that connects the one to the other. These internalized transactions lead to the emergence of higher levels of brain organization which are able to interpret the brain's own lower-level processes as signs of experiences and particular categories of experience – both inner and outer – which occur within and are interpreted within the perspective of the self who undergoes the experience.

Being conscious of something always involves massive neural connectivity and activity. This neural activity is part of the Interaction System perspective on consciousness: consciousness is always embodied in material processes at the same time that it is a higher-scalar reorganization of these processes as meaningful experience or awareness in the perspective of a self. We cannot have consciousness without this material level. The patterns of neural connections have infinite potential possibilities that go beyond what one is aware of as the phenomenological manifestation of a conscious experience. Meaningful experience which can guide our actions and which can anticipate possible future courses of action and also evaluate them in the moral perspective of a self can only occur in the context of the meaning systems that the individual has elaborated along his or her trajectory. Which experiences are meaningful, how we relate to them, and how we evaluate them, are defined in relation to the higher-scalar meaning systems of some ecosocial semiotic system. Yet, consciousness is enacted through our supersystem transactions with our internal and external environments. The meanings that the individual has in his or her system of interpretance enable her to contextualize some of the infinite topological variety of Interaction System processes as conscious experiences of the self.

Consciousness is a highly specified form of Meaning System in the perspective of a self. Furthermore, human consciousness has arisen from prior systems – both biological and social – which in some sense prefigured it. This suggests that consciousness *qua* highly specified Meaning System is founded on the dialectical duality of the Interaction System and the Meaning System perspectives. Consciousness is immanent in Interaction System processes (matter, energy, and information transactions with an environment). At the same time, it is the internalized Meaning System or system of interpretance of the self which makes possible our conscious awareness and experiencing of Interaction System processes. This internalized system of interpretance is a system of contextualizing relations whereby selves are able to perceive or cognize pattern and order in the contexts in which conscious experience occurs. Experience can only be defined in some context and in relation to differentiations, whether topological or typological, that are defined and recognized by a Meaning System of some kind. Perceptual, conceptual, and semiotic categories are all forms of proto-meaning. These proto-meanings form systems of interpretance on various levels of specification in the *Innenwelt* for interpreting phenomena and for acting in relation to them in one's ecosocial environment. Consciousness is a construct for making meaningful the relationships between certain self–nonself transactions in the supersystem and the contexts in which these transactions occur. What is, and what can be contextualized as meaningful, depends on the systems of interpretance which the individual has stored in his or her *Innenwelt*. In humans, this includes systems of interpretance based on perceptual, conceptual, and semiotic categories. These contextualizing relations enable patterned relations on all levels of the specification hierarchy of semiosis to be apprehended in the perspective of the self who undergoes the experience.

2 The self-reflexive structure of (self-)consciousness

Conscious experience and awareness are often treated as forms of referential or cognitive content. Such views tell us little about the contextual character of consciousness. Thus, something is conscious for a self only in relation to a structured context. The structure of this context can be described in terms of the formalism of the metaredundancy contextual hierarchy as follows: content of consciousness / situational context // structure of self–nonself transaction (Thibault 2004a: 26–30). The dialogic or proto-dialogic character of consciousness is implicit even in the highest forms of self-reflexive consciousness. Consciousness is developed and individuated through participation in self–nonself transactions that are integrated to the meta-perspective of a self who interprets these transactions from its own viewpoint. Furthermore, the structure of consciousness is reflected in the essentially dialogical character of these transactions. The earliest forms of self–nonself transactions, as found in the topological flows of affects which characterize the socioaffective exchanges between mother and infant in primary intersubjectivity, are an important source for the development of (self-)consciousness and the self-perspective(s) that this entails. As we shall see in more detail below, the self is discovered and constructed only through the relations it transacts with others. These relations include prelinguistic, linguistic, and non-linguistic forms of self–nonself transactions. Consciousness, rather than arising from within the self, is a consequence of the ways in which self–nonself transactions lead first to a focus on the other before the turn to self and, hence, to (self-)consciousness takes place (see Bogdan 2000: 51–52; chapter 1, section 3).

Take perception, for example. Perception is a first-order structure that picks up information about events in the organism's external and internal environments. The perceiver merely perceives the given phenomenon without also representing the fact that it is the perceiver who perceives the phenomenon. However, the ability to ground the act of perception in the perspective of the SELF as the one who has the perceptual experience is to posit a relationship between the self and the experienced phenomenon (world). That is, a relation between the "self" of (self-)consciousness and the object of perceptual awareness. The positing of a relation between self and object of perceptual awareness is a second-order structure which posits that the self stands in a particular kind of relationship to the object of awareness. In such a relation, the self represents the fact that the perception takes place in the perspective of the self who has the perception. This representation is meta-level or self-reflexive thinking.

Another example is Bateson's description of the man cutting the tree with an axe (see chapter 9, section 6.1.5). The circuit of a transform of differences that connects the man to the tree is a loop which can be schematized as: self-axe-tree-axe-self. This loop is a first-order structure in which the man and the tree are linked by the entire circuit of relations. A first-order structure can be described as the man merely perceiving or experiencing the tree as a consequence of the information which is transformed in the circuit. There is no self-awareness of himself as the experiencer of the tree. In other words, the man has a first-order representation of the tree, though no awareness of that which connects him to the tree. The important point to emphasize here is the circuit of transforms of differences which connects man and tree. Self-awareness or *self*-consciousness is a second-order or meta-level structure whereby the self develops the capacity to represent itself *qua* self as having that particular relation to the given object of consciousness. Bateson's example thus shows that self-consciousness is not consciousness of the self *per se*, but of the self's relations to its environmental milieu. In a first-order relation, the man is aware of the tree, but he is not aware that it is his own self which stands in a particular (perceptual) relation to the tree. There is a first-order experience of the tree, but no second-order experiencing in the perspective of the self of this first-order experiencing by the self.

Thus, self-consciousness is always the recognition that a given "state" of consciousness is a relation between self and experienced world. This reflexive capacity to posit the self (or the other) as the one who undergoes a given experience is a semiotic capacity to interpret self–world relations. It is not and cannot be based on non-inferential access to states of consciousness. Instead, it is a self-reflexive interpretation of some self's relations to the world. The self's relation to the world (nonself) is a dialogic one. On the other hand, the notion that the self has non-inferential access to its own (epistemically private) conscious mental states misses the point that such mental states are relationally linked to the world. Moreover, the evidence is against the notion that self-awareness and self-recognition spring up from within the individual organism. Rather, the evidence indicates that gaze, attention, and agency are, in the initial stages of the child's development, other-directed, rather than self-directed (Bogdan 2000: 151; Trevarthen 1987, 1992; Halliday 1975, 1978a, 1992). Children engage in acts of interpretation of and attempt to influence the actions of others with whom the infant interacts before they develop the ability to interpret their own actions and perceptions from the perspective of the self (chapter 1, section 3). The turn to the self is a later emergence, which is built on the prior acts of other-engagement and other-interpretation. It is in this way that the infant discovers that others stand in particular (perceptual, mental) relations to phenomena in the world. The dialogic and other-directed character of the self's reflexive relation to the world thus derives from the prior re-envoicing in the self-perspective of others and their meanings as standing in particular kinds of relations to the world before this awareness is transferred to the self.

(Self-)consciousness consists of two poles of attention or awareness which are always present in a given state of consciousness. We can focus our attention on the object of consciousness or we can focus our attention on the self as experiencer of the given object of consciousness. In other words, a given state of consciousness always reveals the self in whose perspective the experience occurs whilst the experience is occurring. At its simplest, we can model this relationship as a cascading/collecting cycle involving two poles of proto-awareness, or proto-attention, as shown in Figure 7.1.

Formally, this relationship is akin to the circuit of the transform of differences that Bateson proposed in his discussion of the man cutting a tree with an axe (see chapter 9, section 6.1.5). Figure 7.1 shows a model of what I shall term proto-consciousness. The terms "in here" and

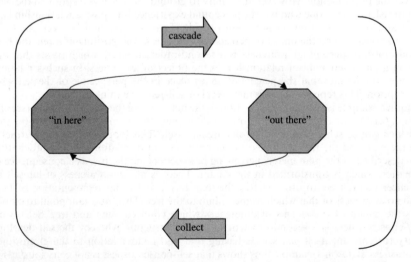

Figure 7.1 Cascading/collecting cycle involving two poles of awareness of proto-self

"out there" are linguistic glosses on the two poles of a simple cascading/collecting cycle (Salthe 1993: 75). The notion of "in here" designates some orderly arrangement of matter, energy, and information which is stored "in here". This means that the "in here" sector refers to the most primordial prototype of what we later come to recognize as an inner perspective. However, the term "in here" implies no strong sense of a self, with its corresponding viewpoint, in Figure 7.1. From "in here", there is a spontaneous, rather than programmed, flow of information or matter-energy, outwards, i.e. towards "out there". This cascading flow towards "out there" is followed by a return to "in here" of information and/or matter-energy which is accumulated and elaborated "in here". It is the convergence and elaboration "in here" of the collected products of its own cascading that gives rise to the emergence of a proto-self-perspective.

3 The foregrounded differentiation and emergence of an inner self-perspective against a background of self–nonself relations and transactions

The notion of intrinsic awareness (Natsoulas) draws attention to the autonomy of individual consciousness. Consciousness is the result of both predictable change (development) and the elaboration of an individual viewpoint (individuation). Consciousness is a system that exhibits organizational closure. The processes which generate individual consciousness are recursively dependent on each other in the generation and maintenance of these same processes. Furthermore, these same processes constitute the system as a unity which is recognizable in the domain in which it operates. Self and nonself are related to each other as a network of interdependent relations that depend on each other in this sense. The organizational closure which characterizes and gives rise to individual consciousness is a meta-loop that closes the cascading/collecting loop linking "in here" and "out there" on the "in here" pole. This may be illustrated as in Figure 7.2.

The closure of the first-order loop gives rise to a (second-order) self-referential perspective. The interdependence of the "in here" and the "out there" processes and the consequent unity of these processes *qua* autonomous system results in a self-referential perspective in which (self-) consciousness is always consciousness of self-in-interaction-with-nonself (other persons, objects, and so on). The emergence of the higher-order meta-loop means that the self on the meta-level can observe and experience its own experiencing of the object. In so doing, the processes on the first level which are experienced are made to correspond to the observational rates of the self-as-observer on the meta-level. For example, if you want to think about the possible consequences of some future course of action, the self can generate a stream of thoughts and reflect on them in consciousness in a matter of minutes or less. A particular pulse of thought, say, in the stream of consciousness is a small-scale model of the larger system in which it is embedded. The reference scale is that of the self and its categories and viewpoints (Salthe 1993: 48). Furthermore, the principle of scalar heterogeneity tells us that the objects of consciousness – recalled, hypothetical, and so on – may be related to very different scales. For this reason, it is necessary that some self-referential connection between self and object be built into the structure of consciousness itself. That is, the self's conscious experiencing of the object system is self-referential to the self such that the self is both intrinsically aware of its own states of consciousness and aware that it is the self who is experiencing them. This self-experiencing of the self's experiencing of the object is intrinsically self-referential.

(Self-)consciousness therefore means (1) being able to attend to and observe one's own states of consciousness and (2) being able to attend to one's self as the agency who is attending to and observing one's own states of consciousness. Observer and observed are intrinsic components of a single overall process. The self collects some of the effects of its own cascading to its own *Innenwelt*. The closing of the meta-loop of the self pole of the circuit of relations described above foregrounds the self component of the self-in-relation-to-nonself. In Flohr's terms (see chapter 1, section 2), very high-order neural mappings create inner meta-representations of self as being progressively differentiated from and foregrounded in relation to what was an earlier, much less differentiated relation between self and nonself. Primary intersubjectivity is characterized by the infant's orientation to the other in the mother–infant

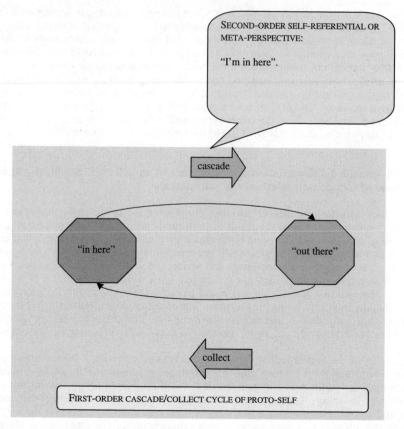

Figure 7.2 The second-order meta-loop that closes the cascading/collecting loop linking "in here" and "out there" on the "in here" pole so as to create a self-referential perspective

dyad, rather than to the self (chapter 3, section 2). That is, to topological representations of other's faces and others as sources of matter, energy, and information relevant to the further development of the (infant) self along its epigenetic trajectory. The transition to the symbolic possibilities of language means that this trajectory becomes progressively more differentiated and determinable. The self's collection of the effects of its own cascading as higher-order meta-representations of the self become ever more symbolically differentiated from others. This increasing self-differentiation goes hand in hand with an increasing commitment to the self's own individuating trajectory *qua* project (Salthe 1993: 243). The inner self who observes its own states of consciousness, and who has a sense of the temporal continuity of its own stream of consciousness, is a semiotic trajectory that is not reducible to the biological organism that supports it. This trajectory is progressively entrained, through epigenesis, to the higher-scalar meaning systems and practices of a given culture.

States of consciousness are larger-scale, time-bound "entities" as compared to the much faster timescales that operate on the lower level of the neural dynamics that support consciousness. In terms of scalar hierarchy theory, states of consciousness occur at the focal level where observer perspectives (i.e. the self in our human case) are also found. The focal level regulates and constrains the lower level at the same time that the lower level provides information which is reinterpreted on the focal level as signs in the perspective of the self (chapter 9, sections 2, 3). Moreover, the focal level is regulated by higher-level processes and constraints which act as boundary conditions that entrain focal level processes to the higher scalar dynamics. Neural dynamics originate in biological initiating conditions which self-organize into higher-order patterns that are entrained to forms of organization on the ecosocial level.

The notion of intrinsic (self-)awareness demonstrates the limitations of the externalist perspective on consciousness. Third person accounts of consciousness look at the self–object relation from the outside, i.e. as a system on the same observational scale as our own and standing beside us (Salthe 1993: 91). But consciousness is a system which we (ourselves) are inside: it is concerned with how we, as observers, give meaning to experience from the perspective of the self that we are (Thibault 2004a: 227–231).

The reentrant closure of the meta-loop on the self pole, along with the progressive differentiation of this with respect to its environment, means that the self and the objects of experience (states of consciousness) are inextricably inside the same system. The ontological firstness of the self ("I think therefore I am") is the result of a culturally particular semiotic polarizing of self-nonself. Studies of early infant proto-semiosis show that the primary reality is the secondness of discovering and expanding the *Umwelt* through signs (chapter 1, section 3). The relevant anti-Cartesian dictum could be: "I am because others interact with and interpret me" or "Others interact with and interpret me therefore I am".

Initial topological vagueness gives way to categorical distinction, nudged along by intrinsic biological values, which are initiating conditions. The child's early sensori-motor exploration and the categorizations that emerge as a result of these explorations are entrained to the higher-order system. The robustness of the supersystem provides boundary conditions which entrain the self along some pathways rather than others. The closing of the meta-loop on the self shows that consciousness is an internalization in the *Innenwelt* of the whole supersystem comprising self and nonself transactions.

Development involves an orderly increase in information as the individual progresses along its ontogenetic trajectory (Salthe 1993: 13–15; Thibault 2004a: 226–227). Moreover, information is produced by energy exchanges. Salthe further points out that information "necessarily must increase (certainly never decrease) in amount if, as is always the case naturally, the observer is in the same supersystem as the objects revealed by the information" (1993: 135). The friction that results from the impact of the material domain on the conscious domain is a source of (self-)organization. The energy transactions that result from the friction between the two modes of experience – the conscious and the material – discussed by Halliday produces information for the observer (the self) who is in the same system as the structures which are a source of information for the observer (chapter 3, section 7).

In the externalist perspective, information refers to the categories and models of the outside observer of the given system. Third person accounts of consciousness rely upon external signs that might provide information about possible *Innenwelt* events of the observed. In the internalist perspective, on the other hand, the *Innenwelt* is the locus of (self-) referential information that the system itself uses to interpret and engage with other systems (nonselves). The increase in information in the *Innenwelt* – e.g. the integration of iconic and indexical semiosis to symbolic semiosis (Thibault 2000a: 301–303) – goes hand in hand with changes in the externally observable body dynamics of the system such that these can be accessed by observers as signs of possible *Innenwelt* states. For example, we interpret external bodily signs of others (gaze, pointing, facial expressions, and so on) as redounding (contextually integrating) with inner mental states and intentions. In the perspective of the self, contextual redundancies are constructed between the experiences of, for example, anger, shame, guilt, and so on, and clusters of bodily states or physical symptoms such as racing heart, tense muscles, erratic breathing, and so on. The *Innenwelt* is the locus of consciousness in the sense that it is the locus of self-referential information, i.e. information which is also grounded in the perspective of the self in intrinsic awareness, and which informs and provides models for possible actions in the world. The self's engagements with its own states of consciousness requires that the self be (1) embedded in the same supersystem as the states (objects) of consciousness that it engages with; and (2) that this supersystem, by virtue of the reentrant looping (closing) of the loop on the self pole, constitutes an *Innenwelt* which regulates the individual's actions and inputs in its *Umwelt*; and (3) the reentrant meta-loop is a higher-scalar level of organization of self that takes into account (experiences) its own lower-scalar experiences of the systems [objects, states of consciousness] that it engages with without, however, necessarily reflecting this "intrinsic awareness" of its own experiences in its external behaviour.

In Flohr's account, the very high-order meta-representations that give rise to an inner per-spective of a self are made possible by lower-level representations. These higher-scalar meta-representations in symbolic neural space contextually integrate and, therefore, reinterpret lower-scalar representations across scalar levels of neural organization in the brain (chapter 9, section 6). The higher-scalar meta-representations of the self-perspective are much more struc-tured (organized) than are the lower-scalar ones that they interpret. Salthe (1993: 167) points out that the lower-scalar components cannot interpret the meta-system in which they are embedded because they lack the structure to do so on account of "scalar limitations" – in this case, neural connectivity. The higher-scalar meta-representation of the self interprets and con-textually integrates lower-scalar processes as signs which it interprets as meanings relevant to its own scale. The higher-scalar self embeds the smaller scale one of self–other transactions within its own observational perspectives such that the self's experiencing of its own experiencing of it own states of consciousness becomes possible.

The self who interprets and experiences its own experiencing of its own states of conscious-ness is necessarily a higher-scalar entity with respect to its observations of its own lower-scalar self-object transactions. The self as observer of its own experiences requires a viewpoint and, hence, information that is not inherent in the meta-self *per se*. Furthermore, the meta-self as experiencer of its own experiencing, is necessarily more extensive than the experiences which it interprets. The higher-scalar self has the benefit of observation of larger timescales that are greater than the smaller-scale of the experiencing of something on a given occasion. The meta-self, by contrast, reflects semiotic-observational moments on the scale of the entire historical-biographical trajectory of the individual and its accumulated meanings in the meta-perspective of the self. In chapter 5, sections 14–15, we saw how this fundamental dynamic emerges.

4 The inner self-perspective as semiotic reorganization across levels of neural networks

Consciousness is a property of a mind that is able to (self-reflexively) take itself into account. Mind is a system of meanings in the individual's *Innenwelt* that is able to reflect upon itself and upon its own experiences. Furthermore, it entails the capacity to reflect upon the self's relations to the world of nonself. For this reason, the relation between self and world is a contextual one. In the specifically human case, our ability to examine and observe our own states of conscious-ness in a purely intrapersonal sense is a case in point. James (1950 [1890]: 125) considered the ability of humans to "look into their own minds" and to "distinguish the mental state as an inward activity or passion, from all the objects with which it may cognitively deal" to be "*the most fundamental of all the postulates of Psychology*" (185; italics in original). The stream of consciousness comprises components that are able to reflect upon and think about other com-ponents in the same stream. According to Natsoulas, one has an intrinsic inner awareness of one's own stream of consciousness (2000a: 330). This means that a given awareness of some-thing in one's own mental life is itself able to be the object of inner awareness. A state of consciousness dually involves: (1) an experience *qua* mental state of a given phenomenon, whether real, hypothetical, fictional, imagined, and so on; and (2) an inner experience or aware-ness of the experiencing of the phenomenon referred to in (1) above. Inner awareness of one's own mental states, as Natsoulas (2000a: 330) points out, is not a form of inner perception. Instead, Natsoulas argues, it is a direct, non-inferential apprehension of one's states of con-sciousness. I have already discussed the reasons why the non-inferential view is inadequate (section 1).

Consider the "in here" and "out there" poles of attention and awareness that I discussed above. The two poles enter into a relationship of dialogical complementarity in the way that I first discussed in chapter 5, section 14. The fact that "in here" and "out there" enter into a relationship of this kind means that in some way they are contextually related to each other. In other words, the probability that the "in here" and the "out there" systems will systematically interact with each other is increased (Thibault 2004a: 34–39). The dialogical complementarity between the two systems irreversibly alters the prior probability landscape of the two systems taken separately. In this kind of (semiotic) regime, the "in here" system can selectively orient to certain "out there" states such that the probability of the "in here" system's orienting to "out there" are internally related to each other. The "out there" system comes to function as a boundary condition which is imported into the internal dynamics of the "in here" system.

The emergent self-organization of the "in here"/"out here" system operates on a single scalar level. However, the dialogical complementarity of the two systems means that the "in here" system's cascading activity favours its selectively orienting to "out there". In turn, this selective orienting to "out there" favours a certain kind of "out there" response, which is, in turn, collected by the "in here" system. In this way, the "in here" system experiences the "out there". The closing of the loop that results from this cascading/collecting cycle gives rise to the emergence of a higher-scalar level or organization which constrains the behaviour of the lower-scalar level. The emergent contextual constraints emanating from the higher-scalar level act as boundary conditions which constrain and entrain the dynamical processes relating "in here" and "out there" on the lower-scalar level.

The newly emergent level of organization, corresponding to the reentrant meta-loop that closes the first-order loop, constitutes an observer perspective on the higher-scalar level. It is an observer who is able to attend to and reflexively interpret its own experiencing of the phenomena of experience "out there" on the first level. This self-reflexive ability to interpret one's own lower-scale experiences is a form of semiotic closure whereby lower-scalar processes and relations are reorganized on the next higher-scalar level as information which is able to be interpreted as meaningful within the perspective of the self on the higher level (see chapter 9, sections 4–5). In other words, there emerges an inner sense of self who observes and develops perspectives on its own states of consciousness. The self just *is* the phenomenological manifestation of this semiotic reorganization across different scalar levels. That is, the self is the phenomenological manifestation of the reentrant entraining of neural maps whose connectivity is massively complex compared to lower-scalar interactions. It is this higher-scalar complexity that explains why the self is able to expand the scope of its dynamical interactions with its environments and invironments to increasingly diverse space-time scales. Moreover, this massive increase in neural connectivity and complexity means that the very high order meta-representations result in a self-perspective which regulates and interprets its own lower-scalar interactions. The higher-scalar self is, with respect to its lower-scalar experiences of phenomena in the world, a system of interpretance. The self's interpretation of its own lower-scalar engagements with the world and the resulting perspectives that it adopts in the central nervous system takes place over a much longer timescale. Moreover, a higher-scalar self-system requires a far greater number of interconnected neuronal networks in order to maintain itself and its meanings in long-term memory in its *Innenwelt*, as well as to interpret its own lower-scalar experiences as meaningful according to its own *Innenwelt* perspectives.

On the first level of schematization, the "out there" pole of the circuit of cascading/collecting relations represented in Figure 7.1 is an environmental integrity which is systematically and internally related to "in here". The dialogical complementarity that exists between the two poles means that there is an ongoing contextual interdependency between them. The first-order interaction of "in here" and "out there" entrains the structure of its own dialogic relations so that a higher-scalar level of organization emerges. The closing of the meta-loop that takes place on the next higher level means that "out there" is imported into the internal dynamics of "in here" (see above). The resulting reorganization across scalar levels of the system's internal dynamics is a source of potential viewpoints which relate the self-system and its own processes and dynamics to those on lower and higher levels. Furthermore, such a system is embedded in a higher-scalar system of interpretance which mediates, enables, and constrains its relations to other levels. In human semiosis, the system of interpretance can be said to be a historically specific higher-scalar social-cultural formation that enables potentially meaningful configurations of information to be interpreted as meaningful in the perspective of the observer. The interpretation of information as meaning is necessarily observer related. In the human case, the observer is a self who has a model of itself in relation to its ecosocial semiotic environment within its *Innenwelt*.

5 Selves, states of consciousness, and the integrating function of the trajectory

The observations made in the preceding paragraph allow us to pose the question of the onto-logical status of the language system in a new way with respect to the way in which language *qua* system is usually posed in linguistics (Thibault 2004a: 49–54). Toolan points out that many linguists have viewed the notion of the language system as a "species-wide and species-specific complex mental program" (1996: 11). Alternatively, we can say that the language system is a semiotic model of the self's environment and invironment relations. It is a semiotic resource that the self has individuated and internalized along its trajectory by virtue of its own agency. A trajectory – historical-biographical in the human case – is, as Salthe (1993: 324) points out, a relatively stable higher-scalar entity which is a constructed source of continuity and coherence for the self's lower-scalar moment-by-moment engagements with the world. Internalized symbolic (e.g. linguistic) models of self–nonself relations and transactions are necessarily lower-scalar categorizations which are based on the system's time-bound transactions with its ecosocial environment. The principle of scalar heterogeneity means that internalized symbolic models increase the scalar reach of the system. The enhanced scalar reach of systems (selves) in possession of symbolic models means that the system – the self – on the focal level of self–nonself transactions, can produce symbolic models of (1) higher-scalar systems on much greater space-time scales than the here-now one of the organism's material interactivity with its immediate environment; and (2) of lower-scalar systems (e.g. sub-atomic particles) that do not exist on the same scale as do our interactions with our ecosocial environment.

In this view, there is not a single global language system for English, Cantonese, and so on, which can be analysed objectively and by means of which each individual can access and exchange its tokens as a free-standing individual in a potentially equal way (Thibault 1992). Rather, trajectories are individuated by selves and their agency on the basis of their participa-tion in and membership of particular social networks, each with their own characteristic ways of orienting to and appropriating the available semiotic and material resources. Unlike the notion of a global language system, the notion of the trajectory explicitly places questions of the self and the self's relationship to the social networks which are traversed by the self at the centre of theoretical concern. There is an explicit link to specification hierarchy thinking here: the making explicit of the self's relationship to its own models of the world and itself necessar-ily embeds the self at the most specified end of the class of integrities to which the self typically relates and in which it typically recognizes itself. This is, I believe, the lesson which Descartes, perhaps unwittingly, teaches us in his discussion of his observations of the people viewed in the square below, as viewed from his own window (see Thibault 2004a: 224–226). The (self-)reflexivity of (self-)consciousness always implicates a model of self-in-relation-to-nonself. Moreover, such a model is never of a unique individual *per se*, but of a highly specified class of semiotic integrities in and through which the self is constituted. This last point suggests, inci-dentally, the possibility that consciousness, in the internalist perspective, is the most highly specified type of Meaning System that we currently know about.

In the perspective outlined in the previous paragraph, (self-)consciousness can be defined as a contextualizing system that provides a necessarily contingent and transient unity to the self-in-relation-to-nonself. A "state" of consciousness in this view is a synchronic moment of the trajectory, as defined by the interacting dynamic variables that are specific to that "state". A given "object" of consciousness is, therefore, richly situated with respect to the class of integri-ties in which it is recognized. Take the case of symbolic consciousness, which is mediated by and constituted by linguistic semiosis. At the outermost level of the specification hierarchy, there are highly schematic categories – i.e. categories which have a very high level of both generality and abstraction – which have been constructed in and through the self's engagements with poten-tially very many instances. Categories originate in discourse, in activity, and in the specific logic of these discourses and activities. For example, the activity of observing and attending to another's gaze vector establishes the target of the other's perceptual awareness or focus of attention. (Self-)consciousness in the individual depends on categories, however vague, that can be fine-tuned as construals of specific material instantiations by virtue of the logic of the specification hierarchy. Individual (self-)consciousness yields, in the perspective or viewpoint of the self, most highly specified models of the "objects" of consciousness. By the same token, these objects can be responded to and acted on because they are traceable back to more schematic categories which the individual has discovered and constructed in the process of engaging with the logic of particular activities or particular discourses.

The uniqueness of individual consciousness is a historical emergence resulting from the contingencies which shape the self's trajectory. This shaping of one's trajectory is achieved by numerous encounters with instances whereby the system constructs its categories through a process of narrowing things down to more schematic details, in the process discovering and/or constructing the systems of interpretance that make such schema possible. As I showed in my book *Brain, Mind, and the Signifying Body* (Thibault 2004a: 224–226), when discussing Descartes' observations in his *Second Meditation* (Descartes 1960 [1641]: 114–115) concerning the people he sees in the square below his apartment, the viewpoint of a self and the consciousness which is grounded at this self-viewpoint can experience a given phenomena when this can be interpreted by the self's categories. The historical emergence of the self therefore reflects robust systems of interpretance in the self's *Innenwelt*. The notion of robustness means that newly contingent experiences can be incorporated to the self's viewpoint without overwhelming the semiotic integrity of the self-system (Thibault 2004a: 63–64). That is, the self adaptively modifies its internal dynamics so as to preserve its (always constructed) continuity and coherence as a trajectory-in-time. (Self-)consciousness is a particular kind of historical emergence on our own scale – one which corresponds to the most highly specified Meaning System that we humans currently know about. In terms of specification hierarchy logic, (self-)consciousness is the most highly specified state of a human Meaning System – one in which the self *qua* observer is self-reflexively related to its own inner processes by a subjective relationship to the most specified (innermost) level of the hierarchy. Just as physical-material processes are regulated and entrained by biological systems and biological systems are regulated and entrained by ecosocial systems, (self-)consciousness is the regulation and entraining of ecosocial constraints and processes to the historically emergent individuating trajectory of the self *qua* agent of its own trajectory.

What is the relationship of particular states of consciousness to the trajectory? This relationship can be explained in scalar hierarchical terms as follows. Particular components of the stream of consciousness may be recorded as states of consciousness. Each such state can be considered as a particulate event in the inner perspective of the self. However, over a given period of time, corresponding to one of our cogent moments (hours, days, weeks, months, or years), these events can be assembled into larger-scale patterns in the perspective of the self. Similarly, these large-scale patterns can be broken down into specific particulate events. The larger-scale pattern is the trajectory, or some given chunk of it, on a particular scalar level and the individual states of consciousness – the particulate events – are lower-scalar entities which constitute information that can be reorganized on higher levels as the trajectory. The self is a still higher-scalar level which functions as a system of interpretance forming boundary conditions which act upon and regulate the lower-scalar levels of the body-brain system. Selves *qua* trajectories can be described as wave functions whilst states of consciousness are lower-scalar particulate components of the wave-like trajectory of the self. Selves are higher-scalar trajectories constructed by the interactions between self and the world, including the lower-scalar components of its own trajectory. Theories of consciousness have concentrated on lower-scalar "states" of consciousness at the expense of the higher-scalar trajectory which is always constructed and interpreted in the inner perspective of the self. The important point to bear in mind is that the wave-particle interpretation represents two different, though complementary, interpretations of the same overall phenomenon – one local, the other global. The self cannot be constructed on the basis of its interactions with lower-scalar particulate states of consciousness *per se*. Selves and the viewpoints that inform selves can only be constructed and interpreted through their interactions with their individuating trajectories. Over time, the particulate states of consciousness are selectively assembled and arranged into larger-scale patterns which reflect the viewpoints and the intrinsic dynamics of the higher-scalar self and its system of interpretance. In terms of the three-level hierarchy, the relations between these scalar levels can be modelled as follows:

L+1   self and its system of interpretance as individuating trajectory
L   wave-like patterning of trajectory over time as reorganization of L–1 particulate events and their integration to a higher-scalar trajectory in the perspective of the self
L–1   states of consciousness as particulate events in stream of consciousness

6 Natsoulas's discussion of the interpersonal meaning of the terms "conscious" and "consciousness"

Natsoulas (1991, 2000a: 335; see also Butterworth 1994: 117; Battacchi 1999: 56) discusses an earlier interpersonal sense of the words "conscious" and "consciousness" with reference to Dewey (1906) and Lewis (1960). Specifically, this interpersonal meaning draws attention to the significance of the prefix "con-" in these two words. Natsoulas points out that the two words once referred to a specifically **interpersonal** dimension of consciousness. Two or more people were conscious of something together "if they shared knowledge about something with each other" (Natsoulas 2000a: 335). Natsoulas summarizes his own earlier treatment of consciousness in the interpersonal sense, or consciousness$_1$, as follows.

> I argued in my previous article [Natsoulas 1991, PJT] that the knowledge involved in consciousness$_1$, rather than being just a passive state of knowledge, must be, at least from time to time, activated and phenomenological. That is, in each one of the individuals who stand in a consciousness$_1$ relation with each other, the specific joint knowledge shared must inform his or her active thought. What their mutual consciousness$_1$ relation is all about and the fact of their sharing with each other knowledge of it must be manifested in each of them, in the occurrent awareness belonging to each individual.
>
> (Natsoulas 2000a: 335)

Natsoulas draws attention to the inadequacies of those views which identify consciousness "simply with having inner awareness of states of consciousness" (2000: 335). The interpersonal aspect of consciousness is relevant here. As already anticipated in previous chapters (see chapter 1, section 3), the interpersonal aspect of consciousness can be connected to the interpersonal dimension of linguistic meaning (chapter 8).

In systemic-functional linguistic theory, the interpersonal dimension of linguistic meaning is defined as language as action as distinct from language as reflection (chapter 5, section 7). Furthermore, (proto-)interpersonal meaning, as we saw in chapter 3, emerges prior to experiential meaning; action precedes reflection in the child's development. However, specification hierarchy logic tells us, and we see, that the earlier stage (action) is integrated to the later stage (experiential reflection) such that the system is globally reorganized along metafunctional lines (chapter 2, section 10). There is no meaning without action. This observation is important to our present discussion of (self-)consciousness because it shows how the dialectical interpenetration of action and reflection implies change and becoming. Thus, a particular experiential construal may imply a given course of action; a given course of action implies values; given certain values we orient to and prefer certain courses of action rather than others. Insofar as (self-)consciousness is a self's orientation to a state or object of consciousness, we can see how the self emerges in relation to its objects of consciousness.

The above considerations land us in the realm of specificity and actual situations. If we can say that a language system, in the individuated sense that I outlined above, is characterized by the quality of concreteness, then (self-)consciousness is characterized by specificity and situatedness – or historical and situational uniqueness – whereas concreteness reflects the logic of an entire specification hierarchy, reaching right back through all the layers of semiosis (iconic, indexical, symbolic), to the vaguest, most general categories that characterized its most primordial stage of being (Thibault 2000a: 301–303; 2003b; 2004: 118–120, 126–134).

The interpersonal sense of consciousness that has been variously discussed by Dewey, Lewis, and Natsoulas has affinities with the interpersonal dimension of linguistic meaning. Thus, Natsoulas, referring to Dewey, argues that two or more people are conscious of something "if they shared knowledge about something with each other" (Natsoulas 2000a: 335). One central way in which this happens is through linguistic interaction. Language does not simply "report" already existing states of consciousness. This view preserves an essentially monological conception of language. It takes the act of reporting one's consciousness as the starting point of a process which emanates from individual consciousness *per se*. However, the dialogical conception of language requires that this view be rejected. Consciousness, too, must be rethought accordingly. This is, of course, the central point of the present chapter (see also chapter 8). I shall argue that language does not report individual consciousness. Instead, it acts on and potentially transforms the consciousness of self and other. If language merely reported individual consciousness, then language would not play a constitutive role in the shaping of consciousness. However, consciousness is the giving of meaning to experience in the perspective of the self. Language plays a constitutive role in the enacting and construing of meaningful relationships. Moreover, what is "reported", so to speak, in the view which I am criticizing here, does not necessarily have its point of origin in individual consciousness. The verbal report is more likely to be part of a much more complex dialogue within individual consciousness as well as between one consciousness and another. We see this principle at work in, for example, the following exchange between Dion and Paul:

> Dion: (// (1) what's he SPILLT it // alREADy?
> // (2) look at the MESS // PAUL // (3) you're gonna have to CLEAN UP // in HERE // (4) it's a PIG STY //
> Paul: // (5) it is RATHer a PIG STY //
> Dion: / (6) YES // WELL // it's YOUR ANimal //

Thus, Dion's move, comprising the clauses, (2) *look at the mess Paul* (3) *you're gonna have to clean up in here* (4) *it's a pig sty*, interpersonally enacts and negotiates a jointly shared consciousness relation between herself and Paul. This is so in the sense that Dion seeks to activate, through her interpersonal negotiation, a joint knowledge frame which informs, to paraphrase Natsoulas (see above quotation), the active thought of both participants in the exchange. Thus, knowledge and the sharing of it in the "concurrent awareness" of the two individuals are manifested in the interpersonal negotiation that takes place in the discourse. In the example, Dion first deploys the imperative clause (a proposal for action) *look at the mess in here Paul* in order to create, in the first instance, a shared frame of perceptual awareness, i.e. by jointly sharing the perceptual awareness of the untidy state of the room. The second clause, *you're gonna have to clean up in here*, proposes a modalized state of consciousness in the form of the proposed action which Dion seeks to create as a concurrent awareness in Paul. The declarative clause *it's a pig sty* is a proposition in which the speaker, in providing her own modal orientation, seeks to conjoin Paul to this same modal framework. That is, she seeks, with this clause, to create in Paul's concurrent awareness a joint frame of knowledge by virtue of their jointly orienting to the same modal evaluation in the proposition, along with the desired course of action which is implied by this particular evaluation of the referent situation (the untidy condition of the room).

The discursive processes described above can occur by virtue of the fact that the brain is a somatic recognition system. Thus, sensori-motor activity *qua* expression stratum enables this specifically interpersonal sense of consciousness to occur. Bodily activity which is projected into the environment provides a shared frame of reference in which one's interlocutor can recategorize in his or her brain vocal tract or other articulatory activity as categories of semantic content in his or her consciousness.

The various mood categories in the interpersonal grammar of English dialogically coordinate the exchange of information (propositions) and/or goods-&-services (proposals) at the same time that they jointly coordinate a modalized stance or evaluation toward these propositions and proposals on the part of the addresser and the addressee. Unlike the child's early protolinguistic exchanges with others, which are concerned with joint engagement in action routines, the metafunctional character of language means that both action and reflection are jointly shared and oriented to. The dialogically coordinated SELF–NONSELF relation allows for joint access to the I–you interpersonal relationship in the form of the jointly dialogically negotiated interacts (chapter 8, section 1) and the stances towards these of interlocutors. At the same time, this dialogical relation allows for joint access to a shared experiential frame of reference which is about some phenomenon that is outside the I-you relation. Moreover, the "physiognomic gaze" of the spoken voice that was identified by Bühler (chapter 2, section 4) provides shared access to the body-states and feelings of interactants towards each other in the exchange. The intersubjective character of SELF–NONSELF exchanges also extends to the textual metafunction. The resources of this metafunction make possible an intersubjectively shareable and textured deictic field, to use Bühler's term, which grounds the joint orientation to both the interaction between them as well as to the experientially construed phenomenon of experience that is being jointly attended to.

Now, the notion that propositions are arguable is a meta-semantic one. The arguability of propositions is founded on the recognition that propositions can be sourced at the semanticized viewpoints or perspectives of some SELF and that this viewpoint can be agreed or disagreed with, believed, disbelieved, affirmed, denied, and so on. That is, the proposition provides access to a determinate viewpoint which emanates from the symbolic neural space where intentionality is sourced (chapter 1, section 3). Furthermore, this viewpoint is interpreted as standing in a particular internal relation to the world vis-à-vis the proposition or proposal which is uttered. For example, the declarative proposition *it's a pig sty* can be understood and responded to as a determinate viewpoint which Dion has regarding the state of the room. Moreover, this viewpoint can be related to an intentional source who evaluates the referent situation in a particular way. This is what it means to say that a given proposition or proposal is grounded in a proximate intention in symbolic neural space (chapter 5, section 13; chapter 8, section 1). As Bogdan (2000: 104) points out, it is the interpretive ability which allows us to recognize the proposition as being about a relation between the proximate intentions (desires, memories, and so on) of the self and some aspect of the world in the perspective of the self. This relation cannot be derived from access to a conscious state *per se* (see section 1).

The prior emergence of proposals in the ontogenesis of language, as we saw in chapter 3, section 6, shows the early concern with other-engagement and other-interpretation before the emergence of self-engagement and self-interpretation. From the child's point of view, a proposed action entails the ability to ascribe to the other the capacity to carry out the particular action. That is, the child develops the ability to interpret the other as having that ability along with the required other–world relation. Propositions, on the other hand, show a tendency to be more concerned with the relation between self and others. This tendency is shown in the fact that propositions either seek to give the addresser's modalized perspective or they appeal to the addressee to give his or hers. This negotiation of perspectives entails engaging with and interpreting self in relation to others. The interpreting of the self in relation to others may go hand in hand with the fact that propositions are concerned with the exchange of **meanings**, rather than goods-and-services. For this reason, propositions enable a focus on the meanings that are ascribed to the perspectives of self and others in contrast to other-centred calculations as to how one's interlocutor can be made to perform a proposed action in order to bring about a given outcome that is desired by the addresser (chapter 1, section 3).

In Dion's move, the declarative sub-moves (1b) and (1c) provide further rationalizations for the proposed action in (1a) from the perspective of herself and her attitudes and values. These explanations are a way of making sense of herself to Paul. That is, she implicitly appeals to higher-order norms or principles of tidiness that are recognized and acted on in certain ways in the relevant local interpersonal moral order (chapter 4, sections 3, 4). By the same token, this appeal entails an interpretation of Paul as another self who is also able to make sense of her attitudes and values – her takes on the world – from his perspective. Paul, too, is held to be an agent who can recognize the implicit connection to the relevant interpersonal moral order. This further suggests that Dion is appealing to criteria of agency and responsibility as to how one should act in relation to states of affairs that one is being held responsible for.

The interpersonal sense of consciousness, as we saw above, implicates modalized evaluations of linguistically realized propositions and proposals in a dialogically coordinated frame of reference pertaining to knowledge and/or action. Dion's move in the above example implicates that her interlocutor, Paul, is a reflexive self who is able to evaluate Dion's proposition from his own standpoint. In other words, Dion's proposition implies the recognition of Paul as a self who is able to adopt a similar stance on her proposition. This recognition further implies that Dion can view her own proposition as others (e.g. Paul) would. In this way, she is able to both anticipate and constrain possible responses from others. It also means that Dion attempts to prick's Paul conscience. Again implicitly, she seeks in the discursive negotiation to elicit in Paul a self-appraisal of his own prior actions and responsibilities in relation to Dion's negative evaluation of the present state of affairs. At the same time, Dion's proposition also anticipates and simulates Paul's inner self-appraisal of his own deeds. Once again, we see how early anticipatory simulation of the other's meanings lays the foundation for the inter- and intra-personal dimensions of moral consciousness (chapter 5, sections 7, 14).

The further step, as we shall see in the following section, is when the self regulates and interprets its own actions and meanings from the perspective of the self in inner speech (Thibault 2004a: 271–275). Self-regulation and self-interpretation entail the kind of inner dialogism identified by Vološinov (1976 [1927]) in which the self provides reasons for its own actions and states of consciousness to internalized others at the same time that it responds to what others think and say about the self. The self-reflexive ability to evaluate one's own actions and states of consciousness from the inner perspective of the self as others see the self is vital for the development of moral consciousness and, hence, to our ability to decide on (right or wrong) courses of action on the basis of the self's evaluation of their goodness or badness, rightness or wrongness, and so on. In this way, the self has developed the ability to morally evaluate and interpret itself as performing/having performed/intending to perform some action or as having or remembering some thought or state of consciousness whereby the self is understood as standing in this or that kind of moral relationship to others and to the interpersonal moral orders in which self and others participate as various categories of social agent (chapter 4, sections 3, 4). The ability self-reflexively to understand and to evaluate (judge) oneself as being in a particular kind of moral relation to one's self (and others) is an interpretive operation of a very high order in symbolic neural space. It is a relation in which the self is able to represent itself as a moral agent who stands in a particular kind of moral relation to the world.

7 Extending the interpersonal sense of consciousness to the intrapersonal domain of conscience and consciousness

As Natsoulas shows, the interpersonal sense of consciousness can be extended into the intrapersonal arena, along lines that hark back to Vygotsky's discussion of the transition from interpersonal to intrapersonal forms of thought (chapter 5, section 4). Natsoulas (2000a: 336) cites Lewis (1960: 187) as follows in order to make this point:

> Man might be defined as a reflexive animal. A person cannot help thinking and speaking of himself as, and even feeling himself to be (for certain purposes), two people, one of whom can act upon and observe the other. Thus he pities, loves, admires, hates, despises, rebukes, comforts, masters or is mastered by, "himself". Above all he can be to himself in the relation that I have called consciring. He is privy to his own acts, is his own *conscius* or accomplice. And of course this shadowy inner accompaniment has all the same properties as an external one; he too is a witness against you, a potential blackmailer, one who inflicts shame and fear.
> (Lewis 1960: 187; quoted in Natsoulas 2000a: 336)

Natsoulas is interested in the further implication, left implicit by Lewis, that the relation of consciring with one's self "would seem to be applicable to one's states of consciousness" (Natsoulas 2000a: 336). It is this implication that I now wish to explore.

As Natsoulas (2000a: 339) points out, the intrapersonal sense of conscience and consciousness involves "a more complex psychological process than the simple undergoing of an immediate apprehension – a perception, as Locke would call it – that has for its object a state of consciousness" (Natsoulas 2000a: 339). The immediate first-hand apprehension of a state of consciousness can be seen to be the self's experiencing of its own experiencing of the given state of consciousness in the way that I discussed above. Natsoulas describes the more complex psychological process as follows:

> However, involved in the more complex process is someone's personally witnessing something of himself or herself. And the individual brings what he or she has witnessed or is witnessing to bear, as such, on a judgement concerning himself or herself. Therefore, inner awareness must be part of what is taking place in each one of these cases.
>
> The psychological process that is consciousness$_t$ [i.e. consciousness in the "together sense", as defined by Natsoulas, PJT] requires it. Suppose, for example, that (a) I have performed or am just now performing a certain action toward another person or animal, (b) I am now remembering or taking notice of doing so, and (c) I am bringing what I remember or am now taking notice of to bear on whether I am cruel or have behaved or am behaving cruelly. In order for me to be conscious of myself as being cruel or behaving cruelly on an occasion past or present, I must consult my stream of consciousness.
>
> (Natsoulas 2000a: 339)

Inner awareness is now further differentiated, as compared to the simple undergoing of an immediate apprehension of a state of consciousness. Whereas such immediate apprehensions can be seen to be an experiencing of experiencing, the further differentiation described by Natsoulas may be seen as a further differentiation of meaning from experiencing, along with the concomitant question of a given self's relation to a given experience. The judgements that the self makes concerning itself and the categories required to make these judgements can only be made through available linguistic resources in some community. Judgements are based on values. Having a stream of consciousness implies, with the further differentiation discussed here, that we can selectively orient to that stream, preferring some things about ourselves, not preferring others, and so on. The value stances that we adopt on our own stream of consciousness may lead us to selectively ignore some aspects of our own stream and, hence, of our own deeds.

Like the interpersonal sense discussed earlier, this intrapersonal sense entails that others can also judge one's own deeds just as one can witness and judge one's own deeds (Natsoulas 2000a: 339). The intrapersonal sense of consciousness entails a form of internalized dialogism: ". . . one is to oneself as though one were another, witnessing one's action and, based on what one has witnessed, making judgments about oneself of the kind that another person also could make" (Natsoulas 2000a: 340). The capacity to look at oneself and one's states of consciousness as others do entails the self-reflexive ability to place oneself in the position of the other. To quote Natsoulas:

> Just as another person can have firsthand knowledge concerning oneself and bring it to bear in forming conclusions regarding the kind of person that one is, so too, one can be to oneself in this regard as another can be to oneself. It is, of course, this "objective" relation to oneself involved in consciousness$_t$ that makes of it the distinct kind of consciousness that it is. As we have seen, Lewis (1960) described the relation in terms of his notion of consciring.
>
> Consciousness in the intrapersonal together sense is analogous to consciousness in the interpersonal sense; one is to oneself as though one were another, witnessing one's actions and, based on what one has witnessed, making judgements about oneself of the kind that another person could also make. There is involved in consciousness$_t$ a duality of awareness: an awareness-with, that goes well beyond the awareness-with that James's stream of consciousness includes and his stream of sciousness lacks. It is as though each of us possesses

two mental lives, and one of these can draw upon the other in order to come to judgements regarding the kind of person that we are. There is the mental life from which our actions emanate and there seems to be a second life observing this process and drawing conclusions about the individual whose mental life it is.

(Natsoulas 2000a: 340)

Natsoulas's duality of awareness expresses (1) the ways in which our actions are entrained along specific trajectories by the higher-scalar neurological dynamics of symbolic possibilities; and (2) the ability to self-reflexively think about and evaluate our own actions and the states of consciousness that are associated with these actions. That is, one can reflect on and be aware of the choices that constrain one's actions (Natsoulas 2000a: 340). Natsoulas's second form of awareness brings in further levels of differentiation at still higher levels of neurological organization which allow the self to differentiate itself from others in increasingly complex ways. The meanings that constrain action trajectories are self-reflexively differentiated in terms of ethical values (Natsoulas 2000a: 341). Natsoulas draws attention to the intimate co-penetration of the two forms of awareness. This co-penetration is so because action, as distinct from mere behaviour, implicates values. The value-laden character of action is reflected in the metafunctional organization of language. The experiential function enables individuals to make language-specific relevant differentiations in the phenomena of experience at the same time that these experiential categories are harnessed to interpersonal ones for acting in the world and interacting with others. The same can be said of lower-level perceptual and conceptual categories, which have proto-metafunctional characteristics. Thus, the perceptual discriminations that an organism is able to make are linked to the ways it can act in the world. Conceptual thinking enables conceptual categories to be linked together as conceptual structures that are not directly linked to behaviour (Edelman 1992: 108–110). The symbolic distinctions of language can be seen as a more specified development of this same logic. The symbolic resources of language enable diverse selves to coordinate and negotiate their viewpoints and actions in discourse across increasingly diverse space-time scales, as compared to the perceptual and conceptual discriminations made on lower integrative levels.

Conscience can, therefore, be seen as the capacity to value some courses of actions rather than others. Values, in turn, implicate choices from among alternative actions, preferring some rather than others. The very higher order meta-representation in symbolic neural space gives rise to an inner perspective of the self and its agency. Agency, in the human case, implies a self whose meanings not only constrain specific action trajectories; it also implies a self who has the ability to self-reflexively choose from and evaluate conflicting courses of action and their associated values. Human selves are embedded in interpersonal moral orders (Harré 1983) as a result of the cross-coupling of individuals to a particular ecosocial semiotic system. As a result of these couplings, the self acquires inner perspectives on its own actions. These perspectives enable the self to act as an agent in the world. That is, its actions can be explained, justified, and accounted for in a given interpersonal order by both self and others in the sense that actions have effects and consequences which can be sourced at the self and its perspectives and values.

The constraining and entraining of the self's action trajectory by semantic alternatives in symbolic neural space can be related to the dialogic properties of semiosis. The perspectives and associated values which the self acquires along its trajectory are selective re-envoicements of voices and their associated values in the system (the state space) of social heteroglossia of some community. The inner voices whereby one evaluates, judges, challenges, commands, exhorts, doubts, questions, praises, and so on, one's own actions and states of consciousness have the form of an internalized dialogue among alternative voices which may represent a potentially conflicting diversity of social viewpoints and values (Vološinov 1976 [1927]). Thus, one can be conscious not merely of some state of consciousness, but also of the fact that one has, in the past, performed, for example, a wrongdoing or some deed that one is ashamed of. It is in this way that an agent comes to be conscious of some wrongdoing in the sense of judging one's actions to be wrong and feeling guilty about it (Natsoulas 2000a: 343). The form of inner awareness of one's deeds that takes the form of judging the rightness or wrongness of one's deeds suggests that the self identifies with the voice of a particular opinion group in the society.

This identification suggests a close link between the notions of conscience and consciousness, as well as between these notions and the system of social heteroglossia in a given context of culture (chapter 2, section 9).

Natsoulas (2000a: 346) draws attention to the semantic connection between the words "conscience" and "consciousness": the former word is defined in terms of the latter in the sense that conscience consists in evaluating, appraising, judging, and so on, one's actions or certain states of consciousness that one experiences (Natsoulas 2000a: 346). Conscience is an intrapersonal form of consciousness coupled with the inner evaluation of the rightness, wrongness, and so on, of one's own actions. Natsoulas (2000a: 347) further posits, following Lewis (1960), that conscience is based on an "inner law giver". The inner law giver is a voice which prescribes courses of action, commands, and directs one's decisions, gives permission to the self to act in a certain way, and so on. The inner law giver is an internalized semantic attractor space which entrains the agent's actions along certain trajectories rather than others (Juarrero 1999: 248). Consciousness of what is right or wrong – i.e. conscience – and the concomitant passing of inner judgements on one's own actions and states of consciousness mean that the agent's (individual) neural dynamics have self-organized into a very high-order semantic space embodying ethical and moral values. The agent acquires ethical perspectives which constrain possible action trajectories. As Juarrero (1999: 248) points out, when action is constrained by meaning and value, the agent is increasingly de-coupled from immediate environmental stimuli (Maritain 1990 [1950]: 36–38). The agent has the capacity to adopt perspectives consisting of choices from among diverse ethical standards and moral values. This capacity means that the agent is able to access an increasing diversity of meanings and values that have the potential to entrain its actions.

The inner awareness of the ethical character or moral value of one's own actions and states of consciousness means that context-dependent reentrant activity in the brain (Edelman 1992: chapter 9) leads to the self-organization of increasingly higher levels of organization in the way theorized by Flohr (1991), for example (chapter 1, section 2; Thibault 2004a: chapter 6). The activities of consciousness are embodied in the brain by a meta-loop of neural organization that is analogous to the way in which, for example, lower down the hierarchy of neural organization, we have an inner awareness of our own experiencing of a given phenomenal experience (see above). The neural meta-loop of conscience (moral consciousness) entails a self-organizing neural dynamics that gives meaning and value to the self's own actions and states of consciousness. The self-organizing dynamics of this semantic level gives rise to further differentiations. Thus, the differential ethical values, moral standards, and the different ways of appraising and judging the self *qua* other mean that the interpersonal moral orders in which the self operates, their perspectives, values, and criteria for the attribution and assignment of agency and responsibility, are imported into and re-envoiced in the self-perspective such that they effectively become the internal dynamics of the individual (chapter 2, sections 5, 6). The ability to internally recognize and appraise one's actions and states of consciousness – i.e. the possession of a conscience – means that higher-scalar contextual constraints embody ethics and values, along with the possibility of selecting from an increasingly differentiated repertoire of moral values. This ability is the phenomenological manifestation of the emergence of self-organizing neural dynamics of conscience, which impose constraints on the lower level dynamics of our own states of consciousness and our own action trajectories.

8 Guilty conscience and the feeling body

Natsoulas makes the further important observation that:

> . . . whenever one's judgements of conscience are of the kind in which one condemns oneself, the judgements are productive of feelings of guilt. The concept of conscience would seem to require that feelings of guilt be an accompaniment of any actual inner self-condemnation. The occurrence of such feelings indicates that self-condemnation has taken place.
>
> (Natsoulas 2000a: 348)

At the every high level of neural organization that we are considering here, we can see how values (Edelman 1992: 132–133) are coupled to particular states of consciousness in ways that influence and modulate our action trajectories. The coupling of the moral condemnation of one's self to particular bodily feelings shows how the body itself modulates states of consciousness, in the process nudging and motivating us in the direction of certain values-action choices rather than others, or else producing adverse or negative affective reactions to other value-action choices in the form of negative somatic feelings.

Affect-laden somatic states, as the research of Damasio (1999) demonstrates, are coupled to states of consciousness and to the judgements of conscience in ways that can select and bias the ethical choices and values which are available to the individual. The selection and biasing of such choices mean that the association of feelings of guilt with certain actions performed or being performed by the self, or with certain states of consciousness which are entertained by the self, entail that bodily feelings can get coupled to one's moral self-evaluation of one's actions (acts of conscience) and states of consciousness. Moreover, these processes occur in ways which have downwardly causal effects on the kinds of interpersonal relations which the self has with others, the different qualities of these, the different kinds of action trajectories which the self chooses from among the available contrast sets of act-types available in a given context. Conscience is inner awareness and evaluation (interpretation) of one's own deeds and the link between these deeds and the bodily feelings they arouse. Lewis's "inner law giver" is a globally stable self-organizing neural structure at a very high level of semantic organization. It regulates and stabilizes the transactions between the individual's internal dynamics and the (external) ecosocial environment of one's exchanges with others.

Body feelings are made meaningful by their contextual redundancies with categories of emotional experience that are recognized and permitted in a given community. The experiencing of particular somatic states as redounding with a particular emotion-category occurs in the perspective of the self. The self is, in turn, coupled to and entrained by higher-scalar social formations and the interpersonal moral orders that are embedded in these (chapter 4, section 3). That is, the self is constructed as a particular type of social identity or personality through its entraining to and positioning in the practices of particular higher-order social formations. Furthermore, social practices such as publicly humiliating another person, shouting angrily at someone, taunting or insulting someone for their sexual or other preferences, scolding a child for a misdemeanour or other form of socially disapproved action, and so on, can produce unpleasant or painful body feelings in individuals and in ways that get linked to and are experienced as contextually redounding with specific emotion-categories. The contextual redundancies between these social practices, their associated social viewpoints and values, emotion-categories, and body feelings are internalized as discourses of control – cf. Lewis's "inner law giver" – that can speak to one's self as the inner voice of conscience which judges and evaluates one actions and states of consciousness in the way discussed by Natsoulas. For example, the hierarchy of metaredundancy relations whereby we make sense of and activate the experience of guilt and its associated body feelings in the perspective of the self, as well as its grounding in the moral values of some interpersonal moral order in some community, may be schematized as follows:

body feeling states/experienced emotion-category: guilt // self /// social practice: e.g. punish other //// interpersonal moral order for assigning criteria of right and wrong actions, thoughts, etc.

If you verbally abuse another person or get angry with someone, then you are doing more than just selecting from a set of contrasting social act-types (e.g. "praise", "encourage", "comfort", and so on). The social acts of verbal abuse and displaying anger play their role as functioning parts in some culturally recognizable activity-structure such as "intimidation", "threat", "harassment", and so on. In so doing, they index some particular contextually relevant value or social situation-type (e.g. gender relations, teacher pupil, relations, employer employee relations, and so on), which is invoked as relevant to the meaning of the verbal abuse or the display of anger. Verbally abusing someone or being angry with someone do all of these things.

However, they can also induce or bring about clusters of physical reactions and symptoms (e.g. racing heart, tense muscles, trembling, upset stomach, increased blood pressure, and so on). Feeling states of the body are contextually integrated to and modulate – or "qualify" in Damasio (1996 [1994]: xvii) – memories, perceptual experiences, social encounters, and so on, in ways that get entrained by higher-scalar ecosocial meanings and constraints. Furthermore, individuals associate these physical responses in complex, discursively mediated ways with culturally recognized emotions such as fear, guilt, intimidation, sadness, and so on. Moreover, these processes of discursive mediation, in turn, index social situations of, say, parent-child or gender domination, teacher-pupil control, and so on, and the participant roles that are involved in these activities. In other words, our ecosocial semiotic practices also induce bodily sensations – both pleasurable and painful – in others. They do so in ways which contextually integrate these somatic states and responses with higher-order emotional states (Harré 1983: 123–126; Scheff 1997; Wierzbicka 1999), which are linked to one's positioning within particular social activity-structures or discourse genres (Harré 1983: 137), as well as to the accumulated bodily memories that the self collects along his or her life trajectory as a result of the various contingencies which constitute his or her historical-biographical emergence as an individual.

8

Interpersonal Meaning, Exchange, and the Dialogic Basis of Consciousness

1 Genre finalization and the dialogic negotiation of semiotic and material friction

The question of ethical values and moral standards as constitutive of the voice(s) of conscience – Lewis's inner law giver – is closely linked to the interpersonal dimension of meaning. Interpersonal meaning always entails meta-perspectives on the dialogic moves that self and other enact in discourse. Mood and modality, for example, are key grammatical resources here. The child does not internalize sentences as such (chapter 5, section 1). Instead, she re-envoices the genre structures and discourse voices in and through which she interacts with others (chapter 5). The elementary speech genres identified by Bakhtin (1986) and Vološinov (1983) provide the means whereby the Meaning System contextualizes supersystem transactions as social activities and social situations. Here is Vološinov's explanation as to how these speech genres "finalize" specific speech situations:

> The finalized question, the exclamation, the command and the request, are the most typical examples of whole utterances in daily use. All of them (especially, for instance, the command and the request) require a non-verbal complement, and, in fact, also a non-verbal beginning. The very type of finalization of these miniature real-life genres is determined by the friction between the word and the non-verbal environment, and between the word and an alien word (another person's word).
>
> Hence the form taken by a command is determined by the obstacles it may meet, the degree of compliance, and so on. The finalization typical for a given genre is a response to the accidental and the non-repeatable features of the real-life situation.
>
> It makes sense to speak of special types of genre finalization in the language of everyday life, only where there are at least some stable forms of everyday communication which have been fixed by life and circumstances.
>
> (Vološinov 1983: 116–117)

The "stable forms of everyday communication" are the various kinds of semantic interact such as Question^Answer, Command^Compliance, Offer^Acceptance, Statement^Response, and so on. In English, the lexicogrammatical resources of the various mood categories, which belong to the interpersonal grammar of the clause, play a key role in the enactment of these semantic interacts. The "friction between the word and the non-verbal environment", on the one hand, and "between the word and an alien word", on the other, corresponds to the basic difference between the social work which is involved in the use of the imperative and indicative moods. This work takes place through processes of discursive negotiation. This negotiation always requires some determinate discourse genre, or semantic interact (Vološinov, *op. cit.*; Halliday 1994 [1985]: 69–70; Martin 1992b; Matthiessen 1995: chap. 5), in order that the meaning exchange may take determinate shape in ecosocial space-time.

The Mood component is concerned with the "clause as exchange" – what Halliday (1994 [1985]: 68) calls an "interact" – in which dialogic moves coordinate both addresser and addressee in relation to the exchange of either information (PROPOSITIONS) or goods-&-services (PROPOSALS). Halliday has defined the notion of "interact" in relation to the exchange of information and goods-&-services as follows:

The most fundamental types of speech role, which lie behind all the more specific types that we may eventually be able to recognize, are just two: (i) giving, and (ii) demanding. Either the speaker is giving something to the listener (a piece of information, for example) or he is demanding something from him. Even these elementary categories already involve complex notions: giving means "inviting to receive", and demanding means "inviting to give". The speaker is not only doing something himself; he is also requiring something of the listener. Typically, therefore, an "act" of speaking is something that might more appropriately be called an "interact": it is an exchange, in which giving implies receiving and demanding implies giving in response.

Cutting across this basic distinction between giving and demanding is another distinction, equally fundamental, that relates to the nature of the commodity being exchanged. This may be either (a) goods-&-services or (b) information. Examples are given in Figure 4.1 [renumbered Figure 8.1]. If you say something to me with the aim of getting me to do something for you, such as "kiss me!" or "get out of my daylight!", or to give you some object, as in "pass the salt!", the exchange commodity is strictly non-verbal: what is being demanded is an object or action, and language is brought in to help the process along. This is an exchange of goods-&-services. But if you say something to me with the aim of getting me to tell you something, as in "is it Tuesday?" or "when did you last see your father?", what is being demanded is information: language is the end as well as the means, and the only answer expected is a verbal one. This is an exchange of information; examples in Figure 4.1 [renumbered Figure 8.1]. These two variables, when taken together, define the four primary speech functions of OFFER, COMMAND, STATEMENT, and QUESTION. These, in turn, are matched by a set of desired responses: accepting an offer, carrying out a command, acknowledging a statement, and answering a question.

Commodity exchanged Role in exchange	(a) goods-&-services	(b) information
(i) giving	"offer" would you like this teapot?	"statement" he's giving her the teapot
(ii) demanding	"command" give me that teapot!	"question" what is he giving her?

Figure 8.1 Halliday's giving or demanding goods-&-services or information

(Halliday 1994 [1985]: 68–69)

The interpersonal grammatical resources of mood in English are a primary resource for the enacting of the various basic types of semantic interact that are defined by Halliday. The centrality of mood in the interpersonal exchange of goods-&-services and information and in the realization of the dialogically organized interactants whereby this takes place enable a fruitful link to be made with Vološinov's observations concerning the negotiation of the semiotic and/or material friction between addresser and addressee in a given exchange.

Imperative mood is the principle interpersonal grammatical resource for negotiating the difference – Vološinov calls it the "friction" – between the position of the addresser and the state of affairs in the material world which the addresser desires to change. The contradiction between the two is a source of friction. This friction gives rise to the meaning which the interactants in the exchange jointly attend to and negotiate in the discourse. The difference to be negotiated in the exchange is both modal and material. It requires the compliance of the addressee to the proposed action in order that the desired state of affairs comes into being. Indicative mood is the primary interpersonal grammatical resource for negotiating the difference between the semiotic-modal viewpoint of the addresser and that of the addressee. That is, between the addresser's "word" and the "alien word" of the addressee. The difference, or the friction, is a modal one between self and other.

The finalization that Vološinov writes about in the above quotation shows how one component of a semantic interact, corresponding to the addresser's contribution to the exchange, anticipates and brings about a complementary response in the addressee. There is no actual exchange of meaning in the sense that meaning does not physically change hands or pass from one interactant to another in the exchange process. The addresser's contribution and the addressee's response result in a change in the internal dynamics of both participants and hence their possibilities for action. The underlying structures of human discourse are, generally speaking, implicit dialogic structures that do not only regulate the contributions – the dialogic moves – of interactants; they also have the capacity to act on and change the consciousness of both self and other.

In my view, the fundamental semantic unit of language is not the clause or the sentence, but the dialogically coordinated interact. Minimally, a dialogic interact is a two-part structure which can be schematized as DIALOGIC MOVE^RESPONSE. More specific forms are QUESTION^ANSWER, COMMAND^COMPLIANCE, OFFER^ACCEPTANCE, STATEMENT^RESPONSE TO STATEMENT. The dialogic basis of language does not mean that all possibilities for responding to a given utterance have been predicted in advance. Rather, it shows that a social agent embodies in his or her central nervous system models of possible and potential responses that are anticipated by the system's own internal dynamics. The dialogic character of language can be seen to be a further specification of Rosen's (1985) notion of anticipatory systems. Anticipatory systems have the capacity to anticipate and to constrain their own futures. This means that anticipation is achieved through internalized models of potential responses from and/or to others. The mood system in the interpersonal grammar can be seen in this light.

According to the traditional view in linguistics, mood refers to a set of basic sentence-types, e.g. declarative, interrogative, exclamative, oblative, and imperative. In systemic-functional linguistic theory, mood is interpreted as a system of resources for creating dialogic moves (utterances and responses to others' utterances) in discourse. The interpersonal grammatico-semantic resources of the mood system constitute a lower-level (to the self) model of self–nonself interpersonal transactions and engagements. This means that the self has a repertoire of interpersonal grammatico-semantic resources for anticipating and, therefore, for responding to actual and potential nonselves and their dialogic moves in the discursive negotiation of meaning. The resources of the mood system in major clauses and the many categories of minor clauses provide a repertoire of possible ways for both initiating and responding to dialogic exchanges (Martin 1981; 1992a: 31–35; Halliday 1994 [1985]: 69–70). The basic categories are presented in Figure 8.2.

Finalization can be reformulated in terms of the ways in which high-order semantic constraints in symbolic neural space regulate and constrain the agent's internal dynamics, along with those originating from the immediate situational context of the utterance, the relevant intertextual systems, and so on. As I said above, an utterance is an action trajectory which flows from and is constrained by an intentional source of meaning in symbolic neural space (chapter 5, sections 14–15). The semantic content of the higher-order intention is transduced (not transformed) and, therefore, preserved (rather than changed) by the motor functions that project the action trajectory into the external context of situation of the individual. The point is that meanings originating in symbolic neural space downwardly constrain motor functions on the expression stratum. In this way, the meaning that has its proximate source in an individual's

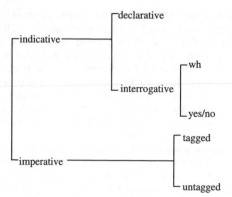

Figure 8.2 Systemic network of basic mood options in the grammar of English, shown as a system of contrasting values; lexicogrammatical stratum

symbolic neural space will flow into and modulate the agent's bodily activity, as well as relevant environmental features along a determinate action trajectory. Juarrero (1999: 188) further points out that the higher-scalar meaning, corresponding to the proximate intention, constrains the semantic state space within which motor activity unfolds such that the resulting motor activity "retains the dynamic organization that identifies the intention" (Juarrero 1999: 188). In discourse, the semantic interacts that organize the exchange of meanings between addresser and addressee show how the proximate intentions of agents are taken up and responded to by interlocutors in ways which negotiate the semantics of the other speaker's trajectory (chapter 5, section 15).

For example, Dion's imperative clause *look at the mess in here Paul*, which I considered in the analysis in chapter 7, section 6, embodies a proximate intention which can be characterized in semantic terms as [DIRECT PAUL'S VISUAL ATTENTION TO THE MESS CAUSED BY THE COCKATOO]. Insofar as Paul complies with this directive by, for example, directing his gaze to the mess (a material bodily response) or responding linguistically in ways which recognize and take up the semantics of Dion's move for the purposes of its further development, we can say that his response – linguistic or non-linguistic – preserves and adaptively modifies the meaning of Dion's intention. The resulting finalization – the local resolution – of the situation in and through the given dialogic interact means that the accidental and non-repeatable contingencies of everyday situations – e.g. the mess made by the cockatoo – that Vološinov refers to have been entrained to the semantic trajectories of the agents involved in the given exchange. The respective semantic trajectories are negotiated in and through the dialogic interact such that a form of socially recognizable closure is achieved. Thus, Paul's visually attending to the mess is an actional response which conforms on the motor level to the semantics of Dion's intention. In this way, material and semiotic contingencies are entrained to the genre forms of determinate social situation-types.

2 The dialogic negotiation of semiotic and material friction: an example from children's play

In this section, I shall briefly analyse a short excerpt from the transcript of a play episode which I first analysed in chapter 4. In the analysis below, I shall focus on phase 5 of the longer episode discussed in chapter 4. The purpose of the analysis below is to reveal the ways in which the contributions of the two playmates connect their interaction to the interpersonal moral orders in which their joint play activity is embedded. Table 8.1 provides a semantic gloss on each speaker's moves in this phase of the overall episode.

Table 8.1 Dialogic moves in Paola–Elena play text

Speaker	Italian text	English translation	Dialogic move: Semantic gloss
Move 1a: Elena-baby	*dobbiamo* fare la mente mamma per oggi per i ghiaccioli di menta	*we have to* prepare the mint mummy for today for the mint paddle pops	Proximate intention: Propose Action
Move 1b:	domani è festa mia che compio dieci anni quindi bisogna fare in fretta	tomorrow it's my birthday when I turn ten so we have to hurry up	Give reason: Condition^Proposed Action
Move 2: Paola-mummy:	è vero sai che quello che stai dicendo è proprio vero	it's true you know that what you're saying is really true	Ratification/Approval
Move 3: Elena-baby:	perché alle feste bisogna fare qualcosa da mangiare altrimenti gli invitati se ne vanno subito	because at parties you must prepare something to eat otherwise the guests will leave straightaway	General principle: Reason^Consequence
Move 4: Paola-mummy:	è vero	it's true	Ratification / Approval

In move 1a, Elena seeks to conjoin Paola to her (Elena's) modal perspective in order to recruit Paola as a co-agent in the carrying out of the desired action that is proposed in this move. Elena's modulated declarative proposition provides the speaker's modal perspective at the same time that she assumes that her addressee lacks the required modal investment in the proposition. In this sense, move 1b seeks to anticipate and constrain Paola's response. Semantically, move 1b is a further elaboration of 1a. In 1b, the speaker provides a specific Reason-Explanation for the desired course of action that was proposed in 1a. In the same move, she also proposes a further related course of action directed toward the same end ("we have to hurry up"), which can be seen as a prosodic amplification and a semantic elaboration of move 1a. In providing the Reason-Explanation structure, Elena demonstrates that she can connect proposed courses of action to rational criteria that are socially shareable and recognizable in a given moral order (Hasan 1992a; Habermas 1984 [1981]; Thibault 1992, 2002). In both cases, we see how Elena's complex discourse move seeks to negotiate both a material lack, corresponding to the desired future state of affairs in the material domain (the paddle pops), and a modal position of [–Lack] ("we must" . . . "need to") in which she has invested at the same time that she attempts to negotiate her addressee's investment in the same modal position. Paola's response in move 2 shows her willingness to take up the modal position articulated by Elena and, therefore, to agree to the proposed course of action. Paola's response in her play role as mother can also be seen as the activation of a parental voice in which she provides ratification of and shows approval of Elena's Reason-Explanation in move 1b.

In move 3, Elena gives voice to a more general, socially grounded, principle for the proposed action. Semantically, this takes the form of a Reason^Consequence structure in which she spells out a general rule of socially correct behaviour towards one's party guests, as well as the negative consequences if this rule is not observed. In both of Elena's moves 1b and 3, we see a focus on the interpretation of herself in relation to Paola, rather than an exclusive imperative-type focus on the other. This focus on self may motivate the use of declarative rather than imperative clauses here (see chapter 7, section 6). This is so on two levels. The first, more immediate level is that of the interaction between the two girls in the play setting. The second level refers to the more implicit voices of those implied others that are associated with the social contexts invoked in the girls' play. Thus, Elena-baby is not only explaining herself to Paola-mother; she is also implicitly responding to and explaining herself to the voices and viewpoints associated with specific norms of social conduct concerned with expectations about birthday parties and how to provide for one's invited guests in the relevant interpersonal moral order. Once again, Paola's response in move 4 partially reiterates the Ratification-Approval semantics of her move 2. It can also be seen as an indication of the ways in which both interactants share and subscribe to the same values with reference to the particular interpersonal moral order that is being indexed here.

In this exchange, the differences to be negotiated by the two interactants are both material and semiotic. These differences are a source of friction in the sense discussed by Vološinov (see section 1). The contradiction (the friction) between Elena's implicitly negative evaluation of the given present state of affairs (no mint to make the paddle pops) and the desired future state of affairs (having the paddle pops ready for the party) is the background friction, so to speak, which generates a particular complex of meanings as a conscious figure against this generalized background. Furthermore, this conscious figure, in the form of, for example, the modulated declarative proposition in move 1a, dialogically coordinates and acts upon the consciousness of **both** interlocutors. Paola's responses in moves 2 and 4 constitute her dialogic uptake of Elena's moves 1a–b and 3. They show how her consciousness has been acted upon and changed in ways that provide a localized resolution or "finalization" of the friction that is posited by Elena's moves. Such resolution is achieved insofar as Paola both agrees to and approves of Elena's proposed actions. Thus, the structure and semantics of Elena's moves brings about a similar modal position in Paola, as evidenced by her responses in moves 2 and 4. There is no actual exchange of meaning between one person and another. The dialogically coordinated nature of the exchange results in a reciprocal modification of Paola's consciousness through the process of her taking up and responding to Elena's moves in the way that she does.

The emergence of these interpersonal resources with the transition from protolanguage to language means that the system is now more effective, more determinable in negotiating interpersonal exchanges with others. In the protolinguistic stage, the infant does not have the resources for enacting sustained dialogic exchanges with others. His or her protolinguistic gestures constituted relatively vague possibilities with respect to the interpersonal resources afforded by language. The interpersonal reach of the child's contributions to early proto-conversations with others were limited to the dyadic engagement of others in here-now contexts of utterance (chapter 3, sections 5, 6). This limited anticipatory reach of the immature system, along with the relative semantic vagueness of its proto-interpersonal contributions to dyadic engagement with others, meant that the agentive determinability of the system was limited. However, the emergence of the interpersonal grammatico-semantic resources of mood and other related systems enables the system to converge on the regularities of the **discursive** negotiation of meaning in determinate discourse genres such that the system's dialogically coordinated anticipatory potential is enhanced and extended.

3 Finiteness, arguability, and the grounding of propositions in the perspective of the self

In English, all major clauses are marked for mood, i.e. declarative, exclamative, interrogative, and imperative. The system of mood is one of the grammatical resources for indicating the interactional status of the clause and more extended units such as the clause complex in discourse. For example, both the declarative and interrogative clauses *School bores me out of my mind* and *Does school bore you out of your mind?* express a proposition which can be argued about as true, false, believable, reliable, and so on. Arguability is an expression of the move's potential for dialogic uptake and negotiation. However, the two clauses are **interpersonally** modified in different ways so as to indicate different interactional perspectives on this proposition. The first clause is declarative mood; the second interrogative mood. Declarative and interrogative mood operators have scope over the entire clause and modify the proposition expressed by the clause (McGregor 1997: 214). Unlike experiential roles such as Actor, Goal, and so on, mood is not a segment or a constituent in the clause. Rather, the structuring principle is **scopal**: the mood element, which in English is placed in initial position in declarative and interrogative propositions, shapes or modifies the clause **as a whole** so as to indicate how it is to be interpreted interpersonally. That is, the mood element holds the entire clause within its scope and modifies it according to the interactional purpose of the addresser. This scopal type of structuring stands outside the constituent structure of experiential meaning and acts on it. For this reason, it can be said to have a meta-semiotic relationship to the experiential meaning of the clause (Thibault 2002: 99–100).

In the first of the two examples above, the mood element indicates that the proposition is being declared or asserted by the speaker; in the second, the mood element indicates the proposition is being interrogated or questioned. The interpersonal structure of the declarative and interrogative clauses above may be represented as DECL (P) and INTER (P), where (P) stands for the proposition SCHOOL BORE ME OUT OF MY MIND, and DECL and INTER stand for the two indicators as to how the proposition is to be interpreted in relation to its role in the interaction (see McGregor 1997: 214). Mood is said to be scopal in character because the mood element extends over or holds in its scope the entire clause, as shown by the arrow extending from DECL to (P) in the example in Figure 8.3.

In English, grammatical Mood is realized by the configuration of Subject + Finite (Halliday 1994 [1985]: 71–75). The remainder of the clause – what is proposed or propositioned – is the Residue (Halliday 1994 [1985]: 74).

The Finite element, Halliday writes:

> . . . has the function of making the proposition finite. That is to say, it circumscribes it; it brings the proposition down to earth, so that it is something that can be argued about. A good way to make something arguable is to give it a point of reference in the here and now; and this is what the Finite does. It relates the proposition to its context in the speech event.
>
> This can be done in one of two ways. One is by reference to the time of speaking; the other is by reference to the judgement of the speaker. An example of the first is *was* in *an old man was crossing the road*; of the second, *can't* in *it can't be true*. In grammatical terms, the first is PRIMARY TENSE, the second is MODALITY.
>
> (Halliday 1994 [1985]: 75)

The finite element in the mood operator of declarative and interrogative clauses functions to ground a predication so that it can be argued about as a proposition which is true, false, certain, possible, probable, believable, and so on (see above). In English, there are two main ways in which the Finite element can ground a proposition. The first is in relation to the time of speaking of the proposition. This is marked by what Halliday (1994 [1985]: 75, 198–199) calls "primary tense". In the clause, *Fujimora began paving the way for these elections years ago*, the past tense marker in the verb *began* indicates that the proposition is grounded in the past with respect to the time of speaking-listening or writing-reading of the addresser. Modal verbs in English can also serve to ground a proposition by relating it to the speaker's evaluation of the

School	bores		me	out of my mind
Subject	Finite: Present Tense	Predicator	Complement	Adjunct
Mood		Residue		
DECL		(P)		→

Figure 8.3 Declarative clause, showing scopal nature of interpersonal modification

proposition. For example, in the clause *Cautious investors may consider staggering their entry into equities*, the modal *may* serves to ground the proposition in relation to the addresser's evaluation of its believability, possibility, and so on. In both kinds of Finite grounding, the proposition is related to an intentional source – the addresser – who invests in the modal success of the proposition. Finiteness functions therefore to ground the proposition in relation to an intentional source. This source is the initiating point of an action trajectory which extends into the environment and is developed or otherwise truncated according to its interactions with other trajectories as well as with factors in the contextual environment of the trajectory. The Finite element thus constructs a meta-semiotic relationship between the intentional source of the action trajectory – e.g. the addresser – and the proposition which is realized in the clause. In doing so, it invests the proposition with the perspective of an intentional self who intervenes in and takes up a perspective on the proposition for the purpose of guiding and modulating the further development of its trajectory in order to bring it to a successful conclusion.

The Subject, Halliday (1994 [1985]: 76) argues, "supplies the rest of what it takes to form a proposition: namely, something by reference to which the proposition can be affirmed or denied". The Subject specifies the entity in which the speaker invests the modal responsibility of the proposition or proposal.

Consider the following exchange, which I have transcribed from an episode of the BBC television science fiction series *Dr. Who*:

The scene: On board the imperial Dalek mother ship in geo-stationary earth orbit over London. The arrival of the Emperor Dalek (Davros) on the ship's bridge is announced, where he confers with a work group on the situation below, in London. There, a renegade Dalek faction has taken possession of the Hand of Omega, which is much sought after by the Imperial Dalek for the opportunities it will provide to control the time-space flow.
Dalek 1: (1) Emperor on the bridge
Emperor Dalek: (2) Report!
Dalek 2: (3) The transmat* is no longer operational
Dalek 3: (4) We have established the position of the Omega device
Emperor Dalek: (5) Prepare the assault shuttle
Dalek 4: (6) Renegade Dalek agents are in the area
Emperor Dalek: (7) They will surrender the Hand of Omega
                              Source: *Dr. Who*, "In Remembrance of the Daleks", Part 3.

* The transmat refers to a device used to beam Dalek attack squads between the orbiting mother ship and a receiving station hidden in the basement of a London school.

Clauses (2) and (5) are imperatives of the jussive type: the speaker – the emperor Dalek – invests the modal responsibility for the clause in the exophorically retrievable second person addressee. In these two clauses, the addressee so designated is selected by the speaker as the one who is being held responsible for carrying out the proposed actions in these two clauses. Clause (7) is declarative mood. In this clause, the speaker invests the modal responsibility for the proposition in this clause in *they*. Thus, the speaker indicates *they* – the renegade Dalek faction – as the entity about which the proposition in this clause is affirmed. In this case, the modal *will* in the Finite element indicates that the speaker is certain that the still hypothetical (future) situation specified by this proposition will come into being. Clauses (1), (3), and (6) are declarative clauses, which invest the modal responsibility of the speaker's assertion in the third person Subject. In clause (4), on the other hand, the speaker – one of the assembled Daleks on the orbiting mother ship – takes responsibility for a group position (speaker + other Daleks assembled, excluding the emperor Dalek).

Halliday argues that the interpersonal grammar of the clause consists of a Mood-Residue structure. Davidse (1997) further argues that the Residue realizes the type-specification of the process, whereas the Mood, consisting of Subject and Finite, functions to instantiate the Residue by grounding it in a specific speech event. The Mood element in the clause consists of Polarity, Subject, and Finite. Polarity quantifies the process instance, the Finite grounds it in terms of temporal and/or modal proximity to the speech event, and the Subject grounds it in terms of person deixis.

These observations show how the Residue is held in the scope of the Mood element in the clause and modified by it for specific interactional-interpersonal purposes in a given speech event. Thus, the Subject has control over Objects, Complements, and Adjuncts. The Predicator is grounded by the Finite. The Polarity not only quantifies the process instance; it also evaluates the Residue that falls within its scope. The difference between positive and negative polarity can imply different evaluations of the Residue, as seen from the point of view of the speaker.

Consider the difference between *join us today* and *don't join us today*. The difference between positive and negative polarity in these two imperative clauses evaluates the Residue differently, implying a positive evaluation of the proposed action in the first instance and a negative one in the second. The evaluation is made by the speaker, yet the listener (the addressee) is the implied second person Subject whom the speaker selects as being modally responsible for carrying out the proposed action. The item selected as Subject is thus grounded as the person who will actualize the proposed action in the Residue.

The Residue, as Davidse points out, is a type-specification of a process. The Subject grounds the Residue in terms of person deixis. In this case, the addressee is the implicit second person Subject that has this function. The absence of a Finite element in imperatives of this kind is due to the fact that at the moment of uttering the proposal, the Residue is ungrounded in terms of the current speech event. The status of the Residue as type-specification means that the speaker has categories of process that can be proposed of different Subjects in different situations. The speaker of an imperative proposal does not rely on currently perceived situations, but can propose situations that have not at the moment of speaking come into being.

How is the distinction between self and nonself punctuated and construed? How are these two levels of "reality" placed in a meta-semiotic relationship with one another? Interpersonal meaning is about the dialogically constituted relations between self and nonself. It is about semiosis as action and dialogically organized interaction between these two poles of experience. For this reason, the nonself is not a passive external reality which is re-processed by the self as information. Rather, the self's active and dialogically constituted relations to the nonself means that the self continually constructs and elaborates its relations with an internalized or virtual other in and through its interactions with specific external nonselves or others (Bråten 1992; Thibault 2000a: 293–296). The various options in the mood system of English thus constitute a system of differentiations for organizing the relations between self and nonself in discourse. In other words, the mood categories are an attractor space for the organization of transactions between self and nonself. As such, they organize and entrain cross-couplings of material and semiotic processes such that disorder in the environment of the self becomes a source of internal order and increasing complexity. The interpersonal grammar allows the individual to orient to experience and to organize his or her responses to it in ways that are not entirely predictable. That is, dialogically organized transactions between self and nonself entail an active and adaptive orientation to the flux of the experienced world. The various mood options constitute a system of symbolic possibilities both for differentiating self and other in dialogically organized exchange (e.g. the speech roles "I" and "you" as opposed to the non-speech roles "it", "he", "she", etc.), as well as for differentiating the kinds of transaction which take place between the two. These transactions are expressed by the wide variety of speech function moves that are made possible through the mapping of mood onto other dimensions of both interpersonal and experiential meaning (see Hasan 1996a).

In propositions, person deixis and finiteness ground the symbolic object of consciousness in a dialogically coordinated frame of reference. Person deixis enables meanings pertaining not only to the first person perspective of SELF, but also meanings pertaining to second and third persons to be made relevant to and to be integrated to the first person observational-evaluative perspectives of SELF. The resources of temporal proximity deixis and attitudinal proximity deixis in the Finite element dialogically coordinate addresser and addressee in terms of the temporal or modal grounding of the proposition. Grounding also means that addressees can re-ground the temporal or modal perspective specified by the Finite in terms of their own perspective. Both of these resources show how, from the point of view of the interpersonal metafunction, there is a dialogical complementarity between the perspectives of SELF and NONSELF. This means that the SELF's awareness that it is the SELF who is conscious of the given object can be re-grounded in the perspective of some other SELF. The dialogic complementarity of SELF and NONSELF in the exchange process refers to the way in which the interpersonal semantic structure of a given dialogic move, as spoken or written by some addresser, potentially results in a corresponding change in the addressee. Thus, the addressee can be internally modified in ways which result in the dialogic coordination of deictic perspectives. The information which is supplied by person deixis and the Finite are principles of order whereby cross-individual dialogic processes integrate individuals to higher-order dialogically coordinated frames of reference. At the same time, they also provide individuals with resources for being conscious of something in the perspective of a self as point of (inter)action and intentionality.

4 The semantic interact as interface between body-brain system and ecosocial semiotic system

The different categories of mood in the grammar of the clause are functional rather than merely formal units. A given mood choice can function to realize a particular speaker's move in a given dialogic exchange. A move is a discourse semantic unit; it refers to the discourse level contextualization of a given mood choice as the interpersonal enactment of an act in the local discourse context. Moves can be both initiating and responding (Halliday 1994 [1985]: 69–70; Martin 1992a: 33–34). Moves are integrated to still larger-scale dialogic frames or semantic interactants. The dialogic or interpersonal character of mood is evident in the ways in which initiating moves are complemented by responding moves. The most schematic category of semantic interact or dialogic frame can therefore be characterized as follows: INITIATING MOVE^RESPONDING MOVE. The participants in dialogue have in their repertoire sets of options for both initiating dialogue with others and for responding to the dialogic moves of others.

Language is interpersonally or dialogically organized such that one participant's move can be responded to by another's participant's move. The second speaker's move complements that of the first speaker. Moreover, the grammar of the mood system is functionally motivated by and adapted to this mutual, dialogically organized, give-and-take of meanings in dialogue. Thus, the participants in dialogue enact complementary dialogic moves in the course of their interaction. A given move also entails the addresser's evaluative orientation to or stance on the proposition or proposal that is uttered.

By the same token, the dialogic character of propositions and proposals affords the addressee's taking up of a stance on the proposition or proposal. Whenever the addresser utters a proposition or proposal, he or she also simultaneously anticipates the other's (the addressee's) response. The addresser enacts his or her dialogic move in relation to the other at the same time that the addresser participates in a complementary other-centred frame of reference whereby the addresser virtually participates in the addressee's response to the addresser. This does not mean that the addresser can necessarily predict the other's exact response. Rather, the addresser, in anticipating the addressee's response, virtually participates in it. Bråten has shown how parents who are spoon feeding babies accompany their own acts of spoon feeding by their virtual participation in the baby receiving the spoonful of food by opening their mouth as they put the spoon in the baby's mouth (Bråten 2002: 280–282). These very earliest forms of infant semiosis are the foundation on which the more specified and elaborate symbolic structures of language emerge (chapter 3). In the case of linguistic propositions and proposals, the addresser accompanies his or her own act of, say, giving information or goods-&-services by mentally simulating or virtually participating in the addressee's act of receiving the information or the commodity (Bråten 2002).

It is important to emphasize here that dialogic structures and transactions are transindividual processes and systems. Whereas the mirror neurons which have been postulated as providing infants with an inborn capacity for dialogic attunement to others' vocalizations and gestures are embodied in the neural dynamics of the individual organism (Rizzolatti and Arbib 1998; Bråten 2002), it is important to emphasize that the dialogue structures and the dyads in which these structures are enacted are higher-scalar transindividual systems. The mirror neuron discharges on their scale that subtend acts of giving and receiving occur within the individual organism. However, it is clear that these organismic processes could not function without their being integrated to higher-scalar transindividual processes and structures which are essentially ecosocial in nature and origin. Rather than falling back on an individual-centred account of mirror neurons as evidence for a putative "theory of mind", it is more fruitful to view mirror neurons as evidence on their scalar level for the essentially ecosocial semiotic nature of the human body-brain system. Mirror neurons can be understood in terms of the intrinsically dialogic and social nature of the individual body-brain system. That is, they can be understood in relation to the higher-scalar ecosocial system to which individual body-brain systems are integrated. Mirror neurons reflect the co-adaptation and the co-evolution of these two levels. This relationship can be expressed in terms of three-level hierarchy thinking as follows:

L+1   Transindividual ecosocial semiotic processes and systems
L   Dyad processes enacted in and through semantic interactants in discourse
L–1   Mirror neuron discharges when individuals orient to and interact with each other

The phenomenon of one participant in a dialogue completing the other participant's utterance is sometimes taken as evidence for a putative "theory of mind" (see Battacchi *et al.* 1998: 140–165), or for evidence of one's virtual participation in one's interlocutor's contribution to the dialogue (Bråten 2002). However, the three-level hierarchy view shows that the meanings that are being negotiated in a particular dialogic exchange often contextually redound with the use of particular linguistic expressions in particular situation-types to such an extent that each participant is able to predict and hence to complete the lexicogrammatical forms that are used by the other to express these meanings.

The participants in the dialogue are not so much attuned to the minds *per se* of each other, but, rather, to the shared contextual redundancies among linguistic forms, meanings, and situations to such an extent that they can predict and complete each other's utterances on the basis of their high level of attunement to an entire system of contextualizing relations which integrate individuals in interaction to its dynamics. In close friendships and very intimate relationships, for example, this ability to complete each other's utterances is an example of the degree to which the individuals have been integrated to the higher-scalar dynamics of the meanings to which their body-brain systems have been entrained along the time-bound trajectory of their relationship.

5 Mood, the semantic interact, and the dialogic frame in action: illustrations from a dispute

The activity which is presented in the transcription in Table 8.2 features two speakers, Noeleen and Laurie, who are involved in a heated discussion about some pens which Laurie cannot get to write for him. The two interactants, Laurie and Noeleen, who are husband and wife, argue about Laurie's inability to make any of the pens he is trying to write with work. The exchange takes place around a bar in the kitchen-dining room area of their home. Throughout the exchange, Laurie is seated at the bar; Noeleen is standing on the opposite side of the bar to Laurie when episode begins. In the particular phase of the overall activity which is presented in Table 8.2, Noeleen is endeavouring to draw Laurie's attention to the particular pen, from among the many on the pen rack, which he had previously used.

In the analysis, I shall focus on the interpersonal meanings of the particular utterances in relation to their meaning and function in the activity as it unfolds in time. In order to do so, I shall refer to three specific levels of analysis, as follows: (1) the lexicogrammatical meaning of each speaker's utterances with specific reference to the interpersonal domain of meaning (e.g. mood); (2) the contextualization of the lexicogrammatical unit as a discourse move in relation

Table 8.2 Transcription of interaction between husband and wife, with a focus on the interpersonal selections in their linguistic utterances and their multimodal integration to discourse-level dialogic frames showing how ego-centred and other-centred facets of each speaker's actions are simultaneously present

Frame 1	Frame 2	Frame 3
N.: (1) *yeah look* L.: (2) *one of those I picked up first* N. turns back towards L. She holds pen in front of him on "yeah", starts writing on "look"	N. leans across bar towards L., pen in hand	N. engages L.'s gaze

Frame 4	Frame 5	Frame 6
N.: (3) *this is the one you had* N. shows pen in her hand to L. N. gaze to L., which is reciprocated very briefly	N. begins writing on paper; L. continues writing on his sheet of paper	L.: (4) *so I picked up one of those first* N.: (5) *right* (on *first*) L. picks up a pen from rack and holds it in front of N. L. gaze to pen rack

to its semantic status as a proposition or proposal; and (3) its integration to a local dialogical frame, including the particular move's relations to non-linguistic dimensions of the overall activity, so that its local discourse meaning can be better approximated.

The analysis has been segmented into a number of visual frames. The utterances of the two interactants along with other relevant details of gaze, movement, posture, and so on, are annotated below each visual frame. Each speaker's linguistic utterance has been identified with number. The names of the two speakers have been abbreviated to L. and N. in the transcription.

Frame 1

Noeleen, who had previously turned away from Laurie, who is seated at the bar, now turns back towards Laurie. In this frame, the utterances of the two speakers overlap to a considerable degree. Noeleen holds the pen in her hand in front of Laurie as she utters the word "yeah" and begins writing on the piece of paper on the bar table in front of Laurie as she utters the imperative clause "look". Laurie's overlapping response is a declarative clause in which he refers to the pens in the pen rack on the bar table.

Clause 1: Noeleen: imperative mood; proposal for action: direct addressee's attention to given phenomenon; Noeleen seeks to coordinate her action of writing on the piece of paper with the pen she has in her hand with Laurie's gaze. In the process, she integrates her action and that of Laurie in a jointly coordinated dialogic frame of shared attention directed to the joint solving of the problem posed by the recalcitrant pens.

Clause 2: Laurie: declarative mood; proposition; Response Statement to Noeleen's proposal for action in clause 1: Laurie clarifies that he had previously used one of the pens in the rack.

Frame 2

Noeleen leans across the bar towards Laurie with the pen still in her hand. In so doing, she creates a closer interpersonal body space between the two participants at the same time that her act of drawing closer to Laurie in this way serves to integrate him to her next move, which her action of drawing closer to Laurie anticipates. Noeleen's act of leaning towards Laurie simultaneously and dialogically activates two frames of reference, viz. the body-centred frame of coordinates pertaining to her own bodily activity in relation to Laurie and a complementary altercentric frame of reference pertaining to her virtual participation in Laurie's anticipated response. Thus, Noeleen's act of converging on Laurie's own body-centred frame of reference and his line of sight means that the bodies of the two participants are increasingly coordinated in a jointly enacted activity.

Frame 3

Frame 3 extends and further develops Frame 2. In Frame 3, Noeleen, who is still holding the pen in her hand, engages in direct face-to-face contact with Laurie on the same physical level. In so doing, she engages with Laurie's line of sight in anticipation of her next utterance move in Frame 4.

Frame 4

Clause 3: Noeleen: declarative mood; proposition; identify the pen she has in her hand in relation to Laurie's previous use of it. The local discourse meaning of clause 3 is definable in terms of the contextual integration of the pen Noeleen has in her hand and which she shows to Laurie. The linguistic expression is a declarative proposition whose experiential meaning identifies the pen specified by the demonstrative pronoun "this" (Identified) by the nominal group "the one you had" (Identifier). Noeleen's here-now act of showing the particular pen she has in her hand to Laurie is accordingly integrated with Laurie's previous use of the same pen.

While uttering this move, Noeleen engages with Laurie's gaze very briefly, thereby reinforcing the interpersonal engagement between them in the act of identifying the pen in question in the way described above.

In the example in Table 8.3, the Mood element, comprising Subject and Finite, grounds the Residue in relation to the here-now speech event. The Subject grounds the Residue "the one you had" as a third person entity specified by the demonstrative pronoun "this", which the addresser and addressee can jointly attend to and evaluate. Moreover, the demonstrative

Table 8.3 Interpersonal grammatico-semantic analysis of the clause *this is the one you had* in the exchange between Laurie and Noeleen

Mood element		Residue	
Subject	Finite	Predicator	Complement
this	IS	IS: Process-type: BE: IDENTIFICATION	the one you had
Subject: demonstrative pronoun: Third person deixis: reference to particular pen	Finite: Tense: Present Polarity: Positive: quantification of Residue as quantifiable occurrence of type-specification; +ve evaluation of Residue		

pronoun "this" in the Subject indexes the pen in question as being spatially proximate to the speaker and therefore grounded as occurring within the here-now-I-you domain of the speech event. The Finite element grounds the Residue by specifying, through the use of present tense, that the Residue is temporally grounded as being simultaneous with respect to the speech event. The positive Polarity indicates that the Residue is grounded as a quantifiable occurrence of its type-specification within the speech event.

The addresser, in grounding the proposition in this way, creates a link between the speech event, the proposition, and the addresser and the addressee who participate in the speech event. The grounding of the proposition by the addresser means that the addresser both takes up a particular (modalized) stance on the proposition at the same time that the proposition affords a complementary stance on the part of the addressee, who may in turn take up and respond to the proposition. In this way, propositions and proposals enable not so much mental sharing or mind reading, but the integration of individual body-brain systems into higher-scalar transindividual ecosocial systems and processes and their meanings.

Frame 5

Having secured Laurie's attention through the shared gaze vector, along with the use of the declarative proposition in Frame 4, Frame 5 extends and further develops Frame 4. Noeleen writes with the pen she has in her hand and which she has just referred to in the way described in Frame 4 in order to show to Laurie that it works. Laurie, for his part, writes with another pen.

Frame 6

Laurie's gaze then shifts from direct engagement with Noeleen to the pen rack on his right as he utters the conjunction "so" in the transition to Frame 6. Laurie's declarative proposition in clause 4 links back to and is semantically integrated with Noeleen's previous utterance in Frame 4 by means of the conjunction "so". Laurie's utterance therefore completes Noeleen's. The conjunction "so" construes a semantic relation of the type EVIDENCE^LOGICAL DEDUCTION between the two speaker's utterances. In this way, the two utterances can be seen as enacting a joint contribution to a discourse-level semantic relationship which the two speakers co-construct: Noeleen provides the material evidence and construes this in relation to

Laurie's past use of the pen through the identifying clause in Frame 4. Laurie, in clause 5, infers a particular logical conclusion on the basis of the evidence provided.

Laurie's uttering of clause 4 overlaps with his action of picking up a pen from the rack and holding it in front of Noeleen at the same time that his gaze vector is also directed away from Noeleen to the pen rack as he performs this action. Once again, we see here that the linguistic utterance is only one dimension of the particular action which the two participants co-construct. The action in question involves, in Frame 6, the coordination of the linguistic utterance with gaze vector and the act of picking up another pen from the rack. In the process, Laurie creates a new, shared vector of interest and attention in response to the one that Noeleen had previously instigated in relation to the pen she had in her hand.

Noeleen's response to Laurie in clause 5 is a minor clause, which Noeleen uses to indicate her agreement with the particular conclusion that Laurie has reached in clause 4. In this clause, Noeleen's uttering of clause 5 overlaps with the word "first" in Laurie's previous move (clause 4).

Throughout this brief episode, we see how the various semiotic modalities (linguistic utterances, gaze vectors, body posture, movement, spatial distance) that the participants co-deploy enable them to create body-centred frames of reference at the same time that the dialogic coordination of each participant's contributions simultaneously entails the ability to take up other-centred frames of reference whereby the self can transcend his or her own perspectives and take up those of the other in the discursive encounter.

The dialogic structures and processes are constitutive parts of higher-scalar ecosocial system processes and structures on level L+1 that both individuals are integrated to. This fact, along with their common biological initiating conditions on level L−1, makes possible the dyadic interaction between the two individuals on level L.

The interpersonal dynamics of the exchange process is largely implicit whereas the experiential content is explicit. However, it is the implicitly dialogic and anticipatory character of each person's contribution to the exchange which enables phenomena such as Laurie's completion of Noeleen's previous utterance to take place. The egocentred frame of reference of Noeleen's move in Frame 4 is accompanied by a complementary altercentric frame of reference, which is more implicit in the exchange process. In this example, Noeleen's utterance (clause 3), her showing of the pen she has in her hand to Laurie, her engagement with Laurie through the gaze vector, and her writing with the pen on the paper in front of Laurie in Frames 4 and 5, point to her virtual participation in Laurie's frame of reference at the same time that she is enacting her move in Frames 4 and 5. That is, she is able to orient to her declarative proposition as Laurie would; she is able virtually to see the pen she is holding from Laurie's perspective, and so on.

In this way, Noeleen's move in Frames 4 and 5 induces a reciprocal modification in Laurie, as evidenced by his response in clause 4. Laurie completes the structure that was initiated by Noeleen because the implicit exchange structure that was initiated by Noeleen is a structure of a type that belongs to the L+1 dynamical processes and structures to which both individuals are integrated even though the explicit experiential content is specific to the particular situation and to the topic (the pens) which is foregrounded in their discussion. The structure of the dialogic exchange process therefore provides the shared resources for the completion of meaningful patterns such as the EVIDENCE∧LOGICAL DEDUCTION type semantic relation referred to on page 198 (see also chapter 2, section 7).

6 The interpersonal enactment of semiotic-material action trajectories in the transactions between self and nonself

Take the exchange between Dion and Paul that I first considered in chapter 7, section 6. The imperative clause *look at the mess Paul* is grounded in a dialogically coordinated frame of reference to which Dion (SELF$_1$) and Paul (SELF$_2$) are integrated. In the first instance, this requires that Dion has the capacity to self-reflexively represent to herself her addressee, Paul, as a SELF$_2$ who can engage in the proposed action in the imperative clause. More generally, the dialogic coordination of perspectives entails that the implied addressee ("you") of the imperative is interpreted by the addresser as an agent who can be made modally responsible for the proposed action and who can, therefore, relate to the world in the required way. In this case, Paul is required to and is therefore assumed to be able to perceptually orient to ("look at") objects in the spatial purview shared by the two interlocutors. This further entails that Dion, as addresser, is able to mentally represent to herself the relevant agent-world relations as being able to bring about desired effects and outcomes in the world prior to her actually uttering the clause in question (Bogdan 2000: 52). The assumption of a shared frame of reference also means that Dion interprets Paul's relatedness to the world in the following three ways. First, Paul is an agent who is in possession of the relevant capacity such that he can fit in to the action schema in the appropriate way. Secondly, Paul's stance can be dialogically coordinated with Dion's modalized stance on the proposed action. Thirdly, Paul is able to self-reflexively take up, respond to, and evaluate the proposed action from his own standpoint.

In the case of the declarative proposition *it's a pig sty*, the dialogically coordinated frame of reference between Dion ($SELF_1$) and Paul ($SELF_2$) may be described as follows. In providing her own modalized stance on the proposition and its correlated referent situation, Dion interprets Paul as an agent who is able to re-ground the proposition in the perspective of his own SELF. That is, he is able to orient to and respond to the proposition from his own perspective. As before, this means that Dion interprets Paul's relatedness to the world in three ways. These are as follows. First, Dion is able to interpret her addressee's (Paul's) relatedness to the world in terms of modalized takes on particular referent situations and/or propositions. Secondly, in giving her modalized take on the proposition, Dion implicitly anticipates Paul's (possible) response(s) to the same proposition, in the process dialogically integrating the two selves to a joint, though always negotiable, modal orientation. Thirdly, as before, Paul is able to self-reflexively take up, respond to and evaluate the proposition and the addresser's modalized stance on it from his own standpoint.

In both cases, we see how proposals and propositions, in their different ways, involve semiotic-material action trajectories which extend from the internal dynamics of a given $SELF_1$ to engage with and attempt to change in some way the internal dynamics of some other $SELF_2$. In our first example, the imperative proposal is part of a semiotic-material trajectory in and through which $SELF_1$ (Dion) mentally represents in symbolic neural space the agent–world relations required to bring about her proximate intention. This intention may be formulated as the desire to materially change (some aspect of) the world in line with her values and preferences by instigating an action trajectory which seeks to entrain another $SELF_2$ to its semantics. In the process, anticipating and constraining the possible responses of this agent. This trajectory may be schematized as follows:

[[[$SELF_1$ self-reflexively represents to herself the agent–world relations → [[$SELF_1$ utters proposed course of action]] → [$SELF_2$ responds]]]

In the second example, the declarative proposition is part of a semiotic trajectory whereby $SELF_1$ (Dion) seeks to integrate $SELF_2$ (Paul) to her modalized propositional stance on a given state of affairs. In the process, $SELF_1$ attempts to act on and to transform Paul's stance on the given state of affairs. In this case, the trajectory can be schematized as follows:

[[[$SELF_1$ self-reflexively represents to herself the relevant agent–world relations → [[$SELF_1$ utters modalized propositional stance on given state of affairs]] → [$SELF_2$'s consciousness transformed in the process of responding to and negotiating $SELF_1$'s modalized stance]]]

In both cases, we can see how the interpersonal semantics of proposals and propositions constrain and entrain the sensori-motor and neural dynamics of selves in order to bring about material changes in the world or changes in the consciousness of individuals. In the first case, $SELF_2$ (Paul) is required to effect a particular bodily action involving perceptual activity so as to attend to a particular feature of the material environment (the untidy condition of the room) which $SELF_1$ seeks to bring to the fore of $SELF_2$'s conscious awareness. In the second case, $SELF_2$ is required to adopt a particular attitudinal stance on a given state of affairs, which

SELF$_1$ seeks to bring to the foreground of conscious attention in order to recruit SELF$_2$ to the desired course of action. In this second example, the choice of a proposition puts the emphasis on the semiotic transformation of conscious awareness and attention, rather than on the bodily activity required to clean up the mess. However, both examples show, though in different ways, and with different emphases, how the semantically constrained trajectories of proposals and propositions have the capacity to entrain bodily actions (sensori-motor activity), neural dynamics (conscious awareness and attention), and selected physical-material features of the world (e.g. cleaning up the room) to their dynamics. The internal neural dynamics of selves generate proximate intentions in the form of proto-meanings that can be sourced at the inner perspective of a given self. By the same token, the higher-scalar ecosocial semiotic system provides boundary conditions which entrain the lower-scalar dynamics of the individual to its dynamics and the action trajectories that result from such processes of entraining.

7 Limitations of the view that higher-order conscious thinking is propositional in the truth-conditional sense

Formal items such as the sentence do not have the capacity that genre structures do to integrate agents to particular social situation-types (section 1). A sentence is a formalism of the written language which is typed and therefore recognized in and through certain practices in our meaning system. Genres, on the other hand, structure meaning-making activity so as to enable it to be situation-specific. The emphasis on higher-order conscious thinking as being propositional in the specifically truth-conditional sense (e.g. Carruthers 1996) is based on a view of language as being about the making of true or false propositions about reality. The truth-conditional semantics of this view is a correspondence theory according to which language forms stand in a picture-like relationship of correspondence to a positivistically defined external reality. This view is then implicitly opposed to the notion of language as action and interaction. In actual fact, all forms of speaking, writing, signing, and so on, are forms of action and interaction that help to create situations by virtue of their occurring. The view that thinking is propositional preserves the idea that one's thoughts may or may not correspond to the "reality" that exists outside our subjective and limited minds. In systemic-functional terms, propositions, like proposals, are forms of action that only exist in the context of dialogic transactions between self and nonself. This means that higher-order linguistically mediated thinking is always and without exception a form of action. Furthermore, it is dialogically coordinated action with others. The other is not necessarily physically present before the thinker. Rather, conscious thinking of this kind is always a form of dialogue with others – with actual, specific others, with imagined others, and so on, across diverse space-time scales. Our consciousness always emerges from and always participates in a social heteroglossia of diverse social voices. The meanings we make within our own consciousness, however idiosyncratic and personal they are, are always part of a larger ecosocial semiotic dialogue. Our minds are not separate, individual entities, but are shaped by the meanings and the patterns of action in which we participate with others along our historical-biographical trajectory.

A further problem with the propositional view of conscious thinking is that it treats "thoughts" as abstract ideas that are separate from, though perhaps in some mysterious way, generated by physical brain processes. Moreover, ideas are seen as "representations" of perceptual and other forms of data about the world "out there" or "in here". But if consciousness is seen as a mode of action, this means that thoughts are **enacted** in relation to bodily and other activities that extend beyond the individual's body (chapter 5, section 8). The emphasis on consciousness as a private and unique experience of the individual's mind is, in actual fact, a limitation on the possibilities of consciousness. Consciousness is borne out of and always exists as a form of highly specified Meaning System in the perspective of a self (chapter 7, section 6). Yet, the self and his or her meanings in consciousness come from interaction. The interaction view stresses that consciousness is always embedded in supersystem transactions which put the self in some kind of (dialogically) organized relation with the nonself. We are conscious of signs of internal and external environmental events to which we respond with action on the basis of the models – the systems of interpretance – that we have in our *Innenwelt* for interpreting energy flows as signs of environmental events. Consciousness necessarily involves interpretation in this sense. Being "closed minded", so to speak, can be seen as an unwillingness to engage with or to interact with and hence to recognize as meaningful a diversity of matter-energy patterns that do not conform to the regular types which we have been led to expect by the kinds of interaction in which we most typically and frequently engage.

8 Agency and Halliday's theory of clause-as-exchange

The ontological realm of mind and its properties is a social semiotic construction arising out of the secondary rationalization and consequent specialization to an "inner" mental domain of the experiential semantics of the mental process verbs (Matthiessen 1993; Thibault 1993). In this view, these verbs are seen as simply referring to or reflecting some pre-existing ontological realm of inner mind. However, we can pose the question as to what might an alternative account of agency and subjectivity look like, i.e. one which is based instead on the interpersonal resources of language. Ontologies of the real and the natural in the western tradition are based on the ideational domain of meaning. The referential projection of mental properties derives from mental process lexemes such as *think*, *believe*, *know*, *want*, and so on. In so doing, it neglects the **implicit** nature of the interpersonal exchange processes whereby agency is enacted. What, then, might an alternative ontology, based on the interpersonal resources of language, look like? Why not a fusion of the interpersonal, instead of the ideational, with the physical-material? What would this entail for a theory of agency? I shall now attempt to provide some preliminary answers to these questions.

The central concept in this attempt is that of *exchange*. Exchange is the central component in the organization of the interpersonal semantic resources in the grammar of the clause, as we saw in section 1. The semiotic-discursive and the physical-material domains are cross-coupled and entrained in and through these exchange processes. This is so for three principal reasons: (1) the two domains cross-couple with each other; (2) the exchange process organizes and constrains the flow of meanings in the semiotic-discursive at the same time that it organizes and constrains matter-energy flows in the physical-material; and (3) language is not simply abstract form, but is also cross-coupled to physical-material processes and dynamics on both the bodily and the ecosocial environmental scales. The problem of finding a linking mechanism between reified psychological causes and material effects vanishes when it is realized that language in use has both semiotic-discursive and physical-material properties. Therefore, the cross-coupling of semiotic-discursive and physical-material processes in the enactment of the ecosocial dynamics requires no mysterious and ethereal link between the two.

The exchange of goods-&-services views language as directly related to the entraining of matter (e.g. commodities) and energy (e.g. getting others to do things). It is language directly related to use value in the sense that the goods-&-services so exchanged are created out of energy and raw materials by social work. The analogue values of matter-energy are digitalized by the semiotic-discursive exchange process. Halliday also describes information as a commodity which is exchanged. But information, as Wilden (1981: 137) points out, is not a substance. Information cannot be reduced to or localized as a commodity because "it involves a relationship between patterns" (Wilden 1981: 138). The exchange of information is related to exchange value. Exchange value is digital in form. The reduction of information to the status of a commodity ends up by reducing it to the status of matter and energy, rather than seeing that information is supported and carried by the former at the same time that it is distinct from its matter-energy base (chapter 9, section 1). The distinction is a critical one. Meaning controls, constrains, and entrains matter-energy flows in the ecosocial system (Wilden 1981: 18; Lemke 1995a: 107).

How can we talk about agency in this model? Harré (1983) has drawn attention to the problems which arise in the traditional philosophical and psychological accounts of agency.

These accounts try to explain agency in causal terms (see also Juarrero 1999: chap. 2). According to Harré, the relevant terms derive from the grammar of "moral necessity" and not that of "causal necessity" (1983: 30), as I showed in chapter 4, section 4. Moral necessity is semantic in character (see Holiday 1988; Thibault 2002). We ascribe agency, autonomy, and the capacity for self-monitoring (reflexivity) to individuals on the basis of the grammar of the interpersonal moral orders in which these qualities are recognized. Harré's notion of interpersonal moral orders can be assimilated to the notion of the semiotic action formations in the conceptual language of ecosocial semiotics.

According to the ontology of efficient causes, agency is described in terms of forces and their impact on things. This ontology is akin to the "billiard-ball physics" discussed by Gregory Bateson: ". . . when ball A hits ball B, A *gives* energy to B, which responds *using* this energy which A gave it" (1980 [1979]: 112). This ontology is grammaticalized in English in the experiential semantics of the Actor + Process: Material Action + Goal model. In Bateson's example, energy is treated like a substance which functions as the linking mechanism for the causal connection to take place. Thus, when I break a window, I do something to the window (i.e. I give energy to it), and the window in turn uses that energy to do something (it breaks). In the mechanical world of cause and effect, according to the classical model, this unilinear sequence of "energetic dependencies" (Bateson 1980 [1979]: 112) between things certainly works. But when I tell someone the time, I do not give my interlocutor some energy which he or she uses to respond. But this is what the causal ontology of agency, in, say, the discourse of mind basically assumes. Harré's account of agency helps us to see that the ascribing of agency to a social being does not depend on the language of forces and impacts. Instead, my performing of some socially recognizable action, in which I am positioned as the agent, means that in the relevant action formation, I am semantically authorized by some socially shared (or disputed) moral/interpersonal norm of action. If necessary, these norms can be evoked and argued over to settle disputes about the rightness or wrongness, goodness or badness, and so on, of particular choices made, intentions, decisions, and courses of action undertaken. Thus, when I say "you must hurry to work now", I am authorizing the action of my addressee – the "you" – with respect to some extrinsic source of authority that is indexed in the relevant interpersonal order. I do not physically give anything to the addressee. Rather, I semantically control or constrain "the energy which is already available in the respondent", as Bateson (1980 [1979]: 113) puts it.

This means that I **semantically** control or restrain the respondent's right or ability to release and channel the energy already available to him or her as a socially positioned agent, or better, as a doee and a potential doer. I do not, therefore, convey or give any energy to the addressee, who then responds by using it, or by virtue of being impacted upon by it. These mechanistic metaphors are decidedly misleading about the real processes involved and, hence, about the real nature of social agency. In authorizing the addressee to do something, I also, by implication, authorize myself or claim the right to do so, again with respect to socially shared interpersonal norms. This means that I, as agent, authorize myself to use a certain amount of the energy which is available to me in doing so. In so doing, I also authorize the addressee to release the particular socially recognized and ascribed tendency or disposition which is assigned to him or her by virtue of his or her positioning in the action formation. When I utter a command, I do not causally force the addressee to carry out the desired action. The social work of carrying out the desired action is done by the "you". The point is that the release of his disposition or tendency to act is authorized by my utterance. I invoke social controls or constraints deriving from particular interpersonal moral orders and their intertexts to achieve this. In so doing, the "you" releases the necessary energy so as to bring about the proposed action, i.e. "hurrying". The source of the flow of energy is the "you". I position myself as Agent in relation to the "you". The "you" is likewise positioned, in and through the socially recognized action formation to partly entrain the flow of matter (the body of the "you") and energy (the "you's" releasing and channelling of the available energy so as to perform the required action, "hurrying"). Information exchange is most explicit; the exchange of structure is most implicit (Lemke 1984d: 7, 9). Information is best understood here as the meaning which is responded to and negotiated in propositions and proposals in discourse. The exchange of structure refers to the ways in which individuals are positioned in various ways at the cross-coupling of matter, energy and meaning flows along specific trajectories in these exchange processes such that they undergo an internal modification of their structure. In this way, consciousness is semantically acted on and entrained to these trajectories (section 4).

Agency entails a complex social semantics in which the agent functions may be distributed across several participants in the action structure (Thibault 1993). In the earlier example, I do not make the "you" hurry in the causal sense of "make". Instead, I semantically authorize the "you" to release the relevant tendency or disposition to do so by claiming the right to do so with respect to a given interpersonal formation. It is the "you" who does the hurrying, and who releases the (stored) tendency to do so. The "I" is the agentive source with the moral authority to authorize or otherwise impose on or constrain the "you" to do so. The "you" may, of course decline or question the moral authority of the "I" or his or her right to do so by challenging the interpersonal formation which is invoked, by asserting a preference for an alternative inter-personal moral order, by citing an alternative construal of the action performed in relation to some other interpersonal criterion other than that in operation, or by challenging the "I's" right to occupy the given agent position.

Agency is not, then, defined on the basis of efficient or linear causality. In an ecosocial semiotic system, there is, as Wilden points out, "no proportionality between a 'cause' ('Look out!') and the energy and the information the message triggers and organizes" (1981: 27). We are not determined by any sort of causal necessity which speaks the language of inevitability. Instead, the language of moral necessity determines what we can and cannot do in a given social situation (chapter 4, section 4). This means that within the relevant system of relations freedom "is the recognition of constraints – some of which can be changed, and some of which cannot" (Wilden 1981: 27). This possibility reintroduces a critical notion of responsibility into our conceptualiza-tion of agency, and in such a way that the social (not individualistic) basis of this is upheld.

9 Exchange, friction, and goal-seeking

In the absence of a theory of the exchange of structure, theorists of agency have tended to look for explicit causal links, rather than the underlying and more implicit structural principles and dynamics of the exchange process. These principles of structuration and their dynamics per-form the following functions: (1) they stabilize and regulate physical-material and semiotic-discursive cross-couplings; (2) they organize, constrain, and direct the flow of meaning and matter-energy; and (3) they position social agents at the intersection of the cross-coupling patterns referred to in (1) in ways that allow the ecosocial dynamics of agency to emerge in the activities whose implicit structure is a condition of their enablement. Halliday distinguishes two basic types of speech role, viz. giving and demanding of either information or goods-&-services. As we have seen, goods-&-services exchange (proposals) emerges much earlier than information exchange (propositions) in ontogenesis (chapter 5, section 7). The prior appearance of goods-&-services exchange parallels the fact that the child must first channel his or her material needs and wants through language in the form of demands for goods-&-services that are other-oriented in the way discussed in section 2. In so doing, the child is inserted into the Symbolic order of language (Wilden (1981: 23). He or she must now discover how and where s/he fits into this order. The insertion into the Symbolic order and the channelling of needs through language as demands generates the fundamental (and unconscious) desire to know. As Wilden points out, "the primary goal of human communication appears to be the INVENTION OF GOALS" (1981: 431). Sartre comes close to such an understanding with his conception of desire and the ontology of the lack, which form the basis of the human project:

> We will not get out of the difficulty by making desire a *conatus* in the manner of a physical force. For the conatus once again, even if we grant it the efficiency of a cause, can not possess in itself the character of reaching out toward another state. The *conatus* as the *producer* of states can not be identified with desire as the *appeal* from a state.
>
> (Sartre 1969 [1943]: 87)

The "appeal from a state" refers to the ways in which desires function as attractors of the dynamics of the system. The desire for a not-yet-existent state of affairs entails a commitment to a project. Projects are pulled into their futures by final causes, which act as the attractors of the system. Desire is always predicated on not-yet-existent future states of affairs towards which the system strives. Such is the logic of goal-seeking systems and their trajectories. That is, desire entails the self's coming up against and having to deal with the contradiction or friction between the self's present, negatively valued position and the desired, positively valued future state of affairs. As we saw in chapter 3, section 7, the projection of the material and semiotic domains into consciousness involves friction. Halliday refers to the "contradiction" between the conscious and the material domains in this same sense. His observations can be related to Vološinov's account of friction that I considered in sections 1 and 2 above. The material (projected) domain is a secondness which impacts upon the firstness of the projecting (conscious) domain. As we have seen, consciousness always implicates a selective attending to the phenomena of experience. The selective or focused nature of this attending to entails the making of choices within an ordered field of possibilities. Friction means that only some of the energy available to the individual can be deployed for the purpose of consciously attending to selected aspects of the material domain. The material and the semiotic are selectively projected into the conscious domain as a conscious figure against a background of generalized friction. Consciousness entails a self-organizing viewpoint which seeks selectively to project the material or the semiotic domains as figures of conscious awareness against a background of friction.

Friction is the energy which must be expended in order that the conscious experience is generated in the form, say, of neural activity. Such a self-organizing viewpoint *qua* firstness seeks to impose itself on secondness and thereby to channel and direct secondness according to the dictates of firstness. In the process, friction is generated. The contradiction between the conscious and material and/or semiotic domains is a source of friction in precisely this sense. Proposals are concerned with the contradiction – the friction – between the conscious and the material domains and the interpersonal negotiation of this. Propositions, on the other hand, are concerned with the contradiction between the conscious and semiotic domains and the negotiation of this. The meaning which this contradiction may generate is the figure against the general background of friction which the contradiction unavoidably entails.

10 Grammatical mood and the negotiation of friction

A given dialogic move – statement, question, offer, command – implies a commitment to a project. Dialogue is driven by semiotic and/or material difference, or friction (Vološinov 1983; Thibault 1995; see also section 1 above). The negotiation of meanings in discourse entails overcoming the oppositions and contradictions which emerge in the course of the dialogue as it unfolds in time. The individual contributions to the negotiation of meaning are entrained to their overall goal-seeking trajectories which, amidst resistances and friction, pull the discourse into its future. Thus, final causes are the projects which entrain the goal-seeking trajectories of agents. Projects are higher-scalar attractors of the dynamics of the trajectories – ontogenetic and logogenetic – of the individual.

Each of the basic mood categories can be seen as a resource for negotiating and "finalizing" this friction. Sartre's "appeal from a state" can be re-formulated in terms of the semantic distinction between [+LACK] and [–LACK] (Thibault 1995). This distinction, as we shall now see, is central to the mood system in English. This distinction can be semiotic and/or material. In relation to the basic mood categories, Table 8.4 shows how each category is associated with a specific intersection of these two factors.

The dialogic basis of mood draws our attention to the systemic basis of goal-seeking in language. The resources of both mood and the various types of minor clause provide the means for either initiating or responding to discourse moves. The fundamental semantic unit in language is not the move *per se*, but the semantic interact (Martin 1981; section 1 above), comprising INITIATING MOVE^RESPONDING MOVE. The primacy of the interact is evidenced by the anticipatory character of the mood categories, which are not self-contained grammatical

Table 8.4 The semantics of the lack in relation to grammatical mood in English

	Modal perspective of self	
Domain of experience	–LACK	+LACK
SEMIOTIC	Declarative	Interrogative
MATERIAL	Oblative	Imperative

units. Instead, they are internally structured as a consequence of the ways in which they function dialogically in discourse either to initiate a move which has as its goal the obtaining of a response from one's interlocutor or to respond to and negotiate someone else's prior move. The view that the declarative is the unmarked point of departure for the monological "reporting" of individual consciousness fails to reveal how the essentially dialogical and anticipatory nature of all dialogic moves in discourse are linked to the modal projects of the selves who negotiate meanings in discourse (chapter 7, section 6). Furthermore, the priority which is given to this view ignores the fact that proposals, in ontogenesis, are more fundamental than propositions in the making and shaping of the self's consciousness as a consequence of the self's dialogical engagements with others (chapter 1, section 3).

Proposals are more fundamental than propositions to the extent that propositions may be subsumed by proposals as the more schematic category of interact. Furthermore, both of these basic categories – proposals and propositions – can be seen as dialogically coordinated forms of action, or interacts, which involve both acting upon the nonself and bringing about change in the nonself. As we shall see below, this change can be both semiotic and material and has important implications for both consciousness and the actions of selves which are regulated by consciousness. It is also concerned with the ways in which selves are semiotically integrated to selected aspects of the material world by their action trajectories. Declaratives can thus be seen to express the self's desire to modalize (the other) at the same time that it is the other (the addressee) whose consciousness is acted upon and potentially transformed in declaratives. The starting point of declaratives is the viewpoint of the self and the self's desire to conjoin others to this viewpoint. Interrogatives are concerned with the self's desire to be modalized at the same time that the self appeals to the other to provide his or her modal perspective on the proposition in the interrogative clause. In this case, the self seeks to conjoin to his or her viewpoint the modal perspective of the addressee. Oblatives express the desire to act on and to change the present social relations between self and nonself by performing a service or giving a commodity to the addressee. Oblatives also act on the consciousness of the addressee by imposing obligations to act in a certain way at some future moment. Imperatives express the speaker's desire to change the way things are in the present by imposing an obligation to act on the addressee. The addressee is, therefore, invited to comply with the addresser's obligation. Both oblatives and imperatives imply a negative evaluation of the given present state of affairs, along with the speaker's desire to change this by bringing into being a desired future state of affairs (see Section 11).

We can see the workings of friction in all four basic mood categories. Each mood category implies a basic form of modal project – a goal-seeking trajectory – for acting on the consciousness of others in order to change it. Moreover, the implications these have for consciousness are always intrinsically connected to possibilities for action. This observation is somewhat different from the view that declarative and interrogative propositions are concerned with the modalized takes of addressers and addressees on objectified states of the affairs in the world whereas oblatives and imperatives are concerned with proposals for acting in the world in order to change it. In my view, all four basic categories have implications for **both** consciousness and action.

Thus, declaratives, in re-modalizing the consciousness of the addressee, can potentially change the attitudes and value orientations of the addressee in ways which regulate future courses of action. In declaratives, friction arises out of the speaker's view that the addressee lacks the modal perspective that the addresser appeals to the addressee to adopt. Interrogatives, on the other hand, stem from the speaker's lack of a modal perspective on the given proposition, along with the desire that the addressee provide his or her perspective to the addresser. In this case, the addresser acts on the addressee in order to be modally transformed by the addressee's response. Again, the implications for action should be clear: as before, a modal change in the speaker's perspective has the potential to regulate future courses of action.

Oblatives are concerned with the addresser's performing of an act – providing a service or giving a commodity to the addressee – which also acts upon the consciousness of the addressee. The addressee is, therefore, invited to feel obliged to act in a certain way towards the addressee at some future moment. Thus, the addresser's act of giving regulates the future actions of the addressee by bringing about a change in his or her consciousness along the lines desired by the addresser. That is, the addresser negotiates this semiotic-material friction by attempting to bring selected aspects of the material world and the consciousness of the addressee into line with a particular desired state of affairs. This change is fundamentally moral in character. Imperatives, on the other hand, negotiate this friction – the gap – between the negatively valued present and the positively valued and desired future state of affairs through the addresser's acting on the consciousness of the addressee with a view to the addressee performing the proposed course of action deemed necessary for bringing this state of affairs into being.

The symbolic-indexical resources of mood enable selves to invent goals whereby modal projects are constituted in discourse. Projects can always be sourced at a viewpoint whose agency generates the action-meaning trajectories which are the concrete manifestation of projects.

11 Proposals, propositions, and the discursive negotiation of moral values

Martin (1992b) has reformulated Halliday's semantic distinction between propositions and proposals as follows:

> From a discourse perspective, this allows us to interpret Questions as demands for modality and Statements as opportunities to modalize . . .
>
> As far as modulation is concerned, Offers express inclination (inviting obligation) whereas Commands assert obligations (inviting inclination) . . .
>
> The relationship of attitude to mood is perhaps less transparent, but modulation and attitude might be related as follows. The desire to act on the world with a proposal (Offer or Command) is in some sense dependent on dissatisfaction with the way things are and a desire to make them better – both from the speaker's point of view. Making a proposal thus implies a negative evaluation of the way things are and a positive evaluation of the way they could be. Or to put this another way – attitude is *realis*; it evaluates what is good or bad. Modulation is *irrealis* – it comments that what is shouldn't be (thereby implicitly evaluating it as bad) and what isn't should be (thereby implicitly evaluating it as good).
>
> (Martin 1992b: 363)

As Wilden (1981: 431) points out, the lack can only belong to the analogue domain of topological-continuous variation, rather than to the domain of digital or typological-categorial distinctions. The analogue domain is a topological continuum; it is concerned with presence and absence – the presence or absence of food, water, sexual gratification, affection, and so on. The channelling and entraining of human needs through language as demands digitally punctuates this domain as a semiotic space in the domain of the semiotic-discursive (typological-categorial). The elementary values described by Edelman (1992) as being necessary for initiating the individual's ontogenetic trajectory, as well as for channelling it along certain preferred developmental pathways rather than others, correspond to the analogue presence referred to here. Hunger, for example, is the absence or the lack of food. Thus, when the organism is hungry something (food) {**should**} be present, but is not. I have placed curly brackets around the word "should" to indicate that it is an ontological and not yet a moral (semantic) "should" (see below). Elementary values like these are essential for the future survival and growth of the organism. The example shows how the idea of something that {should} be present emerges. Therefore, we are in the presence of primordial values in the sense that the absence or lack of food is bad and the presence or availability of food is good. Such lacks correspond to what Maritain (1990 [1950]: 49) calls an "**ontological should, not yet a moral should**". The primordial values described by Edelman are prior to language and are, therefore, prior to the emergence of moral consciousness.

In the interpersonal semantics of clause-as-exchange, the fundamental properties of goal-seeking and the invention of goals emerge. The dialectic between the modalities of "realis" and "irrealis", which Martin discusses in the above quotation, may be reformulated in the following way. From the perspective of propositions, declaratives ground the modalized viewpoint of the addresser in relation to a specific action trajectory that is initiated by the uttering of the proposition; interrogatives seek to ground the addressee's viewpoint. However, it is not just the declarative or interrogative proposition which is modalized. Propositions are dialogically organized interacts which act on and seek to modalize the consciousness of the addressee. Declarative propositions are used to conjoin addressees to the speaker's modalized perspective on the proposition and therefore to influence or change the addressee's knowledge or values in some way. Declarative propositions also elicit and anticipate responses from addressees in the form of agreement or disagreement with the proposition, and so on. Interrogative propositions are used to act on addressees in order to obtain the addressee's modal perspective on the proposition. In this way, the original addresser's modal perspective is acted upon and changed in the process of obtaining a response. Propositions are driven by and negotiate, from the addresser's perspective, a modal lack. Declarative propositions seek to modalize a modal lack on the part of the addressee in the sense that it is the addresser who provides his or her modal perspective and appeals to the addressee to respond to and take up this perspective as his or her own. Interrogative propositions seek to modalize a modal lack on the part of the addresser by appealing to the addressee to provide his or her modal perspective on the proposition. Propositions have the modal status of "realis" because they are grounded in determinate temporal and/or modal perspectives that can be argued about by interactants.

Proposals, on the other hand, are not grounded in the same way and cannot be argued about as to whether they are true, false, believable, possible, sincere, and so on. Proposals are proposals for future courses of action. They have no grounding in a determinate temporal or modal framework that can be argued about. The issue is not whether addresser and addressee are aligned or not around the same axiological orientations, but whether addressees agree or not to proposed courses of action. Proposals are concerned with proposed and/or desired future courses of action in order to change the world. Proposals can be acted upon, complied with, not complied with, accepted, refused, and so on, though they cannot be argued about in the same way that propositions can. Proposals are concerned with the enacting of future-oriented changes in order to bring the material world into line with present desires. The non-finite status of the verbal group in imperatives, for example, signifies that the proposed action in the clause is to be evaluated in terms of its possible future grounding as an action performed by the addressee. That is why modalities of inclination (*would*) and obligation (*should*) characterize proposals.

12 The semantics of the lack in propositions and proposals

From the perspective of propositions, statements have as their primary goal the modalizing of the addresser's take on the proposition (Lack), along with an appeal to the addressee to provide his or hers. Questions have as their primary goal an appeal or demand to the addressee to modalize his or her take on the proposition. In this case, the appeal is driven by the addresser's initial lack of a modal perspective on the same proposition. Propositions are arguable, as we saw earlier. They enact an intersubjective discursive space in which modalized values can be argued about and negotiated in relation to a determinate temporal or modal perspective in which the proposition is grounded. For this reason, propositions have "realis" modality: they evaluate degrees of "is" and "is not" according to different semantic scales of modality and evaluation such as certain-probable-possible, good-bad, ugly-beautiful, and so on.

From the perspective of proposals, Offers have as their primary goal the speaker's enactment of his or her desire to bring about some as yet unfulfilled state of affairs. Commands have as their primary goal the speaker's appeal to the addressee as the one who is to be responsible for bringing about the unfulfilled goal state that is desired by the addresser. Proposals negotiate both ontological and moral "shoulds". Thus, the uttering of a command such as *give me the ball!* entails that, from the speaker's point of view, there is a material (ontological) lack (the ball) and a moral one (the addressee is morally obliged to the addresser to comply with the proposed action). Proposals negotiate degrees of "should" and "should not". Proposals have "irrealis" modality: they negotiate and grade proposals according to what should or should not be. They are concerned with the presence or absence of actions in the fulfilment of moral obligations and inclinations.

Proposals do not simply digitalize an already existing lack. Rather, they digitalize the speaker's desire to act upon the current state of affairs so that the desire may be fulfilled. Given that modulation is "irrealis", what is digitalized as a desire in the semantics of proposals does not exist in the same way that a lack does in the analogue continuum of the pre-semiotic physical-material domain. Wilden (1981: 431) points out that needs can be fulfilled, but semanticized desires cannot. This is so because the semantic categories of the symbolic order of language are not the same as the needs and wants in the analogue domain that they denote. The semantic property of "irrealis" in proposals means that goal-seeking pathways are constantly created by the unstable and morphogenetic dialectic between the speaker's desire to change the way things are into something else which the speaker evaluates positively and would like to bring about. It is through this dialectic that goal-seeking trajectories are articulated in the social semiotics of exchange. In this way, the semantics of clause-as-exchange constitute the basic linguistic resource for the organization and channelling of goal-seeking in and through language. The semantics of Halliday's four basic speech functions can therefore be re-formulated as in Table 8.5.

These basic options and the value-creating semantic distinctions that they create are systemic in character. This systemic character means that the social semantics of goal-seeking is built into the systemic organization of clause-as-exchange as a resource for making meanings in specific contexts. The point is that goal-seeking (desire) is not simply a product of the text or the situationally specific occasion of discourse. It is an inescapable part of the intrinsic organization of the language system and its values (Wilden 1981: 431).

Lemke (1998b) has reformulated Halliday's interpersonal metafunction as the orientational function. As we have seen, interactants dialogically orient both to each other in the exchange process at the same time that they orient to the meaning of the proposition or proposal that is uttered. As we have also seen, both proposals and propositions are centrally concerned with values, rather than with objective states of affairs in reality. Proposals and propositions are a

Table 8.5 A reformulation of Halliday's four basic speech functions in terms of the semantics of the lack

STATEMENT	QUESTION
Addresser (–Lack) gives modalized viewpoint and appeals to addressee (+Lack) to respond to it (I'm telling you, "it is so")	Addresser lacks modal viewpoint (+Lack) appeals to addressee (–Lack) to modalize his or hers (you tell me, "is it so?")
OFFER	COMMAND
Addresser gives goods-&-services (–Lack) and appeals to addressee (+Lack) to respond with an obligation to perform some future act ("I want it to be so")	Addresser lacks desired state of affairs (+Lack) and appeals to addressee to bring it into existence ("I want you to make it so") (–Lack)

resource whereby selves take up (and negotiate) evaluative stances with nonselves. Interpersonal meaning, which we have seen to be primary in ontogenesis, is fundamentally about the motivational values of selves in relation to their ecosocial environment. In this sense, interpersonal values can be seen to be a further specification and reorganization of the most fundamental biological values identified by Edelman (Thibault 2000a: 306–309). The biological values identified by Edelman allow the organism to orient to and evaluate the motivational salience of environment objects and events, including other conspecifics. Thus, will it satisfy my hunger? Will I get affection from it? Can I cuddle it? Is it a source of interpersonal engagement and meaning? Will it hurt me? And so on. (Proto-)imperative exchanges are the most fundamental means whereby the self orients to and takes up an evaluative stance on its negatively valued present state at the same time that this is compared with a not-yet-realized though positively desired future state. The proposed action in the imperative clause is the self's means of actively mediating between the two. This mediation requires the capacity to hypothesize a future goal and to set this against the present such that action is channelled down a specific, value-laden, and semantically modulated trajectory.

Proposals and propositions are semantic resources for orienting to and taking up evaluative stances towards the nonself. They are a means of exploring and intervening in the environment in response to our models of what to expect in determinate situations. They are also a means of interrogating the unexpected in an attempt to assimilate it to the expected and, hence, the known. The conscious attending to phenomena on lower levels of the specification hierarchy – e.g. perception or sensori-motor exploration of the environment – may be seen as a precursor of the kind of exploratory activity that occurs in interpersonal negotiation in discourse (Thibault 2004a: 198–200). For example, the cross-coupling of proposals to physical-material flows means that proposals have direct implication for sensori-motor activity. The addresser of an imperative proposal orients to his or her addressee as an agent with a determinate motivational significance in the exchange, i.e. as someone who is able to fulfil the addresser's desire. The addresser's stance is an exploratory orienting to one's addressee through discursive negotiation in accordance with the capacity to carry out (comply with) the proposed action. At the same time, it is exploration of the moral territory that the two agents inhabit because of the implications that the proposal has for the positioning of addresser and addressee in a given interpersonal moral order.

As we saw in section 9, the "irrealis" modality of proposals enacts a dialectic of "what is: negative" and "what should be: positive" whereby action is channelled along a trajectory on the basis of the axiological salience of these two modal states for the agents who are involved in the transaction. Propositions, in this view, are not directly implicated in sensori-motor activity in the same way that proposals are. They do not mediate the exchange of commodities or the performing of services. Yet, propositions have implications for action at one remove, so to speak. They have evaluative or axiological implications for action. When we take up a declarative stance on something, for instance, we are exploring and orienting to it in the context of the particular discursive exchange in which the proposition occurs. The "realis" modality of propositions means that we can orient to the nonself from our own modalized perspective as something that has been assimilated, to varying degrees, to that perspective. Declarative propositions have this function. On the other hand, we can orient to something as the unknown that needs to be interrogated in order to obtain a desired response that will allow us to assimilate it to our own modal perspective. Both declarative and interrogative propositions therefore constitute a means for dialogically orienting to the expected and/or the unexpected, the known and/or the unknown, and so on, in the process of assigning evaluative significance to the nonself. In assigning value to the nonself, we prescribe incipient courses of action to adopt in relation to it.

13 The self as a totality of integrities in various historically emergent semiotic orders

Consciousness does not emerge in the isolated individual who experiences his or her environment, but on the basis of social and cultural forms of interaction with various types of others, including, most crucially, other conspecifics. Social interaction provides epigenetic information which bootstraps the emergence of a self and the forms of consciousness that this makes possible in the human species. Language and other semiotic modalities play a key role in this process. Further, this is reflected in the intrinsically dialogical nature of semiosis. Studies of child development have long established the critical importance of interpersonal interaction with other human beings for the ontogenetic development of the child (Halliday 1975; Trevarthen 1987; Kaye 1984 [1982]; Bruner 1983; Vygotsky 1986 [1934]). The presence of more senior others (e.g. parents, caretakers, kin) provides the kind of stable higher-order ecosocial environment which is necessary for the imparting of epigenetic information that is essential for the infant's further development. Structured dyadic forms of exchange between infant and adult give rise to the development of the structure of consciousness itself. This is so at all levels of the specification hierarchy. The structured nature of these dyads explains the fact that the structure of individual consciousness and these forms of self–nonself transaction are linked, though this link is not explicit.

The self may come to view itself as having unique conscious experiences and inner states, though without being explicitly aware that this experience is based on implicit dialogical principles which relate self to nonself in larger-scale supersystem transactions. These larger-scale supersystems, for example the mother–infant dyads characteristic of primary intersubjectivity, constitute a regulatory system at a higher-scalar level which regulates the contributions of the individual subsystems (mother and infant) to the organization of the dyad as a whole. Just as the higher-scalar circulatory system in the organism regulates and entrains lower-scalar diffusion to more complex forms of organization (Salthe 1993: 49), the higher-scalar regulatory processes of linguistic and other forms of semiotically mediated interaction on the ecosocial level, regulate and entrain the body-brain of the infant to the meanings and structures of this level. The higher-scalar ecosocial environment is a stable source of material and semiotic processes necessary for the further development of the infant.

For example, more senior members of the culture provide linguistic and other semiotic resources which integrate the child to the higher-scalar dynamical processes of the ecosocial system. The dialogic basis of even the very earliest stages of primary intersubjectivity shows how the infant is oriented to the obtaining of specific kinds of material and semiotic resources at the same time that senior members of the culture have modes of engagement which contact with infants tends to foster. From the point of view of both their common biological inheritance and the social practices of child rearing and bonding between parent and child, there is a reciprocal, dialogically coordinated link between them which makes possible the processes of integration mentioned above. Thus, the infant's earliest attempts to engage with and interpret others are implicit dialogic structures that induce a complementary response in the addressee. This response in turn results in positive feedback such that the addresser's (the infant's) intrinsic dynamics are modified and extended. Thus, the child seeks dyadic engagement with others and, hence, responses from others which it can interpret in ways that will contribute to the further structuring and elaboration of its own developmental trajectory.

Self is a later, more specified emergence than otherness in the sense that the emergence of self and the viewpoints associated with self represent a qualitative leap to a new level of individual organization (chapter 5, section 14). At the same time, self comprises many different integrative levels consisting of increasingly specific constraints (Salthe 1993: 64). In this sense, the closing of the meta-loop on the self-perspective in symbolic neural space can be seen as a contextual integration and consequent reorganization of self–nonself transactions on the lower integrative levels that characterized prior stages of the individual's ontogenetic trajectory. Self is constituted by the simultaneous presence of integrative levels which Salthe (1993: 66), following Buchler (1966), has defined as "the integrities of an object in various semiotic orders". Each developmental emergence, for example, constitutes a semiotic order, which constructs an integrity for the self from the specific point of view of that level. Each integrative level is a construct specifiable in some discourse, i.e. it is an integrity. It is the totality of the integrities which specify the overall shape of the self *qua* trajectory-in-time that constitutes the self. In the case of the self, we can say the self is a construct resulting from the individual's cascading/collecting agency along its trajectory. I have attempted a logical reconstruction of the historical emergence of the self in terms of the developmental emergence of self from historically prior self–other transactions in Table 8.6.

14 The constitutive character of our moral being and the semiotics of exchange

Agency and selfhood are not reducible to the matter-energy needs of human individuals *qua* biological organisms. They are part of an entire ecosocial semiotic dynamic which emerges out of the channelling of primordial needs through language so that they are mediated as demands. In the process, matter-energy and meaning are entrained by the exchange process according to the requirements of the social work which has to be done. In addition, the exchange of structure serves to position individuals as agents – addressers and addressees – at particular cross-couplings of the material and the semiotic. Following Wilden, meaning, as distinct from information, is defined as ". . .the significance of the information to the system processing it" (1981: 233). In terms of the most highly specialized human case, at least from our human point of view, meaning cannot be separated from the perspectives of the selves who make meanings in their interactions with each other. Meaning, then, is at a higher order of logical typing than information. Different agent positions in the same system of relations (the same semiotic formation) entail different subjective investments in, take ups, and construals of information as

Table 8.6 Stages in the semiotic spiral leading to (self-)consciousness and the historical emergence of the self: a logical reconstruction

Stage 1	the infant's engagements with the "virtual other" (Bråten 1992), seen as a general value which is inherent in the infant's neural circuitry from the outset (Edelman 1992) and which acts as a motivating force whereby the infant seeks dialogic engagement with real others, in the process activating the mind as a self-organizing dyad (Bråten 1992: 80).
Stage 2	socioaffective exchanges in primary intersubjectivity: dyadic interaction with actual others
Stage 3	the {self} {interprets} the other's takes on world
Stage 4	the {self} and other exchange proto-signs about jointly attended to objects in world; triadic
Stage 5	the other responds to and interprets the self's takes on world
Stage 6	the self internalizes the other's takes on the world
Stage 7	the self's takes on the world are shared with the other; the self-in-relation-to-other
Stage 8	the self's takes on world and relations to others self-reflexively interpreted by self; emergence of self-referential perspective and on-line self-interpretation of self-in-relation-to-nonself
Stage 9	the self's takes on world and relations to others self-reflexively interpreted by self: off-line self-interpretation and mental rehearsal: emergence of (self-)consciousness and self-closure
Stage 10	re-entrant closing of loop on the self: emergence of self-reflexive consciousness, along with increasing differentiation of self–other categories and relations
Stage 11	the self recursively (self-referentially) interprets the self as others interpret and evaluate the self

Note: the term {self} designates vaguer, less specified, and therefore more general notions of the self before the more highly specified categories that we typically refer to as the self emerge at later stages; later stages are more highly specified than earlier ones, at the same time that later stages integrate prior ones to themselves meaning. Which meanings are construed, when, and how, is a question of the dynamic, open, and probabilistic relations between the relevant system and its environments. Thus, exchange structures and channels the meaning-making practices of human agents as forms of goal-seeking projects. It also organizes and coordinates the interpersonal semantic resources which provide a value orientation (e.g. modality, interpersonal lexis) for particular goal-seeking path-ways. Thus, in the process of channelling needs through language as demands, which in turn generate goal-seeking (desire), needs are modalized as particular axiological orientations which orient the decisions and actions of the agent with respect to the particular kinds of action schemas that are enacted in the exchange process.

Prodi (1989: 101) argues that what we call "morality" is solidary with knowledge and is a constitutive element of the human species. This is not the same as saying that there is a single or universal moral order in the way that the Piaget–Kohlberg developmental schema has sug-gested. This schema confuses the specific (social semiotic) information which is required all along the developmental process with the biological (genetic) information which sets the parameters in which specific developmental pathways may unfold. This specific information is always ecosocial semiotic in character and derives from the meaning-making practices – includ-ing the interpersonal moral orders – of particular social formations. Prodi's point is that a system of linguistic exchange, which is a product of both "natural" and "cultural" evolution, implicates the constitutively moral dimension of our human make up. The exchange process means that human beings *qua* human beings are constituted by other members of the same species. Just as we are regulated by others in the processes of linguistic exchange, so do we internalize these same mechanisms and processes of exchange as part of our own make up as a member of the same species, culture, social group, and so on. The exchange process means that the concept of the individual is meaningless outside the social collectivities which are enacted and which emerge in the exchange process. The fact that this human collectivity is constituted in and through exchange is, Prodi argues, a moral one. The individual cannot depart from his biological inheritance, which means that individual and collective choices may be seen as conforming or not to man's basic constitution, which is fundamentally moral in character.

Prodi's argument shows that the moral dimension of human makeup is no mere epiphenom-enon or external happenstance. The exchange process implicates the joint participation of socially positioned individuals in deeply implicit (unconscious) structures which are enacted by the semiotic formations. The evidence strongly suggests that the genetic heritage of the human species predisposes the developing infant to elicit specific kinds of interactional behaviour from senior others, and that the latter are biologically predisposed to respond in a range of ways which fulfil the needs of the developing individual. Yet, the semiotic-discursive exchange pro-cesses in and through which this takes place will be specific to particular historically specific forms of social organization and the interpersonal moral orders that are embedded in these. (Self-)consciousness may be seen to arise as a consequence of the entraining of the neural dynamics of the individual to the dynamics of these same exchange processes which regulate, orient, and evaluate both self–other and self–self transactions.

9

Dialogic Closure and the Semiotic Mediation of Consciousness in Ecosocial Networks

1 Beaugrande's distinction between the hard-coupling and the soft-coupling of material base and data field in a model of post-classical cognition: implications for the emergence of the semiotic objects of symbolic consciousness and the Principle of Alternation

The stratification of language into the two levels, or strata, that Hjelmslev (1954, 1961 [1943]) called expression and content need not be seen as an unresolved and irresolvable dichotomy between "body" and "mind". Instead, it provides us with a concrete illustration of the general workings of the Principle of Alternation (section 5, page 225). The material matter-energy base of semiosis – e.g. the patterns of acoustic energy or the neuromuscular activity of articulation in the reception and production of speech sounds – is a matter-energy field on one level at the same time that it is information on another level. In this view, matter is inherently also information. Matter and information dialectically interact with each other. The interpretation of waves of acoustic energy by a listener-participant in some discursive event is an interaction between an ecosocial event and the interpreter. The sound waves *qua* ecological event constitute stimulus information that is picked up by the observer-listener.

In this sense, the material event exhibits criteria of observability relative to some observer system (the interpreter). Moreover, the listener interprets this information on the basis of top-down contextual constraints that are not reducible to the matter-energy substrate. Thus, the observer-interpreter brings to bear models of the world which provide contexts for the interpretation of the world. At the same time, the phenomena of experience provide bottom-up material constraints or affordances that specify the nature and the degree of the material constraints. For example, the stream of acoustic energy that constitutes the matter-energy substrate of speech sounds exhibits many degrees of freedom in the form of potentially infinite topological variation. Thus, very many minute differentiations in the material organization of the sound stream are irrelevant to and perhaps not accessible for the purposes of its interpretation as a meaningful linguistic unit.

The relationship between material base and data field in a theory of post-classical cognition has been approached by Beaugrande as follows. In the case of concrete material phenomena such as tables, chairs, kitchen sinks, garden gnomes, ashtrays, rocks, and so on, such concrete phenomena, Beaugrande explains, "are *coarse-grained* in being highly stabilized, and their material base is fairly *hard-coupled* to one data field about them (e.g. size and density). Alternative states of being or alternative data sets have low enough probabilities to be ignored" (1997: 91). Beaugrande elucidates this point with the following example:

> When you enter a room and recognize some chairs, you don't perceive their fine-grained weight, height, width, etc., and you are not disoriented if they vary in shape or if you see them turned at different angles. You "make sense" of the phenomena by determining which relevant data should converge into interobjectivity among your experiences with the same object ... and leaving the rest indeterminate. If the occasion required (e.g. you had to revarnish the chairs), you might determine the size and shape more exactly. Still (like the botanist with the plant in III.18), you would stop at a fairly coarse grain and never go down to the really fine-grained data of, say, molecules.
>
> (Beaugrande 1997: 91)

Beaugrande (1997: 96–97) further points out that phenomena may be characterized by two types of coupling – hard and soft – between their material and informational (data) substrates:

> Phenomena characterized by **hard coupling** have tight, sparse constraints between material and data (Fig. III.16a). Here, we can expect the more classical design of "*lawlike*" connections from part to part (like building blocks) or from cause to effect (like billiard balls) as mandated by the forces of physics (e.g. gravity) or the reactions of chemistry (e.g. bonding). Phenomena characterized by **soft coupling** have loose, rich constraints between material and data. There, we can expect many more "degrees of freedom" through evolving constraints. Sparse data can be **amplified** into rich data, whereas rich data can be **condensed** into sparse data (Fig. III.16b) whilst modifying the material substrate only modestly. For example, sparse, low-energy sound patterns can be hugely amplified by processing them as words of a language being used in a discourse move (e.g. asking a question); and the rich knowledge accessed in this way can be recondensed into similar sound patterns for the next discourse move (e.g. giving an answer). . . .
>
> (Beaugrande 1997: 96–97)

In terms of specification hierarchy thinking, phenomena which are characterized by hard coupling of their material and informational substrates approach a relationship of law-like **necessity** between the two. On the other hand, phenomena characterized by soft coupling of the two substrates are characterized by a relationship of playful **possibility**. In contrast to classical realism, Beaugrande proposes a model of "post-classical cognition" in relation to the dialectical interaction between material substrate and data substrate as follows:

> we can stipulate that an **entity** emerges when that interaction stabilizes its **identity** and determines in what sense or degree the entity has **substantiality** in being endowed with its own boundaries and properties, and has **dimensionality** or **measurability** in being quantifiable in terms of units. Further, the entity has **connectedness** by participating in one or more **contexts** and by persisting through a succession of **states** connected in **temporality** and **locality**. Every change of state constitutes an **event**, while a **process** is a state-event configuration with its **participants**, e.g. agents and targets, and with its accompanying circumstances, e.g. time and location. A relation between co-present entities of a comparable type constitutes a **structure**; a relation between any entity as a means versus the ends it serves is its **function**.
>
> An entity attains **critical mass** when these postulates and the data they supply undergo a convergence among its identity, substantiality, dimensionality, and connectedness via temporality and locality. Henceforth, the entity counts as an **object**, and when **observability** joins the convergence, becomes a **phenomenon**, i.e., a manifestation open to sensory access (e.g. by seeing) (Fig. III.22). The culminating step is the **predictability** through a data convergence rich enough to project connectedness into the temporality of other times and the locality of other places. Whole objects and events in turn converge into the **world-model** that organizes human **knowledge** and **experience**. In this way, all entities emerge from a supportive convergence during which the interaction of material and data is steadily **amplified** with **richer constraints** until it passes thresholds of **critical mass** and takes on **emergent properties**.
>
> (Beaugrande 1997: 104–105; emphasis in original)

In this way, we can see that the phenomena which are on any given level of the specification hierarchy (physical, chemical, biological, semiotic) emerge when the processes and relations that are specific to that particular level stabilize the identity of the given entity relative to some observer perspective. Thus, a linguistic unit emerges and becomes an object of symbolic consciousness *qua* linguistic unit when it is endowed with properties and relations that are specifically linguistic, for example as a lexicogrammatical unit. Thus, a clause is a linguistic unit which has its own emergent properties and relations which are neither reducible to nor wholly explainable in terms of the material substrate of acoustic or optic energy. In this sense, it satisfies Beaugrande's criterion of **substantiality**. A linguistic unit such as the clause also displays criteria of dimensionality: it can be quantified or measured in terms of units.

Moreover, it participates in a range of contexts and therefore exhibits the criterion of connectedness, as well as by persisting through a series of states which are connected in temporality and locality (see also Togeby 2000: 268–271). Thus, a given clause persists in some temporally unfolding discourse context by virtue of its being connected to both prior and succeeding states, as well as occupying a specific position or location in the whole. A given clause is a process-participant configuration, which may also have its attendant circumstances specifying, for example, location, time, manner, and so on. The relations between the various entities such as the various roles which constitute and participate in the whole constitute a dynamical structure at the same time that each component part has its function in relation to the whole. By the same token, the clause as a whole has its function in the still higher-order contexts (co-text, discourse) in which it participates.

Furthermore, the meaning of the specific discourse move in the text in which it occurs, along with the text as a whole *qua* communicative event, converge with the Intertextual Thematic Formations (chapter 2, section 6) and the world-models that organize our knowledge and experience. A spoken linguistic utterance *qua* acoustic event is a material event which can be picked up by the listener's perceptual systems. In this sense, it is a phenomenon which is accessible to perception in primary consciousness. However, the amplification of this material event by richer constraints emanating from the levels of phonology, lexicogrammar, discourse semantics, Intertextual Thematic Formations, and so on, mean that the material acoustic-articulatory event takes on emergent semiotic properties as an object of symbolic consciousness that converges with the world-models that organize human knowledge and experience in symbolic neural space.

2 Lexicogrammar, consciousness, and the three-level hierarchy

In terms of the three levels of organization in the scalar hierarchy, the lexicogrammatical resource systems of a language may be seen as the intermediate level L which reorganizes the relationship between the individual's inner consciousness (level L−1) and the higher-scalar system of interpretance (level L+1) – the semantic patterns, meaning-making conventions, discourse genres – of some ecosocial system. In other words, the lexicogrammar semiotically mediates between the levels above and below it. In this way, the relationship between individual consciousness and the higher-scalar system of interpretance is reorganized. This is a dialectical relationship between the following two principles: (1) Not all variety at level (L−1) remains available for reorganization at level (L+1); there is a *filtering* performed by level L. (2) Conversely, we may say that level (L+1) is *buffered* against variations at level (L−1) by the stabilizing mediations at level L (see Lemke 1999: 7).

The emergence of lexicogrammar at level L thus has a buffering or filtering function such that the flow of information from L−1 to L+1 is stabilized. Moreover, the emergence of level L also adds new kinds of information to the system in the form of the symbolic categories of lexicogrammar. As the discussion of Halliday's theory of language development in chapter 2, section 10 showed, level L units and relations have intrinsic properties and relations and, hence, new informational possibilities which cannot be described in terms of the two previous levels. Moreover, the developmental emergence of lexicogrammar requires the prior bistratal form of protolinguistic organization as its immediate precursor organization. The systemic reorganization entailed by the emergence of lexicogrammar means that the system has attained a new degree of "logical depth" (Lemke 1999) with respect to the specification hierarchy of iconic, indexical, and symbolic modes of semiosis. Furthermore, the emergence of the system's symbolic capacities in the form of a fully-fledged lexicogrammar means that "it is now possible for still newer levels to be interpolated between (N+1) and N, and between N and (N−1)[1]" (Lemke 1999: 2). I shall explore this possibility below with a view to showing how each newly emergent

---

[1]   Lemke's use of the term N and the author's use of the term L in relation to the three-level hierarchy are no more than notational variants of the same basic idea.

level of organization adds new meaning-making potential to the system (see also chapters 10 and 11).

Lemke has proposed, with reference to the scalar hierarchy, that "each new emergent level serves to reorganize one type of semiotic information from the level below it as another type for the level above it" (1999: 2). Consciousness is a meaning-making process (chapter 7, section 6). Typically, consciousness has been discussed in terms of individual experience and awareness of the objects of consciousness. In the present chapter, I shall argue, on the other hand, that consciousness at all levels is fundamentally semiotic in character. It does not follow from this claim that all forms of consciousness can be explained from the point of view of the symbolic resources of language. Consciousness is, in the first instance, a process of construing some mental image as a *sign of some object*, rather than simply interacting with it energetically. In Peirce's terms, the mental image is called the *representamen (R)*, and what we take it to be a sign *of* is called the *object (X)*. Damasio (1999) also recognizes that the mental image (R) does not directly refer to the object (X). Instead, the neural networks which constitute the self engage in interpretative work whereby the self can take up a perspective on the object. Even at the most basic level of core consciousness, there are principles of interpretation which mediate the relationship between mental image and object. This means that there is a system of interpretance – some principle of thirdness – which makes this possible. We shall now see how this same basic principle can be applied to the lexicogrammatical resources of language and their role in the construal of higher-order consciousness.

I shall start by investigating how the principles outlined above can be mapped onto the three-level scalar hierarchy. In this way, we shall be concerned with the place of symbolic, linguistically mediated, meaning-making in the dynamics of higher-order consciousness. Importantly, higher-order consciousness will be seen as a multi-level system in terms of the proposed scalar hierarchy. Lexicogrammatical elements on level L are representamina, R, *of* object-states, X, of phenomena of consciousness on level L–1. The latter dynamically constitute the phenomena at level L, *for* semantic processes or structures at level (L+1), which form the system of interpretance, SI, with respect to which correspondences between Rs and Xs are construed.

Consciousness is more than mere physical interaction between an individual and the world. When an individual picks up stimulus information from the environment – e.g., optical variants and invariants in the ambient optical array – there is physical interaction between these phenomena and the organism's receptor cells on the same molecular scale. But when the organism as a whole mediates the interaction on this lower-scalar level by means of the dynamics of **higher**-scalar sensori-motor and neural dynamics, then the organism is responding to and adapting to information about a given environmental event on the basis of a system of interpretance which is stored in its central nervous system. In this way, the pick up of stimulus energy by the receptors cells is interpreted as a **sign** of an environmental event. Thus, the organism responds not only to the light energy *qua* energy, but as a sign of something on a higher-scalar level than the optical energy which stimulated its receptors. In the case of an organism with symbolic neural space, which is semiotically mediated by the symbolic possibilities of language and other semiotic resource systems in use in a given ecosocial semiotic system, microscopic interactions of the kind mentioned above are not transcended by an immaterial meaning. Transcendental idealism is not the point here.

Semiosis is always cross-coupled to physical-material processes and dynamics in some way. In semiosis, what happens is that the microscopic material interaction is re-interpreted across diverse scalar levels (Thibault 2004a: chapter 2). Information on one level is re-interpreted as information on the next level according to the principle of "semiotic alternation" (Lemke 1999: 6; section 5 below). Neural events can be reorganized at progressively higher levels all the way up to the level of symbolic neural space as particular states of consciousness. In this way, the organism is able to organize a semiotically mediated symbolic response to the original event or to construe a symbolic meaning for it (Thibault 1998c). Higher-order consciousness is, like all forms of consciousness, consciousness *of* something, whether this something be materially present in the here-now environment of the organism or not. If not, it may be consciousness of some proto-meaning – itself subtended by neural activity – which is the focus of attention in memory and which acts in some way as a stimulus to the organism. Stimuli can originate from sources both inside and outside the organism's body. Such stimuli can be re-interpreted across different scales all the way through to the highest scalar level of symbolic neural space in the brain. Semiosis interprets phenomena through a process of contextual integration across scales. The integration of a given phenomenon to the higher-scalar symbolic level of meaning-making in the brain (i.e. symbolic neural space) results in the organism having access to an increased variety of possible symbolic interactions with and construals of the phenomenon in question.

Semiosis is always strongly cross-coupled to physical material processes and flows (Lemke 1995a: 119–120; Thibault 1991a: 6–7). Following Lemke's postulate that semiosis is a material process "in which typically there is a translation or re-interpretation of information from one scale level to another" (1999: 1), I would like to propose that the translation from the expression stratum, which is cross-coupled to bodily processes and dynamics as the environment which it construes, to that of the content stratum, which is cross-coupled to ecosocial phenomena of experience, whether "inner", "outer", imaginary, and so on, entails a move from a relatively more microscopic body scale to a more macroscopic ecosocial one (Thibault 2004a: 39–46). This means that dynamical processes on the scale of the body are reorganized on the higher-scalar level of the content stratum such that the former can have meaningful effects that may ramify across diverse space-time scales. Thus, the same phoneme or sequence of phonemes, entering into different metaredundancy relations in different higher-scale contexts, can lead to different macroscopic effects in the interactions between individuals in some ecosocial system. Meaning-making (semiosis) takes place in human ecosocial systems by "integrating contextual factors across scales" (Lemke 2000a: 182).

The stratal model of semiosis developed by Hjelmslev (1961 [1943]), Halliday (1978b), Lamb (1966), and Martin (1991) shows, in the case of language, how contextual factors which are cross-coupled to the environment of the body on the expression stratum on one relatively microscopic scale are integrated with contextual factors which are cross-coupled to the phenomena of experience on the more macroscopic scale of the ecosocial semiotic environment (Thibault 2004a: 39–46). This integration is possible in the first instance because the two strata do not simply face one way, to their respective environments. Instead, they face two ways such that they are also dynamically cross-coupled to each other in and through the metaredundancy relations that connect the two strata. Furthermore, the emergence of a higher-scalar system of interpretance (SI) entails the emergence of context-sensitive constraints whereby bodily processes and dynamics on the one scale can be causal, though not efficiently so, by virtue of the multi-scale semiotic interdependencies that are created between the individual's body dynamics on the here-now scale and much larger space-time scales.

A given lexicogrammatical form in some discourse context is, to continue the Peircean analysis, a representamen, R; it does not directly cause its object, X. Rather, it construes what Peirce designated as the interpretant of R. In the present discussion, the interpretant of the lexicogrammatical form is the semantic relation which it construes on the discourse semantic stratum. The discourse semantic stratum is realized by the lexicogrammatical stratum (Martin 1991: 114–115; 1992a: 14–21). The discourse stratum is the interface between lexicogrammatical form and the phenomena of experience (physical, imaginary, hypothetical, etc.) that are construed by the semantic stratum. The semantics of the lexicogrammar are construed in the process of meaning-making, or semiosis. Lexicogrammatical choices in discourse are interpreted semantically according to the meaning-making practices of some system of interpretance (SI). That is, the lexicogrammar does not causally determine its semantic interpretant; rather, it is created in and through a given system of interpretance. However, the fact that lexicogrammatical forms do function as signs of specific experiential phenomena – i.e. specific Rs function as signs (semantic construals) of some phenomenon of experience (X) – depends on the way in which the particular lexicogrammatical form is construed, semantically speaking, as a sign of the given object X.

The logic of metaredundancy tells us that the relationship between the lexicogrammatical form and the interpretant which semantically construes its object is not a linear or causal one, but a semiotic one (see also Halliday 1992: 24; Lemke 1984c: 35–39; Thibault 1991a: 91–92). Moreover, the stratal nature of the realizatory relationship between lexicogrammar and semantics means that the semantic stratum, which is the interface between abstract lexicogrammatical form, and the phenomena of experience which lie "outside" language, is an interpretant sign which is, to follow a point made by Lemke (1999: 4), "materially instantiated at a scale level above that of the initial R." In my view, this accords with the way in which the semantic stratum – cf. Peirce's interpretant – is the interface between the intrinsic organization of language form and the higher-scalar ecosocial environment in which language use is always embedded. Thus, the scalar character of this relationship comes clearly into view here for we can see that the objects (X) – e.g. specific referent situations, phenomena of experience, and so on – are, as Lemke puts it, "materially instantiated", as instances of the semantic categories which the system of interpretance construes in and through the lexicogrammatical forms used.

The interpretant sign is "materially instantiated" on a higher-scalar level than that of the lexicogrammatical forms, R. This is in accordance with the stratified nature of the content plane of language into lexicogrammar and semantics. Halliday and Matthiessen (1999: 237) argue that lexicogrammar and semantics constitute two distinct strata rather than simply two facets – i.e. pairings of form and function – of the content plane. This is so because language evolved beyond the original default couplings of given forms and functions as congruent realization (e.g. Process realized by verb, Thing realized by noun) such that the de-coupling of the two enabled an expansion in the experiential semantic resources for construing experience. It was this process which enabled the emergence of grammatical metaphor. In this way, processes, for example, could be de-coupled from their default realization as verbs and realized by nominal groups (chapter 10, section 4).

Semantic interpretants on the level of the system of interpretance are higher-order contextual constraints on the lower-level lexicogrammatical forms. As such, they restrict the degrees of freedom of the lower level, in part because of the interdependency of the various metafunctional semantic regions (chapter 2, section 10). The degrees of freedom of the lower-level are consequently constrained so that it maintains its structural integrity and internal organization. Peirce's notion of "infinite semiosis" refers to the way in which the interpretant sign is a representamen that determines some still further interpretant, and so on. According to Lemke's re-interpretation, Peirce's chain of infinite semiosis is now seen as "the basis of an indefinite (i.e. open-ended) hierarchy of scale levels of systems of interpretance" (1999: 4). A system of this kind is minimally organized in terms of three levels. As we shall see, such an open-ended hierarchy of scale levels enables us to re-interpret the semiotic notion of stratification so as to construct the links between lower-scale bodily dynamics and the ways in which these are contextually integrated on higher scales as signs of symbolic consciousness.

3 The integration of meanings on diverse scalar levels of semiotic organization

Lemke further argues that a higher-scalar system of interpretance on level L+1, which semantically construes the lexicogrammatical (or other semiotic) forms on the lower level L, **doubly** construes. To quote Lemke: "the material reality which is being construed by the SI *as* a representamen is some particular pattern of correlations of material interactions among constituents at level (N–1), but at the same time the interpretant or meaning (at level N+1) of this pattern-as-sign corresponds to an object *at its own (N+1) level*" (1999: 4). Two consequences follow from this. First, "the object X of the original representamen is materially grounded at level (N–1)" (Lemke 1999: 4). Secondly, "the object X corresponding to the interpretant is some phenomenon that has material relevance at level (N+1)" (Lemke 1999: 4). These observations have far-reaching implications for the notion of consciousness. I shall now consider these.

If I utter the clause "Take a look at this picture here" in order to direct my addressee's attention to a specific picture that is within the shared visual purview of both myself (addresser) and my designated addressee, the nominal group *this picture* in this clause functions as a representamen (R) which is construed in and through the relevant system of interpretance as the instantiation of a particular semantic category, as specified by the experiential category of Thing (*picture*), which is realized by the Head noun in the nominal group. A number of factors interact to produce this result. There is a system of interpretance – viz. the English language – which interactants share in varying ways and to varying degrees. There are the indexical practices of selectively pointing to environmental objects (i.e. the picture) in order to indicate that they have specific contextual values or relevancies with reference to the points of view of the interactants in some jointly constructed social event. There is also the socially recognized and jointly made activity (genre) of looking at and commenting on pictures together. The picture is, therefore, doubly construed, as follows.

First, the physical picture referred to in the book is materially grounded at level L–1 as an object (a percept) which is selectively attended to in the unbounded analogue continuum of the perceptual flux which constitutes the visual-spatial purview of addresser and addressee. In this sense, the object in question is a phenomenon of experience which is perceived through the pickup of stimulus information in the environment. Secondly, it is semantically grounded at level L+1 (the higher-scalar system of interpretance) as a material instantiation of a particular experiential semantic category which is recognizable and construable in and through the lexico-grammatical forms of the language system in question in its ecosocial environments. In the terms used by Bateson (1973e [1972]: 381–383, 1973f [1972]), we could say that the object has been logically typed by the system of contextualizing relations in operation as a member of a particular semantic type-category. In this second perspective, the object is an instance of a **symbolically** construed semantic category, or interpretant. As such, a very different kind of object is now available to conscious attention and awareness. This second object is a symbolic one which is constituted in the symbolic neural space of higher-order consciousness as an object in its own right. The relevant hierarchy of relations is set out as follows:

L+1   SI symbolically construes X as an instance of the experiential semantic category [THING: PICTURE]

L   lexicogrammatical form of the representamen (R) – the nominal group [DETERMINER + NOUN]

L–1   object X (the picture) as a perceived phenomenon of experience in the perceptual flux

From the perspective of the L–1 level, the visual perception of the object is, at the lowest anatomical level, an exchange of energy between the radiated photic energy and the receptor cells which are stimulated by light energy as the first stage in sending transforms of difference along nerve fibres to the central nervous system (Gibson 1983 [1966]: 41). However, this is the lowest, or most microscopic, level in what Gibson describes as a hierarchy of organs of sensitivity (Gibson 1983 [1966]: 42). Receptor cells are subordinate to organs of sensitivity such as the eye, "which is a structure containing many energy receptors and many receptive units that can adjust so as to modify the input from cells and units" (1983 [1966]: 41). Lower organs such as the eye are in turn subordinated to higher-order perceptual systems. To quote Gibson:

> The single eye is a system of low order, although it is already an organ with an adjustable lens for sharpening the retinal image and a pupil for normalizing its intensity. The eye with its attached muscles is a system of higher order; it is stabilized in the head relative to the environment with the help of the inner ear, and it can scan the environment. The two eyes together make a dual system of still higher order; the eyes converge for near objects and diverge for far ones. And the two-eyes-with-head-and-body system, in cooperation with postural equilibrium and locomotion, can get around in the world and look at everything.
>
> (Gibson 1983 [1966]: 42)

The photoreceptor cells on the microscopic level interpret light energy through the microscopic interactions between the two by transducing this energy into nerve impulses. However, this is not anything of which I have any kind of conscious experience. Further up the hierarchy, the visual perceptual system actively picks up or obtains information about some environmental event through a process of actively attending to and exploring the environment (Gibson 1983 [1966]: 45). On this more macroscopic level, the information which is actively picked up is information about some object or event on the scale of a system of interpretance which mediates the perceiver's relationship to the information which is picked up and the environmental sources of this information. At this level of self–nonself (environment) relations, the information which is picked up in the ambient optical array is an indexical sign of some environmental object or event. The organism can respond or otherwise adjust its behaviour on the basis of its interpretation of the information picked up as indexing some macroscopic environmental phenomenon which impinges upon its consciousness. For example, the sign may be interpreted as an index of impending danger, a potential sexual partner, food, and so on. The larger point is that the sign is meaningful to its interpreter because it is a sign of something on the scale of the system of interpretance in which the interpreter is embedded (Salthe 1993: 16; Lemke 2000a). In the present example, the indexical sign invokes some contextual value in the here-now environment as an object of conscious experience. However, this invoking of such an object still refers to our primary consciousness of the immediate environment. But what about our symbolic consciousness of phenomena of the there-then kind? I shall now turn to this question.

4 A textual example of semiotically mediated symbolic consciousness and the three-level hierarchy

In order to further explore the question of semiotically mediated symbolic consciousness, let us consider the following text[2]:

> Pinot Grigio Trentino DOC 1994, Cantine Mezzacorona. Pale green in colour, with a delicate milky nose. Soft, fruity, and milky on the palate, with good balance.

This text is an instance of the genre of professional wine tasters' evaluations of commercially sold table wines. In this brief, though complete, text, the wine taster focuses on three aspects of the wine in question: colour, aroma, and taste. I shall confine my analysis to the question of taste, with reference to the adjectival group "Soft, fruity, and milky on the palate, with good balance."

Unlike the previous example, which was about a picture available to visual perception in the immediate environment of the interactants, readers of this text do not necessarily have access to an immediate here-now perceptual purview. Yet, this text is about the wine taster's perceptual experience – visual, olfactory, and taste or palatability. However, there is no direct referential connection between that perceptual experience and the lexicogrammatical choices used in this text; the text cannot be explained away as a verbal report of a conscious experience. Taste, as Gibson (1983 [1966]: 1237) aptly reminds us, is a major perceptual system for reasons connected both to basic survival as well as to the most discriminating values of culture. The social practices of wine tasting, along with the social discourses associated with these practices, amply testify to this.

The linguistic construction "Soft, fruity, and milky on the palate, with good balance" functions as a representamen (R) which is construed in and through the relevant system of interpretance as the instantiation of a series of semantic categories, as specified by the experiential category of Quality in adjectives such as "soft", "fruity", and "milky". In the text, these serve to qualify the nominalized entity "Pinot Grigio Trentino DOC 1994", which is mentioned at the beginning of the text. In the present case, the system of interpretance is defined as follows: (i) the resources of some language system (English, as before); (ii) access to the register-specific semantics of the lexicogrammatical selections in the text; (iii) the indexical practices of invoking specific (perceptual) contents of taste as having specific contextual values or relevancies; and (iv) the socioeconomic practices and values and the discourse genres associated with the activity of wine tasting.

Prototypically, adjectives such as "soft", "fruity", and "milky" construe type-qualities which are attributed, as here, to the experiential category Thing in the nominal group, or the Carrier in

---

[2]   This text was kindly made available to me by Felipe Alcántara Iglesias, though the use that I have made of it here is entirely my own responsibility.

a relational attributive predication. In this way, they further specify the Thing as an instance of the category in question. In the present text, which displays a high degree of ellipsis typical of this genre of text, it would be possible to postulate an attributive clause such as "Pinot Grigio Trentino DOC 1994 is soft, fruity, and milky on the palate, with good balance" in order to reconstruct this more explicit semantic relation between the two textual items. The experiential semantic structure of this relational predication is analysed in Figure 9.1.

Pinot Grigio Trentino DOC 1994	is	soft, fruity, and milky on the palate, with good balance
Carrier / Instance	Process: Relational attributive	Attribute / Schema: Type Quality
nominal group	verb	adjectival group

Figure 9.1 Experiential semantic structure of reconstructed relational: attributive predication

Adjectives specify a semantic class in terms of quality. In the reconstructed relational predication analysed in Figure 9.1, the adjectival group classifies the Carrier in this clause as instantiating a specific class of quality (type-quality). In the present case, this is a complex of several qualities, as specified in the adjectival group. From the perspective of level L–1, adjectives such as "soft", "fruity", and "milky on the palate" qualify an object which is materially grounded in the pick up, by the taste system, of information concerned with the mouth's detection of the wine's texture (soft), the odorous or volatile component of the wine, which stimulates receptors in the olfactory cavity above the mouth (fruity), the sapid component (milky on the palate), and the overall consistency of the wine or its sense of wholeness (with good balance). Now, it is important to bear in mind here that these perceptual properties do not in any way form part of the here-now perceptual purview of the reader of this text. This does not alter the fact that readers may, to varying degrees, be able to construct, on the basis of the dynamic associations in memory of their previous perceptions of wines tasted, along with their perceptions of their own actions (drinking, tasting, etc.) which were concomitant with the taste perception, contextual redundancies between these dynamic associations and the lexicogrammatical selections in the text.

As Gibson (1986 [1979]: 255–256) points out, non-perceptual awareness is explainable in terms of a perceptual system which has become sensitized to higher-order differentiations (invariants) in the stimulus flux such that it can "extract them from the flux and operate without the constraints of the stimulus flux." In this way, contextual metaredundancies may be established in some discourse between non-perceptual awareness (and memory) of invariants and specific lexicogrammatical selections. The linguistic text has the power to invoke an awareness of this kind in those who have had previous experience of and have acquired sensitivity to the perceptual invariants in question. Thus, the taste of the wine may be internally invoked as an object of non-perceptual consciousness even if the adjustment loops for the haptic, olfactory, and other exploratory activity of the receptors in the mouth are shut down, so to speak, when one reads the text in question. In any case, my main point here is that a perceptual object is materially grounded at level L–1 even in the absence of the reader's direct, here-now access to the taste experiences described by the writer of the text. This brings us to the L+1 perspective.

As before, the L+1 level is a system of interpretance which construes lexicogrammatical selections at level L as signs of perceived phenomena level (L–1). These level (L–1) phenomena of experience correspond to the effects of the interaction between the wine taster and the wine in question at level (L–1). This level is not, as was pointed out above, directly accessible by readers of the text. At level L, the lexicogrammatical forms used as their R symbolically construe them as instances of type-categories and type-qualities in a given system of interpretance on level (L+1). In the present case, the causal-material relations between level L–1 and level L+1 are at the very least quite indirect, mediated by intertextual links between this text and particular material social practices of wine tasting, and not given in the text in any way. The point of this discussion is to show how it is on the L+1 level that symbolically construed objects of consciousness are created in and through the semantic resources of language without any direct causal-material connection to the perceptual or other material interactions that are referred to on level L–1.

Secondly, the wine in question is semantically grounded at level L+1 (the higher-scalar system of interpretance) as a material instantiation of a particular experiential semantic category, which is recognizable and construable in and through the lexicogrammatical forms of the language system in question in its ecosocial semiotic environments. In this second perspective, the object is an instance of a **symbolically** construed semantic quality, functioning as interpretant. As such, a very different kind of object is now available to conscious attention and awareness. This second object is a symbolic one which is constituted in the symbolic neural space of higher-order consciousness as an object in its own right. The relevant hierarchy of relations is set out as follows:

L+1 SI symbolically construes X as an instance of the experiential semantic quality-class [QUALITY: SOFT, FRUITY, MILKY . . .]

L lexicogrammatical form of the representamen (R) – the nominal group [ADJECTIVE + ADJECTIVE + ADJECTIVAL GROUP + PREPOSITIONAL PHRASE]

L–1 object X (the taste of the wine) as a perceived phenomenon of experience in the perceptual flux

The semantic type-qualities referred to above are construed by the lexicogrammatical forms. These semantic type-qualities (X) are that which are construed (or "represented", to use the Peircean terminology) by the lexicogrammatical forms (R). Both the semantic type-qualities and the lexicogrammatical class items (the adjectives) which realize them are discrete typological-categorial distinctions. The semantic distinctions in natural languages are defined by their contrasts with other terms in the same system. Thus, the adjective "hard" contrasts with the adjective "soft"; the difference between them is a categorial one. It would take another adjective, expressing yet another categorial distinction, to express a category that lies midway between these two. In language, both the lexicogrammatical forms and the semantic distinctions realized or construed by these are predominantly typological-categorial in nature (Lemke 1998a; chapter 2, section 2).

At the scale of the taste and olfactory perceptual systems which are activated in wine tasting on level L–1, there is, on the other hand, continuous variation among the various kinds of information that are picked about the wine in the wine taster's mouth. At this scale, it is the continuously varying multiple information about factors such as odour, temperature, texture, consistency, etc., all of which are made to covary by the perceptual exploratory activity of the mouth (Gibson 1983 [1966]: 138). In human tasting, what is perceived are not chemical, olfactory, and other sensations, but "nutritive values or affordances" which have gastronomic values (Gibson 1983 [1966]: 139). At the higher scalar level, L, of the lexicogrammatical forms used to represent these values in linguistic semiosis, this multiple, continually varying perceptual information about the taste of the wine is construed, as in our example, by discrete word classes which are, in turn, assigned their categorial semantic meanings on the L+1 level of the system of interpretance which is in operation.

The perceptual information that is picked up in the activity of tasting is continuously varying. However, the lexicogrammatical forms that a speaker or writer uses to describe the experience of wine tasting are exponents of discrete grammatical classes in which only some, and not all, distinctive features make a difference as to which words are used. When a speaker or writer represents the experience of wine tasting using the lexicogrammatical resources of linguistic semiosis, he or she re-construes continuous perceptual variation into discrete linguistic forms. The resulting linguistic text, as in our example, comprises purely linguistic information which is potentially meaningful in some SI. That is, the semantics of these forms, and, hence, the semantic objects, qualities, etc. that are construable in and through these forms, are construed at the L+1 level of the SI. In the process, the infinite variety of the continuous variation of the wine taster's perceptual experience is semiotically translated into the symbolic categories of the higher-scalar SI. The SI categorizes what the wine taster wrote, using the words he did, into a restricted number of discrete and reciprocally contrasting semantic categories, qualities, and so on. In order to do this, the wine taster (and his or her readers) must know the language that is used, its lexicogrammatical resources and their genre-specific semantics and modes of deployment relative to some system of interpretance.

The learning of a language takes place on a much slower ecosocial timescale than the much faster timescale that is involved in the here-now perceptual activity of wine tasting. Learning a language entails a much more massive and interlinked network of neuronal connections over a much larger system scale – that of symbolic neural space – than that involved in the perception of olfactory, textural, and other invariants in the activity of wine tasting. The lexicogrammatical level of the neurological system of language in the brain consists of dynamical attractors, or constrained pathways, in neural semantic space which filter the recognition of typological semantic classes of phenomena from the much shorter, non-criterial, continuous variation of the unbounded topological flux of phenomena perceived through perceptual activity. Thus, we see how the pick up of stimulus information in the ambient flux through active perceptual exploration, the lexicogrammatical forms used, and the relevant semantic categories correspond to the three levels of the scalar hierarchy, seen as a hierarchy of neuro-semiotic functions linking symbolic neural space to lower-scalar sensori-motor exploration.

None of this implies that the semantic construal on level L+1 of the topological-continuous variation on level L–1 is necessarily an impoverishment of the perceptual experience. Rather, it is its further symbolic specification: level L–1 phenomena are contextually integrated to more highly specified symbolic phenomena on level L+1. The genuine wine taster is a connoisseur who is continually fine-tuning and refining his or her perceptual exploration of the stimulus information which the wine affords. The wine provides, potentially, an infinite source of such stimulus information. Just as a good wine improves with age, the activity of wine tasting improves with experience. That is, higher-order variables in taste can be extracted from the flux of stimulus information. This ability is based on differentiation. Gibson (1983 [1966]: 270) points out that this is a matter of "learning what to attend to, both overtly and covertly." Thus, the experienced wine taster knows how to tune into distinctive features in the flux as well as to abstract perceptual invariants under changing stimulation (Gibson 1983 [1966]: 270–271).

So, the pleasures of enjoying a glass or two of a fine wine are not diminished by typological semiotic closure on level L+1. At this level, there is semiotic closure because there is only a finite number of semantic categories, however large this number might be, which constitute available options in meaning in a given language system. Moreover, register- and genre-specific semantic restrictions will impose further, domain-specific limits on the kinds of options that the producers of texts such as the above instance can typically use. But this is not the end of the matter. At a given level of abstraction, all varieties of *Sangiovese*, the still red wine typical of the Emilia-Romagna region of Italy, are alike from the point of view of their typological classification. But the stimulus information which different varieties afford the wine taster in the form of topological-quantitative information enable wine drinkers to detect topological-quantitative distinctions, as well as to abstract general properties, both of which allow wine drinkers to detect new invariants which distinguish one variety from another as individual varieties on the basis of the isolation of many topological features and thus to form at some intermediate level of interpretation a new classification of these newly isolated or extracted invariants.

We see here a concrete illustration of the ways in which perception is not the processing of raw information about an objective world "out there". Instead, perception is embedded in and entrained to the categories of particular social meaning-making practices and their systems of interpretance such that the biomechanical dimensions of the perceptual act are contextually integrated to and consequently reorganized by these meanings and their associated practices. In other words, the material activity of perception is itself dependent on practices of meaning construal that link it to other meanings and practices in the ecosocial semiotic system. Perception is a material activity which is based on biophysical interactions between individual and environmental event in the ecosocial semiotic system at the same time that it is entrained to and construed by the meaning relations of the community as having links with particular social practices in the community (see also Harré and Gillett 1994: 167–172; see especially Goodwin

1996a for an account of how colour perception and classification is integrated to and entrained by the meaning-making practices of archaeologists while excavating a site).

Moreover, a good *Sangiovese* improves with age at the same time that it remains a *Sangiovese*. That is, its type-specific attractors are equifinal insofar as it continues to age along its trajectory as a recognizable *Sangiovese* at the same time that there is still scope for quantitative individuation which future wine tasters can explore and enjoy. Lemke points out that on those levels where only typological difference is relevant, then we have semiotic closure within that level. In the above example, this is the case on the L+1 level of the SI and its semantic categories. However, the Principle of Alternation shows how, across a given triple of levels in a semiotic system, there is always the potential for topological-quantitative openness. It is this topological-continuous variation in degree and quantity which, as our example shows, allows for potential reorganization at some newly emergent higher level as a new typological-semiotic closure. This last point leads us to a consideration of Lemke's Principle of Alternation.

5 Lemke's Principle of Alternation and topological vs typological modes of semiosis

Lemke distinguishes two main classes of semiosis, as follows:

> (a) those cases in which the features of representamen that are criterial for some SI to interpret it as a sign of some X may vary continuously, so that quantitative differences of degree in a feature of R normally lead to differences of degree or kind in the interpretant, *vs.* (b) those in which all representamina are classified by the SI into a discrete spectrum of types, and each R-type is interpreted as a distinct X.

> (Lemke 1999: 4)

The first type is topological-continuous variation; it is quantitative differences of degree that make a difference in this mode. The second type is founded on discrete typological-categorial distinctions. The first type is a generalization of Bateson's (1973g [1972]: 342–344) notion of analogue signalling; the second generalizes his notion of digital signalling. The lexicogrammar and semantics of natural language are, for the most part, based on typological-categorial difference, although, as we shall see in chapters 10 and 11, grammatical metaphor also reveals the topological dimension of natural language semantics. Lemke (1999: 4) further points out that while it is possible to "map continuous variation in X onto continuous variation in R (and vice versa)," (topological) "discrete variants of X onto discrete variants of R (and vice versa)," (typological) there may also be "mixed modes of semiosis in which the continuous is mapped onto the discrete and vice versa." These mixed modes are fundamental to the understanding of the dynamics of multi-scale dynamical systems such as language (Thibault 2003b).

Lemke has proposed the Principle of Alternation as a way of theorizing, in terms of the three-level scalar hierarchy, how semiotic functions are mapped onto dynamical scale levels, and the reorganization of continuous variation into discrete variants. Lemke defines this Principle as follows:

> *Each new, emergent intermediate level N in a complex, hierarchical, self-organizing system functions semiotically to reorganize the continuous quantitative (topological) variety of units and interactions at level (N–1) as discrete, categorial (typological) meaning for level (N+1), and/or to reorganize the discrete, categorial (typological) variety of level (N–1) as continuously variable (topological) meaning for level (N+1).*

> (Lemke 1999: 7; italics in original)

6 The dynamics of higher-order consciousness and the Principle of Alternation

The mapping of semiotic functions onto organizational scales has dynamical implications for the emergence of consciousness. That is, the emergence of a new level in the scalar hierarchy of consciousness can only occur, both phylogenetically and ontogenetically, if, and only if, a new level in the hierarchy of semiotic interpretance emerges. Each higher level in the hierarchy has multiple realizations on lower levels. For example, it is the many-to-one mapping of topological-continuous variety at the L–1 level of taste perception onto the L level of lexico-grammar that allows for the filtering of L–1 non-criterial fluctuations at the L level. Further-more, discrete lexicogrammatical forms at this level can be re-construed at the L+1 level as having an increased variety of meanings, depending on the ways in which constraints on the L level of lexicogrammar are taken up and responded to on the basis of their connections to a culture's intertextual networks on the more global, longer term L+1 level of the SI (see Lemke 1999: 4).

Following Lemke's Principle of Alternation, we see that the semiotic transformation of continuous perceptual information to discrete lexicogrammatical forms and of these to con-tinuous semantic meanings, in the progression from level L–1 to level L+1, constitutes what Lemke defines as "a *semiotic transformation* of the information content of lower levels as *signs* for higher levels, allowing *many-to-one* classifications and *one-to-many* context-dependent reinterpretations" (1999: 9). It is the dynamics of semiotic transformation mapped onto the scalar hierarchy that allows for the emergence of the symbolic neural space of higher-order consciousness.

6.1 Alternation and the reopening of closure

Lemke identifies four different ways in which self-organizing systems are closed in order to establish the relevance of closure to the evolution of complexity. He defines the four ways as follows:

- *material closure*, meaning there is neither matter nor energy flow across the boundary of the system;
- *autocatalytic closure* in the sense that some web of interdependent processes is self-regenerating;
- *informational closure* in the sense that all information critical to the system's behaviour is available internally;
- *semiotic closure*, which entails that in some sense the system's dynamics depends on exhaustive sets of classificatory (paradigmatic) alternatives.

To Lemke's list, I would add two further levels of closure in order to explain the emergence of consciousness. These are:

- *dialogic closure*;
- *self-referential closure*.

The levels of closure referred to here follow the logic of the specification hierarchy. I shall now explore each of these forms of closure in more detail.

6.1.1 Material closure

Systems which are near equilibrium and do not allow flows of matter, energy, and information between the system and its environment undergo predictable change along a uniform trajec-tory. Systems of this kind exhibit no properties of individuation; they are without individual history (Lemke 1995a: 112). In other words, the specific temporal-spatial conditions of the system at its starting point and the specific trajectory that it traverses are irrelevant to the further development of the system's trajectory. Near equilibrium systems are closed systems which do not exhibit properties deriving from their interactions with higher-scalar contexts (Prigogine and Stengers 1985 [1984]: 125–126).

6.1.2 Autocatalytic closure

The closing of the loop on the web of interdependent processes entails the importing of energy from the environment in order to maintain the internal dynamics and organization of the system as a whole. Furthermore, it is the intrinsic organizational dynamics of such systems which regulate the matter-energy flows between the system and its environment whereby the system establishes higher-order parameters whose function it is to maintain the web of inter-dependent processes; in other words, to ensure the ongoing closure of the system. The internal dynamics of the interdependent processes involved thus select and determine which processes are most suitable for the overall maintenance of the autocatalytic web's self-organization instead of being overwhelmed by extrinsic environmental factors. The system as a whole selects only those matter-energy flows which make a difference to the system, that is, those which are relevant to its internal organization and hence conform to its self-organizing "perspective". That is, the system's internal organization – its web of interdependent processes – achieves a relative autonomy from the environment, which allows the given system to achieve informational closure (see Maturana and Varela 1980).

Autocatalytic systems, as Kauffman (1993: 370) observes, integrate their own behaviour in order to form a functional whole. Like the lexicogrammar of a language, the autocatalytic web is defined by a global network of dynamical relations which define the identity and character-istics of the system as a whole as well as its behaviour (chapter 2, section 10). Because of their intrinsic self-organizing dynamics, autocatalytic webs exhibit vectorial directionality towards higher levels of organizational complexity. In this sense, they are self-governing systems whose self-organizing processes are projected towards the future history of the system (Kauffman 1993: 370). For this reason, they can be said to be less specified precursors of teleological systems with conscious, goal-directed behaviour (Juarrero1999: 127). More precisely, autocata-lytic systems are teleonomic or goal-seeking open dynamic systems (Wilden 1981: 27). Kauff-man (1993: 371) proposes "random grammar models" as a further development of the principle of autocatalytic closure. Random grammar models seek to explain how particular couplings of variables arise so as to achieve the functional integration of all the component parts. This is based on "systems of symbol strings" (Kauffman 1993: 371) – strings of symbols standing for chemicals, goods-&-services, and roles in a cultural system (Kauffman 1993: 370) – so that the relations between these grammar rules and the functional integration of the system may be studied. Such models may be seen as less specified precursors of the grammatical organization of natural languages.

6.1.3 Informational closure

Information is a purely quantitative measure of (im)probability, pattern, and order. It refers to the number of bits which a given pattern contains. However, these bits have no semantic content; they are devoid of meaning. Meaning, on the other hand, is always about something, as well as being for someone. In this sense, it is intentional. A bit may be defined as a possible difference, either typological or topological, which is potentially transformable as a meaningful distinction at some higher level. Information refers to the infinite variety of possible differences which may or may not be selected so as to make a difference. Information is coded variety and, like Gibson's environmental information, it is everywhere (Wilden 1980 [1972]: xxix). Informa-tion (coded variety) is distinguished from noise (uncoded variety). The distinction between information and noise is established by context. The probabilistic (quantitative) basis of infor-mation is what Wilden calls "a measure of the degree of (semiotic) freedom, in a given situation, to choose among the available signals, symbols, messages, or patterns to be transmitted (the repertoire), many of which, may be entirely devoid of meaning" (1980 [1972]: 233).

As Halliday's work on probabilities in the grammatical systems of English shows (chapter 2, section 10), if all features in the grammar had an equiprobable frequency of occurrence, the information content of each feature in the grammar would be high. However, the constraints and principles of ordering imposed by the syntagmatic and paradigmatic patterns of the lan-guage skew the probabilities such that some features have more information content than others. Information is not the same as meaning because the purely quantitative basis of information is not concerned with the ways in which information (coded variety) has potential significance for agents within the context of a given ecosocial semiotic system (chapter 8, section 14). The organization of information flows internal to a system may serve to direct and harness the matter-energy flows of autocatalytic processes at the level below.

6.1.4 Semiotic closure

The paradigmatically organized sets of alternatives – the system of semiotically salient differences of values – specify the global organization of a semiotic system such as a language. Depending on the particular semiotic system (language, depiction, gesture, and so on), there can be systems of either typological or topological differences. In the case of language, the paradigmatic organization of the systems of alternative types constitutes its meaning-making potential (Halliday 1978b: 187–188). Halliday and Matthiessen (1999: 14) characterize the global paradigmatic organization of language as "a large semantic 'space' " which is organized in terms of the two dimensions of *delicacy* and *instantiation*. Systemic networks of semantic options may thus be ordered from the least delicate, or most general, to the most delicate, or most specific, type. Instantiation refers to the move from the system's general potential to the instantiation of this potential in particular texts. It is possible to postulate a cline of instantiation which goes from the most general meaning potential, for example, the most general semantic classes of experience, modes of interpersonal engagement, and so on, to the domain specific potential of particular semantic registers and discourse genres (text-types), right through to the instantiation of specific instances of experiential and interactional meaning in text. The semiotic closure that is achieved by the global paradigmatic organization of language and other semiotic systems differentiates the systems of alternatives that comprise the global semantic space. It is this global semantic space which defines the potential significance of information for the ecosocial system, now seen as a system of interpretance in which information flows are re-interpreted as semiotic categories in specific contexts. Semiotic closure defines a system of interpretance in which the information which is determined by the probabilities of lexicogrammar, say, as well as the (meta)redundancy relations of their co-patternings, are construed as semantic interpretants.

6.1.5 Dialogic closure

Dialogic closure entails semiotically mediated interaction between a first and a second, for example between self and nonself. The bringing of a first and a second into a relation which is semiotically mediated by the meaning-making resources of a higher-scalar SI (a third) leads to what I have elsewhere discussed, following Bråten (1992) as "dialogic closure" (Thibault 2000a; see also chapter 3, section 1). Dialogic closure is an emergent consequence of the reciprocal, dialogic processes in and through which a first (self) and a second (nonself) adapt to each other in the context of the dyad which regulates the flow of matter-energy and information-meaning between them. In the process of adapting to each other, there emerge higher-order patterns and constraints which regulate the possible ways in which the two members of the dyad can interact with each other. The resulting dialogic closure consists of emergent order and organization at level L+1. All acts of meaning necessarily entail dialogic closure even in those cases where there is no immediately present other (addressee) with whom one interacts. Face-to-face conversational interaction between two individuals is just one form that dialogic closure can take. Dialogic closure entails some restriction in a determinate context of the global system of meaningful alternatives that are available in a given ecosocial semiotic system. For this reason, it is concerned with the instantiation of specific options in meaning as text which is operational in some context.

Text, as Halliday (1978b: 136–137) has shown, is a semantic unit which is not defined in terms of size, but as an ongoing process of meaningful choice from paradigmatic systems of alternatives. This definition is useful to my present argument because it draws attention to the ways in which social agents make constrained choices from a global semantic space of symbolic possibilities. In this perspective, the logogenetic generation of discourse in context can be seen as the flow of meaning from an intentional source into action (Juarrero 1999: 94). That is, the generation of meaning at an intentional source requires a restriction of the total set of alternatives. Discourse implicates an ongoing dialogically organized encounter between a firstness and a secondness. Such encounters always involve both semiotic and material friction (Thibault 1995). Discourse is the semantically constrained product and/or record of an action trajectory; it is the flowing into action of meaningful structure from an intentional source. Moreover, it is the fact that discourse is an intentional **semantic** (not material) unit which enables it to causally affect the ecosocial environment into which it flows in the entraining of both physical-material and semiotic-discursive processes and flows. The point is that the semantic dependence of text on an intentional source which projects it into its ecosocial environment occurs on the basis of the information which the semantic output "carries about the meaningful content of the intentional source, not its mechanically causal relationship to that source, which is likely to be equivocal" (Juarrero 1999: 96). The central question has to do with how meaning flows into and "causally" entrains both material and semiotic processes. It does not do so, as Juarrero demonstrates, on the basis of mechanical efficient causality.

Rather, the semiotic selections made by an intentional source constrain the textual output so that the latter is construable in some SI as the actualization of the former. It is not the underlying neurological substrate of the neural events which in itself constitutes in the agent's brain the intended meaning. Physical causality has no place here because efficient Newtonian causality "is a relation among externally related events" (Juarrero 1999: 96). The notion of efficient causality presumes the externalist perspective of an agent who observes objectively from a perspective "outside" the event; meaning is not usually assumed to be relevant to this perspective. The flow of meaning from an intentional source out into its ecosocial semiotic environment and that source are **internally** related to each other. They are internally related components of a time-bound trajectory which is constrained by the semantic contents of symbolic neural space, itself constrained by the systems of semiotic alternatives on the higher-scalar level of the SI. This requires an internalist perspective of agents who are inside the relevant system of meanings. From the perspective of ontogenetic time, the processes of both development and individuation along the individual's time-bound trajectory expand semiotic capacity as the infant moves from the proto-semiotic iconicity of the earliest socioaffective exchanges with caregivers through context-bound indexicality to symbolic possibility, in the process accessing new kinds of semiotic alternatives as well as reorganizing the prior ones. The resulting reorganization provides access to an expanding informational-semiotic phase space along the system's developmental trajectory.

Dialogic closure entails a network of relations in terms of which the semiotically mediated relation between a first and a second takes place. It is a system of relations in which no single component can be isolated from the whole in which it belongs and in relation to which it functions. Bateson's example of the man felling a tree with an axe provides a good explanation of the principle of dialogic closure:

> Consider a man felling a tree with an axe. Each stroke of the axe is modified or corrected, according to the shape of the cut face of the tree left by the previous stroke. This self-corrective (i.e., mental) process is brought about by a total system, tree-eyes-brain-muscles-axe-stroke-tree; and it is this total system that has the characteristics of imminent mind.
>
> More correctly, we should spell the matter out as: (differences in tree)-(differences in retina)-(differences in brain)-(differences in muscles)-(differences in movement of axe)-(differences in tree), etc. What is transmitted around the circuit is transforms of difference. And, as noted above, a difference which makes a difference is an *idea* or unit of information.
>
> But this is not how the average Occidental sees the event sequence of tree felling. He says, "I cut down the tree" and he even believes that there is a delimited agent, the "self", which performed a delimited "purposive" action upon a delimited object.
>
> (Bateson 1973a [1972]: 288)

The tree in Bateson's example is the other – the nonself – with which the self interacts. Bateson shows that an entire circuit of relations constitutes the closing of a loop around which successive transforms of difference flow. This circuit is a semiotic-material trajectory which loops through the man's neural and sensori-motor dynamic and which extends out into the environment to the nonself (the tree) and back to the man again. Let us suppose, simplifying matters somewhat, that we have a triadic relationship comprising self-world-other, where self and other are the two dialogically coordinated parties to a dialogue and the world refers to whatever self and other attend to during the dialogic exchange between them. Whether self and other have or do not have perceptual access to the same piece of the world need not concern us here. The point is that the exchange mechanisms regulate the flow of matter, energy, and information between the dialogic loop of relations and its higher-order environment. In this way, the internal structure and dynamics of the self-world-other relation are maintained such that the separate components of the circuit are integrated into the circuit as a whole. Dialogic closure thus entails the maintenance of the structural integrity of the whole circuit, seen as an instance of a dynamic open system which maintains and organizes itself through the exchanges between its internal processes and dynamics and the higher-order environment in which it is embedded. Following Bateson's line of argumentation, dialogic closure shows that there is no self *per se* of which we may be self-aware. Instead, the self is always defined and constituted as a self-in-interaction-with-others-and-world. From the perspective of dialogic closure, a self is a subsystem that collects some of the effects of its own cascading dynamics in the circuit as a whole, in the process building up a self-referential perspective (Salthe 1993: 158). In other words, the emergence of the self-referential perspective amounts to the creating of a further loop – a meta-loop – which closes the loop on the "I" component of the dialogically organized loop (chapter 5, section 14).

6.1.6 *Self-referential closure*

Consciousness, then, is a further level of closure which closes the loop on the "I" (self) sector so as to create a self-referential perspective. It arises when the reentrant connectivity of neural groups creates the meta-loop on the "I" component that I mentioned above. This self-organizing reentrant connectivity of neural groups builds up orderly arrangements which are the effects of an internal perspective (chapter 5, section 2), which is able to be projected into the world and have effects there as meaning-constrained trajectories. Consciousness emerges because the ground of order which is afforded by dialogic closure produces a field of matter, energy, and information-meaning flows within which self-organizing viewpoints can emerge and project their own effects into the world. Bateson's perspective on what I have called dialogic closure is useful because it shows how the definition and behaviour of the various interacting components in the circuit are dependent on and constrained by the successive transforms of difference into information and meaning. Consciousness, at its various levels, is constrained by and dependent on information and meaning.

Furthermore, consciousness is always consciousness *of* something, i.e. it is intentional in Brentano's sense. This means that the self-referential and self-organizing perspective entailed by the further closing of the loop on the "I" component must be sufficiently robust so as to buffer or filter out noise. In this way, conscious awareness and the taking up of perspectives from the "I" point of view can flow into the ecosocial environment as meaningful effects. These effects can be attributed to the meanings the self gives to experience along a time-bound individuating trajectory. This suggests that the crossing of the threshold into consciousness can only take place if the act of consciousness flows from an intentional structure on account of the meaning of that structure. For our present purposes, it does not matter whether this meaning is iconic, indexical, or symbolic. The broader point is that consciousness is semantically grounded at level L+1 (the higher-scalar system of interpretance) as a material instantiation of some interpretant X (see above). It is the semantic structure of the interpretant, rather than the lower-scalar neural events that realize it, which determine how an intentional act of consciousness relates self to its object.

Recall that in Brentano's (1973 [1874]) definition, a mental phenomenon consists of two objects: the object of consciousness (the primary object) and the consciousness of that object (the secondary object). As Battacchi (1998: 8; 1996) points out, only the first can be observed, whereas the second is present only implicitly. The issue at stake here hinges on the way in which agents have immediate awareness of their mental states in the sense that they have consciousness of them – this is what a "state of consciousness" is – at the same time that they are conscious of themselves as having this awareness of their mental states. This draws attention to the creation of the meta-loop that I mentioned above. Thus, self-awareness is never awareness of the self *per se*, as both Brentano and James recognized early in the modern history of consciousness studies. In Brentano's terms, the object of consciousness which is experienced as perceived, remembered, imagined, and so on, is placed in an interactive relationship with the self. Both are present in the act of consciousness; the first explicitly so, the second only implicitly. The self thus undergoes an experience of interacting with, or relating to, the object of consciousness. The object of consciousness can be interpreted as the environment (nonself) with which the self interacts such that the meta-loop is closed on the whole self-in-interaction-with-nonself relation. From this point of view, the self-referential perspective of the self refers, in actual fact, to the capacity to interiorize (re-envoice), through the processes of developmental and historical emergence along the individual's time-bound trajectory, a vast amount of meanings – iconic, indexical, and symbolic – concerning the external and internal environments of the self, as well as to become aware of the thoughts that are so built up. Phenomenologically, this experience of the self's being conscious of some object is an awareness (reentrant loop) of the self's-being-and-doing-in-the-world, where this relationship is still a pre-polarized whole.

7 Rethinking the notion of consciousness as representation

Typically, the tradition of consciousness studies that is traceable back to the pioneering work of Brentano and James talks in terms of the "representation" of the object of consciousness as well as the representation of the representing self. This way of formulating the question suggests the primacy of representation when I think that the notion of self-in-interaction-with-environment invites us to think of the interpersonal-interactive or dialogic dimension as primary. This assumption is borne out by many important studies of infant proto-semiosis in the past few decades (chapter 3). It is not a matter of a self who passively represents to him- or herself already given objects in the external world, but the continually active and dialogic construction of the self's relations to the other (the nonself or second) by way of the reentrant mapping of these self–nonself transactions. As Bateson's discussion of the man felling the tree shows, we tend to construe this in experiential semantic terms as a delimited Actor (the man) performing a delimited action (cut) on a delimited Goal (the tree). Thus, the typological-categorial perspective which is privileged in the idea of representation prevails. Consequently, the event is perceived as being segmented into discrete components which are externally related to each other by way of efficient causality (see also Searle, quoted in Battacchi 1998: 12).

However, the relationship between self and object of consciousness is not an external one; it is not based on efficient causal linkages between the two. As I said earlier, it is a relationship based on meaning (i.e. not on information *per se* in the strict sense, as defined above). The relationship between self and object of consciousness is an internal and dialogic one. Consciousness of some object is consciousness *for* the self at the same time that the self is produced by its own ongoing dialogically oriented activity. The dialogic closure referred to above therefore constitutes the world in which the self acts, rather than merely representing it. Consciousness, in this view, is the active and dialogical construction of the internalized meta-loops which permit a process of progressive differentiation from an earlier undifferentiated (or less differentiated) whole. Consciousness is not a state. Instead, it is a relational trajectory whereby self and object are linked by a flow of meaning. In this way, self and object become parts of an internalized dialogic loop which is reentrantly mapped in the brain. With reference to core consciousness, Damasio provides the following useful insight:

> We become conscious, then, when our organisms internally construct and internally exhibit a specific kind of wordless knowledge – that our organism has been changed by an object –

and when such knowledge occurs along with the salient internal exhibit of an object. The simplest form in which this knowledge emerges is the feeling of knowing, . . .

(Damasio 1999: 169)

In my terms, this process of internal construction is describable as the closing of the dialogic loop on the "I" sector of the loop such that the dialogic interaction between the organism and the object of consciousness is internalized. Furthermore, this interaction is internalized (1) as the self's perspective on the nonself; and (2) the self's relation to the nonself. As Damasio (1999: 169) points out, both organism and object are realized in neural patterns in the brain as first-order maps. The organism's internally mapped sense of a self can be traced back to Damasio's notion of the proto-self. The proto-self is founded on neural patterns which map the moment-to-moment physical integrity of the organism and which are concerned with the self-regulation of all aspects of the organism's internal states as well as its environmental transactions (Damasio 1999: 154). Core self, autobiographical self, and symbolic self are all progressively higher-order mappings of this most primordial sense of a (non-conscious) proto-self, which is seen as both belonging to and being defined by the physical structure of the body. Edelman's concept of reentry provides, in my view, a framework for formulating the ways in which the brain builds up neurally realized maps of both self and object. Reentry is the neuro-anatomical coordination of a number of diverse, though simultaneous, perceptual and motor inputs. It provides an explanation for the coordination across diverse perceptual-motor modalities. Thus, the building up of a neural map of the self, in Damasio's sense, takes place on the basis of the coordination of many different perceptual-motor representations of the inner and outer states of the body. It is the correlation of all of these diverse forms of information from different neural groups as a coherent neural pattern which allows for the neural category of self to emerge (chapter 1, section 2).

Likewise, the mental images of the internalized objects of consciousness are coherent neural patterns which are based on the correlations among diverse forms of information. This information may be perceptual-motor in origin or based on memories of past events which already exist in the brain. In both cases, the information sources which constitute the basis of their correlation in the brain as coherent neural patterns are essentially multimodal in character, i.e. they associate signals deriving from diverse perceptual-motor modalities such as movement, looking, listening, haptic exploration, and so on. This cross-modal linking of signals from diverse sources is achieved by what Edelman (1989, 1992) calls reentry (see chapter 6, section 12; chapter 10, section 2; chapter 11, section 2.2). Thus, each perceptual-motor modality provides the brain with signals which are disjunctively picked up as deriving from independent information sources such as visual perception, haptic exploration, hearing, and so on. These various sources then interact through reentry such that a neural link of the two or more independent sources is created in the form of a higher-order neural map. In turn, the neural maps that constitute the neural self and a given object of consciousness are interrelated by higher-order mapping such that a form of internalized dialogic closure links the two within the body-brain system of the individual.

In the ecosocial semiotic framework of the present study, the neurally realized mappings in the central nervous system of the relationship between self and object which constitute consciousness are a subsystem of a higher-order system, viz. the individual organism at the same time that this is seen as always embedded in higher-order supersystems such as the dyads whereby dialogic closure is attained (see above). From this perspective, consciousness is not independent of the lower- and higher-order systems which embody it and regulate it. The internalized (neurally mapped) relationship between self and object is itself an instance of a dynamic open system, i.e. a system which exchanges matter, energy, and information-meaning with its environment at the same time that it maintains its own structural integrity within that environment. The specific moment-by-moment relationship between self and object in a given act of consciousness is just such a dynamical integrity. Consciousness, I argued above, is a dialogic act which links self and object along a relational trajectory. It involves the exchange of both structure and meaning in the act of consciousness.

Typically, accounts of consciousness speak in terms of the representation of the object (see

Seager 1999: 7–9). Representation involves information construed as meaning by some interpreter (e.g., the self). I believe that this focus prevails because the meaning so represented is explicit. On the other hand, the exchange of structure which makes this "representation" possible is implicit (chapter 8, section 5). The dyadic or dialogic structure which regulates the self-object relationship in the brain tends to be overlooked on account of its essential implicitness. Consciousness depends on the interactions between self and nonself involving the exchange of matter, energy, and information with its environment at the same time that conscious experience maintains its structural integrity. Consciousness is, in the first instance, a putting, through reentry, of the neural maps pertaining to the self and those pertaining to the object into a particular relationship with each other such that a change is brought about in the former (Damasio 1999: 169). For this reason, I argue that the (proto)-interpersonal semiotic function, which is concerned with dialogically organized relations between self and other, is both primary, as well as being ontogenetically prior. This argument has affinities with the view that consciousness is structured around an "objectivating mental act" and an "intrinsic inner awareness" of an embodied self as the subject which knows the objectivating mental act (see Natsoulas 1998, for arguments in support of the notion of "intrinsic inner awareness" as being a constitutive and not merely marginal component of consciousness).

8 Consciousness as integration hierarchy of semiotic levels: iconic, indexical, and symbolic dimensions

Dynamic open systems maintain their structural integrity through the processes of obtaining matter, energy, and information-meaning from a relatively ordered environment and returning to the environment matter and energy in the form of disorder. In this way, the system maintains its own identity and structure in time. We can now ask in what way might this general principle help us to explain neurally realized acts of consciousness in the individual's brain? The immediate internal environment of the higher-order neural maps which realize acts of consciousness are the neural networks in the brain. The hyper-complexity of the neural connections in the human brain entails many degrees of freedom from genetically pre-programmed instinctual behaviours at the same time that it entails that the brain both can cope with and requires a high degree of (internal and external) environmental disorder. It is this complexity which allows the brain to respond to novelty, to change, to environmental contingencies and perturbations in both its external and internal environments in contextually specific ways, rather than according to fixed programmes. The hyper-complexity mentioned above means that the system has the potential for a high degree of symbolic play (Salthe 1993: 267) whereby its (the system's) own agency enables it to be entrained to specific higher-scalar trajectories. As Manghi (1988: 208) observes, the brain requires a high degree of (internal and external) environmental disorder in precisely this sense in order to function. This requirement suggests that dialogically organized acts of consciousness in the brain are a higher-order means of regulation of the neural activity at lower levels. That is, the dialogical nature of the neural maps which realize self–object relations constitute a structuring principle at a higher scalar level of neural organization which functions to contextually integrate the lower-level maps. What is called consciousness can now been seen as an internal dialogic exchange process whereby self–object relations, as an instance of dynamic open systems, emerge and regulate their internal dynamics along with the activities in which the individual organism participates.

Consciousness may be considered as constrained by attractors within the topology of the individual's neural landscape. The notion of a state of consciousness implies that the system does not access all possible regions in its phase space with the same probability. On the other hand, a totally flat landscape would mean that the self entered into relations with no objects of consciousness. Such a landscape would amount to a brain without consciousness. However, the fact that the neurally realized self is attracted to particular regions within its overall neural phase space means that the system has attractor states and, hence, states of consciousness which the system enters into. In this topological landscape, basins of attraction are sharply separated from each other by states which the system tends not to access at the same time that it is attracted to other regions which it is more inclined to access. The specific topography of the neural landscape is itself the result of the system's participation in a time-bound trajectory (both developmental and individuating) such that the neural landscape is sculptured by contextual constraints arising from both the lower-scalar levels of the neurological processes which realize consciousness (L–1) and the higher-scalar ecosocial supersystem contexts (L+1) in which the individual subsystem is embedded. Thus, the neural landscape's propensity for a given attractor state and, hence, particular individual states of consciousness at any given moment are always constrained by factors on all three scalar levels in the three-level hierarchy. The history of the system, its present dynamics, and the ecosocial context all interact as one seamless whole.

Theorists of consciousness frequently emphasize the uniqueness of individual conscious experience. This emphasis poses no difficulties for the above account; nor does it in any way contradict anything I have thus far said. Given the fact that individuals are defined as a time-bound historical-biographical trajectory, this means that both contextual constraints as well as contingent experiences of all kinds work to reset the dynamics of the internal neural landscape such that this incorporates both environmental and historical factors into its dynamics. For these reasons, an individual's neural landscape is constantly self-organizing, responding to new contingencies, and individuating at the same time that it develops according to species-typical biological constraints and socio-cultural ones. The neural phase space of consciousness is constituted by attractors whereby self and object are constrained by meaningful trajectories which, in closing the meta-loop on the neurally realized "I" sector of the dyad, allow the individual to selectively attend to and orient to itself with respect to its inner and outer environments on potentially very diverse space-time scales.

Table 9.1 The integration hierarchy of core, extended, and semantic consciousness

Type of consciousness	Mode of semiosis	Exchange orientation	Stratal organization
core	iconic: no differentiation of meaning from experiencing	socioaffective: an experiencing of self-in-relation-to-other where there is not yet a separation of self from other	none: purely quantitative topological-continuous variation mapped onto same
extended	indexical: an experiencing of experiencing	dyadic: a first soft polarization (weak classification) that established not so much total difference from other as relationship-with-other	bistratal
semantic	symbolic: a meaning of experience that is itself more differentiated from whole to different relationship-qualities, etc.	triadic: emergence of different kinds of more separate others outside I–you dyad	tristratal

The progression from core through extended to semantic consciousness brings about further levels of reentrant looping, as shown in Table 9.1. Each new level entails further differentiation. Thus, there is a progression from no differentiation of meaning from experiencing, to the self's experiencing of experiencing, and thence to the self's giving a meaning to experience. Each level entails increasing differentiation of an original primordial whole in which self and nonself were not sharply differentiated by the continuous topological variation which characterized the relationship between the two to increasingly differentiated relationships and kinds and qualities of relationships between the two.

The first level is a purely **iconic** mapping of topological-quantitative variation onto topological-quantitative variation. For example, intensity, duration, and so on, of movement or sound maps onto waves or surges of affect, interest, attention, and motivation, as in the very earliest proto-conversations between newborn infant and mother. Trevarthen (1992: 105) describes these very early proto-conversations between mother and child as a dialogue between the mother's "intuitive motherese" and "the infant's equally coherent and emotive dynamic expressions – of face movements, coos or frets, hand gestures and body movements." (chapter 3, section 2). Such socioaffective exchanges demonstrate an iconic relationship between physiognomic and kinematic patterns and the reciprocal interpretation of motivation and affect. In this case, it is the socioaffective exchange loop between mother and newborn infant which constitutes the system of interpretance in terms of which the topological-quantitative variation of physiognomic and kinematic patterns (R) is iconically construed as signifying topological-quantitative waves or surges of affect, interest, and so on, as the interpretant, X, which is the object of conscious attention or awareness in the mother–infant dyad.

The second level involves an **indexical** construal of topological-quantitative variation in some environmental phenomenon by means of an indexical sign. Indexical signs are based on topological-quantitative variation such as the child's use of a high-pitched squeak or the act of pointing (chapter 3, section 5), so as to indicate, by means of the pitch intensity of the vocal gesture and/or by the position and vectorial orientation of the hand-arm, some relevant contextual object or value. This stage typically emerges in the period from six to twelve months. It is a stage which is characterized by the dyadic orientation of the infant to other persons (Trevarthen 1992: 113). Trevarthen observes of this period that "infants coordinate their self-centred orientation to events with a partner's other-centred orientation. To do this they must adjust the body-referred *space* of their action to the actions of the other that are related to that other person's body, and they must coordinate moves of attending, manipulating and communicating with the *timing* of the other person's moves" (Trevarthen 1992: 117; italics in original). The proto-signs which are characteristic of this period are essentially indexical in nature. They are expressed by both gestural and vocal means (Halliday 1993: 95) so that the participants in the dyadic exchange can track each other's responses, as well as the objects and events that these signs index as being relevant to the interactive context. Topological-quantitative variation in the spatial deployment and timing of the body functions to index dialogically coordinated moves as well as contextual values of relevance to the protolinguistic exchange (chapter 1, section 3; chapter 3, sections 5, 6).

This indexical phase is characterized by a focus on the interpersonal relationship between "I" and "you". The indexical phase is, if you like, situated mental activity (Bogdan 2000: 103–128), where the "mental" is understood, in my terms, as a meaning-constrained trajectory that loops through the individual's neurological dynamics and out into the environment rather than as some exclusive private affair in the head of the individual (see discussion of Bateson's circuit in section 5 above). In this perspective, internal and external events are internally related to each other by the meaning flows which constrain their dynamics to form an action trajectory, rather than by externally related events, as in efficient causality (Juarrero 1999: 96). The child is able to indexically integrate different domain-specific categories (e.g. objects, people), his or her knowledge of these categories, choices from a repertoire of indexical signs for jointly attending to such objects, and so on (Bogdan 2000: 166). The principle of such integration is, as Trevarthen's observations (cited above) show, essentially sensori-motor. That is, the reentrant mapping of these diverse information sources in the brain is based on the cross-modal integration of information derived from diverse perceptual-motor sources.

The larger point is that the indexical mode does not provide access to long-term memory; it is a here-now perceptual memory able to access the I-you-here-now domain of (inter)action, but not higher-level symbolic reflection (chapter 2, section 10; chapter 3, section 5). In making dialogically coordinated adjustments to the topological-continuous variation in each other's bodies, interactants jointly enact indexical signs which enable them to orient to and construe topological-continuous variation in their shared here-now perceptual purview. For example, indexical resources such as finger pointing, gaze, the use of "a high tone expressing 'curiosity' (construing experience), a low tone 'togetherness' (enacting interpersonal relationship)" (Halliday 1993: 95), and so on, are topological-continuous variations in the body which can function as indexical signs. As such, they enable one's interlocutor to selectively attend to topological-variation in either the perceptual field or the body field of the other as signs which have situation-specific experiential-perceptual or interpersonal-interactive significance. I think it is fair to say here that indexicality, at least in its pure form, involves a dynamic association in working memory of a perceptual category and an action category related to some object of consciousness in the stimulus flux. It seems clear that this is proto-metafunctional in character (chapter 1, section 3).

The third level is the **symbolic** one. It involves the symbolic or semantic construal of topological-quantitative variation in the phenomena of experience as typological-categorial semantic or other distinctions. This phase is characterized by the emergence of a lexicogrammatical stratum between the expression and content of the bi-stratal (indexical) system typical of protolanguage (Halliday 1975: 12–16; 1993: 97; Bates *et al.* 1979: 50–63; see chapter 2, section 10). The move into this symbolic phase is characterized by a move beyond the I–you interpersonal dyad to a triadic I–world–you type of exchange (Trevarthen 1978). It is concerned with the integration of both the interpersonal I–you domain of the prior indexical phase and the phenomena of experience in the world outside this domain that "I" and "you" attend to and interpret. This symbolic phase is therefore outwardly directed to the experiential construal of phenomena of experience outside the I–you dyad. Moreover, the access to these two domains – the interpersonal and experiential – requires their simultaneous mapping onto a shared system of semiotic (lexicogrammatical) forms. Additionally, this means that both the "I" and the "you" have the means for construing and engaging with a plurality of different domains simultaneously. Moreover, there is no longer any requirement that both "I" and "you" have or share the same sensori-motor access to the same domains or even to the same meanings. Scalar heterogeneity increasingly enters the picture here (chapter 6, section 1).

There now exists the possibility of asymmetry of such access, with, for example, one party not having perceptual-motor access to the particular domains in question. The point is that access to a shareable and negotiable system of symbolic forms affords participants the possibility of interpreting domains that they do not perceptually share with the other participant. This possibility allows for "unsituated interpretation" (Bogdan 2000) such that agents can deploy the symbolic resources of language and access specific practices of interpretation (genres, intertextual connections, and so on) so as to elaborate their own semantic interpretation of the given domain, whether this is interpersonal or experiential. Moreover, these symbolic resources allow the self, say, to construe phenomena from the perspective of the consciousness of the other. The symbolic level also allows for the cross-modal integration of different experiential domains (inner, outer, physical, perceptual, mental, emotional, (meta-)semiotic, etc.) by means of shareable symbolic resources which are not tied to specific material instantiations for their interpretation. I have referred to this third level as semantic consciousness in the sense that it is a further extension of the two prior levels of core and extended consciousness, which are derived from Damasio. If the trajectory of consciousness is entrained by symbolic neural space, where semantic meanings self-organize in the brain, then this implies the high level of semantic differentiation that is made possible by the intrinsic metafunctional organization of the lexicogrammatical stratum of the linguistic semiotic.

The progression from iconic to indexical to symbolic consciousness, which the developmental studies cited here bring sharply into focus, does not imply that the lower levels are superseded as the infant progresses from one species-typical developmental stage to another. Instead, the progression illustrated here follows the logic of the implication-cum-specification hierarchy: as one stage is added to the prior one, the more specified later stage integrates the less specified prior ones into its dynamics without, however, totally transcending these (Salthe 1993: 52–74). More specified levels in the hierarchy (e.g. the symbolic level) implicate less specified levels (e.g. the iconic and indexical) levels. The fact of having symbolic consciousness and access to the semiotic resources required for its implementation also means that one has indexical and iconic consciousness. Thus, no use of language is ever uniquely symbolic: iconic and indexical factors and functions are also at play on both the expression and content strata (Thibault 2004a: chapter 3). However, the existence of iconic consciousness in the two-month old infant does not mean he or she has symbolic consciousness.

9 Biological value or mental function?

According to Bogdan (2000: 29), Vygotsky's (e.g. 1986 [1934]: 217–224) concept of semiotic mediation, which is the agency responsible for bringing about the internalization of higher mental functions, requires some prior process of "a give-and-take of mental stances and information", which remains unexplained in Vygotsky's account. Vygotsky's account of semiotic mediation is based, to a large extent, on linguistic semiosis, though he does also make very insightful observations concerning the role of indicative hand-arm gestures in the child's development of reference. However, these observations concerning non-linguistic semiotic modalities do not form part of a more integrated semiotic framework. But before considering what such an integrated framework might look like, I should like to quote at some length from Bogdan's own critique of Vygotsky's opposition between natural (biological) and cultural development, along with his tipping of the explanatory balance in favour of the latter:

> The contrast need not be between biology and culture, with nothing in between. Culture cannot be grafted directly on unsensitized neural functions. Left out are mental functions, however simple. The problem is not that such simple functions are neural; of course they are, in an implementational sense. The problem is that mental functions cannot be reduced to biological or neural functions, insofar as the former (but not the latter) have psychological or mind-world value. That psychological value concerns the relation between organism and world, both physical and social, and the impact of that relation on behavior. This is how psychology (but not biology or neuroscience) looks at organisms.
>
> (Bogdan 2000: 31)

Bogdan's proposed solution to this opposition takes the form of what he calls "*mental* internalizers (not just neural implementers) that secure the engagement and takeover" (2000: 31). In my view, Bogdan's own distinction between neural functions and mental functions only serves to replicate the very opposition he seeks to repudiate, even if at the lower-scalar level of the individual's neurological dynamics in contrast to Vygotsky's focus on the individual-society nexus. This argument may serve to secure a place for a specifically psychological domain of inquiry, though I doubt that it provides the best solution to the problem under discussion here. Neural functions are not simply implementational; they also do the work of interpretation on their own scalar level of organization and functioning. Neural events are, with respect to our scale as observers, on a much faster and much smaller scale, which is not tied to the scales in which our own cogent moments are recognized and defined. Neural events have to be semiotically reorganized across scalar levels as categories of our observer scale *qua* organisms embedded in and entrained to higher-scalar ecosocial dynamics. It is not, therefore, necessary to propose *pace* Bogdan a separate, pre-existing mental function of interpretation as opposed to the "implementational" function of neurological processes.

Edelman's theory of re-entry and his notion of value, along with the dynamically self-organizing character of the system, are all that is needed to start off the process of interpreting the world, including other conspecifics. Thus, the intersubjective sharing of emotions, attending to shared objects of attention, and so on, are joint activities which in themselves provide the basis for the interpretation of both others (e.g. caregivers) and the world (e.g. the objects, events, and so on – the phenomena of experience – jointly attended to by shared gaze vectors). For example, the visual tracking of objects with the eyes, the proprioceptive information provided by the associated movements of the head, neck, and so on, all provide what Edelman calls disjunctive samplings of some environmental event within the purview of the dyad. Thus, two or more distinct neural maps, which are built up by the disjunctive samplings of environmental information, are connected by reentry so that connections are formed between them. The resulting connections form a neural map at a higher order than the first-order mappings which result from the disjunctive sampling of information. In this way, the attending to an object in the world, tracking the object with the visual perceptual system, body movement, and synchronizing one's own activity with that of the other in the dyad work to cross-couple particular neural pathways such that a higher-order perceptual-motor category emerges.

Edelman's theory of neuronal group selection shows that functionally meaningful patterns are construed more globally across first-order neural maps, which are based on the disjunctive samplings of information from distinct sources of stimulus information. In terms of the three-level hierarchy, these first-order maps occur on level L–1. It is the global connections formed through reentry on level L which are interpreted on level L+1 as perceptual-motor categorizations that relate to and in some sense interpret events in the world relative to a system of interpretance on the L+1 level. In terms of the three-level hierarchy idea, these relations can be represented as a triplicate of neuro-semiotic relations across different scalar levels of neural organization, as follows:

L+1   perceptual-motor categorization of objects, events, etc. in world which form the SI in terms of which neural events are related to world events

L   higher-order (global) reentrant mapping of disjunctively sampled neural maps

L–1   first-order neural maps formed by the disjunctive sampling of stimulus information deriving from the environment and/or one's own body

Following Lemke's (1999) lead, Peirce's theory may again be called upon to clarify the broader semiotic questions at issue here. Thus, the reentrant mapping of first-order neural maps on level L are dynamical attractors and separators, R, *of* object-states, X, of environmental stimulus information on level L–1 which dynamically constitute the phenomena at level L, *for* perceptual-motor classifications at level L+1, which form the system of interpretance, SI, with respect to which interpretative correspondences between Rs and Xs are made in neural space.

The three-level hierarchy allows us to see that neural processes are both semiotically mediated and interpretative. There is no need for a dichotomy such as that between neural implementation and mental interpretation. To be sure, we are not talking here in terms of semiotic mediation of the symbolic kind which Vygotsky associated with linguistic activity. Rather, it is semiotic mediation on the very first level of the integration-cum-specification hierarchy of icon, index, and symbol. The perceptual-motor categorizations that are built up through reentry may, in turn, be topologically mapped onto other self-instigated movements such as reaching, grasping, gaze vectors, and so on. These movements themselves afford their interpretation by the other (the caregiver) as iconic-indexical signs of interest, attention, motivation, affect, and so on (see above), such that they are, in turn, attended to and interpreted as contributions – dialogic moves – to the proto-conversation between the two members of the dyad.

As we saw before, the entire process is dialogic from the outset and it is the resulting dialogic closure that allows for progressively more adaptive developmental change to occur. That is, the supersystem which is constituted by dialogic closure provides a system of interpretance in which in-built values in the brain of the infant – e.g. attending to environmental perturbations, exploring with hands, seeking nourishment and affect, responding to other human subsystems (caregivers) with whom the infant already shares a range of socio-biological basic structures – are nudged along certain preferential pathways by the self-organizing activity of the dyad. The conditions required for interpreting the world, including one's conspecifics, spontaneously emerge, only to be, in time, progressively integrated into more specified forms of semiotic mediation. Thus, the originary socio-biological iconic mode of semiotic mediation is integrated to socio-cultural symbolic modes of semiotic mediation. There is no disjunction here between the biological and the cultural. Rather, there is a seamless, time-bound integration of the one to the other.

The progression from iconic to indexical to symbolic forms of consciousness involves increasing meaningful variety as the system self-organizes. Increase in meaningful variety means an increase in the system's autonomy (Salthe 1993: 166). The many degrees of topological-quantitative freedom – the primordial vagueness – of the system's initial stages mean that in this stage the system has many redundancies; its capacity to increase meaningful variety is therefore high. The progressive building up of iconic and indexical variation and symbolic categories means that consciousness emerges from the primordial iconic stage and become progressively determinate through the development of the later stages. As a self-organizing system constrained by a time-bound trajectory, it is important to see that each closing of the loop in the spiral towards symbolic consciousness involves the closing of the loop on the collecting feedback that results from the cascading processes which are the sign of a determinate self with effects in the world (chapter 7, section 3).

10 The metafunctional shape of symbolic consciousness

If symbolic consciousness is constrained by metafunctional semantic space, then the increasing differentiation that characterizes each level in the proposed hierarchy is now clearly seen to semiotically reorganize the primordial wholeness of self–object relations on the first level of core consciousness in terms of:

(1) the interpersonal-dialogic enactment of many more delicately specified categories of interpersonal semiosis along with increasing differentiation in the categories of self and other that participate in this and are related to each other as a consequence of such participation; the intersubjective orientation of the self towards the object of consciousness which it holds in its scope;

(2) the experiential construal of the phenomena of "inner" and "outer" experience in terms of the experiential semantic categories of the various types of semantic role (e.g. Actor-Process-Goal) in the multivariate structure of the clause whereby experience is defined in terms of configurations of discrete elements which are semantically related to each other as a whole figure of experience;

(3) the temporal, causal, and other relations of dependency which link items in a sequence of temporally or causally related items;

(4) the entextualized grounding of semantic consciousness as a textured whole by means of the symbolic resources for creating links between the various components of the act of consciousness and its surrounding milieu.

The systemic-functional theory of language provides us with a model of the linguistic system which includes all four of the above dimensions of meaning as different dimensions of the intrinsic symbolic-indexical-iconic organization of lexicogrammatical form (Thibault 2004a: 126–134). In this, it differs markedly from mainstream linguistic theories, which work with a tripartite division of language into syntax, semantics, and pragmatics, along with a corresponding restriction of semantics to meaning of the denotational or referential kind (Thibault and Van Leeuwen 1996). The removal of those aspects of meaning which are concerned with the relations between language user and the world or the relations between different parts of the same text and the text's relationship to its context, and their relegation to a separate "pragmatic" domain, belong to an epistemology which accords no causal status to context and the ecosocial system, which are seen as secondary or epiphenomenal.

Rather than seeking to explain the intrinsic organizational complexity of lexicogrammatical form in relation to its ecosocial environment, much of twentieth-century linguistics has assumed, in conformity with the mechanistic models of causality derived from classical (Newtonian) science, that linguistic form is comprised of discrete, segmentable particles, seen as the building blocks of language. These particles are combined according to fixed rules whereby the whole was explainable as the sum of its parts. The autocatalytic principles that make something a whole were ignored (chapter 2, section 10; section 6.1.2 above). There was no room for goal-seeking behaviour to be seen as intrinsic to the system's global organization. The principle causal contribution came from the rules which specified how the discrete particles, which were taken to be the primary reality of language, were combined. Only these particles were seen as part of the internal organization of language because they were apparently permanent features of language, independent of any time-bound situation. Situatedness and (inter)subjectivity had no part to play in the explanation of the internal organization of lexicogrammatical form.

Systemic-functional linguistic theory expands the notion of semantics to cover all four of the above mentioned functional regions which are realized in lexicogrammatical form. That is, the experiential, logical, interpersonal, and textual domains of linguistic meaning are different facets of the semantic organization of language, each with its own characteristic modes of symbolic realization in the lexicogrammar. Because the semantics of natural language is, in many ways, symbolic in character, it follows that once an act of consciousness is entrained by the attractors of symbolic neural space, then it is simultaneously constrained by and shaped by all four of the above dimensions of linguistic meaning. The observations I have made here apply to symbolic or higher-order consciousness, in particular. Symbolic or higher-order consciousness is dependent on the individual's being cross-coupled to the higher-scalar ecosocial semiotic level from which the linguistic system derives. However, it is interesting to compare these four symbolic dimensions with the structure of consciousness at lower integrative levels. In doing so, we find that theories of consciousness, irrespective of any questions concerning the nature of language and other semiotic modalities, typically draw attention to four characteristics of acts or states of consciousness, though usually to varying degrees and with different emphases. Table 9.2 suggests some possible correlations between the four semantic metafunctions and the structure of acts of consciousness in general. These correlations suggest that there are proto-metafunctional precursors at lower integrative levels of consciousness even though these precursors are not characterized by the symbolic resources of lexicogrammatical form.

Table 9.2 Correlations between the semantic metafunctions in language and the structure of consciousness

Characteristic of consciousness	Linguistic metafunction
self–object relations resulting in change to self; intrinsic inner awareness of this relation on the part of the experiencing subject; James's "bodily self-awareness"	interpersonal-dialogic enactment and engagement
interdependency and connectedness of events in unfolding sequence; durational component of stream of consciousness	logical interdependency (causal, temporal)
represented object; theme as focus of attention (Gurwitsch 1964 [1953]: 4; quoted in Natsoulas 1998: 9)	experiential
whole or unified character; thematic field as background or horizon out of which theme emerges	textual

The correlations suggested in Table 9.2 suggest that both consciousness, understood here to refer to our primary material interactivity with and awareness of the world prior to meaning, and linguistically mediated discourse as a form of symbolic meaning-making are both implicated in cross-scalar processes. This suggests that consciousness, in the sense intended here, is not limited to the organismic scale. Rather, it, too, occurs on diverse timescales. The proto-metafunctional character of even our primary, essentially topological, awareness of our relations to the world of the nonself shows that consciousness is a dynamical process which is not produced solely on the scale of the organism *per se*. The unified character of conscious awareness is a time-bound phenomenon which arises as a consequence of the organism's interactions with an ecosocial environment that exists on timescales that are very different from those of the organism's immediate interactions with its material environment.

In contrast to the view which privileges the representation of the object of consciousness to the self, the parallels suggested in Table 9.2 between the intrinsic, semantically motivated organization of lexicogrammatical form and the structuring of acts of consciousness allows us to consider the following modification to the Peircean formulation discussed above with respect to the structure of acts of consciousness in symbolic neural space. The resulting Principle of the Symbolic Mediation of Consciousness by the content stratum of the linguistic semiotic is stated in terms of the three-level hierarchy as follows:

> The lexicogrammatical systems and categories on level L are dynamical attractors and separators, R, *of* object-states, X, of neurologically realized phenomena of consciousness on level L–1. These level L–1 processes dynamically constitute the phenomena at level L, *for* discourse semantic processes and relations at level (N+1). The latter form the system of interpretance, SI, with respect to which correspondences between Rs and Xs are symbolically enacted, construed, interrelated, and entextualized as acts of consciousness in metafunctionally organized semantic neural space.

In the theory of language that is assumed here, the content stratum is itself stratified as two layers of organization, viz. lexicogrammar and discourse semantics (Martin 1991: 114). The various metafunctional components of the lexicogrammar do not stand in a fixed relationship with the discourse semantic stratum. The point is that the lexicogrammar is seen as a semiotic resource for making meanings through text, i.e. language which is operational in some discourse context. In this conception, the higher-order discourse semantics at level L+1 re-interprets lexicogrammatical selections on the L level in terms of the meanings they make in the process of making text (Martin 1991: 115). The discourse semantics is the level at which agents jointly co-deploy some constrained set of the available semiotic resources so as to enact a particular occasion of meaning-making. The emergent meaning which arises at any given point in the unfolding text-in-context (the discourse) is a result of the interaction of all the metafunctional components involved. The metafunctions thus constitute a semantic interface between lexicogrammatical form and the discourse semantic level where meanings are made. That is, they are an interface between the intrinsic organization of linguistic form and the phenomena of experience outside language with which they selectively and contextually redound. The notion of the interface here is an important point for it draws attention to the fact that language is a dynamic open system which interacts with and constantly undergoes exchanges with its environment as a consequence of the meaning-making activities of human agents. This last consideration brings me to the relationship between symbolic or semantic neural space and the metafunctional organization of the linguistic system.

Symbolic neural space is not simply locked away within the head of the individual *per se*. Meaning-making resources are distributed across individuals in varying ways on account of their individuating trajectories through the ecosocial system. Peng (1994: 106) has observed that language-in-the-brain enables the individual to make adjustments to his or her internal and external environments. In dynamical terms, self-organizing processes in semantic neural space can enable the individual to respond to disequilibrium either within the individual's own internal dynamics or in the ecosocial environment. Acts of symbolic consciousness may be seen in this light. Thus, a semantically organized act or state of consciousness brings into operation the discourse semantic constraints operating in a given system of interpretance. These constraints work to reorganize or to reset the semantic level of neural organization by creating specific self-organizing trajectories within this space. Given the metafunctional semantic interface which forms a bridge between the individual's semantic neural organization and the higher-scalar system of interpretance on the ecosocial level, the individual's internal dynamics are adjusted in response to specific environmental factors. Therefore, interpretations of meaning made on the discourse semantic level may constitute proximate attractors into which specific courses of action may flow (chapter 5, section 15). The metafunctional bridge that is constructed between symbolic neural space and the higher-scalar system of interpretance means that the latter acts as a set of boundary conditions on the former. In this way, genre conventions, the register specific semantics of particular social situation-types, the typical meaning-making practices of a given community – all of which are located on the higher-scalar level of the system of interpretance – act as constraints on the individual body-brain complex such that the ecosocial semiotic system is internally connected to the individual's neural dynamics (chapter 5, sections 14–15).

In the light of the above observations, the logogenetic instantiation of text in some context can be seen as a control loop which interfaces on the one side with the system of interpretance and, on the other, with the agent's body-brain dynamics. Once a particular proto-meaning has been activated in the brain, this loop "threads through other attractors and self-organized neurological regions such as those embodying psychological and emotional properties" (Juarrero 1999: 198; also see again Bateson's (1973a [1972]: 285–291) notion of the closed circuit of a transform of differences). Furthermore, the unfolding context of situation contributes its own attractor and separator dynamics to the act of consciousness. It is in this way that the dynamics of processes on other levels such as the sensori-motor and feeling states of the body may also be entrained to the higher-order dynamics (chapter 7, section 8). The notion of proto-meaning, which I have borrowed from Peng (1994: 124; see also Thibault 2004a: chap. 6), helps to explain how mental images, memories of past experiences, intentions, desires, inclinations, feelings, and so on, all of which are non-linguistic proto-meanings in the brain, constitute a very broad and shallow attractor basin of vague and indeterminate possibilities. These proto-meanings can be cross-coupled to the more specified symbolic possibilities of language and other semiotic resource systems in order that a more specific, agentively determinate trajectory may be forged in a specific act of meaning. The making of text in context is just such a more specified (logogenetic) trajectory which loops through both the agent's internal dynamics as well as those of the ecosocial environment. In the process, this involves the cross-coupling of semiotic-discursive and physical-material, including bodily, processes and dynamics, so as to entrain these processes and dynamics in some more contextually specified way. It is this process of entraining along a determinate action trajectory that brings about specific effects and consequences, both semiotic and material, in the ecosocial environment.

Now, the proto-meanings in the individual's neural landscape are vague and indeterminate in character. Therefore, the focus on a specific proto-meaning constitutes a very broad and shallow attractor basin in the individual's neural dynamics. Such an attractor basin has very many possibilities of realization as well as very many possibilities of cross-coupling with other neurological and sensori-motor dynamics (see also Juarrero 1999: 199). Proto-meanings are, by definition, vague and unspecified because they are not cross-coupled to the more highly specified symbolic categories and social semiotic resource systems on the ecosocial level. However, the cross-coupling of proto-meanings to the symbolic possibilities of the global semantic space of the linguistic system involves a move along the parameters of both delicacy and instantiation that I discussed above. In the process, the attractor basin is progressively narrowed into a more definite trajectory. In this way, the global semantic space is narrowed to the meaning potential of a particular social domain in which a more restricted subset of meaning selections are chosen and combined according to specific discourse genres and other conventions.

A further narrowing takes place with the logogenetic instantiation of a particular text in a specific context. It is not the case that all this is pushed along from behind by conscious choices and decisions according to the mechanistic principles of efficient causality. Unilinear efficient causality and the mechanistic models this entails have no place here. These models have no place because mental life, as Bateson already understood, is about the meanings which are transformed all along the loop which links body-brain system to environment. Thus, the individual's proto-meanings, which in part constitute his or her neural dynamics, interact with and are entrained by the logogenetic process of text instantiation in a specific environment. Proto-meanings already stored in the individual's brain are no more than initial conditions which may help to start the process going. However, the logogenetic looping of text through both the agent's internal dynamics as well as the ecosocial context mean that higher-order contextual constraints which interface between individual and ecosocial system serve to operationalize the system of interpretance as a specific time-bound trajectory which has determinate effects and identities in the world and which is capable of leaving a trace of these effects in those who engage with it. As we saw in chapter 2, these processes require the semiotic mediation of the intertextual, indexical, and meta-textual meaning-making practices of some community (see also Thibault 2003a).

The contextual constraints that operate here do not bring about or cause their effects on the basis of mechanical push-&-pull. Newtonian causality has no place here. The context-sensitive constraints that operate in the logogenetic unfolding of text along an individuating trajectory entrain physical-material and semiotic-discursive cross-couplings to its dynamics by the ongoing resetting of semiotic probabilities. The probabilistic nature of this process means that other possible pathways are not taken at the same time that a specific trajectory is defined. It also means that the logogenetic loop between the individual's internal dynamics and the semiotic-material context progressively narrows the meaning-making possibilities from the global semantic space to the domain specific semantic space until a particular action trajectory is formed. The particular trajectory which is so formed is the emergent product/process of many interacting dynamical variables. The variables include the proto-meanings in the individual's neural landscape, the sensori-motor dynamics of the body, and the global semantic space that is accessed, along with its progressive narrowing to more determinate domain-type and context-specific selections, whereby the metaredundancy relations that characterize a particular act of meaning-making come into operation.

Self-organizing dissipative structures are local reductions of randomness which lead to increased order and organization. The reduction of the many degrees of freedom of the system's component variables by higher-scalar constraints leads to the emergence of local principles of order as some of the total available energy is used to maintain the internal dynamics of the system at the same time that total entropy production increases in accordance with the second law of thermodynamics. Lemke (1999: 10) points out that the energy required for self-organization is always "vastly less" in scale than that of the global entropic flows which lead to an overall increase in total entropy production. In the context of our present concerns, this is important because consciousness and its dynamics is dependent on larger-scale flows of dissipative energy through the system as well as on higher-scalar contextual constraints which together make possible local far-from-equilibrium sinks of order (Juarrero 1999: 145). Such local sinks represent an entropy decrease which corresponds to the emergence of order in the form of the endogenous creation of selective constraints on just some of the possible relations among the system's dynamic components (Lemke 1999: 10).

In this way, selves and the phenomena they are conscious of co-emerge relative to the scale on which their cogent moments, to use Salthe's phrase, are defined (see section 8). Cogent moments are just such smaller-scale sinks of order relative to an observer perspective on a given scale. On the human ecosocial scale, this includes our acts of meaning and the symbolic objects of consciousness that result from such acts. Only such local sinks of emergent order, always defined against a background of disorder, constitute the phenomena of experience. The orderly relationships that characterize the intrinsic self-organizing dynamics of these local sinks are interpretable in terms of their correlations among fewer dynamic variables on some more macroscopic scale. Therefore, we recognize them, experience them, and give them meaning on our own scale. Our conscious looping back on our experience, of our experiencing, of such correlations means that consciousness is a self-reflexive attributing of meaning to our experience, of our experiencing, of such correlations. It is important to keep in mind here that I am using the term "meaning" to refer to all integrative levels in the semiotic hierarchy. Meaning does not therefore refer to symbolic (e.g. linguistic) meaning *per se*. Selves collect some of the effects of their own cascading; in the process, they build up a self-referential perspective. This fact suggests that the meta-loop formed by the self-referential closure of the "I" sector by means of higher-order neural maps relating self and object is an internalized higher-scalar-scalar system of interpretance in symbolic neural space which mediates self–nonself transactions and relations on lower levels (chapter 5, section 14).

The lexicogrammatical systems and networks of a language are definable in terms of the way that autocatalytic closure selectively constrains the relations among component units, and their internal interdependencies and inter-functional solidarities (chapter 2, section 10). These intrinsic constraints on organization are stronger than their overall dynamic dependency on interactions with their ecosocial environments. It is the relative autonomy – self-organization – of the former which bestows on the system its specific identity at the same time that the latter is the condition of the system's being. The question arises as to whether lexicogrammatical systems at level L are best described in terms of a "spherical" topology of systems or in terms of a network topology. Both Latour (1993 [1991]: 117–122, 1996a, 1996b) and Lemke (2000a: 207–208) have drawn attention to the predominance of the "spherical" topology in the description of human systems. "Spherical" topologies assume that a system's levels of organization are describable as nested levels of increasing (or decreasing) spatial scale (Lemke 2000a: 207–208). In this view, communities of interacting social agents, along with the practices that distinguish such communities, are definable in terms of both spatial nearness and homogeneity. Thus, agents who are spatially near to each other are more likely to interact, and hence to belong to the same community, than are agents who are physically far from each other. However, there is no reason why agents who are spatially distant from each other cannot interact more frequently and more intensively than agents who are spatially near to each other, provided that they are linked by a stable system of shared meaning-making resources along with the necessary technological infrastructures. In this "network" topology, as defined by Latour, agents who share the same network, yet are spatially distant, interact more frequently than agents who are near each other spatially, but not linked by the same network.

There is a widespread tendency to regard consciousness as a function of the individual organism operating in a less structured environment. In this view, consciousness, including higher-order symbolic consciousness, is, phylogenetically speaking, seen as having arisen by natural selection at the level of the individual organism. Thus, there is individual consciousness as possessed by one's self and (the interpretation of) the consciousness of the other selves with whom the self interacts. The focal level in this view corresponds to the unique personal experiences of individual consciousnesses. The problem with this view is that it tends to play down the fact that the interaction between self and nonself is not random or without structure. For example, the stimulus information about environmental events is structured information about these events which the organism, in its environmental niche, has adaptively evolved to pick up. Organism and environmental have co-evolved such that organisms do not live "in" an environment; instead, they are a constitutive part of their environment. The relation between the two is not random, but constitutes a structured, higher-order field of relations (a thirdness) which mediates the relations between organism and environment. This higher-order field of relations provides the organism with systemic criteria for the appropriate interpretation of the stimulus information which is picked up so that appropriate courses of action may be undertaken. Furthermore, our consciousness is, in the first instance, consciousness of our experience of the world on the scale on which we live and perceive the world. We are not normally conscious of the atomic structure of the micro level of reality studied by physics except, of course, through our technological and semiotic extensions of our *Umwelt* to these scales (Harré 1990).

In the first instance, our consciousness evolved as a mediated relation with the ecosocial level of the environmental phenomena – the events, objects, surfaces – about which we pick up stimulus information through our perceptual systems. That is, consciousness, in the first instance, is specific to the scale of the organism's interactions with the nonself. It is symbolic or higher-order consciousness, itself mediated by technological extensions of our techniques of observation, which allows us to be conscious of and to adopt organized viewpoints on material entities such as electrons on the atomic scale. In this way, electrons with semiotic value exist on one (their own?) scale, but are also interpretable on other scales such that they can also exist in symbolic consciousness as interpretants with which we can interact on our own ecosocial scale. Such connections between dynamical processes on the atomic level and the ecosocial level where consciousness resides are not permitted by the adiabatic principle (Lemke 2000b: 279–280; chapter 6, section 1). However, the symbolic resources of language, depiction, and mathematics afford semiotic mediation between processes on vastly different space-time scales such as those mentioned here. In this way, semiotic connectivities can be constructed between symbolic consciousness and interpretants on both the atomic and cosmic scales of, for example, electrons and black holes. Symbolic resources afford semiotic-dynamical interactions between our own scale and these scales that are not part of the environment that we live in.

11 The emergence of new levels of semiotic organization between already existing scalar levels

In the nativist view of language, a purported language gene is seen as the lower-level superveni-ence base on which language depends. This view does not include the relations external to the system under consideration (Bickard and Campbell 2000: 333). But language is a dynamic open system which is, by definition, relational to its environment(s). Language cannot, for this reason, be supervenient to a lower-level genetic or other base. Language exists in the individual, in particular instances of logogenesis, and on the level of the evolution of an entire ecosocial semiotic system as an ongoing organization of matter, energy, and information-meaning across the various scalar levels implicated in its organization. It is not, therefore, reducible to lower-level constituent building blocks. The organization of language-as-process-in-time can only persist through such ongoing system-environment transactions. The metafunctional hypothesis is a hypothesis about the way in which the intrinsic organization of language interfaces with its higher- and lower-scalar levels of organization.

In the nativist hypothesis (Chomsky 1965, 1976; Pinker 1994, 1997), language is already embodied in the individual at the genetic level. In such a "language animal", it is almost as if language were a lower-level initiating condition, rather than a higher-order boundary condition on the ecosocial level which constrains human body-brain dynamics, including consciousness. This hypothesis does not account for the ways in which other individuals also have conscious-ness and that consciousness is mediated and constrained by higher-scalar processes and dynam-ics beyond the individual organism. However, consciousness, from the internalist perspective of the individual, is a matter of interactions with secondnesses in the world; it is this interaction which provides the individual with the information which external observers ascribe to the next level of ecosocial organization. In the perspective of the three-level scalar hierarchy, lower levels provide information which is in some way constitutive of the level in focus; these are in some way functional at the focal level. Higher-scalar levels functionally constrain and contextually integrate information from lower levels (Salthe 1993: 48–49). It is this functional integration (to some system of interpretance) which determines the conditions of interaction of such systems with others on their own scale. Consciousness is always consciousness *of* something. Therefore, it is constituted by the interaction between a first and a second. Beyond this, there is thirdness: higher-scalar systems of interpretance which both depend on and constrain the interactions between the lower-level units (firsts and seconds).

Semiotic closure, Lemke argues, means that a higher scalar system of interpretance on level L+1 is characterized by its own exhaustive paradigms of types (see above). Furthermore, lower-level entities and their interactions, unless amplified as perturbations (Salthe 1993: 45), do not normally affect the structural integrity of the entities and interactions at higher levels. Fluctu-ations at lower levels – for example, the topological-continuous variation of the phenomena of experience that are picked up by our perceptual systems – are attracted to typological-categorial differences in the semantic state space of the higher-scalar system of interpretance. From the perspective of this higher level, lower-level fluctuations have no informational value; they are not typed by the system of interpretance as differences which make a difference. The semantic categories of the system of interpretance are attractors towards which such lower-level fluctu-ations are or are not attracted. It is these attractors in symbolic neural space that constitute the higher-scalar dynamics of the system. Such attractors integrate and complete the lower levels by attracting the phenomena of experience to specific semantic attractor basins, in the process construing them as instantiations of this or that category. In this way, semiotic closure comes into operation at the same time that the system's material and energetic openness is presupposed (Lemke 1999; Juarrero 1999: 168).

Semiotic closure also provides solutions to the question of qualia, which have been central in much of the theoretical discussion of consciousness. The following quotation from Edelman will serve as a starting point:

> Qualia constitute the collection of personal or subjective experiences, feelings, and sensations that accompany awareness. They are phenomenal states – "how things seem to us" as human beings. For example, the "redness" of a red object is a quale. Qualia are discriminable parts of a mental scene that nonetheless has an overall unity. They may range in intensity and clarity from "raw feels" to highly refined discriminanda. These sensations may be very precise when they accompany perceptual experiences; in the absence of perception, they may be more or less diffuse but nonetheless discernible as "visual," "auditory," and so on.
>
> (Edelman 1992: 114)

The phenomenal states called qualia refer to our embodied, subjective experiences, feelings, and sensations that are a constitutive part of our awareness. One of the problems facing those who study consciousness is how to reconcile such uniquely personal experiences with their sharing with others through the use of language and other semiotic systems. Semiotic closure of the typological sort cannot exhaust the topological richness and variety of the qualia that are given to conscious experience. As the discussion of the wine tasting text in section 4 above showed, the typological-categorial distinctions that are construed in and through the lexicogrammatical systems of language filter out or buffer lower-level variation that is not relevant to the semantics of the typological category. From this point of view, differences that do not make a difference are filtered out so that all the phenomena that are assigned to a given semantic category are seen as being of the same type. By the same token, no two tokens of a given type are ever identical from the point of view of their quantitative topological variation. It is this which allows us to distinguish different tokens as individuals and to form, as Lemke points out, "a new intermediate level of interpretance" on the basis of many degrees of quantitative variation so that these patterns may again be classified. Semiotic closure operates at levels where only typological-categorial difference is relevant; when this is so, semiotic closure operates on that level. However, Lemke's Principle of Alternation stipulates the following possibility, which allows for quantitative individuation:

> *At* levels of organization where only typological difference matters, and *for* levels for which this is true, we can speak of semiotic closure *within* a level. But if the Principle of Alternation is a useful guide, then *across* semiotic triples of levels, there is always somewhere a lack of *topological-semiotic* closure, and it is this very source of *potentially* meaningful open variation which is reorganized at some higher level again into a new *typological-semiotic* closure.
>
> (Lemke 1999: 11; italics in original)

According to the three-level paradigm, new emergent levels of organization come into existence *between* already existing scalar levels. For example, emergent social forms of organization exist on a higher-scalar level than the individual body-brain. Social organization entails boundary conditions which amplify sensori-motor movements of the body-brain as signs which function to semiotically mediate the social activities of individuals. Thus, we see how a newly emergent level of (semiotic) organization is added to a prior multi-level system. Ontogenetically, the emergence of a lexicogrammar between the child's elementary vocal and other gestures and the situation-specific semantics which constrain the interpretation of the former illustrates the same general principle. In both cases, we see how lower-scale units and global constraints (e.g. body-brain processes and dynamics and always structured environmental stimulus information, respectively), allow dissipative structures to emerge. In turn, proto-semiosis, in the form of vocal and other gestures and indexically presupposed contextual values, may emerge within this prior system of constraints, with its residual free energy (Lemke 1999: 11). And so on, until the appearance of symbolic systems of meaning-making as a consequence of the emergence of additional intermediate levels of semiotic organization. Figure 9.1 illustrates the emergence of the bistratal indexical mode and the tristral symbolic mode as intermediate levels in a prior multi-level organism-environment system.

The cross-coupling of the diverse scalar levels that emerge semiotically motivates the increasing interdependency of the inter-level relations involved. In each case, additional levels of organization are added to an initial multi-scale system. The typological categories of lexico-grammar, as seen from the point of view of the higher-scalar system of interpretance, retain a "residual quantitative variability" that is filtered out by the system of interpretance on the level above. However, as the example of grammatical metaphor shows (see chapters 10 and 11), it is possible that some patterns within the topological-continuous variation of the lower level come to be construed as making a difference on the level above that of the system of interpretance. This does not mean that new lexicogrammatical categories have been created on the L level of lexicogrammar. Semiotic closure still applies here. However, the newly topological semantic construals of the lower-level lexicogrammatical categories constitute a new immediate level which makes a difference to the system of interpretance on the level above. The principles adumbrated here are diagrammed in Figure 9.2.

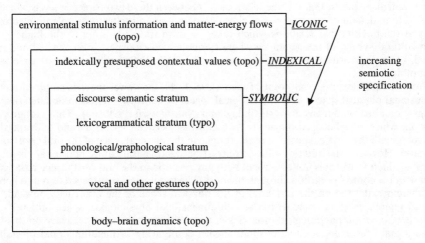

Figure 9.2 Schematized model of emergent levels of semiotic organization from initial multi-level system

Halliday's research on child language development shows that the emergence of lexico-grammar between the prior proto-semantic and expression levels constitutes a newly emergent three-level hierarchy (chapter 2, section 10). Furthermore, the emergence of the new inter-mediate level also entails the reorganization of all the levels in the hierarchy. The L level of lexicogrammar is, of course, the level where the metafunctions are defined and realized. The higher level of the system of interpretance and its semantics is changed because the appearance of a fully-fledged metafunctionally organized lexicogrammar provides new semantic input to the higher level; the system of interpretance is sensitive to simultaneously configured metafunctions, rather than to the discretely realized micro-functions that are characteristic of the infant's protolanguage (chapter 2, section 10). The intermediate lexicogrammatical level is an abstract level of form which is embodied in dynamical attractors which entrain the higher-order semantics to its intrinsic metafunctional organization.

The lower-level expression stratum of articulation is also changed because it is now subject to the new constraints arising from the lexicogrammatical level on the level above. The abstract patterns of lexicogrammatical organization impose their own constraints on the phonetic level of expression such that this, too, is able to access fewer degrees of freedom. In this way, lower-level sensori-motor activities of the body are entrained to emergent phonological patterns which are selected as significant at higher scales. That is, lower-scale body dynamics of the organism are now construed as being semiotically salient, as making a difference, on larger scales that go beyond the here-now dynamics of the organism's body dynamics. In this way, lower-scale body dynamics are seen as the signs of higher-order or symbolic consciousness. Body dynamics are entrained into the meaning-making practices of the higher-scalar system of interpretance where they are construed as having significance across potentially very many space-time scales (see the discussion of scalar heterogeneity in Lemke 2000a; Thibault 2004a: chapter 3). In this way, smaller-, faster-scale articulatory dynamics of the body are construed as making a difference on higher-scalar levels. The lower-scalar articulatory dynamics of the body and its extensions are the system's embodied means of projecting symbolic consciousness across potentially very diverse semiotic scales. It is in this way that consciousness is contextually integrated across different scales of space-time, level by level.

The three-level paradigm applies, in my view, to both the expression and the content strata of semiosis. In saying this, I would also like to suggest that the three-level paradigm enables us to consider the stratified view of semiosis in a new light. As I shall show below, the two strata can be seen as each consisting of a triple of dynamically connected levels of organization. Moreover, I shall also suggest that it is the relationships between these two triples of levels which can allow us to understand the principles of alternation and semiotic closure as operating across all levels in the hierarchy of relations which takes us from the body-brain to the higher-scalar socio-cultural system of interpretance where symbolic consciousness is recognized and interpreted. Let us start with the expression stratum. The notion of a vowel space will serve as our point of departure.

From the physical-material point of view (level L–1), the vowel space is confined to three dimensional physical space. As a physiological space, by contrast, "it accommodates variation along a number of dimensions" (Halliday and Matthiessen 1999: 69). Thus, tongue root position, which is defined typologically as a contrast between "neutral" and "advanced", is congruent with the physical position of the tongue in the physical space of the oral cavity on the L–1 level. However, the addition of the contrast between "nasal" and "non-nasal" is a typological distinction which is not congruent with any position in the oral cavity since nasality has to do with the control of airflow through the nose. The typological contrasts referred to here are not, therefore, defined on the L–1 level of the physical space of the oral cavity; instead, they refer to regions of state space within a multidimensional physiological space on level L. As such, they constrain physiological processes in the multidimensional vowel space on this level. In ways that are analogous to the simultaneous configuring of metafunctional diversity in the lexicogrammar, this multidimensional physiological space simultaneously configures typological features deriving from diverse physiological regions.

This metafunctional analogy is not, in my view, unwarranted. The multidimensional physiological space described above provides the resources for realizing the expression stratum analogue of (1) experiential meaning (i.e. typological-categorial phonological distinctions, or phonemes, and their combining into a constituent hierarchy of larger-scale phonological structures; (2) interpersonal meaning in the form of topological-continuous variation in voice quality, loudness, and so on, as icons and indexes of affect, identity, and so on; and (3) textual meaning in the form of topological-continuous rhythmic pulses functioning as indicators of beginning-end structures (Cléirigh 1998; Thibault 2004a: 86–87, 90–94, 103–104).

The L+1 level of the phonology is characterized by its own exhaustive paradigmatic (systemic) sets of categories which construe the lower-level physiological space in terms of the phonological distinctions that are recognized as making a difference in a given language system. These distinctions impose semiotic (i.e. phonological) closure on the multidimensional physiological space at the level below. That is, the phonological categories, which are typological-categorial in nature, filter out quantitative variability that is not recognized by the higher-scalar phonological system of interpretance as being relevant to the next higher level of the lexicogrammar. However, there is still room for quantitative topological variation on level L to be reorganized at some intermediate level as in some way significant to the higher-level system of interpretance. In my view, the newly topological construals of the lower-level physiological space constitute a new intermediate level which makes a difference to the system of interpretance on the level above, though in a qualitatively different way with respect to the strictly phonological dimension. I would further suggest that such an intermediate level is concerned with the interpretation of quantitative variability deriving from level L as iconic and indexical signs of the speaker's affective states, geographical provenance, personal identity, and so on. The point is that it is the specifically phonological level of the system of interpretance which is concerned with the interpretation of the symbolic significance of level L and, therefore, with the integration of this level into the next higher triple of levels on the content stratum. The three-level hierarchy principle can be used to analyse the semiotic reorganization across levels on the expression stratum as follows:

L+1   system of typological-categorial phonological distinctions as system of interpretance of bodily dynamics

L   multidimensional physiological vowel space

L–1   three-dimensional physical space of oral cavity

The Peircean logic applies to the three-level organization of the expression stratum no less than to the content stratum. Thus, intersections of systemic terms in the vowel space on level L are representamina, R, *of* object-states, X, of physical phenomena on level L–1 which dynamically constitute the phenomena at level L, *for* phonological categories and structures at level (L+1), which form the system of interpretance, SI, with respect to which correspondences between Rs and Xs are construed. Again, it is the phonological objects which are construed on the L+1 level of this SI that are **symbolically** integrated to the next larger scale, as construed by the next triple of levels on the content stratum. On the other hand, topological variation, construed iconically and/or indexically, may or may not be integrated to the next triple of levels. When it is, as in the case of intonation, its topological-continuous modes of prosodic realization are re-interpreted on the level of the system of interpretance as typological-categorial distinctions which are relevant to the making of discourse semantic meanings, for example, by co-patterning with mood selections to realize specific, more delicate categories of speech function (Hasan 1996a; Thibault 2004a: 94–98). This does not imply that the iconic and indexical dimensions of such prosodies have been transcended. Rather, some aspects of their quantitative variation have been integrated to the higher-scalar symbolic level as typological-categorial semantic contrasts.

12 Semiotic-dynamical heterarchy and semiotically mediated consciousness in ecosocial networks

The example of the vowel space draws attention to the dually artifactual and semiotically mediated character of the body-brain itself. For example, the production of vocal tract gestures in the act of speaking entails the utilization of and the entraining of physiological processes to social semiotic purposes. In this way, the materiality of the body is modified by its incorporation into human meaning-making activity (Cole 1996: 117). The body is an artifact in this sense. Artefacts, Cole argues, "are simultaneously *ideal* (conceptual) and *material*. They are ideal in that their material form has been shaped by their participation in the interactions of which they were previously a part and which they mediate in the present" (1996: 117). The notion of the multi-scale hierarchy which has been central in this chapter has explored the idea, following Lemke (1999), of semiosis as an open-ended scalar hierarchy of multi-scale networks. Thus, we see how articulatory processes and dynamics on the body scale of the expression stratum are dually physical-material (physiological, etc.) processes and semiotic-discursive ones in virtue of their having phonological values on that scale.

By the same token, these bodily processes and dynamics on their own scale are re-interpreted on the content stratum as being relevant and meaningful to the higher-scalar ecosocial system whose processes and dynamics have a longer time span than do the much faster dynamics of the lower, body scale (Salthe 1993: 46). In this way, the "ontological isolation" (Salthe 1993: 46), or the separability of entities and processes on different scalar levels, is broken. Ontological isolation entails that processes and entities on a given level in the overall scalar hierarchy, while coherent or homogeneous on their own level, are relatively isolated from processes and entities on other levels. There is no direct interaction between levels. Different levels can only be *constitutive* (L–1 to L) or *constraining* (L+1 to L) in relation to one another (see Lemke 2000a on scalar homogeneity vs scalar heterogeneity; also see Thibault 2000a).

In the first instance, words are material artifacts whose articulatory properties on the body-scale are interpreted semiotically by the brain as having meanings that are relevant to very different timescales with respect to the fast, short timescale of the articulatory dynamics of the speaker's body. Rather than mapping linguistic utterances onto neurological tokens that reconstitute symbolic reference in the way described by Deacon (1997: 266; see Cowley 2002: 86–87 for a critique of Deacon's token-realism), we can argue that linguistic utterances are bodily produced and perceived material artifacts that circulate in ecosocial networks and are construed as meaningful in specific situations. This means that, in the first instance, linguistic utterances are material objects and/or events that exist in an ecosocial environment, rather than uniquely emanating from within the head of the speaker. It is the particular material affordances of these events that enable discourse participants to construct meaningful structures that exist in what Goodwin (1996b: 399) calls "a distributed field of action" among the various participants rather than being uniquely attributable to any single individual as their sole author or origin of the meaning of the utterance. The stratification of language as expression and content can be re-interpreted in the light of these considerations as referring to the integration of the timescale of articulatory events and their interpretation to the very different timescale of the systems of interpretance in terms of which articulatory events on the body scale have the meanings they do (Thibault 2004a: 39–46). The relevant focal level scale here is that of the organism. This level is the scale of our production and perception of voluntary acts of articulation. It is the scale of the immediate motor activity on which much of human interaction, especially interaction between infants and adults, takes place. Moreover, the organism scale is closely linked to that of our agency and our interactions with other agents who share the same observer perspectives and the same cogent moments. Deacon (1998 [1997]: 109) has pointed out that languages have adapted to children's spontaneous assumptions about interaction. By virtue of their own developing agency, children are entrained, through their interactions with adults *qua* environmental affordances for social interaction, to higher-scalar ecosocial levels through processes of selection by consequences. That is, in using and interpreting their own and others' bodies as semiotic artifacts, they expand and individuate their agentive capacity and, hence, their capacity to link their use of their bodies to the meanings which circulate in social networks (chapters 4–6). The notion of selection by consequences, which I have borrowed from Salthe (1993: 267), puts the emphasis on the role that the individual's own agency plays in both evolution and development. Rather than subscribing to the view that it all depends on bottom-up sub-organismic mechanisms, we can say that children's agency plays a key role in their entraining to the dynamics of the higher-scalar ecosocial level. Their own growing repertory of bodily dynamics on the organismic scale selects for interactions with conspecifics. This process of selection means that they discover – are entrained to – the processes on very different timescales in and through which bodily actions are interpreted as meaningful in relation to the observer perspectives afforded by the organism scale. These observer perspectives are themselves implicated in the integration hierarchy of perception, conceptual thinking, and symbolic meaning-making.

Lemke argues in this respect that timescales are the most relevant parameter for understanding cross-scale semiotic relations and constraints (2000a, 2000b). The processes of semiotic mediation break with the ontological isolation of different scales such that there can be semiotic mediation between very different timescales in ways not normally allowed by the adiabatic principle (Lemke 2000b: 279–280). Semiotic mediation across diverse timescales has important implications for the notion of semiotically mediated consciousness. It shows how each level of semiotic mediation – iconic, indexical, symbolic – in the specification hierarchy of consciousness introduces the possibility of new semiotic-dynamical connectivities between the individual's internal body-brain dynamics (neurological landscape, sensori-motor activity, affective dispositions, etc.) and entities and processes, including other human and nonhuman agents, on very different space-time scales beyond that of the here-now scale where proximate information about environmental events is picked up by our perceptual systems. In this way, higher-order or symbolic consciousness can be seen as embedded in and participating in multi-scale networks of interdependent semiotic-dynamical processes. The embodied viewpoints of individual consciousnesses and their resulting trajectories loop through both the individual's internal dynamics as well as, potentially, through large-scale cultural-historical processes. This emergent semiotic-dynamical "heterarchy" should have much to tell us about the ontogenesis and phylogenesis of human consciousness and the body-brain systems which support it.

PART IV
Metaphor and System Complexity

10

Metaphor as Multiplication of Meaning Potential and its Implications for Consciousness

0 Preliminary observations

Metaphor raises fundamental questions about the relationship between semiotics and the dynamics of complex self-organizing ecosocial semiotic systems. Metaphor can help us to understand how the complexity of such systems arises from the emergence of new levels of organization. With respect to the Principle of Alternation developed by Lemke (1999; see chapter 9, section 2), metaphor is a newly emergent level of organization in the dynamics of the language system. It functions to reorganize variety on the level below as meaning for the level above. In ways suggested by the Principle of Alternation, the emergence of metaphor in semiotic systems means that both the semiotic and the dynamical closure of system levels are reopened to allow the development and evolution of greater complexity and therefore of new possibilities of consciousness, action, and meaning. The two chapters in Part IV will explore these issues.

1 Lakoff and Johnson's theory of metaphor as conceptual mapping from one domain to another

Lakoff and Johnson (1999) define metaphor as a mapping from one conceptual domain to another. These authors explain their notion of primary metaphor as follows:

> Primary metaphors, from a neural perspective, are neural connections learned by coactivation. They extend across parts of the brain between areas dedicated to sensori-motor experience and areas dedicated to subjective experience. The greater inferential complexity of the sensory and motor domains gives the metaphors an asymmetric character, with inferences flowing in one direction only.
>
> From a conceptual point of view, primary metaphors are cross-domain mappings, from a *source domain* (the sensori-motor domain) to a *target domain* (the domain of subjective experience), preserving inference and sometimes preserving lexical representation. Indeed, the preservation of inference is the most salient property of conceptual metaphors.
>
> We will be using two conventional notations for conceptual metaphors interchangeably throughout the remainder of this book, for example, Similarity is Proximity, with the target domain in subject position (Similarity), the source domain in predicate nominal position (Proximity), and the mapping represented by the capitalized copula (Is). This takes the superficial form of an English sentence just to make it easier to read. But technically, it is intended not as a sentence in English, but as a name for a metaphorical mapping across conceptual domains.
>
> (Lakoff and Johnson 1999: 57–58)

The question arises as to whether metaphor is an inferential mapping from one domain to another in the way that Lakoff and Johnson suggest. Is the notion of mapping the best way of explaining the kind of semiotic reorganization across levels that metaphor entails? In order to answer this question, I shall first briefly consider some of the semiotic implications of the map as a form of pictorial sign. A map is a kind of iconic sign which represents continually varying (territorial) shape by continually varying (pictorial) shape in some kind of relationship of relation-preserving correspondence. In other words, topological-continuous variation is mapped onto topological-continuous variation. There is an iconic relationship between "map" (cf. Source) and "territory" (cf. Target). Lakoff and Johnson posit that the mapping from Source to Target is asymmetrical, rather than bi-directional: Similarity is Proximity (but **not** Proximity is Similarity). This amounts to saying that the metaphor is about a primary domain (Similarity) and that the metaphorical domain (Proximity) is merely an alternative means of expressing the primary domain. An alternative way of considering how this metaphor is relatable to and derivable from sensori-motor experience may be developed through a con-sideration of recent work in developmental psychology and neurobiology concerning the ways in which young children achieve an understanding of the potential for spatial relations in the physical world to have symbolic meaning. I shall now turn to these considerations so as to develop an alternative sensori-motor and neural understanding of the underlying processes involved. It will be clear in the ensuing discussion that I diverge from Lakoff and Johnson on a number of critically important issues.

2 Towards an alternative: children's symbolic construal of spatial proximity as categorial similarity as semiotic reorganization across levels

A number of researchers have noted children's use of space as a means for classifying phenom-ena. Thus, the ability to put objects of one kind close together in one group and objects of some other kind together in another, physically separate group leads children to construe space symbolically, viz. proximity stands for similarity; farness stands for difference (Thelen and Smith 1994: 337; also see Inhelder and Piaget 1964). It is not difficult to reconstruct a schematic representation of the neural activities which carry out this act of categorization in accordance with Edelman's theory of reentry. In this case, the input stimulus information to the central nervous system arises from the child seeing the objects belonging to the same category as being grouped close together. It is important to emphasize here that this situation has arisen through the child's **activity** of placing the objects into the two different, spatially segregated groups. One pattern of neural activation occurs on the basis of visual information which detects the similarities among the objects in the same group. A second pattern occurs on the basis of information concerning the spatial separation into two groups of dissimilar objects. A third pattern is activated on the basis of the child's own sensori-motor activity of placing the objects into the two separate groups.

Now, the child's activity of placing the objects into the two distinct groups is a form of participation in a social practice. It is participation in this practice which brings about the patterns of neural activation in the brain that enhance symbolic and metaphorical modes of meaning-making (see also Cowley 2002: 80). The point is that the neural dynamics of the brain on their own do not achieve this. Instead, participation in social practices selects patterns of neural activation which, when cross-coupled to the articulatory (vocal, gestural, kinesic, and so on) dynamics of the body, favour the emergence of symbolic modes of meaning-making. It is by virtue of this activity-mediated cross-coupling that the self-organizing dynamics of symbolic neural space entrain bodily dynamics along specific action trajectories (chapter 4, section 4; chapter 9, section 6.1.5). Thus, the child's external manipulation of objects and physical space creates relationships between different contextual domains (e.g. spatial proximity and categorial similarity) such that his or her neural dynamics are entrained to new reentrant mappings. Rather than acting on and manipulating internal symbol representations, it is the individual's external use of symbolic forms and artifacts which has the power to reorganize neural dynamics around metaphor as a mode of brain organization.

Each of the patterns of neural activation mentioned above leads to the abstraction of features derived from their respective disjunctive samplings of the input perceptual-motor information. The two sets of features which are so abstracted may be glossed as VISUAL LIKENESS and SPATIAL PROXIMITY, respectively. These two sets of features are independently transmitted to distinct sets of degenerate neural maps and then connected through reentry to form a higher-order mapping. The formation of this higher-order or reentrant mapping leads to the emergence of a network of neural connections. Consequently, the two originally disjunctive samplings of the same input information as separate perceptual-motor information are now correlated in real time. The establishing of the correlations between the two sets of samplings leads to the emergence of a dynamic categorization, which can be glossed as PROXIMITY IS CONSTRUED AS SIMILARITY. Contrary to Lakoff and Johnson's view of an asymmetric mapping across conceptual domains, Edelman's notion of reentry suggests that the conceptual metaphor which I have glossed here as PROXIMITY IS CONSTRUED AS SIMILARITY arises from the **two-way** interconnectivity of the first-order disjunctive mappings by the higher-order reentrant mapping. Moreover, rather than a simple mapping of topological-continuous variation onto topological-continuous variation, the higher-order reentrant mapping makes possible a symbolic reorganization of the lower-level topological variation. In terms of the three-level hierarchy, these relations are as follows:

L+1   higher-order reentrant mapping leads to the symbolic construal through correlation of PHYSICAL PROXIMITY AS CATEGORIAL SIMILARITY (topological)

L   first-order disjunctive multimodal sampling of stimulus information as two distinct sets of features, viz. VISUAL LIKENESS and SPATIAL PROXIMITY (typological)

L–1   input stimulus information (topological)

It is important to remember here that we are not talking about language, but about the **symbolic construal** of physical space on the basis of the disjunctive perceptual-motor sampling of the physical environment. The emergent categorization on level L+1 is a topological symbolic reorganization of the lower levels such that the reentrant mapping correlates the two first-order mappings in a single global topological relation. Physical proximity symbolizes a categorial distinction (similarity), rather than a real-world event *per se*. This symbolic distinction means that physical proximity can, in time, be construed as symbolizing similarity on different occasions, irrespective of the particular objects that happen to be grouped together. Moreover, physical proximity is seen to contrast with the symbolic value of other relations such as physical distance, which could be construed as symbolizing dissimilarity. In this way, the child builds up a system of contrasting items which have the potential for symbolic values. They are symbolic because there is no necessary relation between physical proximity, for example, and the categorial distinction "similarity". For instance, there is no relationship of physical (iconic) resemblance between physical proximity and similarity. Rather, the symbolic relationship between the two terms is established on the basis of the particular relationship's place in an emerging system of symbolic possibilities which are not tied to the world in fixed ways. Thus, the child's external manipulation of the symbolic relationship between physical proximity and similarity in turn entrains patterns of neural activation in the formation of categories of experience. The relationship between physical proximity and similarity is metaphorical because an already meaningful relationship, viz. physical proximity, is made to symbolize a new domain of meaning or experience other than that which it had already meant prior to the creation of the metaphorical relation between the previously disjunctive two domains. Physical proximity is already meaningful in the child's experience before it is newly made to symbolize the new meaning that I have glossed as categorial similarity. The resulting metaphor combines the meanings of both terms in the creation of the new metaphorical meaning.

The fundamental question posed by the above example is not just what physical proximity means, but, rather, how is the categorial similarity of items expressed? In this perspective, we can say that it is expressed congruently as perceived visual likeness between objects, or metaphorically as the placing of these same objects into a single group of physically proximate objects. Therefore, the domain of physical proximity (action, viz. spatial juxtaposition of objects) is mapped onto the domain of visual likeness (perception). This operation results in an intersection of two previously disjunctive domains and it is this intersection which creates the metaphorical meaning.

In my view, the emergence of what Lakoff and Johnson call primary metaphor is more convincingly seen in the way I have described here. My approach has the advantage of (1) preserving the two-way nature of metaphorical relationships; (2) avoiding the suggestion that topological-continuous variation is simply mapped onto topological-continuous variation without undergoing further reorganization at higher levels; and (3) providing a neurologically more realistic account of the ways in which such symbolic reconstruals of, for example, physical space depend on the time-bound and dynamic reentrant mappings of perception, bodily action, and neural activity during the individual's embodied exploration of and interaction with the physical environment. This alternative proposal avoids the simplifying assumptions of a presumed one-way mapping of sensori-motor experience to subjective experience. It is better able to show that the presumably "subjective" experience of the idea of, for example, similarity is itself grounded in the agent's perceptual-motor engagements with the world as a secondness rather than existing subjectively in the agent as a firstness *per se*.

The children referred to above are agents who, through their own activity, bring about the neural reorganization on which the symbolic connection between visual likeness and spatial proximity is made. Thus, the child's participation in the social practice of classifying phenomena in this way suggests that activities of this kind can affect phenotypes and, in time, the gene pool of a given population such that a particular symbolic capacity is selected. In this case, the child's participation in the activity of grouping similar objects close together and dissimilar ones far apart entrains neural activity that favours symbolically mediated action. Thus, participation in social activities helps to select and entrain individuals to develop contextualizing capacities that allow human beings to make symbolic connections through their participation in semiotically mediated activity. In the case of the example discussed here, we see how the activity itself induces the children to treat visual likeness and spatial relations as potentially symbolic. In so doing, the symbolic connection that is made across the two domains through the child's activity leads to the reorganization of neural maps. This symbolic connection is not intrinsic to neural dynamics *per se*. Instead, it arises on the basis of a contextualizing relation that is not isolable in terms of any single component, but is implicated in the entire loop which links the individual's neural dynamics, his or her sensori-motor activity, and selected environmental affordances as one continuous circuit of relations.

Lakoff and Johnson's projection of the traditional Subject-Predicate relationship onto their notion of cross-domain mapping may help, at least in part, to account for the problems that arise in their theory. I will explain this as follows. The assumption that the target (e.g. Similarity) is in Subject position and that the Source is in Predicate position, on analogy with the traditional grammatical relation, leads to the notion that the Subject is that which sub-stands some quality, which is embodied in the Predicate. Thus, the formulation Similarity is Proximity suggests that Proximity-as-Predicate exists as something which is separable from the more substantive Similarity-as-Subject. In the traditional view, substance is that which has no qualities insofar as it only supports qualities which are separable from it (Bateson 1987 [1951]: 243–244; Whorf 1956: 241).

As Whorf points out, the Subject-Predicate relation predisposes one to assume that the more substantive and thing-like Subject exists in its own right. Therefore, it is able to be referentially projected onto the world "out there" *as if* it stood in a relationship of direct correspondence with an objective world that can be referred to and predicated of. Lakoff and Johnson end up objectifying this relationship by assuming, for instance, that Similarity is Proximity is a relationship between that which is predicated of the Subject (i.e. Proximity) and the substantive nature of the Subject (Similarity) which embodies the former at the same time that it (the Subject) is seen as directly corresponding to something "out there". The real point, to paraphrase Bateson (1987 [1951]: 244), is that the formulation SIMILARITY IS CONSTRUED AS PROXIMITY is information about the **relationship** between the speaker/observer's categories and the given phenomenon of experience. This is, I believe, precisely the point underlying my reconstruction (see above) of the symbolic construal of physical proximity as similarity. Both visual likeness and spatial proximity are categories belonging to the observer's system. Their metaphorical reconstrual on some higher level of organization is always dependent on the categories of some observer system. It is the observer system which construes a relationship between the two previously disjunctive sets of first-order categorizations by virtue of the perspectives afforded by the system's categorial reach. Consider the following examples:

There is a close connection between fear and stress
Elizabeth bears a close resemblance to her mother
The kangaroo is closely related to the wallaby
John closely resembles his younger brother

In these examples, the disjunctive meanings [PHYSICAL PROXIMITY] and [SIMILARITY] are metaphorically brought together, or hybridized, in the Epithet *close* in the nominal groups *a close connection* and *a close resemblance* in the first two examples. In the third example, the manner circumstance *closely* performs the same function. In all three examples, the meaning "similarity" is metaphorically re-construed as the meaning "physical proximity".

3 The two-way and hybrid nature of metaphor as multiplication of meaning potential

The metaphorical meaning is not paraphraseable in the primary domain because the second domain itself adds new dimensions of meaning potential. It does not simply substitute an alternative meaning for one which was there previously. It is not a one-way path leading from source to target. The point is that the mapping, as Lakoff and Johnson call it, is not additive, but multiplicative (Bateson 1973d [1972]: 319–320; Lemke 1998a). It is the **product**, not simply the sum, of the meanings it brings into correspondence. To say that it is the product and not merely the sum means that when lexicogrammatical resources congruently used to construe one kind of meaning (e.g. "close" → spatial proximity) also and simultaneously construe another (e.g. "close" → similarity), we have a **multiplication** of the meaning potential of both possibilities such that the resulting metaphor means both "spatial proximity" and "similarity", simultaneously.

In the alternative perspective I have just outlined, the Token-Value relation in identifying *be*-clauses provides a useful semantic analogy for modelling the two-way character of metaphorical relations. This analogy also serves as an alternative to the Subject-Predicate relation used by Lakoff and Johnson. In identifying *be*-clauses there is a semantic relation between two semantic entities, which Halliday (1994 [1985]: 124–128) has described as the Token-Value relationship. The first term is the less abstract or more concrete form; the second term is the more abstract value which is realized by the form. That is, the first term realizes the value expressed by the second term. The first term is the Token; the second the Value. The relationship between these two terms is a two-way and reversible one of semiotic realization. It is possible to adopt two different perspectives on this relationship, depending on the particular direction which informs one's perspective. Thus, (1) a given Token realizes a Value; and (2) a given Value is realized by a Token. In identifying *be*-clauses, the interaction of both the Identified-Identifier and the Token-Value variables within the same clause produces a meaning which may be glossed as follows with respect to the following example of an identifying *be*-clause: *A fitness landscape is the distribution over protein space of the capacity to carry out one specific reaction.* Thus, *A fitness landscape* (Identified/Token) is identified by realizing *the distribution over protein space of the capacity to carry out one specific reaction* (Identifier/Value). The perspective can be reversed in the following way: *The distribution over protein space of the capacity to carry out one specific reaction* (Identified/Value) *is a fitness landscape* (Identifier/Token). Thus, *The distribution over protein space of the capacity to carry out one specific reaction* identifies by being realized by *a fitness landscape*.

This reversibility is borne out by the fact that identifying clauses distinguish between the "decoding" and the "encoding" types (Halliday 1967a: 228; 1967b; 1968; Davidse 1992: 110). That is, the experiential grammar and semantics of identifying clauses give rise to both an identifying function and a coding, or realization, function. These two distinct functions entail different possible mappings of the semantic functions Identified/Identifier and Token/Value. The different possible mappings produce the distinction between "encoding" and "decoding" structures in identifying clauses. If the Identified is mapped onto the Token, then the less abstract participant which this produces is decoded into a Value. If, on the other hand, the Identifier is mapped onto the Token, the more abstract participant which results is re-construed and identified in terms of the less abstract one. In other words, the identifying clause specifies by which Token the Value is being encoded. The metaphorical relationship between Source and Target in Lakoff and Johnson can be reformulated so as to take account of these two different, though complementary, perspectives, as follows:

- the Source/Token (e.g. Proximity) is identified by realizing the Target/Value (e.g. Similarity)
- the Target/Value (e.g. Similarity) identifies by being realized by the Source/Token (e.g. Proximity)

The relationship between Source and Target does not, therefore, come down to a choice between asymmetry as opposed to bi-directionality. Instead, there is a move between two different levels of symbolic abstraction, i.e. between more concrete Token (cf. Source) and more abstract Value (cf. Target), as this comparison with the terminology proposed by Lakoff and Johnson shows. This move is formally analogous to the semantics of identifying relational clauses. For this reason, it is more coherent to see the metaphorical relationship as an overlapping or intersection of two semantic domains on analogy with the two-way and reversible nature of the Token-Value relationship in identifying *be*-clauses. Rather than saying that inferencing flows in just one direction, this way of modelling metaphorical relations – both lexical and grammatical – shows that metaphor involves a two-way process of symbolic construal. Typically, this process involves two levels of abstraction, as expressed by the semantic functions Token and Value in identifying clauses. The comparison with identifying processes further suggests that metaphorical relations in language always implicate a two-way process of symbolic construal along the lines modelled by the grammar and semantics of identifying clauses. For this reason, a metaphor such as the example cited above from Lakoff and Johnson is more accurately glossed as SIMILARITY IS SYMBOLICALLY RE-CONSTRUED AS PROXIMITY. The relationship "is re-construed as" reminds us that metaphor is always a re-construal across semantic or other semiotic domains. Furthermore, reconstrual always implicates the activity of an agent who does the re-construing. This is so both for novel metaphors as well as for those grammatical metaphors (e.g. nominalization in English) that are so thoroughly naturalized that we do not usually think of them as being metaphorical in spite of the difficulties of interpretation they often pose for language users precisely because of their metaphorical character (section 4).

4 Extending the view of metaphor as two-way construal of semiotic domains: Halliday's theory of grammatical metaphor

In Halliday's (1994 [1985]: 342) theory of grammatical metaphor, a process is congruently realized by a verb or verbal group functioning within the structure of the next highest grammatical rank, viz. the clause. It is at this level of grammatical organization that the process in a clause is assigned its temporal or modal grounding, along with its semantic dependence on one or more participant roles (e.g. Actor, Goal, Agent, Medium, Senser, Phenomenon). Grounding may be realized by a temporal or modal element in a finite verbal group. A process is said to be congruently coded if it is realized by a verb or verbal group at clause level. When a process is congruently realized in this way, the participants are coded as directly relating to the process in the clause. Likewise, a noun congruently realizes a semantic category of "thing". These congruent realizations (e.g. verb → Process; noun → Thing) emerge first in the child's language development. For this reason, they are perceived as more naturally construing the semiotic reality in which the self is embedded. This perception of naturalness does not mean that there is some kind of necessary connection between, for example, a given instance of the grammatical class "noun" and real-world things. Rather, the relationship is between the grammatical class noun and the semantic category of "thing". This semantic relationship is a functionally motivated or non-arbitrary one in the sense that the grammatical class has evolved to express the particular semantic (not natural kind or real-world) category (Halliday 1988; Beaugrande 1997: 43). The fact that congruent realizations are prior in the ontogenesis of language means that they can be considered a typical pattern of developmental emergence for users of English. Thus, children learn to use common nouns to name things in the world as belonging to or instantiating a given semantic class of "thing" before they progress to the more abstract meanings of the grammatical class noun and the expanded metaphorical potential of the nominal group (Halliday 1993: 98). In so doing, semantic categories of "thing" emerge from the multiple disjunctive takes on reality that occur through the child's contextualized use of linguistics forms to name things in the world in his or her always time-bound interactions with others. Furthermore, it is the ongoing, time-bound nature of this process which later enables the meaning potential of the nominal group to be expanded so as to include metaphorical construals of figures – i.e. process-participant configurations in the clause – as things.

A process may be nominalized. This means that it is realized at nominal group rank, rather than at clause rank. In other words, a semantic process is now construed by the grammatical resources which evolved in the first instance to construe semantic things. Things are semantic entities which can be classified into taxonomic hierarchies. The realization of a process by a nominalization is a non-congruent or metaphorical coding. It is metaphorical because there has been a metaphorical shift from the congruent to the non-congruent realization in which the process is now seen as Thing-like. Halliday (1994 [1985]: 352–353) has referred to the reconstrual of a particular semantic configuration by a non-congruent lexicogrammatical resource as grammatical metaphor. The same basic principles which operate in lexical metaphor are also seen to apply to the grammatical level. For example, the clause is a grammatical unit which realizes a semantic configuration called a figure (Halliday 1998: 190–191). A figure comprises a process and one or more participants. The nominal group is a grammatical unit which realizes an element which has the semantic status of "thing". When the resources of the nominal group are used to re-construe a figure as a thing, then we have an instance of grammatical metaphor. The metaphor is a complex semantic relation which produces a hybrid meaning relation that cannot be reduced to either the "thing" or the "figure" readings. Instead, the meanings pertaining to the previously disjunctive domains of "thing" and "figure" produce a new meaning relation in which both semantic construals are simultaneously present, as shown in Figure 10.1.

Take an example of grammatical metaphor such as *heart failure*. This metaphor can be related to a congruent (non-metaphorical) realization at clause rank such as *the heart fails* or *his heart failed*. The metaphorical meaning is explainable in terms of both the semantic categories associated with the congruent realization of processes at clause rank ("event") and the semantic categories associated with the congruent realization of a "thing" at (nominal) group rank. The metaphorical meaning of *heart failure* results from the multiplying effect of construing the given phenomenon as "figure-as-thing". In symbolic neural space, we might postulate, initially, two mappings. The first maps the lexicogrammatical unit *heart failure* to the congruently coded categories of the nominal group, viz. Classifier^Thing. The second maps the same lexicogrammatical unit to the congruently coded categories "figure-coded-at-clause-rank", viz. Medium^Process: Event. The third mapping, the reentrant one, maps the two preceding mappings onto each other. Thus, the two disjunctive mappings of the input lexicogrammatical unit to the semantic categories available in symbolic neural space entail two different semantic construals of that unit. Their mutual correlation by virtue of the higher-order reentrant map creates a topological semantic space in which the two first-order semantic construals intersect to create the double perspective, viz. "figure-as-thing", which is made possible by the input unit, as shown in Figure 10.2.

Consider the following example of grammatical metaphor: *The war's action may be shifting south*. I shall focus on the initial nominal group *The war's action* as an example of grammatical metaphor. In this case, the grammatical metaphor involves the re-construal of a figure as a nominalized participant (see Halliday 1998: 190–191; Halliday and Matthiessen 1999: 241 for discussion of the notion of semantic figure). In the terms used by Lakoff and Johnson, we can

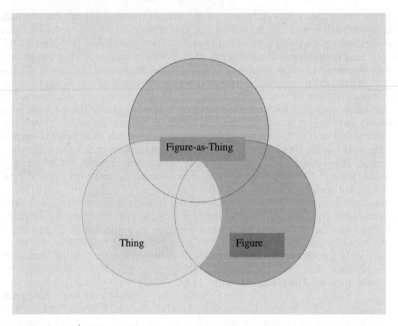

Figure 10.1 Grammatical metaphor showing multiplying effect of construing Figure-as-Thing

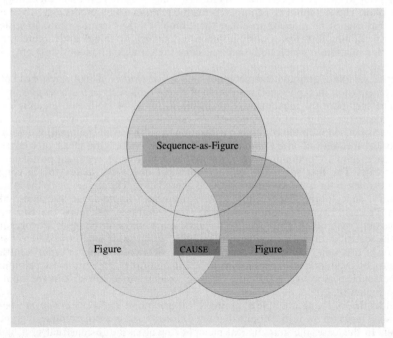

Figure 10.2 Metaphorical re-construal of a sequence of two figures as a figure, showing topological semantic merging of Sequence-as-Figure

say that a figure has been mapped onto a participant. Figures are congruently realized by clauses whereas participants are congruently realized by nominal groups. When a figure is mapped onto a participant function and realized by a nominal group instead of by a clause, grammatical metaphor results. In the example under consideration here, the figure that is expressed in the nominal group *the war's action* can be unpacked into its congruent form, as follows:

the opposing sides in the war are acting in ways such that their actions may be causing the war to shift south

My unpacking of this metaphor draws attention to the ways in which (1) the nominal group *the war's action* is a metaphorical reconstrual of a clausally realized figure which can be approximately re-constructed by the clause *the opposing sides in the war are acting*; and (2) the entire clause *the war's action may be shifting south* is itself a metaphorical re-construal of a sequence of two clauses in which, in the congruently realized sequence, one clausally realized figure causes or makes the event construed by the second figure happen. The clause *the war's action may be shifting south* can be unpacked as a sequence of two figures linked by a causal relation, as analysed in Figure 10.3.

Congruent:

the opposing sides are acting →(as a result of their actions) →the war may shift south

sequence:　　 figure 1　　　　　　　　　 +　　　　　　　　 figure 2

Metaphorical:

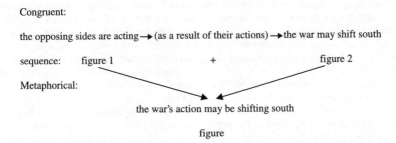

the war's action may be shifting south

figure

In the case of the nominal group, *the war's action*, the grammatical metaphor may, in turn, be unpacked into its approximate congruent form as follows:

Congruent:

(the opposing sides in / those who are waging) the war are acting (figure)

Metaphorical:

the war's action (participant)

Figure 10.3 Unpacking of a grammatical metaphor

Schematically, this metaphor can also be analysed, on analogy with the Token-Value relation in the semantics of identifying *be*-clauses, as follows:

FIGURE IS CONSTRUED AS PARTICIPANT or PARTICIPANT CONSTRUES AS FIGURE
Value　　　　　　　　　　　　 Token　　　　 Token　　　　　　　　　　 Value

The two schematizations illustrate the two-way nature of the symbolic process of construal between the grammatico-semantic domains of "figure" and "participant". The Token-Value relation draws attention to the two different levels of symbolic abstraction that are involved on analogy with the interstratal relationship of realization (Davidse 1992: 108). In this example, the participant function *the war's action* is the more concrete Token – the form – which realizes/construes the more abstract figure as its Value. The two-way, or reversible, nature of this relationship is exemplified by the fact that the Value is realized/construed by the Token.

In natural language, the semantics of inferential processes are also implicated in identifying processes, as illustrated by identifying clauses such as the following:

The evidence acquired so far implies his innocence
Token   Value

Fighting inside means major losses
Token   Value

In these two examples, the significance of the concrete Token is diagnosed as a symptom of larger principles or tendencies which can be inferred from the observable facts. In such examples, we see how the lexicogrammar of identifying clauses provides a model for organizing logical reasoning. In this case, the grammar of identifying clauses provides a resource for relating – through their respective processes *implies* and *means* – an inferred Value to the concrete Token, which is the basis for deriving a particular inference.

The distinction between congruent and non-congruent (metaphorical) realizations should not be confused with the traditional distinction between "literal" and "metaphorical" meaning. The term "congruent" does not mean "literal". Halliday's notion of congruency refers to the way in which language first evolved such that clauses construe figures and elements of clauses such as the nominal group, the verbal group, and the adverbial group congruently construe elements such as participants, processes, and circumstances, respectively (see Halliday and Matthiessen 1999: 237). This means, for example, that the grammatical class item "nominal group" is strongly coupled to the semantic function "participant". Grammatical metaphor entails a de-coupling of this congruent relation between form and function and a re-coupling of the form – e.g. the grammatical class of nominal group – to a new semantic function. Re-coupling of this kind occurs in the example discussed in the preceding paragraphs. This example of nominalization illustrates the fact that the schematic meaning "figure" can be realized congruently as a clause or non-congruently (metaphorically) as a nominal group. This is the view "from above", so to speak. This view starts with the meaning and then looks at the (variable) ways in which the meaning is realized in grammatical form. Alternatively, one could start with the view "from below" and ask: what does the grammatical class of "nominal group" mean? To this question one could answer that, congruently, a nominal group means a participant, and metaphorically it can mean a figure.

The advantage of the two perspectives – from above and from below – is that they help us to see more clearly how grammatical form and meaning are soft-coupled rather than hard-coupled (chapter 9, section 1). Therefore, they can be de-coupled and re-coupled in ways that expand and reorganize the meaning potential of language. In the traditional view, there is a fixed "literal" or core meaning which is presumed to remain invariant from context to context and there are metaphorical extensions of the form's literal meaning. On the other hand, the notion of congruency means that the congruent coupling of, say, nominal group to participant constitutes just one domain of that element's meaning potential. In turn, this meaning potential can be related to the different intertextual formations in which these forms are used and in relation to which their meanings are assigned to them (chapter 2, sections 5–8). Furthermore, the metaphorical re-coupling of the nominal group to the domain of meaning associated with the figure represents an expansion of the nominal group's meaning potential to another semantic domain. By the same token, the metaphorical meaning preserves its derivational history, albeit in a suitably transformed way. The metaphor implies possible congruent forms from which it could be derived and with which it intersects whereas the congruent form does not lead us to infer a metaphorical counterpart. Thus, a metaphorical Figure-as-Participant implies that it can be unpacked into a congruently realized Figure in a clause. On the other hand, a congruently realized Figure in a clause does not imply its nominalization as Figure-as-Participant.

5 Congruency and non-congruency with respect to lexical metaphor: lexicogrammatical and semantic aspects

Let us first consider some examples of lexical metaphor in order to explore this point in a little more detail. Both of the examples that I shall discuss below are from speeches by former American President, Ronald Reagan. Here is the first example:

> This year, relations between the United States and the Soviet Union advanced.
> [Source: President Ronald Reagan, untitled radio address, The Oval Office, 27 December 1986, p. 18]

The above example may be compared with the congruent meaning of *advance* in the following example:

> "We [= the northern alliance's army in the war in Afghanistan] will advance to the gates of Kabul within two weeks," predicts a senior rebel officer.
> [Source: *TIME*, 19 November 2001, p. 31]

The first of these examples metaphorically construes the political relationship between the United States and the former Soviet Union in terms of physical movement forward. In Lakoff and Johnson's terms, we can say that a primary sensori-motor domain concerning our embodied experience of locomotion in the physical environment is used to understand a secondary domain, that of a change in the international political situation. Furthermore, the use of the lexical verb *advanced* also entails the positive appraisal of this movement. Thus, the positive change in the relations between the United States and the Soviet Union is metaphorically construed as movement forward. The metaphorical meaning here is not so much a transfer from one semantic domain to another, but, rather, an intersection of the two domains such that a metaphorical relationship is constructed between them. In the process, a new hybrid meaning relation, viz. the metaphor, is created through the joint contextualization of the two domains. This joint contextualization further implies that the newly emergent metaphorical meaning is not reducible to the meaning associated with either of the previously separate domains.

Instead, the notion of a hybrid contextualization indicates that the metaphor is a new joint contextualizing relation which is qualitatively different from the previously disjunctive domains. The metaphorical meaning of "advanced", i.e. "made (positively valued) progress" does not, therefore, simply stand for or replace the congruent meaning "moved forward". Rather, the intersection of the previously disjunctive meanings, which I shall gloss here as MAKE PROGRESS and MOVE FORWARD, forms a new joint contextualizing relation. The metaphorical meaning is the product, not the mere sum, of the contextualizing relation which is created between the two domains (see above). In the present example, the metaphor lies principally in the lexical verb *advanced* at word rank. Rather than a stratal tension between alternative grammatical realizations, the metaphorical correspondence is established between two distinct, though related, domains of meaning within the same stratum. The lexical metaphor realized in the verb *advanced* brings two different experiential domains into a relation of correspondence at the same time that the secondary (political) domain is positively valued by the primary one.

According to Lakoff and Johnson, the primary domain in examples such as the present one is based on or derived from our embodied sensori-motor experience of the world. This may well be the case and I see no reason to contest this claim, albeit in the suitably modified form that I outlined above. However, I would point out that the metaphorical meaning of the linguistic unit *advanced* in the present example is based on the possibility afforded by the metaphor of simultaneously construing two distinct experiential **semantic** domains which are symbolized by the linguistic unit (the verb *advanced*) in question. The relationship to the sensori-motor domain is a derived one; it is not direct because the metaphor entails a **linguistic** construal of the sensori-motor domain. Another way of looking at the relation between the congruent and metaphorical meanings of *advanced* can be found at the level of the clausally realized figure

[Medium + Process: Material] in which *advanced* is the lexical verb which realizes the process. The metaphorical meaning very much depends on the kind of participant role(s) with which the process contracts a relation of semantic dependency in the clause. The semantic relation between the process and participant role helps to clarify the relation between the congruent and metaphorical meanings. Thus, the congruent meaning of *advanced* is associated with and is sensitive to the semantic characteristics of the participant role in the clause to which both elements belong. In this respect, Table 10.1 compares metaphorical and congruent meanings of the lexical verb *advanced* in relation to the clauses in which they occur. The analysis in Table 10.1 shows that the congruent meaning of *advanced* occurs in the semantic environment of participants such as *we* (= the northern alliance's army), which have the feature [+concrete].

Table 10.1 Congruent and metaphorical construals of *advanced* in relation to clausally realized figure

Metaphorical	relations between the United States and the Soviet Union	advanced
	Medium: – concrete participant; – animate; + self-instigative; + volitive	Process: abstract movement forward; instigated process; abstract change-of-state (location) of Medium
Congruent	we (= army)	advanced
	Medium: + concrete participant; + animate; + self-instigative; + volitive	Process: physical movement forward; instigated process; concrete change of state (location) of Medium

The analysis proposed in Table 10.1 suggests that the congruent and metaphorical meanings of lexical items, which function as elements in clausally realized figures, are definable with reference to the clausally realized semantic figures in which these elements occur. Thus, *advanced* has no inherent metaphorical meaning as such; the metaphorical meaning can only be construed on the basis of the semantic characteristics of the participant(s) it relates to in the clausally realized figure as a whole. This fact in itself highlights the point that what is at stake is not a distinction between "literal" versus "non-literal" meanings. Instead, it is a question of which dimensions of the given item's meaning potential are activated in accordance with the semantic relations it enters into at clause rank.

In the present example, the nominal participant *relations between the United States and the Soviet Union* is an abstract thing; it is this fact which allows for the metaphorical construal. This suggests that the congruent or metaphorical status of elements is defined in relation to the environment of the figure in which they occur. It is at this level that the distinction between, for example, physical and abstract domains is established, as the present example shows. In the present case, the congruent meaning is concerned with the construal of the physical domain, viz. "movement forward", as illustrated by the example on page 265 about the war in Afghanistan. Nevertheless, it is a semantic construal of this domain. This connection to the physical domain appears to be consistent with Halliday's argument that congruency is prior in ontogenesis. That is, our first experiential semantic construals consist of the names which we assign to phenomena in the **physical** world which impact upon our perceptual systems. Abstract things come later. In the case of lexical metaphor, the congruent meaning derives from the fact that our sensori-motor interactions with the world are the primitives of human experience from the very outset of infant semiosis (chapter 3). These primitives precede and therefore constitute the basis for the emergence of more specified forms of semiosis: generalization, abstraction, and metaphor come later in the child's linguistic development (Halliday 1993: 111; see below for further discussion). Again, there is no suggestion here that "congruent" is equivalent to the notion of "literal" meaning (see Thibault 1986c, 1999b: 582–584 for a critique of "literal" meaning). The point is that both the "congruent" and "non-congruent" (metaphorical) construals of a given linguistic or other semiotic form constitute different facets of that form's overall meaning potential. Non-congruent realizations are only definable in contrast to congruent ones. Congruent form-meaning construals emerge first in ontogenesis, i.e. before metaphorical ones (Halliday and Matthiessen 1999: 235; see section 4). This is probably the case because these early contextualizing activities are based on perceptual-motor exploration. They are semiotic construals of the phenomena of experience which derive from the ways in which we are continuously cross-coupled to our physical-material environment through our perceptual-motor activity and therefore to the categories that are reentrantly mapped in the brain by means of this activity.

In any case, it is impossible to establish whether congruent realizations came before the non-congruent ones in phylogenesis (Halliday 1994 [1985]: 343). Nevertheless, the pervasiveness of metaphor not only in symbolic modalities of semiosis such as language and depiction, but also in the conceptual models that precede language (Edelman 1992: 246–247), strongly suggests that metaphor is fundamental to the way in which the brain elaborates meanings at all levels. Edelman's claims concerning the reentrant and degenerate nature of category formation lend strong support to this view (see also chapter 6, section 12). Once the emphasis in the understanding of metaphor is shifted to seeing it as variation in meaning, rather than limiting it to variation in the form used, it is possible to extend this notion of variation in meaning to the conceptual structures based on embodied sensori-motor schemata on the lower integrative levels that are central to Lakoff and Johnson's theory.

The same argument applies to the second example that I discussed above. In both cases, we are dealing with meanings which are symbolically construed by lexicogrammatical units in the English language. The question of the relationship between the symbolic meanings which arise in linguistic forms and the less specified iconic and indexical meanings based on sensori-motor (perception-action) category formation through our physical interactions with the world cannot be answered on the basis of a direct causal link between the two. Instead, I would suggest that the answer lies in the ways in which less specified levels may be integrated to more specified ones according to the logic of the specification hierarchy (chapter 1, section 3). The experiential categories of clause grammar do not simply sit "above" the less specified levels. Nor are the semantic categories of language supervenient on lower-level sensori-motor ones. The logic of the specification hierarchy indicates that the symbolic categories of natural language do not transcend or leave behind the categorizations that have their basis in the prior iconic and indexical modes. The fact that the latter continue to exist and also that they may be integrated to the symbolic level means that meaning-making is a seamless web which reaches back from the most specified symbolic to the least specified, most primordial iconic and indexical levels of our earliest socioaffective and sensori-motor engagements with the world of the nonself. In examples such as those under consideration here, the congruent meaning is concerned with the **linguistically mediated** construal (symbolization) of a given physical domain. This suggests that congruency is definable with reference to the kind of sensori-motor experience mentioned by Lakoff and Johnson, rather than by some alternative, non-congruent grammatical coding. The congruent starting point, so to speak, can be traced back to prior, non-symbolic forms of semiosis which constitute the primitives of human experience. These have their basis in our sensori-motor interactions with the physical world in the way discussed by Lakoff and Johnson. The metaphorical end point is the metaphorical construal of an abstract meaning – e.g. thing or process – in symbolic neural space.

Let us now consider a second example of lexical metaphor from another political address by Ronald Reagan:

Six years ago we began our country on the path to greater growth and opportunity.
[Source: President Ronald Reagan, Federal Budget radio address, The Oval Office, 3 January 1987, p. 19]

The second example again illustrates the metaphor of "change = movement along a path" (see Lakoff and Johnson 1999: 179). In this case, the change is that implied in the economic growth and opportunity of the United States relative to how things were six years prior to the time of President Ronald Reagan's uttering these words on 3 January 1987. Again, the metaphor is lexical and hinges on the noun *path*. Thus, the path referred to by President Reagan is the means along which the country's journey towards the goal of "greater growth and opportunity" takes place. In actual fact, the example involves a whole cluster of lexical metaphors which together create a semantic syndrome for expressing the complex meaning involved in the above example. These metaphors can be summarized as follows:

> our country = a traveller on a journey
> the path along which the journey takes place = the means to the desired purpose
> the aim or purpose of greater growth and opportunity = the destination of the journey
> we (the American people) as cause = forceful mover of our country along its journey

The metaphorical meaning "the means towards the desired end" stands for or represents the congruent meaning "the physical way along which locomotion takes place". In this example, the metaphor lies principally in the lexical noun *path* at word rank. Rather than a stratal tension between alternative (congruent and non-congruent) grammatical realizations, the metaphorical correspondence is established between two distinct domains of experiential meaning within the same grammatical stratum, i.e. at word rank. The word *path* is a count noun. It designates a discrete, spatially bounded entity. However, the definition of a thing used here is semantic; it does not designate physical objects *per se* "out there" in the world in any objectivist or truth-conditional sense (Halliday 1994 [1985]: 189–190; Langacker 1987: 183). It is not necessary for one to have a perceptual experience of a given physical path in order to use the noun *path*. If this were so, then the metaphorical meaning would be impossible. Instead, the symbolic construal of a semantic entity "path" instantiates a type-category of semantic Thing which can be jointly attended to by addresser and addressee as an object of conscious attention in symbolic neural space.

The semantic entity in question here is construed as having continuous physical extension along some parameter, e.g. through a forest; along a river; from location, or point of departure, *a*, to location, or point of arrival, *b*, and so on. Moreover, there is a functional relationship between the starting point and the end point of the spatially bounded entity which is symbolically construed by the noun *path*. These observations apply, in the first instance, to the congruent meaning of *path* as symbolizing a physical entity which has the properties described here. The metaphorical meaning lies in the correspondence that is established between the physical meaning of "path" and the more abstract meaning of "path" as an abstract spatial entity, as in the above example. It is in this way that the meaning of "path = means" can be derived through the setting up of a metaphorical relation between the physical and abstract meanings of this count noun. Once again, the metaphorical meaning arises as a result of the way in which language forms are used to create contextualizing relations between different domains of meaning and experience such that a symbolic relation is created between the meanings associated with "path" and "means". The metaphor arises through the agent's symbolically mediated action that connects domains of experience at the same time that co-activation and entraining of neural maps results from this same activity.

The above examples show that a given metaphor is a hybrid semiotic construct whereby people give structure and meaning to their actions and experience in particular social domains. Intertextually retrievable semantic patterns which are typically associated with one domain of human practice and experience are overlaid on or hybridized with (see Thibault 1991a: 10–11, 81–82) the semantic patterns of some other domain in order to produce insights, perspectives, and evaluations about the particular domain to hand. What President Reagan does with these and the many other metaphors that run through his political addresses (Thibault 1986d) is to enable his listeners to "see" the dense and richly intertwined web of physical-material processes, texts, institutions, political meetings, and so on, that we normally black-box (Latour 1993 [1991]). The result of such black-boxing is that the texture of the experience construed by the metaphor is difficult to "see" (Bowker and Star 2000: 158–159). This metaphorical "seeing" frequently consists in moving between the concrete and the abstract, as in the above examples. It

is, of course, a collective "seeing" which is looped through the symbolic neural space of potentially very many listeners. What President Reagan creates in so doing is a sense of a textured
landscape of those otherwise opaque political and economic processes such that both he and
his listeners can "see" and "feel" them together. President Ronald Reagan, of course, had
an orator's knack, a convenient rhetorical trick, of making the complexity and intricacy of
political-economic processes look easy. The question then becomes one of reopening the black
box of the metaphor so as to discover the meaning-making work which has gone into its
construction. In so doing, the textual products of this work may no longer look quite so
seamless.

Metaphorical meanings arise in the ways in which language mediates and contextually connects different domains of human experience and practice. The use of language forms to
metaphorical ends entrains and reorganizes our neural dynamics such that human semiotic
capacities can be reorganized and expanded in response to the body-brain's need to adaptively
modify the ecosocial semiotic environment in which it is embedded.

6 Experiential and interpersonal grammatical metaphor in a text

I shall now analyse a specific example of a text featuring both experiential and interpersonal
grammatical metaphor. The example in question occurs in the following exchange between a
young female writer and an agony aunt and was published in the problem pages of *Cleo*
(Australia) magazine (September 1985, p. 155). I have elsewhere undertaken a detailed analysis
of interpersonal meaning in this exchange (Thibault 2002). The present, rather more selective
use of the same text, does not reproduce this analysis, but serves a different purpose. The two
texts have been reproduced in full here in order to better contextualize the clause which I shall
shortly focus on. For the purposes of the discussion, the two texts have been segmented below in
terms of clauses and clause complexes. Arabic numerals refer to the clause complex and lower-
case Roman letters designate the constituent clauses in each complex. The two texts, referred to
as A and B, are assumed to be components of a single entextualized social activity, comprising a
young female writer's Letter to Agony Aunt and the Agony Aunt's Reply. Thus, A1a-b refers to
the clause complex comprising clauses 1a and 1b in Text A. This notation will be used throughout the ensuing discussion in order to identify the clauses and clause complexes in the two texts.

Text A

Q. 1a. I am a 17-year-old virgin
    1b. and am very scared.
    2a. I have never been brave enough
    2b. to try sexual intercourse.
    3a. Could you please give me some idea
    3b. as to how I will feel,
    3c. what will happen
    3d. and what to expect
    3e. when I finally share my body with another?
    4. Reader, Vic.

Text B

R. 1a. I can't tell you
    1b. how you'll feel about your first experience of intercourse.
    2. So much depends on how ready you are emotionally for the experience, and the type
        of relationship you have with your partner.
    3a. From the sound of things you have not been in a situation

3b. where you are ready
3c. to proceed to a more intense sexual relationship.
4a. There is nothing brave
4b. about trying sex –
5a. it often takes more courage
5b. to wait
5c. until you know
5d. the time is right for you.
6a. In the right relationship, a loving sensitive male will take things gradually,
6b. and you will progress naturally.
7a. You may care
7b. to take a look at the excellent book *Will I like it?* by Peter Mayle (Hutchinson, 1978).

In particular, the analysis and related discussion below focus on clause A3a.

Experiential metaphor

Experientially, clause A3a is construable as either a congruently realized material action process or a non-congruent (metaphorical) construal of a verbal process. The two interpretations are presented in Figure 10.4.

Metaphorical:	Could	you	please	give	me	some idea a to...
Material process		Actor		Process: Material Action	Beneficiary: Recipient	Goal
Congruent:	Could	you	please	tell	me	how I will feel...
Verbal process		Sayer		Process: Verbal	Receiver: Addressee	Verbiage: Projected Locution

Figure 10.4 Metaphorical and congruent experiential construals of clause A3a

In the clause *could you please give me some idea . . .*, in Figure 10.4, two different experiential semantic domains are related. In the first instance, a verbal process of "telling" is metaphorically re-construed as a material process of "giving". In this way, the metaphorical construction provides a further perspective on the phenomenon, though without taking anything away from the congruent perspective. Thus, *could you please give me some idea* is like the congruently realized material process clause *could you please give me a glass of water?* at the same time that it is different from it on account of its metaphorical status. As Figure 10.4 shows, the metaphorical clause also evokes a non-metaphorical agnate *could you please tell me how I will feel . . . ?* From this point of view, it is significant that the agony aunt in her reply in clause B1a re-construes the metaphorical encoding in A3a as the non-metaphorical agnate *I can't tell you.* . . . The significance of this shift probably relates to her contrasting perspective on the exchange and their respective participant roles in it with respect to the young female writer. Whereas the latter desires to have the agony aunt act upon her consciousness, so to speak, the agony aunt takes up the perspective of the one who is required to tell. There are a number of grammatical distinctions between the metaphorical and non-metaphorical agnates, as shown by the lack of any systematic proportionality of the following kind:

could you give me a glass of water?: could you give a glass of water to me?
could you give me some idea . . . ?: could you give some idea to me?

Once again, we see that the metaphorical meaning is not paraphraseable in the primary domain (material process) because the experiential semantics of the second domain entails new dimensions of meaning potential. The second domain does not simply substitute a prior meaning or add on an alternative wording for something already there. Again, the newly hybridized semantic relation is a multiplicative one. It is the overall product of the metaphorical bringing together of the semantics of the material and verbal process-types. In this case, the lexicogrammatical resources that are congruently used to construe one kind of semantic function (Material Process → Action) also and simultaneously construe another (Semiotic Process → Saying). It is this double construal which produces the multiplication of the meaning potential of both construals: something is seen, simultaneously, as both a material action in the world and as a mental activity abstracted from the external world.

The metaphorical meaning of *could you please give me some idea . . . ?* can be explained as follows. First, the projected (reported) locution in the congruent realization is an entire clause in its own right which is metaphorically re-construed as a participant *some idea*; it therefore assumes the experiential semantic status of a Thing, rather than of a figure. Moreover, the semantic figure realized by the projected clause in the congruent realization is a projected second-order metaphenomenon (Halliday 1994 [1985]: 252–253). It has the status of a meaning (specifically, a locution) which is projected – reported as indirect discourse in the traditional terminology – by the Sayer, *you*, in the projecting clause. On the other hand, the metaphorical construal of this projected locution as a Thing relocates it as belonging to the first-order level of physical reality which directly impacts on our perceptual systems, rather than to the second-order reality of semiotic metaphenomena which are attributed to symbolic sources of consciousness, i.e. as verbal and mental processes that are symbolically projected from Sayers and Sensers, respectively. In this way, a semiotic metaphenomenon is construed as having an objectified, Thing-like status, i.e. as something existing in first-order reality and which can be materially acted upon. Its first-order status is shown by the fact that this clause is a material process in which *some idea* is treated as a commodity to be disposed of. A further aspect of the metaphorical meaning of this clause is that the nominal participant *some idea* can function as the unmarked locus of information by virtue of its appearing in final, culminative position in its clause, rather than having the status of a separate, projected figure, as in the congruent realization.

In this case, a material process metaphorically construes the verbal transaction between the two participants as the transfer of a Thing – the Verbiage, *some idea* – from the Actor to the Beneficiary. Significantly, the Thing which is so transferred is not a material entity, but an abstract **mental** one. Thus, the verbal process of telling is metaphorically construed as a material process of transferring a mental – not material – entity to the Beneficiary. Furthermore, it is a mental entity which has to do with knowledge, i.e. something which the agony aunt is presumed to know, but which the girl does not, and which the girl wants the agony aunt to tell her. The writer of A3a requires her addressee to **do** something, i.e. to **tell** the writer something that the agony aunt is presumed to know.

Let us consider some further experiential implications of the choice of the nominal group *some idea* in the clause under consideration. The experiential type-category denoted by the Head noun *idea* lies, of course, within the class of abstract mental, rather than concrete material, things (see above). Moreover, the verbal action of telling someone something that they did not previously know implicates a cognitive transformation of the semantic Receiver of the verbal process (chapter 6, section 2). Thus, verbal processes of, for instance, saying, telling, persuading, convincing, explaining, and so on, imply the possibility of the manipulation and transformation of the addressee's cognitive competence (Greimas 1983: 123). This observation now allows us to re-cast the experiential predication "you give me some idea . . ." as also implicating a metaphorical construal of a causal **mental** process of cognition "you make me know it" by virtue of the act of telling. More precisely, it is a verbal process which has the potential to transform the cognitive status of the Recipient from an initial state of [–KNOWLEDGE] to a desired end state of [+KNOWLEDGE] such that the Recipient – *me* – is, then, reconstruable as the Senser in a mental process of the cognition subtype. The relationship between the verbal and mental meanings in this structure can be unpacked as follows:

[[You tell me   [I know]]
[[Instigating verbal process → [Instigated mental process]]

The experiential metaphor in this example, in bringing together the material, verbal, and mental domains, provides a concrete example of how action adapts to constraints in the ongoing development of the situation. The metaphor is not a fixed property of the form, but is an emergent property of the ways in which linguistic choices on the discourse stratum are interfaced with and adapted to contextual constraints such that verbal action and cognitive domains are acted upon. The topological nature of this metaphor is illustrated in Figure 10.5.

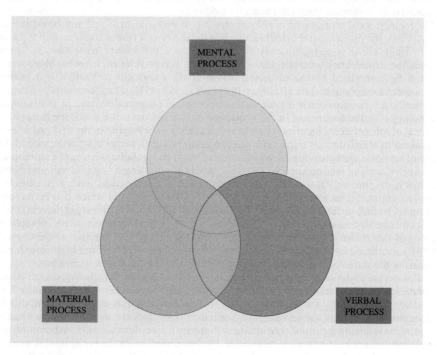

Figure 10.5 Experiential grammatical metaphor showing topological semantic continuum among the material, verbal, and mental process domains

The creation of the metaphor, which relates two typologically distinct domains of experiential meaning – viz. material and verbal processes – in a single overall topological semantic space, illustrates the Principle of Semiotic Alternation (chapter 9, sections 3, 4). This metaphor can be modelled in terms of the three-level hierarchy as follows: the discrete, typological-categorial variety of the lexicogrammatical level L, functions to reorganize the continuous topological variation of proto-meanings corresponding to the writer's desire to know on level L–1 as a topological-continuous semantic space on level L+1 in which two semantic construals provide a double perspective on the object of consciousness in symbolic neural space. In terms of the three-level hierarchy, these relations are presented as follows:

L+1   metaphorical construal of intersecting experiential – verbal-material – semantic categories as a continuously varying topological semantic space in which a semantic object of symbolic consciousness is construed in some SI

L   lexicogrammatical typology of discrete categories of process-types (material, verbal, and mental)

L–1   topological-continuous variation of proto-meanings in writer's neural dynamics

The L–1 level where vague, indeterminate proto-meanings are to be found constitutes the intentional source of the meaningful trajectory which is generated and which flows into the ecosocial context of the interaction. Thus, a proto-semiotic intention must be constrained and entrained by meaning along a trajectory if it is to flow into action (Juarrero 1999: 95; chapter 5, section 15). It is the meaning so defined and constructed along a trajectory that determines the efficacy of the action structure relative to its ecosocial environment. Systemic-functional linguistics is well placed to offer some elegant and powerful solutions to this question. The instance of grammatical metaphor discussed above was of the experiential kind. I shall now consider the same example as an instance of interpersonal metaphor.

Interpersonal metaphor

In Halliday's account, the interpersonal semantics of dialogic moves combines selections from two basic systems, viz. (1) the speech roles taken by the interactants in the exchange; and (2) the nature of the commodity – information or goods-&-services – which is being exchanged (chapter 8, section 8). The combining of selections from the two subsystems gives us the basic speech functions of statement, question, offer, and command. Dialogic moves involving the exchange of information (statements and questions) are propositions. Those involving the exchange of goods-&-services (offers and commands) are proposals. The basic speech functions are interpersonal semantic categories corresponding to various basic types of discourse move. Each of these basic types is congruently realized by a particular mood selection. For example, the congruent grammatical realization of a question is interrogative mood; in the case of a command it is imperative mood.

Speech function categories may also be realized metaphorically. For example, a command may be realized by a modulated interrogative, as shown by the difference between the imperative *Give me some more wine!* and the modulated interrogative *Could you give me some more wine?* Proposals are proposals for action. The congruent realization of a command by imperative mood in English reflects the way in which commands realized in this way are concerned with negotiating the entraining of physical-material flows along an action trajectory involving addresser and addressee. The action trajectory is cross-coupled to and coordinated by the imperative mood choice. This trajectory extends from the speaker through the mood choice to the designated addressee and the possible future outcome of the addresser's proposal for action. Semantically, the meaning of a command may be glossed as: "I want this to happen; you do it for me". The addresser invests the responsibility for the proposed action in the addressee, who is required to carry out the designated action. Propositions (statements and questions) are concerned with the modalized perspectives of addresser and addressee on the clausally realized proposition. In statements, the addresser provides his or her own modal perspective on the proposition; in questions, the addresser seeks the addressee's modal perspective on the proposition. Propositions are oriented to the negotiating of linguistically realized meanings, rather than using linguistic means to coordinate and entrain physical-material flows along an action trajectory, as in proposals.

Metaphor arises in this area of the grammar when the grammatical resources of mood which are congruently used to enact one kind of dialogic move (e.g. interrogative → question) also and simultaneously enact another kind of dialogic move (e.g. imperative → command). As with experiential metaphor, the resulting semantic intersection of meanings associated, respectively, with propositions and proposals produces a multiplying effect in which the interpersonal metaphor both combines the two meanings at the same time that the resulting metaphorical meaning is not reducible to either one of these. Again, the semantic product of this intersection is a hybrid interpersonal construct which often has a somewhat indeterminate semantic status. This hybrid semantic status is shown by the fact that interpersonal mood metaphors are liable to be negotiated from both perspectives – proposition and proposal – on the discourse level (see Martin 1991). Unlike experiential grammatical metaphor (e.g. nominalization), interpersonal metaphor of this kind does not have implications for the ways in which information is organized in discourse. This is so because interpersonal meaning, unlike experiential meaning, is not based on constituency. A nominalized figure can be slotted into Theme position in the clause and therefore backgrounded as Given (Halliday and Matthiessen 1999: 270). Thematization of semantic figures is possible because the nominal group is a constituent in clause structure. However, interpersonal mood metaphor has other kinds of implications for the discourse level of organization owing to its prosodic and scopal nature. For this reason, the semantic effects of interpersonal metaphor can be spread over stretches of discourse of indeterminate length. The prosodic spreading of interpersonal meaning may be explained as follows (chapter 8, section 3).

First, the mood selection in the clause is a formal grammatical unit which realizes a dialogically coordinated move on the discourse stratum. The move may extend over several clauses or it may coincide with the clause in which the mood selection is realized. The point is that the mood selection holds an entire discourse move within its semantic scope. Secondly, mood *qua* grammatical category is the realization of a grammatical level of meaning which is specific to the kind of mood selection (declarative, interrogative, exclamative, optative, imperative, and so on) irrespective of how it functions on the higher-level discourse stratum. In other words, the mood choice makes its own contribution to the meaning of the dialogue on its own level. Thirdly, the specific contribution which mood *qua* grammatical category makes is also a resource, along with other choices (e.g. modality, attitudinal lexis), for the negotiating of interpersonal meaning on the discourse level. In this way, we can see how mood functions in interpersonal metaphor. It is one of the grammatical means which interactants use and respond to in the negotiating of their variously converging and diverging orientations to the meanings that are at risk in discourse. The indeterminacies of interpersonal metaphor – viz. proposition or proposal? – create an expanded phase space of possibilities for enacting such negotiation.

A particular experiential meaning selection in the clause correlates with a particular dialogic exchange relationship between the interactants. This latter aspect corresponds to the interpersonal dimension of the clause's meaning. In systemic-functional linguistic theory, the mood system is one of a number of interpersonal systems in the grammar of English which regulate and coordinate dialogic exchange relationships between interactants. The basic mood system constitutes a general potential which can realize many more delicate semantic moves and their corresponding speech roles, such as giving and/or demanding information or goods-&-services (Halliday 1994 [1985]: chapter 4; see Hasan 1996a for an account of the more delicate semantic categories that can be derived from these basic distinctions). This general interpersonal semantic potential is then restricted according to semantic register along the dimensions of power, affect, solidarity, and so on. In the text under consideration here, the interpersonal relationship between the young female writer and the agony aunt may be described as unequal in power, low in familiarity, and so on. Furthermore, the interpersonal context has implications for the experiential choices in the sense that choices in one semantic metafunction co-determine or constrain choices in others. In the example, the young female writer demands information about a specific experiential domain, i.e. sexual relations, and the agony aunt responds by providing information and advice about that domain.

What we see here is how the lexicogrammatical choices on level L constrain and channel the proto-meaning on level L–1. The latter is variably realized by neurological processes in the brain and sensori-motor interactions with the material world. It is the content, however vague and ill-defined, of the proto-meaning (e.g. pre-linguistic desires, intentions, etc.) which defines the intentional source (of consciousness) rather than the neural events which these realize (Juarrero 1999: 96). It is the reorganization of the topological variety – the vagueness and indeterminacy – of L–1 proto-meanings as a more determinate typological-categorial variety by the dynamics attractors on the L level of lexicogrammar which enables the L–1 proto-meanings of the intentional source to be functionally integrated to a larger action trajectory. In turn, this trajectory flows into the higher-scalar ecosocial environment as a text which is construed as deriving from a source of symbolic consciousness and which can be discursively taken up, negotiated, and responded to, and acted upon by others. The metafunctional organization of lexicogrammar also suggests how proto-meanings which have to do with cognition, affect, intention, and so on, may be integrated in the brain and then entrained by the higher-order dynamics of symbolic neural space. Context-sensitive entraining of cognitive, affective, and other factors occurs at all levels of neural organization, i.e. from proto-meanings all the way up to higher-scalar symbolic neural space. In this way, the neural landscape of the individual's consciousness is, at all levels, the result of the entraining of many different self-organizing neural dynamics to the attractors in operation at a specific moment, relative to a given context. The metafunctional organization of semiosis on levels L and L+1 entrains and reorganizes the neurally realized proto-meanings on level L–1 along a time-bound individuating trajectory such that higher-scalar semantic constraints are imposed on lower-scalar neural processes.

It is the interpersonal dimension of the clause's meaning which makes possible the dialogic coordination of what the addresser and the addressee do in some interaction. The interpersonal structure and meaning of a given move do not, in my view, lead to an "exchange" of meaning in the sense of a literal transfer from one person to another of information. Instead, the choice of a particular move by a given interactant induces the taking up and negotiating of the move by means of other moves by the other parties to the interaction such that a particular unfolding meaningful trajectory is further individuated and, perhaps, completed or "finalized", as Bakhtin (1986: 76–77) expressed it (chapter 8, section 1). Thus, the different contributions to a dialogue, say, by different participants – viz. the different moves realized by the interpersonal grammar – result in a reciprocal and ongoing modification of both the meanings that are made along a given action trajectory and the internal dynamics of the participants involved.

The interpersonal grammar of our example also exhibits grammatical metaphor. In this case, the metaphor is associated with the mood choice in the clause. The mood metaphor in this case yields the possibility of both a congruent and a metaphorical interpretation of the semantic status of the clause as a dialogic move in the text. That is, the clause may be negotiated as a congruent demand for information and/or a metaphorical demand for action (goods-&-services) given that imperative mood (e.g. *give me some idea* . . . !) is the congruent realization of a demand for action. In the first possibility, the focus of the interpersonal negotiation is on the choice of polar interrogative mood; the addressee is positioned as having to take up and respond to the meaning of this aspect of the interpersonal status of the move by either affirming or negating the polarity. In this reading, the addressee treats the clause as a question concerning her ability (could you? / couldn't you?) to perform the action specified in the Residue. That is, as a "demand for information", in Halliday's terms. According to the second possibility, the focus of the negotiation is on the action which the addresser desires the addressee to perform. In this case, the focus is on the meaning potential of the type-specification of the action which is lexicalized in the Residue ("give me some idea . . ."). The addressee has the possibility of negotiating the clause as a demand or request to perform the specified action. The semantic tension between the two interpretations again yields a topo-logical semantic space. Consequently, the interactional status of this dialogic move lies in the fuzzy or indeterminate area between the congruent and metaphorical readings, as shown in Figure 10.6. The metaphor derives from this hybridization of the "demand information" and "demand action" meanings.

could	you	please	give me some idea as to ...
Finite: Modality	Subject	Adjunct: Modal	Residue
Mood: Polar interrogative			

Congruent	Proposition: Demand information ^ ("Yes, I can"/"No, I can't"): negotiate Polarity
Metaphorical	Proposal: Demand goods-&-services ^ (Give goods: some idea): negotiate action specified in Residue

Figure 10.6 Metaphorical and congruent interpersonal semantics of clause A3a

7 Interpersonal metaphor and symbolic consciousness

The further question is: why has the interpersonal semantics of natural language evolved the kind of complexity that is adduced by grammatical metaphor? The answer lies, in least in part, in the nature of higher-order or symbolic consciousness. This form of consciousness is best defined as an ecosocial semiotic neural space. It has evolved in the human species in response to the complexities of social life. Ontogenetically, this is evidenced by the fact that (proto-)imperative mood emerges prior to (proto-)indicative mood in early infant semiosis. The (proto-)imperative is concerned with the entraining of physical-material entities and processes in the ecosocial semiotic environment. The congruent realization of commands by imperatives ties in with the way in which the grammar of the imperative is strongly cross-coupled to specific physical-material processes and entities in its immediate context. This focus on the entraining of physical-material processes is, to be sure, a form of social interaction; however, the orientation to the physical-material domain means that this form is not, in the first instance, concerned with negotiating the complexities of social life (see also Bogdan 2000: 17). That is, the physical-material world in itself is not likely to be a stimulus for more complex forms of social interaction in complex social forms of organization. Instead, this stimulus arises from other social agents with whom one interpersonally engages in a wide range of different social and institutional contexts, with their different interactional-interpersonal demands on individuals, the diverse interactional roles they engage in, and so on.

Social life and its complexities require a considerably enlarged mental space in comparison with the relatively simpler demands made by mechanical relations between entities in the physical world. In the domain of social exchange relations, the evolution of interpersonal grammatical metaphor may be seen as a response to the complexities of the expanded phase space of social life. Put simply, a complex social environment requires enlarged and increasingly complex interpersonal semantic resources for negotiating its intricacies. This complexity also entails, as I said before, an enlarged symbolic neural space. Interpersonal metaphor has evolved to meet this requirement and, hence, to negotiate one's way through this space. Interpersonal metaphor has evolved to negotiate the complexities and indeterminacies of social life and therefore the problems and complexities in interpreting others (chapter 1, section 3). Consequently, the potential for the topological overlap of different speech functions within the same discourse move interfaces with the often fluctuating and uncertain nature of the status and power relations between interlocutors in the unfolding discourse situation. In this way, the complexity of social encounters and their interpersonal negotiation can be traded off with increasing semantic indeterminacy through the use of interpersonal metaphor.

In their theory, Lakoff and Johnson (1999) have stressed how primary metaphor emerged from sensori-motor representations concerning the body's interactions with the physical environment. The notion of cognition which Lakoff and Johnson most stress in their work is ideationally based. Furthermore, the social domain is overwhelmingly represented in ideational terms, rather than in interpersonal-interactive ones. However, it is the interpersonal-interactive domain, along with the semiotic resources that have evolved to enable this, which are most fundamental in engaging with others as distinct from our ideational construals of our sensori-motor interactions with the physical world (chapter 1, section 3). The physical world and the relations of efficient causality that are observable or inferable in it are not in themselves a sufficient basis for higher-order consciousness. The emergence of higher-order consciousness entails a self-reflexive sense of a self who is dialogically related to others in a complex social space where it is possible to adopt meta-perspectives on one's own perspective as well as the perspectives of others (chapter 8, section 1). This reflexivity is possible because the individual's symbolic neural space loops through a wider heteroglossic system of possible social viewpoints and evaluative stances in relation to which social agents position and orient themselves, their texts, and their interlocutors. The interpersonal semantic resources of mood, modality, and evaluation are crucial in this respect (Lemke 1998b; Martin 1992b; Thibault 1992, 1999b: 570–574, 2000a: 304–305, 2002; see also chapter 8). Interpersonal, dialogically coordinated, engagements with others in the social world require the ability to interpret the social actions of others, to attribute motives and intentions to these, and the self-reflexive ability to view things from the point of view of the other, i.e. to put one's self in the position of the other (Habermas 1984 [1981]; Trevarthen 1992). Mead's (1934) discussion of the interiorization of the distinction between "I" and "me" is an early formulation of this ability in the tradition of American pragmatism (see chapter 5, section 14). It is the development of these abilities which leads to the capacity to mentally rehearse, as Bogdan (2000: 21) puts it, these same abilities off-line, i.e. when not interacting with an actual other in some social context. With the above considerations in mind, I shall now consider some further questions concerning the interpersonal semantics of our example.

The interpersonal negotiation between the young female writer and the agony aunt is about much more than a simple request for information or goods-&-services. Instead, it involves the negotiation of complex social relations between the two within the social space which is constituted by this genre of text. Furthermore, it is a form of interpersonal negotiation which implicates diverse space-time scales, along with the ability to project beyond one's own perspective in order to imagine the likely or possible response of the other. For example, the choice of interrogative mood, in shifting the modal responsibility for the arguability of the proposition to the addressee, entails a meta-semiotic ability on the part of the addresser to self-reflexively project onto the addressee the mental capacity to take up and respond to the proposition from her own perspective. This ability requires that the addresser is able to "see" things from the other's perspective and, hence, to see the addressee as an agent who can adopt a particular (modalized) perspective on the proposition (chapter 7, section 6). Furthermore, it is this ability to take up the other's perspective which is implicated in the fundamentally intersubjective character of the interpersonal resources of language whereby social agents negotiate meanings, attitudes, values, affect, status, power, and so on, that go beyond interaction for purely here-now utilitarian goals and purposes (Bogdan 2000: 22).

Take the case of proto-imperative mood in early infant semiosis (chapter 3, section 6). The dyadic interaction that this coordinates is strongly cross-coupled to here-now scale perceptions, needs, and wants relating to the physical-material world, including one's own body. The indexical basis of proto-imperative interaction is topological in character, based on the here-now mapping of body processes to processes (events, other people's actions, and so on) in the ecosocial environment. It is a form of interaction which is based on sensori-motor mappings between self and world. It is procedural knowledge of the kind, "I want this; you get it for me". The dyadic, as opposed to triadic, character of this type of interaction (see Halliday 1978a, Trevarthen 1978), derives from the fact that explicit experiential construal of the world, and therefore the possibility for reflection, is absent; the primary form of knowledge is based on direct enactment and is, for this reason, implicit. The indexical basis of this form of consciousness is tied to perceptual-motor interactions on the here-now scale. Halliday has described this early protolinguistic form of engagement with the infant's social environment in terms of a number of discrete micro-functions which emerge in the protolinguistic phase. These micro-functions are essentially indexical-procedural in character. They represent the mapping of discrete micro-functions onto vocal and other gestural activity. For this reason, they do not have the property of a lexicogrammar (chapter 2, section 10; chapter 3, section 6). They cannot, therefore, create information or construct discourse (Halliday 1993: 96). Halliday describes some of these micro-functions as follows:

> Semantically, the systems develop around certain recognizeable functions (the micro-functions, as I have called them): instrumental and regulatory, where the sign mediates in some other, nonsymbolic act (e.g. "give me that!", "sing to me!"); interactional, where the sign sets up and maintains an intimate relationship ("let's be together"); and personal, where the sign expresses the child's own cognitive and affective states (e.g. "I like that", "I'm curious about that"). There may also be the beginnings of an imaginative play function, a "let's pretend!" sign, often accompanied with laughter.
>
> (Halliday 1993: 96)

The proto-imperative mode of dyadic interaction in early infant semiosis is concerned with the situation-specific entrainment of the physical-material world. However, it also always entails the recruiting of others as co-agents in the fulfilling of the addresser's aims and desires. For this reason, the very earliest manifestations of proto-imperative sign-making are intrinsically social from the outset. By the same token, it seems unlikely that proto-imperative dialogic engagement involves the same kind of self-reflexive understanding of the other as an agent who is able to adopt a modalized take on the proposal. Instead, the much more situated understanding of the addresser in proto-imperative engagement is limited to the indexical-procedural understanding of the addressee as a (potential) co-agent who can be harnessed to one's project so as to bring about physical, causal change in the world. A social agent who does not progress beyond this stage will not develop the kind of self-reflexive higher-order consciousness that I discussed above. Indexicality *per se* mitigates against the possibility of progressing beyond perceptual-motor forms of knowledge. The possibility of progressing further lies in the emergence of the indicative mode. It is this mode which enables the eventual progression to unsituated forms of consciousness and self-reflexivity (chapter 5, section 7). As Halliday's (1975, 1993, 1978a) research on child language development shows, the indicative mode affords the exchange of information both about "I" and "you" as well as the "third person" experiential domains which lie outside the early I–you forms of dyadic engagement which are characteristic of the indexical form of consciousness.

It is the indicative exchange of information which allows for the emergence of those forms of interpersonal engagement based on the expanded phase space of symbolic consciousness. Interactants are thus able to attribute self-reflexive consciousness to each other and, hence, to engage in the interpersonal negotiation and interpretation of each other's modal takes on particular propositions. In its later stages, the indicative exchange of information also allows for the possibility that agents can self-reflexively project themselves into the perspective – the dialogic position – of the other (real or imagined) off-line.

The observations made above may help to provide a glimpse into the reasons for the emergence of interpersonal grammatical metaphor and its relations to higher-order consciousness. The example analysed above, in keeping with my previous observations about metaphor, enacts a topological semantic space which provides a double perspective on the dialogic move in this clause, i.e. it is both a proposition and a proposal. This dual perspective shows how grammatical metaphor creates an enlarged semantic phase space which functions to constrain and direct intentional acts along a trajectory. In the example, the action trajectory is constrained by intrinsic neural dynamics embodying the desire to know something from the agony aunt. The complex grammatical metaphor enacts a trajectory through semantic space which attracts to it the material, verbal, and mental experiential construals that we have considered above. At the same time, these are correlated with the interpersonal grammar of the clause and thus organized as an action trajectory emanating from an intentional source and directed towards an addressee.

11

Metaphor as Semiotic Reorganization across Levels

1 Lakoff and Johnson's theory of embodied realism

Some theoretical criticisms from the perspective of ecosocial semiotics

Lakoff and Johnson (1999) approach the question of categorization in terms of their theory of "embodied realism". The central tenets of this approach are summarized by these authors as follows:

> Living systems must categorize. Since we are neural beings, our categories are formed through our embodiment. What this means is that the categories we form are *part of our experience*. They are the structures that differentiate aspects of our experience into discernible kinds. Categorization is thus not a purely intellectual matter, occurring after the fact of experience. Rather, the formation and use of categories is the stuff of experience. It is part of what our bodies and brains are constantly engaged in. We cannot, as some meditative traditions suggest, "get beyond" our categories and have a purely uncategorized and unconceptualized experience. Neural beings cannot do that . . . we form extraordinarily rich conceptual structures for our categories and reason about them in many ways that are crucial for our everyday functioning. All of these conceptual structures are, of course, neural structures in our brains. This makes them embodied in the trivial sense that any mental construct is realized neurally. But there is a deeper and more important sense in which our concepts are embodied. What makes concepts concepts is their inferential capacity, their ability to be bound together in ways that yield inferences. *An embodied concept is a neural structure that is actually part of, or makes use of, the sensori-motor system of our brains. Much of conceptual inference is, therefore, sensori-motor inference.*
>
> (Lakoff and Johnson 1999: 19–20; italics in original)

Lakoff and Johnson emphasize the sensori-motor interaction between embodied individuals and the world as the source of what they call "basic level categories". These categories are derived from Gestalt perception, sensori-motor interaction, and so on. In spite of this interactionist perspective, the individual body-brain remains the level of first focus. From the point of view of the ecosocial semiotic theory in the present study, the embodied realism espoused by Lakoff and Johnson derives from a non-semiotic conception of language. Moreover, their focus on the individual body-brain suggests that the individual body-brain *qua* firstness is prior. According to the ecosocial perspective of the present study, it is the world *qua* secondness, understood as the ecosocial environment in which body-brains are embedded, which is prior both phylogenetically and ontogenetically, though this is not so in any objectivist sense. My point is that the ecosocial environment precedes the self and provides the self with something to interact with, in the process discovering and elaborating its own sense of self. I am in full agreement with Lakoff and Johnson in their arguments against what they call objectivist accounts of meaning, which derive, in their terms, from "disembodied realism" (1999: 94–96). My point is that the Gestalt, sensori-motor and other embodied basic level categories discussed by Lakoff and Johnson are the derived result of the emerging agency of the individual. Furthermore, in the process of deriving and constructing these categories, the individual agent also constructs the principles of interpretation – the system of interpretance – in which the categories so derived have their meaning (Salthe 1993: 15; Thibault 1999a: 32). The problems I have with Lakoff and Johnson's approach are summarized as follows:

- Their emphasis is on bottom-up first-order or enabling constraints which exist at the level of organization of organisms, i.e. within the neural and sensori-motor dynamics of the individual (Juarrero 1999: 142–3). There is no account of how individual–world interactions, through autocatalysis, bring about the emergence of second order or top-down contextual constraints which function as the boundary conditions on the various elements which comprise the lower level entity (Juarrero 1999: 141). Consequently, there is no account of how the internal dynamics of the individual are entrained to the dynamics of higher-scalar ecosocial levels; it is in this way that the probability distributions of the individual's interactions with the world are altered so that its degrees of freedom are reset by higher-scalar boundary conditions;
- Furthermore, there is no account of the ways in which the categories at all levels – perceptual-motor, conceptual, and social semiotic – are built up as a result of the fact that the individual is only a part of a larger supersystem. The individual human subsystem is maintained on the basis of the ongoing exchanges of matter, energy, and information between the individual subsystem and its supersystem environment. The Gestalt, sensori-motor, and other categorizations discussed by Lakoff and Johnson are meaningful structures whereby individuals understand and interpret their embodied existence in the world. In the ecosocial semiotic view, such structures are built up and maintain their integrity as a result of the individual's structured exchanges with the environment. It is only through such thermodynamic-like exchanges that meaningful structure is built up in the organism. The individual system progresses beyond perceptual-motor categorization to conceptual and then symbolic categorization because the historically prior level and the exchange processes which enabled its structure to emerge are integrated into structured structuring exchange processes at higher levels of organization. For this reason, it is important to understand how the embodied image schemata, sensori-motor, Gestalt and other categorizations proposed by Lakoff and Johnson are regulated by exchange structures at the ecosocial semiotic level of organization of human systems;
- In terms of the previous observation, it is noteworthy that the theory of language espoused by Lakoff and Johnson is inherently biased towards experiential categorization (see also Halliday and Matthiessen 1999: 428). Consequently, there is no account of the intersubjective processes of exchange and the interpersonal grammatical categories that enact these. There is no account of language as action and interaction. The interpersonal dimension of language is a no less intrinsic part of the semantic organization of language and other semiotic modalities than are the ideational categories that Lakoff and Johnson privilege;
- The focus on individual embodiment *per se* provides us with little bottom-up slices of the overall trajectory of individuals. However, it is unable to show how the individual is only definable in terms of a time-bound trajectory, rather than by its moment-by-moment embodiments (Lemke 1995a: 113–115; Salthe 1993: 260). Our material embodiment locates us in the primary structure (Harré 1983: 66) of Newtonian space-time; in this perspective, the individual is a mere point location on a physical grid. The work of Lakoff and Johnson goes to considerable lengths to discuss the internal dynamics of the neural architecture of individuals. However, the focus on embodiment *per se*, rather than on time-bound trajectories as the seat of individual identity and agency, prevents the theory of embodied realism from considering the ways in which trajectories, unlike our moment-by-moment embodiment, can interact with other trajectories so that trajectories are able to dialogically engage with and interpenetrate with each other across diverse semiotic scales in ecosocial space-time;
- The text-time of logogenesis would be a local cogent moment of a trajectory in which, as in a conversation between two or more individuals, the trajectories of the individuals involved are dialogically intertwined with each other. Any text which results from this

interaction can be seen as a textual record or product of this encounter between trajector-ies. From the higher-scalar vantage point of someone who is in a position "not available to us mortals" to observe the entire trajectory of an individual, along with its dialogically constituted entwinements with others' trajectories, the life-span trajectory which would come into view, now seen from its beginning to its end as a single totalizing "moment", could be seen as an heteroglossic assemblage of that trajectory's engagements with and adaptive modifications of the discursive voices articulated and engaged with along the trajectory. Any given act of meaning-making can be seen as a local twist or turn in the overall trajectory. It is the organism *qua* dissipative structure which embodies its trajectory. Moreover, it is this material embodiment, which is the dissipative structure, which enables one's trajectory – i.e. the self – to be connected to other such structures through the yet higher-scalar trajectory in terms of which they cohere;

• The progressive integration along an individual's trajectory of perceptual-motor, con-ceptual, and social semiotic categories means that the individual is able to access more phase states. In other words, he is she is able to access and enter into meaningful relations with other trajectories. The possession of symbolic categories means that the individual can access a greater variety of structures than can an organism which is in possession of iconic and indexical categories only. That is, the trajectory integrates increasing levels of specification (e.g. the presupposition-cum-implication hierarchy of icon, index, and symbol) so that less specified Gestalt, sensori-motor, and other forms of embodied cat-egorization are integrated with the symbolic categories emanating from the higher-scalar ecosocial semiotic level and its much slower dynamics.

2 Towards an ecosocial semiotic account of metaphor

2.1 Rethinking the implications of embodied realism for metaphor in language: a systemic-functional view

Lakoff and Johnson (1999: 58–59) argue that metaphor is not so much a mode of speech as a mode of thought. Thus, linguistic metaphors are manifestations of sensori-motor schemata and the resulting thought processes, which can, in themselves, be metaphorical. I do not disagree with the argument that metaphor is not specific to language as a semiotic modality, or that meanings on lower integrative levels – e.g. our sensori-motor interactions with the world and the resulting conceptual structures – can be metaphorical in character. Indeed, the evidence provided by Lakoff and Johnson convincingly shows that metaphor is a pervasive mode of organization of our ways of making sense of our embodied relations to our material and social environments at all levels in the specification hierarchy of iconic, indexical, and symbolic modes of meaning making. Nevertheless, there are a number of areas in which the relationship between language and sensori-motor schemata requires more careful theoretical elaboration. I shall now summarize these areas of concern as follows.

Linguistic metaphor does not derive from or merely manifest more basic conceptual struc-tures. This formulation assumes that linguistic metaphor depends on lower-level sensori-motor properties without explaining how the higher-level properties of language themselves constitute a reorganization of the lower levels. Furthermore, higher levels cannot be reduced to lower levels. Lakoff and Johnson's theory seems to regard the sensori-motor level as a supervenience base which includes sensori-motor schemata and subjective experience. Conceptual metaphor is explained in terms of these components and the relationships between them. However, lin-guistic metaphor is not supervenient on this lower level. The implicit assumption that linguistic metaphor exists in a relation of supervenience dependency to this lower level cannot explain how language, and, therefore, linguistic metaphor, is dependent on the relations between lan-guage system and its higher-scalar ecosocial environment. Metaphor in language is dependent on its ecosocial environment and cannot be reduced to – either causally or explanatorily – its lower-level sensori-motor schemata.

The problem raised in the previous paragraph raises the question as to the relationship between the conceptual structures discussed by Lakoff and Johnson and metaphor in semiotic modalities such as language and depiction. The primary metaphors based on sensori-motor interactions with the world and linguistic metaphor can be viewed in terms of the specification hierarchy of integrative levels (chapter 1, section 3). Thus, conceptual structures are located on the less specified inner integrative levels whereas fully symbolic semiotic systems such as language and depiction are located on more specified outer integrative levels. Higher levels are more specified levels in which increasingly specific constraints come into view (Salthe 1993: 64). The emergence of higher levels such as language always presupposes the existence of lower, more general conceptual levels. With respect to the conceptual level, language is an outermost level which is conceptually subordinated to the more schematic categories of the inner level of the conceptual structures based on sensori-motor experience (Salthe 1993: 64).

The meanings – the conceptual structures – derived from sensori-motor experience are largely implicit, procedural forms of knowledge. Procedural knowledge, which is based on activity, is iconic and indexical in character (chapter 3, section 5). On the other hand, language and depiction implicate symbolic systems of possibilities which are not tied to the organism's here-now interactivity with its material environment. Instead, the symbolic possibilities of language provide the organism with increased categorial reach over diverse space-time scales. In this regard, it is important to insist on the fact that language, unlike sensori-motor activity, is discourse.

Linguistic metaphor does not simply manifest lower-level conceptual structures. Instead, metaphor in language and depiction semiotically reorganizes and integrates lower-level conceptual structures to principles of organization that are specific to the higher-level ecosocial semiotic system. In terms of the Principle of Alternation (chapter 9, section 5), sensori-motor interactions and schemata constitute lower-level informational variety which is reorganized as meaning on the higher level of language or depiction. Such reorganization takes place in terms of the properties which are specific to the higher level. The fact that linguistic form and function interfaces with and is in many respects organized in terms of the discourse level of organization further implicates that linguistic metaphor is integrated to the discourse functions of language. For this reason, metaphor cannot be adequately explained in terms of sentence-based linguistic formalisms such as the traditional Subject-Predicate relation. Halliday and Matthiessen (1999: 238–242) show how the ideational grammatical form that is characteristic of nominalization has implications that go beyond the experiential meaning of the metaphor *per se* (e.g. Figure-as-Participant). For example, the construing of a figure as a participant has implications for the textual organization of discourse and therefore for the ways in which discourse organizes the knowledge states of interactants through choices in Theme-Rheme and Given-New.

Consider, for example, the following passage in which the example from *Time* that I analysed earlier occurs. Once again, I shall focus on the nominal group which I analysed above as an instance of experiential metaphor with the meaning figure-as-participant. Here is the text in question:

A senior Alliance official told TIME that the Alliance now controls the northwest and has advanced as far south as Pul-I-Khumri – 100 miles away from the capital, Kabul. The official said Taliban soldiers stranded in Kunduz and further east in Taloquan have been cut off from fresh supplies. On Saturday the Alliance launched an assault near Taloquan, hoping to seize the heavily defended city and then coordinate its forces with those moving east from Mazar to strangle the Taliban in Kunduz. If Kunduz falls, the rebels will hold nearly all of northern Afghanistan.

The war's action may be shifting south. Late last week both sides mobilized in preparation for a trench battle for control of the air base at Bagram – the front north of Kabul.

[Source: "The Afghan way of war" by Romesh Ratnesar, *TIME*, 19 November 2001, p. 31]

The nominal group *The war's action* is Theme in its clause. The metaphorical packaging of a figure in a nominal group enables the meaning of a figure to be mapped onto the textual meaning that Halliday and Matthiessen (1999: 239) gloss as "backgrounded as point of departure". This is the meaning associated with Theme in the English clause. The grammatical resources of nominalization therefore allow an entire semantic figure to be used as the point of departure for the further informational development of the clause in its discourse context. The choice of a given item as Theme (realized by first position in the English clause) also positions that item as Given. That is, the given item is presented as something which is already known and can therefore be used as the local point of departure in the clause for the development of the new information in the remainder of the clause (Halliday and Matthiessen 1999: 239). In the text cited above, we can see this principle at work. The thematized nominal group *The war's action* is the local point of departure for the development of new information not only in its clause, but also in the paragraph which this clause initiates. The nominal group *The war's action* refers to a series of military actions by both the rebel northern alliance and the Taliban forces in the war in Afghanistan between October and November 2001. The nominal group refers to a series of actions by both sides which were introduced as new information in the preceding paragraph. When we get to the beginning of the new paragraph, this information is no longer presented as new, but as given. It is placed in Theme position as a nominalized figure which condenses the various actions referred to previously in a number of different clauses into a single nominalized figure. This thematized figure in turn serves to background the information from the previous paragraph as a stable point of anchorage for the development of a further pulse of new information in the remainder of this clause. In this case, the choice of *The war's action* as Theme serves to foreground the selection of *shifting south* at the end of this clause as the new information which is being presented in the discourse context for the first time. And this is what happens in the remainder of this paragraph, which focuses on presenting and developing further aspects of the meanings associated with *shifting south*.

Finally, the view that metaphor in language is merely a manifestation of non-linguistic thought or conceptual structures fails to account for the ways in which language itself is deeply and non-trivially implicated in many – not all – forms of higher-order or symbolic thought and action to the extent that much of our conscious higher-order thinking takes place in and through language. This further implies that symbolic thought and consciousness are structured by and mediated by our participation in discursive activities involving language and other symbolic modalities of semiosis.

2.2 From Edelman's general cognitive mechanisms as providing the basis for linguistic structures to a three-level account of language as emergent between the body-brain and the ecosocial system

Edelman claims that "linguistic categories naturally show strong structural resemblances to their underlying cognitive models" (1992: 247). Edelman bases this claim on the ways in which linguistic structures are built up from the pre-existing conceptual structures that are embodied in individuals in the theory of cognitive semantics developed by Lakoff and Johnson (e.g. 1999):

> In this view of cognitive semantics, linguistic categories naturally show strong structural resemblances to their underlying cognitive models. Language makes use of general cognitive mechanisms to construct propositional models, image schematic models, metaphoric models, and metonymic models. As we have said, metaphoric models involve a mapping from a structure in one domain to a corresponding structure in another domain. This mapping involves either propositional or image schemas. Metonymic models use these schemas and metaphor to map a function from one element of a model to another (for example, a part-whole relationship).
>
> (Edelman 1992: 247)

Presumably, embodied pre-conceptual structures of the kind proposed by Edelman are high-level cognitive schemas which have a neural basis and which generalize over the linguistic schemas which ultimately derive from these, according to this theory. The linguistic schemas, so derived, are lower-level, more specific instantiations of these embodied pre-linguistic conceptual schemas. The high-level schemas are both more abstract and more general than their lower-level, more specific instantiations (Langacker 1987: 68; Davidse 1991: 12). Edelman's high-level conceptual or cognitive structures are fully functional structures in their own right. However, their schematic status means that they are less "semantically" specified than the more detailed lower-level linguistic structures that derive from them. While it is correct to say that the conceptual structures postulated by Lakoff and Johnson generalize over a number of more specific, lower-level experiential constructions in the experiential grammar of the clause, this schematic relationship between high-level sensori-motor schema (conceptual structures) and lower-level linguistic ones, still does not tell us **how** the lower-level linguistic categories derive from the conceptual structures based on sensori-motor schemata. For instance, how are the latter re-categorized or reorganized as specifically linguistic schemas? Where does lexicogrammar come into the picture?

The argument that "Language makes use of general cognitive mechanisms to construct propositional models" suggests that language emerges from lower-level embodied sensori-motor schemas as their further progression. This argument further implies that individuals progress from being isolated organisms who undergo sensori-motor interactions with the world to organisms who possess language. This is a two-level view in which language is focal on level L at the same time that level L–1 sensori-motor interactions are the lower-level constituents on which language is founded. However, this view neglects the ways in which higher-scalar ecosocial semiotic processes on level L+1 represent selectional constraints on the ways in which linguistic processes on level L make use of the affordances they have on account of their lower-level L–1 constituents. The point is that there is not a progression – either phylogenetic or ontogenetic – from sensori-motor schemata to linguistic ones as such; instead, the progression is from lower-scalar sensori-motor dynamical processes (level L–1) to higher-scalar ecosocial dynamical processes (level L+1) to the emergence of a more specified **intermediate** level of linguistic organization (level L) between these two. The progression is not from the sensori-motor dynamics of the isolated organism to the emergence of language in the organism. Instead, there are **already existing** higher-scalar ecosocial environments which constrain and select the ways in which language emerges as an intermediate level of organization **between** lower-scalar bodily processes and higher-scalar ecosocial ones (chapter 9, section 11). Language is, then, a more specified intermediate level of organization involving the emergence of more organized levels of expression and content between sensori-motor and ecosocial dynamical processes. Therefore, the logical progression is not from the sensori-motor level to the linguistic level, but from the sensori-motor-ecosocial to the sensori-motor-phonological-lexicogrammatical-semantic-ecosocial. In this way, we can see how both the expression stratum of phonology and content stratum of lexicogrammar are more specified intermediate levels of organization which emerge between the organismic and the ecosocial scales as a consequence of the ways in which sensori-motor and neural dynamics on the organismic scale are entrained to higher-scalar ecosocial dynamics and consequently reorganized.

The fact that language has evolved in our species, along with the fact that some design parameters – e.g. stratification and metafunctionality – appear to be universal features of all human languages can therefore be seen not as the result of a lower-scalar genetic or other cause, but because our body-brain dynamics have co-evolved with these higher-scalar ecosocial systems and in ways which entrain the former to the latter. In such a view, it becomes easier to see how features like stratification and metafunctionality have evolved in relation to (1) the ways in which language connects body-brain processes to larger-scale ecosocial semiotic ones (stratification) (see Thibault 2004a: 39–46) and (2) the functionally diverse ways in which language acts on and construes its environment (metafunctionality) (Halliday 1979a; chapter 1, section 3). This view contrasts with the focus on rule-governed syntactical constraints in formalist theories of language. Such theories emphasize the relatively sparse connections between the "frozen islands" of "sparse standing constraints such as 'article + noun' in English" (Beaugrande 1997: 37, 52). Such formal constraints, isolated from both body-brain and ecosocial system, do not connect up with the ways in which language emerged as an intermediate level of organization between the organismic and ecosocial levels (chapter 2, section 10; chapter 9, section 11).

The first point I should like to draw attention to here is the experiential bias of the model of language in question. That is, the various up-down, part-whole, container, and link schemas postulated by Lakoff and Johnson as being rooted in human bodily experience and as constituting the pre-existing conceptual structures on which linguistic categories are modelled are overwhelmingly derived from just one of the functions which motivate linguistic and other semiotic forms, viz. the experiential or representational function of language. This aspect of meaning is concerned with the way reality is semantically analysed into a number of parts which function together to form some larger experiential whole. Lakoff's proposed image schemas are considerably less concerned with **interpersonal** interaction. That is, the experiential bias of the proposed image schemas does not account for those aspects of meaning which are specifically concerned with interacting with and orienting to others. They do not specify how the schemas are deployed in interaction so as to act on and affect other persons. Finally, Lakoff's image schemas do not specify how these are connected to context through the use of linking relationships.

A further problem lies in the fact that the conceptual structures postulated by Lakoff and Johnson, along with Edelman's incorporation of these into his biological theory of consciousness, remain static and tied to the individual self. They do not show how bodily schemas are dynamically organized in temporally unfolding interaction as bodies orient to and interact with each other in socially defined space-time. In other words, they are insufficiently dialogic or other-oriented at the same time that there is insufficient attention to temporal dynamics.

The processes involved are fundamentally dialogic or interpersonal in character. This means that "individual" consciousness is integrated to shared dialogic structures which enable the construction of joint perceptions through individuals' entrainment to and participation in the same higher-scalar system of interpretance. Moreover, the existence of socially coordinated dialogic structures implicates the fact that individual participants have differing perceptions and viewpoints. The proto-semiotic dialogue structures of primary intersubjectivity suggest that the newborn's consciousness is continuous with that of the mother. There is, at this stage, no clear cut distinction between the two: the infant's developing consciousness is closely dependent on the socioaffective flows characteristic of the mother–infant dyad (chapter 3, section 2). The dyad is based on topological-continuous variation such that there is no strong insulation of the child's self from the mother's. It is only when the child begins to be entrained into the typological-categorial distinctions of language and other symbolic resource systems that he or she develops a consciousness of him- or herself as having a distinct consciousness which is separate from that of the mother (chapter 3, section 3).

The emphasis that Lakoff and Johnson place on our embodied interactions with the physical environment as being primary is fundamentally misplaced. In the words of Lakoff and Johnson: "Meaning has to do with the ways in which we function meaningfully in the world and make sense of it via bodily and imaginative structures" (1999: 78). Earlier in the same book, Lakoff and Johnson argued that "most [of our categories, PJT] are formed automatically and unconsciously as a result of functioning in the world" (1999: 18). Moreover, Lakoff and Johnson argue: "it is not just that our bodies and brains determine *that* we will categorize; they also determine what kinds of categories we will have and what their structure will be" (1999: 18). The "world" remains an underspecified notion in Lakoff and Johnson's account. There is no sense of the "world" *qua* ecosocial semiotic system or *Umwelt* which acts as a system of contextual constraints or boundary conditions on the lower-scalar level of the body-brain so as to give rise to categorizations as a consequence of the self-organizing processes that are engendered by the interaction of higher-scalar contextual constraints (cf. the world) and lower-scalar biological initiating conditions (cf. body and brain). Rather, Lakoff and Johnson use a strongly causal language to argue that bodies and brains "determine" both *that* we categorize and *what* we categorize. The fact that the body-brain complex and its functioning is contextually dependent on its higher-scalar environments is underplayed to the point of being a negligent factor in Lakoff and Johnson's account. Instead, categories are seen as supervenient with respect to bodies and brains *qua* supervenience base. However, categories are no less dependent on a higher-scalar environment *qua* thirdness which mediates the body-brain's transactions with the world. The (re)organization of neural activity across diverse timescales can only be meaningful to the self if the appropriate self-environment transactions occur and are maintained over the time-bound trajectory of the self.

Human cognitive and semiotic structures and processes are, above all, founded on our earliest, always embodied, **interpersonal** transactions with other, more senior members of our species (see chapter 1, section 3; chapter 3, section 2), as well as the body-brain's predisposition to interpersonal transactions from the outset of the individual's life. That is, category formation is an emergent consequence of essentially transindividual processes. Lakoff and Johnson remain focused on experiential categorization, which may (wrongly) suggest an individual basis to category formation. This experiential and individual bias is evident in the arguments that Lakoff and Johnson propose as to how we develop an "embodied realism" of basic level categories:

> Why has metaphysical realism been so popular over the centuries? Why is it so common to feel that our concepts reflect the world as it is – that our categories of mind fit the categories of the world? One reason is that we have evolved to form at least one important class of categories that optimally fit our bodily experiences of entities and certain extremely important differences in the natural environment – what are called *basic-level categories*.
>
> Our perceptual systems have no problem distinguishing cows from horses, goats from cats, or elephants from giraffes. In the natural world, the categories we distinguish among most readily are the folk versions of biological general categories, namely, those that have evolved significantly distinct shapes so as to take advantage of different features of their environments. Go one level down in the biological hierarchy and it is a lot harder to distinguish one species of elephant from another . . . It's the same for physical objects. It's easy to tell cars from boats or trains, but a lot less easy to tell one kind of car from another.
>
> Consider the categories *chair* and *car*, which are "in the middle" of the category hierarchies *furniture-chair-rocking chair* and *vehicle-car-sports car*. In the mid–1970's, Brent Berlin, Eleanor Rosch, Carolyn Mervis, and their coworkers discovered that such mid-level categories are cognitively "basic" – that is, they have a kind of cognitive priority, as contrasted with "superordinate" categories like *furniture* and *vehicle* and with "subordinate" categories like *rocking chair* and *sports car*.
>
> (Lakoff and Johnson 1999: 26–27)

The mid-level categories of differences in the physical world reflect an experiential bias which requires correction. Whether the categories in question are perceptual-motor or symbolic (e.g. semantic) categories, it is important to point out that they are built up through processes of interacting with a given ecosocial environment. The notion of basic-level categories certainly makes it clear that categories do not randomly vary from biological individual to biological individual; nor are they exactly the same for all individuals. However, perceptual categories, like symbolic (e.g. semantic) categories, reflect patterns of interactions between individuals and the higher-scalar environments in which they are embedded. Perceptual categories, for example, will reflect patterns which are typical of the kinds of environment-organism transactions that a given species engages in. For this reason, it is not entirely accurate to insist in any absolute way on the "uniqueness" of conscious experience for such experience always involves higher-order representations in the individual's brain of the environment-organism patterns referred to above.

Human consciousness at all levels from perceptual to symbolic is embedded in, and is a part of, higher-scalar ecosocial semiotic systems and their dynamical, time-bound processes. Individual consciousness is not simply the result of a body-brain interacting with the physical world. Instead, it is constrained by higher-scalar biological (epigenetic and evolutionary) constraints that integrate individuals to the physical-material and semiotic-discursive dimensions of their ecosocial semiotic environments. An overemphasis on the "uniqueness" of individual consciousness can only fail to take account of the higher-scalar systems in which consciousness is necessarily embedded and in terms of which it makes sense. Human beings do not in the first instance develop ideational categorizations of the world. Humans develop initially in and through their participation in **interpersonal-social** relations. Furthermore, cognition and meaning are founded on the increasingly higher-order representations of these always situated interpersonal transactions. Humans are epigenetically adapted to interact with other humans; their interaction with nonhuman objects emerges from and is built upon the early interpersonal dyads which semiotically mediate the infant's interactions with the social environment. Moreover, linguistic and other modalities of symbolic projection constitute resources for operating on representations of interpersonal relations involving self and other, as well as the possibilities for ideationalizing or interpersonalizing self–other transactions.

3 The metaphorical reopening of embodiment across scalar levels: creating links between body-brain system, meaning, and world

In this section, I shall propose, with reference to the example examined in chapter 10, section 6, some possible relationships between the sensori-motor and symbolic levels of interaction. I shall begin by noting that the act of giving something to another person in the material sense entails some sort of forceful interaction, as the Giver acts on the object and transfers it to the Receiver. That is, it is based on sensori-motor activity. To give something means generating the right kinds of movements in particular situations in order to accomplish the desired goal. The act of giving some object provides the individual organism with information about his or her movements in interaction with the world of the nonself. Through processes of neuronal group selection, the reiterative, correlated reentry of movements and their perceptual consequences, infants in the first instance come to apply categories of knowledge. They learn, for example, how much force is required to extend their hand towards some object, in synergy with movements of their legs, heads, and postural stability, all of which entail the scaling of forces in order to bring about some forceful interaction with the environment, including social others. In learning to control forces through the sensori-motor activity of the body, more general categories such as that of "force in general" emerge. In this way, we build up sensori-motor schemata which pervade and are integrated to higher-order symbolic thinking and language. We come to understand and categorize the world through our sensori-motor explorations of and interactions with it.

In the first instance, we understand the experiential structure of the act of giving something because we have acted upon and felt such acts and their consequences. But these embodied experiences and the categories – the schemata – built up and elaborated on the basis of these experiences carry over into other domains of experience and activity. This is where metaphor comes into the picture. In the example examined in chapter 10, section 6, we see how the use of hand-arm movement in the physical act of giving extends to the mental domain. Mental processes and the phenomena of higher-order consciousness are related to bodily activities. As I said earlier, the meaning-making resources afforded by our bodies – in particular the many degrees of topological differentiation that the hands and face are capable of making – can be reorganized on higher levels such that emergent new levels of meaning enable us to elicit new categorial distinctions and new possibilities for (inter)action from previously stable and predictable domains of experience. Through the many degrees of freedom of these embodied capacities, human beings can analyse and then synthesize in novel and creative ways selected aspects of their environments. This extended semiotic capacity – linguistic, visual, kinesic – has brought about an enormous expansion in our exploratory capacity and hence in our possibilities for creative adaptation and modification. As we shall see more fully below, this is due to the semiotic reorganization that takes place across levels in the scalar hierarchy of semiotic relations.

In this view, thinking can be regarded as an abstracted form of exploration and manipulation, **without** the need for sensori-motor activity. Thought is semiotic activity, realized by neural processes, in which sensori-motor activity is inhibited and reentrantly turned "inwards" to what we construe in our folk-psychological accounts as an epistemically private mental domain. Nevertheless, thinking **is** activity (Thelen and Smith 1994: 336–337). Thought is neither abstract nor de-contextualized; it does not exist separately from the meaning-making practices in which the body-brain is embedded in its higher-scalar ecosocial environment (chapter 5, section 7). The metaphorical expansion of the meaning potential of our example from the realm of concrete sensori-motor activity to that of abstract mental activity highlights the way in which language brings new phenomena, new domains of experience into existence. In enabling differentiated action and thought, language transforms and renews human experience. The mental and the psychological domains are thus seen as metaphorical transforms and further specifications of embodied sensori-motor activity and the schemata that are derived from this.

This process enables us to make the world we share with others out of the undifferentiated and unlabelled topological-continuous variation in which we are immersed. We make both our *Innenwelt* and our *Umwelt* in and through our semiotically mediated interactions with the unknown – in the first instance, with the resources of our hands and face – in order to differentiate and hence to manipulate things, to alter their perceptual-action characteristics and possibilities, and, above all, to endow them with value. When Ilyenkov observes that "Thinking is not the *product* of an action but the *action itself*, considered at the moment of its performance" (1977 [1974]: 35; italics in original), I believe that he is drawing attention to the embodied and contextualized nature of thought. The fact that, in thinking, overt sensori-motor activity is inhibited leads one wrongly to suppose that thought itself is abstract. However, both concrete sensori-motor action and intervention in the physical environment and abstract action and intervention in thought – e.g. thought about action and its consequences in the absence of action and its consequences – are always part of a larger loop which extends beyond the individual into a higher-scalar ecosocial environment (chapter 5, section 7). Further, as the experiential structure of the metaphor in the example in chapter 10, section 6 reveals, the manner in which we conduct our abstract exploration appears to be tightly linked to the material and verbal actions in and through which we mediate our interactions with both the material world and the social world of other persons. This link between abstract and concrete modes of exploration is also shown in the ways in which "thinking" is tightly linked to physiological structures of the brain as is the manner in which we move and interact with the physical environment, as evidenced by the relatively high proportion of the cerebral cortex devoted to the face and hands (Thelen and Smith 1994: 136–137).

Rather than the computational and cognitivist view of concepts as symbolic structures that transcend specific experience, but which interpret and classify experience, Edelman's Theory of Neuronal Group Selection allows for a view in which context and diversity are the basis of acting, knowing, and meaning. In Edelman's theory, it is time-bound reentrant maps that make and manifest knowledge and meaning in the individual. Perceptual-motor categories are the foundation of cognitive and semiotic development and are a specific case of pattern formation. The task facing the infant is to reduce the many degrees of freedom of the external world – the potentially indeterminate and undifferentiated mass of stimuli – by forming perceptual categories. They must do the same for their internal worlds – the no less indeterminate nature of their joints and muscles – by seeking patterns of motor coordination and control. At the same time, they must match their internal dynamics to those of the world around them. In other words, they must make their perceptual categories and their action categories congruent in order to function in flexible, adaptive ways.

Thus, pattern formation or categorization refers to the processes whereby heterogeneous elements self-organize to produce coherence in time and space. Such patterns are dynamic – whether fleeting or stable, they are time-dependent. Metaphor is crucial to this process. Saying that the process is time-dependent means that it has not only a here-now, but also a past (a history) and a future. Metaphor emerges on the basis of the dynamics of perception, action, and meaning-making in real time (chapter 10, section 2). The neural processes – the cross-modal reentrant mappings of actions and perceptions – constitute a form of dynamic pattern formation. In this way, the categories of sensori-motor activity and exploration form the developmental core of higher mental functions, including language and its metaphorical expansions.

In my view, the pervasive nature of metaphor as a means of construing experience and interacting with others probably has its basis in the following claims made by Edelman (1989, 1992) concerning the nature of category formation in the central nervous system. First, the degenerate nature of the system ensures that a diversity of disjunctive samplings of some perceptual or other stimulus are mapped together in the real-time pick up of environmental information. It is this diversity of possible input which constitutes the primitive basis on which cross-domain connectivity can occur. Secondly, categories emerge on the basis of the reentrant (second-order) mapping of these separate samplings of the stimulus. Thirdly, reentrant mapping is based on the perceptual cross-modal correlations that exist in real time among the disjunctive inputs. Fourthly, in reentry both perception and activity are entirely inter-dependent such that the perceptual pick up of stimulus information depends on the organism's active exploration of the environment. Perception and action are, therefore, always tightly cross-coupled as one seamless overall process in time. In my view, it is this cross-coupling of perception and action which is the precursor of the metafunctional organization of more specified symbolic forms of semiosis. I shall develop this point more fully below. Fifthly, the overall system of relations always entails variation at all levels. In many respects, chapter 6 is an extended exploration of these five points.

On the L–1 level of the initiating conditions, there are many-to-one interactions with the L level; on the L+1 level of the boundary conditions there are also many-to-one interactions with the L level. The inherently cross-modal nature of the disjunctive samplings itself provides a means whereby, through reentry, a given domain can be understood in terms of another. For example, a material process of giving an object to another person can be used as a metaphor for the mental process of acquiring an understanding of something (see chapter 10, section 6).

The key to this principle is that mutually disjunctive maps derived from independent sam-plings – e.g. action and perception – are connected by reentry to form a higher-order mapping. For example, tracking with the eyes and moving the head-body in the same direction. Features of the tracked object are correlated with features of the sensori-motor activity involved in the movement that is deployed to track the object. The two sets of features are, in turn, correlated so that a new higher-order mapping is assembled from the two independent, first-order dis-junctive mappings. This higher-order mapping selectively strengthens the connections between the two pathways and leads to the building up of sensori-motor schemata or perception-action categories. The neural dynamics described here are a concrete illustration of ways in which a newly emergent level of organization in the dynamics of the system functions to reorganize variety on the level below as meaning for the level above. Thus, the ambient stimulus flux of energy on level L–1 is a vague and indeterminate source of stimulus information about environmental events. On level L, independent sensori-motor samplings of this environmental information yield mutually disjunctive mappings of perceptual information. On level L+1, these separate, modality-specific samplings are reentrantly correlated so as to produce a higher-scalar reentrant mapping in the way described above. The building up of perception-action categories in this way is therefore shown to be an example of semiotic reorganization across a given triplicate of levels.

Recent research in neurophysiology and developmental studies questions the view that the primary developmental task is the construction of an integrated reality from distinct and modu-lar perceptual-motor sources of stimulus information (Thelen and Smith 1994: 189). Instead, there is rich interconnectivity between modalities from the very earliest stages of development. This interconnectivity does not imply that perceptual information is not also separated into separate modalities in diverse functional areas in the brain. The point is that a growing body of evidence indicates that there is no localized region in the brain where multimodal representa-tions are stored; instead, this is achieved by on-line communication between diverse modal systems in the brain. The observations made by Thelen and Smith indicate that inter-modal connections are a fundamental feature of neural functioning and design from the very earliest stages, both phylogenetically and ontogenetically. The evidence marshalled by Thelen and Smith, both from their own research, as well as that of many other researchers, suggests that both the elementary mental functions and the elementary forms of proto-semiosis that infants engage in have a biogenetic foundation (Hasan 1992b: 522). Moreover, both these elementary mental functions and the elementary forms of semiosis are fundamentally multimodal in char-acter. Thelen and Smith point out that a growing body of evidence indicates "strong intermodal linkages in newborns and young infants, long before the gradual process of assimilation and accommodation posited by Piaget would allow these coordinations to develop" (1994: 191).

Examples include the ways in which newborns orient to the spatial location of a heard sound. It is the cross-modal integration of "brightness" and "loudness" which orients the infant to the stimulus (see also Halliday 1993: 95). Furthermore, it is, Thelen and Smith point out, with reference to the research of Turkewitz and colleagues, quantitative variation in the intensity of stimuli "e.g. loudness, brightness, and so on" which is the basis of this cross-modal unity.

Intensity is a question of topological-continuous variation, which is iconic in character. Thelen and Smith sum up these findings in the following way:

> there are two truths about the organization of the perceptual system. First are the separate qualitatively dissimilar "takes" on the physical world that are the separate modalities. Second, up and down the system, at all levels of complexity, and from the beginning of development, are the multiple interactions between these parallel and disjunctive processing systems. The developmental significance lies in the two truths considered jointly. The engine behind development must be the reciprocal education of the heterogeneous yet continuously interacting systems, and the generation of new forms made possible by the self-organizing dynamics of such a system.
>
> (Thelen and Smith 1994: 191)

For Thelen and Smith, inter-modal integration of perceptual-motor information is the very engine of development, rather than its by-product (1994: 192). It is the cross-modal integration of such information in the real-time performance of some activity in context which explains how perception-action categories are built up. Drawing on Edelman's theory of neuronal group selection, Thelen and Smith propose that "cross-modal features that are continually and reliably associated in the real world will become stable and persistent basins of attraction" (1994: 193). In this way, features which are regularly associated are strengthened in the neural connections and consequently built up in memory as integrated categories of perception and action. These multimodal neural connections therefore constitute the primordial foundation on which multiple contextual redundancies are built up in multimodal forms of textual and discursive activity.

We can conjecture at this point that the metaphorical shift from the material to the verbal and mental domains in the example which was the focus of the discussion in chapter 10, section 6, itself provides us with a glimpse into the emergence of symbolic thought. But let us start from the material end and trace this chain of logical implications through from beginning to end. The material (not linguistic) act of giving an object to another person brings about concrete physical changes which both the giver and the receiver, along with other observers, can perceive. The end result of that activity is both the physical displacement of some object or commodity along a trajectory (from Giver to Receiver) as well as a change in both the person who gives the object and the person who comes to possess it. It is in the perceiving of this result and the reentrant mapping of this perception back onto the activity which engendered the perception that we develop an awareness of the potential significance of such perception-action complexes for our interactions with others. In the first instance, this awareness is founded on our understanding that more than Newtonian causality is involved. The action *qua* action is not reducible to the physical movements whereby an object is physically displaced from one position to another. The physical movement alone does not explain the way in which the behaviour is constrained by meaningful mental content which can be relatable to an intentional source (Juarrero 1999: 96). In other words, the material action in question is semantically construable as an instance of an act-type which is recognizable in the culture.

The next step concerns the shift from the material process to the verbal process in the example that I first analysed in chapter 10, section 6. Once again, acts of speaking are material activities which bring about perceivable concrete changes in the world. There is a difference, however. The act of saying something to another person brings about physical-material responses in other persons; it also brings about internal neuronal activity called thinking, which is not the same as the activity of speaking (or listening) *per se*. Speaking may bring about inner mental changes in others which we cannot observe directly, but which we attribute to others as intentional agents on the basis of what they say and do, including the many often unconscious icons and indexes of inner mental states that we observe in others. In perceiving the consequences of our verbal exchanges for others and reentrantly mapping these back onto our acts of saying, we create signs of inner mental life in our self and in other's bodily activities. Speaking is, of course, much more than the making of physical sounds. Rather, the vocal tract gestures and the resulting speech sounds on level L are understood as semiotically mediated and constrained activity (level L+1) which has its proximate origin at an intentional source in the neurally realized proto-meanings of the agent on level L−1.

The fact that it is so sourceable means that the signs we create of the mental domain are understood to relate intentional source, spoken output (text), and listener as internally related components of a larger relational trajectory in which both inner neural activity and observable activity are understood as being shaped by semiotically mediated mental life which constrains and modulates our actions. The fact that there are a large number of metaphors – lexical and grammatical – in language illustrating the shift I mentioned above from the material domain to the mental domain suggests that, in the first instance, people develop their understanding of the mental domain through the symbolic construal of the physical-material domain, including the observable signs of the body as people engage in reciprocal acts of giving and receiving objects. In the process, they construe contextual redundancies between these observable signs and internal states of the body such that these first-order contextual redundancies are reentrantly mapped as inner mental states. Similarly, the physical ownership by one person of some object and its transfer to another person comes to stand for and is transformed, metaphorically, into a symbolic mental space such that thoughts-cum-commodities are "shared" between minds. In this way, the symbolic construal of mental space in one's self and others may have originally emerged from the observable characteristics of sensori-motor activity and the reentrant mapping of the results of such activity onto the agent's intrinsic neural dynamics. In this way, metaphorical signs can be exchanged between agents about emergent non-symbolic activities of thinking, perceiving, and so on, which are the products of the organism's ongoing interactions with its environment. Here are some examples – again courtesy of President Ronald Reagan – to illustrate this particular semantic syndrome:

> And with this spirit of Thanksgiving *in mind*, I thought I'd speak with you . . . (p. 1)
>   I thought it would be a good opportunity to think and reflect *with you* about those crucial foreign policy matters so much in the news lately. It's also a chance to do something I've wanted to do throughout the course of these events – and that's *share some personal thoughts with you* . . . (p. 7)
>   . . . family is very much *on our minds* during the holidays, . . . (p. 13)
>   Our administration will be *giving these recommendations serious consideration* in the days ahead. (p. 14)
>   . . . we might all do well to *keep our families in mind* . . . (p. 14)
>   Source: President Ronald Reagan, untitled radio address, The Oval Office, 27 December 1986

In the text which we used as the main basis of our discussion in chapter 10, section 6, clause A3a construes a complex experiential semantic space in which distinct type-categories of processes – viz. material, verbal, and mental – are related in an overall topological semantic space. Lakoff and Johnson might say that this complex symbolic construal is itself based on a primary metaphor whereby the act of giving something to someone is modelled on our sensori-motor experience of bodily transactions with and experiences of our physical environment. According to this argumentation, higher-order symbolic meanings are based on and are extensions of our bodily interactions with the physical world that surrounds us. Thus, "giving someone an idea" would have its origins in a sensori-motor schema involving the experience of the physical handing over of some commodity to another person, as well as the physical experience of receiving the object of this physical act. On one level of analysis, the physical movement involved is a global physical stimulus. One set of disjunctive samplings of informational stimuli constitutes an analysis of the various components of the overall visual stimulus, i.e. hand-arm, directional movement of hand-arm, object held in hand, designated recipient of object. A further set of samplings constitutes an analysis of the overall shape of the movement itself rather than its component parts. This second mapping is concerned with the overall action sequence, its vectorial directionality, and its intentionality. Furthermore, the action sequence can be viewed both from the point of view of the person who performs the action and the person who is the recipient. In this way, a model – both analytic and global – is simultaneously constructed in real-time performance by both performers and receivers of the action. As we saw earlier, these two disjunctive samplings of stimulus information are then reentrantly mapped so that a sensori-motor schema – a perception-action category – is formed by the brain. A third mapping, the reentrant one, relates the two mappings to each other.

What we see emerging here is a picture of the ways in which independent, disjunctive samplings of environmental stimulus information yield qualitatively distinct interpretations of this information at the same time that the correlation of the two in real time gives rise to a higher-order mapping of the sensori-motor activity as corresponding to the intentional act of someone giving something to someone else at the same time that the other person (the recipient) responds to this act. The first level – the perceptual stimulus information – is iconic in the sense already defined. That is, stimulus information in the ambient array is iconic to an environmental event. This is stimulus information about a physical event. The intentional content or otherwise of this event is not at issue here. All that matters is the perception of physical movement and its physical consequences according to the tenets of Newtonian efficient causality. On the other hand, the reentrant mapping described above produces an indexical sign of a purposeful social act: the hand-arm movement indexes an intention and a social context of cooperation or mutual give-&-take. This last point serves to highlight a problem in the view that primary metaphor is based on the understanding of subjective experience in terms of sensori-motor experience (Lakoff and Johnson 1999: 45). My point is that the indexical understanding of the sensori-motor act of, say, handing an object to another person, is itself an intentional social-interpersonal act. It is not reducible to the physical interaction between organism and environment *per se*. Moreover, the two disjunctive mappings – respectively, analytic and global – described above reveal the vague outlines of what will later become the distinctive metafunctions on the symbolic level of organization of natural language.

To illustrate this last point, I shall refer once more to our earlier example. The physical act of giving an object to someone may create the conditions for emergent category formation. In visually tracking the object as the hand extends towards the other person, the infant links features of the perceived world with felt bodily movement. In so doing, he or she maps the correlated features of the objects in view – e.g. HAND-ARM MOVEMENT, OBJECT IN HAND, RECIPIENT OF OBJECT, RESPONSE OF RECIPIENT. In this sensori-motor schema, we see the precursors of both the experiential and interpersonal meanings which are realized in the clause grammar of natural language. This analysis is presented in Figure 11.1.

HAND-ARM	MOVEMENT TOWARDS RECIPIENT	SOLID OBJECT HELD IN HAND	RECIPIENT OF OBJECT
Proto-experiential analysis into component parts, based on disjunctive sampling of visual input:			
ACTOR	PROCESS: MATERIAL ACTION	GOAL	BENEFICIARY
Proto-interpersonal synthesis of global shape of intentional act, based on disjunctive sampling of movement performed:			
INTENTIONAL SOURCE / SUBJECT	HERE-NOW GROUNDING OF VECTORIAL INTENTIONAL ACT OF GIVING GOODS-&-SERVICES TO ADDRESSEE		

Figure 11.1 Proto-experiential and proto-interpersonal meaning in hand-arm movement analytically construed in terms of its perceived component parts and globally synthesized as intentionally sourced act of giving

It is the reentrant or second-order mapping of the two disjunctive samplings of the visual and movement modalities which leads to the emergence of the proto-metafunctional organization I have postulated in Figure 11.1. I have not specified the proto-textual metafunction here because this would entail an analysis of the here-now spatio-temporal milieu in which the given act occurs. Clearly, the abstract and de-contextualized nature of the present analysis does not permit this step to be taken. In any case, my main concern is to show how metafunctional organization in symbolic modes of semiosis can be related to less specified perception-action categories on lower integrative levels in the specification hierarchy. The mapping illustrated in Figure 11.1 in turn creates the possibility over time of further mappings. For example, the grasping in the hand and the spatial displacement from one location to another of solid objects or commodities as contrasted with that of non-solid commodities may lead to the formation of the category SOLID vs. NON-SOLID COMMODITIES that can be given. Such category distinctions constitute the ontological basis for the further development of distinctions such as those between the external world of concrete material things and the internal world of abstract thoughts and ideas.

We have already seen that the grammatical metaphor in the clause I analysed in chapter 10, section 6 is based on the multiplying effect of two semantic construals operating simultaneously, viz. material and verbal process-types. The two construals suggest that many cases of grammatical metaphor are higher-order linguistic restructurings of less specified meanings derivable from multiple disjunctive takes on perceptual-action categories at lower, less specified levels of semiosis, as shown in Figure 11.1. This interesting possibility will now be considered in relation to Table 11.1.

Table 11.1 The multiplication of meaning potential in an experiential metaphor, showing levels of implication from stimulus information to mental level

Stimulus information; iconic sign of environmental event				
Sensori-motor schema; embodied indexical sign comprising component parts and global action schema	HAND-ARM	MOVEMENT OF HAND-ARM IN DIRECTION OF OTHER	RECIPIENT OF OBJECT	OBJECT HELD IN HAND
Experiential structure of material process [+ SOLID; EXTERIOR]	[can] you ACTOR	give PROCESS: MATERIAL ACTION	me BENEFICIARY: RECIPIENT	some idea RANGE
Experiential structure of verbal process [–SOLID; EXTERIOR]	[can] you SAYER	tell PROCESS: VERBAL	me TARGET	some idea VERBIAGE/ RANGE
Experiential structure of mental process [– SOLID; INTERIOR]	you AGENT/ KNOWER	make PROCESS: CAUSAL	me SENSER/ KNOWEE	know PROCESS: MENTAL

Table 11.1 is an example of a specification hierarchy. The progression from the first row to the bottom row of the table signifies the integration of vaguer, more general categories to increasingly more specified ones. The vaguer, iconic level of the stimulus information is integrated to the next, more specified, indexical level, where the sensori-motor act is construed as having a more specified contextual significance. The indexical level, in turn, is integrated to the more highly specified symbolic level of the grammatical metaphor under discussion here. In this way, we see more clearly that much of the conventional mental imagery derivable from

sensori-motor experience is already integrated by constraints deriving from the higher-scalar ecosocial level. This integration illustrates the more general principle that lower-level sensori-motor interactions with the physical world cannot directly bring about the higher-scalar symbolic level. The emergence of the latter requires higher-scalar ecosocial boundary conditions which amplify and reorganize lower-scalar sensori-motor activity in ways which lead to the emergence of more specified, intermediate levels of organization. Metaphor is an example of how the self-organizing dynamics of ecosocial semiotic systems yield more specified intermediate levels of organization such as the complex metaphorical space referred to here. Subjective mental experience, according to Lakoff and Johnson, is based to a large extent on the primary metaphors that are construed through the interaction between sensori-motor activity and the physical world. Thus, "understanding an idea" (a subjective experience) can be (metaphorically) understood in terms of "grasping an object" (sensor-motor experience) (Lakoff and Johnson 1999: 45). The component parts of this explanation are a subjective mental component, a biological sensori-motor component, and the physical environment. For Lakoff and Johnson, the fundamental organizational role of intersubjective and dialogical processes is absent (chapter 1, section 3).

What is not explained here is how these variables are anything but proximate activities constituting lower-scalar constraints on behaviour. There is no corresponding explanation as to how the higher-scalar constraints on lower-scalar dynamical processes attract the dynamics of the system to metaphorical transformations on the symbolic level. In order that this may occur, there must be ecosocial semiotic constraints entraining the dynamics of lower levels. The specification hierarchy I have postulated in Table 11.1 does not mean that the lower levels "upwardly" cause the higher ones. Instead, higher levels integrate and reorganize the lower levels on the basis of an overall system of constraints arising from the interactions among all levels. On the other hand, an explanation of metaphor which locates the causal basis of metaphor in the lower levels *per se* is unable to construct the necessary theoretical bridges between the lower- and higher-scalar levels of relations which are required to bring about metaphor in language and other semiotic modalities. In the following section, I shall consider how children's ludic activity functions as a higher-scalar constraint which facilitates metaphorical transformations of action and experience.

4 Proto-metaphor in children's symbolically mediated play activity

In this section, I shall offer some further observations on the instance of "egocentric" speech that I examined in chapter 5. I shall begin by drawing attention to the fact that in that episode no physical-material object in the spatio-temporal purview of the child actually corresponds to the thing which the experiential semantics of the nominal group construes. The child does not use any real cooking oil to add to the imaginary food she is preparing. This fact is of major importance for understanding what is going on in exchanges such as the one under consideration here. (See chapter 5, section 12.2 for the linguistic analysis of the example under consideration.)

The experiential structure of this nominal group construes an instance of a formless and quantifiable substance (cooking oil). However, no such substance is materially present in the physical-material context of the utterance. The absence of any such substance poses no problem for the child; the relationship between the lexicogrammatical form and the (non-existent) substance is a fully motivated one. In other words, the experiential resources of this nominal group are used to construe such a relationship with something that does not, materially speaking, exist. What is going on here? How is the play context relevant to this?

To answer these questions, we need to inquire into a number of grammatical and semantic characteristics of the nominal group. Silverstein (1987) has proposed a two-dimensional hierarchical referential space of noun phrase (nominal group) types in order to specify the systemic possibilities of the nominal group for referring to the universe of extensionables. Silverstein has formulated this referential space in terms of binary intersections of features, as shown in Figure 11.2.

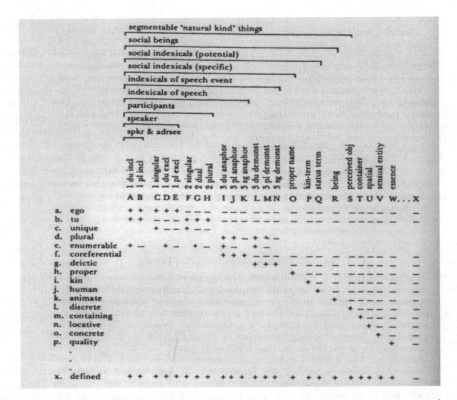

Figure 11.2 Two-dimensional hierarchical referential space of noun phrase types; reproduced from Silverstein 1987: 138

The left-most categories distinguish the categories of PERSON PRONOUNS, specifically the various categories of first and second person. The further to the right we go, the more we move away from such categories of specifically social beings to increasingly abstract entities. The existence of the right-most entities is established by the symbolic coding potential of lexicogrammar itself, rather than by any relationship to indexically presupposable existents in the social and physical-material domains. The nominal group *un po' di olio* does not lie this far to the right in the proposed array. According to Silverstein's schema, its categorial feature specification may be best approximated as [+ discrete; + perceivable, quantifiable, manipulable and edible object]. In comparison, the first person singular pronoun in both English and Italian – viz. *I* and *io* – indexically presupposes the person who utters a token of this pronoun. The first person singular pronoun would have the feature specification [+ ego; + singular]. In terms of the overall referential space of the nominal group, this means that the first person pronouns are maximally transparent to their denoted objects (the persons they refer to in the act of speaking). Maximal transparency means that there is maximal "functional overlap" of both the "indexically presupposing" (endophoric deixis) and the "denotation" (experiential construing) functions (Silverstein, 1987: 160–163). As Silverstein explains, "the person deictics denote by virtue of the fact that they unavoidably index their denotata, which are therefore characterizable as the pragmatic conditions presupposed by these forms" (1987: 161).

There is, however, a further dimension to this question of maximal transparency of sign form. Silverstein distinguishes between the pragmatic and metapragmatic dimensions of extensional reference, as follows:

Indexically, we should note that there are certain indexical presuppositions on the occurrence of a signal *qua* felicitous referring expression and certain indexical entailments as well (empirically testable by the nature of further reference to the object extended, for example, linguistically, with TOPICAL expressions). Metapragmatically, we should note identification of an entity as referent – in this sense, picking it out – distinguishes linguistic extension in particular from any other kind of semiotic act of extension; hence, crucially, the intentional/ purposive signaling act of supplying information (description) about the entity delicately sufficient to the task but not over rich (the latter having its own indexical and metapragmatic characterization along distinct dimensions, such as interpersonal relations, discourse chunking, etc.). It should be clear that, for any act of referring, its reconstruction as a supplying of information of sufficient delicacy so as to identify and hence pick out an entity is a description of an indexically signaling event; that is, it is truly a metapragmatics of a particular sort for the pragmatics of referring, a kind of metalanguage in terms of which the pragmatics of felicitous reference events can be characterized, and hence felicitous extensions *regimented*, at the intentional/purposive level.

(Silverstein 1987: 159)

The issue is the extent to which "pragmatic code" and "metapragmatic code" can be brought into "approximation" in particular instances (Silverstein 1987: 160). In other words, the extent to which the metapragmatic code is transparent to its pragmatic object code. In Silverstein's own words, the former is concerned with "metapragmatic characterizability conditions, in terms of which felicitous identification of referents can be guaranteed as an entailment of use" (1987: 160). Now, it is clear that what we have here is a number of different levels of relationships, proceeding from lower to higher levels of abstraction – from object code to meta-code – or vice versa.

There is no such transparency of metapragmatic-to-pragmatic coding in the case of nominal groups such as *un po' di olio*, which are somewhat more rightward in Silverstein's referential feature space. Nor is there any coincidence of indexical and denotational functions. The Thing element *olio* denotes a particular experiential category of Thing. However, the Thing does not both indexically presuppose and denote its object of reference. Instead, the Thing symbolically construes (names) a type-category of Thing rather than a specific instance which is extendable by the contextualized use of the form. In the present case, there is no indexically presupposed existent in the context which is extendable by the use of the form. In the example, the deictic element and the quantifier function to ground the Thing element as an arbitrary instance of a gradable quantity of the type-category of Thing. Moreover, the nominal group, rather than indexically presupposing the prior existent of its referent in the discourse context, indexically **creates** it. Thus, the referent of the nominal group is brought into existence by the interplay of the symbolic and indexical (deictic) functions within the grammatical structure of the nominal group itself.

The example demonstrates the symbolic, rather than merely indexical, potential of lexicogrammatical forms to create discourse referents in their contexts of use. Linguistics forms are no longer tied to the real-world things they presuppose in a relationship of indexical presupposition (Silverstein 1985: 231). In the example under discussion here, the child has grasped the use of linguistic structures as **symbolic** (not just indexical) means to ends. This is so in two senses. First, the nominal group in question experientially construes its semantically denoted object. That is, the child's uttering of this nominal group indexically creates the object as a discursively grounded instance of the category of Thing denoted by the head noun. The lexicogrammatical form is the means whereby the semantic object-of-consciousness is brought into existence and hence accessed in its context of use. Secondly, the interpersonal-actional semantics of the utterance treats the experientially construed object as the goal of the action which the child performs or enacts by virtue of uttering this token as a form of self-command. That is, the experientially construed oil becomes the goal of the action of self-commanding her self to add the oil to the imaginary meal which she is preparing.

The linguistic act of referring is indexical in the sense that the deictic resources of language point to a particular entity – real or imaginary – in the discourse context as a grounded instance of the type-category of Thing in the nominal group which is selected for the purposes of being referred to and tracked through the discourse as a participant. By the same token, the act of referring is metapragmatic because the resources of the nominal group are being used to categorize and identify the given entity as the instantiation of the type-category of Thing which is specified by the nominal group. In this sense, the nominal group "describes", as Silverstein puts it, the entity which is being referred to. Thus, the indexical event of pointing to a given entity is also a metapragmatic act of categorizing and identifying the given entity as an instantiation of the type-category of Thing which is construed by Thing element in the nominal group. The experiential construal of the entity as an instance of this or that category is thus reconstructable as an intentional/purposive act of supplying information about that entity by virtue of naming or classifying it as an instance of a semantic category of Thing. In this way, the entity is symbolically specified at the same time that it is deictically grounded in some context.

Silverstein's metapragmatic "characterizability conditions" are rules of use which specify the contextual conditions in which "felicitous" acts of referring, in the Austinian parlance, can take place. These conditions are not, for Silverstein, "in" the code of language, but act on it, from the "outside". They are, precisely, "conditions" of use of linguistic forms. In my view, there is a systematic and internal relationship between the stratum of the lexicogrammar and that of the "higher" level discourse semantics and the genre conventions which regulate this. Metapragmatic rules of use can be related to this level.

The "characterizability conditions" are specifiable as genre-specific principles of discourse-level organization, their attendant meaning-making practices, and how these constrain choices on the lexicogrammatical stratum (Thibault and Van Leeuwen 1996). What Silverstein calls "purposive/intentional reconstructability" refers, in actual fact, to the way in which functional semantic distinctions which are construed on the lexicogrammatical stratum are not simply projected in a one-to-one way onto the discourse stratum. No feature on the lexicogrammatical stratum *qua* lexicogrammatical stratum directly participates in the constructing or construing of its context. This level is always mediated by the higher-level discourse semantic stratum. Potentially meaningful selections on the lexicogrammatical stratum are re-combined and re-construed as more global co-patternings of meaning relations on the discourse stratum. This is a dynamic and contingent process, as seen from the real-time perspective of the participants who are jointly making and negotiating meanings in some discourse event. It is a dynamic process of construal and reconstrual of the meaning-making resources of the lower strata at the same time that the resources of these are co-deployed by participants in the making of that social occasion of discourse and/or textual product(s) which result from it (chapter 8, section 5).

In primary intersubjectivity, communication between infant and caretaker is inward directed; it is focused on the socioaffective exchanges between the "you" and the "me" in the dyad (chapter 3). Primary intersubjectivity is characterized by "statements" of emotion based on the "you" and "me" that comprise the dyad (Trevarthen 1987: 187). The primary reality is the embodied connectedness of the "you" and "me" in and through the socioaffective exchange processes which the dyad organizes. Trevarthen describes the emergence of secondary intersubjectivity, which typically occurs around the age of five to six months, as follows:

This is triadic and cooperative play with other things and experiences shared. No longer is communication merely between the two partners [i.e. typically mother and infant, PJT]; it now has an outward direction as well, and functions to bring in topics.

(Trevarthen 1978: 127)

With the emergence of secondary intersubjectivity, the "outward direction" of the communication also entails a reorganization of the implicit meta-rules that govern the communication. This change requires a metacommunicative, if unconscious, awareness that the protolinguistic, and later, the linguistic, signs used to construe "outer" reality (cf. the third person) as instances of semantic categories are of a different level of logical typing than the physical-material objects, events, happenings, and so on, that they construe (chapter 5, section 11). It is significant that Trevarthen, in the above quotation, characterizes secondary intersubjectivity in terms of "triadic and cooperative" play. Triadic play displays proto-experiential characteristics on account of its orientation to third person objects and events. The development described by Trevarthen involves a partial and gradual objectification with respect to the metacommunicative rules which operated in primary intersubjectivity. Play, I argue, provides the ecosystemic mechanism whereby this objectification emerges and further develops (chapter 4, section 1). The emergence of the outward directed proto-experiential metafunction prepares the way for the semiotic reorganization of the material world as symbolically construed objects of reflection and thought.

With the onset of the experiential resources of language, the child's ability to attend to and control these "external" events is massively enhanced and expanded. Outward directed secondary intersubjectivity entails an increasing orientation to social practices, their learning, and re-envoicement in the self-perspective. Linguistically, this means, with the transition to language, an orientation to the "third person" domain of persons, objects, and events that do not constitute the dialogic relationship between "I" and "you" (Halliday 1992: 22). The experiential grammar plays a crucial role here in naming and classifying the phenomena of experience "out there" in the third person domain. This transition represents a significant expansion of the child's world at the same time that some effects of overall "compression" occur in the reorganization of the ecosocial semiotic system inhabited by the child. The semantic resources of the experiential grammar mean that the child is now able to construe and interpret material perturbations in the ambient flux – including the child's own body – in and through a symbolic resource for interpreting reality which the child shares with others. Moreover, the unhinging of the indexically presupposing and denotational functions of the nominal group means that this outward orientation is, in time, extended to semantic things which are created by the lexicogrammatical resources of the nominal group itself, rather than relying on the prior existence of their referents in the material world. Ludic activity has a fundamental role to play in the making of this discovery (chapter 4, section 1).

In all forms of meaning-making, implicit meta-levels function to give the participants instructions as to the appropriate ways in which to understand the meanings made on the first level. It also provides participants with rules for dealing with the paradoxes of logical typing which arise when relating language, say, to the world of objects, events, and so on, which language denotes. In this way, participants understand that a given activity is not what it seems to "denote" – e.g. a task-oriented social act such as preparing a real meal – but is pretence or play (Bateson 1973h [1972]: 153–155). Therefore, individuals learn that language is not identical with the objects, things, persons, actions, happenings, events, and so on, that it denotes. Language and the phenomena that it denotes exist on two different levels of abstraction, or two different levels of logical typing (chapter 5, section 11). Bateson (1973h [1972]: 153) uses Korzybski's (1941) distinction between map and territory to explain how language relates to the objects which it denotes:

> language bears to the objects which it denotes a relationship comparable to that which a map bears to a territory. Denotative communication as it occurs at the human level is only possible *after* the evolution of a complex set of metalinguistic (but not verbalized) rules which govern how words and sentences shall be related to objects and events.
>
> (Bateson 1973h [1972]: 153)

The map is a semiotic reorganization of the territory according to the largely implicit meta-rules of interpretation that specify how the map relates to the territory. This reorganization is possible because map and territory exist on two different orders of abstraction. Bateson (1973h [1972]) has drawn attention to the paradoxical nature of ludic activity. Play has evolved as a mechanism for helping us to deal with and live with the paradoxes which are the stuff of everyday forms of communication. Bateson has shown that play is a prototypical form of activity in humans and other species in which "the actions of 'play' are related to, or denote, other actions of 'not play' " (1973h [1972]: 153). The child learns that map and territory are not the same and that the map itself can be remapped onto the territory in new ways. In the inward looking phase of primary intersubjectivity, map and territory coincide in the sense that topological-continuous variation in the "territory" (socioaffective flows in the dyad) is mapped to topological-continuous in the "map" (iconic signs of interest, attention, mood, and so on). The move into the outward-looking phase of secondary subjectivity brings about a reorganization of the relations between map and territory: topological-continuous variation in the territory is reorganized as typological-categorial distinctions in the map through the intermediate level of linguistic organization. The relationship between these two orders of abstraction can be reconfigured in play so that the signs and actions of play denote signs and actions of "not play". In reconfiguring the map in this way, the territory is itself reconfigured. Just as a map relates to the territory it denotes according to semiotic meta-rules that connect the two levels, the relationship between words and the phenomena of experience is mediated by higher-order meta-rules which implicitly specify (1) that words and the objects and events in the world that words denote are not the same; and (2) how agents can relate the words they use to the world.

In our example, the nominal group *un po' di olio* does not denote a real instance of the type-category of Thing (cooking oil) which is specified in this nominal group. Moreover, the child's activity, itself mediated by this linguistic form, is not a real act of meal preparation, but a pretend act, just as the oil in question is pretend oil, rather than real. The play context suggests that the implicit meta-rules of contextualization for relating words to objects and actions are reorganized. Bateson's discussion of the distinction between map and territory can be reformulated in terms of the three-level hierarchy as follows:

L+1   SI of metalinguistic rules governing how words and sentences relate to objects and events

L   words and sentences of language (map)

L–1   objects and events in the world (territory)

Play is a form of symbolically mediated activity which reorganizes the rules governing the ways in which linguistic and other semiotic forms relate to their objects. It does so by metaphorically connecting words to domains of experience other than those that are normally denoted by the words used. Furthermore, it implies a specific meta-modalization of this relationship as one of pretence. The metaphorical power of this kind of symbolic play lies in the way it exploits the soft coupling of lexicogrammar to semantics (chapter 9, section 1). That is, it exploits the power of the grammar to symbolically construe phenomena of experience as semantic categories rather than directly referring to objects and events in the world. In our example, the child, who was aged just 04.10 when she produced this utterance, has not yet moved into grammatical metaphor. However, she has a sufficient command of the generalizing power of grammatical form such that she can not only construe real physical-material phenomena as instances of this or that semantic category, but she can also use the lexicogrammar to reconstrue phenomena which have no material existence in the situation, or to cross-couple phenomena from different domains of action and experience.

In the animal play discussed by Bateson, the playful nip denotes the bite, but it does not denote what would be denoted by the bite (e.g. aggression). The protolinguistic forms of communication which various nonhuman species have in common with pre-linguistic infants are iconic-indexical in character. Unlike human language, there is no system of lexicogrammatical forms which can be integrated to discourse forms of organization and manipulated to achieve a variable range of contextual effects. The congruent meaning of the nip is "bite" (aggression) in non-play situations. On the other hand, the non-congruent meaning of the nip is "not what the bite denotes". The forms of communication that are evidenced by animal play show only a limited capacity for reflexivity. That is, there is limited scope for metapragmatic criteria of what Silverstein calls "purpose/intentional reconstructability" (see above). On the other hand, the young child in our example uses and contextually manipulates a lexicogrammatical form which allows for the metapragmatic criteria that Silverstein refers to. For this reason, both the child and external observers have the capacity to attribute criteria of intentionality or purposefulness to the speaker of the utterance. In the example, the utterance is perceived as a self-command which functions to coordinate and entrain the child's activity along a particular action trajectory. These observations refer to the interpersonal dimension of the utterance's meaning. In parallel fashion, the experiential semantics of this linguistic form are not limited to the immediate here-now context. If the congruent meaning of *un po' di olio* names an instance of a particular formless and perceivable substance that is used in cooking, the play context exploits the possibilities for symbolic manipulation of this linguistic form to mean things that are not named by the congruent meaning. In this way, the potential for the form to connect with – to contextually redound with – other domains of social practice is enhanced.

Halliday (1998: 192–193) has pointed out that metaphor in language (both lexical and grammatical) is a re-mapping of the semantics onto the lexicogrammar. The metaphorical transformations that occur as a result of these re-mappings depend, as Halliday shows, on the stratal organization of the content plane of language into semantics and lexicogrammar. The stratification of the content plane into semantics and lexicogrammar also involves two different orders of symbolic abstraction, as discussed in chapter 10, section 3 in relation to the Token-Value relation in identifying clauses. Like the map-territory relationship discussed by Bateson, though in infinitely more variable and flexible ways, the relationship between the two levels of abstraction in the content plane of language can be reconfigured or remapped (Halliday 1998: 190). From this point of view, the symbolically mediated play that children engage in may be seen as proto-metaphoric. This is so in the sense that lexicogrammatical forms such as *un po' di olio* in our example, which congruently map the names of instances of perceivable and manipulable real-world phenomena, can also allow non-congruent mappings of pretend objects and pretend acts. This is not grammatical metaphor in Halliday's sense. That comes later in the child's semiotic development. The point is, rather, that the power of lexicogrammatical categories to transform the phenomena of experience into meaning is being extended so that these same categories can be used to create hypotheses about and to experiment on pretend realms of experience. To paraphrase Bateson, the nominal group *un po' di olio* in the child's play activity denotes – symbolically construes – the cooking oil, but it does not denote what is denoted by the cooking oil (e.g. a real cooking ingredient). Instead, it invokes a symbolic object at the same time that it specifies that this is a "pretend-object-in-a-pretend-activity". In my view, this is the essential point underlying the child's manipulation of linguistic forms to create pretend contexts.

The example also suggests how the child's own agency actively contributes to the entraining of her own neural dynamics. The play context provides an extended range of possibilities for acting in symbolically mediated ways that go beyond the here-now to encompass pretence and the "not real". Play facilitates the exploration of and experimentation with an expanded range of symbolically mediated activities without any of the existential risks to the self that characterize non-play activities (chapter 5, section 4). Play is a domain of human activity in which agents can actively explore an expanded range of such possibilities. In turn, these possibilities entrain the individual's neural dynamics in ways which favour the cross-coupling of the individual to an increasing diversity of social practices. Play thus serves an adaptive function in selecting and entraining brains to an expanded range of ecosocial semiotic possibilities that go beyond the here-now scale. The "egocentric" nature of this example means that the child is immersed, by virtue of her own activity, in information derived from both proprioceptive and exteroceptive sources that stimulates and modulates her own perceptual-motor systems in ways that, in time, affect patterns of neural connectivity in the brain. Thus, the individual's own activity – i.e. the cross-modal coupling in real-time of body movements associated with preparing the meal, the use of language, and non-linguistic vocalizations to imitate specific actions – can act on and entrain brain dynamics and functions.

Play is of critical importance in our phylogenetic and ontogenetic makeup because it is the prototypical form in early life of what Lukács in his *Aesthetics* (1973 [1970]) calls "objectification". Play provides a space-time in which participants can attain a degree of relative abstraction from the immediate (unmediated) experience of their day-to-day praxis. For Lukács, it is scientific and aesthetic forms of activity which attain the highest level of mediation, or objectification, with respect to our day-to-day praxis. Play is a necessary form of communicative activity in both the evolution of the ecosystem (phylogenesis) and in the individual's development (ontogenesis).

The ludic has a major role to play in the child's developing capacity for objectification, a capacity which only develops through the socially shared and "outward directed" resources of experiential meaning. The child's increasing ability to objectify the phenomena of experience in this way means, in effect, that the world which becomes newly accessible to him or her is a world open to hypothesis formation and experimental manipulation (Prodi 1977: 128–131, 230–231). The extended analysis in chapter 6 is a concrete illustration of this ability. The capacity to generalize, abstract from, and metaphorize experience depends on this ability to objectify. The world can be interpreted and re-interpreted by the successive operations which are performed on it. Ludic communication provides the ecosystemic space-time in which the child learns to move from hypothesis to "reality" and back to hypothesis again through a continual process of experimentation. This experimentation is always and necessarily a dialogically organized and oriented process. It is not a question of the child, as subject, acting on an objectified "outer" world, as object. The interpersonal grammar shows us that this is always a dialogically organized operation relative to some "point of action". The physical-material world is the other in relation to which these operations are oriented and on which they are performed. In other words, the child learns, dialogically, self-reflexively to connect him- or herself to the nonself at the same time that he or she learns how to construe this experientially and to act on its interpersonally. Experiential construal affords the possibility of objectification and explicit reflection that is not possible with the implicit nature of interpersonal-procedural forms of knowledge. The child learns that the world may be a centre for the operations which the child wishes to perform on it and for the child's subjective (modal) investments. It is the "friction" (Vološinov 1983), both semiotic and material, with the physical-material which gives rise to the necessarily dialogic processes in and through which the self learns to detach itself from the world. There is a self-reflexive aspect to this. In detaching things from the self, and in construing relevant distinctions between "self" and "nonself", the self is also distinguished from the "nonself". The distinction between "self" and "nonself" is the basis for constructing a dialogically organized relation between them. It is the basis whereby self is connected to nonself.

The selective attending to and interpreting of physical-material perturbations in the ambient flux is never a disinterested activity. The dialogic processes of objectification mean that the world is constructed as a hypothesis in which modal investments by socially positioned agents can be made. In detaching the world from the self, the self constructs it as a hypothesis (a subjective modal investment) which can be shared, contested, and so on, with others. The "friction" between self and nonself generates a modal project. Egocentric speech is a means whereby the child learns to experiment this discovery and to centre him- or herself in relation to the hypothesis-building power of language. This power is a consequence of the "outward directed" and, hence, objectifying breakthrough into experiential meaning. The motor which drives this is the semiotic and material friction which the child encounters and has to negotiate by virtue of the cross-coupling of the material and the discursive which arises as a consequence of his or her embodied social being. The child, in so doing, enters into a system of signs which does not have to be invented, but which is already available. It is a system which is shared by other social beings at the same time that the child learns to take up and invest in specific subjective positions in it. The ludic provides a space in which this development can occur without the risks or commitments which are entailed by either task-oriented or existential forms of communication.

The self-reflexive character of egocentric speech means that the child is looking at his or her own developing social praxis through his or her own praxis. In this way, the child learns (1) that there is a system of social meanings to which he or she has differential access; (2) that he or she is connected to this meaning-making potential; and (3) that he or she can use this potential both to reflect on and to act on his or her relationship to this potential. This capacity is necessary in the process of social learning and hence in the development and individuation of consciousness and agency.

Egocentric speech, like all speech, is socially organized and oriented; it is dialogic through and through. The self-reflexive character of egocentric speech may be formulated in terms of the semantic metafunctions. First, the child learns to deploy his or her expanding access to the resources of the experiential grammar so as to reflect on the self-activity which the child is performing. In other words, the child learns to use the resources of the experiential grammar so as to construe the activity he or she is performing NOW. It is categorized as being an activity of a certain type in relation to a system of types which are recognized in that community. Thus, the child's self-activity is connected to the wider system of act-types in the community. Secondly, interpersonally, it is a comment on (1) the child's modal investment, or positioning, in relation to the activity so construed; and (2) a meta-semiotic comment on the dialogic exchange relationship in which the child is implicated with some social other. In other words, the child learns, through his or her self-activity, to act on the other.

The transactions which the child participates in are, therefore, self-reflexively linked to the wider community's ways of talking about these, i.e. for talking about what that community recognizes as acts of a certain type. The hypothetical and experimental character of egocentric speech is, I argue, about the progressive "clarification", in Vološinov's sense, of the relation of the self to the nonself. It is, thus, an explicit foregrounding of BOTH self-reflection and self-activity, i.e. the social praxis of the self in relation to the group. There are several aspects to this: (1) the self is located at a number of socially recognized person-places, or points of action; (2) the self links its own positioning to the social group's system of available categories of social action; and (3) the self orients to and relates to the nonself (the other) in dialogically coordinated ways. For these reasons, a more suitable term than "egocentric speech" might be SELF-ACTIVITY CENTRED SPEECH.

Semiotically speaking, the above observations also mean that the child is learning that any contingent, socially organized deployment of the available semiotic and material resources in a given activity is not the result of an arbitrary relation between a signifier and a signified. This is so both from the point of view of the socially positioned speaker and from the point of view of the "object" which the sign construes (Kress 1992). Kress points out that the sign always encodes the speaker's interest in the object. The notion of interest would be equivalent to the notion of subjective modal investment in the present account. From the point of view of the "object", that which is experientially construed may, at first sight, appear to be up against a paradox. In the present case, there is **no** such "object" to which the sign "refers". This is so only if one restrictedly thinks of objects as physical-material entities in the ambient flux which our perceptual systems can pick up. Things are more complex than this, as we have seen. In our example, we are dealing with the construal of the very activity in which the child is engaged in the real-time deployment of the discourse. Her activity is construed as an instance of a certain category of event relative to the child's developing, always socially defined, self-awareness. The speaker's interest in the "object" also determines those characteristics of the object which will be so construed.

In her play, the child acts out the parental role of preparing a meal for the baby. Abstract symbolic understanding of language tokens is hardly the point here. As I showed in chapter 5, section 12.1–12.2, the use of the lexicogrammatical form is integrated with the child's sensori-motor activity. That is, with the child's bodily activity of preparing the pretend meal. Understanding here is of the most primary kind. The child acts out in her play activities that are typically associated with parents and grandparents and in this way she embodies the parent role in her sensori-motor activity. What is significant about the choice of the nominal group is the way it produces a subjective motivational stance at the same time that it has implications for action. The experiential category construed by the nominal group is, from the child's point of view, relevant insofar as it can be used and incorporated to action without necessarily entailing any explicit system of symbolic categories. From the child's point of view, the category "oil" is something that is embodied in behavioural routine so that it can be used – in cooking, for example. The lexicogrammatical form is treated as naming something which is perceptible and manipulable. It therefore serves as the basis for initial categorization before the development of more abstract categories. The further point is that such basic categories are not only learned and named first; they are also understood in association with actions such as cooking a meal which characterize the category.

As I said in chapter 5, section 9.2, the child's acting out in play of the preparing-a-meal-routine re-constitutes an activity which is valued in the society and culture in question. Meaning for the child is implication for embodied activity, rather than abstract symbol manipulation.

The linking of a category to action constitutes a link to a contextual value, which is itself linked to specific social practices. The lexicogrammatical form she uses in this episode integrates a desired future goal (the pretend meal for the baby) to the present state of affairs. The linking of the two domains means that the language she uses serves as a means by which the present state might be transformed into the desired future state. The external manipulation and use of the symbolic construct and its integration to the child's embodied activity suggests that the brain, as Cowley (2002: 92) argues, is designed so that "for bodies, things happen". The insinuation of language into the child's body-brain is based on a socially fostered belief that language provides a resource not so much for the manipulation of abstract and disembodied symbolic tokens, but for actively positing future goals for our behaviour in relation to our understanding of the present such that experience is provided with a framework for the ongoing evaluation of events (chapter 4, section 6).

In the present case, the goal exists in the child's fantasy as a desirable end state – e.g. preparing a meal for her baby – such that an implicit belief system concerning the relative value of various affective and motivational states, both desirable and undesirable, is acted out. The child's socialization into language, and therefore the latter's insinuation into her brain, is assisted by her subscribing to a myth of the known and the familiar which connects her to the familiar and established adult world and its meanings that she metaphorically acts out in her fantasy play. The myth finds metaphorical expression in the lexicogrammatical form construing the cooking oil. In this case, the metaphorical meaning arises from the reentrant mapping of the child's linguistically mediated sensori-motor activity to meanings associated with the parental role of preparing a meal for one's baby. The metaphor is, from the child's perspective, implicit in the integration of language to embodied activity, rather than in any abstract symbolic awareness of how language can metaphorically bring together two distinct experiential domains as metaphor.

The metaphorical potential is built into the pretend character of the play context. Whilst the nominal group *un po' di olio* is hardly an instance of grammatical metaphor, it does, nevertheless, function to connect different domains of experience and activity. In particular, it connects the social practices of preparing a meal and caring for children with the child's own embodied activity in the play context. This entails a de-locating of meanings and practices from a given domain and their re-location in some other domain such that meanings and practices from more than one domain are hybridized in the play context itself. Moreover, the de-location of meanings and practices from the domain in which they are congruently acted out in practice constitutes a step along the path of generalization and abstraction discussed by Halliday (1993). In the particular example under consideration here, we see that the child's external manipulation of a lexicogrammatical form in this little episode of "egocentric" speech reentrantly maps specific domains of social practice and their associated meanings (i.e. their intertextually retrievable semantic patterns), patterns of vocalization, and the bodily activity of manipulating the objects, and so on, that she uses to prepare the meal.

The play context therefore facilitates and extends the capacity to cross-contextualize diverse domains of meaning and experience in the process of experimenting with and extending the child's power over reality. This capacity requires powers of generalization and abstraction which are, in time, further reorganized as metaphor. For this reason, the child's ability to both abstract from specific contexts and to hybridize diverse contexts in her play is, in my view, proto-metaphorical. Another way of formulating this may be to say that metaphor is already implicit in the sensori-motor schemata which are instantiated in her bodily actions which bring together and embody different domains of experience. As I have said before, such schema are implicit in bodily activity and are not subject to reflective thinking. The use of the linguistic form – the nominal group – as an explicit object of both external manipulation *qua* pretend oil and vocalization *qua* articulatory activity connects bodily activity to higher-scalar ecosocial practices. In so doing, the symbolic forms of activity that this necessarily entails open up the possibility of the further reorganization of the child's meaning-making potential that is entailed by metaphor. In this case, bodily activity is cross-coupled to a discourse level of organization such that the body-brain itself is interfaced with an increasing diversity of contextual domains.

5 Grammatical metaphor as semiotic reorganization of lexicogrammatical potential in discourse

The primary metaphors analysed by Lakoff and Johnson may be seen to derive from a bio-genetic line of development, viz. in the infant's earliest multimodal interactions with the world. However, these pre-symbolic, largely iconic and indexical modes of proto-semiosis, which are based on sensori-motor experience, do not in themselves explain how the complex metaphors – lexical and grammatical – of language emerge. For this reason, the higher-scalar ecosocial level is required in order to explain the historical emergence of language in the individual. There cannot, for this reason, be any form of direct causal connection between multimodal sensori-motor experience and language, unmediated by the higher scalar level. It is worth considering Halliday's observations on the developmental significance of the emergence of grammatical metaphor in the child. Halliday (1993: 111) points out that children do not begin to unravel the complexities of grammatical metaphor until around age 9. Grammatical metaphor, unlike the primary metaphors discussed by Lakoff and Johnson, is not based on or derived from sensori-motor experience in any direct way. Rather, it constitutes a "gateway" which enables the child to gain access to the specialized meanings of technical and scientific discourse. Such access can only be obtained once the child has understood the discourse practices for construing the metaphors in the grammar. Halliday postulates a "three-step model of human semiotic development" (1993: 111) to explain where grammatical metaphor fits in after the onset of language, viz. (protolanguage →) generalization → abstractness → metaphor.

The indexical character of the child's protolinguistic signs means that these are strongly cross-coupled to specific physical-material phenomena in the child's purview. The sensori-motor basis of protolinguistic gestures strongly cross-couples these to determinate experiences that the child undergoes in specific situations (chapter 1, section 3). Protolinguistic signs are themselves relatively indeterminate – i.e. vague – as is the potentially infinite topological-quantitative variation of the phenomena of perceptual-motor experience which they index. The child's early uses of nouns to name phenomena are hard coupled to specific instances of the particular phenomenon that is named. The naming of instances precedes the ability for generalization and abstraction. The use of nouns to generalize and abstract means that the noun is increasingly soft-coupled to the phenomena of experience. The emergence of lexico-grammar enhances the child's capacity for generalization and abstraction in the sense that the more determinate lexicogrammatical categories of language enable the child to filter out much of the topological vagueness and indeterminacy of the phenomena of experience (chapter 9, section 4). The potentially infinite variety of experience can be handled by a smaller number of linguistic categories which are semiotically salient and socially functional in a given community. The ability to generalize and abstract entails just this ability to manage the indeterminacy and vagueness of experience in terms of linguistic generalization and abstraction. By the same token, the reduction of the topological richness and ineffability of the phenomena of experience to a more determinate set of linguistic categories also means that a price is paid. This price takes the form of a reduction of experience to a semiotically more closed, though still very complex, set of categories. This price would reach its theoretical maximum if the use of linguistic categories to generalize about and abstract from experience resulted in total closure such that a given category generalized, say, about just one domain. Generalization and abstraction implicate the integration of diversity to a specific semantic domain. A discrete lexicogrammatical form (noun) is mapped to a discrete semantic category (Thing).

(Grammatical) metaphor reorganizes the typological determinateness of linguistic categorization such that complex semantic interactions can occur across different semantic domains and the contexts these pertain to. The point is, I think, that grammatical metaphor reorganizes discrete categories such as "Thing" and "Figure" such that an open-ended and creative adaptiveness to the complexities of the diversity of contextual domains and the interactions between these is enhanced. This means that grammatical metaphor reintroduces on a higher level of semiotic (re)organization an increase in semantic complexity along with a corresponding decrease in semantic determinacy. Generalization and abstraction entail the increasing soft-coupling of specific linguistic categories to any specific detail pertaining to a particular concrete phenomenon of experience. In this perspective, the semiotic reorganization of this potential through the emergence of grammatical metaphor means that the semantic complexity of metaphor is increasingly soft-coupled with respect to determinate linguistic categories. The semiotic gain lies in the enhanced power of language to integrate meanings specialized to diverse contextual domains (e.g. material → mental) or to different ranks in lexicogrammar (e.g. noun-Thing → verb-Process) such that the functional adaptation of language to the world is extended and enriched.

The congruent construal of Things by nouns means that the intermediate level L of lexicogrammatical form – specifically the noun – serves to reorganize the topological-continuous variation of the phenomena of experience at level L–1 as discrete semantic categories of Thing on level L+1. In terms of the three-level hierarchy, the reorganization across levels that this entails can be schematized as follows:

L+1   discrete semantic categories of Thing (typological)
L   discrete lexicogrammatical forms (nouns) that congruently realize Things (typological)
L–1   vague and indeterminate flux of phenomena of experience (topological)

In terms of the three-level hierarchy, nominalization is an emergent intermediate level of lexicogrammatical form between Things and Figures. In their respective congruent realizations, a noun realizes a discrete Thing and a clause realizes a discrete Figure. This helps us to see how nominalization metaphorically reorganizes discrete typological categories on level L (lexicogrammar) as topologically continuous intersections such as Figure-as-Thing on level L+1 (discourse).

The reorganization across levels that is entailed by nominalization may be schematized as follows:

L+1   metaphorical semantic space: Figure-as-Thing (nominalization)
L   discrete lexicogrammatical categories: Thing (noun) and Figure (clause)
L–1   topological indeterminacy and vagueness of phenomena of experience

In this case, the lexicogrammatical form – the nominalization – on level L is mapped to a complex topological intersection of semantic domains on level L+1.

The cognitive loss lies in the increased processing burden which the semantic "unpacking" of grammatical metaphor necessarily places on those individuals who have not been apprenticed into the specialized meanings and practices of the social domain in question (e.g. scientific discourse). However, both semiotic and cognitive loss may also result when, for example, the semantic complexity of grammatical metaphor, especially nominalization, is used, as it regularly is in technocratic discourse (see Lemke 1990b; Thibault 1991b) to obfuscate and render opaque the functional relation between form and meaning and language and world. In this case, the increased cognitive burden does not yield any corresponding semiotic gain in the form of an enriched creative adaptation to new contextual domains. Contemporary bureaucratic and managerial forms of discourse are clear examples of this and are rightly disdained by many people as forms of de-humanizing gobblede-gook.

Grammatical metaphor is a pervasive feature of modern English and many other languages. This is so to such an extent that grammatical metaphor has ramified well beyond the discourses of science and technology, which were the original historical reason for the emergence of this phenomenon in English (Halliday 1998). Consequently, grammatical metaphor has become a feature of many other forms of institutionalized discourse such as administration, economics, education, bureaucracy, and so on. These observations point to the fact that grammatical metaphor crucially depends upon the interface between discourse and the higher-scalar eco-social level for its interpretation. It cannot be solely explained in terms of or causally derived from lower-scalar sensori-motor experience in any straightforward way; instead, the sensori-motor level is integrated to the more specified symbolic level where grammatical metaphor resides as part of the meaning-making potential of language as an ecosocial semiotic system. Grammatical metaphor is characterized by a semantic drift towards "thinginess" on account of the way it re-construes sequences and figures as nominalizations. Consequently, the phenomena of experience are objectified and viewed as things, rather than as actions and events.

For this reason, grammatical metaphor, along with the developmentally prior stages of generalization and abstraction identified by Halliday, may appear to represent a shift away from the rich, on-line multimodal integration of diverse sensory modalities that are the driving force, so to speak, of early infant semiosis. In my view, the difference is not one of kind *per se*, but of degree. The developmental progression sketched by Halliday involves, at all stages, the integration of real-time processes and developmental change. When children encounter written scientific texts for the first time, there is no genetic rule for grammatical metaphor which will provide the key to the solution to the new problems encountered. Rather, grammatical metaphor, like other developmental problems, is resolved by the child constructing a match between his or her intrinsic dynamics and the contextually constrained problem to hand. The constructing of such a match will be illustrated below with respect to a school child's efforts to construe the scientific discourse of blood and its transportation in the body through the co-deployment of the semiotic resources of language and depiction.

6 Linguistic and visual metaphor in a child's multimodal construal of white blood cells

The text to be analysed in this section is that of an Italian schoolboy aged approximately eight years. The text, which is a short verbal-visual essay on white blood cells, is taken from his school copy book. The entire text is re-produced as Figure 11.3.

The verbal text and the image text both play their part in the building up and development in this text of a wider multimodal thematic formation and its meanings that can be glossed as [WHITE BLOOD CELL] (see also Thibault 2000b). In other words, the meanings of this thematic formation are jointly constructed on the basis of verbal and visual semiotic resources. Whilst there is very little integration of the linguistic and pictorial texts, which are kept fairly distinct in terms of the spatial layout of the page, the relationship between the two is not simply one of spatial juxtaposition of image and linguistic text on the same page. Both the image and the main verbal text play their part in the development of a joint verbal-visual thematic formation. In this case, the image selectively instantiates and develops part of the thematic concerned with the function of white blood cells in the blood transportation system of vertebrates (specifically humans).

This joint visual-verbal thematic formation may be modelled as in Figure 11.4, which shows how the thematic formation [WHITE BLOOD CELL] is built up on the basis of a trade-off between verbal and visual elements such that the two semiotic modalities jointly create this thematics. In the verbal text, the clause complex *siamo come la polizia perché il nostro compito è uccidere o ingoiare tutti gli individui dannosi "virus" i batteri che possono danneggiare il corpo* ["we are like the police because our task is to kill or swallow all the harmful individual viruses and bacteria that can harm the body"] is a fragment of a wider intertextual thematic formation which fits with the superordinate pattern /WHITE BLOOD CELLS-DESTROY-HARMFUL FOREIGN GERMS/. This example is co-hyponymic to the clause *devo battere i virus* ["I must beat the viruses"] in the same text. The two examples are, in turn, hyponyms in relation to the more superordinate ITF [WHITE BLOOD CELLS-DESTROY-HARMFUL FOREIGN GERMS], which is retrievable from the text and which the specific items both instantiate and index.

The specific examples in the child's text are also co-hyponymic to examples from other texts such as the following: "white corpuscles fight and destroy germs and bacteria" and "human white corpuscles take in bacteria", which are taken from school science textbooks analysed by myself in a separate study (Thibault 2001). While the specific wording may differ in each case, it is not difficult to see how each of these examples instantiates the same meaning within the wider ITF to which it is assigned. In this sense, the specific examples referred to above are typical instantiations of the more general meaning of the ITF in question.

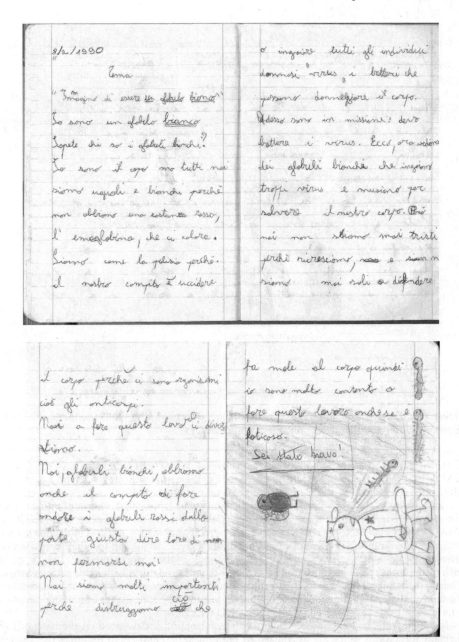

Figure 11.3 Joint verbal-visual text about white blood cells by nine-year-old Italian schoolboy

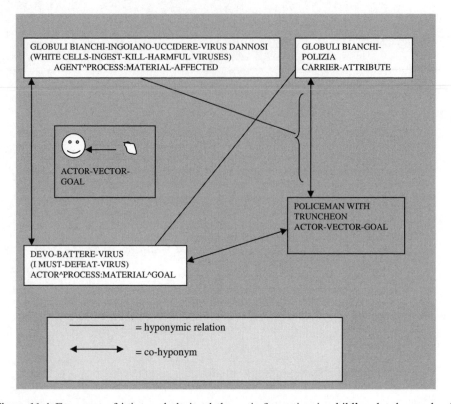

Figure 11.4 Fragment of joint verbal-visual thematic formation in child's school copy book, showing multimodal thematic connections and meanings

In the visual text, the meaning that I glossed above as /WHITE BLOOD CELLS-DESTROY-HARMFUL FOREIGN GERMS/ is expressed by the visual transitivity relation of Actor-Material Action-Goal in the form of the policeman-white blood cell, who is connected by a visual vector to the nasty small green participants who represent the harmful viruses. This visual transitivity relation is as follows: ACTOR (white blood cell-policeman)-ACTION: SWALLOW (visual vector)-GOAL (small green participants). Other features of the image such as the truncheon in the policeman's right hand, his badge, and his cap together form a set of visual collocates which serve to index the policeman role of the figure in question. In turn, items such as the truncheon enter into more specific co-thematic relations with items such as *battere* ["beat"] in the verbal text. Each of these individual thematic items, along with the links between them, instantiate, both individually and jointly, some more specific aspect of the superordinate intertextual thematic formation [WHITE BLOOD CELL].

In actual fact, the joint verbal-visual thematic formation is developed on the basis of two thematic formations which are hybridized by both the verbal and visual resources that are co-deployed in the child's multimodal text. The two intertextual thematic formations in question may be glossed as [WHITE BLOOD CELL] and [POLICE ENFORCE LAW & ORDER]. Clearly, the two formations derive from very different domains of social life. The point is that the child's multimodal text constructs and elaborates both a metaphorical relationship and a heteroglossic alliance (see below) between these two heteroglossically diverse domains. Moreover, the metaphor operates in both the linguistic and visual components of this text. I pointed out in chapter 10, section 5 that metaphor works by overlaying intertextually retrievable semantic patterns from one domain of human practice and experience on the semantic patterns of some other domain in order to produce insights, perspectives, and evaluations about the particular domain to hand.

In the ITF glossed above as [WHITE BLOOD CELL], the clause *human white cells take in bacteria*, which is attested in a school science book that I have analysed elsewhere (Thibault 2001), instantiates a fragment of the thematic meanings that are derived from that particular ITF. On the other hand, the clause *They [white corpuscles] are the troops of the body, rushed to the battle with the invaders (germs)*, in the same school science textbook, can be assigned its meaning in relation to the ITF glossed as [SOLDIERS FIGHT INVADERS], which, in turn, can be related to the ITF glossed above as [POLICE ENFORCE LAW & ORDER]. However, I pointed out previously that the metaphorical hybridizing of the two domains in the child's text is quite typical of the ways in which the scientific meanings concerned with blood and its trans-portation in the body are constructed in primary school and junior high school texts for young apprentices to the specialist meanings of the scientific discourse. These meanings are not, on the other hand, typical of the specialist discourses of scientific experts in the field in question (see Thibault 2001 for an extended discussion). My point is that the child's multimodal meta-phorical construction is not unique to the child, but is assignable to a typical ITF in terms of which the specific meanings of the child's text are made.

/LAW & ORDER: POLICE-FIGHT-CRIMINALS:; POSITIVE EVALUATION/

↕

metaphorically hybridized with / heteroglossically allied with

↕

/BIOLOGICAL: WHITE CELLS-TAKE IN-BACTERIA; POSITIVE EVALUATION/

In both the verbal and visual semiotic, the metaphor is based on a heteroglossic alliance which is construed between these two ITFs. In so doing, this child, as we also saw in a different context in chapter 5, section 12.2, identifies with a particular social voice and its associated values in the wider system of social heteroglossia. There is a positively valued relationship of complemen-tarity between the /BIOLOGICAL: WHITE CELL/ and the /SOCIAL: LAW & ORDER/ formations. It is this complementarity which gives voice to this particular textual meaning and the social positions associated with it when the child positions himself in relationship to them. This last point can now be discussed in relation to the distinction between the ideational and interpersonal sourcing of meanings in discourse (Thibault 1999b: 576–580).

The linguistic text of the child foregrounds the interpersonal enactment and negotiation of the meanings that are sourced at the first person writer of the text in the form of *io* (I) and *noi* (we). In other words, the interpersonal frame of reference is the intersubjective relationship between writer and reader, where the writer metaphorically takes up the speaking position of a white blood cell – sometimes as individual (*io*); sometimes as one of a group or team who work together (*noi*). By the same token, the ideational meanings of the text belong to the heteroglos-sically diverse /BIOLOGICAL/ and /SOCIAL/ domains referred to above. That is, the child writer-depicter: (1) is the addresser who enacts interpersonal negotiation between himself *qua* white cell-policeman and the reader; **and** (2) who ideationally construes the relations between these two thematic formations.

The point is that the diverse ideational sources of the meaning pertaining to these two ITFs are not relativized to their own discursive domains and the validity claims that operate in these. Instead, they are assimilated to the perspective of the young writer as interpersonal (though not ideational) source of the meanings that his text negotiates. As such, the meanings of the text are recounted as personal experience, rather than generic scientific truths and values that are detached from particular first person speaking and writing positions. Ideation-ally, these meanings are sourceable in the thematic domains of various categories of third person other, i.e. the meanings of science, its practitioners and spokespersons and related intertexts, on the one hand, and the meanings, practitioners, and spokespersons of law enforcement, along with related intertexts, on the other. The same processes are evidenced in the child's picture, where the metaphorical condensation of the two thematic domains results in the conflation of the experiential construal of the meanings associated with white blood cells and their functions with the child as interpersonal enactor of these meanings in the form of the policeman.

7 Visual semiosis and visual metaphor

Visual semiosis is a topological semiotic modality which is based on continuous variation in colour, visual intensity, size, shape, and position. Visual semiosis shows very well that if information, in Bateson's famous phrase, is "a difference that makes a difference" (1973a [1972]: 286), then it is possible to have difference of kind (typological) and difference of degree (topological). Both types of difference can then be interpreted as making a difference in the object X for which some representamen (R) stands for in a particular system of interpretance. In actual fact, visual semiosis is probably a mixed-mode case where we can represent quantitatively variable phenomena (X) on the expression plane by discrete or typological criteria on the content plane. In "seeing images" we are often "seeing" visual cues that are not actually there visually; as the visual information which is picked up by our receptor cells is matched to the most likely or only possible image, higher-level networks that correspond to whole patterns are activated. This is, of course, the sense of Gestalt pattern completion phenomena for visual perception.

In a given visual text, some features will be perceived to be more salient than others and, hence, to have greater informational prominence in the text or some part of it. Visual salience is related to the articulation of the relationship between figure and ground, as studied by researchers of visual perception in the Gestalt tradition. Kanizsa (1980: 41) points out that, in a given visual field, a figure emerges with respect to a ground on the basis of a number of interacting factors. The most important of these include the relative size of the parts, their topological relations, their types of margin, as well as spatial orientation (Kanizsa 1980: 41–43). Salient objects tend, overall, to occupy a smaller proportion of the total volume of the visual field than does the background. Furthermore, salient objects tend to be more substantial and distinct with respect to their background, both in terms of solidity and colour. The background, by contrast, may be relatively indistinct, lacking in detail, and exhibiting less compactness of colouring. These are generalizations only and each individual case may make use of these in different ways, or it may make use of only some of these possibilities.

The visual field is topological in nature. However, the processes of perception and assigning meaning to a given visual field additionally mean that this must be segmented and categorized such that the objects, events and so on, that are recognized in the visual field are assigned a meaning (Kanizsa 1991: 113).

The visual invariants that are applied to a treated surface such as the page and which constitute the basis for our perception of the information that is displayed on this surface are in the first instance composed of the following classes of elements:

- points
- lines
- colours
- light-shadow.

These elements are always organized into larger patterns and in my view constitute the expression stratum of visual semiosis. The elements referred to above are not in themselves visual invariants. The perceptual-informational variants are comprised of nestings – intersections, combinations, and so on – of these. It is these nestings which are the basic building blocks of all forms of visual semiosis. Visual semiosis is essentially topological-continuous in character in contrast to the predominantly typological-categorial nature of linguistic semiosis (Lemke 1998a). Consequently, the nestings identified by Gibson are constructed on the basis of factors such as degree, quantity, gradation, continuous change, topological relations of varying nearness and farness, the interpenetration of different dimensions, and so on. On a treated surface such as the page, the visual invariants that constitute the frozen array of the visual image remain "invariant under a changing perspective of surfaces" (Gibson 1986 [1979]: 288). This means that no matter how much the reader or viewer of the page may change his angle of viewing, alter his distance from the page, selectively attend to one part of the page rather than others, follow a particular reading path, and so on, these invariants do not in themselves alter.

The nesting of the four kinds of element identified above to form informational invariants occurs on a number of different scalar levels relative to the page as a whole. In saying this, we are assuming that the page is the largest unit of visual analysis for our present purposes.

As Gibson points out, the information is specified by the connections between lines rather than by the lines themselves. Furthermore, some areas are nested within other areas. It is these connections and nestings of lines and regions, rather than the lines *per se*, that produce the meaning of the drawing as a whole. The relations between lines and between different scalar levels of organization are topological-continuous in character rather than discrete, linear, and segmental. Figure 11.5 reproduces a drawing by the author's daughter when she was aged 2:4. The drawing is of her father (the author).

The drawing consists of a number of traces on various scalar levels. Some of these traces come back to where they started to produce closure (e.g. the eyes and the face as a whole). Some traces intersect with others. An example is the way in which the brown traces intersect with the top part of the outermost grey trace to depict the hair on top of the head. It is not difficult to recognize the drawing as a face. The tracings on various scalar levels, their nestings and intersections, in some cases, their closures, produce visual invariants which the child has extracted from the stimulus flux of the ambient optic array. That is, the child perceives invariants and their topological relations which amount to an eyes-nose-mouth-hair, etc. invariant. As Gibson points out, a picture makes available a delimited optic array of "arrested structures with underlying invariants of structure" (1986 [1979]: 272).

In terms of the three-level hierarchy, the visual text can be seen in terms of the following levels of organization:

L–1   topological-continuous field of patterns of points, lines, colours, and light-shadow on different scalar levels of organization by virtue of nestings of these to produce informational invariants in the arrested optical array of the page

L   informational invariants categorially segmented as volumes, vectors, and so on

L+1   volumes, vectors, and so on, construed as depicted participants, objects, actions, events, and so on; complex topological relations of degree, quantity, gradation, continuous change, relative nearness and farness, non-linear relations of dynamical emergence between objects, actions, and so on, in depicted world of visual text

In visual semiosis, metaphor arises by virtue of the fact that volumes, vectors, and so on, may be interpreted on level L+1 in terms of an intersection of two (or more) visual thematic domains. For example, the child's depiction of the white blood corpuscle as policeman, which I discussed in section 6, shows this topological merging of visual domains. In this case, the relevant volume maps visual features associated with policemen to the participant that depicts the white blood corpuscle defending the body from potentially dangerous bacteria. As in linguistic metaphor, there is a topological hybridizing of distinct visual thematic domains. The hybrid meaning which results cannot be seen as the mere sum of the two domains, but as the newly emergent product of their metaphorical intersection. In terms of the three-level hierarchy, this means that on level L–1 lines, points, colours, and light-shadow and their nestings and intersections, and so on, constitute information which is reorganized on level L as underlying invariants of structure deriving from two, say, categorially distinct objects of perception. In turn, these two objects constitute information for the system of interpretance on L+1, where the metaphorical meaning is interpreted.

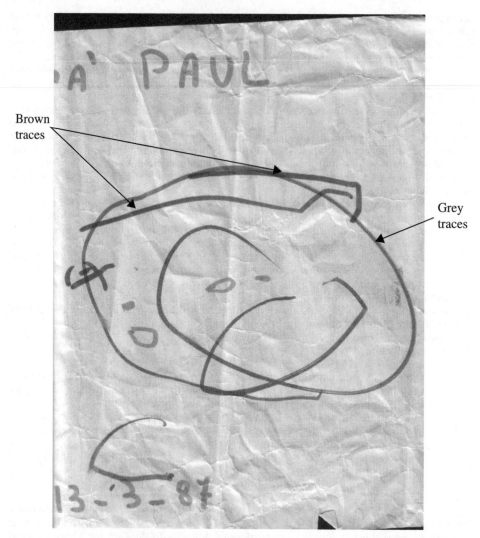

Figure 11.5 A young child's (aged 2.4) drawing of her father's face, showing tracings on various scalar levels, and how their nestings, intersections, and closures produce visual invariants.

8 Metaphor and Lemke's Principle of Alternation

The three-level hierarchy paradigm provides a model of how semiotic functions are mapped onto dynamical scale levels. I analysed above some instances of both linguistic and visual metaphor. In accordance with Lemke's Principle of Alternation (see chapter 9, section 5), these examples show the reorganization of continuous variation as discrete variants, and of discrete variants as continuous variation.

Each new, emergent intermediate level L in a complex, hierarchical, self-organizing system functions semiotically (1) to reorganize the continuous quantitative (topological) variety of units and interactions at level L–1 as discrete, categorial (typological) meaning for level

L+1; and/or (2) to reorganize the discrete, categorial (typological) variety of level L–1 as continuously variable (topological) meaning for level L+1.

Level L+1 functions in both cases as the system of interpretance which construes entities and phenomena at level L as signs of the system at level L–1. Sensori-motor experience (Lakoff and Johnson) can thus be seen as states and interactions which correspond to the effects of interaction with the environment at level L–1. Level L–1 states and interactions are not linguistic phenomena as such. It is higher levels of the system which respond to them as signs at level L of phenomena in the environment of symbolic neural space at level L+1, relative to the discourse semantic level of some system of interpretance. It does not follow that there is necessarily any direct causal-material relationship between the L+1 level of the semantic objects construed in symbolic neural space and the sensori-motor interactions on level L–1, i.e. visual invariants which have been extracted from the flux of the ambient visual array.

In language, congruent codings (e.g. noun → Thing) entail the mapping of discrete lexico-grammatical items to discrete semantic categories at the next level. If language were limited to such codings, we would have simple, automatized form-function couplings in which the semantic construal of experience would be restricted to such pre-determined couplings (Halliday and Matthiessen 1999: 237). The emergence of a topological metaphorical space on level L+1 allows for the expansion of the grammar's meaning potential such that genuine creativity and innovation are possible. Thus, nouns need not automatically function solely as the names of semantic things. If this were the case, then the relationship between grammatical class and semantic function would be merely tautologous. Likewise, semantic construals of the material domain can serve as the basis for the construal of the mental domain.

The creativity and meaning-expanding potential of metaphor lies in the fact that the many degrees of freedom on the L–1 level of our sensori-motor interactions with the world provide for many-to-one classifications (L–1 to L) which are filtered at the L level of lexicogrammar. It is in this way that discrete, categorial items (e.g. nouns, verbs) on the L level of the lexicogrammar can be re-construed on the discourse semantic level of L+1 in an expanded phase space of metaphorical possibilities. These possibilities are themselves dependent on the lexicogrammatical constraints of the L level, which can be integrated into the L+1 level as experiential construals and interpersonal negotiations in a complex higher-scalar ecosocial semiotic space. The opening up of a metaphorical space on level L+1 thus shows how typological-categorial lexicogrammatical distinctions on level L are re-interpreted on level L+1 as a qualitatively new kind of topological-continuous variation. This would appear to be a concrete working out of the "alternation between topological and typological semiotic relationships of adjacent levels" (Lemke 1999: 8) in terms of the logic of the three-level hierarchy.

In conformity with the Principle of Alternation, we see that the transformations of sensori-motor interactions (continuous) to lexicogrammatical construals (discrete) and metaphorical meanings (continuous) across levels in the hierarchy entails a semiotic transformation of the information content of lower levels as signs for higher levels, allowing many-to-one classifications and one-to-many context-dependent experiential re-construals and possibilities for interpersonal negotiation. Such a system of dynamical transformations across scales of semiosis thus allows for the emergence of genuine creativity and innovation.

The emergence of metaphor affords the possibility for de-construing and re-construing the categorial distinctions of the lexicogrammar of natural language as topological-continuous variation. This variation can, in turn, be related back to less specified, less differentiated levels of semiosis in the specification hierarchy of iconic, indexical, and symbolic modes of semiosis. In this way, the typological-categorial distinctions made by lexicogrammar can be related back to antecedent semiotic primitives. Therefore, lexicogrammar itself is seen to have emerged from the primordial many degrees of freedom of the prior, sensori-motor based modalities of semiosis which constitute our earliest, always embodied, always semiotically mediated, transactions with the topological richness and variety of the social and physical-material processes and flows of the world in which we are immersed.

Appendix I (chapter 4)

Transcription of the Play Episode

Phase No.	Speaker	Italian Text	English Translation
Phase 1	Paola	(1) senti (2) ti dico una cosa (3) giociamo a mamma (4a) te la piccola che mi aiutavi a fare le faccende (4b) eh?	(1) listen (2) I'll tell you something (3) let's play mummies (4a) you the little baby who helps me to do things (4b) eh?
	Elena	(5) no	(5) no
	Paola	(6a) allora dopo questa facciamo finta (6b) che il mangiare . . . (6c) che dopo giociamo a mamma (6d) eh?	(6a) well after this let's pretend (6b) that the eating . . . (6c) that afterwards we play mummies (6d) eh?
	Elena	(7) però sono la bimba grande	(7) yet I'm the big baby
	Paola	(8) va bene (9) adesso però che mi aiutavi	(8) alright (9) now however you help me
	Elena	(10) la bimba piccola in scuola (11a) quando c'è la bimba piccola (11b) facciamo un pò di giochi con la bimba piccola	(10) the baby girl in school (11a) when there's the baby girl (11b) let's play some games with the baby girl
Phase 2	Paola	(12) ma che potevi anche cantare Sings:	(12) but you could sing too Sings:
		(13) con gocce d'acqua vuole il capitano	(13) with drops of water the captain wants
		un reggimento un battaglione formare	to form a regiment a battalion
		è soltanto un chicco	he's only a grain of rice
		ma si sente eroe	but he feels himself a hero
		fiumi e mari vuole conquistare	rivers and seas he wants to conquer
Phase 3	Paola	(14) sai da dove l'ho imparata?	(14) do you know where I learned it?
	Elena	(15) che cosa?	(15) what?
	Paola	(16) questa canzone	(16) this song
	Elena	(17a) dal maesto (17b) anch'io l'ho imparata dal maestro	(17a) from the teacher (17b) I too learned it from the teacher
	Paola	(18) sì	(18) yes

Phase No.	Speaker	Italian Text	English Translation
Phase 4	Paola	(19a) un pò di olio (19b) ch ch (20a) questo è l'olio (20b) se ti serve (20c) ch ch (20d) e l'olio . . . (21) vado a prendere il sale [exits bedroom to get salt from kitchen; returns after a long interval of some minutes]	(19a) a little oil (19b) ch ch (20a) this is oil (20b) if it's useful to you (20c) ch ch (20d) and oil . . . (21) I'll go and get the salt
Phase 5	Elena	(22) dobbiamo fare la mente mamma per oggi per i ghiaccioli di menta (23a) domani è festa mia (23b) che compio dieci anni (23c) quindi bisogna fare in fretta	(22) we have to make the mint mummy for today for the mint paddle pops (23a) tomorrow it's my birthday (23b) when I turn ten (23c) so we have to hurry up
	Paola	(24) è vero (25a) sai che (25b) quello che stai dicendo è proprio vero	(24) it's true (25a) you know that (25b) what you're saying is really true
	Elena	(26a) perchè alle feste bisogna fare qualcosa da mangiare	(26a) because at parties you have to prepare something to eat
	Paola	(27) è vero	(27) it's true
	Elena	(26b) altrimenti gli invitanti se ne vanno subito via	(26b) otherwise the guests will go away straightaway
Phase 6	Paola	(28a) allora questa è la forchetta per fare così (28b) eh? (28c) per schiacciare . . .	(28a) well then this is the fork for doing this (28b) eh? (28c) for crushing . . .

Appendix II (chapter 4)

Linguistic Analysis and Interpretation of the Transcription in Appendix I

Phase 1

Clauses 1 to 4b enact a complex dialogic move, which can be more delicately described as a sequence of five sub-moves. Each of these is realized by the sequence of clauses which together comprise the more global move referred to here. We shall consider these shortly. The overall move may be glossed as PROPOSAL: DIRECTIVE. It is a complex move, which seeks, in clause 3, to conjoin the addressee to the speaker as joint Subject of this clause, thereby positioning the addressee as an agent who will jointly carry out the action that is proposed by the speaker. Clause 4a semantically extends clause 3 by adding information that further specifies the distribution of roles in the play that the speaker has proposed in clause 3. The two clauses together index a particular intertextually defined moral order, which can be glossed as /MOTHERHOOD: ROLE RELATIONS: MOTHER-CHILD/.

Clauses 1 to 6 are each describable in terms of the local semantics of clause-as-exchange. Each of these clauses enacts a distinctive dialogic move. We shall look at the contribution of each taken as a separate unit shortly. The overall sequence is a form of Command-Explanation complex in which Paola seeks to elicit Elena's willingness and cooperation in the playing of the game, as well as to explain the way the game is to be played and the allocation of roles in the activities that the two girls perform.

Semantically, clause 2 has the features Pre-announce Communicative Intent. The speaker positions herself as the "point of action", to use Harré's (1983: 104) term, from which certain agentive effects will flow. This move constructs an axiological orientation to the addressee as a social being who can be addressed in the terms recognized by the relevant moral order. The speaker does not simply impart information to her addressee. Rather, her move positions the other as a social being who can be addressed in the terms recognized in the local moral order. This also means that the addressee will have certain rights of reply.

Clause 3 can be sub-classified as Directive. The second person pronoun *noi*, which is morphologically conflated with the verb, realizes the inclusive first person plural pronoun (speaker + addressee) as Subject of this clause. The speaker therefore proposes this joint Subject, comprising the two participants, as the agent that is modally responsible for carrying out the proposed action. In clause 3, the speaker seeks to construct a joint agent position out of the semantic conjunction of the two participants to a proposed joint activity, which requires both participants for its successful execution.

Clause 4a is a dialogic move in which the speaker gives information concerning the respective roles to be taken up by the two participants in the proposed joint activity. This activity has to do with the allocation and distribution of the social roles of "mother" and "young child" with respect to local social norms concerning the division of labour in the home. Clause 4b has strongly rising (Tone 2) intonation; it functions as a kind of prosodically realized tag whereby the speaker seeks the addressee's assent for the proposals previously made.

In clause 5, Elena responds by declining the action proposed by Paola. She then seeks to renegotiate her initial proposal. There is a subtle difference, however, in the way that she does this. Clause 6a is a projecting (reporting) clause. Paola now construes the activity from a meta-level position through the mental process verb *facciamo finta* ("let's pretend that"). In using clause 6a, she seeks both to renegotiate the earlier bid at the same time that she gives it a new experiential construal. Again, the first person inclusive plural imperative clause seeks to bind both participants as the joint Subject who is modally responsible for carrying out the proposed action at the same time that the two participants are also construed as the joint Senser of the mental process of cognition that the experiential semantics of the projecting clause expresses. In so doing, Paola seeks to position the two participants both at the same point of action and at the same meta-level point of view. She not only seeks to position Elena as a co-agent in the performance of the proposed action; she also seeks to co-opt Elena to the same meta-level experiential construal of a joint mental process of consciousness in relation to the projected clauses 6b and 6c. Clause 6b is incomplete, though its mention of *mangiare* ("eating") may be an anticipation of the further development of this theme in Phase 4 and Phase 6. The projected clause 6c re-proposes the joint activity that Paola first proposed in clause 3. Clause 6d is a further use of the prosodic tag, common in this girl's speech in this period, and discussed in relation to clause 4b. The function is the same in both instances.

In clause 7, Elena now accepts Paola's proposal, though not without making a successful bid partially to redefine and to re-appropriate the situation in her favour. That is, to be the big girl instead of the little one. In 8, Paola accepts Elena's redefinition of her identity and status, though not without a further attempt to redefine this in clause 9. The thematized adverbial adjunct of time *adesso* ("now") in 9 grounds this dialogic move in the present. Paola's concern is with maintaining control over the point of action from which she attempts to influence the regularities of the discursive event. Secondly, the adversative conjunction *però* both echoes its prior use in Elena's clause 7 and signals the heteroglossic opposition between the positions of the two girls.

In 10, Elena initiates a further (partial) redefinition of the situation first defined by Paola at the beginning of this episode. Now that she has successfully redefined herself as the "big girl", the "little girl" role is reintroduced by Elena as a potential third (imaginary) participant in the discourse. In clause 10, the imaginary "little girl" is said to be *in scuola* ("at school"). Clause 10 therefore indexes a specific aspect of the social networks shared by the two girls at the same time that her evocation of the "little girl" can be seen as a strategic bid on her part to renegotiate to some extent the nature of the play activity first proposed by Paola. In the complex comprising clauses 11a and 11b, Elena construes an imaginary or hypothetical situation in which she and Paola are jointly positioned in relation to the imaginary "little girl" with whom they can play.

Phase 2

Clause 12 marks a transition into a qualitatively different activity-sequence. Paola proposes an alternative activity to Elena, i.e. singing. Clause 15a signals the transition not only in the shift to a new activity, but also through the adversative conjunction *ma* (but). Paola then sings the song, which will not be further analysed here.

Phase 3

Clauses 14 to 18 constitute a question-answer sequence which is focused on the song which Paola has just sung. Hasan (1988: 78) has distinguished two basic types of question, depending on the kind of information which is sought by the speaker. These two types can be more delicately subclassified as a system network of more specific options. In terms of the basic distinction, the speaker either seeks to confirm, which is realized by a yes/no question; or she seeks the answer to a wh-type question.

The clause complex represented by clauses 14a and 14b realizes features of both types of question. Clause 14a projects 14b through the mental process verb *sai* ("do you [T] know?"). On this basis, the clause complex may be analysed as follows: *sai* [projecting clause = "do you know"] + *da dove l'ho imparata* [projected clause = "from where I learned it"]. The respondent could take up and negotiate either the projecting (reporting) or the projected (reported) clause, or both, when giving his answer. For example, in the invented response *sì, dal maestro* ("yes, from the teacher"), *sì* responds to and negotiates the meaning "do you know?" in the projecting clause and *dal maestro* responds to and negotiates the meaning "from where I learned it?" in the projected clause.

Clause 14a is a question of the type [demand; information; confirm: ask: non-assumptive: represent] (see Hasan 1988). This type of question does not assume that the relevant knowledge is shared by addresser and addressee. Clause 14b is a question of a different type. Its semantics can be specified as [demand; information: apprize: precise: circumstance]. It, too, has the semantic feature [non-assumptive]. Paola, in selecting this complex of semantic features in her question, indicates her assumption that her addressee does not share the knowledge which Paola is "in possession of". The two-part nature of this question may be glossed as CONFIRM + SPECIFY. It is important to bear in mind that the song to which the question refers is very much a part of the shared knowledge of the two girls. However, the semantics of the question which Paola asks puts a very different construction on this. I shall develop this point shortly.

Elena's response in 15 seeks further interpretation of the discourse reference item *l'* ("it") in order to establish the referent of this pronoun. Its semantics can be delicately subclassified as [specify: apprize: precise: participant: interpretative]. It seeks further interpretation of the participant in the developing referential chain. Clause 16 specifies the referent, and in 17a, Elena's response, *dal maestro*, gives the answer which is semantically most congruent with *da dove* in 14. The song has now been sourced, but in such a way that the definite article *il* (fused with *da + il*) uses presuming reference. Elena, in 17b, assumes her answer to be knowledge which both girls share. The shared basis of the source of the knowledge, as assumed in her response, is further elaborated and supported in 17b. She, too, learned it from the same teacher.

We can now return to the significance of the school as the relevant interpersonal moral order here. We have seen that the song, which is a shared piece of knowledge by virtue of the common school experience of the two girls, is constructed as non-shared knowledge in Paola's question. Furthermore, Paola's question in 14 uses the mental process verbs *sai* ("know") and *imparata* ("learned"), whose semantics are already specialized to the abstract processes of interpretation – the process of knowledge construction (definition, classification, interpretation) – which are an essential part of the pedagogic context (Hasan 1988: 80).

This kind of knowledge, as Hasan points out, is created on the basis of making one's assumptions explicit and on not assuming a shared basis for experience. It is that form of knowledge which is valued as objective, rationalist, abstract and individualistic. Thus, the basis of formal reasoning is already present in the meaning-making practices of the two girls *qua* apprentice pedagogic subjects. The question-answer sequence in clauses 14 and 18 functions to make this explicit. Having done so, it is interesting that Elena's response in 17b takes the teacher to be the mutually shared piece of knowledge. In 17b, the thematization of *anch'io* ("I too") focuses on the inner based and self-directed nature of the learning process – the *maestro* is the source from whom the knowledge was acquired. Thus, in 17b, Elena exactly parallels Paola's semantic construction of this process in 14. That is, both girls are the centre of ego-based mental processes (*imparare*) in which the teacher is semantically coded as a Circumstance: Location, i.e. the source for this ego-based or self-directed acquisition process. Clause 21 closes this discourse phase with Paola providing a positive evaluation of Elena's response.

Phase 4

Clauses 19 to 20d instantiate a different type of activity-structure. In this phase, Paola linguistically monitors a non-linguistic activity sequence, which she enacts at the same time as this self-monitoring takes place. In other words, the activity sequence is realized by the non-linguistic actions she performs, as well as by her self-monitoring of these actions in her speech. The two occur simultaneously as seamlessly interwoven strands of a single activity. Generically, the activity sequence derives from the social activity of preparing a meal in the kitchen, a task whose role allocation can be related to the division of labour in the home. The linguistic activity is organized around an unfolding action in experiential time and space. This explains the particular clustering of linguistic selections here: conjunction is mainly implicit, participant identification is exophoric, the experiential selections construe the action sequence as it unfolds, the temporal orientation is to the present, i.e. the real time of the unfolding activity, deixis is oriented to the here-and-now, the participant orientation is primarily first person. The prosodic realizations (intonation, rhythm, voice dynamics) of this phase are also different from the previous phase.

Clause 19a can be subclassified as a [Proposal: Command: Self-guidance / Self-Monitoring]. Paola is here telling herself what to do; she is directing her own non-linguistic action of adding the oil to the imaginary recipe, which she is preparing. The non-linguistic sound realized in 19b completes this exchange unit with a move that can be glossed as [Compliance to (Self-) Directive]. In other words, Paola commands herself in 19a and then complies with this self-command in 19b. 19a may also be construed as a Statement that functions as a commentary on the activity sequence. The two interpretations are not exclusive. Rather, they are complementary interpretations of different factors at play in the semantics of this situation.

Clause 20a may also be interpreted in two ways. As a Statement, it constitutes part of the commentary on – i.e. explaining and evaluating – the ongoing activity. More precisely, it identifies the object which is being attended to here, i.e. the oil, as shown by the exophoric use of *questo* ("this") and the identifying relational process. Clause 20a may also be construed as a [Proposal: Offer: Goods Exchange]. It is that kind of Offer whose semantics mediate and enact the handing over of some goods – the oil, in this case. Clause 20b is hypotactically dependent on 20a. For this reason, it has no independent mood structure. It qualifies 20a by specifying a condition that applies to it.

Clause 20c finalizes this exchange. It may function as Acceptance of Offer. It may also signify the handing over of the oil to some non-specific other. Again, it is not possible to decide in any definitive way. As before, this unit also has a self-monitoring function. We have seen that it may be construed as experiential commentary on the object being attended to (identifying the oil) in relation to the action sequence.

I have argued elsewhere (Thibault 1993, 1995) that Offers function to release the social agent's disposition or tendency to perform social actions (goods-&-service exchange) in the public domain of ethical commitments and responsibilities. The agent is located at a person-place – a point of action – in relation to which he or she is authorized to perform the action (Harré 1983: 104). In the egocentric speech of this child, the utterance token which I have interpreted as an Offer is not, of course, located in the public domain in quite the same way, precisely because it is a self-monitoring speech act.

What, then, is the function of this offer in 20a–b? My hypothesis is that the child is, in this case, monitoring her capacity to locate herself at certain person-places in the public realm of interpersonal commitments and responsibilities. It is discourse which the child has re-envoiced from the ecosocial semiotic system. The child is monitoring her own developing agentive capacity; a capacity which requires the agent to occupy the socially authorized person-places which entitle one to release one's own tendencies and dispositions to act, or those of others.

I have already referred to the semantic slippage which these tokens demonstrate between language as action and language as reflection. This distinction is grammaticalized as the distinction between the imperative ("telling self or other what to do") and indicative ("telling self or other what is going on") moods. Experientially, the self-monitoring characteristics of egocentric speech may be seen as reflection turned outwards as externalized commentary on one's own activity. It is speech which is not yet "internalized" as "thought".

Phase 5

In clause 22, Elena both informs and seeks to negotiate a joint activity or team performance involving addresser and addressee. It is the selection of the modulation *dobbiamo* ("we must"), which lies in the semantic area of moral necessity, which is of most interest here. Such modulations impose an external constraint of the moral-practical or the moral-normative kind on participants.

The speaker has the power to release the relevant agentive tendency or disposition with reference to the appropriate moral order. It is in relation to the relevant moral order that reasons may be appealed to in order to justify, explain, or rationalize a given action. This is what social psychologists refer to as the warranting or accounting for the actions of the self and others. The Subject of the clause is the entity in which the speaker modally invests the success or failure of the proposition. In this case, the Subject specifies the one whom the speaker seeks to make responsible for the carrying out of the action. The speaker does this by transferring to the Subject and therefore investing in the Subject the modal competence that authorizes the Subject to undertake the particular course of action. Initially, the Subject does not have the moral authority to release the tendency or the disposition to do so. That authority is external to the Subject and resides in the speaker; it is the speaker who transfers this authority to the Subject in the process of uttering the clause. In this way, the Subject is modalized with the required modal competence of the moral-practical kind for performing the action desired by the speaker.

The modulation in 22 evokes some interpersonal moral order – some normative reason – which is not made explicit in that clause. As Hasan (1988: 70) has pointed out, elaborated code speakers of English tend to justify dialogic moves such as commanding, offering, generalizing, and so on, by reference to some inherent logical reason, rather than to some irrational or external factor such as bribe, threat, or community norm. These justifications constitute forms of warranting or accounting for speech acts in relation to interpersonal norms or moral orders, which can also be specified in terms of particular intertextual formations.

In 23a–23c, the speaker goes on to provide such an inherent reason. This clause complex further enhances 22 by making explicit just such an inherent logical reason by way of an explanation or reason for the action specified in 22. However, I think it is also true here that "behind" the inherent reason provided, we can also postulate some general community norm which clauses 23a–23c make explicit. There are general community norms concerning children's birthday parties and the socially appropriate ways of celebrating them. Such norms are intertextually adduced activity-structures. What is of further interest here is that Elena, in the role of the "big girl", addresses her "mother" from the point of view of her being a unique individual – *domani è festa mia che compio dieci anni* ("tomorrow is my birthday when I turn ten"). Consistent with the elaborated coding orientation, the semantic orientation is to the uniqueness of the self over and above general social/communal norms. It is a self which is strongly ego-centred and strongly insulated from others (Hasan 1988: 74). The argumentative structure in this complex is of the type Cause: Reason, as shown below.

23a–23b   +   23c
because P   so result Q

Clause 26c realizes the second instance of a modulation in the semantic area of necessity – *bisogna* ("need"). Again, the speaker constructs the situation in such a way that a constraint deriving from the appeal to some reason is imposed on the speaker. The sense of moral necessity is enhanced by the logical structure: BECAUSE P SO RESULT Q IS NECESSARY. The two modulations reinforce each other, though it should be pointed out that *bisogna* in 23c shifts to a more impersonal mode.

In 24, Paola, in her play role as mother, accomplishes two main social purposes in this dialogic move. Clause 24 can be said to support or affirm the previous speaker's dialogic move. In so doing, it does something very typical of mothers who speak the elaborated coding orientation. First, it provides a positive evaluation of the child's speech act. Elaborated coding mothers invest a good deal of time in showing interest in, in supporting, in positively evaluating the child's discourse (Hasan 1988: 78). In this way, mothers invest in and channel the motivations of the child. From this point of view, Paola, as "mother", has re-envoiced the social voice of the mother in her social role as empathizing with and positively evaluating the discourse of the child. Secondly, and this point is clearly related to the first one, Paola places great stress on Elena (in her role as the "big girl") as the possessor of a unique subjectivity, with a capacity for unique thoughts, needs, feelings, and a unique capacity and right to voice these. Thus, Paola, in 24–25b, voices two distinct interpersonal moral orders in constructing the mother–child dyad in this way. The close tie up between 24–25b is illustrated in the interpersonal grammatical prosodies: *vero* and *proprio vero*, which run like an interpersonal motif through this stretch of the discourse. The prosody is further extended in 30, in response to 29.

In 26a–b, Elena further develops the semantic feature [inherent logical reason] by way of a still higher-level generalization about birthday parties in general. In 26a, the third occurrence of the semantic feature moral necessity is realized in *bisogna*. At this point, the modulation is strongly prescriptive about the general social norm to be followed. This interpretation is supported by the logical structure of the paratactic clause complex linked by the adversative conjunction *altrimenti* ("otherwise"), comprising 26a and 26b, i.e. "if you don't do P, then the undesirable consequence Q will follow".

Phase 6

In response to this injunction, Paola, as "mother", once again takes up the kitchen activities which we have already examined in relation to Phase 4.

Appendix III (Chapter 6)

Transcript and Observations of Child's Solo Performance (20 April 1991, age 06.04)

Italian text	English translation	Observations on activity
Phase 1		
(1) aspettate che adesso prendo il quaderno e vi canto questa	(1) wait till I get the exercise book and I'll sing you this one	addresses imaginary audience: announces intention to audience and seeks joint attention of audience
(2) adesso vi canto una canzone	(2) now I'll sing you a song	
(3) allora ve ne canto . . . una tre . . .	(3) right I'll sing you . . . one three . . .	as above
(4) ah no questo no	(4) ah no this one no	self-correction: changes choice of song
(5) su cantiamo su giochiamo	(5) come on let's sing come on let's play	sings as lead singer, addressing other classmates by name
il tuo nome sai tu dir qual è – Paola	your name do you know what it is? – Paola	
guarda bene la mia mano	take a good look at my hand	
stai attento adesso tocca a te – Andrea	pay attention now it's your turn – Andrea	
vado avanti e arrivo fino a te	I'll go on and I'll come to you	
conto conto il tuo nome qual è – Ginevra	I count I count what's your name – Ginevra	
cerco i nomi con la mano	I'll look for the names with my hand	
su cantiamo – Alice	come on let's sing – Alice	end of song
(6) aspettate che adesso prendo il quaderno (7) e vi canto questa	(6) wait till I get the exercise book and (7) I'll sing you this one	address imaginary audience: direct action + seek joint attention + announce intention to sing next song
(8) guardate che è troppo bella che la voglio proprio registrare	(8) look it's so beautiful that I really want to record it	evaluates own performance and seeks to orient audience to share same evaluation
(9) ah allora è qui	(9) ah then it's here	self-monitoring of own
(10) è quello (11) lo prendo (12) eccola eccola l'ho presa	(10) it's this one (11) I'll get it (12) here it is here it is I've got it	activity as she looks

Italian text	English translation	Observations on activity
(13) che è su questo quaderno scritta . . . questo quaderno	(13) it's written in this exercise book . . . this exercise book	for song in exercise book
(14) adesso sentite il fruscio de . . . ascoltate la carta	(14) now hear the crackling of . . . listen to the paper	addresses imaginary audience: directs their attention to proposed action of crumpling paper and crumples paper so that they can listen to the sound:
(15) sound of paper being crumpled		SOUND OF PAPER BEING CRUMPLED
Phase 2		
(16) no questa è bella	(16) no this is nice	evaluation of / affective reaction towards song;
(17) ve la canto tutta allora	(17) I'll sing all of it to you then	address audience + states intention to act
(18) le cose d'ogni giorno	(18) everyday things	sings song
raccontano segreti	tell secrets	
a chi le sa guardare	to whomever knows how to look at them	
ed ascoltare	and to listen (to them)	
per fare un tavolo	to make a table	
ci vuole il legno	you need wood	
per fare il legno	to make the wood	
ci vuole l'albero	you need a tree	
per fare l'albero	to make a tree	
ci vuole il seme	you need a seed	
per fare il seme	to make a seed	
ci vuole il frutto	you need the fruit	
per fare il frutto	to make the fruit	
ci vuole il fiore ci vuole il fiore	you need the flower you need the flower	
per fare un tavolo ci vuole un fiore	to make a table you need a flower	
per fare un fiore	to make a flower	
ci vuole un ramo	you need a branch	
per fare il ramo	to make the branch	
ci vuole l'albero	you need the tree	
per fare l'albero	to make the tree	
ci vuole il bosco	you need the forest	
per fare il bosco	to make the forest	
ci vuole il monte	you need the hill	
per fare il monte	to make the hill	

Italian text	English translation	Observations on activity
ci vuol la terra	you need the earth	
per far la terra	to make the earth	
ci vuole un fiore	you need a flower	
per fare tutto	to make everything	
ci vuole un fiore	you need a flower	
Phase 3		
(19) adesso adesso vi canto questa	(19) now now I'll sing you this one	addresses audience: announces intention to sing new song
(20) su cantiamo su balliamo	(20) come on let's sing come on let's dance	(20) sings song
batti le tue mani insieme a me	clap your hands together with me	
prendi presto la mia mano	quick take my hand	
fai due passi avanti e uno indietro	take two steps forward and one back	
su una gamba e con le braccia in su	one leg up and arms raised	
gira gira e non fermarti più	turn turn and don't ever stop	
piano piano ci fermiamo	slowly slowly we are coming to a stop	
ascoltiamo	let's listen	
suona suona il tamburello	the tambourine is playing is playing	
le maracas scuoti insieme a me	the maracas is shaking together with me	
il triangolo che bello!	the triangle – how beautiful!	
fa din din a tempo insieme a te	it goes ding ding in time with you	
il tamburo batte e fa bum bum	the drum beats and goes bum bum	
le bacchette battono tic tac	the drumsticks beat tic tac	
e i sonagli piano piano	and the rattles softly softly	
su balliamo	come on let's dance	end of song
Phase 4		
(21) adesso ce ne dovrebbe essere un altro, no?	(21) now there should be another one of these, shouldn't there?	addresses self: self-monitoring speech as she turns pages of copy book
(22) vi è piacuta vero? sì?	(22) you liked it, didn't you? yes?	addresses audience: seeks audience evaluation of previous song
(23) però adesso forse . . .	(23) but now maybe . . .	addresses self: self-monitoring speech as she looks for song
(24) ecco sì	(24) here it is yes	

Italian text	English translation	Observations on activity
(25) vi canto tutte le canzoni	(25) I'll sing you all the songs	addresses audience: announces intention to sing to audience
Phase 5		
(26) una presentazione a tempo di musica e con ritmo	(26) a presentation in time with music and rhythm	reads from exercise book
(27) adesso più avanti adesso più avanti c'è ne un'altra che è bella questa . . . me lo ricordo anche da sola	(27) now further on now further on there's another one, which is nice . . . I even remember this one on my own	self-monitoring and self-evaluation + evaluation of song
(28) bene . . . adesso via	(28) good . . . now on with it	self-command: regulates own performance
Phase 6		
(29) per cantare insieme	(29) for singing together	reads exercise book
(30) tre bambini con un contrabasso	(30) three children with a double bass	sings song
stavan chiacchierando sopra un sasso	were chattering on a stone	
passò la polizia	the police came by	
"cos'è questo fracasso?"	"what's this noise?"	
(31) e se vuoi diverti puoi cantarla usando ogni volta una sola vocale	(31) and if you want to have fun you can sing it using a single vowel each time	reads from exercise book
(32) bene	(32) good	self-evaluation
Phase 7		
(33) adesso vi canto questo	(33) now I'll sing you this one	addresses audience: announces intention to sing next song
(34) uno febbraio venerdi 1991	(34) first of February Friday 1991	reads date from exercise book
(35) dalla musica alla favola	(35) from music to story	reads title of lesson in exercise book
(36) scegli il titolo	(36) choose the title	reads instruction in exercise book
(37) autunno nel bosco	(37) autumn in the forest	reads title in exercise book
(38) qual personnagio preferisci interpretare?	(38) which character do you prefer to perform?	reads question and answer sequence in text book or copy book
		Teacher's Question
(39) mi piace fare l'albero	(39) I like to be the tree	Pupil's Response
(40) perchè?	(40) why?	Teacher's Question
(41) mi fa venire allegria	(41) it makes me happy	Pupil's Response
(42) bravissima	(42) very good	Teacher's Evaluation

Italian text	English translation	Observations on activity
Phase 8		
(43) bene (44) adesso vi dico questi . . .	(43) good (44) now I'll tell you these . . .	addresses audience: announces next intention and explains current activity
(45) aspetta che li cerco	(45) wait while I look for them	
(46) ecco . . . questi	(46) here they are . . . these ones	self-monitoring as she locates page in exercise book with pictures and written sound scripts, Appendix IVa
(47) venti cinque febbrario lunedi	(47) twenty-fifth February Monday	reads from exercise book, Appendix IVa
(48) impariamo ad ascoltare	(48) let's learn to listen	
(49) i suoni e i rumori dentro la scuola	(49) the sounds and noises in school	
(50) C!!!CICECI!! BLA!BLA!	(50)	Performs the sounds and noises referred to in the exercise book, Appendix IVa
SSSS!!		
SBAM! BABAM		
etc.		
Phase 9		
(51) adesso questi	(51) now these ones	self-monitoring as she locates table in copy book, Appendix IVb;
(52) vent'otto febbraio giovedi	(52) twenty-eighth February Thursday	reads from exercise book, Appendix IVb
(53) che cosa intendiamo per suoni e rumori	(53) what do we mean by sounds and noises?	reads from exercise book: attempts to re-envoice teacher's voice, but uses falling intonation, Appendix IVb
(54) cosa intendiamo per suoni e rumori?	(54) what do we mean by sounds and noises?	self-corrects previous attempt; reads from exercise book; replicates teacher's voice of interrogation: rising intonation
(55) suoni	(55) sounds	reads from table in exercise book, Appendix IVb
(56) la campanella	(56) the door bell	Column 1, "suoni", Appendix IVb
una canzone	a song	
i bambini che cantano	the children singing	
(57) rumori	(57) noises	Column 2, "rumori", Appendix IVb
(58) parlare tutti insieme	(58) everyone talking together	
il "ssss" della maestra	the "ssss" of the teacher	

Italian text	English translation	Observations on activity
la porta che sbatte	the door that slams	
una sedia trascinata	a chair dragged along	
una sedia che cade	a chair that falls	
la matita che scrive	the pencil that writes	
il gesso che si spezza	the chalk that breaks	
il calenaccio della porta	the broken door hinge	
Phase 10		
(59) allora adesso tutti gli strumenti	(59) well now all the instruments	addresses audience
(60) anche gli strumenti musicali hanno un timbro	(60) musical instruments too have a timbre	reads from exercise book falling intonation, Appendix IIIa
(61) anche gli strumenti musicali hanno un timbro?	(61) don't musical instruments have a timbre too?	reads from exercise book: teacher's question to class: rising intonation
(62) sì perchè ad occhio chiuso possiamo riconoscerli	(62) yes because we can recognize them with our eyes closed	Pupil's response
(63) tamburelli	(63) tambourines	reads list of musical instruments in exercise book, Appendix IIIa
triangolo	triangle	
sonaglio	rattle	
na . . . nacchere	castanets	
metallofono	xylophone	
marocas	maracas	continues to read list of musical instruments in exercise book, Appendix IIIb
bacchette	drum sticks	
piatti	cymbals	
flauto	flute	
Phase 11		
(64) venti cinque . . . venti cinque febbraio 1991	(64) twenty-fifth . . . twenty-fifth February [really March]	reads date in exercise book
(65) conosciamo altri strumenti musicali	(65) we know other musical instruments	reads from exercise book
una fiaba musicale	a musical tale	
(66) "Pierino e il lupo" di Se –	(66) "Peter and the Wolf" by Se –	reads but is unable to pronounce the name "Serge Prokoviev"
(67) questo nome è un po' difficile e quindo non lo dico	(67) this name is a bit difficult so I won't say it	self-evaluation and self-explanation of difficulty reading from exercise book
(68) è fatta di parole e musica	(68) it's made of words and music	

Italian text	English translation	Observations on activity
(69) i personaggi	(69) the characters	reads list of characters from exercise book
(70) Pierino	(70) Peter	
il lupo	the wolf	
il gatto	the cat	
l'anatra	the duck	
l'uccellino	the little bird	
il nonno	the grandfather	
i cacciatori	the hunters	
Phase 12		
(71) gli strumenti della fiaba	(71) the instruments of the tale	reads from exercise book
Phase 13		
(72) adesso questo	(72) now this one	self-monitoring as she locates and attends to new item in exercise book
(73) abbiamo visto il film di "Pierino e il Lupo"	(73) we saw the film of "Peter and the Wolf"	reads from exercise book at the same time that she addresses her audience
(74) chi ha la voce più grossa?	(74) who has the biggest voice?	reads question and answer sequence in exercise book
– il nonno di Pierino	– Peter's grandfather	
(75) chi ha la voce più fine, sottile?	(75) who has the finest, smallest voice?	
– l'uccellino, amico di Pierino	– the little bird, Peter's friend	
(76) il fagotto, cioè la voce del nono ha un suono **grave**	(76) the bassoon, that is, the voice of the grandfather, has a grave (flat) voice	very low pitched voice on the word "grave"
(77) il flauto, cioè la voce del nonno ha un suono **acuto**	(77) the flute, that is, the voice of the little bird has an acute (sharp) voice	very high-pitched voice on the word "acuto"
Phase 14		
(78) adesso vi leggo tutto	(78) now I'll read you everything	addresses audience
(79) ascoltiamo le nostri voci	(79) let's listen to our voices	reads from exercise book
(80) tutti abbiamo detto la frase "sulla finestra c'era un piccione"	(80) all of us said the sentence "on the window there was a pigeon"	
(81) phew . . . no	(81) phew . . . no	self-monitoring: signals termination of performance + resulting physical fatigue
		indeterminate sounds; end of episode; tape recorder is switched off

Appendix IVa

first (left) page of double page from child's school copy book

Appendix IVb

second (right) page of double page from child's school copy book

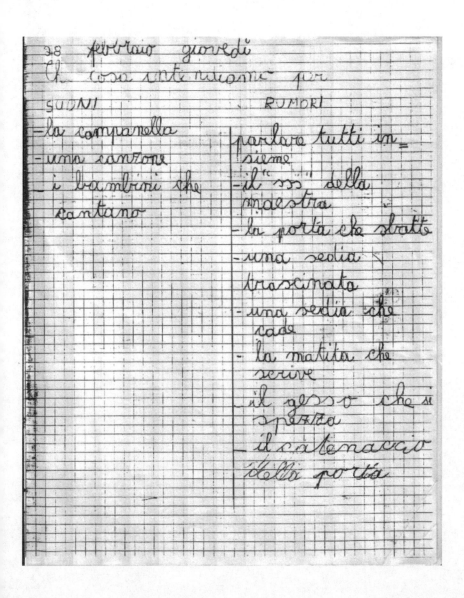

References

Abercrombie, David 1967. *Elements of General Phonetics*. Edinburgh: Edinburgh University Press.

Andersen, Peter Bøgh 2000. "Genres as self-organising systems". In Peter Bøgh Andersen, Claus Emmeche, Niels Ole Finnemann, and Peder Voetmann Christiansen (eds.), *Downward Causation: Minds, bodies and matter*, 214–260. Aarhus: Aarhus University Press.

Baars, Bernard J. and McGovern, Katharine 1996. "Cognitive views of consciousness. What are the facts? How can we explain them?" In Max Velmans (ed.), *The Science of Consciousness: Psychological, neuropsychological and clinical reviews*, 63–95. London and New York: Routledge.

Bakhtin, Mikhail M. 1981 [1975]. "Discourse in the novel". In Michael Holquist (ed.), *The Dialogic Imagination: Four Essays*, 259–422. Austin: University of Texas Press.

Bakhtin, Mikhail M. 1986. "The problem of speech genres". In Caryl Emerson and Michael Holquist (eds.), *Speech Genres & Other Late Essays*, 60–102. Trans. Vern W. McGee. Austin: University of Texas Press.

Bates, Elizabeth 1979 (with the collaboration of Laura Benigni, Inge Bretherton, Luigia Camaioni, Vicki Carlson, Karlana Carpen, and Marcia Rossner). *The Emergence of Symbols: Cognition and communication in infancy*. New York and London: Academic Press.

Bateson, Gregory 1973a [1972]. "The cybernetics of 'self': a theory of alcoholism". In Gregory Bateson, *Steps to an Ecology of Mind*, 280–308. London and New York: Granada.

Bateson, Gregory 1973b. "Style, grace, and information in primitive art". In Gregory Bateson, *Steps to an Ecology of Mind*, 101–125. London and New York: Granada.

Bateson, Gregory 1973c [1972]. "Towards a theory of schizophrenia". In Gregory Bateson, *Steps to an Ecology of Mind*, 173–198. London and New York: Granada.

Bateson, Gregory 1973d [1972]. "The role of somatic change in evolution". In Gregory Bateson, *Steps to an Ecology of Mind*, 316–333. London and New York: Granada.

Bateson, Gregory 1973e [1972]. "Cybernetic explanation". In Gregory Bateson, *Steps to an Ecology of Mind*, 375–386. London and New York: Granada.

Bateson, Gregory 1973f [1972]. "Redundancy and coding". In Gregory Bateson, *Steps to an Ecology of Mind*, 387–401. London and New York: Granada.

Bateson, Gregory 1973g [1972]. "Problems in cetacean and other mammalian communication". In Gregory Bateson, *Steps to an Ecology of Mind*, 334–348. London and New York: Granada.

Bateson, Gregory 1973h [1972]. "A theory of play and fantasy". In Gregory Bateson, *Steps to an Ecology of Mind*, 150–166. London and New York: Granada.

Bateson, Gregory 1980 [1979]. *Mind and Nature: A necessary unity*. London: Fontana.

Bateson, Gregory 1987 [1951]. "Information and codification: a philosophical approach". In Jurgen Ruesch and Gregory Bateson, *Communication: The social matrix of psychiatry*, 168–211. London: Norton.

Battacchi, Marco W. 1996. "Conscience de soi e connaissance de soi dans l'ontogenèse". *Enfance* 2: 156–164.

Battacchi, Marco W. 1999. "Consciousness, awareness, and experience". *Teorie & Modelli* IV(3): 55–63.

Battacchi, Marco W. 1998. "Self-knowledge and self-consciousness". Dipartimento di Psicologia, Università degli Studi di Bologna: Mimeo.

Battacchi, Marco, Battistelli, Piergiorgio, and Celani, Giorgio 1998. *Lo Sviluppo del Pensiero Metarappresentativo e della Coscienza*. Milan: Franco Angeli.

Beaugrande, Robert de 1997. *New Foundations for a Science of Text and Discourse: Cognition, communication and the freedom of access to knowledge and society*. Norwood, NJ: Ablex.

Bereiter, Carl 1997. "Situated cognition and how to overcome it". In David Kirshner and James A. Whitson (eds.), *Situated Cognition: Social, semiotic, and psychological perspectives*, 281–300. Mahwah, New Jersey, and London: Lawrence Erlbaum.

Berne, Eric 1988 [1974]. *What Do You Say After You Say Hello?* London: Corgi Books.

Bernstein, Basil 1971. *Class, Codes and Control, Volume I: Theoretical studies towards a sociology of language*. London and Boston: Routledge & Kegan Paul.

Bernstein, Basil 1990. *Class, Codes and Control, Volume IV: The Structuring of Pedagogic Discourse*. London and New York: Routledge.

Bickhard, Mark H. and Campbell, Donald T. 2000. "Emergence". In Peter Bøgh Andersen, Claus Emmeche, Niels Ole Finnemann, and Peder Voetmann Christiansen (eds.), *Downward Causation: Minds, bodies and matter*, 322–348. Aarhus: Aarhus University Press.

Bogdan, Radu J. 2000. *Minding Minds: Evolving a reflexive mind by interpreting others*. Cambridge, MA and London: The MIT Press.

Bouissac, Paul 1999. "The semiotics of facial transformations and the construction of performing identities". *Journal of Comparative Cultures*, (Sapporo University), 3: 1–17.

Bowker, Geoffrey C. and Star, Susan Leigh 2000. "Invisible mediators of action: classification and the ubiquity of standards". *Mind, Culture, and Activity* 7(1&2): 147–163.

Bråten, Stein 1992. "The virtual other in infants' minds and social feelings". In A. Heen Wold (ed.), *The Dialogical Alternative: Towards a theory of language and mind*, 77–97. Oslo: Scandinavian University Press.

Bråten, Stein 1998. "Intersubjective communion and understanding: development and perturbation". In Stein Bråten (ed.), *Intersubjective Communication and Emotion in Early Ontogeny*, 372–382. Cambridge and Paris: Cambridge University Press and Editions de la Maison des Sciences de l'Homme.

Bråten, Stein 2002. "Altercentric perception by infants and adults in dialogue: Ego's virtual participation in Alter's complementary act". In Maxim I. Stamenov and Vittorio Gallese (eds.), *Mirror Neurons and the Evolution of Brain and Language*, 273–294. Amsterdam/Philadelphia: John Benjamins.

Brentano, Franz 1973 [1874]. O. Kraus (ed.), *Psychology from the Empirical Standpoint*. Trans. A. Rancurello, D. Terrell, and L. McAllister. London: Routledge and Kegan Paul.

Bruner, Jerome 1983. *Child's Talk: Learning to Use Language*. Cambridge, MA: Harvard University Press.

Bruner, Jerome 1999. "The intentionality of referring". In Philip D. Zelazo, Janet W. Astington, and David R. Olson (eds.), *Developing Theories of Intention: Social understanding and self-control*, 329–339. Mahwah, NJ: Lawrence Erlbaum.

Buchler, J. 1966. *Metaphysics of Natural Complexes*. New York: Columbia University Press.

Bühler, Karl 1990 [1934]. *Theory of Language: The representational function of language*. Trans. Donald Fraser Goodwin. Amsterdam/Philadelphia: Benjamins.

Butterworth, George 1994. "Theory of mind and the facts of embodiment". In Charlie Lewis and Peter Mitchell (eds.), *Children's Early Understanding of Mind: Origins and development*, 115–132. Hove, UK and Hillsdale, USA: Lawrence Erlbaum.

Carruthers, Peter 1996. *Language, Thought and Consciousness: An essay in philosophical psychology*. Cambridge and New York: Cambridge University Press.

Chomsky, Noam 1965. *Aspects of the Theory of Syntax*. Cambridge, MA: The MIT Press.

Chomsky, Noam 1976. *Reflections on Language*. London: Fontana.

Cléirigh, Chris 1998. *A Selectionist Model of The Genesis of Phonic Texture: Systemic phonology & universal Darwinism*. Department of Linguistics, University of Sydney: Unpublished Ph.D. thesis.

Cole, Michael 1996. *Cultural Psychology: A once and future discipline.* Cambridge, MA and London: Harvard University Press.

Cook-Gumperz, Jenny and Corsaro, William 1976. "Social-ecological constraints on children's communicative strategies". In Jenny Cook-Gumperz and John Gumperz (eds.), *Papers on Language and Context* (Working Paper 46). Berkeley: Language Behaviour Research Laboratory, University of California.

Cook-Gumperz, Jenny 1986. 'Keeping it together: Text and context in children's language socialization'. In J. Alatis and D. Tannen (eds.), *Language and Communication in Context.* Washington, D.C.: Georgetown University Press.

Cook-Gumperz, Jenny 1991. 'Children's construction of childness'. In M. Almy, S. Ervin-Tripp, A. Nicolipoulou, and B. Scales (eds.), *Play and the Social Context of Development.* New York: Teacher's College Press.

Cook-Gumperz, Jenny 1992. [This reference could not be traced, but any information which would help with the correct and complete acknowledgement of this reference would be greatly appreciated by the author and publisher.]

Coulthard, Malcolm 1992. "The significance of intonation in discourse". In Malcolm Coulthard (ed.), *Advances in Spoken Discourse Analysis*, 35–49. London and New York: Routledge.

Cowley, Stephen J. 2001. "The baby, the bathwater, and the 'language instinct' debate". *Language Sciences* 23: 69–91.

Cowley, Stephen J. 2002. "Why brains matter: an integrational perspective on *The Symbolic Species*". *Language Sciences* 24: 73–95.

Cowley, Stephen J., Moodley, S. and Fiori-Cowley, Agnese. In press. "Grounding signs of culture: primary intersubjectivity in social semiosis". *Mind, Culture, and Activity.*

Damasio, Antonio R. 1996 [1994]. *Descartes' Error: Emotion, reason and the human brain.* London and Oxford: Papermac.

Damasio, Antonio 1999. *The Feeling of What Happens: Body, emotion and the making of consciousness.* London: William Heinemann.

Dascal, Marcelo 2002. "Language as a cognitive technology". *Cognition and Technology* 1(1): 35–61.

Davidse, Kristin 1991. "Categories of Experiential Grammar". Ph.D. thesis. Leuven: Department of Linguistics, Katholieke Universiteit.

Davidse, Kristin 1992. "A semiotic approach to relational clauses". *Open Papers in Systemic Linguistics* (OPSL) 6: 99–131.

Davidse, Kristin 1997. "The Subject-Object versus the Agent-Patient asymmetry". Paper presented at the congress "Objects, grammatical relations and semantics", University of Gent, 23–24 May 1997.

Deacon, Terrence 1998 [1997]. *The Symbolic Species: The co-evolution of language and the human brain.* London and New York: Penguin.

Descartes, René 1960 [1641]. "Meditations". In *Discourse on Method and Other Writings*, 101–169. Trans. Arthur Wollaston. Harmondsworth, Middlesex: Penguin.

Dewey, J. 1906. "The terms 'conscious' and 'consciousness' ". *Journal of Philosophy, Psychology and Scientific Method* 3: 39–51.

Dore, John 1989. "Monologue as reenvoicement of dialogue". In K. Nelson (ed.), *Narrative from the Crib*, 231–259. Cambridge, MA: Harvard University Press.

Edelman, Gerald M. 1989. *The Remembered Present: A biological theory of consciousness.* New York: Basic Books.

Edelman, Gerald M. 1992. *Bright Air, Brilliant Fire: On the matter of the mind.* London and New York: Penguin.

Edelman, Gerald M. and Tononi, Giulio 2000. *A Universe of Consciousness: How matter becomes imagination.* New York: Basic Books.

Elman, Jeffrey L. 1995. "Language as a dynamical system". In Robert F. Port and Timothy van Gelder (eds.), *Mind as Motion: Explorations in the dynamics of cognition*, 195–225. Cambridge, MA and London: The MIT Press.

Fawcett, Robin P. 1988. "What makes a 'good' system network good? – four pairs of concepts for such evaluations". In James D. Benson and William S. Greaves (eds.), *Systemic Functional Approaches to Discourse*, 1–28. Norwood, NJ: Ablex.

Flohr, Hans 1991. "Brain processes and phenomenal consciousness: a new and specific hypothesis". *Theory & Psychology* 1(2): 45–262.

Gee, James Paul 1992. *The Social Mind: Language, ideology, and social practice*. Bergin & Garvey: New York and London.

Gee, James Paul 1997. "Thinking, learning, and reading: the situated sociocultural mind". In David Kirshner and James A. Whitson (eds.), *Situated Cognition: Social, semiotic, and psychological perspectives*, 235–259. Mahwah, New Jersey and London: Lawrence Erlbaum.

Gendlin, Eugene 1962. *Experiencing and the Creation of Meaning: A philosophical and psychological approach to the subjective*. Evanston, Illinois: Northwestern University Press.

Gibson, James J. 1983 [1966]. *The Senses Considered as Perceptual Systems*. Westport, Connecticut: Greenwood Press.

Gibson, James J. 1986 [1979]. *The Ecological Approach to Visual Perception*. Hillsdale, NJ and London: Lawrence Erlbaum.

Goffman, Erving 1981. *Forms of Talk*. Oxford: Basil Blackwell.

Goodwin, Charles 1996a. "Practices of color classification". *Ninchi Kagaku* (Cognitive Studies: Bulletin of the Japanese Cognitive Science Society). 3(2): 62–82. [Also published as Goodwin, Charles 2000. "Practices of color classification". *Mind Culture and Activity* 7(1&2): 19–36].

Goodwin, Charles 1996b. "Transparent vision". In Elinor Ochs, Emanuel A. Schegloff, and Sandra Thompson (eds.), *Interaction and Grammar*, 370–404. Cambridge: Cambridge University Press.

Gregory, Michael 1995. "Generic expectancies and discoursal surprises: John Donne's 'The Good Morrow'". In Peter H. Fries and Michael Gregory (eds.), *Discourse in Society: Systemic Functional Perspectives*, 67–84. Norwood, NJ: Ablex.

Gregory, Michael 2002. "Phasal analysis within communication linguistics: two contrastive discourses". In Peter Fries, Michael Cummings, David Lockwood, and William Spruiell (eds.), *Relations and Functions within and around Language*, 316–345. London and New York: Continuum.

Greimas, Algirdas J. 1983. "Le savoir e le croire: un seul univers cognitif". In *Du Sens II: Essais sémiotiques*, 115–133. Paris: Seuil.

Gurwitsch, A. 1964 [1953]. *The Field of Consciousness*. Pittsburgh: Pennsylvania: Duquesne University Press.

Habermas, Jürgen 1984 [1981]. *The Theory of Communicative Action: Volume 1: Reason and the rationalization of society*. Trans. Thomas McCarthy. London: Heinemann.

Haken, H. 1984. *Synergetics: An introduction*. Heidelberg: Springer-Verlag.

Haken, H. 1988. *Information and Self-organization. A macroscopic approach to complex systems*. Heidelberg: Springer-Verlag.

Halliday, M. A. K. 1967a. "Notes on transitivity and theme in English I". *Journal of Linguistics* 3(1): 37–81.

Halliday, M. A. K. 1967b. "Notes on transitivity and theme in English II". *Journal of Linguistics* 3(2): 199–244.

Halliday, M. A. K. 1968. "Notes on transitivity and theme in English III". *Journal of Linguistics* 4(2): 179–215.

Halliday, M. A. K. 1975. *Learning How to Mean: Explorations in the development of language*. London: Arnold.

Halliday, M. A. K. 1976 [1970]. "Modality and modulation in English". In G. Kress (ed.), *Halliday: System and Function in Language* 189–213. Oxford and London: Oxford University Press.

Halliday, M. A. K. 1978a. "Meaning and the construction of reality in early childhood". In Herbert L. Pick and Elliot Saltzman, (eds.), *Modes of Perceiving and Processing Information*. Hillsdale, 67–96. N.J.: Erlbaum.

Halliday, M. A. K. 1978b. *Language as Social Semiotic: The social interpretation of language and meaning*. London: Edward Arnold.

Halliday, M. A. K. 1979a. "Modes of meaning and modes of expression: types of grammatical structure and their determination by different semantic functions". In D. J. Allerton, Edward Carney and David Holdcroft (eds.), *Function and Context in Linguistic Analysis: A Festschrift for William Haas*, 57–79. Cambridge: Cambridge University Press.

Halliday, M. A. K. 1979b. "One child's protolanguage". In M. Bullowa (ed.), *Before Speech: The beginning of interpersonal communication*, 171–190. Cambridge: Cambridge University Press.

Halliday, M. A. K. 1983. "On the transition from child tongue to mother tongue". *Australian Journal of Linguistics* 3: 201–216.

Halliday, M. A. K. 1984. "Listening to Nigel: Conversations of a very small child". Unpublished manuscript, University of Sydney, Linguistics Department, Sydney, Australia.

Halliday, M. A. K. 1988. "On the ineffability of grammatical categories". In James D. Benson, Michael J. Cummings, and William S. Greaves (eds.), *Linguistics in a Systemic Perspective*, 27–51. Amsterdam/Philadelphia: Benjamins.

Halliday, M. A. K. 1991. "Towards probabilistic interpretations". In Eija Ventola (ed.), *Functional and Systemic Linguistics: Approaches and uses*, 39–61. Berlin: Mouton de Gruyter.

Halliday, M. A. K. 1992. "How do you mean?" In Davies, Martin and Ravelli, Louise (eds.), *Advances in Systemic Linguistics: Recent theory and practice*, 20–35. London and New York: Pinter.

Halliday, M. A. K. 1993. "Towards a language-based theory of learning". *Linguistics and Education* 5: 93–116.

Halliday, M. A. K. 1994 [1985]. *Introduction to Functional Grammar*. 2nd edition. London and Melbourne: Arnold.

Halliday, M. A. K. 1995. "On language in relation to the evolution of human consciousness". In S. Allen (ed.), *Of Thoughts and Words: Proceedings of Nobel Symposium 92: "The relation between language and mind"*. Stockholm, 8–12 August 1994, 45–84. River Edge, NJ: Imperial College Press.

Halliday, M. A. K. 1998. "Things and relations: regrammaticising experience as technical knowledge". In J. R. Martin and Robert Veel (eds.), *Reading Science: Critical and functional perspectives on discourses of science*, 187–235. London and New York: Routledge.

Halliday, M. A. K. and Hasan, Ruqaiya 1976. *Cohesion in English*. London: Longman.

Halliday, M. A. K. and Matthiessen, Christian 1999. *Construing Experience through Meaning: A language-based approach to cognition*. London and New York: Cassell.

Halliday, M.A. K., Mcintosh, Angus, and Streven, Peter 1964. *The Linguistic Sciences and Language Teaching*. Longman: London.

Handel, Stephen 1989. *Listening: An introduction to the perception of auditory events*. Cambridge, MA and London: The MIT Press.

Hanks, William F. 1996. *Language and Communicative Practices* [Critical Essays in Anthropology Series]. Boulder, CO: Westview Press.

Harré, Rom 1983. *Personal Being: A theory for individual psychology*. Oxford: Blackwell.

Harré, Rom 1989. "Language games and the texts of identity". In John R. Shotter and Kenneth J. Gergen, (eds.), *Texts of Identity* 20–35, London and New Delhi: Sage.

Harré, Rom 1990. "Exploring the human Umwelt". In Roy Bhaskar (ed.), *Harré and His Critics. Essays in honour of Rom Harré with his commentary on them*. 297–364. Oxford: Basil Blackwell.

Harré, Rom and Gillett, Grant 1994. *The Discursive Mind*. Thousand Oaks, CA and New Delhi: Sage.

Harris, Roy 2001 [2000]. *Rethinking Writing*. London and New York: Continuum.

Hasan, Ruqaiya 1980. "The texture of a text". In Halliday, M. A. K. and Hasan, Ruqaiya, *Text and Context: Aspects of language in a social-semiotic perspective*, 43–59. Sophia University, Tokyo, The Graduate School of Languages and Linguistics, Linguistic Institute for International Communication: Working Papers in Linguistics, No. 6.

Hasan, Ruqaiya 1985. "The structure of a text". In *Language, Context, and Text: A social-semiotic perspective*, M. A. K. Halliday and Ruqaiya Hasan, 52–69. Geelong, Victoria: Deakin University Press.

Hasan, Ruqaiya 1988. "Language in the processes of socialisation: home and school". In Linda Gerot, Jane Oldenburg and Theo van Leeuwen (eds.), *Language and Socialisation: Home and school. Proceedings from the Working Conference on Language in Education, Macquarie University 17–21 November 1986, 36–95.* Macquarie University, Sydney.

Hasan, Ruqaiya 1992a. "Rationality in everyday talk: from process to system". In Jan Svartik (ed.), *Directions in Corpus Linguistics: Proceedings of Nobel Symposium 82 Stockholm, 4–8 August 1991,* 257–307. Berlin and New York: Mouton de Gruyter.

Hasan, Ruqaiya 1992b. "Speech genre, semiotic mediation and the development of the higher mental functions". *Language Sciences* 14(4): 489–528.

Hasan, Ruqaiya 1996a. "Semantic networks: a tool for the analysis of meaning". In Carmel Cloran, David Butt, and Geoff Williams (eds.), *Ways of Saying: Ways of Meaning,* 104–131. London and New York: Cassell.

Hasan, Ruqaiya 1996b [1986]. "The ontogenesis of ideology: an interpretation of mother-child talk". In Carmel Cloran, David Butt, and Geoff Williams (eds.), *Ways of Saying: Ways of Meaning,* 133–151. London and New York: Cassell.

Hasan, Ruqaiya 1998. "Educating the language teacher: a social semiotic perspective". In Barry Asker, (ed.), *Teaching Language and Culture: Building Hong Kong on education,* 209–231. Hong Kong: Addison Wesley Longman China Limited.

Hasan, Ruqaiya 1999. "Speaking with reference to context". In Mohsen Ghadessy (ed.), *Text and Context in Functional Linguistics,* 219–328. Amsterdam/Philadelphia: John Benjamins.

Hjelmslev, Louis 1954. "La stratification du langage". *Word* 10(2–3): 163–188.

Hjelmslev, Louis 1961 [1943]. *Prolegomena to a Theory of Language.* Trans. Francis J. Whitfield. Revised English edition. Madison, Milwaukee and London: The University of Wisconsin Press.

Holiday, Anthony 1988. *Moral Powers: Normative necessity in language and history.* London: Routledge.

Ilyenkov, E. V. 1977 [1974]. *Dialectical Logic: Essays on its history and theory.* Trans. H. Campbell Creighton. Moscow: Progress Publishers.

Inhelder, B. and Piaget, J. 1964. *The Early Growth of Logic in the Child.* London: Routledge & Kegan Paul.

James, William 1950 [1890]. *The Principles of Psychology, Volume 1.* New York: Dover.

Johnson, M. H. and Morton, J. 1991. *Biology and Cognitive Development: The case of face recognition.* Oxford: Blackwell.

Juarrero, Alicia 1999. *Dynamics in Action: Intentional behavior as a complex system.* Cambridge, MA and London: The MIT Press.

Kanizsa, Gaetano 1980. *Grammatica del Vedere: Saggi su percezione e gestalt.* Bologna: Il Mulino.

Kanizsa, Gaetano 1991. *Vedere e Pensare.* Bologna: Il Mulino.

Kauffman, S. 1993. *The Origins of Order: Self-organization and selection in evolution.* New York and Oxford: Oxford University Press.

Kaye, Kenneth. 1984 [1982]. *The Mental and Social Life of Babies: How parents create persons.* London: Methuen.

Kinsbourne, Marcel 2000. "Inner speech and the inner life". *Brain and Language* 71: 120–123.

Korzybski, A. 1941. *Science and Sanity.* New York: Science Press.

Kress, Gunther 1992. "Against arbitrariness: the social production of the sign as a foundational issue in critical discourse analysis". *Discourse & Society* 4(2): 169–191.

Kress, Gunther and Van Leeuwen, Theo 1996. *Reading Images: The grammar of visual design.* London and New York: Routledge.

Lakoff, George and Johnson, Mark 1999. *Philosophy in the Flesh: The embodied mind and its challenge to western thought.* New York: Basic Books.

Lamb, Sydney M. 1966. "Epilegomena to a theory of language". *Romance Philology* Vol. XIX, No. 4, 531–573.

Langacker, Ronald W. 1987. *Foundations of Cognitive Grammar. Volume I: Theoretical prerequisites.* Stanford, CA: Stanford University Press.

Langacker, Ronald W. 1991. *Foundations of Cognitive Grammar. Volume II: Descriptive application.* Stanford, CA: Stanford University Press.

Latour, Bruno 1993 [1991]. *We Have Never been Modern*. Trans. Catherine Porter. London and Singapore: Prentice Hall.
Latour, Bruno 1996a. "On interobjectivity". *Mind, Culture, and Activity* 3(4): 228–245.
Latour, Bruno 1996b. "Pursuing the discussion of interobjectivity". *Mind, Culture, and Activity* 3(4): 266–269.
Lave, Jean 1997. "The culture of acquisition and the practice of understanding". In David Kirshner and James A. Whitson (eds.), *Situated Cognition: Social, semiotic, and psychological perspectives*, 17–35. Mahwah, NJ: Lawrence Erlbaum.
Lemke, Jay L. 1983. "Thematic analysis: systems, structures, and strategies". *Recherches Sémiotiques/Semiotic Inquiry* (RSSI) 3(2): 159–187.
Lemke, Jay L. 1984a. "Making trouble". In J. L. Lemke, *Semiotics and Education*, 94–149. Victoria University, Toronto: Toronto Semiotic Circle Monographs, Working Papers and Prepublications, No. 2.
Lemke, Jay L. 1984b. "Action, context, and meaning". In J. L. Lemke, *Semiotics and Education*, 63–93. Victoria University, Toronto: Toronto Semiotic Circle Monographs, Working Papers and Prepublications, No. 2.
Lemke, Jay L. 1984c. "The formal analysis of instruction". In J. L. Lemke, *Semiotics and Education*, 23–62. Victoria University, Toronto: Toronto Semiotic Circle Monographs, Working Papers and Prepublications, No. 2.
Lemke, Jay L. 1984d. "Towards a model of the instructional process". In J. L. Lemke, *Semiotics and Education*, 6–22. Victoria University, Toronto: Toronto Semiotic Circle Monographs, Working Papers and Prepublications, No. 2.
Lemke, Jay L. 1985 [1982]. "Ideology, intertextuality, and the notion of register". In James D. Benson and William S. Greaves (eds.), *Systemic Perspectives on Discourse, Volume I*, 275–94. Norwood, NJ: Ablex.
Lemke, Jay L. 1990a. *Talking Science: Language, learning, and values*. Norwood, NJ: Ablex.
Lemke, Jay L. 1990b. "Technical discourse and technocratic ideology". In J. Gibbons, H. Nicholas and M. A. K. Halliday (eds.), *Learning, Keeping and Using Language: Selected papers from the 8th World Congress on Applied Linguistics*, 435–460. Amsterdam/Philadelphia: John Benjamins.
Lemke, Jay L. 1995a [1993]. "Discourse, dynamics, and social change". In J. L. Lemke, *Textual Politics: Discourse and social dynamics*, 100–129. London and Bristol, PA: Taylor & Francis.
Lemke, Jay L. 1995b. "The social construction of the material subject". In J. L. Lemke, *Textual Politics: Discourse and social dynamics*, 80–99. London and Bristol, PA: Taylor & Francis.
Lemke, Jay L. 1997. "Cognition, context, and learning: a social semiotic perspective". In David Kirshner and James A. Whitson (eds.), *Situated Cognition: Social, semiotic, and psychological perspectives*, 37–55. Mahwah, NJ: Lawrence Erlbaum.
Lemke, Jay L. 1998a. "Multiplying meaning: visual and verbal semiotics in scientific texts". In J. R. Martin and R. Veel (eds.), *Reading Science: Critical and functional perspectives on discourses of science*, 87–113. London and New York: Routledge.
Lemke, Jay L. 1998b. "Resources for attitudinal meaning: Evaluative orientations in text semantics". *Functions of Language* 5(1): 33–56.
Lemke, Jay L. 1999. "Opening up closure: semiotics across scales". Paper presented at the conference, "Closure: Emergent Organizations and their Dynamics", University of Ghent, Belgium; May 1999; Web site: *http://academic.brooklyn.cuny.edu/education/jlemke/index.htm*
Lemke, Jay L. 2000a. "Material sign processes and emergent ecosocial organization". In Peter Bøgh Andersen, Claus Emmeche, Niels Ole Finnemann, and Peder Voetmann Christiansen (eds.), *Downward Causation: Minds, bodies and matter*, 181–213. Aarhus: Aarhus University Press.
Lemke, Jay L. 2000b. Across the scales of time: artifacts, activities, and meanings in ecosocial systems'. *Mind, Culture, and Activity* 7(4): 273–290.
Lewis, C. S. 1960. *Studies in Words*. Cambridge: Cambridge University Press.
Lord, Albert B. 1960. *The Singer of Tales*. Cambridge, MA.: Harvard University Press.
Lukács, György 1973 [1970]. *Estetica*, Vol. I. Abridged edition, Ferenc Fehér (ed.). Italian translation, Anna Solmi. Turin: Einaudi.

Lukács, György (1980 [1978]. *The Ontology of Social Being 3: Labour*. Trans. David Fernbach. London: Merlin.

Lyons, John 1977. *Semantics*. Cambridge: Cambridge University Press.

Malinowski, Bronislaw 1923. "The problem of meaning in primitive languages". Supplement I in "The Meaning of Meaning", C. K. Ogden and I. A. Richards. London: Kegan Paul Trench.

Malinowski, Bronislaw 1935. "An ethnographic theory of language: Part IV". In *Coral Gardens and their Magic*, Vol. 2. London: Allen & Unwin.

Manghi, Sergio 1988. "Il soggetto ecosistemico: Identità e complessità biosociale". In Ferruccio Andolfi (ed.), *Figure d'Identità: Ricerche sul soggetto moderno*, 173–227. Milan: Franco Angeli.

Mann, William A., Matthiessen, Christian M. I. M., and Thompson, Sandra A. 1992. "Rhetorical structure theory and text analysis". In W. A. Mann and S. A. Thompson (eds.), *Discourse Description: Diverse analyses of a fundraising text*, 39–78. Amsterdam/Philadelphia: John Benjamins.

Maritain, Jacques 1990 [1950]. *An Introduction to the Basic Problems of Moral Philosophy*. Trans. Cornelia N. Borgerhoff. Albany, NY: Magi Books.

Martin, James R. 1981. "How many speech acts?" *UEA Papers in Linguistics* 14–15: 52–77.

Martin, James R. 1991. "Intrinsic functionality: implications for contextual theory". *Social Semiotics* 1(1): 99–162.

Martin, James R. 1992a. *English Text: System and structure*. Philadelphia and Amsterdam: John Benjamins.

Martin, James R. 1992b. "Macro-proposals: meaning by degree". In W. C. Mann and S. A. Thompson (eds.), *Discourse Description: Diverse analyses of a fundraising text*, 359–396. Amsterdam and Philadelphia: Benjamins.

Matthiessen, Christian 1993. "The object of study in cognitive science in relation to its construal and enactment in language". In M. A. K. Halliday (guest ed.), *Language as Cultural Dynamic. Cultural Dynamics* 6(1).

Matthiessen, Christian 1995. *Lexicogrammatical Cartography: English systems*. Tokyo: International Language Sciences Publishers.

Maturana, R. and Varela, F. 1980. *Autopoiesis and Cognition*. Dordrecht: Reidel.

McGregor, William B. 1997. *Semiotic Grammar*. Oxford: Clarendon Press.

Mead, George Herbert 1934. *Mind, Self, and Society. From the standpoint of a social behaviourist*. Chicago: Chicago University Press.

Miettinen, Reijo 1999. "The riddle of things: activity theory and actor-network theory as approaches to studying innovations". *Mind, Culture, and Activity* 6, 3: 170–195.

Natsoulas, Thomas 1991. "The concept of consciousness$_1$: The interpersonal meaning". *Journal for the Theory of Social Behaviour* 21: 63–89.

Natsoulas, Thomas 1998. "The case for intrinsic theory: III. Intrinsic inner awareness and the problem of straightforward objectivation". *The Journal of Mind and Behavior* 19(1): 1–19.

Natsoulas, Thomas 2000a. "Consciousness and conscience". *The Journal of Mind and Behavior* 21(4): 327–352.

Natsoulas, Thomas 2000b. "On the intrinsic nature of states of consciousness". *Consciousness & Emotion* 1(1): 139–166.

Nöth, Winfried 1990. *Handbook of Semiotics*. Bloomington and Indianapolis: Indiana University Press.

Oldenburg, Jane 1987. "From Child Tongue to Mother Tongue: a case study of language development in the first two and a half years". Ph.D. thesis. University of Sydney, Department of Linguistics.

Olson, David R. 1995. "Writing in the mind". In James V. Wertsch, Pablo del Río, and Amelia Alvarez (eds.), *Sociocultural Studies of Mind*, 95–123. Cambridge and Melbourne: Cambridge University Press.

Ono, Tsuyoshi and Thompson, Sandra A. 1995. "The dynamic nature of conceptual structure building: evidence from conversation". In Eija Ventola and Anna Solin (eds.), *The New Courant* No. 4, Department of English, University of Helsinki, 25–34.

Painter, Clare 1984. *Into the Mother Tongue: A case study in early language development.* Open Linguistics Series. London: Pinter.

Painter, Clare 1989. "Learning language: a functional view of language development". In R. Hasan and J. R. Martin (eds.), *Language Development: Learning language, learning culture. Meaning and choice in language, Vol. 1*, 18–65. Norwood, NJ: Ablex.

Peng, Fred C. C. 1994. "Language disorders and brain function". *Acta Neurologica Sinica* 3(3): 103–130.

Perinat, Adolfo and Sadurní, Marta 1999. "The ontogenesis of meaning: an interactional approach." *Mind, Culture, and Activity* 6(1): 53–76.

Piaget, Jean 1940. *The Mental Development of the Child.* Reprinted in Six Psychological Studies by Jean Piaget. New York: Vintage Books.

Piaget, Jean 1946. *La Formation du Symbole chez l'Enfant.* Neuchâtel: Delachaux et Niestlé.

Piaget, Jean 1952. *Origins of Intelligence in Children.* New York: Norton.

Piaget, Jean 1953. *La Naissance de l'Intelligence chez l'Enfant.* Neuchâtel: Delachaux et Niestlé.

Piaget, Jean 1959. *The Language and Thought of the Child.* London: Routledge and Kegan Paul.

Pinker, Stephen 1994. The *Language Instinct: The new science of language and mind.* Harmondsworth, Sussex: Penguin.

Pinker, Stephen 1997. *How the Mind Works.* London: Norton.

Prigogine, Ilya and Stengers, Isabelle 1985 [1984]. *Order out of Chaos. Man's new dialogue with nature.* London: Fontana.

Prodi, Giorgio 1977. *Le Basi Materiali della Significazione.* Milan: Bompiani.

Prodi, Giorgio 1987. *Alla Radice del Comportamento Morale.* Genoa: Marietti.

Prodi, Giorgio 1989. *L'Individuo e La Sua Firma.* Bologna: Il Mulino.

Rizzolatti, G, and Arbib, M. A. 1998. "Language within our grasp". *Trends in Neuroscience* 21(5):188–194.

Rizzolatti, Giacomo, Craighero, Laila and Fadiga, Luciano 2002. "The mirror system in humans". In Maxim I. Stamenov and Vittorio Gallese (eds.), *Mirrors and the Evolution of Brain and Language*, 37–59. Amsterdam/Philadelphia: John Benjamins.

Rogoff, Barbara 1995. "Observing sociocultural activity on three planes: participatory appropriation, guided participation, and apprenticeship". In James V. Wertsch, Pablo del Río, and Amelia Alvarez (eds.), *Sociocultural Studies of Mind*, 139–164. Cambridge and Melbourne: Cambridge University Press.

Rosen, R. 1985. *Anticipatory Systems: Philosophical, mathematical and methodological foundations.* Oxford: Pergamon.

Salthe, Stanley N. 1993. *Development and Evolution: Complexity and change in biology.* Cambridge, MA and London: The MIT Press.

Sartre, Jean-Paul 1969 [1943]. *Being and Nothingness: An essay on phenomenological ontology.* Trans. Hazel E. Barnes. London: Methuen.

Saussure, Ferdinand de 1971 [1915]. *Cours de Linguistique Générale.* Paris: Payot.

Saussure, Ferdinand de 1993. Eisuke Komatsu (ed.), *Cours de Linguistique Générale: Premier et troisième cours d'après les notes de Reidlinger et Constantin.* Collection Recherches Université Gaskushuin n° 24. Tokyo: Université Gakushuin.

Scheff, Thomas J. 1997. *Emotions, the Social Bond, and Human Reality: Part/whole analysis.* Cambridge and Paris: Cambridge University Press and Editions de la Maison des Sciences de l'Homme.

Seager, William 1999. *Theories of Consciousness: An introduction and assessment.* London and New York: Routledge.

Searle, John R. 1992. *The Rediscovery of the Mind.* Cambridge, MA: The MIT Press.

Shanker, Stuart G. 1996. "Autism and the theory of mind". Department of Philosophy and Psychology, York University, Toronto: Mimeo.

Shannon, Claude E. and Weaver, Warren 1949. *The Mathematical Theory of Communication.* Urbana, IL: University of Illinois Press.

Silverstein, Michael 1976. "Shifters, linguistic categories, and cultural description". In K. H. Basso and H. A. Selby (eds.), *Meaning in Anthropology*, 11–55. Albuquerque: University of New Mexico Press.

Silverstein, Michael 1985. "The functional stratification of language and ontogenesis". In James V. Wertsch (ed.), *Culture, Communication, and Cognition: Vygotskian perspectives*, 205–235. Cambridge and Melbourne: Cambridge University Press.

Silverstein, Michael 1987. "Cognitive implications of a referential hierarchy". In Maya Hickmann (ed.), *Social and Functional Approaches to Language and Thought*, 125–164. New York and London: Academic Press.

Silverstein, Michael 1997. "The improvisational performance of culture in realtime discursive practice". In R. Keith Sawyer (ed.), *Creativity in Performance*, 265–312. Greenwich, CT: Ablex.

Thelen, Esther and Smith, Linda B. 1994. *A Dynamic Systems Approach to the Development of Cognition and Action*. Cambridge, MA and London: The MIT Press.

Thelen, Esther 1995. "Time-scale dynamics and the development of an embodied cognition". In Robert F. Port and Timothy van Gelder (eds.), *Mind as Motion: Explorations in the dynamics of cognition*, 69–100. Cambridge, MA and London: The MIT Press.

Thibault, Paul J. 1986a. "The cognitive hypothesis: a critical comment". In *Text, Discourse, and Context: A social semiotic perspective*, 26–45. Victoria University, Toronto: Monographs, Working Papers and Prepublications of the Toronto Semiotic Circle, Vol. 3.

Thibault, Paul J. 1986b. "Thematic system analysis and the construction of knowledge and belief in discourse: the headlines in two Italian newspaper texts". In *Text, Discourse, and Context: A social semiotic perspective*, 44–91. Victoria University, Toronto: Monographs, Working Papers and Prepublications of the Toronto Semiotic Circle, Vol. 3.

Thibault, Paul J. 1986c. "The literal meaning hypothesis: a critical comment". In *Text, Discourse, and Context: A social semiotic perspective*, 92–100. Victoria University, Toronto: Monographs, Working Papers and Prepublications of the Toronto Semiotic Circle, Vol. 3.

Thibault, Paul J. 1986d. "Metaphor and political oratory in Ronald Reagan's acceptance speech". In R. M. Bollettieri Bosinelli (ed.), *U.S. Presidential Election 1984: An interdisciplinary approach to the analysis of political discourse*, 149–68. Bologna: Pitagora Editrice.

Thibault, Paul J. 1989. "Semantic variation, social heteroglossia and intertextuality: thematic and axiological meanings in spoken discourse". *Critical Studies* 1(2): 181–209.

Thibault, Paul J. 1990. "Questions of genre and intertextuality in some Australian television advertisements". In R. Rossini Favretti (ed.), *The Televised Text*, 89–131. Bologna: Pàtron.

Thibault, Paul J. 1991a. *Social Semiotics as Praxis. Text, social meaning making and Nabokov's "Ada"*. Theory and History of Literature series, Vol. 74, Wlad Godzich and Jochen Schulte-Sasse, (eds.), Minneapolis and Oxford: University of Minnesota Press.

Thibault, Paul J. 1991b. "Grammar, technocracy and the noun: technocratic values and cognitive linguistics". In Eija Ventola (ed.), *Recent Systemic and Other Functional Views on Language*, 281–305. Trends in Linguistics Studies and Monographs. Berlin: Mouton de Gruyter.

Thibault, Paul J. 1992. "Grammar, ethics, and understanding: functionalist reason and clause as exchange". *Social Semiotics* 2(1): 135–175.

Thibault, Paul J. 1993. "Using language to think interpersonally: experiential meaning and the cryptogrammar of subjectivity and agency in English". In M. A. K. Halliday (guest ed.), *Language as Cultural Dynamic: Cultural Dynamics* 6(1–2): 131–186.

Thibault, Paul J. 1994. "Text and/or context?: an open question". State-of-the-Art article. In *The Semiotic Review of Books* (Toronto) 5, 2, May 1994.

Thibault, Paul J. 1995. "The interpersonal grammar of Mood and the ecosocial dynamics of the semiotic exchange process". In Ruqaiya Hasan and Peter Fries (eds.), *On Subject and Theme: From the perspective of functions in discourse*, 51–89. Amsterdam and Philadelphia: Benjamins.

Thibault, Paul J. 1997. *Re-reading Saussure: The dynamics of signs in social life*. London and New York: Routledge.

Thibault, Paul J. 1998a. "Inner speech". In Paul Bouissac (ed.), *The Encyclopedia of Semiotics*, 312–314. Oxford and New York: Oxford University Press.

Thibault, Paul J. 1998b. "Embodiment, perception, consciousness, personhood: The cascading/collecting dialectic of *langue* and *parole* in the individual". Cyber Semiotics Institute,

University of Toronto (Canada); website: *http://www.chass.utoronto.ca/epc/srb*, Lecture No. 8 in the course "Saussure and Beyond" (1996–98).

Thibault, Paul J. 1998b. "Metasemiosis". SRB Insights. *The Semiotic Review of Books* 9.2 May 1998: 8–12.

Thibault, Paul J. 1999a. "Putting Humpty Dumpty's theory of meaning back together again: can Saussure help?" *Belgian Essays on Language and Literature* 9: 7–34. Liège: Belgian Association of Anglicists in Higher Education.

Thibault, Paul J. 1999b. "Communicating and interpreting relevance through discourse negotiation: an alternative to relevance theory". *Journal of Pragmatics* 31: 557–594.

Thibault, Paul J. 2000a. "The dialogical integration of the brain in social semiosis: Edelman and the case for downward causation." *Mind, Culture, and Activity* 7(4): 291–311.

Thibault, Paul J. 2000b. "The multimodal transcription of a television advertisement: theory and practice". In Anthony Baldry (ed.), *Multimodality and Multimediality in the Distance Learning Age*, 311–85. Campo Basso: Lampo.

Thibault, Paul J. 2001. "Multimodality and the school science textbook". In Carol Taylor Torsello, Giuseppe Brunetti, and Nicoletta Penello (eds.), *Corpora Testuali per Ricerca, Traduzione e Apprendimento Linguistico*, 293–335. Padova: Unipress.

Thibault, Paul J. 2002. "Interpersonal meaning and the discursive construction of action, attitudes and values: the Global Modal Program of one text". In Peter Fries, Michael Cummings, David Lockwood, and William Spruiell (eds.), *Relations and Functions within and around Language*, 56–116. London and New York: Continuum.

Thibault, Paul J. 2003a. "Contextualization and social meaning-making practices". In Susan Eerdmans, Carlo Prevignano, and Paul J. Thibault (eds.), *Discussing John J. Gumperz*, 41–61. Amsterdam and Philadelphia: Benjamins.

Thibault, Paul J. 2003b. "Body dynamics, social meaning-making, and scale heterogeneity: re-considering contextualization cues and language as mixed-mode semiosis". In Susan Eerdmans, Carlo Prevignano, and Paul J. Thibault (eds.), *Discussing John J. Gumperz*, 127–147. Amsterdam and Philadelphia: Benjamins.

Thibault, Paul J. 2004a. *Brain, Mind, and the Signifying Body: An ecosocial semiotic theory*. London and New York: Continuum.

Thibault, Paul J. 2004b. "Agency, individuation, and meaning-making: reflections on an episode of bonobo-human interaction". In Geoffrey Williams and Annabelle Lukin (eds.), *Language Development: Functional Perspectives on Evolution and Ontogenesis*, 108–132. London and New York: Continuum.

Thibault, Paul J. and Van Leeuwen, Theo 1996. "Grammar, society, and the speech act: renewing the connections". *Journal of Pragmatics* 25: 561–585.

Togeby, Ole 2000. "Anticipated downward causation and the arch structure of texts". In Peter Bøgh Andersen, Claus Emmeche, Niels Ole Finnemann, and Peder Voetmann Christiansen (eds.), *Downward Causation: Minds, bodies and matter*, 261–277. Aarhus: Aarhus University Press.

Toolan, Michael 1996. *Total Speech: An integrational linguistic approach to language*. Durham and London: Duke University Press.

Trevarthen, Colwyn 1978. "Modes of perceiving and modes of acting". In Herbert L. Pick and Elliot Saltzman (eds.), *Modes of Perceiving and Processing Information*, 99–136. Hillsdale, NJ: Erlbaum.

Trevarthen, Colwyn 1987. "Sharing makes sense: intersubjectivity and the making of an infant's meaning". In Ross Steele and Terry Threadgold (eds.), *Language Topics: Essays in honour of Michael Halliday, Vol. I*, 177–199. Amsterdam and Philadelphia: John Benjamins.

Trevarthen, Colwyn 1992. "An infant's motives for speaking and thinking in the culture". In Astri Heen Wold (ed.), *The Dialogical Alternative: Towards a theory of language and mind*, 99–137. Oslo: Scandinavian University Press.

Trevarthen, Colwyn 1998. "The concept and foundations of infant intersubjectivity". In Stein Bråten (ed.), *Intersubjective Communication and Emotion in Early Ontogeny*, 15–46. Cambridge and Paris: Cambridge University Press and Editions de la Maison des Sciences de l'Homme.

Van Leeuwen, Theo 1999. *Speech, Music, Sound*. London: Macmillan.

Vološinov, V. N. 1973 [1930]. *Marxism and the Philosophy of Language*. Trans. Ladislav Matejka and I. R. Titunik. New York and London: Seminar Press.

Vološinov, V. N. 1976 [1927]. *Freudianism: A marxist critique*. Trans. and ed. I. R. Titunik and Neal H. Bruss. New York and London: Academic Press.

Vološinov, V. N. 1983. "The construction of the utterance". Trans. Noel Owen. In Ann Shukman (ed.), *Bakhtin School Papers: Russian poetics in translation, No. 10*, 114–137. Oxford: RPT Publications (in association with Department of Literature, University of Essex, Colchester).

Vygotsky, Lev 1986 [1934]. *Thought and Language*. Trans. Alex Kozulin. Cambridge, MA and London: The MIT Press.

Vygotsky, L. S. 1987 [1934]. "Thinking and speech". In R. W. Rieber and A. S. Carton (eds.), *The Collected Works of L. S. Vygotsky, Vol. 1. Problems of general psychology*, 37–285. New York: Plenum Press.

Waddington, C. H. 1977. *Tools for Thought*. London: Jonathan Cape.

Walkerdine, Valerie 1997. "Redefining the subject in situated cognition theory". In David Kirshner and James A. Whitson (eds.), *Situated Cognition: Social, semiotic, and psychological perspectives*, 57–70. Mahwah, NJ: Lawrence Erlbaum.

Wells, Gordon 1999. *Dialogic Inquiry: Towards a sociocultural practice and theory of education*. Cambridge and New York: Cambridge University Press.

Wertsch, James V. 1991. *Voices of the Mind: A sociocultural approach to mediated action*. London and Singapore: Harvester Wheatsheaf.

Wertsch, James V. 1995. "The need for action in sociocultural research". In James V. Wertsch, Pablo del Río, and Amelia Alvarez (eds.), *Sociocultural Studies of Mind*, 56–74. Cambridge and Melbourne: Cambridge University Press.

Whitson, James A. 1997. "Cognition as a semiotic process: from situated mediation to critical reflective transcendence". In David Kirshner and James A. Whitson (eds.), *Situated Cognition: Social, semiotic, and psychological perspectives*, 97–149. Mahwah, NJ and London: Lawrence Erlbaum.

Whorf, Benjamin Whorf 1956 [1941]. "Languages and logic". In John B. Carroll (ed.), *Language, Thought & Reality*, 233–245. Cambridge, MA: The M.I.T. Press.

Wierzbicka, Anna 1999. *Emotions across Languages and Cultures: Diversity and universals*. Cambridge and Paris: Cambridge University Press and Editions de la Maison des Sciences de l'Homme.

Wilden, Anthony 1980 [1972]. *System and Structure: Essays in communication and exchange*. Second edition. London: Tavistock.

Wilden, Tony 1981. "Semiotics as praxis: strategy and tactics". *Recherches Sémiotiques/ Semiotic Inquiry* 1(1): 1–34.

Zelazo, Philip D. 1999. "Language, levels of consciousness, and the development of intentional action". In Philip D. Zelazo, Janet W. Astington, and David R. Olson (eds.), *Developing Theories of Intention: Social understanding and self-control*, 95–117. Mahwah, NJ: Lawrence Erlbaum.

Subject Index

Index of Names